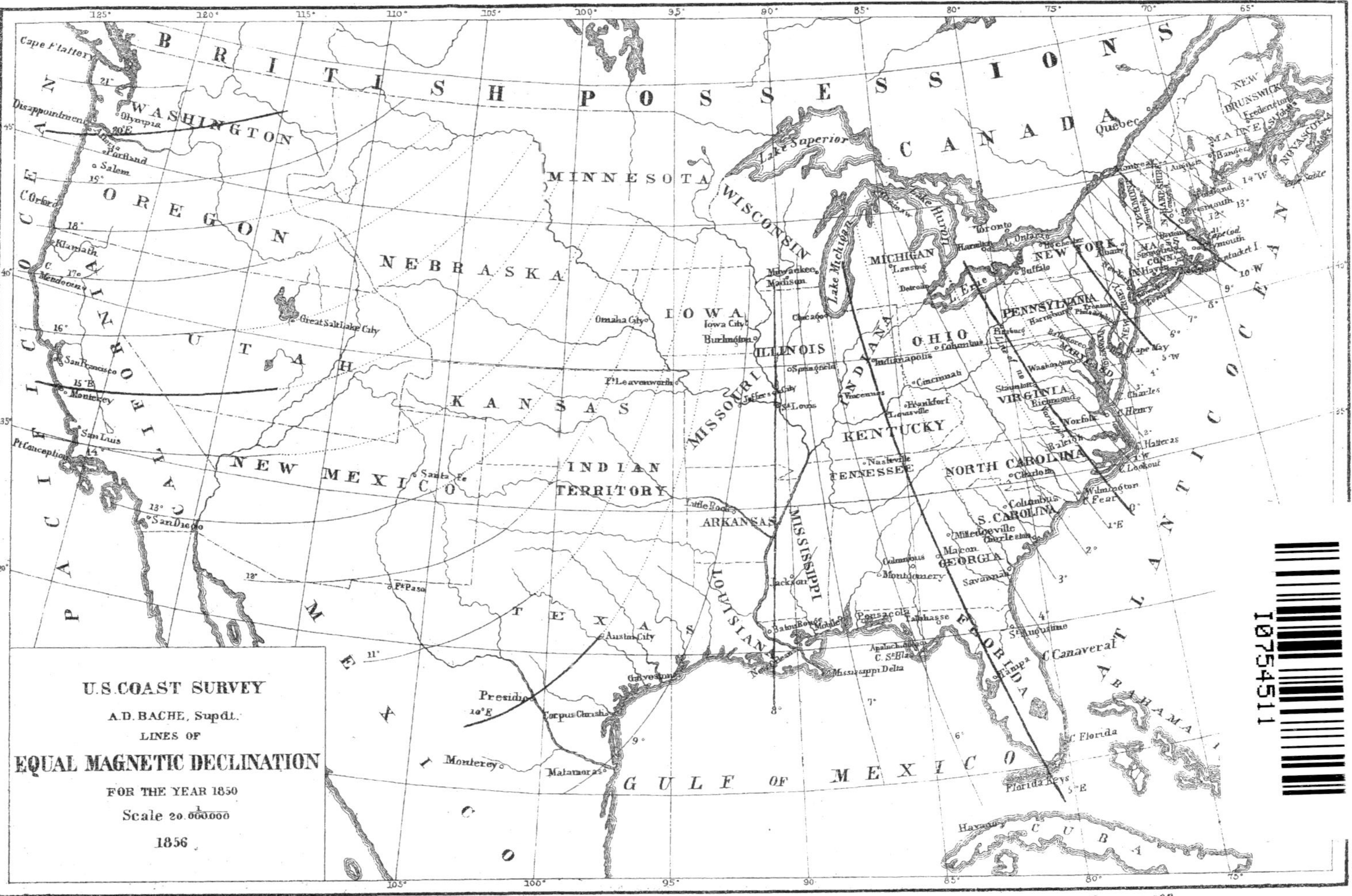

Am. Photo-Lithographic Co. N.Y. (Osborne's Process.)

See page 199

A

TREATISE

ON

LAND-SURVEYING:

COMPRISING

THE THEORY

DEVELOPED FROM FIVE ELEMENTARY PRINCIPLES;

AND THE PRACTICE

WITH THE CHAIN ALONE, THE COMPASS, THE TRANSIT, THE THEODOLITE, THE PLANE TABLE, &c.

ILLUSTRATED BY

FOUR HUNDRED ENGRAVINGS,

AND A MAGNETIC CHART.

BY W. M. GILLESPIE, LL. D., CIV. ENG.,

PROFESSOR OF CIVIL ENGINEERING IN UNION COLLEGE.

AUTHOR OF "A MANUAL OF ROAD-MAKING," ETC.

EIGHTH EDITION.

NEW YORK:

D. APPLETON AND COMPANY,

90, 92 & 94 GRAND STREET.

LONDON: 16 LITTLE BRITAIN.

1868.

PREFACE.

LAND-SURVEYING is perhaps the oldest of the mathematical arts. Indeed, Geometry itself, as its name—"Land-measuring"—implies, is said to have arisen from the efforts of the Egyptian sages to recover and to fix the land-marks annually swept away by the inundations of the Nile. The art is also one of the most important at the present day, as determining the title to land, the foundation of the whole wealth of the world. It is besides one of the most useful as a study, from its striking exemplifications of the practical bearings of abstract mathematics. But, strangely enough, Surveying has never yet been reduced to a systematic and symmetric whole. To effect this, by basing the art on a few simple principles, and tracing them out into their complicated ramifications and varied applications (which extend from the measurement of "a mowing lot" to that of the Heavens), has been the earnest endeavor of the present writer.

The work, in its inception, grew out of the author's own needs. Teaching Surveying, as preliminary to a course of Civil Engineering, he found none of the books in use (though very excellent in many respects) suited to his purpose. He was therefore compelled to teach the subject by a combination of familiar lectures on its principles and exemplifications of its practice. His notes continually swelling in bulk, gradually became systematized in nearly their present form, and in 1851 he printed a synopsis of them for the use of his classes. His system has thus been fully tested, and the present volume is the result.

A double object has been kept in view in its preparation; viz. to produce a very plain introduction to the subject, easy to be mastered by the young scholar or the practical man of little previous acquirement the only pre-requisites being arithmetic and a little geometry; and at the same time to make the instruction of such a character as to lay a foundation broad enough and deep enough for the most complete superstructure which the professional student may subsequently wish to raise upon it

For the convenience of those wishing to make a hasty examination of the book, a summary of some of its leading points and most peculiar features will here be given.

I. *All the operations of Surveying are deduced from only five simple principles.* These principles are enunciated and illustrated in Chapter 1, of Part I. They will be at once recognized by the Geometer as familiar systems of "Co-ordinates;" but they were not here arbitrarily assumed in advance. They were arrived at most practically by analyzing all the numerous and incongruous methods and contrivances employed in Surveying, and rejecting, one after another, all extraneous and non-essential portions, thus reducing down the operations, one by one and step by step, to more and more general and comprehensive laws, till at last, by continual elimination, they were unexpectedly resolved into these few and simple principles; upon which it is here attempted to build up a symmetrical system.

II. The three operations common to *all* kinds of Land-surveying, viz. Making the Measurements, Drawing the Maps, and Calculating the Contents, are fully examined *in advance*, in Part I, Chapters 2, 3, 4; so that when the various methods of Surveying are subsequently taken up, only the few new points which are peculiar to each, require to be explained.

Each kind of Surveying, founded on one of the five fundamental principles, is then explained in its turn, in the successive Parts, and each carefully kept distinct from the rest.

III. A complete system of Surveying with only a chain, a rope, or any substitute, (invaluable to farmers having no other instruments,) is very fully developed in Part II

IV. The various Problems in Chapter 5, of Part II, will be found to constitute a course of practical Geometry on the ground. As some of their demonstrations involve the "Theory of Transversals, etc," (a beautiful supplement to the ordinary Geometry), a carefully digested summary of its principal Theorems is here given, for the first time in English. It will be found in Appendix B.

V. In Compass Surveying, Part III, the Field work, in Chapter 3, is adapted to our American practice; some new modes of platting bearings are given in Chapter 4, and in Chapter 6, the rectangular method of calculating contents is much simplified.

VI. The effects of the continual change in the Variation of the magnetic needle upon the surveys of old lines, the difficulties caused by it, and the means of remedying them, are treated of with great minuteness of practical detail. A new table has been calculated for the time of "greatest Azimuth," those in common use being the same as the one prepared by Gummere in 1814, and consequently greatly in error now from the change of place of the North Star since that date.

VII. In Part IV, in Chapter 1, the Transit and Theodolite are explained in every point; in Chapter 2, all forms of Verniers are shewn by numerous engravings; and in Chapter 3, the Adjustments are elucidated by some novel modes of illustration.

VIII. In Part VII, will be found all the best methods of overcoming obstacles to sight and to measurement in angular Surveying.

IX. Part XI contains a very complete and systematic collection of the principal problems in the Division of Land.

X. The Methods of Surveying the Public Lands of the United States, of marking lines and corners, &c., are given in Part XII, from official documents, with great minuteness; since the subject interests so many land-owners residing in the Eastern as well as in the Western States.

XI. The Tables comprise a *Traverse Table*, computed for this volume, and giving increased accuracy in one-fifteenth of the usual space; a *Table of Chords*, appearing for the first time in English, and supplying the most accurate method of platting angles; and a Table of natural *Sines and Tangents.* The usual Logarithmic Tables are also given. The tables are printed on tinted paper, on the eye-saving principle of Babbage.

XII. The great number of engraved illustrations, most of them original, is a peculiar feature of this volume, suggested by the experience of the author that one diagram is worth a page of print in giving clearness and definiteness to the otherwise vague conceptions of a student.

XIII. The practical details, and hints to the young Surveyor, have been made exceedingly full by a thorough examination of more than fifty works on the subject, by English, French and German writers, so as to make it certain that nothing which could be useful had been overlooked. It would be impossible to credit each item (though this has been most scrupulously done in the few cases in which an American writer has been referred to), but the principal names are these: Adams, Ainslie, Baker, Begat, Belcher, Bourgeois, Bourns, Brees, Bruff, Burr, Castle, Francoeur, Frome, Galbraith, Gibson, Guy, Hogard, Jackson, Lamotte, Lefevre, Mascheroni, Narrien, Nesbitt, Pearson, Puille, Puissant, Regnault, Richard, Serret, Simms, Stevenson, Weisbach, Williams.

Should any important error, either of printer or author, be discovered (as is very possible in a work of so much detail, despite the great care used) the writer would be much obliged by its prompt communication.

The present volume will be followed by another on Levelling and Higher Surveying: embracing *Levelling* (with Spirit-Level, Theodolite, Barometer, etc.); its applications in *Topography* or Hill-drawing, in *Mining* Surveys, etc.; the *Sextant*, and other reflecting instruments; *Maritime* Surveying; and *Geodesy*, with its practical Astronomy.

GENERAL DIVISION OF THE SUBJECT.

[*A full Analytical Table of Contents is given at the end of the volume.*]

TO TEACHERS AND STUDENTS.

As it is desirable to obtain, at the earliest possible period, a sufficient knowledge of the general principles of Surveying to commence its practice, the Student at his first reading may omit the portions indicated below, and take them up subsequently in connection with his review of his studies. The same omissions may be made by Teachers whose classes have only a short time for this study.

In PART I, omit only Articles (46), (47), (48), (51), (72), (84), (85).

In PART II, omit, in Chapter IV, (127), (128), (129), (130); *and in Chapter V, learn at first under each Problem, only one or two of the simpler methods.*

In PART III, omit only (225), (226), 232), (233), (244), (251), (280), (297), (322)

Then pass over PART IV; and in PART V, take only (379), (380); *and* (391) *to* (395).

Then pass over PART VI; and go to PART VII, (if the student has studied Trigonometry), and omit (423); (431) *to* (438); *and all of Chapter IV, except* (439) *and* (440).

PART VIII may be passed over; and PARTS IX and X may be taken in full.

In PART XI, take all of Chapter I; and in Chapters II and III, take only the simpler constructions, not omitting, however, (517), (518) *and* (538).

In PART XII, take (560), (561), (565), (566).

Appendix C, on LEVELLING, may conclude this abridged course.

LAND-SURVEYING

PART I.

GENERAL PRINCIPLES

AND

FUNDAMENTAL OPERATIONS.

CHAPTER I.

DEFINITIONS AND METHODS.

(1) SURVEYING is the art of making such measurements as will determine the relative positions of any points on the surface of the earth; so that a *Map* of any portion of that surface may be drawn, and its *Content* calculated.

(2) The position of a point is said to be *determined*, when it is known how far that point is from one or more given points, and in what direction there-from; or how far it is in front of them or behind them, and how far to their right or to their left, &c; so that the place of the first point, if lost, could be again found by repeating these measurements in the contrary direction.

The "points" which are to be determined in Surveying, are not the mathematical points treated of in Geometry; but the corners of fences, boundary stones, trees, and the like, which are mere points in comparison with the extensive surfaces and areas which they are the means of determining. In strictness, their centres should be regarded as the points alluded to.

(3) A straight *Line* is "determined," that is, has its length and its position known and fixed, when the points at its extremities are determined; and a plane *Surface* has its form and dimensions determined, when the lines which bound it are determined. Consequently, the determination of the relative positions of *points* is all that is necessary for the principal objects of Surveying; which are to make a *map* of any surface, such as a field, farm, state, &c., and to calculate its *content* in square feet, acres, or square miles. The former is an application of Drafting, the latter of Mensuration.

(4) The position of a point may be determined by a variety of methods. Those most frequently employed in Surveying, are the following; all the points being supposed to be in the same plane.

(5) **First Method.** *By measuring the distances from the required point to two given points.*

Fig. 1.

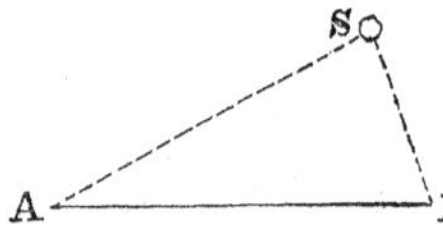

S
A B

Thus, in Fig. 1, the point S is "determined," if it is known to be one inch from A, and half an inch from B: for, its place, if lost, could be found by describing two arcs of circles, from A and B as centres, and with the given distances as radii. The required point would be at the intersection of these arcs.

In applying this principle in surveying, S may represent any station, such as a corner of a field, an angle of a fence, a tree, a house, &c. If then one corner of a field be 100 feet from a second corner, and 50 feet from a third, the place of the first corner is known and determined with reference to the other two.

There will be two points fulfilling this condition, one on each side of the given line, but it will always be known which of them is the one desired.

In *Geography*, this principle is employed to indicate the position of a town; as when we say that Buffalo is distant (in a straight line) 295 miles from New-York, and 390 from Cincinnati, and thus convey to a stranger acquainted with only the last two places a correct idea of the position of the first.

In *Analytical Geometry*, the lines AS and BS are known as "*Focal Co-ordinates;*" the general name "co-ordinates" being applied to the lines or angles which determine the position of a point.

(6) Second Method. *By measuring the perpendicular distance from the required point to a given line, and the distance thence along the line to a given point.*

Fig. 2.

Thus, in Fig. 2, if the perpendicular distance SC be half an inch, and CA be one inch, the point S is "determined": for, its place could be again found by measuring one inch from A to C, and half an inch from C, at right angles to AC, which would fix the point S.

The Public Lands of the United States are laid out by this method, as will be explained in Part XII.

In *Geography*, this principle is employed under the name of Latitude and Longitude.

Thus, Philadelphia is one degree and fifty-two minutes of longitude east of Washington, and one degree and three minutes of latitude north of it.

In *Analytical* Geometry, the lines AC and CS are known as "*Rectangular Co-ordinates.*" The point is there regarded as determined by the intersection of two lines, drawn parallel to two fixed lines, or "*Axes,*" and at a given distance from them. These *Axes*, in the present figure, would be the line AC, and another line, perpendicular to it and passing through A, as the origin.

(7) Third Method. *By measuring the angle between a given line and a line drawn from any given point of it to the required point; and also the length of this latter line.*

Thus, in Fig. 3, if we know the angle BAS to be a third of a right angle, and AS to be one inch, the point S is determined; for, its place could be found by drawing from A, a line making the given angle with AB, and measuring on it the given distance.

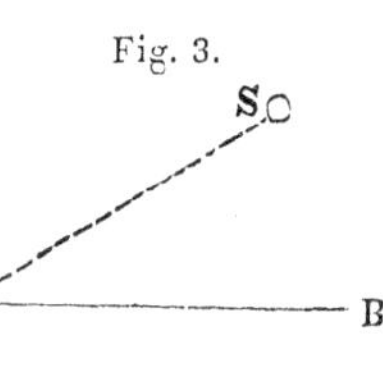

Fig. 3.

In applying this principle in surveying, S, as before, may represent any station, and the line AB may be a fence, or any other real or imaginary line.

In "Compass Surveying," it is a north and south line, the direction of which is given by the magnetic needle of the compass.

In *Geography*, this principle is employed to determine the relative positions of places, by "Bearings and distances"; as when we say that San Francisco is 1750 miles nearly due west from St. Louis; the word "west" indicating the *direction*, or angle which the line joining the two places makes with a north and south line, and the number of miles giving the *length* of that line.

In *Analytical Geometry*, the line AS, and the angle BAS, are called "*Polar Co-ordinates.*"

(8) Fourth Method. *By measuring the angles made with a given line by two other lines starting from given points upon it, and passing through the required point.*

Thus, in Fig. 4, the point S is determined by being in the intersection of the two lines AS and BS, which make respectively angles of a half and of a third of a right angle with the line AB, which is one inch long; for, the place of the point could be found, if lost, by drawing from A and B lines making with AB the known angles.

Fig. 4.

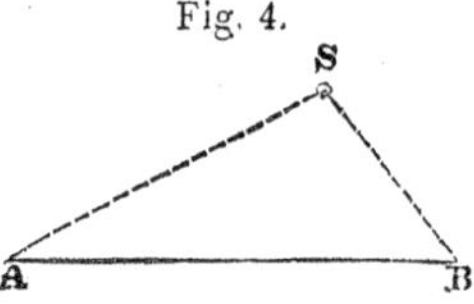

In *Geography*, we might thus fix the position of St. Louis, by saying it lay nearly due north from New-Orleans, and due west from Washington.

In *Analytical Geometry*, these two angles would be called "*Angular Co-ordinates.*"

(9) In Fig. 5, are shown together all the measurements necessary for determining the same point S, by each of the four preceding methods. In the *First* Method, we measure the distances AS and BS; in the *Second* Method, the distances AC and CS, the latter at right angles to the former; in the *Third* Method, the distance

Fig. 5.

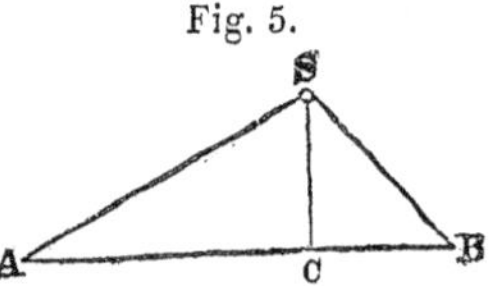

AS, and the angle SAB; and in the *Fourth* Method, the angles SAB and SBA. In all these methods the point is really determined by the intersection of two lines, either straight lines or arcs of circles. Thus, in the First Method, it is determined by the intersection of two circles; in the Second, by the intersection of two straight lines; in the Third, by the intersection of a straight line and a circle; and in the Fourth, by the intersection of two straight lines.

(10) Fifth Method. *By measuring the angles made with each other by three lines of sight passing from the required point to three points whose positions are known.*

Fig. 6.

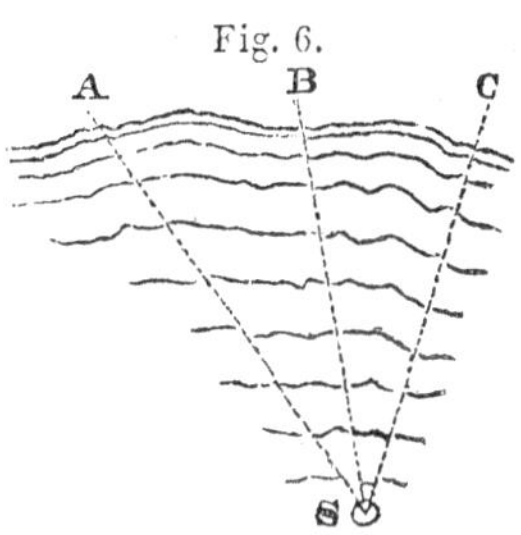

Thus, in Fig. 6, the point S is determined by the angles, ASB and BSC, made by the three lines SA, SB and SC.

Geographically, the position of Chicago would be determined by three straight lines passing from it to Washington, Cincinnati, and Mobile, and making known angles with each other; that of the first and second lines being about one-third, and that of the second and third lines, about one-half of a right angle.

From the *three lines* employed, this may be named the Method of *Trilinear* co-ordinates.

(11) The position of a point is sometimes determined by the intersection of two lines, which are themselves determined by their extremities being given. Thus, in Fig. 7, the point S is determined by its being situated in the intersection of AB and CD. This method is sometimes employed to fix the position of a Station on a Rail-Road line, &c., when it occurs in a place where a stake cannot be driven, such as in a pond; and in a few other cases; but is not used frequently enough to require that it should be called a *sixth* principle of Surveying.

Fig. 7.

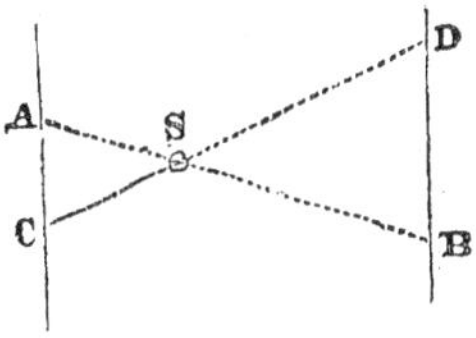

(12) These five methods of determining the positions of points, produce five corresponding systems of Surveying, which may be named as follows:

I. DIAGONAL SURVEYING.
II. PERPENDICULAR SURVEYING.
III. POLAR SURVEYING
IV. TRIANGULAR SURVEYING.
V. TRILINEAR SURVEYING.

(13) The above division of Surveying has been made in harmony with the principles involved and the methods employed.

The subject is, however, sometimes divided with reference to the *instruments* employed; as the chain, either alone or with cross-staff; the compass; the transit or theodolite; the sextant; the plane table, &c.

(14) Surveying may also be divided according to its *objects.*

In *Land* Surveying, the content, in acres, &c., of the tract surveyed, is usually the principal object of the survey. A map, showing the shape of the property, may also be required. Certain signs on it may indicate the different kinds of culture, &c. This land may also be required to be divided up in certain proportions; and the lines of division may also be required to be set out on the ground. One or all of these objects may be demanded in Land Surveying.

In *Topographical* Surveying, the measurement and graphical representation of the inequalities of the ground, or its "relief," i. e. its hills and hollows, as determined by the art of "Levelling," is the leading object.

In *Maritime* or *Hydrographical* Surveying, the positions of rocks, shoals and channels are the chief subjects of examination.

In *Mining* Surveying, the directions and dimensions of the subterranean passages of mines are to be determined.

(15) Surveying may also be divided according to the *extent* of the district surveyed, into *Plane* and *Geodesic*. Geodesy takes into account the curvature of the earth, and employs Spherical Trigonometry. *Plane* Surveying disregards this curvature, as a needless refinement except in very extensive surveys, such as those of a State, and considers the surface of the earth as plane, which may safely be done in surveys of moderate extent.

(16) *Land Surveying* is the principal subject of this volume; the surface surveyed being regarded as *plane;* and each of the five Methods being in turn employed. For the purposes of instruction, the subject will be best divided, partly with reference to the Methods employed, and partly to the Instruments used. Accordingly, the *First* and *Second* Methods (Diagonal and Perpendicular Surveying) will be treated of under the title "Chain Surveying," in Part II. The *Third* Method (Polar Surveying) will be explained under the titles "Compass Surveying," Part III, and "Transit and Theodolite Surveying," Part IV. The *Fourth* and *Fifth* Methods will be found under their own names of "Triangular Surveying," and "Trilinear Surveying," in Parts V and VI.

(17) In all the methods of Land Surveying, there are three stages of operation:

1° *Measuring* certain lines and angles, and recording them;

2° *Drawing them* on paper to some suitable scale;

3° *Calculating* the content of the surface surveyed.

The three following chapters will treat of each of these topics in their turn.

CHAPTER II.

MAKING THE MEASUREMENTS.

(18) THE *Measurements* which are required in Surveying, may be of lines or of angles, or of both; according to the Method employed. Each will be successively considered.

MEASURING STRAIGHT LINES.

(19) The lines, or distances, which are to be measured, may be either actual or visual.

Actual lines are such as really exist on the surface of the land to be surveyed, either bounding it, or crossing it; such as fences, ditches, roads, streams, &c.

Visual lines are imaginary lines of sight, either temporarily measured on the ground, such as those joining opposite corners of a field; or simply indicated by stakes at their extremities or otherwise. If long, they are "ranged out" by methods to be given.

Lines are usually measured with chains, tapes or rods, divided into yards, feet, links, or some other unit of measurement.

(20) Gunter's Chain. This is the measure most commonly used in Land surveying. It is 66 feet, or 4 rods long.* Eighty such chains make one mile.

Fig 8.

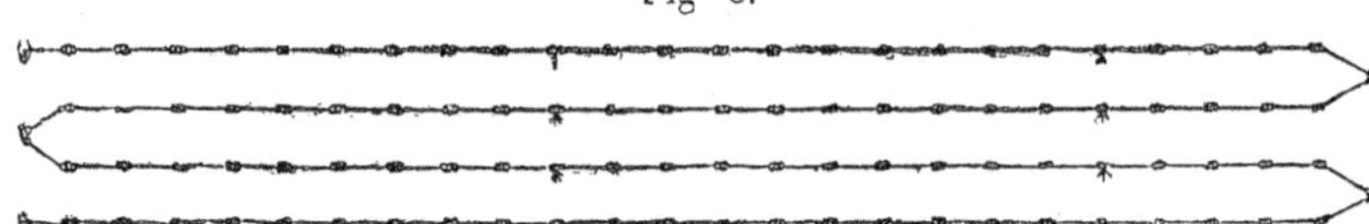

It is composed of one hundred pieces of iron wire, or links, each bent at the end into a ring, and connected with the ring at the end of the next piece by another ring. Sometimes two or three rings are placed between the links. The chain is then less liable to

* This length was chosen (by Mr. Edward Gunter) because 10 square chains of 66 feet make one acre, (as will be shown in Chapter IV,) and the computation of areas is thus greatly facilitated. For other Surveying purposes, particularly for Rail-road work, a chain of 100 feet is preferable. On the United States Coast Survey, the unit of measurement (which at some future time will be the universal one) is the French *Metre*, equal to 3.281 feet, nearly.

twist and get entangled, or "kinked." Two or more swivels are also inserted in the chain, so that it may turn around without twisting. Every tenth link is marked by a piece of brass, having one, two, three, or four points, corresponding to the number of tens which it marks, counting from the nearest end of the chain.* The middle or fiftieth link is marked by a round piece of brass.

The hundredth part of a chain is called a link.† The great advantage of this is, that since links are decimal parts of a chain, they may be so written down, 5 chains and 43 links being 5.43 chains, and all the calculations respecting chains and links can then be performed by the common rules of decimal Arithmetic. Each link is 7.92 inches long, being $= 66 \times 12 \div 100$.

The following Table will be found convenient:

CHAINS INTO FEET.				FEET INTO LINKS.			
CHAINS.	FEET.	CHAINS.	FEET.	FEET.	LINKS.	FEET.	LINKS.
0.01	0.66	1.00	66.	0.10	0.15	10.	15.2
0.02	1.32	2.	132.	0.20	0.30	15.	22.7
0.03	1.98	3.	198.	0.25	0.38	20.	30.3
0.04	2.64	4.	264.	0.30	0.45	25.	37.9
0.05	3.30	5.	330.	0.40	0.60	30.	45.4
0.06	3.96	6.	396.	0.50	0.76	33.	50.0
0.07	4.62	7.	462.	0.60	0.91	35.	53.0
0.08	5.28	8.	528.	0.70	1.06	40.	60.6
0.09	5.94	9.	594.	0.75	1.13	45.	68.2
0.10	6.60	10.	660.	0.80	1.21	50.	75.8
				0.90	1.36	55.	83.3
0.20	13.20	20.	1320.	1.00	1.52	60.	90.9
0.30	19.80	30.	1980.	2.	3.0	65.	98.5
0.40	26.40	40.	2640.	3.	4.5	70.	106.1
0.50	33.00	50.	3300.	4.	6.1	75.	113.6
0.60	39.60	60.	3960.	5.	7.6	80.	121.2
0.70	46.20	70.	4620.	6.	9.1	85.	128.8
0.80	52.80	80.	5280.	7.	10.6	90.	136.4
0.90	59.40	90.	5940.	8.	12.1	95.	143.9
1.00	66.00	100.	6600.	9.	13.6	100.	151.5

* To prevent the very common mistake, of calling forty, sixty; or thirty, seventy; it has been suggested to make the 11th, 21st, 31st and 41st links of *brass;* which would at once show on which side of the middle of the chain was the doubtful mark. This would be particularly useful in Mining Surveying.

† This must not be confounded with the pieces of wire which have the same name, since one of them is shorter than the "link" used in calculation, by half a ring, or more, according to the way in which the chain is made.

To reduce links to feet, subtract from the number of links as many units as it contains hundreds; multiply the remainder by 2 and divide by 3.

To reduce feet to links, add to the given number half of itself, and add one for each hundred (more exactly, for each ninety-nine) in the sum.

The chain is liable to be lengthened by its rings being pulled open, and to be shortened by its links being bent. It should therefore be frequently tested by a carefully-measured length of 66 feet, set out by a standard measure on a flat surface, such as the top of a wall, or on smooth level ground between two stakes, their centres being marked by small nails. It may be left a little longer than the true length, since it can seldom be stretched so as to be perfectly horizontal and not hang in a curve, or be drawn out in a perfectly straight line.* Distances measured with a perfectly accurate chain will always and unavoidably be recorded as longer than they really are. To ensure the chain being always strained with the same force, a spring, like that of a spring-balance, is sometimes placed between one handle and the rest of the chain.

If a line has been measured with an incorrect chain, the true length of the line will be obtained by multiplying the number of chains and links in the measured distance by 100, and dividing by the length of the standard distance, as given by measurement of it with the incorrect chain. The proportion here employed is this: *As* the length of the standard given by the incorrect chain *Is to* the true length of the standard, *So is* the length of the line given by the measurement *To* the true length. Thus, suppose that a line has been measured with a certain chain, and found by it to be ten chains long, and that the chain is afterwards found to have been so stretched that the standard distance, measured by it, appears to be only 99 links long. The measured line is therefore longer than it had been thought to be, and its true length is obtained by multiplying ten by 100, and dividing by 99.

* The chain used by the Government Surveyors of France, which is 10 Metres, or about half a Gunter's chain in length, is made from one-fifth to two-fifths of an inch longer than the standard. An inaccuracy of one five hundredth of its length (= 1½ inches on a Gunter's chain) is the utmost allowed not to vitiate the survey

(21) Pins. Ten iron pins or "arrows," usually accompany the chain.* They are about a foot long, and are made of stout iron wire, sharpened at one end, and bent into a ring at the other. Pieces of red and white cloth should be tied to their heads, so that they can be easily found in grass, dead leaves, &c.

They should be strung on a ring, which has a spring catch to retain them. Their usual form is shown in Fig. 9. Fig. 10 shows another form, made very large, and therefore very heavy, near the point, so that when held by the top and dropped, it may fall vertically. The uses of this will be seen presently.

Fig. 9. Fig. 10.

(22) On irregular ground, two stout stakes about six feet long are needed to put the forward chain-man in line, and to enable whichever of the two is lowest, to raise his end of the chain in a truly vertical line, and to strain the chain straight.

A number of long and slender rods are also necessary for "ranging out" lines between distant points, in the manner to be explained hereafter; in Part II, Chapter V.

(23) How to Chain. Two men are required; a forward chain-main, and a hind chain-man; or leader and follower. The latter takes the handles of the chain in his left hand, and the chain itself in his right hand, and throws it out in the direction in which it is to be drawn. The former takes a handle of the chain and one pin in his right hand, and the other pins (and the staff, if used,) in his left hand, and draws out the chain. The follower then walks beside it, examining carefully that it is not twisted or bent. He then returns to its hinder end, which he holds at the beginning of the line to be measured, puts his eye exactly over it, and, by the words "Right," "Left," directs the leader how to put his staff, or the pin which he holds up, "in line," so that it may seem to cover and hide the flag-staff, or other object at the end of the line.

* Eleven pins are sometimes used, one being of brass. Nine of iron, with four or eight of brass, may also be employed. Their uses are explained in Articles (23) and (24).

The leader all the while keeps the chain tightly stretched, and his end of it touching his staff. Every time he moves the chain, he should straighten it by an undulating shake. When the staff (or pin) is at last put "in line," the follower says "Down." The leader then puts in the single pin precisely at the end of the chain, and replies "Down." The follower then (and never before hearing this signal that the point is fixed) loosens his end of the chain, retaining it in his hand. The leader draws on the chain, making a step to one side of the pin just set, to avoid dragging it out. He should keep his eye steadily on the object ahead, or, in a hollow, should line himself approximately by looking back. The follower should count his steps, so as to know where to look for the pin in high grass, &c. As he approaches the pin, he calls "Halt." On reaching it, he holds the handle of the chain against it, pressing his knee against both to keep the pin firm. He then, with his eye over the pin, "lines" the leader as before. When the "Down" has been again called by the follower, and answered by the leader, the former pulls out the pin with the chain-hand, and carries it in his other hand, and they go on as before.* The operation is repeated till the leader has arrived at the end of the line, or has put down all his pins.

When the leader has put down his tenth pin, he draws on the chain its length farther, and after being lined, puts his foot on the handle to keep it firm, and calls "Tally." The follower then drops his end of the chain, goes up to the leader and gives him back all the pins, both counting them to make sure that none have been lost. One pin is then put down at the forward end of the chain, and they go on as before.

Some Surveyors cause the leader to call "tally" at the tenth pin, and then exchange pins; but then the follower has only the hole made by the pin, or some other indefinite mark, to measure from.

Eleven pins are sometimes preferred, the eleventh being of brass, or otherwise different from the rest, and being used to mark the

* When a chain's length would end in a ditch, pool of water, &c. and the chainmen are afraid of wetting their feet, they can measure part of a chain, to the edge of the water, then stretch the chain across it, and then measure another portion of a chain, so that with the former portion, it may make up a full chain.

end of the eleventh chain; another being substituted for it before the leader goes on.

The two chain-men may change duties at each change of pins, if they are of equal skill, but the more careful and intelligent of two laborers should generally be made "follower."

When the leader reaches the end of the line, he stops, and holds his end of the chain against it. The follower drops his end and counts the links beyond the last pin, noting carefully on which side of the "fifty" mark it comes. Each pin now held by the follower, including the one in the ground, represents 1 chain; each time "tally" has been called, and the pins exchanged, represents 10 chains, and the links just counted make up the total distance.

(24) Tallies. In chaining very long distances, there is danger of miscounting the number of "tallies," or tens. To avoid mistakes, pebbles, &c., may be changed from one pocket into another at each change of pins; or bits of leather on a cord may be slipped from one side to the other; or knots tied on a string; but the best plan is the following. Instead of ten iron pins, use nine iron pins, and four, or eight, or ten pins of brass, or very much longer than the rest. At the end of the tenth chain, the iron pins being exhausted, a brass pin is put down by the leader. The follower then comes up, and returns the nine iron pins, but retains the brass one, with the additional advantage of having this pin to measure from. At the end of the twentieth chain, the same operation is repeated; and so on. When the measurement of the line is completed, each brass pin held by the follower counts ten chains, and each iron pin one, as before.

(25) Chaining on Slopes. All the distances employed in Land-surveying must be measured horizontally, or on a level; for reasons to be given in chapter IV. When the ground slopes, it is therefore necessary to make certain allowances or corrections. If the slope be gentle, hold the up-hill end of the chain on the ground, and raise the down-hill end till the chain is level. To ensure the elevated end being exactly over the desired spot, raise it along a staff kept vertical, or drop a pin held by the point with the ring downwards, (if you have not the heavy pointed ones shown in Fig. 10), or, which is better, use a plumb-line. A person standing beside the chain, and at a little distance from it, can best tell if it be nearly level. If the hill be so steep that a whole chain cannot be held up level, use only half or quarter of it at a time. Great care is necessary in this operation. To measure down a steep hill, stretch the whole chain in line. Hold the upper end fast on the ground. Raise up the 20 or 30 link-mark, so that that portion of the chain is level. Drop a plumb-line or pin. Then let the follower come forward and hold down that link on this spot, and the leader hold up another short portion, as before. Chaining down a slope is more accurate than chaining up it, since in the latter case the follower cannot easily place his end of the chain exactly over the pin.

Fig. 11.

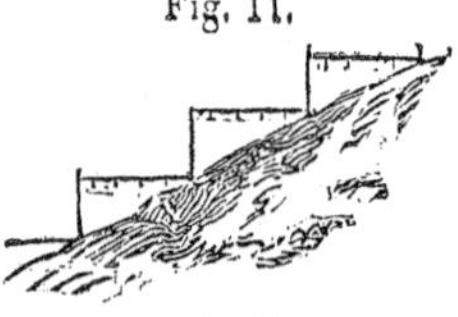

(26) A more accurate, though more troublesome, method, is to measure the angle of the slope; and make the proper allowance by calculation, or by a table, previously prepared. The correction being found, the chain may be drawn forward the proper number of links, and the correct distance of the various points to be noted will thus be obtained at once, without any subsequent calculation or reduction. If the survey is made with the Theodolite, the slope of the ground can be measured directly. A "Tangent Scale," for the same purpose, may be formed on the sides of the sights of a Compass. It will be described when that instrument is explained.

In the following table, the first column contains the angle which the surface of the ground makes with the horizon; the second column contains its slope, named by the ratio of the perpendicular to the base; and the third, the correction in links for each chain measured on the slope, i. e. the difference between the hypothenuse, which is the distance measured, and the horizontal base, which is the distance desired.

TABLE FOR CHAINING ON SLOPES.

ANGLE.	SLOPE.	CORRECTION IN LINKS.	ANGLE.	SLOPE.	CORRECTION IN LINKS.
3°	1 in 19	0.14	13°	1 in 4½	2.56
4°	1 in 14	0.24	14°	1 in 4	2.97
5°	1 in 11½	0.38	15°	1 in 4	3.41
6°	1 in 9½	0.55	16°	1 in 3¾	3.87
7°	1 in 8	0.75	17°	1 in 3½	4.37
8°	1 in 7	0.97	18°	1 in 3¼	4.89
9°	1 in 6½	1.23	19°	1 in 3	5.45
10°	1 in 6	1.53	20°	1 in 2¾	6.03
11°	1 in 5¼	1.84	25°	1 in 2	9.37
12°	1 in 4¾	2.19	30°	1 in 1¾	13.40

(27) Chaining is the fundamental operation in all kinds of Surveying. It has for this reason been very minutely detailed. The "follower" is the most responsible person, and the Surveyor will best ensure his accuracy by taking that place himself. If he has to employ inexperienced laborers, he will do well to cause them to measure the distance between any two points, and then remeasure it in the opposite direction. The difference of their two results will impress on them the necessity of great carefulness.

To "do up" the chain, take the middle of it in the left hand, and with the right hand take hold of the doubled chain just beyond the second link; double up the two links between your hands, and continue to fold up two double links at a time, laying each pair obliquely across the others, so that when it is all folded up, the handles will be on the outside, and the chain will have an hour-glass shape, easy to strap up and to carry.

(28) Tape. Though the chain is most usually employed for the principal measurements of Surveying, a *tape-line*, divided on one side into links, and on the other into feet and inches, is more convenient for some purposes. It should be tested very frequently, particularly after getting wet, and the correct length marked on it at every ten feet. A "Metallic Tape," less liable to stretch, has been recently manufactured, in which fine wires form its warp. When the tape is being wound up, it should be passed between two fingers to prevent its twisting in the box, which would make it necessary to unscrew its nut to take it out and untwist it. While in use, it should be made portable by being folded up by arm's lengths, instead of being wound up.

(29) Substitutes for a chain or a tape, may be found in leather driving lines, marked off with a carpenter's rule, or in a cord knotted at the length of every link. A well made rope, (such as a "patent wove line," woven circularly with the strands always straight in the line of the strain), when once well stretched, wetted and allowed to dry with a moderate strain, will not vary from a chain more than one foot in two thousand, if carefully used.

(30) Rods. When unusually accurate measurements are required, rods are employed. They may be of well seasoned wood, of glass, of iron, &c. They must be placed in line very carefully end to end; or made to coincide in other ways; as will be explained in Part V, under the title of "Triangular Surveying," in which the peculiarly accurate measurement of one line is required, as all the others are founded upon it.

(31) Pacing, Sound, and other approximate means, may be used for measuring the length of a line. They will be discussed, in Part IX. The *Stadia* is described in Art. (375.)

(32) A *Perambulator*, or "Measuring Wheel," is sometimes used for measuring distances, particularly Roads. It consists of a wheel which is made to roll over the ground to be measured, and whose motion is communicated to a series of toothed wheels within the machine. These wheels are so proportioned, that the index wheel registers their revolutions, and records the whole distance passed over. If the diameter of the wheel be $31\frac{1}{2}$ inches, the circumference, and therefore each revolution, will be $8\frac{1}{4}$ feet, or half a rod. The roughnesses of the road and the slopes necessarily cause the registered distances to exceed the true measure.

MEASURING ANGLES.

(33) The angle made by any two lines, that is, the difference of their directions, is measured by various instruments, consisting essentially of a circle divided into equal parts, with plain sights, or telescopes, to indicate the directions of the two lines.

As the measurement of angles is not required for "Chain Surveying," which is the first Method to be discussed, the consideration of this kind of measurement will be postponed to Part III.

NOTING THE MEASUREMENTS.

(34) The measurements which have been made, whether of lines, or of angles, require to be very carefully noted and recorded. Clearness and brevity are the points desired. Different methods of notation are required for each of the systems of surveying which are to be explained, and will therefore be given in their appropriate places.

CHAPTER III.

DRAWING THE MAP.

(35) A MAP of a survey represents the lines which bound the surface surveyed, and the objects upon it, such as fences, roads, rivers, houses, woods, hills, &c., in their true relative dimensions and positions. It is a miniature copy of the field, farm, &c., as it would be seen by an eye moving over it; or as it would appear, if from every point of its irregular surface, plumb lines were dropped to a level surface under it, forming what is called in geometrical language, its *horizontal projection.*

(36) Platting. A *plat* of a survey is a skeleton, or outline map. It is a figure "similar" to the original, having all its angles equal, and its sides proportional. Every inch on it represents a foot, a yard, a rod, a mile, or some other length, on the ground;

all the measured distances being diminished in exactly the same ratio.

PLATTING *is repeating on paper, to a smaller scale, the measurements which have been made on the ground.*

Its various operations may therefore be reduced, in accordance with the principles established in the first chapter, to two, viz: drawing a straight line in a given direction and of a given length; and describing an arc of a circle with a radius whose length is also given. The only instruments absolutely necessary for this, are a straight ruler, and a pair of "dividers," or "compasses." Others, however, are often convenient, and will be now briefly noticed.

Fig. 12

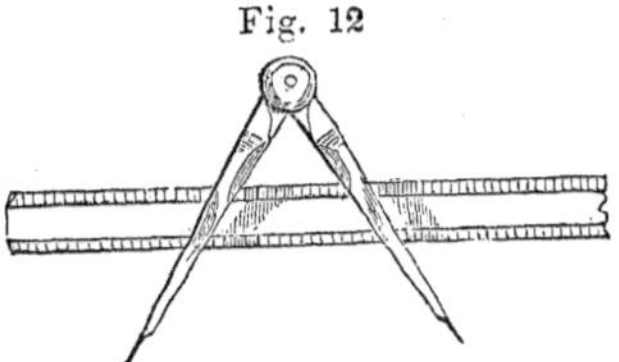

(37) Straight Lines. These are usually drawn by the aid of a straight-edged ruler. But to obtain a very long straight line upon paper, stretch a fine silk thread between any two distant points, and mark in its line various points, near enough together to be afterwards connected by a common ruler. The thread may also be blackened with burnt cork, and snapped on the paper, as a carpenter snaps his chalk line; but this is liable to inaccuracies, from not raising the line vertically.

(38) Arcs. The arcs of circles used in fixing the position of a point on paper, are usually described with compasses, one leg of which carries a pencil point. A convenient substitute is a strip of pasteboard, through one end of which a fine needle is thrust into the given centre, and through a hole in which, at the desired distance, a pencil point is passed, and can thus describe a circle about the centre, the pasteboard keeping it always at the proper distance. A string is a still readier, but less accurate, instrument.

(39) Parallels. The readiest mode of drawing parallel lines is by the aid of a triangular piece of wood and a ruler. Let AB be the line to which a parallel is to be drawn, and C the point through which it must pass. Place one side of the triangle against the line, and place the ruler against another side of the triangle. Hold the ruler firm and immovable, and slide the triangle along it till the side of the triangle which had coincided with the given line, passes through the given point. This side will then be parallel to that given line, and a line drawn by it will be the line required.

Fig 13.

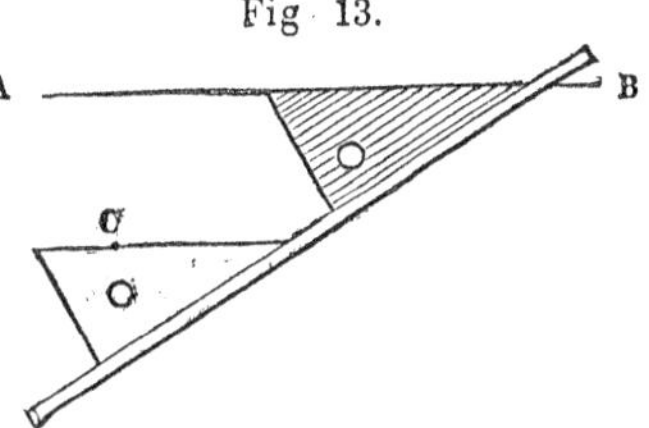

Another easy method of drawing parallels, is by means of a T square, an instrument very valuable for many other purposes. It is nothing but a ruler let into a thicker piece of wood, very truly at right angles to it. For this use of it, one side of the cross-piece must be even, or "flush," with the ruler. To use it, lay it on the paper so that one edge of the ruler coincides with the given line AB. Place another ruler against the cross-piece, hold it firm, and slide the T square along, till its edge passes through the given point C, as shown by the lower part of the figure. Then draw by this edge the desired line parallel to the given line.

Fig. 14.

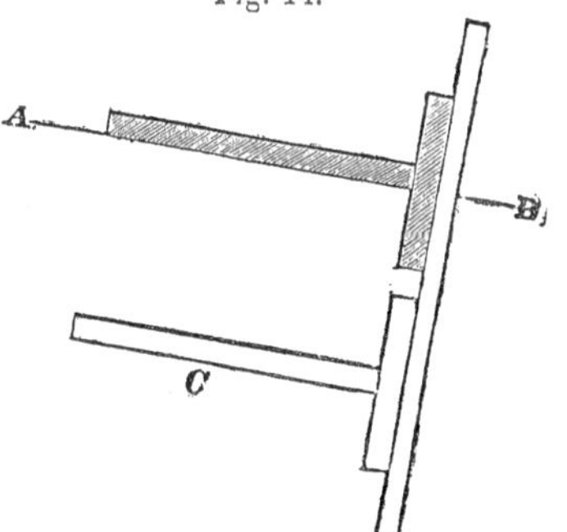

(40) Perpendiculars. These may be drawn by the various problems given in Geometry, but more readily by a triangle which has one right angle. Place the longest side of the triangle on the given line, and place a ruler against a second side of the triangle. Hold the ruler fast, and turn the triangle so as to bring its third side against the ruler. Then will the long side be perpendicular to the

Fig. 15.

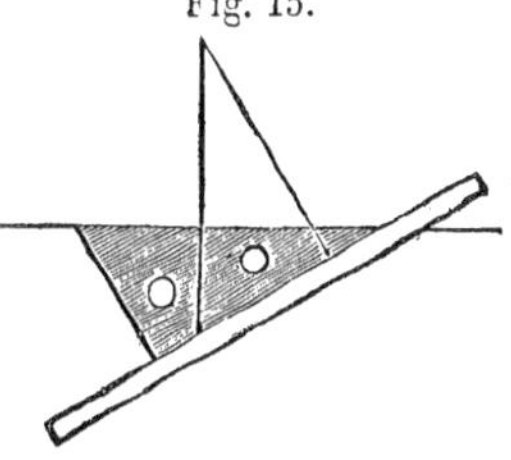

given line. By sliding the triangle along the ruler, it may be used to draw a perpendicular from any point of the line, or from any point to the line.

(41) Angles. These are most easily set out with an instrument called a Protractor, usually a semi-circle of brass. But the description of its use, and of the other and more accurate modes of laying off angles, will be postponed till they are needed in Part III, Chapter IV.

(42) Drawing to Scale. The operation of drawing on paper lines whose length shall be a half, a quarter, a tenth, or any other fraction, of the lines measured on the ground, is called "Drawing to Scale."

To set off on a line any given distance to any required scale, determine the number of chains or links which each division of the scale of equal parts shall represent. Divide the given distance by this number. The quotient will be the number of equal parts to be taken in the dividers and to be set off.

For example, suppose the scale of equal parts to be a common carpenter's rule, divided into inches and eighths. Let the given distance be twelve chains, which is to be drawn to a scale of two chains to an inch. Then six inches will be the distance to be set off. If the given distance had been twelve chains and seventy five links, the distance to be set off would have been six inches and three-eighths, since each eighth of an inch represents 25 links.

If the desired scale were three chains to an inch, each eighth of an inch would represent $37\frac{1}{2}$ links; and the distance of 1275 links would be represented by thirty-four eighths of an inch, or $4\frac{1}{4}$ inches.

A similar process will give the correct length to be set off for any distance to any scale.

If the scale used had been divided into inches and tenths, as is much the most convenient, the above distances would have become on the former scale $6\frac{37}{100}$ inches, or nearly $6\frac{4}{10}$ inches; and on the latter scale $4\frac{25}{100}$ inches, coming midway between the 2d and 3d tenth of an inch.

(43) *Conversely*, to find the real length of a line drawn on paper to any known scale, reverse the preceding operation. Take the length of the line in the dividers, apply it to the scale, and count how many equal parts it includes. Multiply their number by the number of chains or links which each represents, and the product will be the desired length of the line on the ground.

This operation and the preceding one are greatly facilitated by the use of the scales to be described in Art. (48)

(44) Scales. The choice of the scale to which a plat should be drawn, that is, how many times smaller its lines shall be than those which have been measured on the ground, is determined by several considerations. The chief one is, that it shall be just large enough to express clearly all the details which it is desirable to know. A Farm Survey would require its plat to show every field and building. A State Survey would show only the towns, rivers, and leading roads. The size of the paper at hand will also limit the scale to be adopted. If the content is to be calculated from the plat, that will forbid it to be less than 3 chains to 1 inch.

Scales are named in various ways. *They should always be expressed fractionally;* i. e. they should be so named as to indicate what fractional part of the real line measured on the ground, the representative line drawn on the paper, actually is. When custom requires a different way of naming the scale, both should be given. It would be still better, if the denominator could always be some power of 10, or at least some multiple of 2 and 5, such as $\frac{1}{500}$, $\frac{1}{1000}$, $\frac{1}{2000}$, $\frac{1}{2500}$, &c. For convenience in printing, these may be written thus: 1:500, 1:1000, 1:2000, 1:2500, &c.

Plats of *Farm Surveys* are usually named as being so many chains to an inch.

Maps of *Surveys of States* are generally named as being made to a scale of so many miles to an inch.

Maps of *Rail-road Surveys* are said to be so many feet to an inch, or so many inches to a mile.

(45) Farm Surveys. If these are of small extent, two chains to one inch (which is $= \frac{1}{2 \times 66 \times 12} = \frac{1}{1584} = 1:1584$) is convenient

A scale of one chain to one inch (1 : 792) is useful for plans of build ings. Three chains to one inch (1 : 2376) is suitable for larger farms. It is the scale prescribed by the English Tithe Commissioners for their first class maps.

In France, the *Cadastre* Surveys are lithographed on a scale about equivalent to this, being 1 : 2500. The original plans are drawn to a scale of 1:5000. Plans for the division of property are made on the former scale. When the district exceeds 3000 acres, the scale is 1:10,000. When it exceeds 7,500 acres, the scale is 1:20,000. A common scale in France for small surveys is 1:1000; about $1\frac{1}{4}$ chains to 1 inch.

Fig. 16.

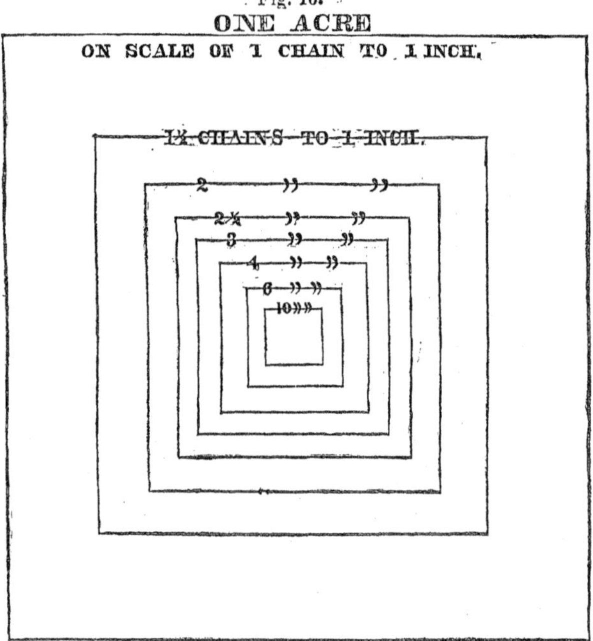

The choice of the most suitable scale for the plat of a farm survey, may be facilitated by the Figure given above, which shows the actual space occupied by *one acre*, (the customary unit of land measure), laid out in the form of a square, on maps drawn to the various scales named in the figure.

(46) State Surveys. On these surveys, smaller scales are necessarily employed.

On the admirable *United States* Coast Survey, all the scales are expressed fractionally and decimally. "The surveys are generally platted originally on a scale of one to ten or twenty thousand, but in some instances the scale is larger or smaller.

These original surveys are reduced for engraving and publication, and when issued, are embraced in three general classes. 1°, small Harbor charts; 2°, charts of Bays, Sounds, and 3°, of the Coast General Charts.

The scales of the first class vary from 1:10,000 to 1:60,000, according to the nature of the Harbor and the different objects to be represented.

Where there are many shoals, rocks, or other objects, as in Nantucket Harbor and Hell-Gate, or where the importance of the harbor makes it necessary, a larger scale of 1:5,000, 1:10,000, and 1:20,000 is used. But where, from the size of the harbor, or its ease of access, a smaller one will point out every danger with sufficient exactness, the scales of 1:40,000 and 1:60,000 are used, as in the case of New-Bedford Harbor, Cat and Ship Island Harbor, New-Haven, &c.

The scale of the second class, in consequence of the large areas to be represented, is usually fixed at 1:80,000, as in the case of New-York Bay, Delaware Bay and River. Preliminary charts, however, are issued, of various scales from 1:80,000 to 1:200,000.

Of the third class, the scale is fixed at 1:400,000, for the General Chart of the Coast from Gay Head to Cape Henlopen, although considerations of the proximity and importance of points on the coast, may change the scales of charts of other portions of our extended coast."*

The National Survey of *Great Britain* is called, from the corps employed on it, the "Ordnance Survey."

The "Ordnance Survey" of the southern counties of England was platted on a scale of 2 inches to 1 mile, (1:31,680), and reduced for publication to that of one inch to a mile, (1:63,360). The scale of 6 inches to a mile (1:10,560) was adopted for the

* Communicated from the U. S. Coast Survey office.

northern counties of England and for the southern counties of Scotland. The same scale was employed for platting and engraving in outline the "Ordnance Survey" of Ireland. But a map on a scale of 1 inch to 1 mile (1:63,360) is about to be published, the former scale rendering the maps too unwieldy and cumbrous for consultation.

The Ordnance Survey of Scotland was at first platted on a scale of six inches to one mile, (1:10,560). That scale has since been abandoned, and it is now platted on a scale of two inches to 1 mile, (1:31,680), and the general maps are made to only half that scale.

The Ordnance Survey scale for the maps of London and other large towns, is 5 feet to 1 mile, (1:1056), or $1\frac{1}{3}$ chains to one inch.

In the "Surveys under the Public Health act" of England, the scale for the general plan is two feet to one mile, (1:2,640); and for the detailed plan, ten feet per mile, (1:528), or two-thirds of a chain per inch.

The Government Survey of *France* is platted to a scale of 1:20,000. Copies are made to 1:40,000; and the maps are engraved to a scale of 1:80,000, or about $\frac{3}{4}$ inch to 1 mile.

Cassini's famous map of France was on a scale of 1:86,400.

The French War Department employ the scales of 1:10,000; 1:20,000; 1:40,000; and 1:80,000; for the topography of France.

(47) Rail-road Surveys. For these the New-York General Rail-road Law of 1850 directs the scale of maps which are to be filed in the State Engineer's Office, to be five hundred feet to one-tenth of a foot, (= 1 : 5000.)

For the New-York Canal Maps a scale of 2 chains to 1 inch (1 : 1584) is employed.

The Parliamentary "standing orders" prescribe the plans of Rail-roads, prepared for Parliamentary purposes, to be made on a scale of not less than 4 inches to the mile, (1 : 15840) : and the enlarged portions (as of gardens, court-yards, &c.) to be on a scale not smaller than 400 feet to the inch, (1 : 4800.) Accordingly the practice of English Railway Engineers is to draw the whole plan to a scale of 6 chains, or 396 feet to the inch, (1 : 4752) as being just within the Parliamentary limits.

In France, the Engineers of "Bridges and Roads" (Corps des Ponts et Chaussees) employ for the general plan of a road a scale of 1 : 5000, and for appropriations 1 : 500.

(48) In the United States Engineer service, the following scales are prescribed:

General plans of buildings, 1 inch to 10 feet, (1;120).
Maps of ground, with horizontal curves one foot apart, 1 inch to 50 feet, (1:600)
Topographical maps, one mile and a half square, 2 feet to one mile, (1:2,640).
Do. comprising three miles square, 1 foot to one mile, (1:5,280).
Do. between four and eight miles square, 6 inches to one mile, (1:10,560).
Do. comprising nine miles square, 4 inches to one mile, (1:15,840).
Maps not exceeding 24 miles square, 2 inches to one mile, (1:31,680).
Maps comprising 50 miles square, 1 inch to one mile, (1:63,360).
Maps comprising 100 miles square, ½ inch to one mile, (1:126,720.)
Surveys of Roads, Canals, &c., 1 inch to 50 feet, (1:600).

(49) The most convenient scales of equal parts are those of box-wood, or ivory, which have a *fiducial* or feather edge, along which they are divided, so that distances can be at once marked off from this edge, without requiring to be taken off with the dividers; or the length of a given line can be at once read off. Box-wood is preferable to ivory as much less liable to warp, or to vary in length with changes in the moisture in the air.

The student can, however, make for himself platting scales of drawing paper, or Bristol board. Cut a straight strip of this material, about an inch wide. Draw a line through its middle, and set

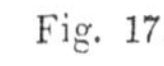
Fig. 17.

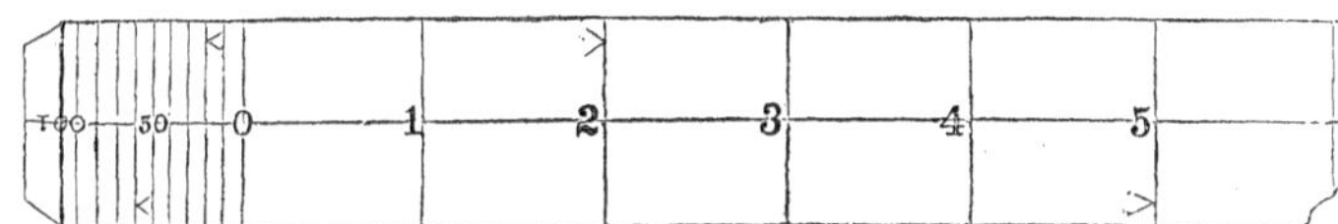

off on it a number of equal parts, each representing a chain to the desired scale. Sub-divide the left hand division into ten equal parts, each of which will therefore represent ten links to this scale. Through each point of division on the central line, draw (with the T square) perpendiculars extending to the edges, and the scale is made. It explains itself. The above figure is a scale of 2 chains to 1 inch. On it the distance 220 links would extend between the arrow-heads above the line in the figure; 560 links extends between the lower arrow-heads, &c.

A paper scale has the great advantage of varying less from a plat which has been made by it, in consequence of changes in the weather, than any other. The mean of many trials showed the difference between such a scale and drawing paper, when exposed alternately to the damp open atmosphere, and to the air of a warm dry room, to be equal to .005, while that between box-wood scales and the paper was .012, or nearly $2\frac{1}{2}$ times as much. The difference with ivory would have been even greater.

Some of the more usual platting scales are here given in their actual dimensions.

In these five figures, different methods of drawing the scales have been given, but each method may be applied to any scale. The first and second, being the most simple, are generally the best. In the third the subdivisions are made by a diagonal line: the distances between the various pairs of arrow heads, beginning with the uppermost, are, respectively, 310, 540, and 270 links.

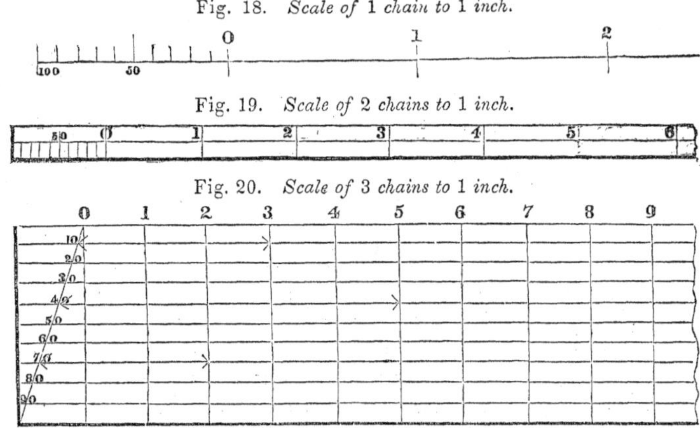

Fig. 18. *Scale of* 1 *chain to* 1 *inch.*

Fig. 19. *Scale of* 2 *chains to* 1 *inch.*

Fig. 20. *Scale of* 3 *chains to* 1 *inch.*

In the fourth figure the distances between the arrow heads are respectively 310, 270, and 540 links.

Fig. 21. *Scale of* 4 *chains to* 1 *inch.*

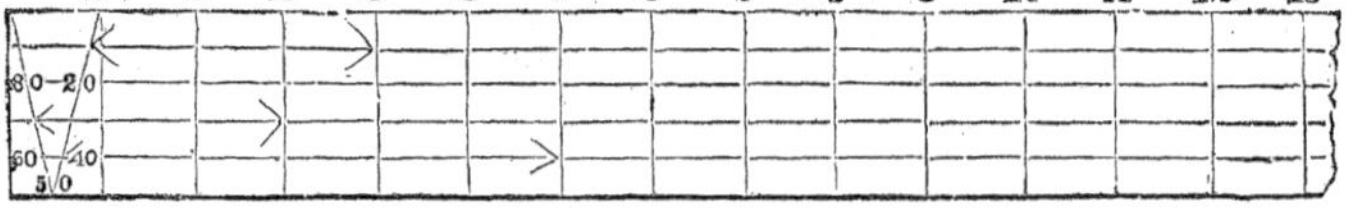

In the fifth figure the scale of 5 chains to 1 inch is subdivided diagonally to only every quarter chain, or 25 links. The distance between the upper pair of arrow-heads on it is $12\frac{1}{4}$ chains, or 12.25; between the next pair of arrow-heads, it is 6.50; and between the lower pair, 14.75.

Fig. 22. *Scale of* 5 *chains to* 1 *inch.*

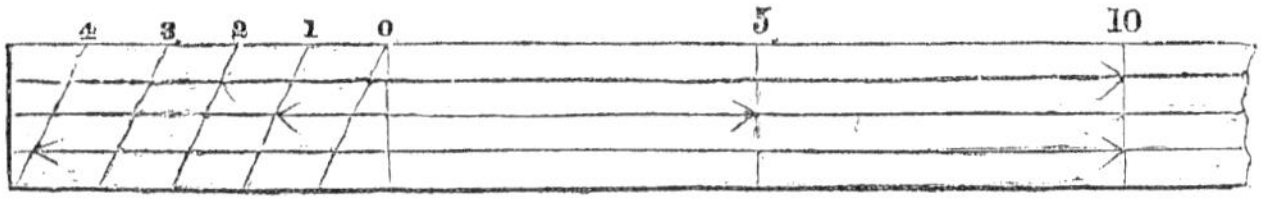

A diagonal scale for dividing an inch, or a half inch, into 100 equal parts, is found on the "Plain scale" in every case of instruments.

(50) Vernier Scale. This is an ingenious substitute for the diagonal scale. The one given in the following figure divides an inch into 100 equal parts, and if each inch be supposed to represent a chain, it gives single links.

Fig. 23.

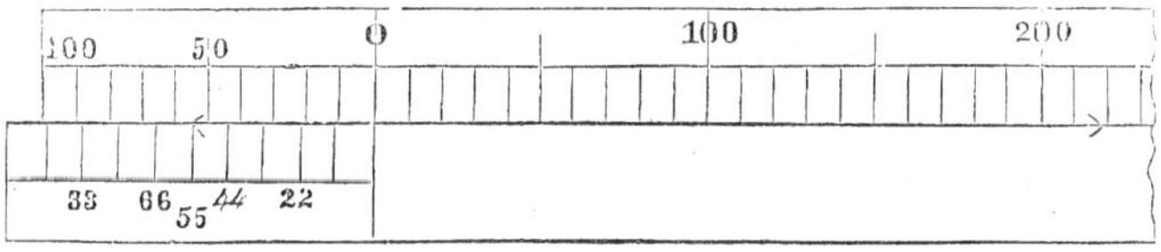

Make a scale of an inch divided into tenths, as in the upper scale of the above figure. Take in the dividers eleven of these divisions, and set off this distance from the 0 of the scale to the left of it. Divide the distance thus set off into 10 equal parts. Each of them will be one tenth of eleven tenths of one inch; i. e. eleven hundredths, or a tenth and a hundredth, and the first division on the short, or vernier scale, will overlap, or be longer than the first division on the long scale, by just *one* hundredth of an inch; the second division will overlap *two* hundredths, and so on. The principle will be more fully developed in treating of "Verniers," Part IV, Chapter II.

Now suppose we wish to take off from this scale 275 hundredths of an inch. To get the last figure, we must take five divisions on the lower scale, which will be 55 hundredths, for the reason just given. 220 will remain which are to be taken from the upper scale, and the entire number will be obtained at once by extending the dividers between the arrow-heads in the figure from 220 on the upper scale (measuring along its lower side) to 55 on the lower scale, 254 would extend from 210 on the upper scale to 44 on the lower. 318 would extend from 230 on the upper scale to 88 on the lower. Always begin then with subtracting 11 times the last figure from the given number; find the remainders on the upper scale, and the number subtracted on the lower scale.

(51) A plat is sometimes made by a nominally reduced scale in the following manner. Suppose that the scale of the plat is to be ten chains to one inch, and that a diagonal scale of inches, divided into tenths and hundredths, is the only one at hand. By dividing all the distances by ten, this scale can then be used without any further reduction. But if the content is measured from the plat to the same scale, in the manner explained in the next chapter, the result must be multiplied by 10 times 10. This is called by old Surveyors "Raising the scale," or "Restoring true measure."

(52) Sectoral Scales. The *Sector*, (called by the French "Compass of Proportion"), is an instrument sometimes convenient for obtaining a scale of equal parts. It is in two portions, turning on a hinge, like a carpenter's pocket rule. It contains a great number of scales, but the one intended for this use is lettered at its ends L in English instruments, and consists of two lines running from the centre to the ends of the scale, and each divided into ten equal parts, each of which is again subdivided into 10, so that each leg of the scale contains 100 equal parts. To illustrate its use, suppose that a scale of 7 chains to 1 inch is required. Take 1 inch in the dividers, and open the sector till this distance will just reach from the 7 on one leg to the 7 on the other. The sector is then "*set*" for this

Fig. 24.

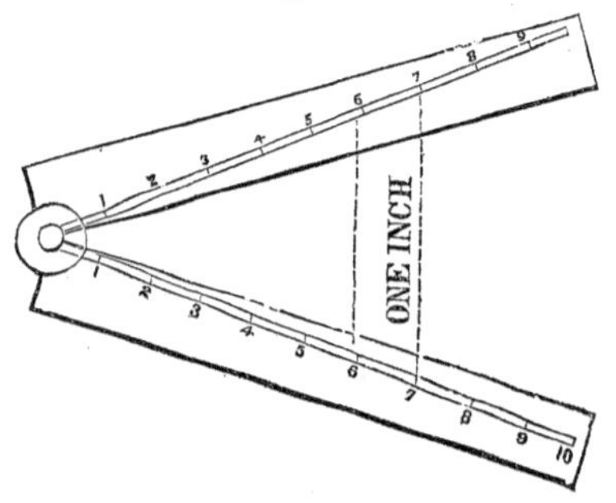

scale, and the angle of its opening must not be again changed. Now let a distance of 580 links be required. Open the dividers till they reach from 58 to 58 on the two legs, as in the dotted line in the figure, and it is the required distance. Again, suppose that a scale of $2\frac{1}{2}$ chains to one inch is desired. Open the sector so that 1 inch shall extend from 25 to 25. Any other scale may be obtained in the same manner.

Conversely, the length of any known line to any desired scale can thus be readily determined.

(53) Whatever scale may be adopted for platting the survey, it should be drawn on the map, both for convenience of reference, and in order that the contraction and expansion, caused by changes in the quantity of moisture in the atmosphere, may affect the scale and the map alike. When the drawing paper has been wet and glued to a board, and cut off when the map is completed, its contractions have been found by many observations to average from one-fourth to one-half per cent. on a scale of 3 chains to an inch, (1:2376), which would therefore require an allowance of from one-half perch to one perch per acre.

A scale made as directed in Art. (49), if used to make a plat on unstretched paper, and then kept with the plat, will answer nearly the same purpose.

Such a scale may be attached to a map, by slipping it through two or three cuts in the lower part of the sheet, and will be a very convenient substitute for a pair of dividers in measuring any distance upon it.

(54) Scale omitted. It may be required to find the unknown scale to which a given map has been drawn, its superficial content being known. Assume any convenient scale, measure the lines of the map by it, and find the content by the methods to be given in the next chapter, proceeding as if the assumed scale were the true one. Then make this proportion, founded on the geometrical principle that the areas of similar figures are as the squares of their corresponding sides: *As* the content found *Is* to the given content *So is* the square of the assumed scale *To* the square of the true scale.

CHAPTER IV.

CALCULATING THE CONTENT.

(55) The CONTENT of a piece of ground is its superficial *area*, or the number of square feet, yards, acres, or miles which it contains.

(56) Horizontal Measurement. All ground, however inclined or uneven its surface may be, should be measured horizontally, or as if brought down to a horizontal plane, so that the surface of a hill, thus measured, would give the same content as the level base on which it may be supposed to stand, or as the figure which would be formed on a level surface beneath it by dropping plumb lines from every point of it.

This method of procedure is required for both Geometrical and Social reasons.

Geometrically, it is plain that this horizontal measurement is absolutely necessary for the purpose of obtaining a correct plat. In Fig. 25, let ABCD, and BCEF, be two square lots of ground, platted horizontally. Suppose the ground to slope in all directions from the point C, which is the summit of a hill. Then the lines BC, DC, measured on the slope, are longer than if measured on a level, and the field ABCD, of Fig. 25, platted with these long lines, would take the shape ABGD in Fig. 26; and the field BCEF, of Fig. 25, would become BHEF of Fig. 26. The two adjoining fields would thus overlap each other; and the same difficulty would occur in every case of platting any two adjoining fields by the measurements made on the slope.

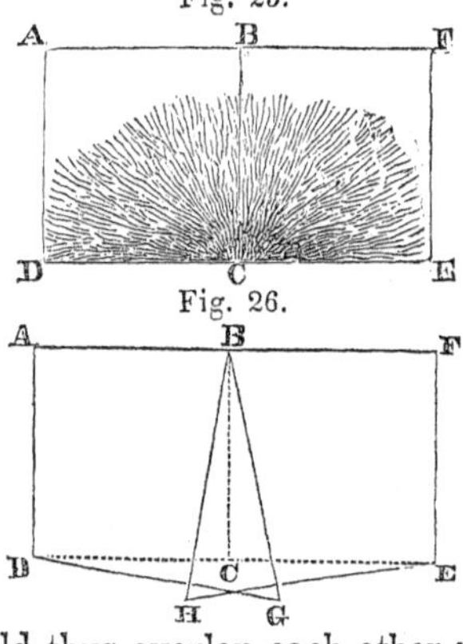

Let us suppose another case, more simple than would ever occur in practice, that of a three-sided field, of equal sides and composed of three portions each sloping down uniformly, (at the rate of one to one) from one point in the centre, as in Fig. 27. Each slope being accurately platted, the three could not come together, but would be separated as in Fig. 28.

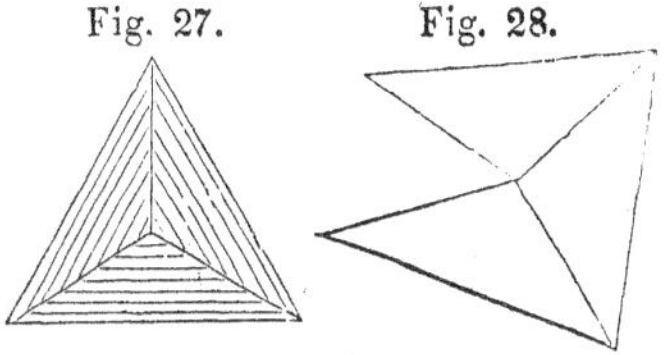
Fig. 27. Fig. 28.

We have here taken the most simple cases, those of uniform slopes. But with the common irregularities of uneven ground, to measure its actual surface would not only be improper, but impossible.

In the *Social* aspect of this question, the horizontal measurement is justified by the fact that no more houses can be built on a hill than could be built on its flat base; and that no more trees, corn, or other plants, which shoot up vertically, can grow on it; as is represented by the vertical lines in the Figure.* Even if a side hill should produce more of certain creeping plants, the increased difficulty in their cultivation might perhaps balance this. For this reason the surface of the soil thus measured is sometimes called *the productive base* of the ground.

Fig. 29.

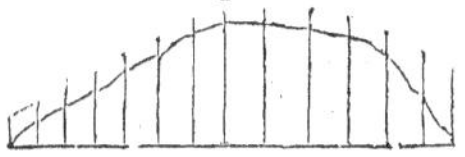

Again, a piece of land containing a hill and a hollow, if measured on the surface would give a larger content than it would after the hollow had been filled up by the hill, while it would yet really be of greater value than before.

Horizontal measurement is called the "Method of Cultellation," and Superficial measurement, the "Method of Developement."†

An act of the State of New-York prescribes that "The acre, for land measure, shall be measured horizontally."

* This question is more than two thousand years old, for Polybius writes, "Some even of those who are employed in the administration of states, or placed at the head of armies, imagine that unequal and hilly ground will contain more houses than a surface which is flat and level. This, however, is not the truth. For the houses being raised in a vertical line, form right angles, not with the declivity of the ground, but with the flat surface which lies below, and upon which the hills themselves also stand."

† The former from *Cultellum*, a knife, as if the hills were sliced off; the latter so named because it strips off or unfolds, as it were, the surface.

(57) Unit of Content. The *Acre* is the unit of land-measurement. It contains 4 Roods. A *Rood* contains 40 Perches. A *Perch* is a square Rod; otherwise called a Perch, or Pole. A *Rod* is $5\frac{1}{2}$ yards, or $16\frac{1}{2}$ feet.

Hence, 1 acre = 4 Roods = 160 Perches = 4,840 square yards = 43,560 square feet.

One square mile = 5280 × 5280 feet = 640 acres.

Since a chain is 66 feet long, a square chain contains 4356 square feet; and consequently *ten square chains make one acre.**

In different parts of England, the acre varies greatly. The statute acre, as in the United States, contains 160 square perches of $16\frac{1}{2}$ feet, or 43,560 square feet. The acre of Devonshire and Somersetshire, contains 160 perches of 15 feet, or 36,000 square feet. The acre of Cornwall is 160 perches of 18 feet, or 51,840 square feet. The acre of Lancashire is 160 perches of 21 feet, or 70,560 square feet. The acre of Cheshire and Staffordshire, is 160 perches of 24 feet, or 92,160 square feet. The acre of Wiltshire is 120 perches of $16\frac{1}{2}$ feet, or 32,670 square feet. The acre in Scotland consists of 10 square chains, each of 74 feet, and therefore contains 54,760 square feet. The acre in Ireland is the same as the Lancashire. The chain is 84 feet long.

The French units of land-measure are the *Are* = 100 square *Metres*, = 0.0247 acre, = one fortieth of an acre, nearly; and the *Hectare* = 100 *Ares* = 2.47 acres, or nearly two and a half. Their old land-measures were the "Arpent of Paris," containing 36,800 square feet; and the "Arpent of Waters and Woods," containing 55,000 square feet.

(58) When the content of a piece of land (obtained by any of the methods to be explained presently) is given in square links, as is customary, cut off four figures on the right, (i. e. divide by 10,000), to get it into square chains and decimal parts of a chain; cut off the right hand figure of the *square chains*, and the remaining figures will be *Acres*. Multiply the remainder by 4, and the figure, if any, outside of the new decimal point will be *Roods.*

* Let the young student beware of confounding 10 square chains with 10 chains square. The former make one acre; the latter space contains ten acres.

Multiply the remainder by 40, and the outside figures will be *Perches*. The nearest round number is usually taken for the Perches; fractions less than a half perch being disregarded.*

Thus, 86.22 square chains = 8 Acres 2 Roods 20 Perches.
Also, 64.1818 do. = 6 A. 1 R. 27 P.
" 43.7564 do. = 4 A. 1 R. 20 P.
" 71.1055 do. = 7 A. 0 R. 18 P.
" 82.50 do. = 8 A. 1 R. 0 P.
" 8.250 do. = 0 A. 3 R. 12 P.
" 0.8250 do. = 0 A. 0 R. 13 P.

(59) The following Table gives by mere inspection the Roods and Perches corresponding to the Decimal parts of an Acre. It explains itself.

Decimal parts of an acre.	ROODS.				Perches.
	0	1	2	3	
	.000	.250	.500	.750	+ 0
	.006	.256	.506	.756	+ 1
	.012	.262	.512	.762	+ 2
	.019	.269	.519	.769	+ 3
	.025	.275	.525	.775	+ 4
	.031	.281	.531	.781	+ 5
	.037	.287	.537	.787	+ 6
	.044	.294	.544	.794	+ 7
	.050	.300	.550	.800	+ 8
	.056	.306	.556	.806	+ 9
	.062	.312	.562	.812	+10
	.069	.319	.569	.819	+11
	.075	.325	.575	.825	+12
	.081	.331	.581	.831	+13
	.087	.337	.587	.837	+14
	.094	.344	.594	.844	+15
	.100	.350	.600	.850	+16
	.106	.356	.606	.856	+17
	.112	.362	.612	.862	+18
	.119	.369	.619	.869	+19
	.125	.375	.625	.875	+20

Decimal parts of an acre.	ROODS.				Perches.
	0	1	2	3	
	.131	.381	.631	.881	+21
	.137	.387	.637	.887	+22
	.144	.394	.644	.894	+23
	.150	.400	.650	.900	+24
	.156	.406	.656	.906	+25
	.162	.412	.662	.912	+26
	.169	.419	.669	.919	+27
	.175	.425	.675	.925	+28
	.181	.431	.681	.931	+29
	.187	.437	.687	.937	+30
	.194	.444	.694	.944	+31
	.200	.450	.700	.950	+32
	.206	.456	.706	.956	+33
	.212	.462	.712	.962	+34
	.219	.469	.719	.969	+35
	.225	.475	.725	.975	+36
	.231	.481	.731	.981	+37
	.237	.487	.737	.987	+38
	.244	.494	.744	.994	+39
	.250	.500	.750	1.000	+40

(60) Chain Correction. When a survey has been made, and the plat has been drawn, and the content calculated; and after-

* To reduce square yards to acres, instead of dividing by 4840, it is easier, and very nearly correct, to multiply by 2, cut off four figures, and add to this product one-third of one-tenth of itself.

wards the chain is found to have been incorrect, too short or too long, the true content of the land, may be found by this proportion: *As* the square of the length of the standard given by the incorrect chain *Is to* the square of the true length of the standard *So is* the calculated content *To* the true content. Thus, suppose that the chain used had been so stretched that the standard distance measured by it appears to be only 99 links long; and that a square field had been measured by it, each side containing 10 of these long chains, and that it had been so platted. This plat, and therefore the content calculated from it, will be smaller than it should be, and the correct content will be found by the proportion $99^2 : 100^2 :: 100$ sq. chains : 102.03 square chains. If the chain had been stretched so as to be 101 *true* links long, as found by comparing it with a correct chain, the content would be given by this proportion: $100^2 : 101^2 ::$ 100 square chains : 102.01 square chains. In the former case, the elongation of the chain was $1\frac{1}{99}$ true links; and $100^2 : (101\frac{1}{99})^2 ::$ 100 square chains : 102.03 square chains.

(61) Boundary Lines. The lines which are to be considered as bounding the land to be surveyed, are often very uncertain, unless specified by the title deeds.

If the boundary be a brook, the middle of it is usually the boundary line. On tide-waters, the land is usually considered to extend to low water mark.

Where hedges and ditches are the boundaries of fields, as is almost universally the case in England, the dividing line is generally the top edge of the ditch farthest from the hedge, both hedge and ditch belonging to the field on the hedge side. This varies, however, with the customs of the locality. From three to six feet from the roots of the quickwood of the hedges are allowed for the ditches.

METHODS OF CALCULATION.

(62) The various methods employed in calculating the content of a piece of ground, may be reduced to four, which may be called *Arithmetical*, *Geometrical*, *Instrumental*, and *Trigonometrical*.

(63) FIRST METHOD.—ARITHMETICALLY. *From direct measurements of the necessary lines on the ground.*

The figures to be calculated by this method may be either the shapes of the fields which are measured, or those into which the fields can be divided by measuring various lines across them.

The familiar rules of mensuration for the principal figures which occur in practice, will be now briefly enunciated.

(64) Rectangles. If the piece of ground be rectangular in shape, its content is found by multiplying its length by its breadth.

(65) Triangles. When the given quantities are one side of a triangle and the perpendicular distance to it from the opposite angle; the content of the triangle is equal to half the product of the side and the perpendicular.

When the given quantities are the three sides of the triangle; add together the three sides and divide the sum by 2; from this half sum subtract each of the three sides in turn; multiply together the half sum and the three remainders; take the square root of the product; it is the content required. If the sides of the triangle be designated by a, b, c, and their sum by s, this rule will give its area $= \sqrt{[\frac{1}{2}s\,(\frac{1}{2}s - a)\,(\frac{1}{2}s - b)\,(\frac{1}{2}s - c)]}$.*

Fig. 30.

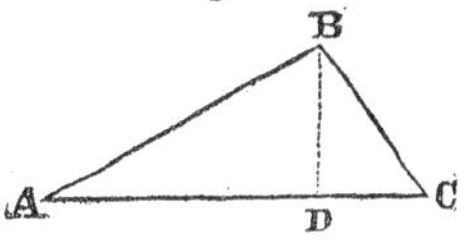

* When two sides of a triangle, and the included angle are given, its content equals half the product of its sides into the sine of the included angle. Designating the angles of the triangle by the capital letters A,B,C, and the sides opposite them by the corresponding small letters a,b,c, the area $= \frac{1}{2}\, bc$ sin. A.

When one side of a triangle and the adjacent angles are given, its content equals the square of the given side multiplied by the sines of each of the given angles, and divided by twice the sine of the sum of these angles. Using the same symbols as before, the area $= a^2 \dfrac{\text{sin. B . sin. C}}{2\,\text{sin. (B + C)}}$

When the three angles of a triangle and its altitude are given, its area, referring to the above figure, $= \frac{1}{2}\,\text{BD}^2 \cdot \dfrac{\text{sin. B}}{\text{sin. A . sin. C}}$.

(66) **Parallelograms**; or four-sided figures whose opposite sides are parallel. The content of a Parallelogram equals the product of one of its sides by the perpendicular distance between it and the side parallel to it.

(67) **Trapezoids**; or four-sided figures, two opposite sides of which are parallel. The content of a Trapezoid equals half the product of the sum of the parallel sides by the perpendicular distance between them.

If the given quantities are the four sides a, b, c, d, of which b and d are parallel; then, making $q = \frac{1}{2}(a + b + c - d)$, the area of the trapezoid will $= \frac{b+d}{b-d}\sqrt{[q(q-a)(q-c)(q-b+d).]}$*

(68) **Quadrilaterals, or Trapeziums**; four-sided figures, none of whose sides are parallel.

A very gross error, often committed as to this figure, is to take the average, or half sum of its opposite sides, and multiply them together for the area: thus, assuming the trapezium to be equivalent to a rectangle with these averages for sides.

In practical surveying, it is usual to measure a line across it from corner to corner, thus dividing it into two triangles, whose sides are known, and which can therefore be calculated by Art. (65).†

* When two parallel sides, b and d, and a third side, a, are given, and also the angle, C, which this third side makes with one of the parallel sides, then the content of the trapezoid$=\frac{b+d}{2} \,.\, a \,.\, \text{sin. C}$.

† *When two opposite sides, and all the angles are given*, take one side and its adjacent angles, (or their supplements, when their sum exceeds 180°), consider them as belonging to a triangle, and find its area by the second formula in the note on page 43. Do the same with the other side and its adjacent angles. The difference of the two areas will be the area of the quadrilateral.

When three sides and their two included angles are given, multiply together the sine of one given angle and its adjacent sides. Do the same with the sine of the other given angle and its adjacent sides. Multiply together the two opposite sides and the sine of the supplement of the sum of the given angles. Add together the first two products, and add also the last product, if the sum of the given angles is more than 180°, or subtract it if this sum be less, and take half the result. Calling the given sides, p, q, r; and the angle between p and q = A; and the angle between q and r = B; the area of the quadrilateral

$$= \tfrac{1}{2}\,[p \,.\, q \,.\, \text{sin. A} + q \,.\, r \,.\, \text{sin. B} \pm p \,.\, r \,.\, \text{sin.}\,(180^\circ - \text{A} - \text{B})].$$

When the four sides and the sum of any two opposite angles are given, proceed thus: Take half the sum of the four given sides, and from it subtract each side in turn Multiply together the four remainders, and reserve the product. Multiply together the four sides. Take half their product, and multiply it by the cosine of the given sum of the angles increased by unity. Regard the sign of

(69) *Surfaces bounded by irregularly curved lines.* The rules for these will be more appropriately given in connection with the surveys which measure the necessary lines; as explained in Part II, Chap. III.

(70) SECOND METHOD.—GEOMETRICALLY. *From measurements of the necessary lines upon the plat.*

(71) Division into Triangles. The plat of a piece of ground having been drawn from the measurements made by any of the methods which will be hereafter explained, lines may be drawn upon the plat so as to divide it into a number of triangles. Four

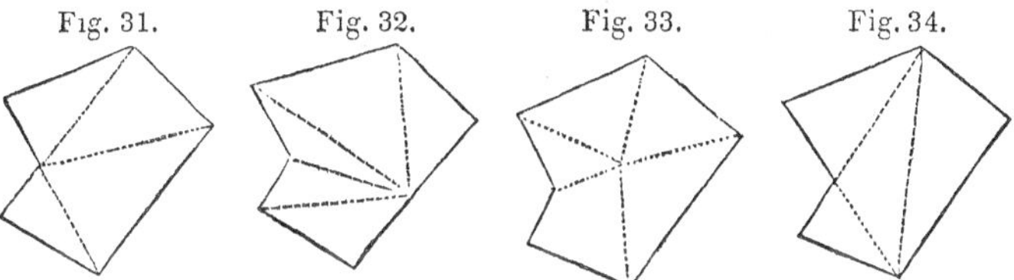
Fig. 31. Fig. 32. Fig. 33. Fig. 34.

ways of doing this are shown in the figures: viz. by drawing lines from one corner to the other corners; from a point in one of the sides to the corners; from a point inside of the figure to the corners; and from various corners to other corners. The last method is usually the best. The lines ought to be drawn so as to make the triangles as nearly equilateral as possible, for the reasons given in Part V.

One side of each of these triangles, and the length of the perpendicular let fall upon it, being then measured, as directed in Art. (43,) the content of these triangles can be at once obtained by multiplying their base by their altitude, and dividing by two.

The easiest method of getting the length of the perpendicular, without actually drawing it, is, to set one point of the dividers at the angle from which a perpendicular is to be let fall, and to

the cosine. Subtract this product from the reserved product, and take the square root of the remainder. It will be the area of the quadrilateral.

When the four sides, and the angle of intersection of the diagonals of the quadrilateral are given; square each side; add together the squares of the opposite sides; take the difference of the two sums; multiply it by the tangent of the angle of intersection, and divide by four. The quotient will be the area.

When the diagonals of the quadrilateral, and their included angle are given, multiply together the two diagonals and the sine of their included angle, and divide by two. The quotient will be the area.

open and shut their legs till an arc described by the other point will just touch the opposite side.

Otherwise; a platting scale, (described in Art. **(49)** may be placed so that the zero point of its edge coincides with the angle, and one of its cross lines coincides with the side to which a perpendicular is to be drawn. The length of the perpendicular can then at once be read off.

The method of dividing the plat into triangles is the one most commonly employed by surveyors for obtaining the content of a survey, because of the simplicity of the calculations required. Its correctness, however, is dependant on the accuracy of the plat, and on its scale, which should be as large as possible. Three chains to an inch is the smallest scale allowed by the English Tithe Commissioners for plats from which the content is to be determined.

In calculating in this way the content of a farm, and also of its separate fields, the sum of the latter ought to equal the former. A difference of one three-hundredth ($\frac{1}{300}$) is considered allowable.

Some surveyors measure the perpendiculars of the triangles by a scale half of that to which the plat is made. Thus, if the scale of the plat be 2 chains to the inch, the perpendiculars are measured with a scale of one chain to the inch. The product of the base by the perpendicular thus measured, gives the area of the triangle at once, without its requiring to be divided by two.

Another way of attaining the same end, with less danger of mistakes, is, to construct a *new* scale of equal parts, longer than those by which the plat was made in the ratio $\sqrt{2}:1$; or $1.414:1$. When the base and perpendicular of a triangle are measured by this new scale and then multiplied together, the product will be the content of the triangle, without any division by two. In this method there is the additional advantage of the greater size and consequent greater distinctness of the scale.

When the measurement of a plat is made some time after it has been drawn, the paper will very probably have contracted or expanded so that the scale used will not exactly apply. In that case a correction is necessary. Measure very precisely the present length of some line on the plat, of known length originally. Then make this proportion: *As* the square of the present length of this line *Is to* the square of its original length, *So is* the content obtain ed by the present measurement *To* the true content.

(72) *Graphical Multiplication.* Prepare a strip of drawing paper, of a width exactly equal to two chains on the scale of the plat; i. e. one inch wide, as in the figure, for a scale of two chains to 1 inch; two-thirds of an inch wide for a scale of 3 chains; half an inch for 4 chains; and so on. Draw perpendicular lines across the paper at distances representing one-tenth of a chain on the scale of the triangle to be measured, thus making a platting scale. Apply it to the triangle so that one edge of the scale shall pass through one corner, A, of the triangle, and the other edge through another

Fig. 35.

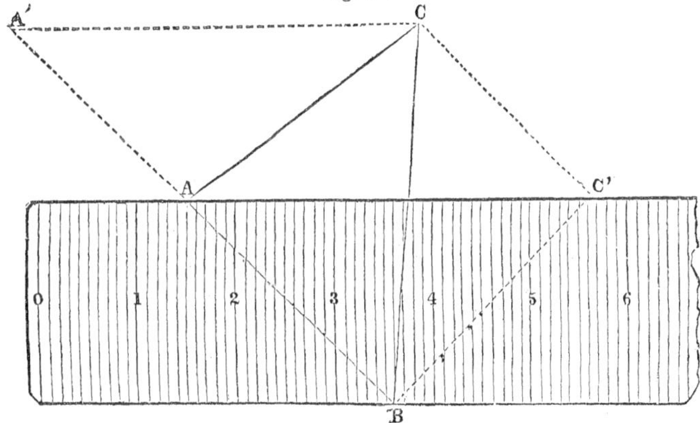

corner, B; and note very precisely what divisions of the scale are at these points. Then slide the scale in such a way that the points of the scale which had coincided with A and B, shall always remain on the line BA produced, till the edge arrives at the point C. Then will A'C, that is, the distance, or number of divisions on the scale, from the point to which the division A on the scale has arrived, to the third corner of the triangle, express the area of the triangle ABC in square chains.*

*For, from C draw a parallel to AB, meeting the edge of the scale in C', and draw C'B. Then the given triangle ABC = ABC'. But the area of this last triangle = AC' multiplied by half the width of the scale, i. e. = AC' × 1 = AC'. But, because of the parallels, A'C = AC'. Therefore the area of the given triangle ABC = A'C i. e. it is equal in square chains to the number of linear chains read off from the scale. This ingenious operation is due to *M. Cousinery.*

(73) Division into Trapezoids. A line may be drawn across the field, as in Fig. 36, and perpendiculars drawn to it. The field will thus be divided into trapezoids, (excepting a triangle at each end), and their content can be calculated by Art. (67).

Fig. 36.

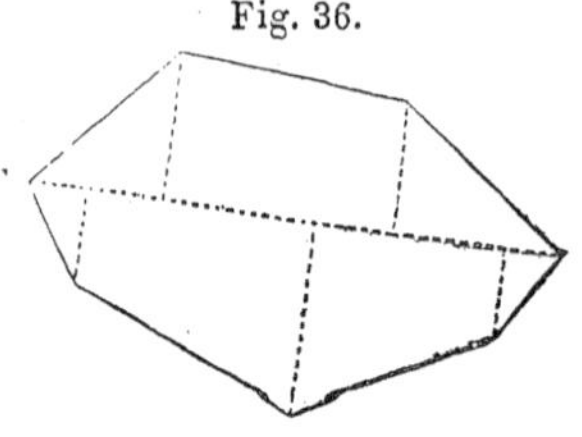

Otherwise; a line may be drawn outside of the figure, and perpendiculars to it be drawn from each angle. In that case the difference between the trapezoids formed by lines drawn to the outer angles of the figure, and those drawn to the inner angles, will be the content.

Fig. 37.

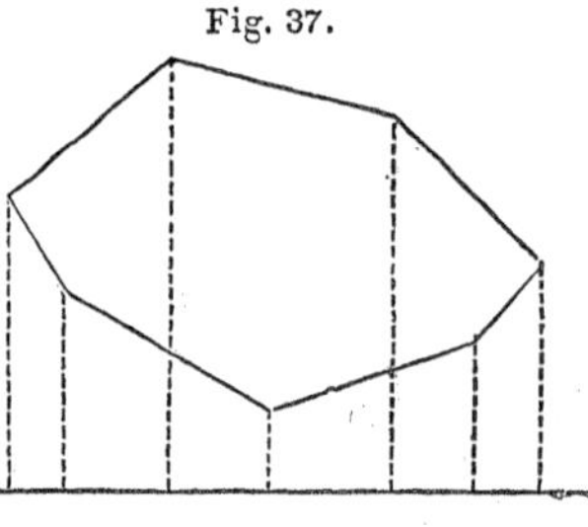

This method is very advantageously applied to surveys by the compass; as will be explained in Part III, Chap. VI.

(74) Division into Squares. Two sets of parallel lines, at right angles to each other, one chain apart (to the scale of the plat) may be drawn over the plat, so as to divide it into squares, as in the figure. The number of squares which fall within the plat represent so many square chains; and the triangles and trapezoids which fall outside of these, may then be calculated and added to the entire square chains which have been counted.

Fig. 38.

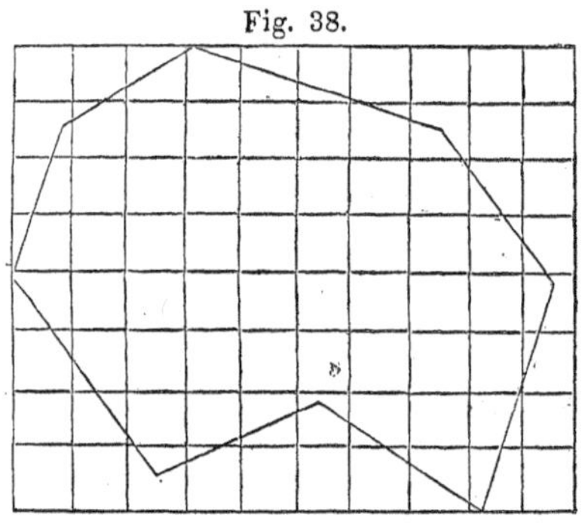

Instead of drawing the parallel lines on the plat, they may better be drawn on a piece of transparent "tracing paper," which is simply laid upon the plat, and the squares counted as before. The same paper will answer for any number of plats drawn to the same scale. This method is a valuable and easy check on the results of other calculations.

To calculate the fractional parts, prepare a piece of tracing paper, or horn, by drawing on it one square of the same size as a square of the plat, and subdividing it, by two sets of ten parallels at right angles to each other, into hundredths. This will measure the fractions remaining from the former measurement, as nearly as can be desired.

(75) Division into Parallelograms. Draw a series of parallel lines across the plat at equal distances depending on the scale. Thus, for a plat made to a scale of 2 chains to 1 inch, the distance between the parallels should be $2\frac{1}{2}$ inches; for a scale of 3 chains to 1 inch, $1\frac{1}{9}$ inch; for a scale of 4 chains to 1 inch, $\frac{5}{8}$ inch; for a scale of 5 chains to 1 inch, $\frac{4}{10}$ inch; and for any scale, make the distance between the parallels that fraction of an inch which would be expressed by 10 divided by the square of the number of chains to the inch. Then apply a common inch scale, divided on the edge into tenths, to these parallels; and every inch in length of the spaces included between each pair of them will be an acre, and every tenth of an inch will be a square chain.*

To measure the triangles at the ends of the strips between the parallels, prepare a piece of transparent horn, or stout tracing paper, of a width equal to the width between the parallels, and draw a line through its middle longitudinally. Apply it to the oblique line at the end of the space between two parallels, and it will bisect the line, and thus reduce the triangle to an equivalent rectangle, as at A in the figure. When an angle occurs between two parallels, as at B in the figure, the fractional part may be measured by any of the preceding methods.

Fig. 39.

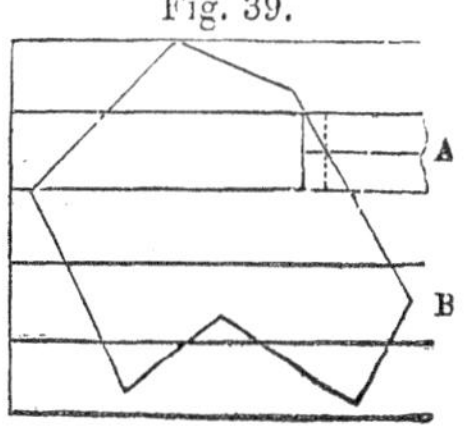

* For, calling the number of chains to the inch, $= n$, and making the width between the parallels $\frac{10}{n^2}$ inch, this width will represent $\frac{10}{n^2} \times n = \frac{10}{n}$ chains; and as the inch length represents n chains, their product, $\frac{10}{n} \times n = 10$ square chains $= 1$ acre.

A somewhat similar method is much used by some surveyors, particularly in Ireland: the plat being made on a scale of 5 chains to 1 inch, parallel lines being drawn on it, half an inch apart, and the distances along the parallels being measured by a scale, each large division of which is $\frac{8}{10}$ inch in length. Each division of this scale indicates an acre; for it represents 4 chains, and the distance between the parallels is $2\frac{1}{2}$ chains. This scale is called the "Scale of Acres."

(76) Addition of Widths. When the lines of the plat are very irregularly curved, as in the figure, draw across it a number of equi-distant lines as near together as the case may seem to require. Take a straight-edged piece of paper, and apply one edge of it to the middle of the first space, and mark its length from one end; apply the same edge to the middle of the next space, bringing the mark just made to one end, and making another mark at the end of the additional length; so go on, adding the length of each space to the previous ones. When all have been thus measured, the total length, multiplied by the uniform width, will give the content.

Fig. 40.

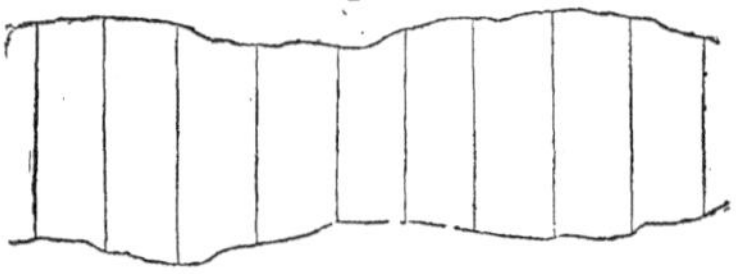

(77) THIRD METHOD.—INSTRUMENTALLY. *By performing certain instrumental operations on the plat.*

(78) *Reduction of a many sided figure to a single equivalent triangle.* Any plane figure bounded by straight lines may be reduced to a single triangle, which shall have the same content. This can be done by any instrument for drawing parallel lines, such as those described in Art. (39). Let the trapezium, or four sided figure, shown in Fig. 41, be required to be reduced to a single equivalent triangle. Produce one side of the figure, as 4——1. Draw a line from the first to the third angle of

Fig. 41.

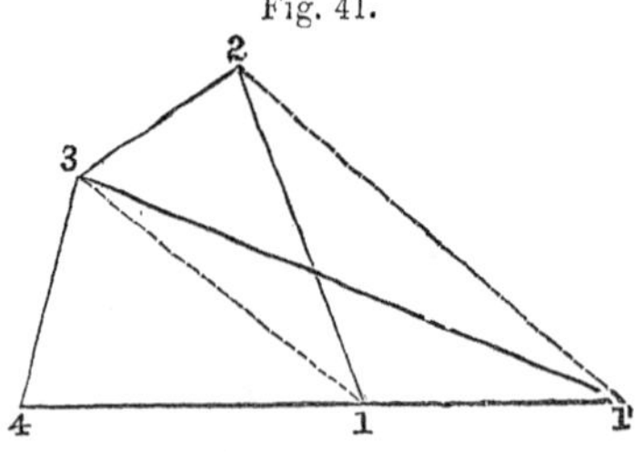

the figure. From the second angle draw a parallel to the line just drawn, cutting the produced side in a point 1′. From the point 1′ draw a line to the third angle. A triangle (1′—3—4 in the figure) will thus be formed, which will be equivalent to the original trapezium.*

The content of this final triangle can then be found by measuring its perpendicular, and taking half the product of this perpendicular by the base, as in the first paragraph of Art. (65).

(79) Let the given figure have five sides, as in Fig. 42. For brevity, the angles of the figure will be named as numbered in the engraving. Produce 5—1. Join 1—3. From 2 draw a parallel to 1—3, cutting the produced base in 1′. Join 1′—4. From 3 draw a parallel to it, cutting the base in 2′. Join 2′—4. Then will the triangle 2′—4—5 be equivalent to the five sided figure 1—2—3—4—5, for similar reasons to those of the preceding case.

Fig. 42.

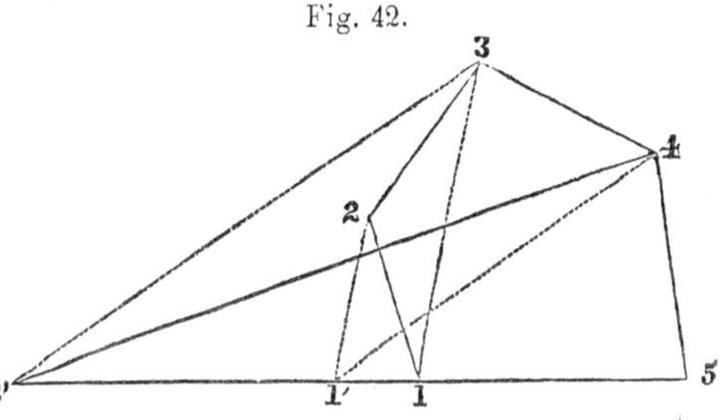

(80) Let the given figure be 1—2—3—4—5—6—7—8, as shown in Fig. 43, given at the top of the following page. All the operations are shown by dotted lines, and the finally resulting triangle 5′—7—8, is equivalent to the original figure of eight sides.

It is best, in choosing the side to be produced, to take one which has a long side adjoining it on the end not produced; so that this long side may form one side of the final triangle, the base of which will therefore be shorter, and will not be cut so acutely by the final line drawn, as to make the point of intersection too indefinite.

* For, the triangle 1—2—3 taken away from the original figure is equivalent to the triangle 1′—1—3 added to it; because both these triangles have the same base and also the same altitude, since the vertices of both lie in the same line parallel to the base.

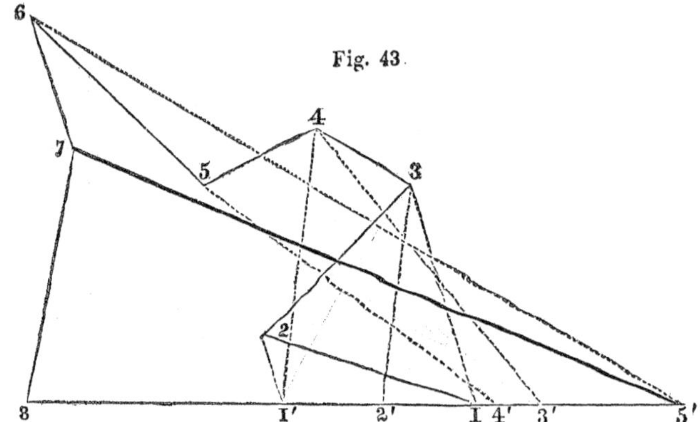

Fig. 43.

(81) *General Rule.* When the given figure has many sides, with angles sometimes salient and sometimes re-entering, the operations of reduction are very liable to errors, if the draftsman attempts to reason out each step. All difficulties, however, will be removed by the following *General Rule:*

1. Produce one side of the figure, and call it a base. Call one of the angles at the base the first angle, and number the rest in regular succession around the figure.

2. Draw a line from the 1st angle to the 3d angle. Draw a parallel to it from the 2d angle. Call the intersections of this parallel with the base the 1st mark.

3. Draw a line from the 1st mark to the 4th angle. Draw a parallel to it from the 3d angle. Its intersection with the base is the 2d mark.

4. Draw a line from the 2d mark to the 5th angle. Draw a parallel to it from the 4th angle. Its intersection with the base is the 3d mark.

5. In general terms, which apply to every step after the first, draw a line from the last mark obtained to the angle whose number is greater by three than the number of the mark. Draw a parallel to it through the angle whose number is greater by two than that of the mark. Its intersection with the base will be a mark whose number is greater by one than that of the preceding mark.*

* In the concise language of Algebra, draw a line from the nth mark to the $n+3$ angle. Draw a parallel to it through the $n+2$ angle, and the intersection with the base will be the $n+1$ mark.

6. Repeat this process for each angle, till you get a mark whose number is such that the angle having a number greater by three is the last angle of the figure, i. e. the angle at the other end of the base. Then join the last mark to the angle which precedes the last angle in the figure, and the triangle thus formed will be the equivalent triangle required.

In practice it is *unnecessary* to actually draw the lines joining the successive angles and marks, but the parallel ruler is merely laid on so as to pass through them, and the points where the parallels cut the base are alone marked.

(82) It is generally more convenient, for the reasons given at the end of Art. **(80)**, to reduce half of the figure on one side and half on the other, as is shown in Fig. 44, which represents the same field as Fig. 42. The equivalent triangle is here 1′—3—2′.

Fig. 44.

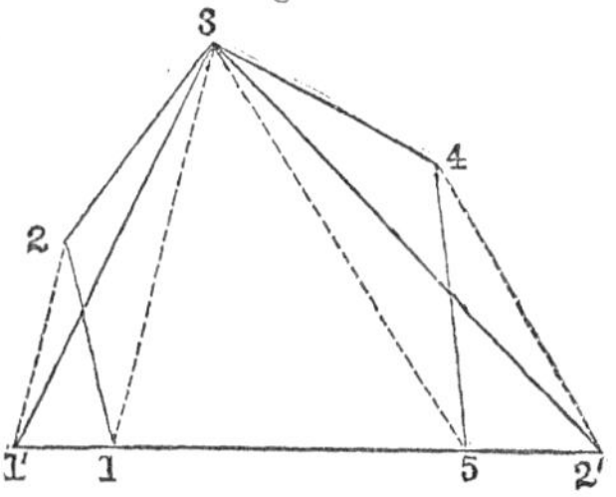

When the figure has many angles, they should not be numbered consecutively all the way around, but, after the numbers have gone around as far as the angle where it is intended to have the vertex

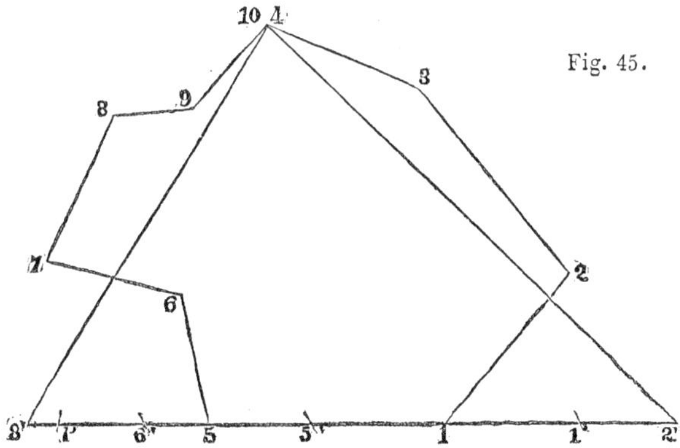

Fig. 45.

of the final triangle, the numbers should be continued from the other angle of the base, as is shown in Fig. 45. In it only the intersections are marked.*

(83) It is sometimes more convenient, not to produce one of the sides of the figure, but to draw at one end of it, as at the point 1 in Fig. 46, an indefinite line, usually a perpendicular to a line

Fig. 46.

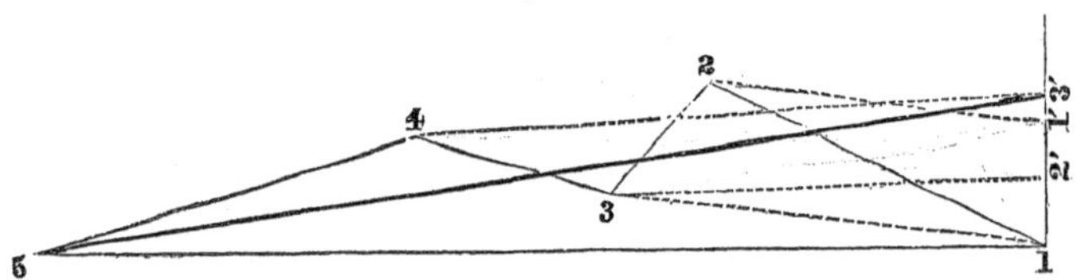

joining two distant angles of the figure, and make this line the base of the equivalent triangle desired. The operation is shown by the dotted lines in the figure. The same General Rule applies to it, as to the previous figures.

(84) Special Instruments. A variety of instruments have been invented for the purpose of determining areas rapidly and correctly. One of the simplest is the "*Computing Scale*," which is on the same principles as the Method of Art. (75). It is represented in Fig. 47, given on the following page. It consists of a scale divided for its whole length from the zero point into divisions, each representing $2\frac{1}{2}$ chains to the scale of the plat. The scale carries a slider, which moves along it, and has a wire drawn across its centre at right angles to the edges of the scale. On each side of this wire, a portion of the slider equal in length to one of the primary, or $2\frac{1}{2}$ chain, divisions of the scale, is laid off and divided into 40 equal parts.

This instrument is used in connection with a sheet of transparent paper, ruled with parallel lines at distances apart each equal to one chain on the scale of the plat. It is plain, that when the

* A figure with curved boundaries may be reduced to a triangle in a similar manner. Straight lines must be drawn about the figure, so as to be partly in it and partly out, giving and taking about equal quantities, so that the figure which these lines form, shall be about equivalent to the curved figure. This having been done, as will be further developed in Art. (124), the equivalent straight lined figure is reduced by the above method.

instrument is laid on this paper, with its edge on one of the parallel lines, and the slider is moved over one of the divisions of $2\frac{1}{2}$ chains, that *one rood*, or a quarter of an acre, has been measured between two of the parallel lines on the paper (since 10 square chains make one acre); and that one of the smaller divisions measures *one perch* between the same parallels. Four of the larger divisions give one acre. The scale is generally made long enough to measure at once five acres.

Fig 47.

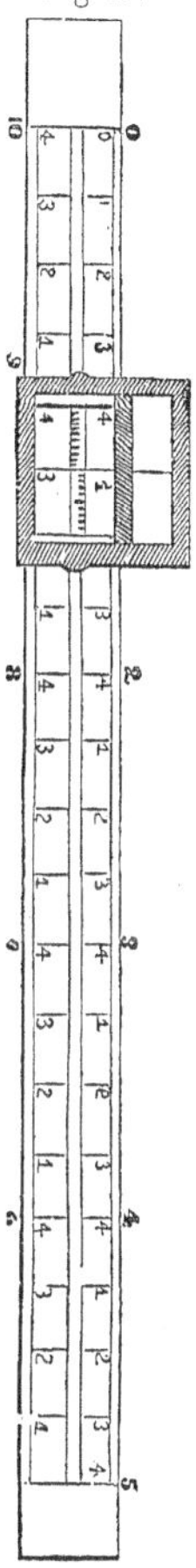

To apply this to the plat of a field, or farm, lay the transparent paper over it in such a position that two of the ruled lines shall touch two of the exterior points of the boundaries, as at A and B. Lay the scale, with the slide set to zero, on the paper, in a direction parallel to the ruled lines, and so that the wire of the slide cuts the left hand oblique line so as to make the spaces *c* and *d* about equal. Hold the scale firm, and move the slider till the wire cuts the right hand oblique line in such a way as to equalize the spaces *e* and *f*. Without changing the slide, move the scale down the width of a space, and to the left hand end of the next space; begin there again, and proceed as before.

Fig. 48.

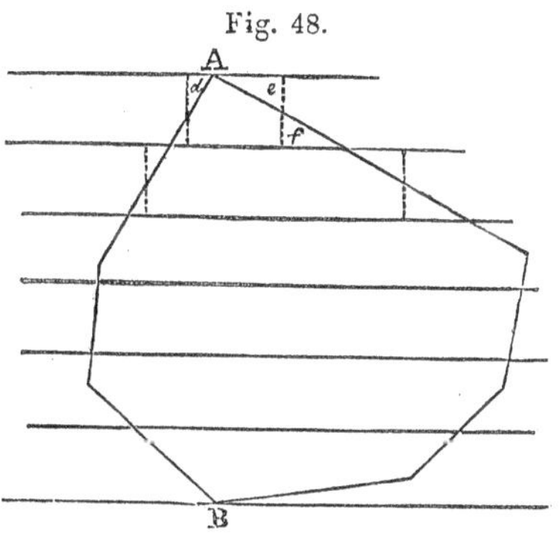

So go on, till the whole length of the scale is run out, (five acres having been measured), and then begin at the right hand side and work backwards to the left, reading the lower divisions, which run up to 10 acres. By continuing this process, the content of plats of any size can be obtained.

A still simpler substitute for this is a scale similarly divided, but without an attached slide. In place of it there is used a piece of horn having a line drawn across it and rivetted to the end of a short scale of box-wood, divided like the former slide. It is used like the former, except that at starting, the zero of the short scale and not the line on the horn is made to coincide with the zero of the long scale. The slide is to be held fast to the instrument when this is moved.

The *Pediometer* is another less simple instrument used for the same object. It measures any quadrilateral directly.

(85) Some very complicated instruments for the same object have been devised. One of them, Sang's *Planometer*, determines the area of any figure, by merely moving a point around the outline of the surface. This causes motion in a train of wheel work, which registers the algebraic sum of the product of ordinates to every point in that perimeter, by the increment of their abscissas, and therefore measures the included space.

Instruments of this kind have been invented in Germany by Ernst, Hansen, and Wetli.

(86) A purely mechanical means of determining the area of any surface by means of its *weight*, may be placed here. The plat is cut out of paper and weighed by a delicate balance. The weight of a rectangular piece of the same paper containing just one acre is also found; and the "Rule of Three" gives the content. A modification of this is to paste a tracing of the plat on thin sheet lead, cut out the lead to the proper lines and weigh it.

(87) FOURTH METHOD.—TRIGONOMETRICALLY. *By calculating, from the observed angles of the boundaries of the piece of ground, the lengths of the lines needed for calculating the content.*

This method is employed for surveys made with angular instruments, as the compass, &c., in order to obtain the content of the land surveyed, without the necessity of previously making a plat, thus avoiding both that trouble and the inaccuracy of any calculations founded upon it. It is therefore the most accurate method; but will be more appropriately explained in Part III, Chapter VI, under the head of "Compass Surveying."

PART II.

CHAIN-SURVEYING;

By the First and Second Methods:

OR

DIAGONAL AND PERPENDICULAR SURVEYING.

(88) The chain alone is abundantly sufficient, without the aid of any other instrument, for making an accurate survey of any surface, whatever its shape or size, particularly in a district tolerably level and clear. Moreover, since a chain, or some substitute for it, formed of a rope, of leather driving reins, &c., can be obtained by any one in the most secluded place, this method of Surveying deserves more attention than has usually been given to it in this country. It will, therefore, be fully developed in the following chapters.

CHAPTER I.

SURVEYING BY DIAGONALS:

OR

By the First Method.

(89) *Surveying by Diagonals* is an application of the *First Method* of determining the position of a point, given in Art. (5,) to which the student should again refer. Each corner of the field or farm which is to be surveyed is "determined" by measuring its distances from two other points. The field is then "platted" by repeating this process on paper, for each corner, in a contrary order, and the "content" is obtained by some of the methods explained in Chapter IV of Part I.

The lines which are measured in order to determine the corners of the field are usually *sides* and *diagonals* of the irregular polygon which is to be surveyed. They therefore divide it up into triangles; whence this mode of surveying is sometimes called "Chain Triangulation."

A few examples will make the principle and practice perfectly clear. Each will be seen to require the three operations of *measuring*, *platting*, and *calculating*.

(90) A three-sided field; as Fig. 49.

Fig. 49.

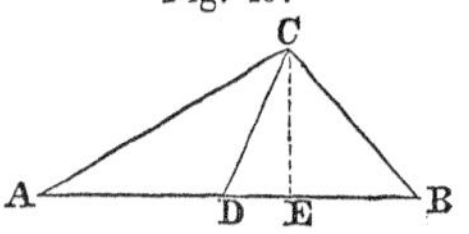

Field-work. Measure the three sides, AB, BC, and CA. Measure also, as a proof line, the distance from one of the corners, as C, to some point in the opposite side, as D, at which a mark should have been left, when measuring from A to B, at a known distance from A. A stick or twig, with a slit in its top, to receive a piece of paper with the distance from A marked on it, is the most convenient mark.

Platting. Choose a suitable scale as directed in Art. (44). Then, by Arts. (42) and (49), draw a line equal in length, on the chosen scale, to one of the sides; AB for example. Take in the compasses the length of another side as AC, to the same scale, and with one leg in A as a centre, describe an arc of a circle. Take the length of the third side BC, and with B as a centre, describe another arc, intersecting the first arc in a point which will be the third corner C. Draw the lines AC and BC; and ABC will be the *plat*, or miniature copy — as explained in Art. (35) — of the field surveyed.

Instead of describing two arcs to get the point C, two pairs of compasses may be conveniently used. Open them to the lengths, respectively, of the last two sides. Put one foot of each at the ends of the first side, and bring their other feet together, and their point of meeting will mark the desired third point of the triangle.

To "prove" the accuracy of the work, fix the point D, by setting off from A the proper distance, and measure the length of the line

DC, by Art. (43). If its length on the plat corresponds to its measurement on the ground, the work is correct.*

Calculation. The content of the field may now be found as directed in Art. (65), either from the three sides, or more easily though not so accurately, by measuring on the plat, by Art. (43), the length of the perpendicular CE, let fall from any angle to the opposite side, and taking half the product of these two lines.

Example 1. Figure 49, is the plat, on a scale of two chains to one inch, of a field, of which the side AB is 200 links, BC is 100 links, and AC is 150 links. Its content by the rule of Art. (65), is 0.726 of a square chain, or 0A. 0R. 12P. If the perpendicular CE be accurately measured, it will be found to be $72\frac{1}{2}$ links. Half the product of this perpendicular by the base will be found to give the same content.

Ex. 2. The three sides of a triangular field are respectively 89.39, 54.08, and 45.98. Required its content.

Ans. 100A. 0R. 10P.

(91) A four-sided field; as Fig. 50.

Fig. 50.

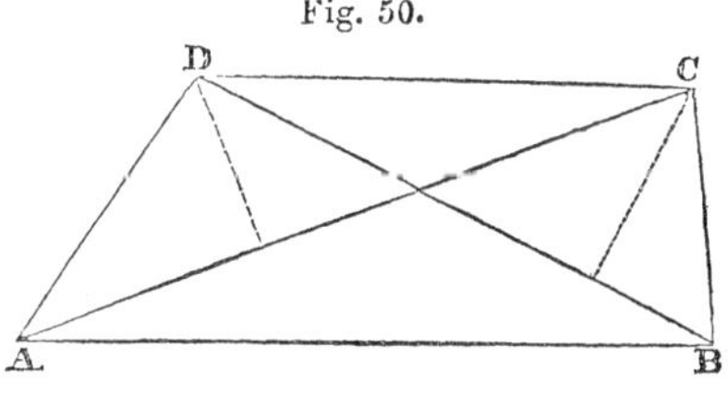

Field-work. Measure the four sides. Measure also a diagonal, as AC, thus dividing the four-sided field into two triangles. Measure also the other diagonal, or BD, for a "Proof line."

Platting. Draw a line, as AC, equal in length to the diagonal, to any scale, by Arts. (42) and (19). On each side of it, construct a triangle with the sides of the field, as directed in the preceding article.

To prove the accuracy of the work, measure on the plat the length of the "proof line," BD, by Art. (43), and if it agrees with the length of the same line measured on the ground, the field work and platting are both proved to be correct.

* It is a universal principle in all surveying operations, that the work must be tested by some means independent of the original process, and that the same result must be arrived at by two different methods. The necessary length of this proof line can also easily be calculated by the principles of Trigonometry.

Calculation. Find the content of each triangle separately, as in the preceding case, and add them together; or, more briefly, multiply either diagonal (the longer one is preferable) by the sum of the two perpendiculars, and divide the product by two.

Otherwise: reduce the four-sided figure to one triangle as in Art. (78); or, use any of the methods of the preceding chapter.

Example 3. In the field drawn in Fig. 50, on a scale of 3 chains to the inch, AB = 588 links, BC = 210, CD = 430, DA = 274, the diagonal AC = 626, and the proof diagonal BD = 500. The total content will be 1A. 0R. 17P.

Ex. 4. The sides of a four-sided field are AB = 12.41, BC = 5.86, CD = 8.25, DA = 4.24; the diagonal BD = 11.55, and the proof line AC = 11.04. Required the content.

Ans. 4A. 2R. 38P.

Ex. 5. The sides of a four-sided field are as follows: AB = 8.95, BC = 5.33, CD = 10.10, DA = 6.54; the diagonal from A to C is 11.52; the proof diagonal from B to D is 10.92. Required the content. *Ans.*

Ex. 6. In a four-sided field, AB = 7.68, BC = 4.09, CD = 10.64, DA = 7.24, AC = 10.32, BD = 10.74. Required the content. *Ans.*

(92) A many-sided field, as Fig. 51.

Fig. 51.

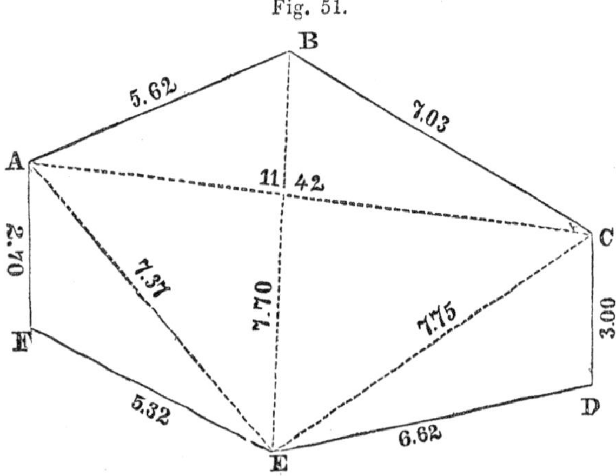

Field-Work. Measure all the sides of the field. Measure also diagonals enough to divide the field into triangles; of which there will always be two less than the number of sides. Choose such diagonals as will divide the field into triangles as nearly equilateral as possible. Measure also one or more diagonals for "Proof lines." It is well for the surveyor himself to place stakes in advance at all the corners of the field, as he can then select the best mode of division.

Platting. Begin with any diagonal and plat one triangle, as in Art. (**90**). Plat a second triangle adjoining the first one, as in Art. (**91**). Plat another adjacent triangle, and so proceed, till all have been laid down in their proper places. Measure the proof lines as in the last article.

Calculation. Proceed to calculate the content of the figure, precisely as directed for the four-sided field, measuring the perpendiculars and calculating the content of each triangle in turn; or taking in pairs those on opposite sides of the same diagonal; or using some of the other methods which have been explained.

Example 7. The six-sided field, shown in Fig. 51, has the lengths of its lines, in chains and links, written upon them, and is divided into four triangles, by three diagonals. The diagonal BE is a "proof-line." The Figure is drawn to a scale of 4 chains to the inch. The content of the field is 5A. 3R. 22P.

Ex. 8. In a five-sided field, the length of the sides are as follows: AB = 2.69, BC = 1.22, CD = 2.32, DE = 3.55, EA = 3.23. The diagonals are AD = 4.81, BD = 3.33. Required its content. *Ans.*

(**93**) A field may be divided up into triangles, not only by measuring diagonals as in the last figure, but by any of the methods shown in the four figures of Art. (**71**). The one which we have been employing, corresponds to the last of those figures.

Still another mode may be used when the angles cannot be seen from one another, or from any one point within. Take three or more convenient points within the field, and measure from them to the corners, and thus form different sets of triangles.

KEEPING THE FIELD NOTES.

(94) By Sketch. The most simple method is to make a sketch of the field, as nearly correct as the unassisted hand and eye can produce, and note down on it the lengths cf all the lines, as in Fig. 51. But when many other points require to be noted, such as where fences, or roads, or streams are crossed in the measurement, or any other additional particulars, the sketch would become confused, and be likely to lead to mistakes in the subsequent platting from it. The following is therefore the usual method of keeping the Field-notes. A long narrow book is most convenient for it.

(95) In Columns. Draw two parallel lines about an inch apart from the bottom to the top of the page of the field-book, as in the margin. This column, or pair of lines, may be conceived to represent the measured line, *split in two*, its two halves being then separated, an inch apart, merely for convenience, so that the distances measured along the line, may be written between these halves.

Hold the book in the direction of the measurement. At the *bottom* of the page write down the name, or number, or letter, which represents the station at which the survey is to begin.

A "station" is marked with a triangle or circle, as in the margin. The latter is more easily made.

In the complicated cases, which will be hereafter explained, and in which one long base line is measured, and also many other subordinate lines, it will be well, as a help to the memory, to mark the stations on the Base line with a triangle, and the stations on the other lines with the ordinary circle.

The station from which the measurements are made is usually put on the left of the column; and the station which is measured to, is put on the right.

	⊙	*to* B
	562	
From A	⊙	

But it is more compact, and avoids interfering with the notes of "offsets" (to be explained hereafter) to write the name or number of the station *in* the column, as in the margin.

B
562
A

The measurements to different points of a line are written above one another. The numbers all refer to the beginning of the line, and are counted from it.

B
400
250
100
A

The end of a measured line is marked by a line drawn across the page above the numbers which indicate the measurements which have been made.

If the chaining does not continue along the adjoining line, but the chain-men go to some other part of the field to begin another measurement, *two* lines are drawn across the page.

When a line has been measured, the marks ┌ or ┐ are made to show whether the following line turns to the right or to the left.

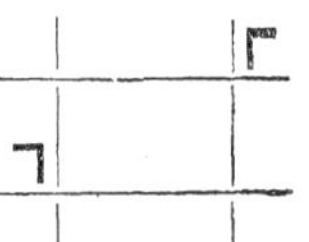

A line is named, either by the names of the stations between which it is measured, as the line AB; or by its length, a line 562 links long, being called the line 562; or it is recorded as Line No. 1, Line No. 2, &c; or as Line on page 1, 2, &c., of the Field-book.

When a mark is left at any point of a line, as at D, in Fig. 49, with the intention of coming back to it again, in order to measure to some other point, the place marked is called a *False Station*, and is marked in the Field-book F. S.; or has a line drawn around it, to distinguish it; or has a station mark △ placed outside of the column, to the right or left, according to the direction in which the measurement from it is to be made. Examples of these three modes are given in the margin.

562	
200	F. S.
0	
562	
(200)	
0	
562	
200	△
0	

A False Station is named by its position on the line where it belongs; as thus—“200 on 562.”

When a gate occurs in a measured line, the distance from the beginning of the line to the side of the gate first reached, is the one noted.

When the measured line crosses a fence, brook, road, &c., they are drawn on the field-notes in their true direction, as nearly as possible, but not in a continuous line across the column, as in the first figure in the margin, but as in the second figure, so that the two parts would form a continuous straight line, if the halves of the “split line” were brought together.

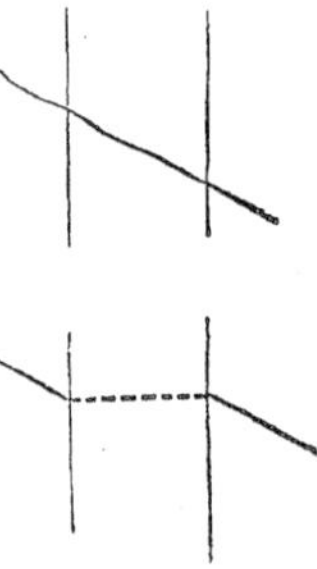

It is convenient to name the lines, in the margin, as being Sides, Diagonals, Proof lines, &c.

(96) The Field-notes of the triangular field platted in Fig. 49, are given below, according to both the methods mentioned in the preceding Article, pages 62 and 63.

In the Field-notes in the column on the right hand, it is not absolutely necessary to repeat the B and C.

PROOF LINE.		89	*to* C
	From D	F. S.	
SIDE.		150	*to* A
	From C	⊙	┐
SIDE.		100	*to* C
	From B	⊙	┐
SIDE.		200	*to* B
		80	F. S
	From A	⊙	

PROOF LINE.		C 89	
	From	(80)	*on* 200
SIDE.	┐	A 150 C	
SIDE.	┐	C 100 B	
SIDE.		B 200 (80) A	

(97) The Field-notes of the survey platted in Fig. 51, are given below. They begin at the bottom of the left hand column.

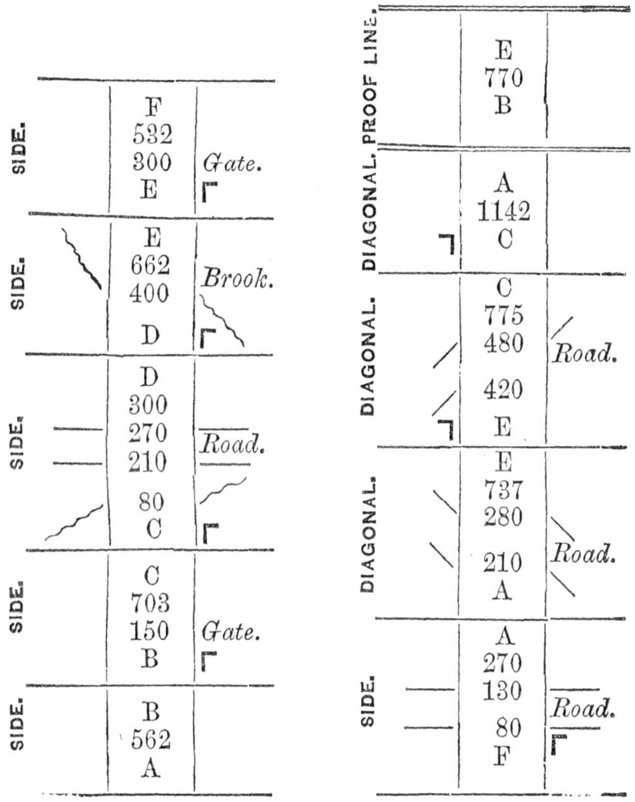

CHAPTER II.

SURVEYING BY TIE-LINES.

(98) *Surveying by Tie-lines* is a modification of the method explained in the last chapter. It frequently happens that it is impossible to measure the diagonals of a field of many sides, in consequence of obstacles to measurements, such as woods, water, houses, &c. In such cases, "*Tie-lines*," (so called because they *tie* the sides together), are employed as substitutes for diagonals.

Thus, in the four-sided field shown in the Figure, the diagonals cannot be measured because of woods intervening. As a substitute, measure off from any convenient corner of the field, as B, any distances, BE, BF, along the sides of the field. Measure also the "tie-line" EF. Measure all the sides of the field as usual.

Fig. 52.

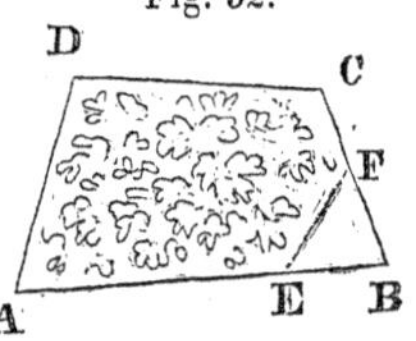

To plat this field, construct the triangle BEF, as in Art. (**90**). Produce the sides BE and BF, till they become respectively equal to BA and BC, as measured on the ground. Then with A and C as centres, and with radii respectively equal to AD and CD, describe arcs, whose intersection will be D, the remaining corner of the field.

(99) It thus appears that one tie-line is sufficient to determine a four-sided field; two, a five-sided field, and so on. But, as a check on errors, it is better to measure a tie-line for each angle, and the agreement, in the plat, of all the measurements will prove the accuracy of the whole work.

Since any inaccuracy in the length of a tie-line is increased in proportion to the greater length of the sides which it fixes, the tie-lines should be measured as far from the point of meeting of these sides as possible, that is, they should be, as long as possible.

The radical defect of the system is that it is "working from less to greater," (which is the exact converse of the true principle), thus magnifying inaccuracies at every step.

A tie-line may also be employed as a "proof line," in the place of a diagonal, and tested in the same manner.

Fig. 53.

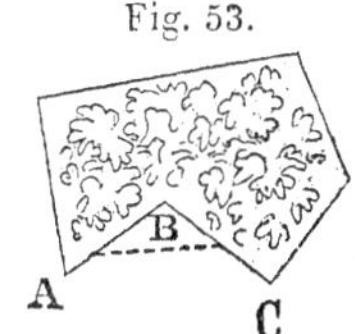

If any angle of the field is re-entering, as at B in the figure, measure a tie-line across the salient angle ABC.

(100) Chain Angles. It is convenient, though not necessary, to measure equal distances along the sides; BE, BF, in Fig. 52, and BA, BC, in Fig. 53. "Chain Angles" are thus formed.*

(101) Inaccessible Areas. The method of tie-lines can be applied to measuring fields which cannot be entered.

Fig. 54.

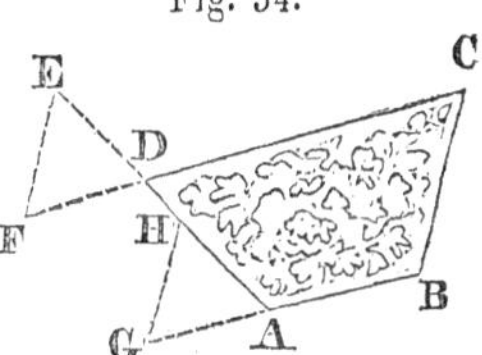

Thus, in the Figure, ABCD is an inaccessible wooded field, of four sides. To survey it, measure all the sides, and at any corner, as D, measure any distance DE, in the line of AD produced. Measure also another distance DF in the line of CD produced. Measure the tie-line EF, and the figure can be platted as in the case of the field of Fig. 52, the sides of the triangle being produced in the contrary direction.

The same end would be attained by prolonging only one side, as shown at the angle A of the same figure, and measuring AG, AH, and GH. It is better in both cases to tie *all* the angles in a similar manner.

This method may be applied to a figure of any number of sides by prolonging as many of them as are necessary; all of them, if possible.

* Chain angles may be reduced to angles measured in degrees, by observing that the tie-line is the chord of the angle to a radius equal to one of the equal distances measured on the sides. Therefore, divide the length of the tie-line by the length of this distance. The quotient will be the chord of the angle to a radius of *one*. In the TABLE OF CHORDS, at the end of this volume, find this quotient and the number of degrees and minutes corresponding to it gives the angle re quired. Otherwise; since the chord of any angle equals twice the sine of half the angle, we have this rule: Divide half the tie-line by the measured distance find in a table of natural sines the angle corresponding to the quotient, and mul tiply this angle by two, to get the angle desired.

(102) If the sides CD and AD were prolonged by their full length, the content of the figure could be calculated without any plat; for the new triangle DEF would equal the triangle DAC; and the sides of the triangle ACB would then be known.

This principle may be extended still farther. For a five-sided field, as in Fig. 55, produce two pairs of sides, a distance equal to their length, forming two new triangles, as shown by the dotted lines, and measure the sides B′D′, and A′D″. The three sides of each of these triangles will thus be known, and also the three sides of the triangle BAD, since AD = A′D″, and BD = B′D′.

The method of this article may be employed for a figure of six sides as shown in Fig. 56, (in which the dotted lines within the wooded field have their lengths determined by the triangles formed outside of it,) but not for figures of a greater number of sides.

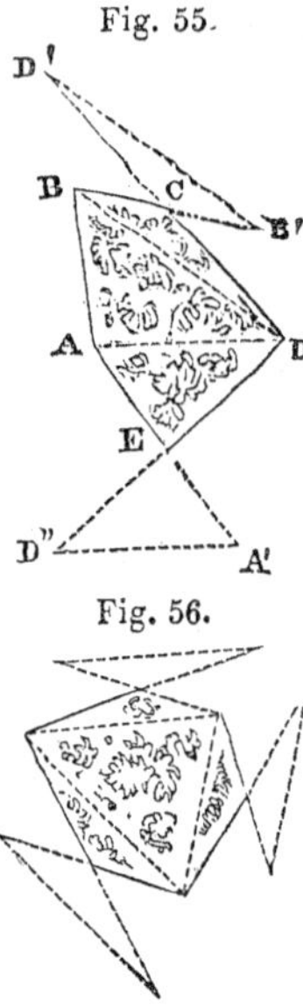

Fig. 55.

Fig. 56.

CHAPTER III.

SURVEYING BY PERPENDICULARS:

OR

By the Second Method.

(103) THE method of *Surveying by Perpendiculars* is founded on the *Second Method* of determining the position of a point, explained in Art. (6). It is applied in two ways, either to making a complete Survey by "*Diagonals and Perpendiculars*," or to measuring a crooked boundary by "*Off-sets*." Each will be considered in turn.

The best methods of getting perpendiculars on the ground must, however, be first explained.

TO SET OUT PERPENDICULARS.

(104) Surveyor's Cross. The simplest instrument for this purpose is the *Surveyor's Cross*, or *Cross-Staff*, shown in the figure. It consists of a block of wood, of any shape, having in it two saw-cuts, made very precisely at right angles to each other, about half an inch deep, and with centre-bit holes made at the bottom of the cuts to assist in finding the objects. This block is fixed on a pointed staff, on which it can turn freely, and which should be precisely 8 links ($63\frac{1}{3}$ inches) long, for the convenience of short measurements.

Fig. 57.

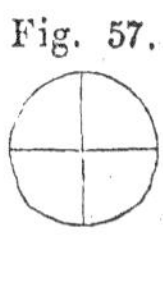

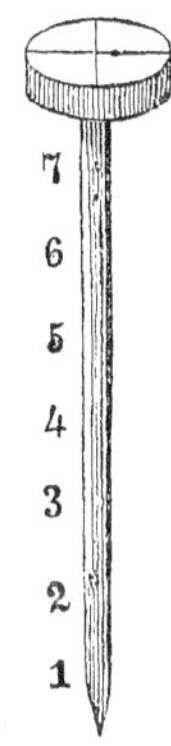

To use the Cross-staff to erect a perpendicular, set it at the point of the line at which a perpendicular is wanted. Turn its head till, on looking through one saw-cut, you see the ends of the line. Then will the other saw-cut point out the direction of the perpendicular, and thus guide the measurement desired.

To find where a perpendicular to the line, from some object, as a corner of a field, a tree, &c., would meet the line, set up the cross-staff at a point of the line which seems to the eye to be about the spot. Note about how far from the object the perpendicular at this point strikes, and move the cross-staff that distance; and repeat the operation till the correct spot is found.

(105) To test the accuracy of the instrument, sight through one slit to some point A, and place a stake B in the line of sight of the other slit. Then turn its head a quarter of the way around, so that the second slit looked through, points to A. Then see if the other slit covers B again, as it will if correct. If it does not do so, but sights to some other point, as B′, the apparent error is double the real one, for it now points as far to the right of the true point, C as it did before to its left.

Fig. 58.

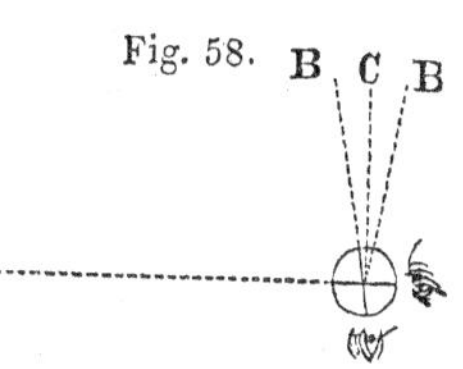

This is the first example we have had of the invaluable principle of *Reversion*, which is used in almost every test of the accuracy of Surveying and Astronomical instruments, its peculiar merit being that it doubles the real error, and thus makes it twice as easy to perceive and correct it.

(106) The instrument, in its most finished form, is made of a hollow brass cylinder, which has two pairs of slits exactly opposite to each other, one of each pair being narrow and the other wide, with a horse-hair stretched from the top to the bottom of the latter. It is also, sometimes, made with eight faces, and two more pairs of slits added, so as to set off half a right angle.

Fig. 59.

Another form is a hollow brass sphere, as in the figure. This enables the surveyor to set off perpenpendiculars on very steep slopes.

Fig. 60

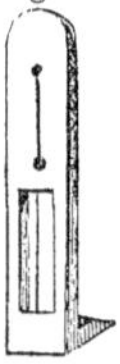

Another form of the surveyor's cross consists of two pairs of plain " Sights," each shaped as in the figure, placed at the ends of two bars at right angles to each other. The slit, and the opening with a hair stretched from its top to its bottom, are respectively at the top of one sight and at the bottom of the opposite sight.* This is used in the same manner as the preceding form, but is less portable and more liable to get out of order.

A temporary substitute for these instruments may be made by sticking four pins into the corners of a square piece of board; and sighting across them, in the direction of the line and at right angles to it.

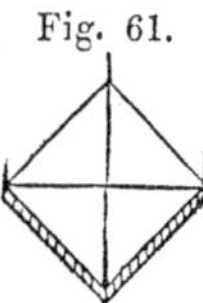

Fig. 61.

(107) Optical Square. The most convenient and accurate instrument is, however, the Optical Square. The figures give a perspective view of it, and also a plan with the lid removed. It is a small circular box, containing a strip of looking-glass, from the upper half of which the silvering is removed. This glass is placed

* The French call the narrow opening *œilleton*, and the wide one *croisée*.

so as to make precisely half a right angle with the line of sight, which passes through a slit on one side of the box, and a vertical hair stretched across the opening on the other side, or a mark on the glass. The box is held in the hand over the spot where the perpendicular is desired, (a plumb line in the hand will give perfect accuracy) and the observer applies his eye to the slit A, looking through the upper or unsilvered part of the glass, and turns the box till he sees the other end of the line B, through the opening C. The assistant, with a rod, moves along in the direction where the perpendicular is desired, being seen in the silvered parts of the glass, by reflection through the opening D, till his rod, at E, is seen to coincide with, or to be exactly under, the object B. Then is the line DE at right angles to the line AB, by the optical principle of the equality of the angles of incidence and reflection.

Fig. 62.

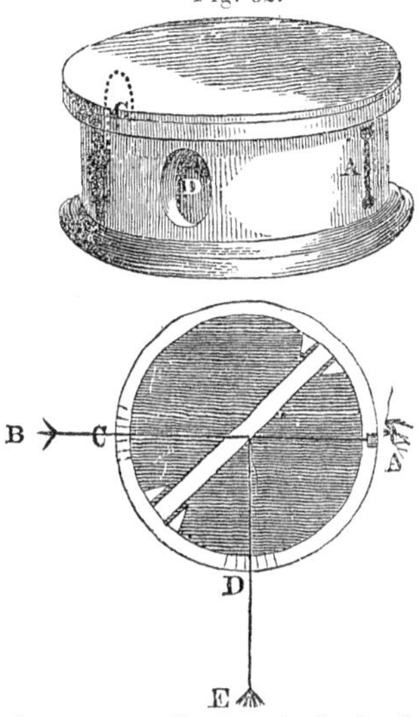

To find where a perpendicular from a distant object would strike the line, walk along the line, with the instrument to the eye, till the image of the object is seen, in the silvered part of the glass, to coincide with the direction of the line seen through the unsilvered part.

The instrument may be tested by sighting along the perpendicular, and fixing a point in the original line; on the principle of "Reversion."

The surveyor can make it for himself, fastening the glass in the box by four angular pieces of cork, and adjusting it by cutting away the cork on one side, and introducing wedges on the other side. The box should be blackened inside.

Another form of the optical square contains two glasses, fixed at an angle of 45°, and giving a right angle on the principle of the Sextant.

(108) **Chain Perpendiculars.** Perpendiculars may be set out with the chain alone, by a variety of methods. These methods generally consist in performing on the ground, the operations executed on paper in practical geometry, the chain being used, in the place of the compasses, to describe the necessary arcs.

As these operations, however, are less often used for the method of surveying now to be explained, than for overcoming obstacles to measurement, it will be more convenient to consider them in that connection, in Chapter V.

DIAGONALS AND PERPENDICULARS.

(109) In Chapter I, of this Part, we have seen that plats of surveys made with the chain alone, have their contents most easily determined by measuring, on the plat, the perpendiculars of each of the triangles, into which the diagonals measured on the ground have divided the field. In the *Method of Surveying by Diagonals and Perpendiculars*, now to be explained, the perpendiculars are measured *on the ground*. The content of the field can, therefore, be found at once, (by adding together the half products of each perpendicular by the diagonal on which it is let fall,) without the necessity of previously making a plat, or of measuring the sides of the field. This is, therefore, the most rapid and easy method of surveying when the content alone is required, and is particularly applicable to the measurement of the ground occupied by crops, for the purpose of determining the number of bushels grown to the acre, the amount to be paid for mowing by the acre, &c.

Fig. 63.

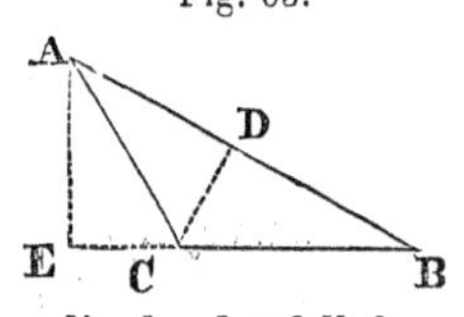

(110) **A three-sided field.** Measure the longest side, as AB, and the perpendicular, CD, let fall on it from the opposite angle C. Then the content is equal to half the product of the side by the perpendicular. If obstacles prevent this, find the point, where a perpendicular let fall from an angle, as A, to the opposite side produced, as BC, would meet it, as at E in the figure. Then half the product of AE by CB is the content of the triangle.

(111) A four-sided field. Measure the diagonal AC. Leave marks at the points on this diagonal at which perpendiculars from B and from D would meet it; finding these points by trial, as previously directed in Arts. (**104**) and (**107**). The best marks at these "False Stations," have been described in Art. (**90**). Return to these false stations and measure the perpendiculars. When these perpendiculars are measured before finishing the measurement of the diagonal, great care is necessary to avoid making mistakes in the length of the diagonal, when the chainmen return to continue its measurement. One check is to leave at the mark as many pins as have been taken up by the hind-chainman in coming to that point from the beginning of the line.

Fig. 64.

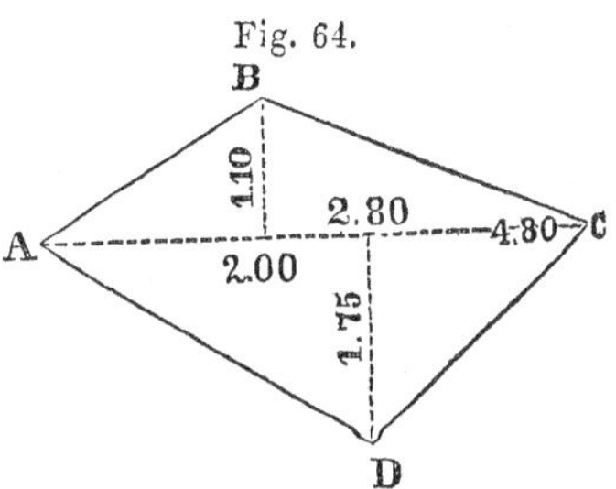

Example 9. Required the content of the field of Fig. 64.

Ans. 0A. 2R. 29P.

The field may be platted from these measurements, if desired, but with more liability to inaccuracy than in the first method, in which the sides are measured. The plat of the figure is 3 chains to 1 inch.

The field-notes may be taken by writing the measurements on a sketch, as in the figure; or in more complicated cases, by the column method, as below. A new symbol may be employed, this mark, ⊢, or ⊣, to show the False Station, from which a perpendicular is to be measured.

PERP.		110	*to* B
	From 200 *on* 480	F. S.	⊣
PERP.		175	*to* D
	From 280 *on* 480	F. S.	⊢
DIAGONAL.		480	*to* C
		280	⊢
	⊣	200	
	From A	⊙	

Example 10. *Calculation.*

sq. lks.

$$ABC = \tfrac{1}{2} \times 480 \times 110 = 26400$$

$$ADC = \tfrac{1}{2} \times 480 \times 175 = 42000$$

sq. chains 6.8400

Acres 0.684

It is still easier to take the two triangles together; multiplying the diagonal by the sum of the perpendiculars and dividing by two.

(112) A many-sided field. Fig. 65, and the accompanying field-notes represent the field which was surveyed by the First Method and platted in Fig. 51.

Fig. 65.

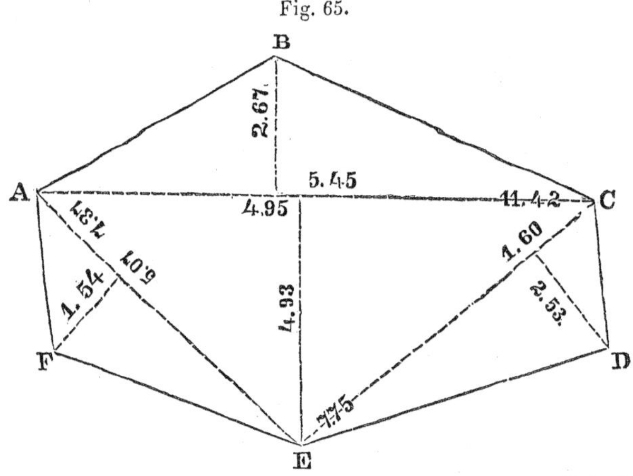

	1.54	*to* F
From 5.07 *on* 7.37	F. S.	
	2.53	*to* D
From 1.60 *on* 7.75	F. S.	
	4.93	*to* E
From 5.45 *on* 11.42	F. S.	
	2.67	*to* B
From 4.95 *on* 11.42	F. S.	
	7.37	*to* A
┤	5.07	
From E	⊙	┌
	7.75	*to* E
┤	1.60	
From C	⊙	┌
	11.42	*to* C
	5.45	├
┤	4.95	
From A	⊙	

Example 11. *Calculation.* The content of the triangles may be expressed thus:

sq. lks.

$$ABC = \tfrac{1}{2} \times 1142 \times 267 = 152457$$
$$AEC = \tfrac{1}{2} \times 1142 \times 493 = 281503$$
$$CDE = \tfrac{1}{2} \times 775 \times 253 = 98037$$
$$AEF = \tfrac{1}{2} \times 737 \times 154 = 56749$$

sq. chains 58.8746

Acres 5.88746

or, 5A. 3R. 22P.

The first two triangles might have been taken together, as in the previous field.

Content calculated from the perpendiculars will generally vary slightly from that obtained by measuring on the plat.

(113) A small field which has many sides, may sometimes be conveniently surveyed by taking one diagonal and measuring the perpendiculars let fall on it from each angle of the field, and thus dividing the whole area into triangles and trapezoids ; as in Fig. 36, page 48.

The line on which the perpendiculars are to be let fall, may also be outside of the field, as in Fig. 37, page 48.

Such a survey can be platted very readily, but the length of the perpendiculars renders the plat less accurate.

This procedure supplies a transition to the method of "Offsets," which is explained in the next article.

OFFSETS.

(114) Offsets are short perpendiculars, measured from a straight line, to the angles of a crooked or zigzag line, near which the straight line runs. Thus, in the figure, let ACDB be a crooked fence, bounding one side of a field. Chain along the straight line AB, which runs from one end of the fence to the other, and, when opposite each corner, note the distance from the beginning, or the point A, and also measure and note the perpendicular distance of each corner C and D from the line. These corners will then be "determined" by the *Second Method*, *Art.* (**6**).

Fig. 66.

The Field-notes, corresponding to Fig. 66, are as in the margin. The measurements along the line are written in the column, as before, counting from the beginning of the line, and the offsets are written beside it, on the right or left, opposite the distance at which they are taken. A sketch of the crooked line is also usually made in the Field-notes, though not absolutely necessary in so simple a case as this. The letters C and D would not be used in practice, but are here inserted to show the connection between the Field-notes and the plat.

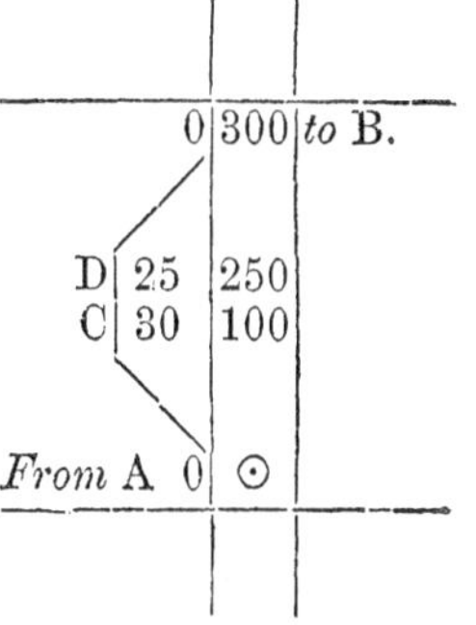

In taking the Field-Notes, the widths of the offsets should not be drawn proportionally to the distances between them, but the breadths should be greatly exaggerated in proportion to the lengths.

(115) A more extended example, with a little different notation, is given below. In the figure, which is on a scale of 8 chains to one inch for the distances along the line, the breadths of the offsets are exaggerated to four times their true proportional dimensions.

	B	
	1500	0
	1250	20
0	1000	0
30	750	
50	500	
40	250	
	0	
	A	

Fig. 67.

(116) The plat and Field-notes of the position of two houses, determined by offsets, are given below on a scale of 2 chains to 1 inch.

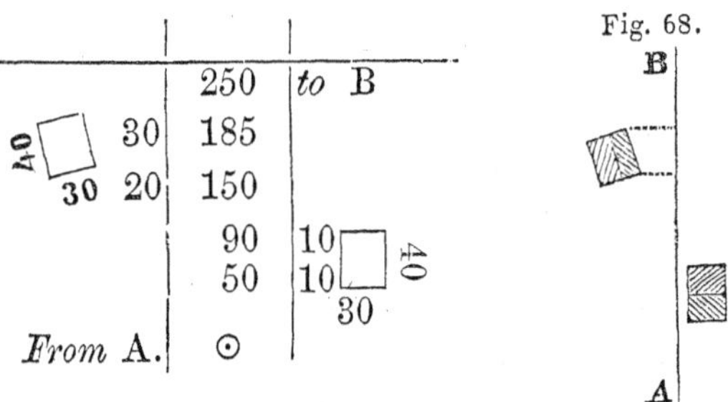

Fig. 68.

(117) Double offsets are sometimes convenient; and sometimes triple and quadruple ones. Below are given the notes and the plat, 1 chain to 1 inch, of a road of varying width, both sides of which are determined by double offsets. It will be seen that the line AB crosses one side of the road at 160 links from A, and the other side of it at 220.

Two methods of keeping the Field-notes are given. In the first form, the offsets to each side of the road are given separately and connected by the sign +. In the second form, the total distance of the second offset is given, and the two measurements connected by the word "*to*." This is easier both for measuring and platting.

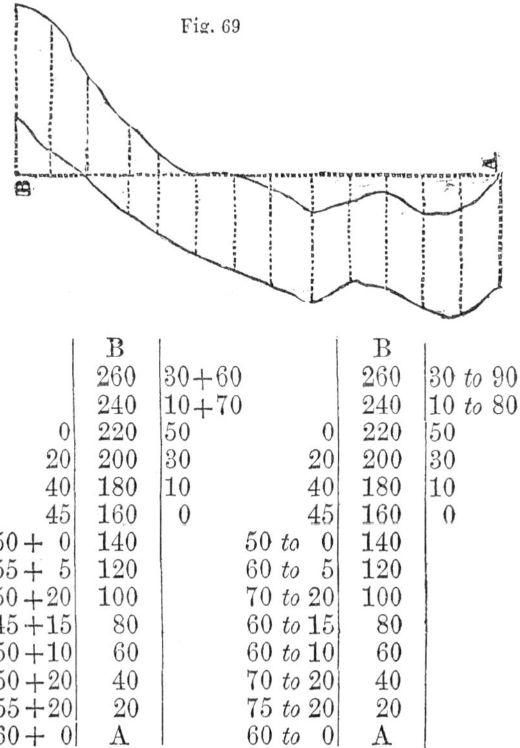

Fig. 69

	B	
	260	30+60
	240	10+70
0	220	50
20	200	30
40	180	10
45	160	0
50+ 0	140	
55+ 5	120	
50+20	100	
45+15	80	
50+10	60	
50+20	40	
55+20	20	
60+ 0	A	

	B	
	260	30 *to* 90
	240	10 *to* 80
0	220	50
20	200	30
40	180	10
45	160	0
50 *to* 0	140	
60 *to* 5	120	
70 *to* 20	100	
60 *to* 15	80	
60 *to* 10	60	
70 *to* 20	40	
75 *to* 20	20	
60 *to* 0	A	

(118) These offsets may generally be taken with sufficient accuracy by measuring them as nearly at right angles to the base line as the eye can estimate. The surveyor should stand by the chain, facing the fence, at the place which he thinks opposite to the corner to which he wishes to take an offset, and measure "square" to it by the eye, which a little practice will enable him to do with much correctness.

The offsets may be measured, if short, with an *Offset-staff*, a light stick, 10 or 15 links in length, and divided accordingly; or if they are long, with a tape. They are generally but a few links in length. A chain's length should be the extreme limit, as laid down by the English "Tithe Commissioners," and that should be employed only in exceptional cases. When the "Cross-staff" is in use, its divided length of 8 links, renders the offset-staff needless.

When offsets are to be taken, the method of chaining to the end of a line, described in Art. (23), page 21, is somewhat modified. After the leader arrives at the end of the line, he should draw on the chain till the follower, with the back end of the chain, reaches the last pin set. This facilitates the counting of the links to the places at which the offsets are taken.

The offsets are to be taken to every angle of the fence or other crooked line; that is, to every point where it changes its direction. These angles or prominent bends can be best found by one of the party walking along the crooked fence and directing another at the chain what points to measure opposite to. If the line which is to be thus determined is *curved*, the offsets should be taken to points so near each other, that the portions of the curved line lying between them may, without much error, be regarded as straight. It will be most convenient, for the subsequent calculations, to take the offsets at equal distances apart along the straight line from which they are measured.

In the case of a crooked brook, such as is shown in the figure given below, offsets should be taken to the most prominent angles, such as are marked *a a a* in the figure, and the intermediate bends may be merely sketched by eye.

Fig. 70.

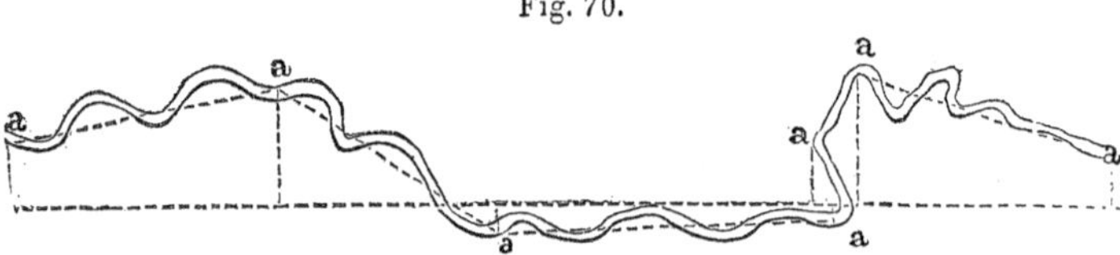

When offsets from lines measured around a field are taken inside of these bounding lines, they are sometimes distinguished as *Insets*.

(119) Platting. The most rapid method of platting the offsets, is by the use of a *Platting Scale* (described in Art. 49) and an *Offset Scale*, which is a short scale divided on its edges like a platting scale, but having its zero in the middle, as in the figure.

Fig. 71

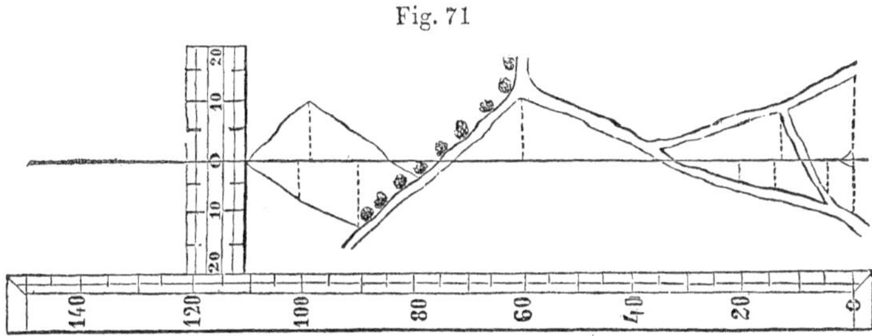

The platting scale is placed parallel to the line, with its zero point opposite to the beginning of the line. The offset scale is slid along the platting scale, till its edge comes to a distance on the latter at which an offset had been taken, the length of which is marked off with a needle point from the offset scale. This is then slid on to the next distance, and the operation is repeated. If one person reads off the field-notes, and another plats, the operation will be greatly facilitated. The points thus obtained are joined by straight lines, and a miniature copy of the curved line is thus obtained; all the operations of the platting being merely repetitions of the measurements made on the ground.

If no offset scale is at hand, make one of a strip of thick drawing paper, or pasteboard; or use the platting scale itself, turned crossways, having previously marked off from it the points from which the offsets had been taken.

In plats made on a small scale, the shorter offsets are best estimated by eye.

On the Ordnance Survey of Ireland, the platting of offsets is facilitated by the use of a combination of the offset scale and the platting scale, the former being made to slide in a groove in the latter, at right angles to it.

(120) Calculating Content. When the crooked line determined by offsets is the boundary of a field, the content, enclosed between it and the straight line surveyed, must be determined, that it may be added to, or subtracted from, the content of the field bounded by the straight lines. There are various methods of effecting this.

The area enclosed between the straight and the crooked lines is divided up by the offsets into *triangles and trapezoids*, the content of which may be calculated separately by Arts. (**65**) and (**67**), and then added together. The content of the plat on page 75, will, therefore, be 1500 + 4125 + 625 = 6250 square links = 0.625 square chain. The content of the plat on page 76, will in like manner be found to be, on the left of the straight line 30,000 square links, and on its right 5,000 square links.

(**121**) *When the offsets have been taken at equal distances*, the content may be more easily obtained by adding together half of the first and of the last offset, and all the intermediate ones, and multiplying the sum by one of the equal distances between the offsets. This rule is merely an abbreviation of the preceding one.

Thus, in the plat of page 76, the distances being equal, the content of the offsets on the left of the straight line will be 120 × 250 = 30,000 square links, and on the right 20 × 250 = 5,000 square links; the same results as before.

When the line determined by the offsets is a curved line, "Simpson's rule" gives the content more accurately. To employ it, an *even* number of *equal* distances must have been measured in the part to be calculated. Then add together the first and last offset, four times the sum of the even offsets, (i. e. the 2d, 4th, 6th, &c.,) and twice the sum of the odd offsets, (i. e. the 3d, 5th, 7th, &c.,) not including the first and the last. Multiply the sum by one of the equal distances between the offsets, and divide by 3. The quotient will be the area.

Example 12. The offsets from a straight line to a curved fence, were 8, 9, 11, 15, 16, 14, 9, links, at equal distances of 5 links. What was the content included between the curved fence and the straight line? *Ans.* 371.666

(122) Many erroneous rules have been given on this part of the subject. *One rule* directs the surveyor to divide the sum of all the offsets by one less than their number, and multiply the quotient by the whole length of the straight line; or, what is the same thing, to multiply the sum of all the offsets by the common distance between them. This will be correct only when the offsets at each end of the line are nothing, i. e. when the curved line starts from the straight line and returns to it at the beginning and end of one of the equal distances. In all other cases it will give too much. *A second rule* directs the surveyor to divide the sum of all the offsets by their number, and then to multiply the quotient by the whole straight line. This may give too much, or too little, according to circumstances.

Suppose offsets of 10, 30, 20, 80, 50, 30, links, to have been taken at equal distances of a chain. The correct content of the enclosed space is $200 \times 100 = 2$ square chains. The first of the above rules would give 2.2 square chains, and the second would give 1.8333 chains.

(123) *Reducing to one triangle* the many-sided figure which is formed by the offsets, is the method of calculation sometimes adopted. This has been fully explained in Part I, Art. (78), &c. The method of Art. (83) is best adapted for this purpose.

(124) *Equalizing*, or *giving and taking*, is an approximate mode of calculation much used by practical surveyors. A crooked line, determined by offsets, having been platted, a straight line is drawn on the plat, across the crooked line, leaving as much space outside of the straight line as inside of it, as nearly as can be estimated by the eye, "Equalizing" it, or "Giving and taking" equal

Fig. 72.

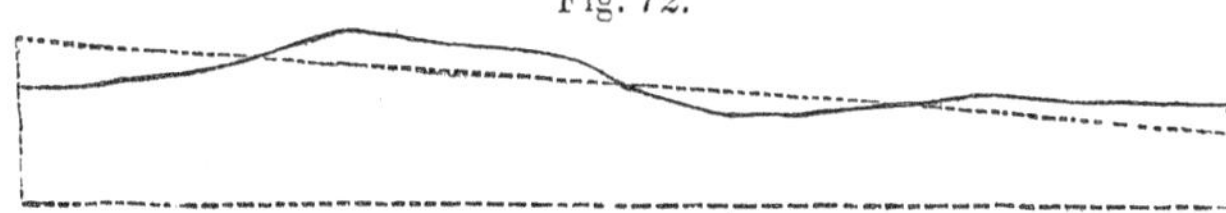

portions. The straight line is best determined by laying across the irregular outline the straight edge of a piece of transparent horn, or tracing paper, or glass, or a fine thread or horse-hair streτched straight by a light bow of whalebone. In practical hands, this method is sufficiently accurate in most cases. The student will do well to try it on figures, the content of which he has previously ascertained by perfectly accurate methods.

Sometimes this method may be advantageously combined with the preceding; short lengths of the croooked boundary being "Equalized," and the fewer resulting zigzags reduced to one line by the method of Art. (78), &c.

CHAPTER IV.

SURVEYING BY THE PRECEDING METHODS COMBINED.

(125) All the methods which have been explained in the three preceding chapters—Surveying by *Diagonals*, by *Tie-lines*, and by *Perpendiculars*, particularly in the form of offsets—are frequently required in the same survey. The method by *Diagonals* should be the leading one; in some parts of the survey, obstacles to the measurement of diagonals may require the use of *Tie-lines;* and if the fences are crooked, straight lines are to be measured near them, and their crooks determined by *Offsets.*

(126) *Offsets* are necessary additions to almost every other method of surveying. In the smallest field, surveyed by diagonals, unless all the fences are perfectly straight lines, their bends must be determined by offsets. The plat (scale of 1 chain to 1 inch), and field-notes, of such a case are given below. A sufficient number of the sides, diagonals, and proof-lines, to prove the work, should be platted before platting the offsets.

Fig. 73.

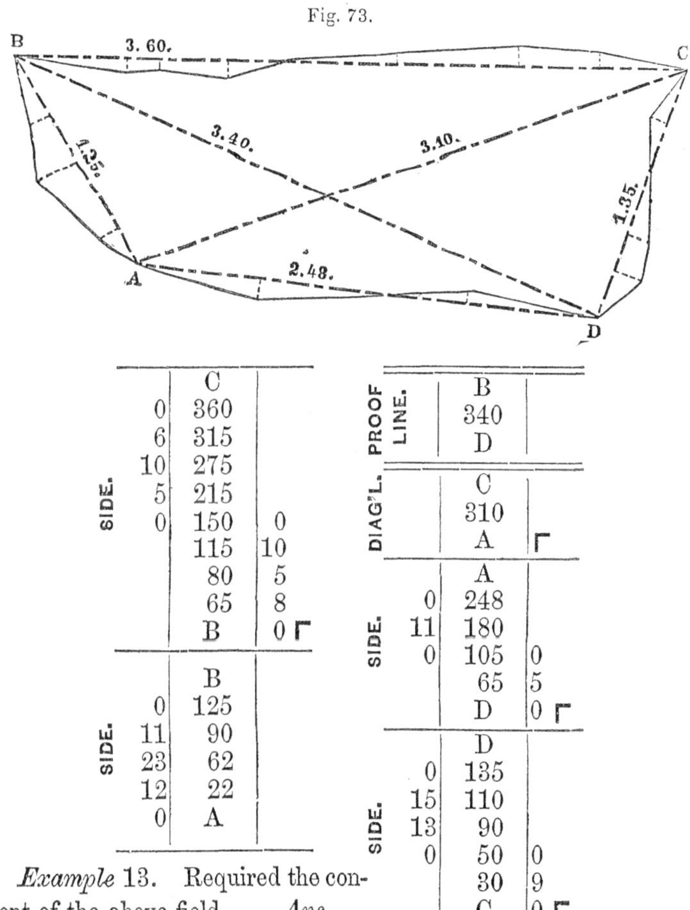

	Left	Station	Right
SIDE.		C	
	0	360	
	6	315	
	10	275	
	5	215	
	0	150	0
		115	10
		80	5
		65	8
		B	0 ┌
SIDE.		B	
	0	125	
	11	90	
	23	62	
	12	22	
	0	A	

	Left	Station	Right
PROOF LINE.		B	
		340	
		D	
DIAG'L.		C	
		310	
		A	┌
SIDE.		A	
	0	248	
	11	180	
	0	105	0
		65	5
		D	0 ┌
SIDE.		D	
	0	135	
	15	110	
	13	90	
	0	50	0
		30	9
		C	0 ┌

Example 13. Required the content of the above field. *Ans.*

(127) Field-books. The difficulty and the importance of keeping the Field-notes clearly and distinctly, increase with each new combination of methods. For this reason, three different methods of keeping the Field-notes of the same survey will now be given, (from Bourns' Surveying), and a careful comparison by the student of the corresponding portions of each will be very profitable to him.

FIELD-BOOK No. 1.

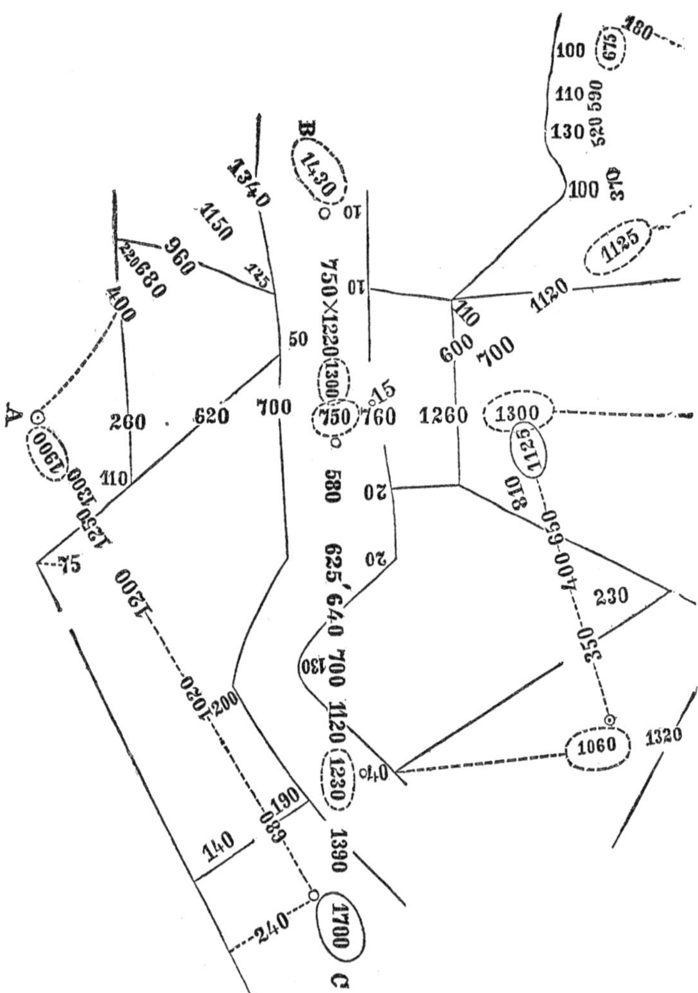

Field-Book No. 1 (Fig. 74) shews the Sketch method, explained in Art. (94).

FIELD-BOOK No. 2.

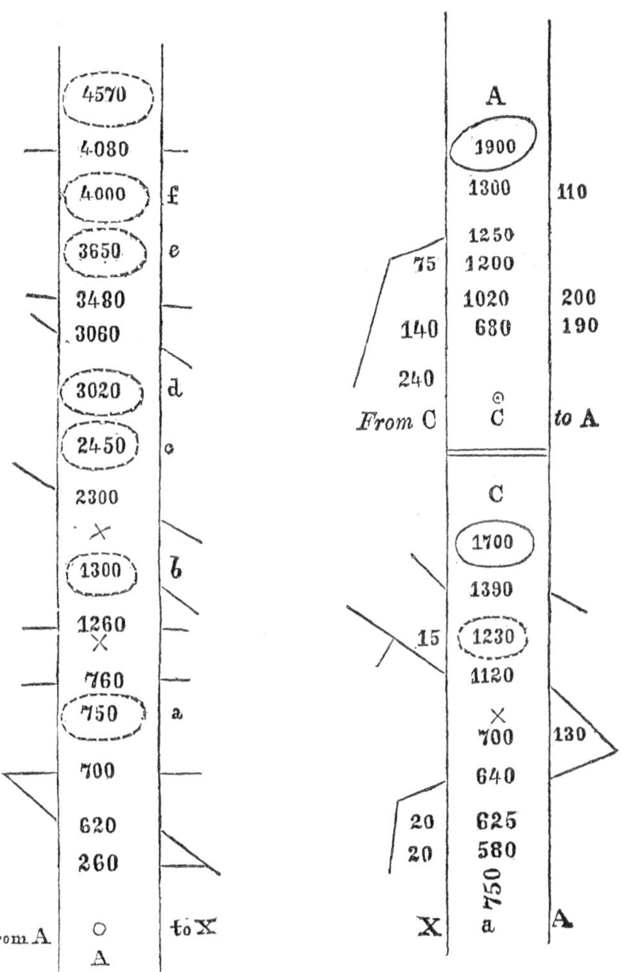

Field-Book No. 2 (Fig. 75) shews the Column method, explained in Art. (95).

FIELD-BOOK No. 3.

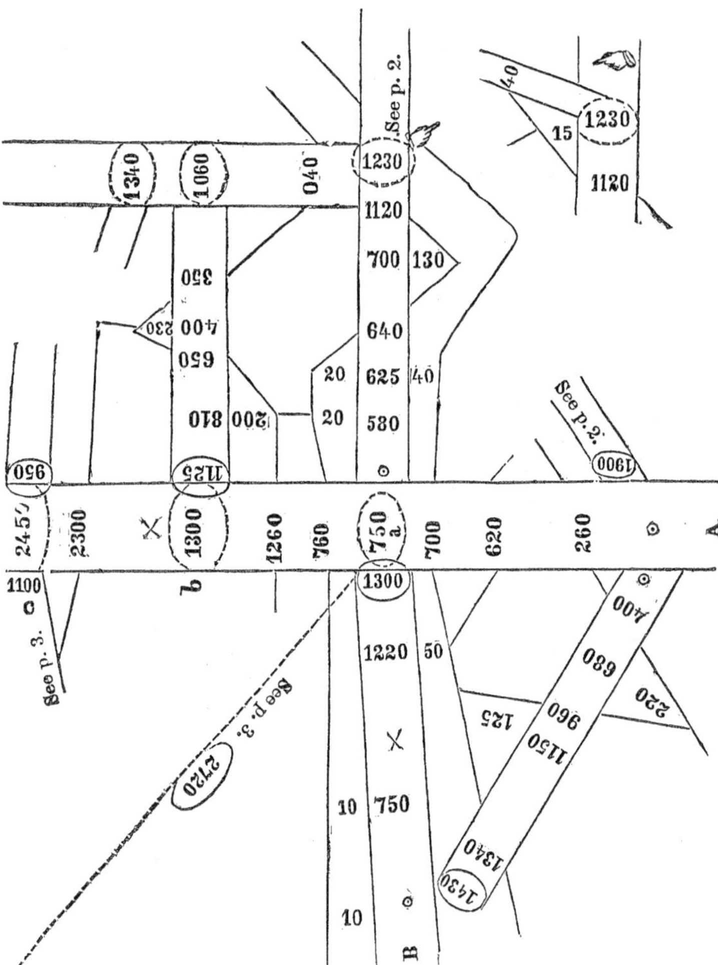

Field Book No. 3 (Fig. 76) is a convenient combination of the two preceding methods. The bottom of the Book is at the side of this figure, at A.

(128) It will easily appear from the sketch of Field-book No. 1, how much time and labor may be saved, or lost, by the manner of doing the work. Thus, beginning at A, and measuring 750 links, a pole should be left there, and the line to the right measured to 17 chains, or C, leaving a pole at 12.30 as a new starting point by and by. Then from C measure 19 chains to A again; then measure from A to B, and from B back to the pole left at 7.50 on the main line.

(129) The example which will now be given shows part of the Field-notes, the plat, (on a scale of 6 inches to 1 mile [1:10,560]), and a partial calculation of the "Filling up" of a large triangle, the angular points of which are supposed to have been determined by the methods of Geodesic Surveying. They should be well studied.*

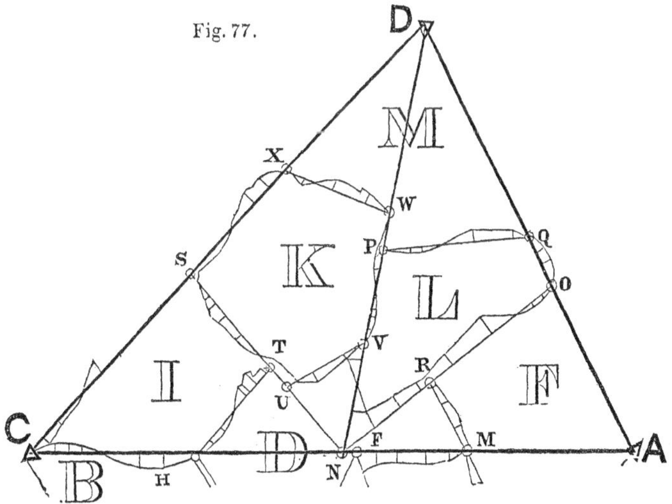

Fig. 77.

* Capt. FROME, in his "Trigonometrical Survey," from which this example has been condensed, remarks, "It may, perhaps, be thought that too much stress is laid on *forms*; but *method* is a most essential part of an undertaking of magnitude: and without excellent preliminary arrangements to ensure uniformity in all the most trifling details, the work never could go on creditably."

	2564	80
F	2452	
N	2324	
H	1264	0
	1240	52
	1140	86
	950	100
	772	60
0	604	0
34	502	
50	450	
70	342	
82	220	
From C	△	*to* A
	C	

	D	
	△ 3398	
Q	1700	0
	1530	84
	1420	40
O	1340	0
From A	△	*to* D
	A	

	A	
	△ 4454	
M	3296	0
	3275	54
	3120	62
	2940	85
	2572	60

	C	
	△ 4250	
100	4050	
62	3890	
42	3730	
0	3540	0
	3420	30
72	2484	S
40	2332	
60	2206	
0	2056	0
	1805	40
	1550	50
X	1442	0
From D	△	*to* C.
	D	

In the above specimen of a field-book, (which resembles that on page 85), all offsets, except those having relation to the boundary lines, are purposely omitted, to prevent confusion, the example being given solely to illustrate the method of calculating these larger divisions. Rough diagrams are drawn in the field-book not to any scale, but merely bearing some sort of resemblance to the lines measured on the ground, for the purpose of showing, at any period of the work, their directions and how they are to be connected; and also of eventually assisting in laying down the diagram and content plat. On these rough diagrams are written the distinctive letters by which each line is marked in the field-book, and also its length, and the distances between points marked upon it, from which other measurements branch off to connect the interior portions of the district surveyed.

(130) Calculations. The calculation of one of the figures, M, is given below in detail. It is composed of the triangle DPQ, with offsets along the sides PQ; and of the triangle DWX, with offsets along the sides PW and WX. From the content thus obtained must be subtracted the offsets on PQ, belonging to the figure L, and those on WX belonging to the figure K. When the offsets are triangles, (right angled, of course), the base and perpendicular are put down as two sides; when they are trapezoids, the two parallel sides and the distance between them occupy the columns of "sides."

DIVISION.	TRIANGLE OR TRAPEZOID.	1ST SIDE.	2D SIDE.	3D SIDE.	CONTENT IN CHAINS.
	DPQ	1680	1698	1078	86.2650
	PQ	—	52	250	.6500
		52	30	80	.3280
		30	—	216	.3240
					1.3020
M *Additives.*	DWX	1370	1442	770	51.8339
	PW	30	—	310	.4650
	WX	—	56	114	.3192
		56	36	104	.4784
		36	—	90	.1620
					.9596
		Total Additives,			140.8255
	PQ	—	50	174	.4350
		50	30	292	1.1680
		30	—	66	.0990
					1.7020
	WX	—	52	142	.3692
M *Subtractives.*		52	64	232	1.3456
		64	—	88	.2816
					1.9964
	Total Subtractives,				3.6984
	Total Additives,				140.8255
	Difference,				137.1271

The other figures, comprised within the large triangle, are recorded and calculated in a similar manner. An abridged register of the results is given below.

DIVISION.	ADDITIVES.	SUBTRACTIVE.	DIFFERENCE IN SQUARE CHAINS.
K	DNS and offsets.	DWX NUV and offsets.	140.4893
L	DNO and offsets.	DPQ and offsets.	100.1882
F	ANO and offsets.	NRM and offsets.	103.9778
D	HTN NUV NRM and offsets.	Offsets.	81.6307
I	CNS and offsets.	HTN and offsets.	109.5064
M	DPQ DWX and offsets.	Offsets.	137.1271
Total, - - - - - -			672.9195

The accuracy of the preceding calculations of the separate figures must now be tested by comparing the sum of their areas with that of the large triangle ACD, which comprises them all. Their area must previously be increased by the offsets on the lines CS and CH, which had been deducted from I, and which amount respectively to 3.5270 and 2.8690. The total areas will then equal 679.3155 square chains. That of the triangle ACD is 679.5032; a difference of less than a fifth of a square chain, or a fiftieth of an acre; or about one-fortieth of one per cent. on the total area.

(131) The six lines. In most cases, great or small, *six fundamental lines* will need to be measured; viz. four approximate boundary lines, forming a quadrilateral, and its two diagonals. Small triangles, to determine prominent points, can be formed within and without these main lines by the FIRST METHOD, Art. (5), and the lesser irregularities can be determined by offsets.

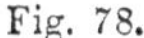

Fig. 78.

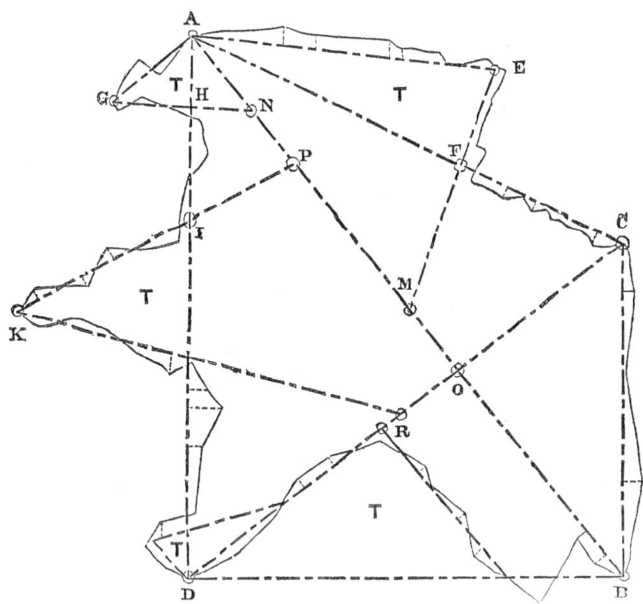

Thus, in the above figure, two straight lines AB and CD are measured through the entire length and breadth of the farm, or township, which is to be surveyed. The connecting lines AC, CB, BD and DA are also measured, uniting the extremities of the first two lines. The last four lines thus form a quadrilateral, which is divided into two triangles by one of the first measured lines, while the second serves as a proof-line. The distance from the intersection of the two diagonals to the extremities of each, being measured on the ground and on the plat, affords an additional test.

Other points of the district surveyed (as E, G, K., &c., in the figure,) are determined by measuring the distances from them to known points (as M, N, P, R, &c., in the figure) situated on some of the six fundamental lines, thus forming the triangles T, T.

The intersection O of the main diagonals, and also the intersections of the various minor lines with the main lines and with each other, should all be carefully noted, as additional checks when the work comes to be platted.

The larger figures are determined first, and the smaller ones based upon them, in accordance with this important principle in all surveying operations, always to work from the whole to the parts, and from greater to less. The unavoidable inaccuracies are thus subdivided and diminished. The opposite course would accumulate and magnify them.

These additional lines, which form secondary triangles, should be so chosen and ranged as to pass through and near as many objects as possible, in order to require as few and as short offsets as the position of the lines will permit; the smaller irregularities being determined by offsets as usual. It is better to measure too many lines than too few, and to establish unnecessary "false stations," rather than not to have enough.

(132) Exceptional cases. The preceding arrangement of lines, though in most cases the best, may sometimes be varied with advantage. Unless the farm surveyed be of a shape nearly as broad as long, the two diagonals will cross each other obliquely, instead of nearly at right angles, as is desirable.

When the farm is much longer than it is wide, two systems, of six lines each, may be used with much advantage, as in Fig. 79. Several such may be combined when necessary.

Fig. 79

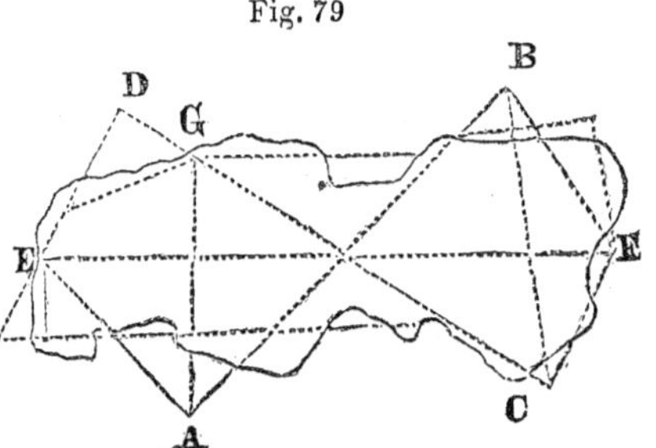

Fig. 80.

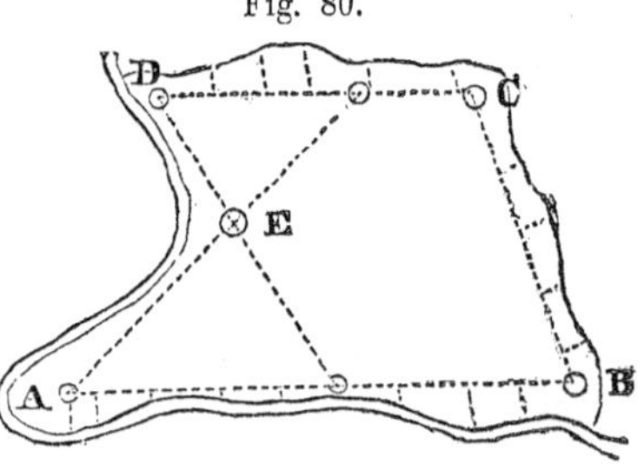

In a case like that in Fig. 80, five lines will be better than six, and will tie one another together, their points of intersection being carefully noted.

Fig. 81

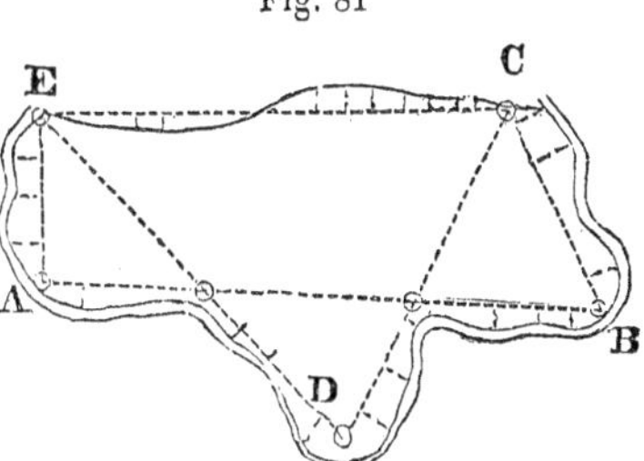

In the farm represented in Fig. 81, the system of lines there shown is the best, and they will also tie one another.

(133) Much difficulty will often be found in ranging and measuring the long lines required by this method in extensive surveys. Various contrivances for overcoming the obstacles which may be met with, will be explained in the following chapter. It will often be convenient to measure the minor lines along roads, lanes, paths, &c., although they may not lie in the most desirable directions. Steeples, chimneys, remarkable trees, and other objects of that character, may often be sighted to, and the line measured towards them, with much saving of time and labor. The point where the measured lines cross one another should always be noted, and they will thus form a very complete series of tie-lines.*

A view of the district to be surveyed, taken from some elevated position, will be of much assistance in planning the general direction of the lines to be measured.

(134) Inaccessible Areas. A combination of offsets and tie-lines supplies an easy method of surveying an *inaccessible area*, such as a pond, swamp, forest, block of houses, &c., as appears from the figure; in which external bounding lines are taken at will and

Fig. 82.

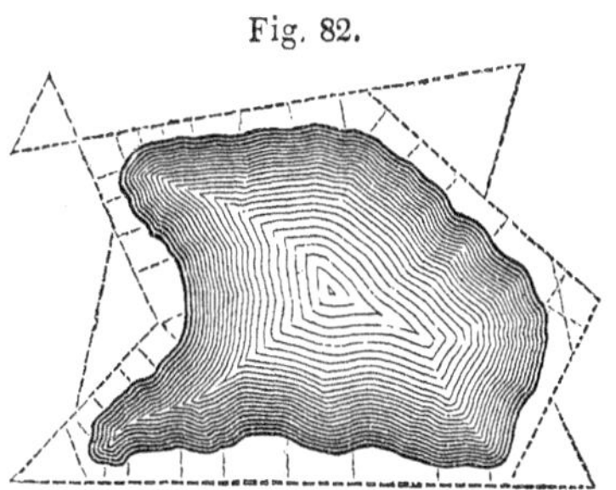

* To find the exact point of intersection of these lines, which are only "visual lines," (explained in Art. (19),) three persons are necessary: one stands at some point of one of the lines and sights to some other point on it; a second does the same on the second line; by signs they direct, to right or left, the movements of a third person, who holds a rod, till he is placed in both of the lines and thus at their intersection, on the principle of Art. (11).

measured, and tied by "tie-lines" measured between these lines, prolonged when necessary, as in Art. (**101**), while offsets from them determine the irregularities of the actual boundaries of the pond, &c.

These *offsets* are *insets*, and their content is, of course, to be subtracted from the content of the principal figure.

Even a circular field might thus be approximately measured from the outside.

If the shape of the field admits of it, it will be preferable to measure four lines about the field in such directions as to enclose it in a rectangle, and to measure offsets from the sides of this to the angles of the field.

Fig. 83.

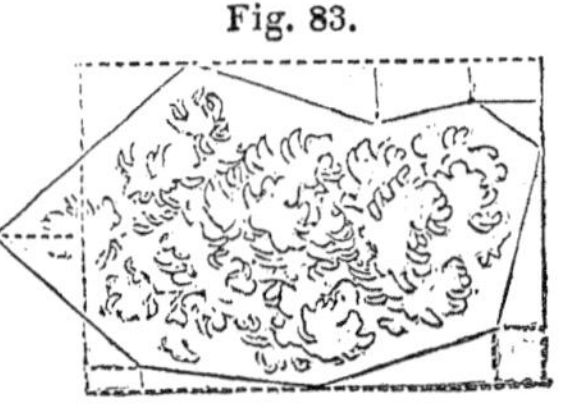

(135) When one of the lines with which an inaccessible field is surrounded, as in the last two figures, cuts a corner of the field, as in Fig. 84, the triangle ABC is to be deducted from the content of the enclosing figure, and the triangle CDE added to it. The triangle DEF is also to be added, and the triangle FGH deducted. To do this directly, it would be necessary to find the points of intersection C and F. But this may be difficult, and can be dispensed with by obtaining the difference of each pair of triangles. The difference of ABC and CDE will be obtained at once by multiplying the difference of the offsets AB and DE by half of BE; and the difference of DEF and FGH by multiplying the difference of DE and GH by half of EG.*

Fig. 84

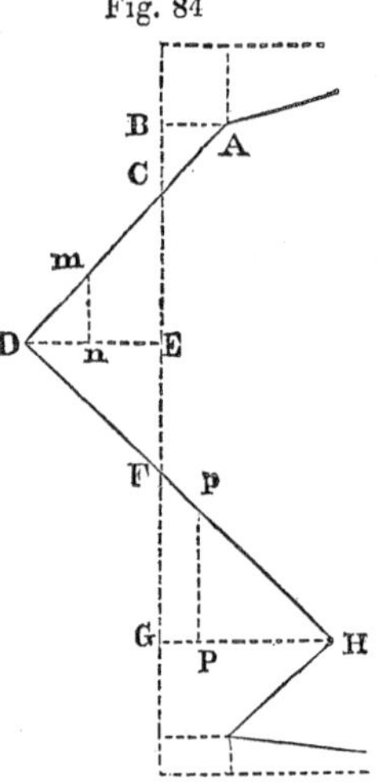

* For, making the triangle $Dmn = ABC$, then $mnEC = En \times \frac{1}{2}(mn + CE) = (DE - AB) \times \frac{1}{2} EB$; and so with the other pair of triangles.

(136) Roads. A winding Road may also be surveyed thus, as is shown in Fig. 85; straight lines being measured in the road,

Fig. 85.

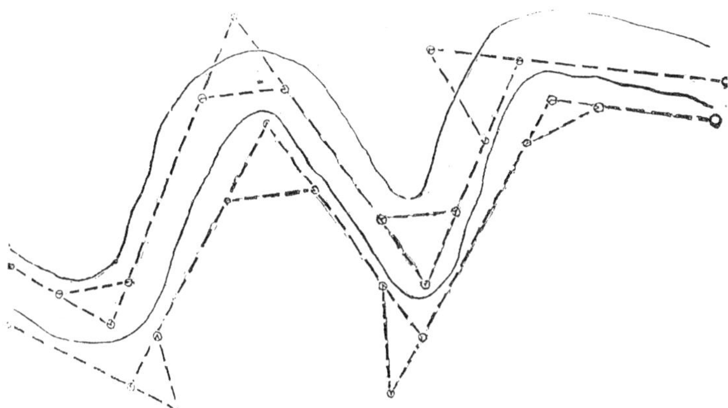

their changes in direction determined by tie-lines, tying one line to the preceding one prolonged, as explained in Chapter II, of this Part, and points in the road-fences, on each side of these straight lines, being determined by offsets.

A **River** may also be supposed to be represented by the above winding lines; and the lower set of lines, tied to one another as before, and with offsets from them to the water's edge, will be sufficient for making an accurate survey of one side of the river.

(137) Towns. A town could be surveyed and mapped in the same manner, by measuring straight lines through all the streets, determining their angles by tie-lines, and taking offsets from them to the blocks of houses.

CHAPTER V.

OBSTACLES TO MEASUREMENT IN CHAIN SURVEYING.

(138) In the practice of the various methods of surveying which have been explained, the hills and valleys which are to be crossed, the sheets of water which are to be passed over, the woods and houses which are to be gone through—all these form *obstacles* to the measurement of the necessary lines which are to join certain points, or to be prolonged in the same direction. Many special precautions and contrivances are, therefore, rendered necessary; and the best methods to be employed, when the chain alone is to be used, will be given in the present chapter.

(139) The methods now to be given for overcoming the various obstacles met with in practice, constitute a LAND-GEOMETRY. Its problems are performed on the ground instead of on paper: its *compasses* are a chain fixed at one end and free to swing around with the other; its *scale* is the chain itself; and its *ruler* is the same chain stretched tight. Its advantages are that its single instrument, (or a substitute for it, such as a tape, a rope, &c.) can be found anywhere; and its only auxiliaries are equally easy to obtain, being a few straight and slender rods, and a plumb-line, for which a pebble suspended by a thread is a sufficient substitute.

Many of these problems require the employment of perpendicular and parallel lines. For this reason we will commence with this class of Problems.

The Demonstrations of these problems will be placed in an Appendix to this volume, which will be the most convenient arrangement for the two great classes of students of surveying; those who wish merely the practice without the principles, and those who wish to secure both.

The elegant "Theory of Transversals" will be an important element in some of these demonstrations. All of them will constitute excellent exercises for students.

PROBLEMS ON PERPENDICULARS.*

Problem 1. *To erect a perpendicular at any point of a line.*

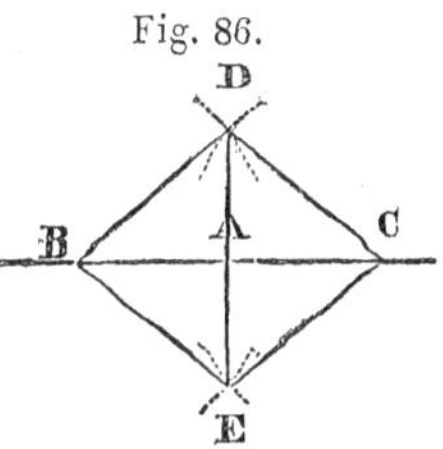

(140) *First Method.* Let A be the point at which a perpendicular to the line is to be set out. Measure off equal distances AB, AC, on each side of the point. Take a portion of the chain not quite $1\frac{1}{2}$ times as long as AB or AC, fix one end of this at B, and describe an arc with the other end. Do the same from C. The intersection of these arcs will fix a point D. AD will be the perpendicular required. Repeat the operation on the other side of the line. If that is impossible, repeat it on the side with a different length of chain.

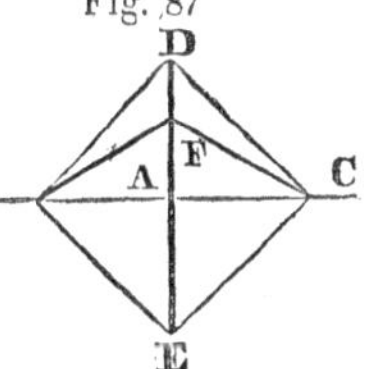

(141) *Second Method.* Measure off as before, equal distances AB, AC, but each about only one-third of the chain. Fasten the ends of the chain with two pins at B and C. Stretch it out on one side of the line and put a pin at the middle of it, D. Do the same on the other side of the line, and set a pin at E. Then is DE a perpendicular to BC. If it is impossible to perform the operation on both sides of the line, repeat it on the same side with a different length of chain, as shown by the lines BF and CF in the figure, so as to get a second point.

(142) *Other Methods.* All the methods to be given for the next problem may be applied to this.

* Many of these methods would seldom be required in practice, but cases sometimes occur, as every surveyor of much experience in Field-work has found to his serious inconvenience, in which some peculiarity of the local circumstances forbids any of the usual methods being applied. In such cases the collection here given will be found of great value.

In all the figures, the given and measured lines are drawn with fine full lines, the visual lines, or lines of sight, with broken lines, and the lines of the result with heavy full lines. The points which are centres around which the chain is swung, are enclosed in circles. The alphabetical order of the letters attached to the points shows in what order they are taken.

Problem 2. *To erect a perpendicular to a line at a given point, when the point is at or near the end of the line.*

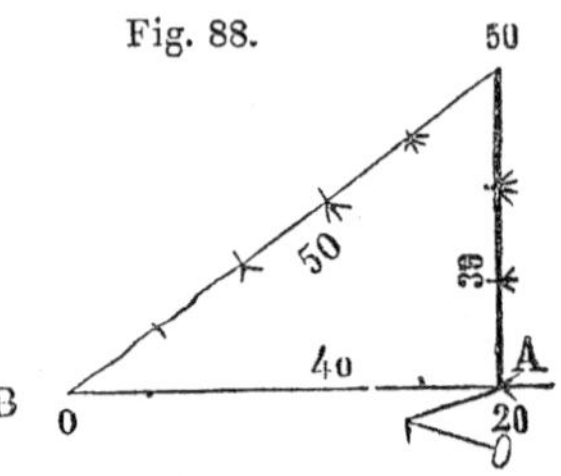

(143) *First Method.* Measure 40 links along the line. Let one assistant hold one end of the chain at that point; let a second hold the 20 link mark which is nearest the other end, at the given point A, and let a third take the 50 link mark, and tighten the chain, drawing equally on both portions of it. Then will the 50 link mark be in the perpendicular desired. Repeat the operation on the other side of the line so as to test the work.

The above numbers are the most easily remembered, but the longer the lines measured the better; and nearly the whole chain may be used, thus: Fix down the 36th link from one end at A, and the 4th link from the same end on the line at B. Fix the other end of the chain also at B. Take the 40th link mark from this last end, and draw the chain tight, and this mark will be in the perpendicular desired. The sides of the triangle formed by the chain will be 24, 32 and 40.

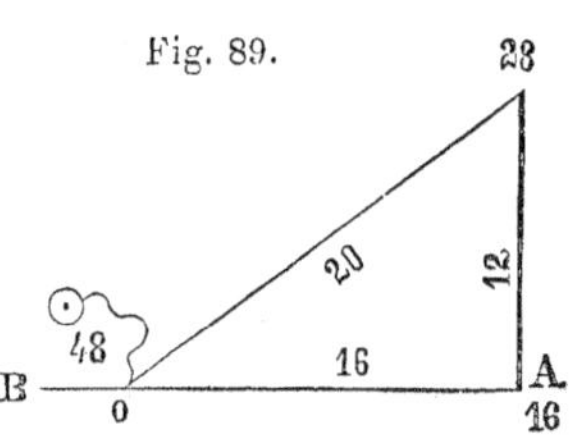

(144) Otherwise: using a 50 feet tape, hold the 16 feet mark at A; hold the 48 feet mark and the ring-end of the tape together on the line; take the 28 feet mark of the tape, and draw it tight; then will the 28 feet mark be in the perpendicular desired.

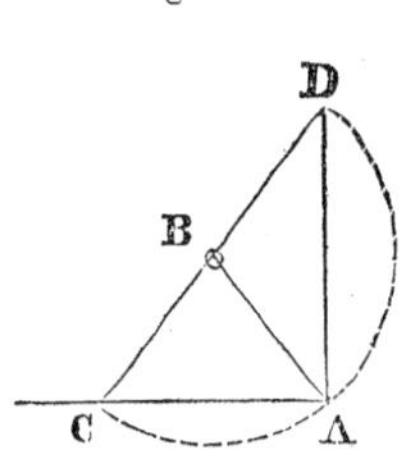

(145) *Second Method.* Hold one end of the chain at A and fix the other end at a point B, taken at will. Swing the chain around B as a centre, till it again meets the line at C. Then carry the same end around (the other end remaining at B) till it comes in the line of CB at D. AD is the perpendicular required.

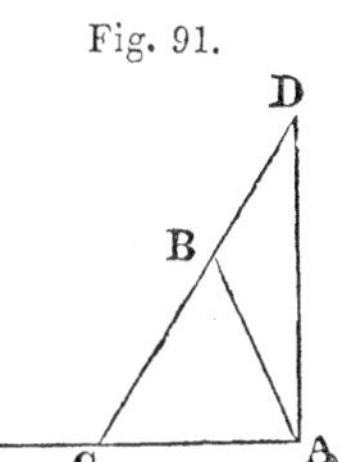

Fig. 91.

(146) *Third Method.* Let A be the given point. Choose any point B. Measure BA. Set off, on the given line, AC = AB. On CB produced set off from C, a distance $= \frac{2\ AC^2}{CB}$. This will fix the point D, and AD will be the perpendicular required.

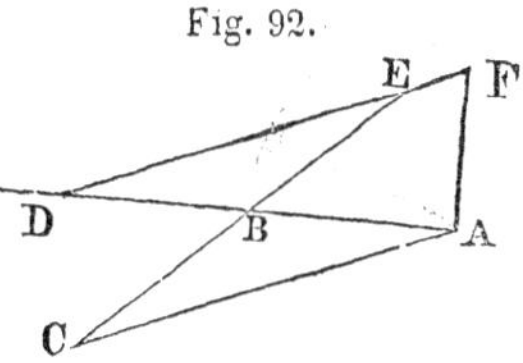

Fig. 92.

(147) *Fourth Method.* From the given point A set off on the given line any distance AB. From B, in any convenient direction, set off BC = AB. Then on the given line, set off AD = AC. On CB prolonged, set off CE = AD. Join DE; and on DE, from D, set off DF = 2 AB. Then will the line AF be perpendicular to the line AD at the point A.

Problem 3. *To erect a perpendicular to an inaccessible line, at a given point of it.*

(148) *First Method.* Get points in the direction of the inaccessible line prolonged, and from them set out a parallel to the line, by methods which are given in Art. (165), &c. Find by trial the point in which a perpendicular to this second line (and therefore to the first line) will pass through the required point.

(149) *Second Method.* If the line is not only inaccessible, but cannot have its direction prolonged, the desired perpendicular can be obtained only by a complicated trigonometrical operation.

Problem 4. *To let fall a perpendicular from a given point to a given line.*

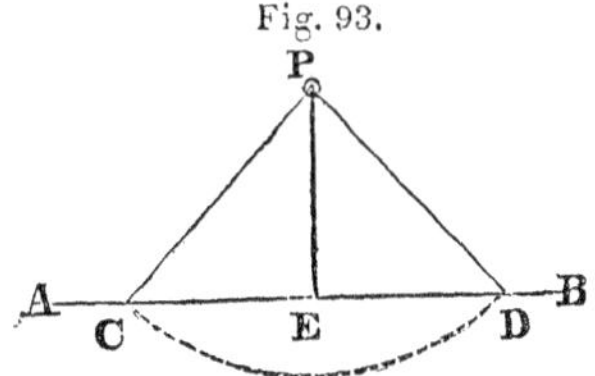

Fig. 93.

(150) *First Method.* Let P be the given point, and AB the given line. Measure some distance, a chain or less, from C to P, and then fix one end of the chain at P, and swing it around till the same distance meets the line at some point D. The middle point E of the distance CD will be the required point, at which the perpendicular from P would meet the line.

(151) *Second Method.* Stretch a chain, or a portion of it, from the given point P, to some point, as A, of the given line. Hold the end of the distance at A, and swing round the other end of the chain from P, so as to set off the same distance along the given line from A to some point B. Measure BP. Then will the distance BC from B to the foot of the desired perpendicular $= \frac{BP^2}{2\,AB}$.

Fig. 94.

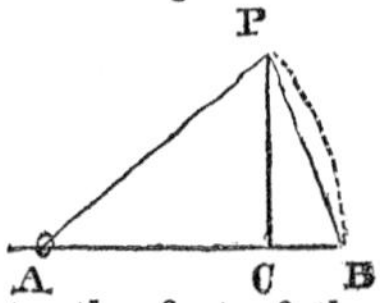

(152) *Other Methods.* All the methods given in the next problem can be applied to this one.

Problem 5. *To let fall a perpendicular to a line, from a point nearly opposite to the end of the line.*

(153) *First Method.* Stretch a chain from the given point P, to some point, as A, of the given line. Fix to the ground the middle point B of the chain AP, and swing around the end which was at P, or at A, till it meets the given line in a point C, which will be the foot of the required perpendicular.

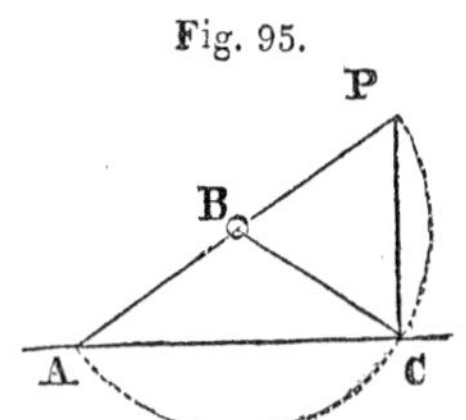

Fig. 95.

(154) *Second Method.* Take any point, as A, on the given line. Measure a distance AB. Let the end of this distance on the chain be held at B, and swing around the end of the chain, till it comes in the line of AP at some point C, thus making BC = AB. Measure AC and AP. Then the distance AD, from A to the foot of the perpendicular required $= \frac{AP \times AC}{2\,AB}$.

Fig. 96

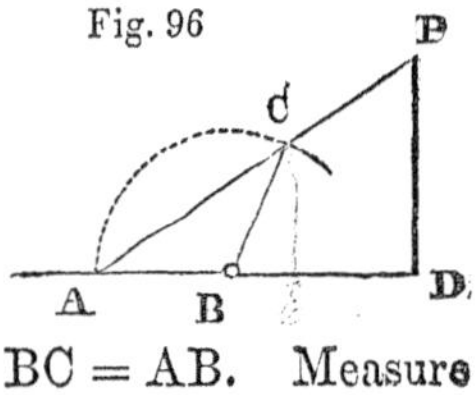

(155) *Third Method.* At any convenient point, as A, of the given line, erect a perpendicular, of any convenient length, as AB, and mark a point C on the given line, in the line of P and B. Measure CA, CB and CP. Then the distance from C to the foot of the perpendicular, i. e. $CD = \frac{CA \times CP}{CB}$.

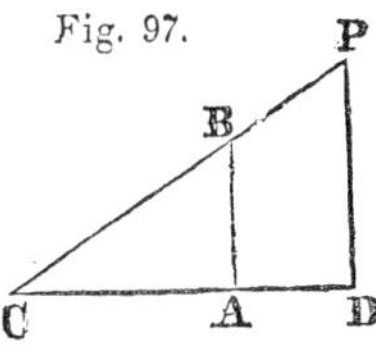

Fig. 97.

Problem 6. *To let fall a perpendicular to a line, from an inaccessible point.*

(156) *First Method.* Let P be the given point. At any point A, on the given line, set out a perpendicular AB of any convenient length. Prolong it on the other side of the line the same distance. Mark on the given line a point D in the line of PB; and a point E in the line of PC. Mark the point F at the intersection of DC and BE prolonged. The line FP is the line required, being perpendicular to the given line at the point G.

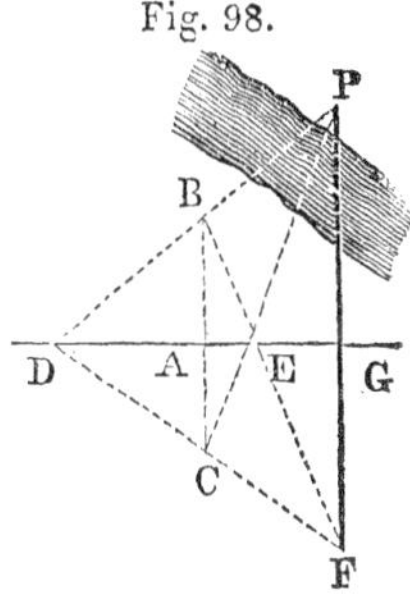

Fig. 98.

(157) *Second Method.* Let A and B be two points of the given line. From A let fall a perpendicular, AC, to the visual line BP; and from B let fall a perpendicular, BD, to the visual line AP. Find the point at which these perpendiculars intersect, as at E (see Art. (**133**)), and the line PE, prolonged to F, will give the perpendicular required.

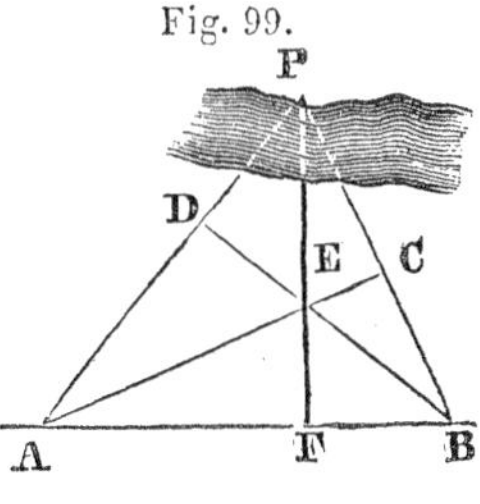

Fig. 99.

Problem 7. *To let fall a perpendicular from a given point to an inaccessible line.*

(158) *First Method.* Let P be the given point and AB the given line. By the preceding problem, let fall perpendiculars from A to BP, at C; and from B to AP, at D; the line PE, passing from the given point to the intersection of these perpendiculars, is the desired perpendicular to the inaccessible line AB.

Fig. 100.

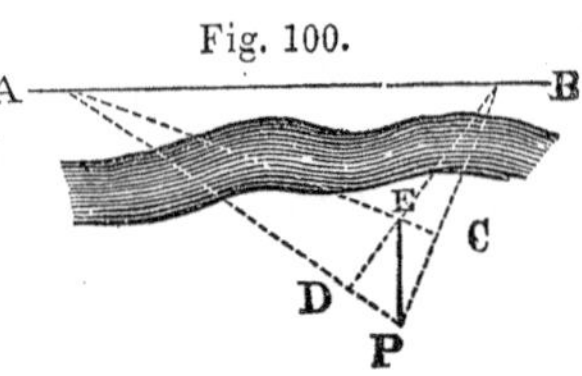

This method will apply when only two points of the line are visible.

(159) *Second Method.* Through the given point, set out, by the methods of Art. **(165)**, &c., a line parallel to the inaccessible line. At the given point erect a perpendicular to the parallel line, and it will be the required perpendicular to the inaccessible line.

PROBLEMS ON PARALLELS.

Problem 1. *To run a line, from a given point, parallel to a given line.*

(160) *First Method.* Let fall a perpendicular from the point to the line. At another point of the line, as far off as possible, erect a perpendicular, equal in length to the one just let fall. The line joining the end of this line to the given point will be the parallel required.

(161) *Second Method.* Let AB be the given line, and P the given point. Take any point, as C, on the given line, and from it set off equal distances, as long as possible, CD on the given line, and CE, on the line CP. Measure DE. From P set off PF = CE; and from F, with a distance = DE, and from P, with a distance = CD, describe arcs intersecting in G. PG will be the parallel required. If it is more convenient, PC may be prolonged, and the equal triangle, CDE, be formed on the other side of the line AB.

Fig. 101.

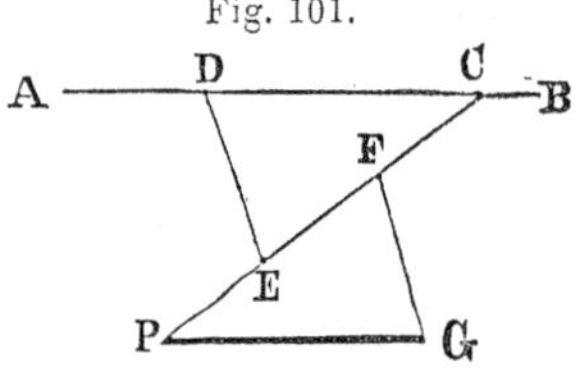

(162) *Third Method.* Measure from P to any point, as C, of the given line, and put a mark at the middle point, D, of that line. From any point, as E, of the given line, measure a line to the point D, and continue it till DF = DE. Then will the line PF be parallel to AB.

Fig. 102.

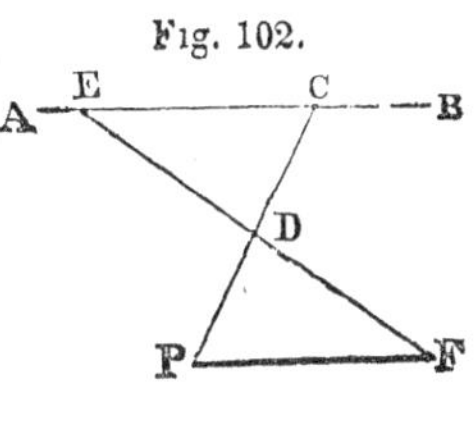

(163) *Fourth Method.* Measure from P to any point C, of the given line, and continue the measurement till CD = CP. From D measure to any point E of the given line, and continue the measurement till EF = ED. Then will the line PF be parallel to AB. If more convenient, CD may be made one-half, or any other fraction, of CP, and EF be then made twice, &c., DE.

Fig. 103.

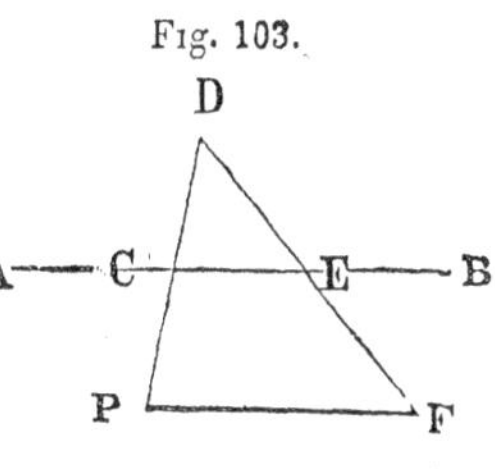

(164) *Fifth Method.* From any point, as C, of the line, set off equal distances along the line, to D and E. Take a point F, in the line of PD. Stake out the lines FC and FE, and also the line EP, crossing the line CF in the point G. Lastly, prolong the line DG, till it meets the line EF in the point H. PH is the parallel required.

Fig. 104.

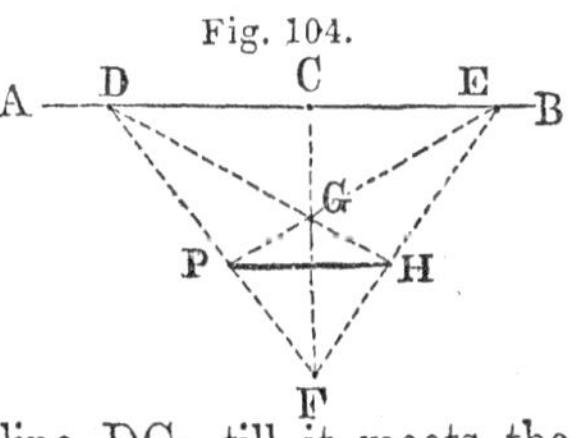

Problem 2. *To run a line from a given point parallel to an inaccessible line.*

(165) *First Method.* Let AB be the given line, and P the given point. Set a stake at C, in the line of PA, and another at any convenient point, D. Through P, set out, by the preceding problem, a parallel to DA, and set a stake at the point, as E, where this parallel intersects DC prolonged. Through E

Fig. 105.

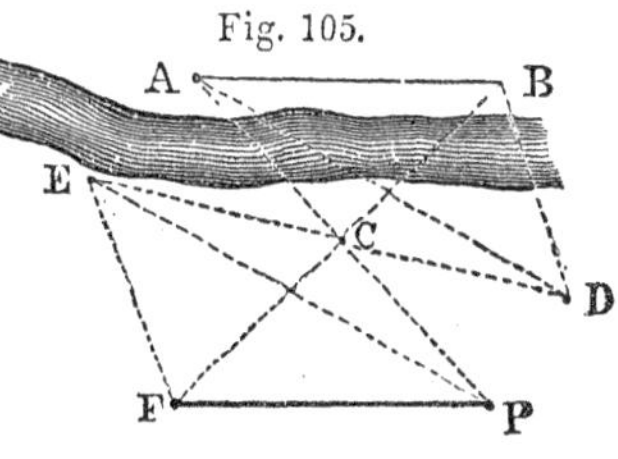

set out a parallel to BD, and set a stake at the point F, where this parallel intersects BC prolonged. PF is the parallel required

Fig. 106.

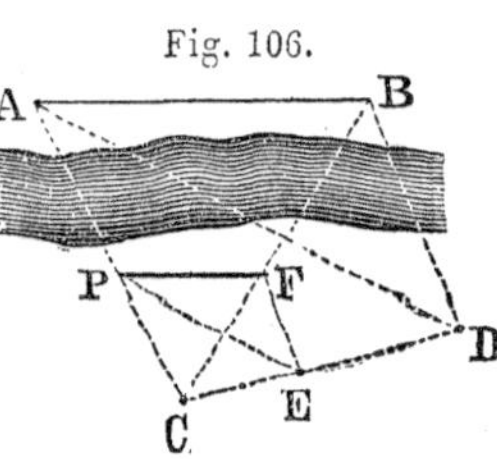

(166) *Second Method.* Set a stake at any point, C, in the line of AP, and another at any convenient place, as at D. Through P set out a parallel to AD, intersecting CD in E. Through E set out a parallel to DB, intersecting CB in F. The line PF will be the parallel required.

(167) Alinement and Measurement. We are now prepared, having secured a variety of methods for setting out Perpendiculars and Parallels in every probable case, to take up the general subject of overcoming Obstacles to Measurement.

Before a line can be measured, its direction must be determined. This operation is called *Ranging* the line; or *Alining* it; or *Boning* it.* The word *Alinement*† will be found very convenient for expressing the direction of a line on the ground, whether between two points, or in their direction prolonged.

This branch of our subject naturally divides itself into two parts, the first of which is preliminary to the second; viz:

I. Of Obstacles to Alinement; *or how to establish the direction of a line in any situation.*

II. Of Obstacles to Measurement; *or how to find the length of a line which cannot be actually measured.*

I. OBSTACLES TO ALINEMENT.

(168) All the cases which can occur under this head, may be reduced to two; viz:

A. To find points in a line *beyond* the given points, i. e. to *prolong* the line.

B. To find points in a line *between* two given points of it, i. e. to *interpolate* points in the line.

* This word, like many others used in Engineering, is derived from a French word, *Borner*, to mark out, or limit; indicating that the Normans introduced the art of Surveying into England.

† Slightly modified from the French *Alignement.*

A. TO PROLONG A LINE

(169) By ranging with rods. When two points in a line are given, and it is desired to prolong the line by ranging it out with rods, three persons are required, each furnished with a straight slender rod, and with a plumb-line, or other means of keeping their rods vertical. One holds his rod at one of the given points, A, in the figure, and another at B. A third, C, goes forward as far as he can without losing sight of the first two rods, and then, looking back, puts himself "in line" with A and B, i. e. so that when his eye is placed at C, the rod at B hides or covers the rod at A. This he can do most accurately by holding a plumb-line before his eye, so that it shall cover the first two rods. The lower end of the plumb-bob will then indicate the point where the third rod should be placed; and so with the rest. The first man, at A, is then signalled, and comes forward, passes both the others, and puts himself at D, "in line" with C and B. The man at B, then goes on to E, and "lines" himself with D and C: and so they proceed, in this "hand over hand" operation, as far as is desired. Stakes are driven at each point in the line, as soon as it is determined.

Fig. 107.

(170) The rods should be perfectly straight, either cylindrical or polygonal, and as slender as they can be without bending. They should be painted in alternate bands of red and white, each a foot, or link, in length. Their lower ends should be pointed with iron, and a projecting bolt of iron will enable them to be pressed down by the foot into the earth, so that they can stand alone. When this is done, one man can range out a line. A rod can be set perfectly vertical, by holding a plumb-line before the eye at some distance from the rod, and adjusting the rod so that the plumb-line covers it from top to bottom; and then repeating the operation in a direction at right angles to the former. A stone dropped from top to bottom of the rods will approximately attain the same end.

When the lines to be ranged are long, and great accuracy is required, the rods may have attached to them plates of tin with open ings cut out of them, and black horse-hairs stretched from top to bottom of the openings. A small telescope must then be used for ranging these hairs in line. In a hasty survey, straight twigs, with their tops split to receive a paper folded as in the figure, may be used.

Fig. 108

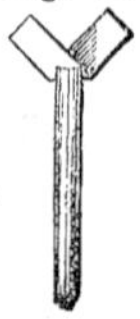

(171) By perpendiculars. The straight line, AB in the figure, is supposed to be stopped by a tree, a house, or other obstacle, and it is desired to prolong the line beyond this obstacle. From any two points, as A and B, of the line, set off (by some of the methods which have been given) equal perpendiculars, AC and BD, long enough to pass the obstacle. Prolong this line beyond the obstacle, and from any two points in it, as E and F, measure the perpendiculars EG and FH, equal to the first two, but in a contrary direction. Then will G and H be two points in the line AB prolonged, which can be continued by the method of the last article. The points A and B should be taken as far apart as possible, as should also the points E and F. Three or more perpendiculars, on each side of the obstacle, may be set off, in order to increase the accuracy of the operation. The same thing may also be done on the other side of the line, as another confirmation, or test, of the accuracy of the prolonged line.

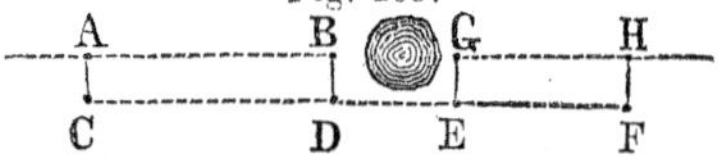

Fig. 109.

(172) By equilateral triangles. The obstacles, noticed in the last article, may also be overcome by means of three equilateral triangles, formed by the chain. Fix one end of the chain, and also the end of the first link from its other end, at B; fix the end of the 33d link at A; take hold of the 66th link, and draw the chain tight, pulling equally on each part, and put a pin at the point thus found, C, in the figure. An equilateral triangle will thus be formed, each side being 33 links. Prolong the line AC, past the obstacle, to some point, as D. Make another

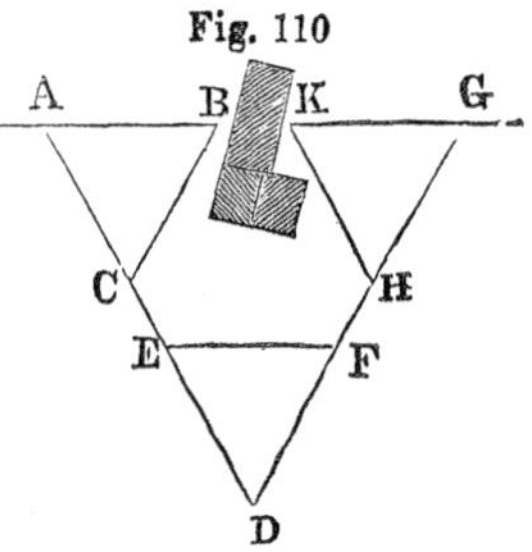

Fig. 110

equilateral triangle, DEF, as before, and thus fix the point F. Prolong DF, to a length equal to that of AD, and thus fix a point G. At G form a third equilateral triangle GHK, and thus fix a point K. Then will KG give the direction of AB prolonged.

(173) By symmetrical triangles. Let AB be the line to be prolonged. Take any convenient point, as C. Range out the line AC, to a point A′, such that CA′ = CA. Range out CB, so that CB′ = CB. Range backwards A′B′, to some point D, such that DC prolonged will pass the obstacle. Find, by ranging, the intersection, at E, of DB and AC. From C, measure, on CA′, the distance CE′ = CE. Then range out DC and B′E′ to their intersection in P, which will be a required point in the direction of AB prolonged. The symmetrical points are marked by corresponding letters. Several other points should be obtained in the same manner.

Fig. 111.

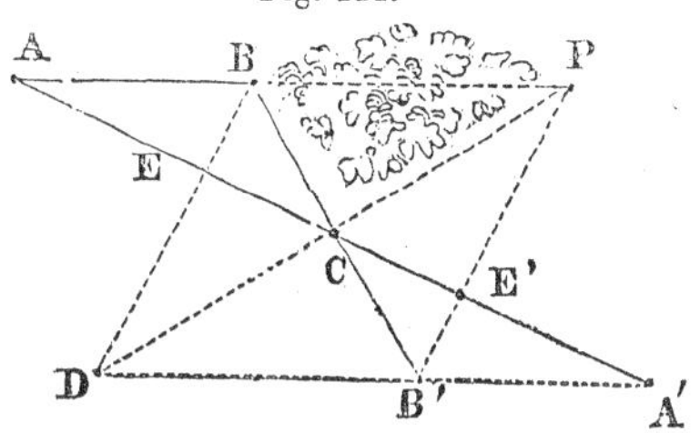

In this, as in all similar operations, very acute intersections should be avoided as far as possible.

(174) By transversals. Let AB be the given line. Take any two points C and D, such that the line CD will pass the obstacle. Take another point, E, in the intersection of CA and DB. Measure AE, AC, CD, BD and BE. Then the distance from D to P, a point in the required prolongation, will be

$$DP = \frac{CD \times BD \times AE}{BE \times AC - BD \times AE}.$$

Fig. 112.

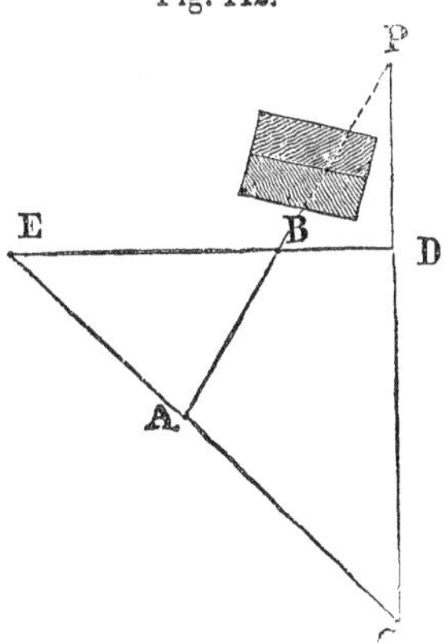

Other points in the prolongation may be obtained in the same manner, by merely moving the single point C, in the line of EA; in which case the new distances CA and CD will alone require to be measured.

If AE be made equal to AC, then is $DP = \frac{CD \times BD}{BE - BD}$.

If BE be made equal to BD, then is $DP = \frac{CD \times AE}{AC - AE}$.

The *minus* sign in the denominators must be understood as only meaning that the difference of the two terms is to be taken, without regard to which is the greater.

(175) By harmonic conjugates. Let AB be the given line. Set a stake at any point C. Set stakes at points, D, on the line CA, and at E, on the line CB; these points, D and E, being so chosen that the line DE will pass beyond the obstacle. Set a fourth stake, F, at the intersection of the lines AE and DB. Set a fifth stake, G, anywhere in the line CF; a sixth stake, H, at the intersection of CB and DG prolonged; and a seventh, K, at the intersection of CA and EG prolonged. Finally, range out the lines DE and KH, and their intersection at P, will be in the line AB prolonged.

Fig. 113.

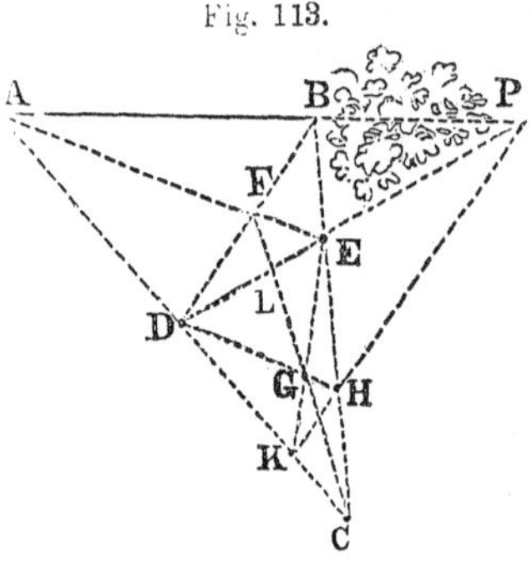

(176) By the complete quadrilateral. Let AB be the given line. Take any convenient point C; measure from it to B, and onward, in the same line prolonged, an equal distance to D. Take any other convenient point, E, such that CE and DE produced will clear the obstacle. Measure from E to A, and onward, an equal distance, to F. Range out the lines FC and DE to their intersection in G. Range out FD and CE to intersect in H. Measure GH. Its middle point, P, is the required point in the line of AB prolonged. The unavoidable acute intersections in this construction are objectionable.

Fig. 114

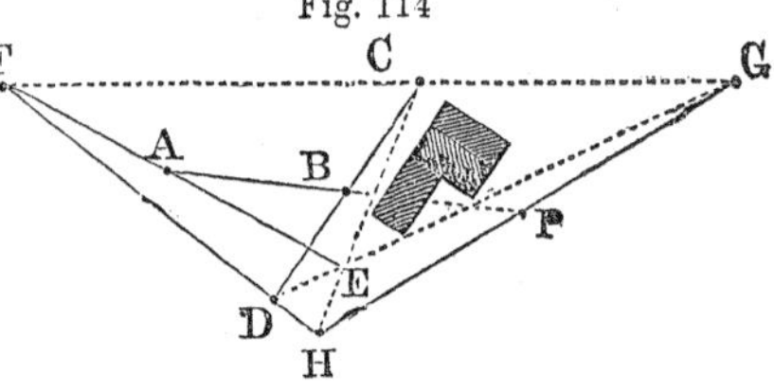

B. TO INTERPOLATE POINTS IN A LINE.

(177) The most distant given point of the line must be made as conspicuous as possible, by any efficient means, such as placing there a staff, bearing a flag; red and white, if seen against woods, or other dark back-ground; and red and green, if seen against the sky.

A convenient and portable signal is shown in the figure.

Fig. 115.

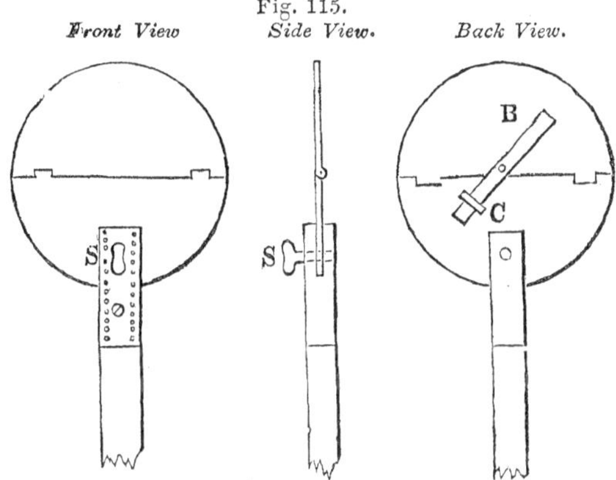

The figure represents a disc of tin, about six inches in diameter, painted white and hinged in the middle, to make it more portable. It is kept open by the bar, B, being turned into the catch, C. A screw, S, holds the disc in a slit in the top of the pole.

Another contrivance is a strip of tin, which has its ends bent horizontally in contrary directions. As the wind will take strongest hold of the side which is concave towards it, the bent strip will continually revolve, and thus be very conspicuous. Its upper half should be painted red and its lower half white.

A bright tin cone set on the staff, can be seen at a great distance when the sun is shining.

178) Ranging to a point, thus made conspicuous, is very simple when the ground is level. The surveyor places his eye at the nearest end of the line, or stands a little behind a rod placed on it, and by signs moves an assistant, holding a rod at some point as nearly in the desired line as he can guess, to the right or left, till his rod appears to cover the distant point.

(179) Across a valley. When a valley, or low spot, intervenes between the two ends of the line, A and Z in the figure, a rod held in the low place, as at B, would seldom be high enough to be seen, from A, to cover the distant rod at Z. In such a case, the surveyor at A should hold up a plumb-line over the point, at arm's length, and place his eye so that the plumb-line covers the rod at Z. He should then direct the rod held at B to be moved till it too is covered by the plumb-line. The point B is then said to be "in line" between A and Z. In geometrical language, B has now been placed in the vertical plane determined by the vertical plumb-line and the point Z. Any number of intermediate points can thus be "interpolated," or placed in line between A and Z.

Fig. 116.

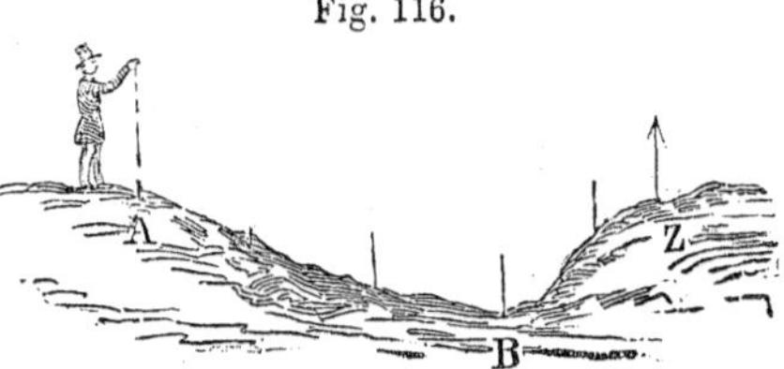

(180) Over a hill. When a hill rises between two points and prevents one being seen from the other, as in the figure, (the upper

Fig. 117.

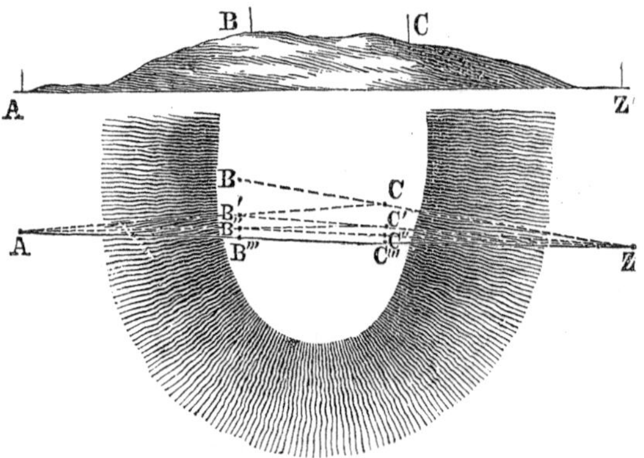

of which shows the hill in "Elevation," and the lower part in "Plan"), two observers, B and C, each holding a rod, may place themselves on the ridge, in the line between the two points, as nearly as they can guess, and so that each can at once see the other and the point beyond him. B looks to Z, and by signals puts C "in line." C then looks to A, and puts B in line at B′. B repeats his operation from B′, putting C at C′, and is then himself moved to B″, and so they alternately "line" each other, continually approximating to the straight line between A and Z, till they at last find themselves both exactly in it, at B‴ and C‴.

(181) A single person may put himself in line between two points, on the same principle, by laying a straight stick on some support, going to each end of it in turn, and making it point successively to each end of the line. The "Surveyor's Cross," Art. **(104)**, is convenient for this purpose, when set up between the two given points, and moved again and again, until, by repeated trials, one of its slits sights to the given points when looked through in either direction.

(182) On water. A simple instrument for the same object, is represented in the figure. AB and CD are two tubes, about $1\frac{1}{2}$ inches in diameter, connected by a smaller tube EF. A piece of looking-glass, GH, is placed in the lower part of the tube AB, and another, KL, in the tube CD. The planes of the two mirrors are at right angles to each other. The eye is placed at A, and the tube AB is directed to any distant object, as X, and any other object behind the observer, as Z, will be seen, apparently under the first object in the mirror GH, by reflection from the mirror KL, when the observer has succeeded in getting in line between the two objects. M, N, are screws by which the mirror KL may be adjusted. The distance between the two tubes will cause a small parallax, which will, however, be insensible except when the two objects are near together.

Fig. 118.

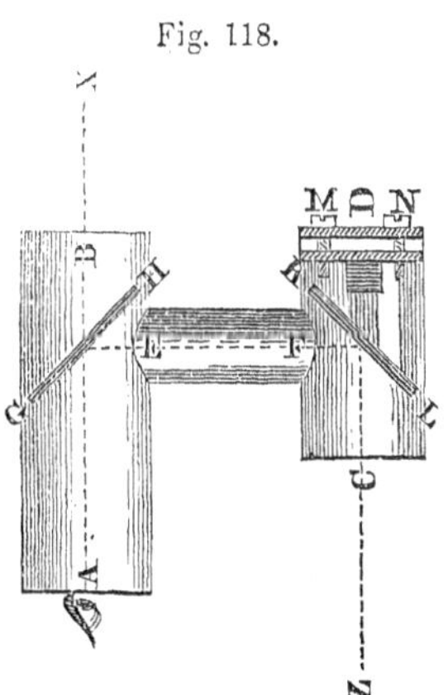

(183) Through a wood. When a wood intervenes between any two given points, preventing one from being seen from the other, as in the figure, in which A and Z are the given points, proceed thus.

Fig. 119.

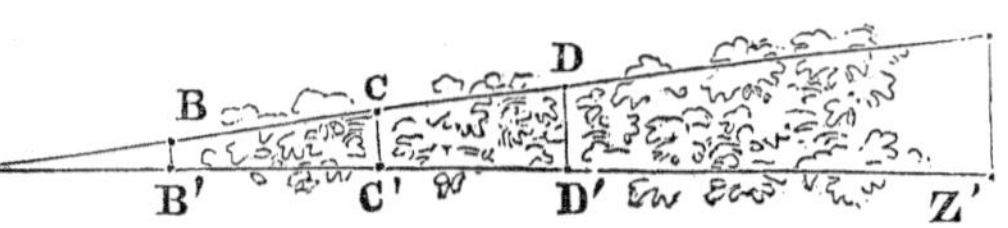

Hold a rod at some point B′ as nearly in the desired line from A as can be guessed at, and as far from A as possible. To approximate to the proper direction, an assistant may be sent to the other end of the line, and his shouts will indicate the direction; or a gun may be fired there; or, if very distant, a rocket may be sent up after dark. Then range out the "random line" AB′, by the method given in Art. (169), noting also the distance from A to each point found, till you arrive at a point Z′, opposite to the point Z, i. e. at that point of the line from which a perpendicular there erected would strike the point Z. Measure Z′Z. Then move each of the stakes, perpendicularly from the line AZ′, a distance proportional to their distances from A. Thus, if AZ′ be 1000 links, and Z′Z be 10 links, then a stake B′, 200 links from A, should be moved 2 links to a point B, which will be in the desired straight line AZ; if C′ be 400 links from A, it should be moved 4 links to C, and so with the rest. The line should then be cleared, and the accuracy of the position, of these stakes tested by ranging from A to Z.

(184) To an invisible intersection. Let AB and CD be two lines, which, if prolonged, would meet in a point Z, invisible from either of them; and let P be a point, from which a line is required to be set out, tending to this invisible intersection.

Fig. 120.

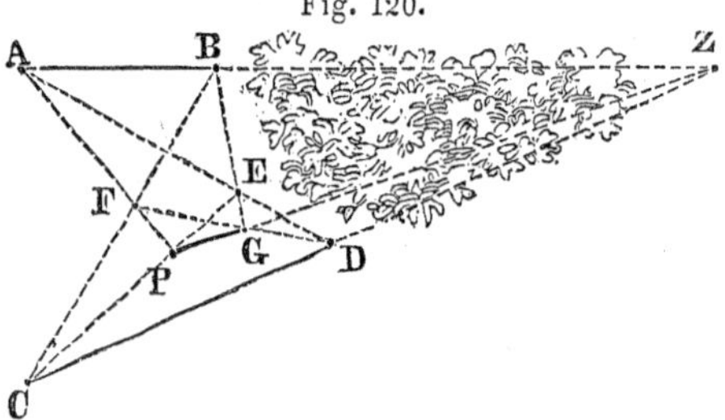

Set stakes at the five given points, A, B, C, D, P. Set a sixth stake at E, in the alinements of AD and CP; and a seventh stake at F, in the alinements of BC and AP. Then set an eighth stake at G, in the alinements of BE and DF. PG will be the required line.

Otherwise; Through P range out a parallel to the line BD. Note the points where this parallel meets AB and CD, and call these points Q and R. Then the distance from B, on the line BD, to a point which shall be in the required line running from P to the invisible point, will be $= \frac{BD \times QP}{QR}$.

II. OBSTACLES TO MEASUREMENT.

(185) The cases, in which the direct measurement of a line is prevented by various obstacles, may be reduced to three.

A. When both ends of the line are accessible.

B. When one end of it is inaccessible.

C. When both ends of it are inaccessible.

A. WHEN BOTH ENDS OF THE LINE ARE ACCESSIBLE.

(186) By perpendiculars. On reaching the obstacle, as at A in the figure, set off a perpendicular, AB; turn a second right angle at B, and measure past the obstacle; turn a third right angle at C; and measure to the original line at D. Then will the measured distance, BC, be equal to the desired distance, AD.

Fig. 121.

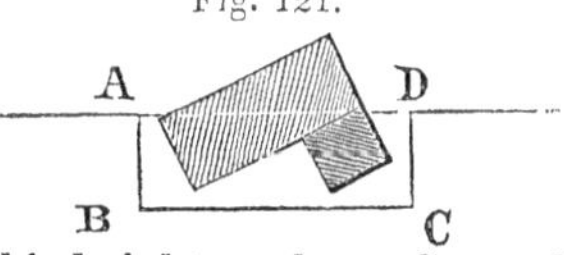

If the direction of the line is also unknown, it will be most easily obtained by the additional perpendiculars shown in Fig. 109, of Art. (171).

(187) By equilateral triangles. The method given in Art. (172), for determining the direction of a line through an obstacle, will also give its length; for in Fig. 121′ (Fig. 110 repeated) the desired distance AG is equal to the measured distances AD, or DG.

Fig. 121′.

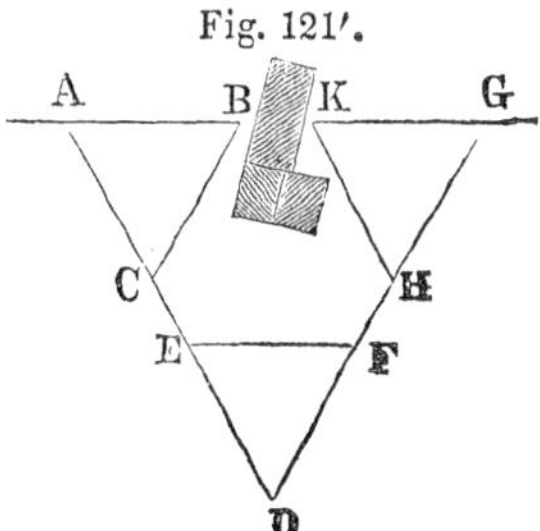

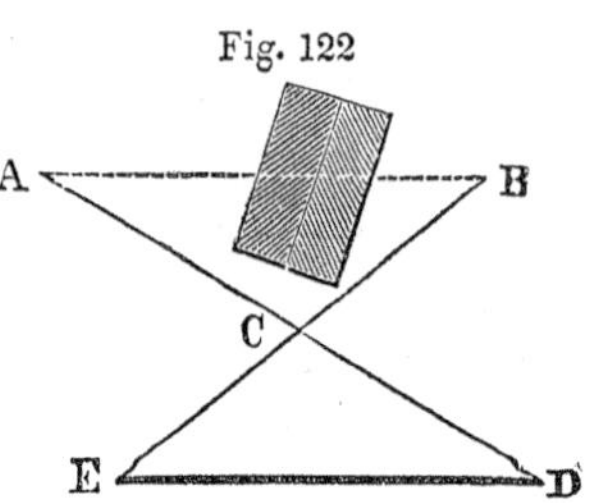

Fig. 122

(188) By symmetrical triangles. Let AB be the distance required. Measure from A obliquely to some point C, past the obstacle. Measure onward, in the same line, till CD is as long as AC. Place stakes at C and D. From B measure to C, and from C measure onward, in the same line, till CE is equal to CB. Measure ED, and it will be equal to AB, the distance required. If more convenient, make CD and CE equal, respectively, to half of AC and CB; then will AB be equal to twice DE.

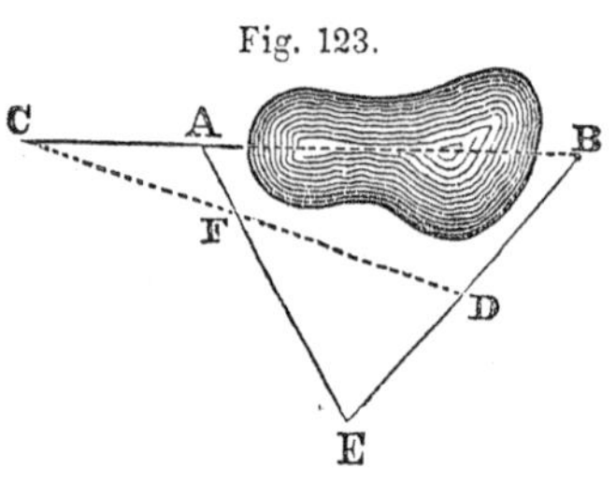

Fig. 123.

(189) By transversals. Let AB be the required distance. Set a stake, C, in the line prolonged; set another stake, D, so that C and B can be seen from it; and a third stake, E, in the line of BD prolonged, and at a distance from D equal to the distance from D to B. Set a fourth stake, F, at the intersection of EA and CD. Measure AC, AF and FE. Then is $AB = \frac{AC}{AF}$ (FE—AF).

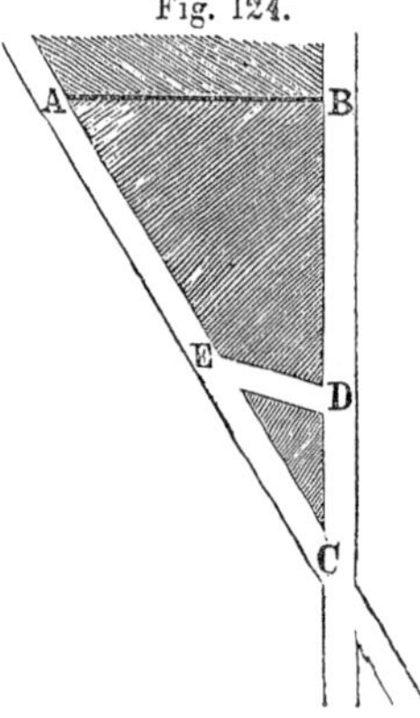

Fig. 124.

(190) In a Town. Cases may occur, in the streets of a compactly built town, in which it is impossible to measure along any other lines than those of the streets. The figure represents such a case, in which is required the distance, AB, between points situated on two streets which meet at the point C, and between which runs a cross-street, DE. In this case measure AC, CE, CD, DE and CB. Then is the required distance

$$AB = \sqrt{\left\{ (AC - BC)^2 + \left[DE^2 - (CE - CD)^2\right] \frac{AC \times BC}{CD \times CE} \right\}}$$

As this expression is somewhat complicated, an example will be given: Let AC = 100, CE = 40, CD = 30, DE = 21, and CB = 80; then will AB = 51.7.

B. WHEN ONE END OF THE LINE IS INACCESSIBLE.

(191) By perpendiculars. This principle may be applied in a variety of ways. In Fig. 125, let AB be the required distance. At the point A, set off AC, perpendicular to AB, and of any convenient length. At C, set off a perpendicular to CB, and continue it to a point, D, in the line of A and B. Measure DA. Then is $AB = \frac{AC^2}{AD}$.

Fig. 125.

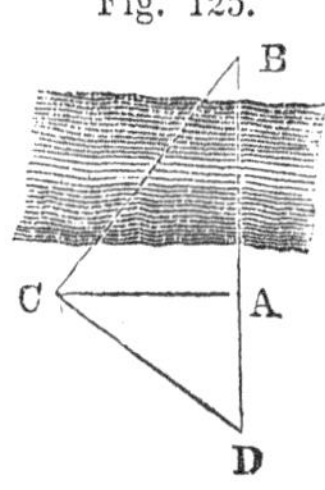

(192) *Otherwise:* At the point A, in Fig. 126, set off a perpendicular, AC. At C set off another perpendicular, CD. Find a point, E, in the line of AC, and BD. Measure AE and EC. Then is $AB = \frac{AE \times CD}{CE}$.

Fig. 126

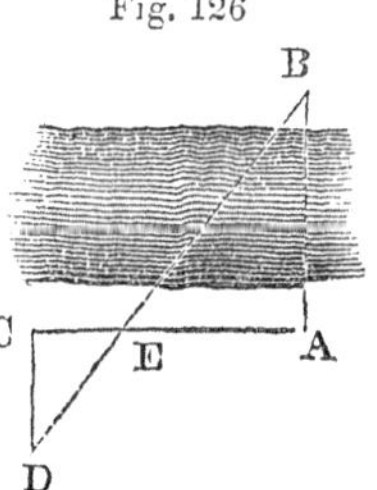

If EC be made equal to AE, and D be set in the line of BE, and also in the perpendicular from C, then will CD be equal to AB.

If $EC = \frac{1}{2} AE$, then $CD = \frac{1}{2} AB$.

(193) *Otherwise:* At A, in Fig. 127, measure a perpendicular, AC, to the line AB; and at any point, as D, in this line, set off a perpendicular to DB, and continue it to a point E, in the line of CB. Measure DE and also DA. Then is $AB = \frac{AC \times AD}{DE - AC}$.

Fig. 127.

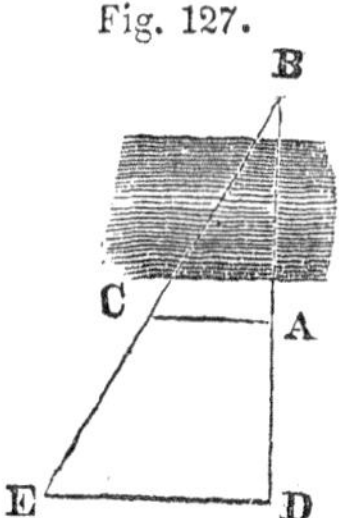

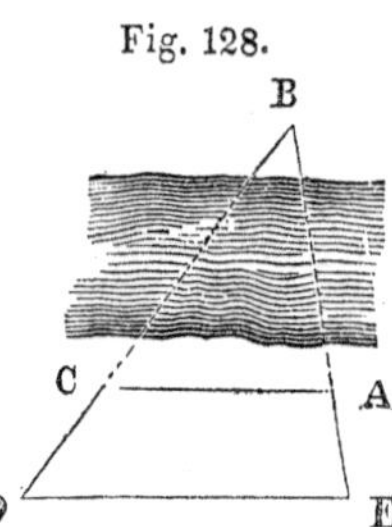

Fig. 128.

(194) By parallels. From A measure AC, in any convenient direction. From a point D, in the line of BC, measure a line parallel to CA, to a point E, in the line of AB. Measure also AE.

Then is $AB = \frac{AC \times AE}{DE - AC}$.

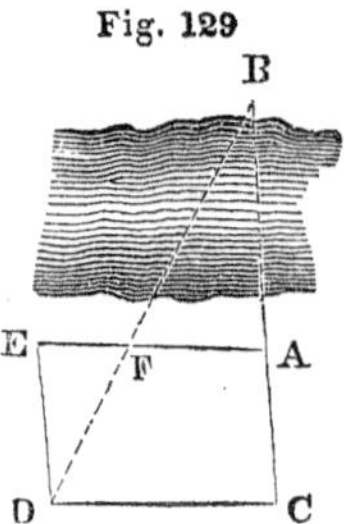

Fig. 129

(195) By a parallelogram. Set a stake, C, in the line of A and B, and set another stake, D, wherever convenient. With a distance equal to CD, describe from A, an arc on the ground; and, with a distance equal to AC, describe another arc from D, intersecting the first arc in E. Or, take AC and CD, so that together they make one chain; fix the ends of the chain at A and D; take hold of the chain at such a link, that one part of it equals AC, and the other CD, and draw it tight to fix the point E. Set a stake at F, in the intersection of AE and DB. Measure AF and EF. Then is $AB = \frac{AC \times AF}{EF}$; or, $CB = \frac{AC \times CD}{EF}$.

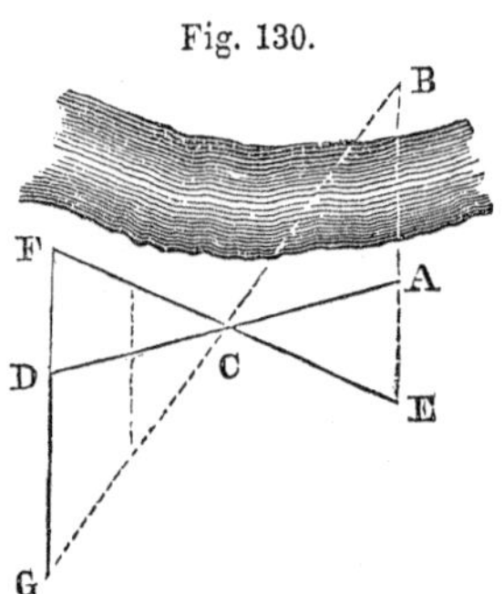

Fig. 130.

(196) By symmetrical triangles. Let AB be the required distance. From A measure a line, in any convenient direction, as AC, and measure onward, in the same direction, till CD = AC. Take any point E in the line of A and B. Measure from E to C, and onward in the same line, till CF = CE. Then find by trial a point G, which shall be at the same time in the line of C and B, and in the line of D and F. Measure the distance from G to D, and it will be equal to the required distance from A to B. If more convenient, make $CD = \frac{1}{2} AC$, and $CF = \frac{1}{2} CE$, as shown by the finely dotted lines in the figure. Then will $DG = \frac{1}{2} AB$.

(197) *Otherwise:* Prolong BA to some point C. Range out any convenient line CA′, and measure CA′ = CA. The triangle CA′B, is now to be reproduced in a symmetrical triangle, situated on the accessible ground. For this object, take, on AC, some point D, and measure CD′ = CD. Find the point E, at the intersection of AD′ and A′D. Find the point F, at the intersection of A′B and CE. Lastly, find the point B′, at the intersection of AF and CA′. Then will A′B′ = AB. The symmetrical points have corresponding letters affixed to them.

Fig. 131.

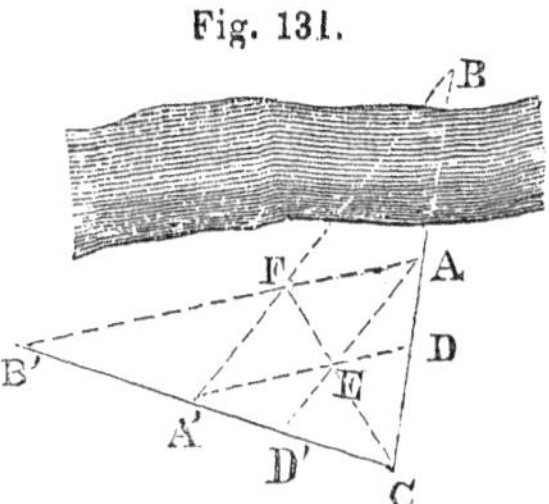

(198) By transversals. Set a stake, C, in the alinement of BA; a second, D, at any convenient point; a third, E, in the line CD; and a fourth, F, at the intersection of the alinements of DA and EB. Measure AC, CE, ED, DF and FA. Then is

$$AB = \frac{AC \times AF \times DE}{CE \times DF - AF \times DE}.$$

Fig. 132.

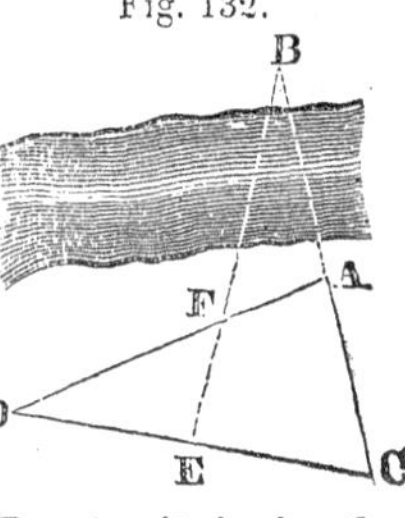

If the point E be taken in the middle of CD, (as it is in the figure) then $AB = \frac{AC \times AF}{DF - AF}$.

If the point F be taken in the middle of AD, then $AB = \frac{AC \times DE}{CE - DE}$.

The *minus* signs must be interpreted as in Art. (**174**).

(199) By harmonic division. Set stakes, C and D, on each side of A, and so that the three are in the same straight line. Set a third stake at any point, E, of the line AB. Set a fourth, F, at the intersection of CB and DE; and a fifth, G, at the intersection of DB and CE. Set a sixth stake, H, at the intersection of AB and FG. Measure AE and EH. Then is $AB = \frac{AE \times AH}{AE - EH}$.

Fig. 133.

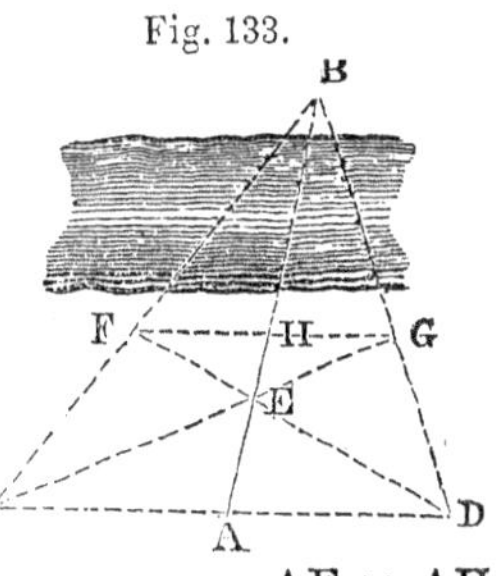

(200) To an inaccessible line. The shortest distance, CD, from a given point, C, to an inaccessible straight line AB, is required. From C let fall a perpendicular to AB, by the method of Art. (**158**). Then set a stake at any point, E, on the line AC; set a second, F, at the intersection of EB and CD; a third, G, at the intersection of AF and CB; and a fourth, H, at the intersection of EG and CD. Measure CH and HF. Then is

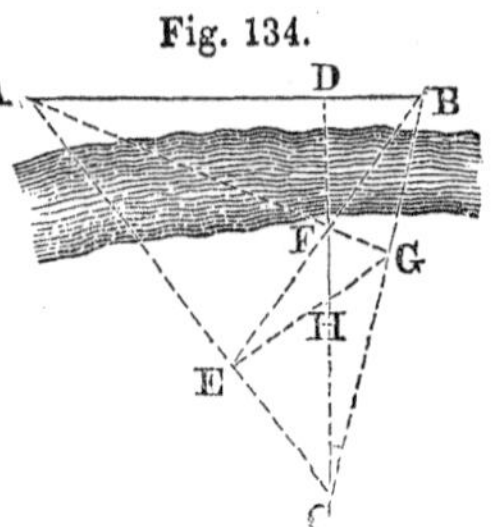

Fig. 134.

$$CD = \frac{CH \times CF}{CH - HF}; \text{ or, } CD = CH \cdot \frac{CH + HF}{CH - HF}; \text{ or, } CD = \frac{CH \times CF}{2CH - CF}$$

Otherwise; When the inaccessible line is determined by the method of Art. (**205**) or (**206**), the distance from any point to it, can be at once measured to its symmetrical representative.

(201) To an inaccessible intersection. When two lines (as AB, CD, in the figure) meet in a river, a building, or any other inaccessible point, the distance from any point of either to their intersection, DE, for example, may be found thus. From any point B, on one line, measure BD, and continue it, till DF = DB. From any other point, G, of the former line, measure GD, and continue the line till DH = GD. Continue HF to meet DC in some point K. Measure KD. KD will be equal to the desired distance DE.

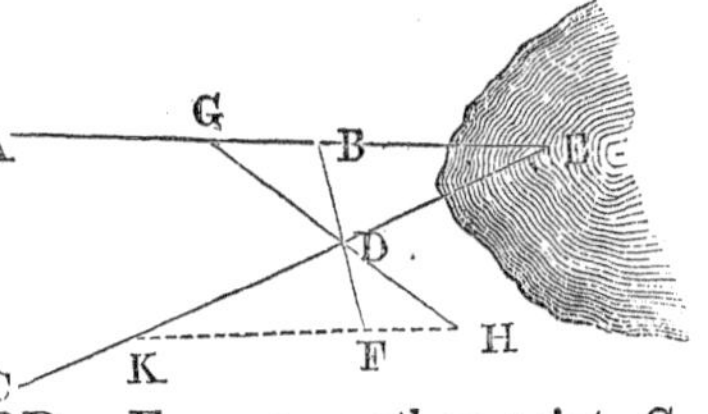

Fig. 135.

BE can be found by measuring FK, which is equal to it.

If DF and DH, be made respectively equal to one-half, or one-third, &c., of DB and DG, then will KD and KF be respectively equal to one-half or one-third, &c., of DE and BE.

C. WHEN BOTH ENDS OF THE LINE ARE INACCESSIBLE.

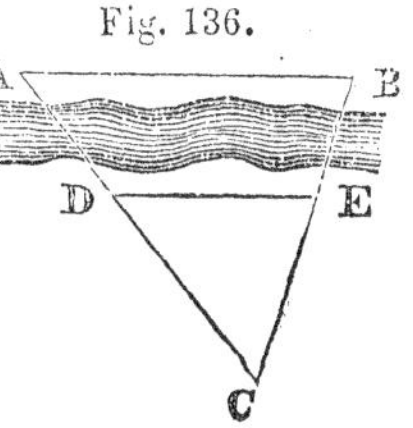

Fig. 136.

(202) By similar triangles. Let AB be the inaccessible distance. Set a stake at any convenient point C, and find the distances CA and CB, by any of the methods just given. Set a second stake at any point, D, on the line CA. Measure a distance, equal to $\frac{CB \times CD}{CA}$, from C, on the line CB, to some point E. Measure DE. Then is $AB = \frac{AC \times DE}{CD}$.

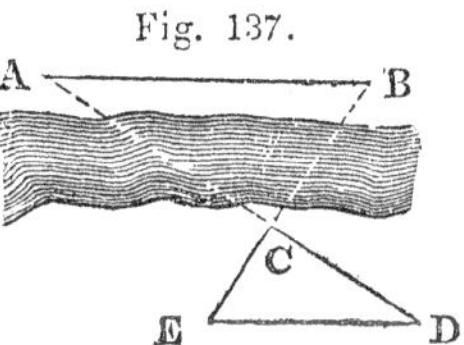

Fig. 137.

If more convenient, measure CD in the contrary direction from the river, as in Fig. 137, instead of towards it, and in other respects proceed as before.

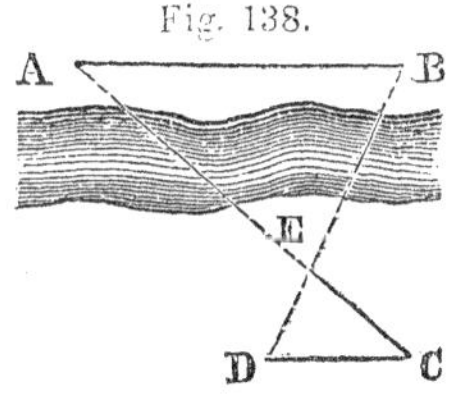

Fig. 138.

(203) By parallels. Let AB be the inaccessible distance. From any point, as C, range out a parallel to AB, as in Art. (165), &c. Find the distance CA, by Art. (191), &c. Set a stake at the point E, the intersection of CA and DB, and measure CE. Then is $AB = \frac{CD \times (AC - CE)}{CE}$.

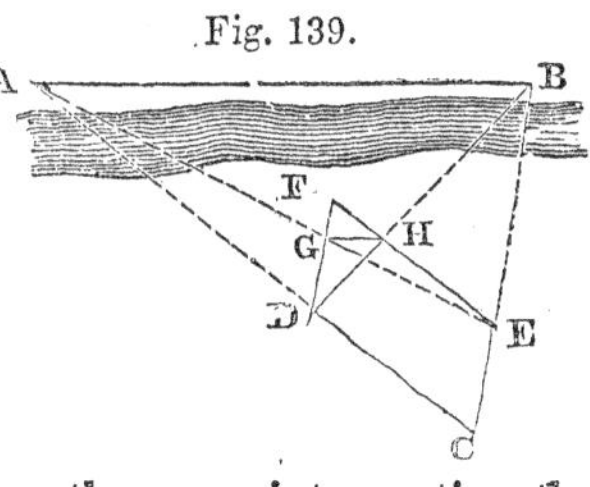

Fig. 139.

(204) By a parallelogram. Set a stake at any convenient point C. Set stakes D and E, anywhere in the alinements CA and CB. With D as a centre, and a length of the chain equal to CE, describe an arc; and with E as a centre, and a length of the chain equal to CD, describe another arc, intersecting the former one at F. A parallelogram, CDEF, will thus be formed. Set stakes at G and H, where the alinements DB and EA intersect the sides of this parallelogram. Measure CD, DF, GF, FH, and HG. The inaccessible distance $AB = \frac{CD \times DF \times GH}{FG \times FH}$.

If $CD = CE$, then $AB = \frac{CD^2 \times GH}{FG \times FH}$.

(205) **By symmetrical triangles.** Take any convenient point, as C. Set stakes at two other points, D and D′, in the same line, and at equal distances from C. Take a point E, in the line of AD; measure from it to C, and onward till CE′ = CE. Take a point F in the line of BD; measure from it to C, and onward till CF′ = CF. Range out the lines AC and E′D′, and set a stake at their intersection, A′. Range out the lines BC and F′D′, and set a stake at their intersection, B′. Measure A′B′. It will be equal to the desired distance AB.

Fig. 140.

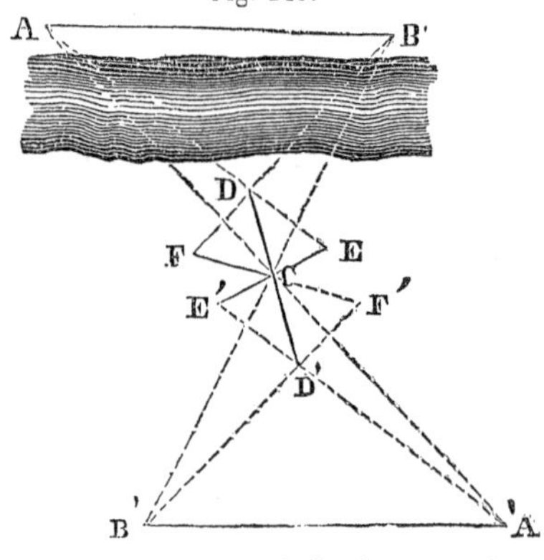

(206) *Otherwise:* Take any convenient point, as C, and set off equal distances on each side of it, in the line of CA, to D and D′. Set off the same distances from C, in the line of CB, to E and E′. Through C, set out a parallel to DE, or D′E′, and set stakes at the points F and F′ where this parallel intersects AE′ and BD′. Range out the lines AD′ and EF′, and set a stake at their intersection A′. Range out the lines BE′ and DF, and set a stake at their intersection B′. Measure A′B′, and it will be equal to the desired distance AB.

Fig. 141.

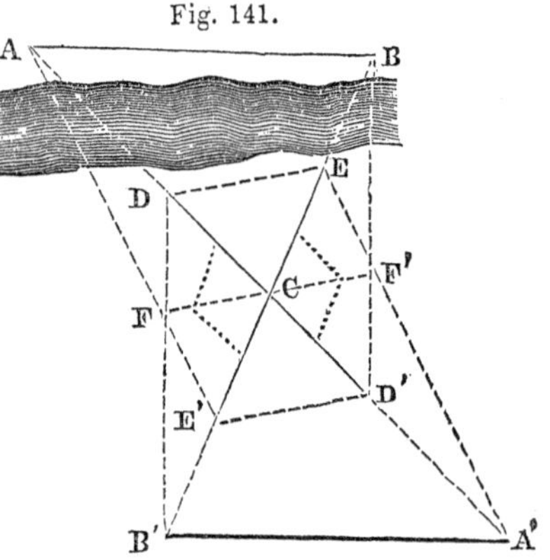

The easiest method of setting out the parallel in the above case, is to fix the middle of the chain at the point C, and its ends on the lines CD, CE′; then carry the middle of the chain from C towards F, and mark the point to which it reaches; and repeat this on the other side of C, as shown by the finely dotted lines in the figure.

INACCESSIBLE AREAS.

(207) Triangles. In the case of a triangular field, in which one side cannot be measured, or determined by any of the methods just given, the two accessible sides may be prolonged to their full length, and an equal symmetrical triangle formed, all of whose sides can be measured. Thus in Fig. 102, page 103, if CDE be the original triangle, of which the side EC is inaccessible, DFP will be equal to it. But if this also be impossible, portions of the sides may be measured, as AD, AE, in the figure in the margin, and also DE, and the area of this triangle found by any of the methods which have been given. Then is the desired area of the triangle ABC = area of $ADE \times \frac{AB \times AC}{AD \times AE}$.

Fig. 142.

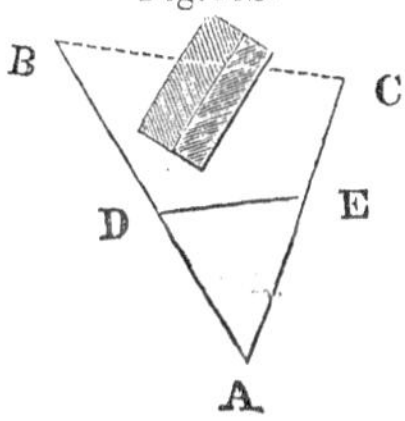

(208) Quadrilaterals. In the case of a four-sided field, whose sides cannot be measured, or prolonged, but whose diagonals can be measured, the area may be obtained thus. Measure the diagonals AC and BD; and also the portions AE, EC, into which one of them is divided by the other. Calculate the area of the triangle BCE, by the preceding method, or any of those heretofore given. Then the area of the quadrilateral ABCD = area of $BCE \times \frac{AC \times BD}{BE \times CE}$.

Fig. 143.

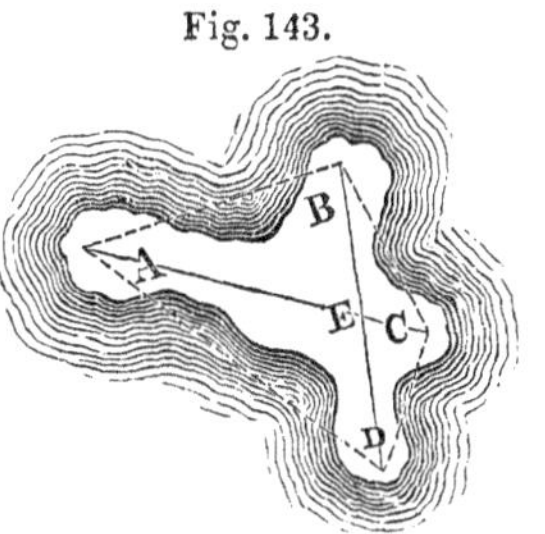

(209) Polygons. Methods for obtaining the areas of inaccessible fields of more than four sides, have been given in Arts. **(101,)** &c.

PART III.

COMPASS SURVEYING:

OR

By the Third Method.

CHAPTER I.

ANGULAR SURVEYING IN GENERAL.

(210) *Angular Surveying* determines the relative positions of points, and therefore of lines, on the THIRD PRINCIPLE, as explained in Art. (7), which should now be referred to.

(211) When the two lines which form an angle lie in the same horizontal or level plane, the angle is called a *horizontal angle.**

When these lines lie in a plane perpendicular to the former, the angle is called a *vertical angle.*

When one of the lines is horizontal and the other line from the eye of the observer passes above the former, and in the same vertical plane, the angle is called an *angle of elevation.*

When the latter line passes below the horizontal line, and in the same vertical plane, the angle is called an *angle of depression.*

When the two lines which form an angle, lie in other planes which make oblique angles with each of the former planes, the angle is called an *oblique angle.*

Horizontal angles are the only angles employed in common land surveying.

* A plane is said to be *horizontal,* or *level,* when it is parallel to the surface of standing water, or perpendicular to a plumb-line. A line is horizontal when it lies in a horizontal plane.

(212) The angles between the directions of two lines, which it is necessary to measure, may be obtained by a great variety of instruments. All of them are in substance mere modifications of the very simple one which will now be described, and which any one can make for himself.

(213) Provide a circular piece of wood, and divide its circumference (by any of the methods of Geometrical Drafting) into three hundred and sixty equal parts, or "Degrees," and number them as in the figure. The divisions will be like those of a watch face, but six times as many. These divisions are termed *graduations*. The figure shows only every fifteenth one. In the centre of the circle, fix a needle, or sharp-pointed wire, and upon this fix a straight stick, or thin ruler placed edge-wise, (called an *alidade*), so that it may turn freely on this point and nearly touch the graduations of the circle. Fasten the circle on a staff, pointed at the other end, and long enough to bring the alidade to the height of the eyes. The instrument is now complete. It may be called a *Goniometer*, or Angle-measurer.

Fig. 144.

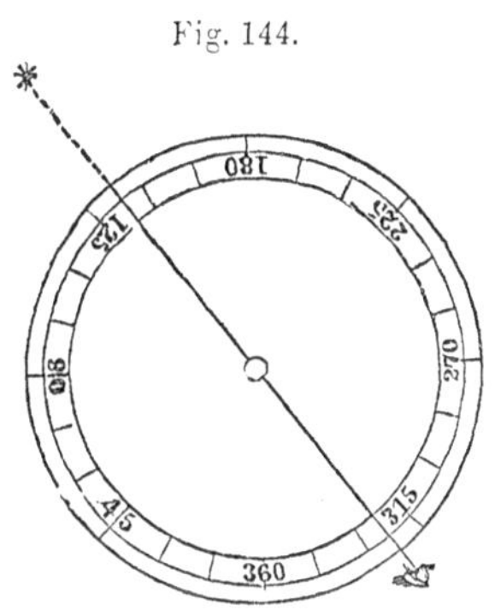

(214) Now let it be required to measure the angle between the lines AB and AC. Fix the staff in the ground, so that its centre shall be exactly over the intersection of the two lines. Turn the alidade, so that it points, (as determined by sighting along it) to a rod, or other mark at B, a point on one of the lines, and note what degree it covers, i. e. "The Reading." Then, without disturbing the circle, turn the alidade till it points to C, a point on the other line. Note the new reading. The difference of these readings, (in the figure, 45 degrees), is the difference in the directions of the two lines, or is the angle which one makes with the other. If the dis-

Fig. 145.

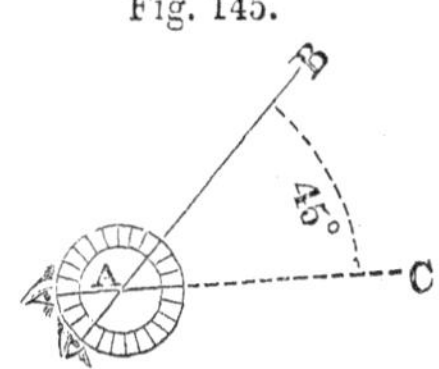

tance from A to C be now measured, the point C is "determined," with respect to the points A and B, on the *Third Principle*. Any number of points may be thus determined.

(215) Instead of the very simple and rude alidade, which has been supposed to be used, needles may be fixed on each end of the alidade; or sights may be added, such as those described in Art. **(106)**; or a small straight tube may be used, one end being covered with a piece of pasteboard in which a very small eye hole is pierced, and threads, called "cross-hairs," being stretched across the other end of it, as in the figure; so that their intersection may give a more precise line for determining the direction of any point.

Fig 146.

(216) When a telescope is substituted for this tube, and supported in such a way that it can turn over, so as to look both backwards and forwards, the instrument (with various other additions, which however do not affect the principle), is called the *Engineer's Transit.*

With the addition of a level, and a vertical circle, for measuring vertical angles, the instrument becomes a *Theodolite;* in which, however, the telescope does not usually admit of being turned over.

(217) The *Compass* differs from the instruments which have been described, in the following respect. They all measure the angle which one line makes with another. The compass measures the angle which each of these lines makes with a third line, viz: that shown by the magnetic needle, which always points (approximately) in the same direction, i. e. North and South, in the *Magnetic Meridian*. Thus, in the figure, the line AB makes an angle of 30 degrees with the line AN, and the line AC makes an angle of 75 degrees with AN. The difference of these angles, or 45 degrees, is the angle which AC makes with AB, agreeing with the result obtained in Art. **(214)**.

Fig. 147.

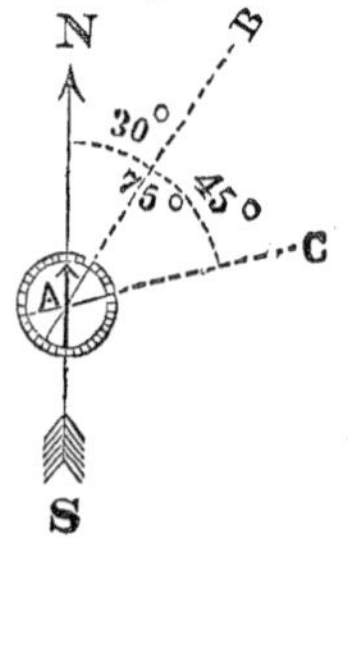

(218) Surveying with the compass is, therefore, a less direct operation than surveying with the Transit or Theodolite. But as the use of the compass is much more rapid and easy (only one sight and reading at each station being necessary, instead of two, as in the former case), for this reason, as well as for its smaller cost, it is the instrument most commonly employed in land surveying in this country, in spite of its imperfections and inaccuracies.

As many may wish to learn "Surveying with the Compass," without being obliged to previously learn "Surveying with the Transit," (which properly, being more simple in principle, though less so in practice, should precede it, but which will be considered in Part IV), we will first take up COMPASS SURVEYING.

(219) Angular Surveying in general, and therefore Compass Surveying, may employ either of the 3d, 4th and 5th methods of determining the position of a point, given in Part I; that is, any instrument which measures angles may be employed for *Polar*, *Triangular*, or *Trilinear* Surveying. The first of these, Polar Surveying, is the one most commonly adopted for the compass, and is therefore the one which will be specially explained in this part.

The same method, as employed with the Transit and Theodolite, will be explained in the following part.

The 4th and 5th methods will be explained in the next two parts.

(220) The method of *Polar Surveying* embraces two minor methods. The most usual one consists in going around the field with the instrument, setting it at each corner and measuring there the angle which each side makes with its neighbor, as well as the length of each side. This method is called by the French the method of *Cheminement.* It has no special name in English, but may be called (from the American verb, To progress), the *Method of Progression.* The other system, the *Method of Radiation*, consists in setting the instrument at one point, and thence measuring the direction and distance of each corner of the field, or other object. The corresponding name of what we have called Triangular Surveying is the *Method of Intersections;* since it determines points by the intersections of straight lines.

THE COMPASS.
Fig. 198.

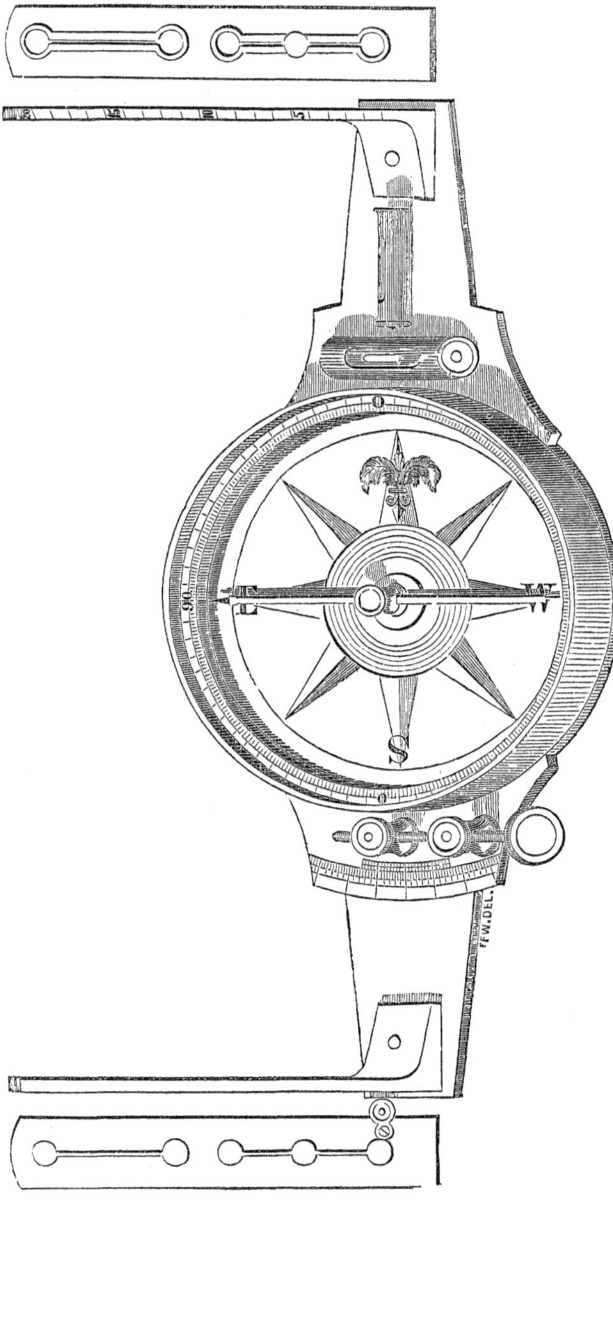

CHAPTER II.

THE COMPASS.

(221) The Needle. The most essential part of the compass is the magnetic needle. It is a slender bar of steel, usually five or six inches long, strongly magnetized, and balanced on a pivot, so that it may turn freely, and thus be enabled to continue pointing in the same direction (that of the "*Magnetic Meridian*," approximately North and South) however much the "Compass Box," to which the pivot is attached, may be turned around.

As it is important that the needle should move with the least possible friction, the pivot should be of the hardest steel ground to a very sharp point; and in the centre of the needle, which is to rest on the pivot, should be inserted a cap of agate, or other hard material. Iridium for the pivot, and ruby for the cap, are still better.

If the needle be balanced on its pivot before being magnetized, one end will sink, or "Dip," after the needle is magnetized. To bring it to a level, several coils of wire are wound around the needle so that they can be slid along it, to adjust the weight of its two ends and balance it more perfectly.

The North end of the needle is usually cut into a more ornamental form than the South end, for the sake of distinction.

The principal requisites of a compass needle are, intensity of directive force and susceptibility. "Shear steel" was found by Capt. Kater to be the kind capable of receiving the greatest magnetic force. The best form is that of a rhomboid, or lozenge, cut out in the middle, so as to diminish the extent of surface in proportion to the mass, as it is the latter on which the directive force depends. Beyond a certain limit, say five inches, no additional power is gained by increasing the length of the needle. On the contrary, longer ones are apt to have their strength diminished by several consecutive poles being formed. Short needles, made very hard, are therefore to be preferred.

Fig. 149.

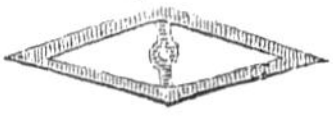

The needle should not come to rest very quickly. If it does, it indicates either that it is weakly magnetized, or that the friction on the pivot is great. Its sensitiveness is indicated by the number of vibrations which it makes in a small space before coming to rest.

A screw, with a milled head, on the under side of the plate which supports the pivot, is used to raise the needle off this pivot, when the instrument is carried about, to prevent the point being dulled by unnecessary friction.

(222) The Sights. Next after the needle, which gives the direction of the fixed line, whose angles with the lines to be surveyed are to be measured, should be noticed the Sights, which show the directions of these last lines. At each end of a line passing through the pivot is placed a "Sight," consisting of an upright bar of brass, with openings in it of various forms; usually either slits, with a circular aperture at their top and bottom*; or of the form described in Art. (**106**); all these arrangements being intended to enable the line of sight to be directed to any desired object, with precision.

(223) A Telescope which can move up and down in a vertical plane, i. e. a plunging telescope, or one which can turn completely over, is sometimes substituted for the sights. It has the great advantage of giving more distinct vision at long distances, and of admitting of sights up and down very steep slopes. Its accuracy of vision is however rendered nugatory by the want of precision in the readings of the needle. If a telescope be applied to the compass, a graduated circle with vernier should be added, thus converting the compass into a "Transit." The Telescope will be found minutely described in Part IV, "Transit Surveying."

(224) The divided circle. We now have the means of indicating the directions of the two lines whose angle is to be measured. The number of degrees contained in it is to be read from a circle, divided into degrees, in the centre of which is fixed the

* An inside and an outside view, or "Elevation," of such sights, are given on each side of the figure of the Compass, on page 126. It is itself drawn in "Military Perspective."

pivot bearing the needle. The graduations are usually made to half a degree, and a quarter of a degree or less can then be "estimated." The pivot and needle are sunk in a circular box, so that its top may be on a level with the needle. The graduations are usually made on the top of the surrounding rim of the box, but should also be continued down its inside circumference so that it may be easier to see with what division the ends of the needle coincide.

The degrees are not numbered consecutively from 0° around to 360°; but run from 0° to 90°, both ways from the two diametrically opposite points at which a line, passing through the slits in the middle of the sights, would meet the divided circle.

The lettering of the Surveyor's Compass has one important difference from that of the Mariner's Compass.

When we stand facing the North, the East is on our right hand, and the West on our left. The graduated card of the Mariner's Compass which is fastened to the needle, and turns with it, is marked accordingly. But, in the Surveyor's compass, one of the 0 points being marked N, or North, (or indicated by a fleur-de-lis,) and the opposite one S, or South, the 90-degrees-point on the *right* of this line, as you stand at the S end and look towards the N, is marked W, or West; and the *left* hand 90-degrees-point is marked E, or East. The reason of this will be seen when the method of using the compass comes to be explained in the following chapter.

(225) The Points. In ordinary land surveying, only four points of the compass have names, viz: North, South, East and West; the direction of a line being described by the angle which it makes with a North and South line, to its East or to its West. But for nautical purposes, the circle of the compass is divided into 32 points, the names of which are shown in

Fig. 150.

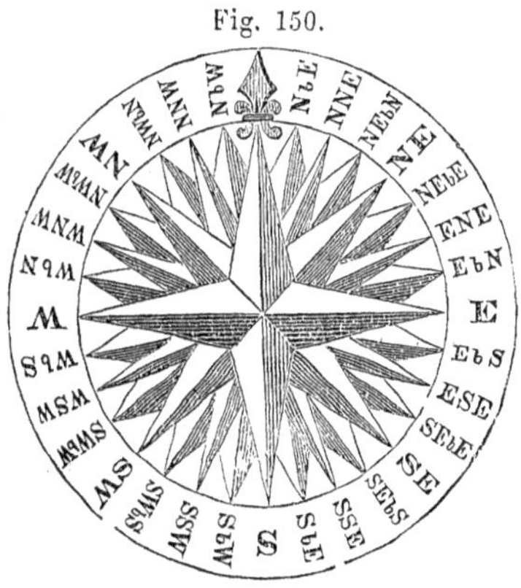

the figure. Two rules embrace all the cases. 1° When the letters indicating two points are joined together, the point half way between the two is meant; thus, N. E. is half way between North and East; and N. N. E. is half way between North and North East. 2° When the letters of two points are joined together with the intermediate word *by*, it indicates the point which comes next after the first, in going towards the second; thus, N. by E, is the point which follows North in going towards the East; S. E. *by* S. is the next point from South East, going towards the South.

(226) Eccentricity. The centre-pin, or pivot of the needle, ought to be exactly in the centre of the graduated circle; the needle ought to be straight; and the line of the sights ought to pass exactly through this centre and through the 0 points of the circle. If this is not the case, there will be an error in every observation. This is called the *error of eccentricity*.

When the maker of a compass is about to fix the pivot in place, he is in doubt of two things; whether the needle is perfectly straight, and whether the pivot is exactly in the centre. In figures 151 and 152, both of these are represented as being excessively in error.

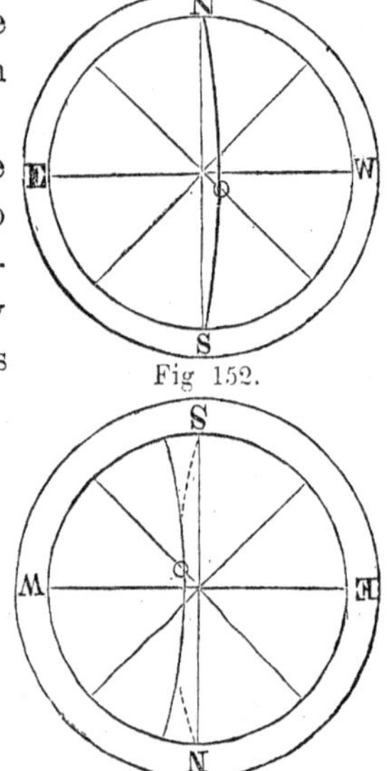

Firstly, to examine if the needle be straight. Fix the pivot temporarily, so that the ends of the needle may cut opposite degrees, i. e. degrees differing by 180°. The condition of things at this stage of progress, will be represented by Fig. 151. Then turn the compass-box half way around. The error will now be doubled, as is shown by Fig. 152, in which the former position of the needle is indicated by a dotted line.* Now bend the needle, as in Fig. 153, till it cuts divisions midway between those cut by it in

* This is another example of the fruitful principle of *Reversion*, first noticed in Art. (105).

its present and in its former position This makes it certain that the needle is straight, or that its two ends and its centre lie in the same straight line.

Fig 153.

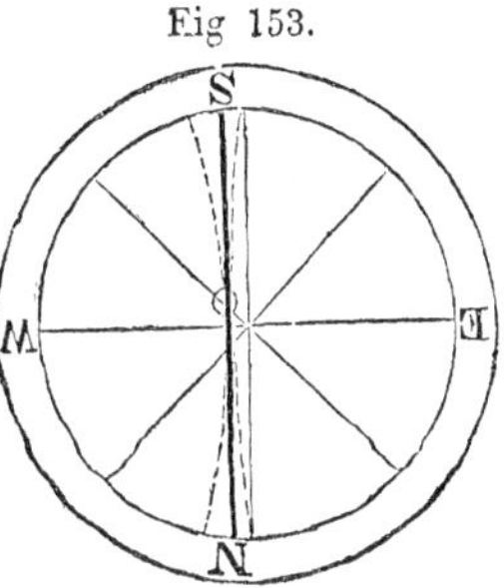

Secondly, to put the pivot in the centre. Move it till the straightened needle cuts opposite divisions. It is then certain that the direction of the needle passes through the centre. Turn the compass box one-quarter around, and if the needle does not then cut opposite divisions, move the pivot till it does. Repeat the operation in various positions of the box. It will be a sufficient test if it cuts the opposite divisions of 0°, 45° and 90°.

To fix the sights precisely in line, draw a hair through their slits and move them till the hair passes over the 0 points on the circle.

The surveyor can also examine for himself, by the principle of Reversion, whether the line of the sights passes through the centre or not. Sight to any very near object. Read off the number of degrees indicated by one end of the needle. Then turn the compass half around, and sight to the same object. If the two readings do not agree, there is an error of eccentricity, and the arithmetical mean, or half sum of the two readings is the correct one.

Fig. 154.

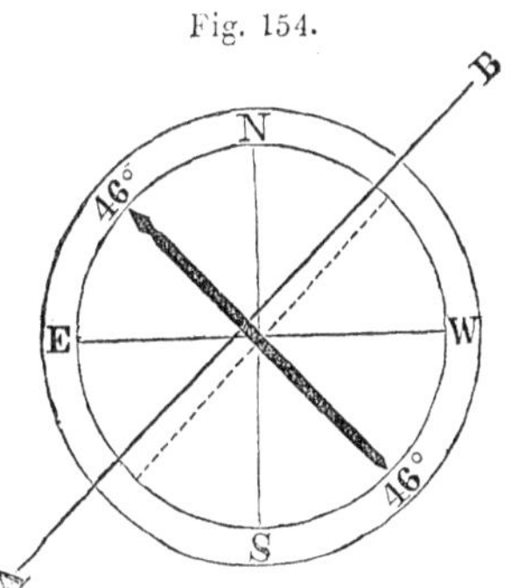

Fig. 155.

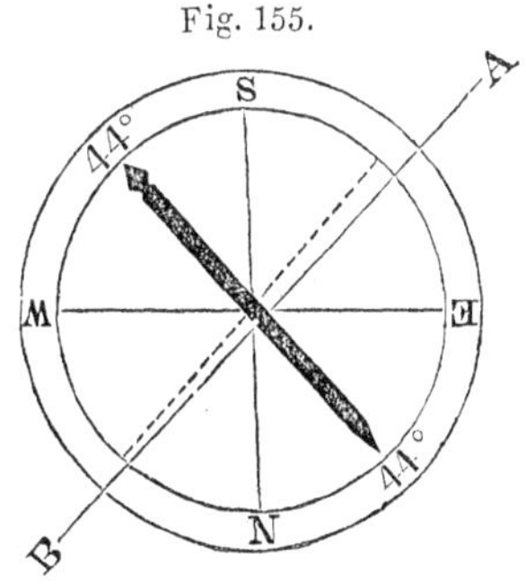

In Fig. 154, the line of sight AB is represented as passing to one side of the centre, and the needle as pointing to 46°. In Fig. 155, the compass is supposed to have been turned half around and the other end of the sights to be directed to the same object. Suppose that the needle would have pointed to 45°, if the line of sight had passed through the centre. The needle will now point to 44°, the error being doubled by the reversion, and the true reading being the mean.

This does not, however, make it certain that the line of the sights passes through the 0 points, which can only be tested by the hair, as mentioned above.

(227) Levels. On the compass plate are two small spirit levels. They consist of glass tubes, slightly curved upwards, and nearly filled with alcohol, leaving a bubble of air within them. They are so adjusted that when the bubbles are in the centres of the tubes, the plate of the compass shall be level. One of them lies in the direction of the sights, and the other at right angles to this direction.

(228) Tangent Scale. This is a convenient, though not essential, addition to the compass, for the purpose of measuring the slopes of ground, so that the proper allowance in chaining may be made. In the figure of the compass, page 126, may be seen, on the edge of the left hand sight, a small projection of brass with a hole through it. On the edge of the other sight are engraved lines numbered from 0° to 20°, the 0° being of the same height above the compass plate that the eye-hole is. To use this, set the compass at the bottom of a slope, and at the top set a signal of exactly the height of the eye-hole from the ground. Level the compass very carefully, particularly by the level which lies lengthwise, and, with the eye at the eye-hole, look to the signal and note the number of the division on the farther sight which is cut by the visual ray. That will be the angle of the slope; the distances of the engraved lines from the 0° line being tangents (for the radius equal to the distance between the sights) of the angles corresponding to the numbers of the lines.

(229) Vernier. The compass box is connected with the plate, which carries it and the sights, so that it can turn around on this plate. This motion is given to it by a screw, (called a slow-motion, or Tangent screw), the head of which is the nearest one in the figure on page 126. If two marks be made opposite to each other, one on the projecting part of the compass box, and the other on the plate to which the sights are fastened, these marks will separate when the slow-motion screw is turned. Their distance apart (in angular measurement, i. e. fractions of a circle), in any position, is measured by a contrivance called a *Vernier*, which is the minutely divided arc of a circle seen between the left hand sight and the compass box. It will be better to defer explaining the mode of reading the vernier for the present, since it is rarely used with the compass, and an entire chapter will be given to it in Part IV. Its principle is similar to that of the Vernier Scale, described in Art. (50). Its applications in "Field-work" will be noticed under that head.

(230) Tripod. The compass, like most surveying instruments, is usually supported on a Tripod, consisting of three legs, shod with iron, and so connected at top as to be movable in any direction. There are many forms of these. Lightness and stiffness are the qualities desired. The most usual form is shewn in the figures of the Transit and the Theodolite, at the beginning of Part IV. Of the two represented in Figs. 156 and 157, the first has the advantage of being very easily and cheaply made ; and the second that of being light and yet capable of very firmly resisting horizontal torsion.

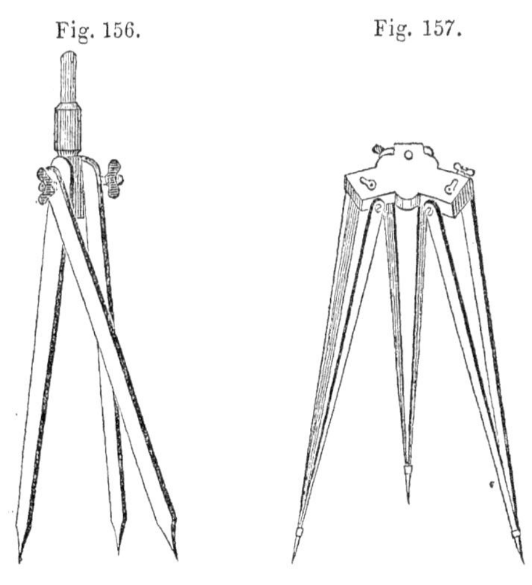
Fig. 156. Fig. 157.

The joints, by which the instrument is connected with the tripod, are also various. Fig. 158 is the "Ball-and-socket joint," most usual in this country. It takes its name from the ball, in which

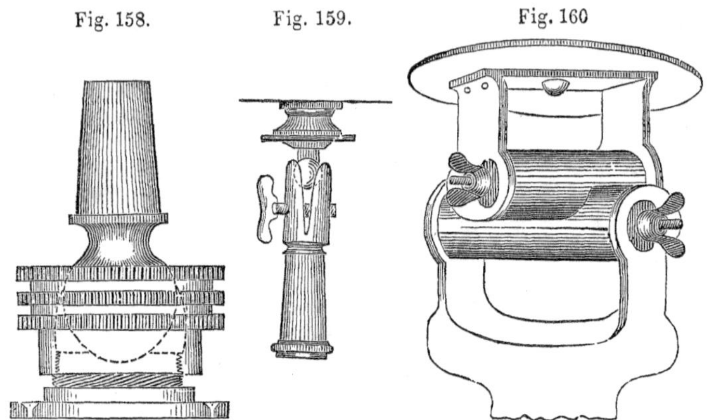

Fig. 158. Fig. 159. Fig. 160

terminates the covered spindle which enters a corresponding cavity under the compass plate, and the socket in which this ball turns. It admits of motion in any direction, and can be tightened or loosened by turning the upper half of the hollow piece enclosing it, which is screwed on the lower half. Fig. 159 is called the "Shell-joint." In it the two shell-shaped pieces enclosing the ball are tightened by a thumb-screw. Fig. 160, is "Cugnot's joint." It consists of two cylinders, placed at right angles to each other, and through the axes of which pass bolts, which turn freely in the cylinder and can be tightened or loosened by thumb-screws at their ends. The combination of the two motions which this joint permits, enables the instrument which it carries, to be placed in any desired position. This joint is much the most stable of the three.

(231) Jacob's Staff. A single leg, called a "Jacob's Staff," has some advantages, as it is lighter to carry in the field, and can be made of any wood on the spot where it is to be used, thus saving the expense of a tripod and the trouble of its transportation. Its upper end is fitted into the lower end of a brass head which has a ball and socket joint, and axis above. Its lower end should be shod with iron, and a spike running through it is useful for pressing it into the ground with the foot. Of course it cannot be conveniently used on frozen ground, or on pavements. It may, however, be set before or behind the spot at which the angle is to be measured, provided that it is placed very precisely in the line of direction from that station to the one to which a sight is to be taken.

(232) The Prismatic Compass. The peculiarity of this instrument (often called Schmalcalder's) is that a glass triangular prism is substituted for one of the sights. Such a prism has this peculiar property that at the same time, it can be seen through, so that a sight can be taken through it, and that its upper surface reflects like a mirror, so that the numbers of the degrees immediately under it, can be read off at the same time that a sight to any object is taken. Another peculiarity, necessary for profiting by the last one, is, that the divided circle is not fixed, but is a card fastened to the needle and moving around with it, as in the Mariner's Compass. The minute description, which follows, is condensed from Simms.

Fig. 161.

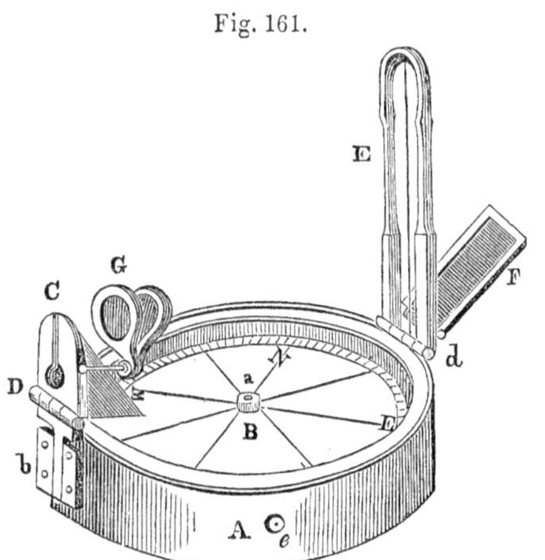

In the figure, A represents the compass box, and B the card, which, being attached to the magnetic needle, moves as *it* moves, around the agate centre, *a*, on which it is suspended. The circumference of the card is usually divided to $\frac{1}{4}$ or $\frac{1}{2}$ of a degree. C is a prism, which the observer looks through. The perpendicular thread of the sight-vane, E, and the divisions on the card, appear *together* on looking through the prism, and the division with which the thread coincides, when the needle is at rest, is the "Bearing" of whatever object the thread may bisect, i. e. is the angle which the line of sight makes with the direction of the needle. The prism is mounted with a hinge joint, D. The sight-vane has a fine thread stretched along its opening, in the direction of its length, which is brought to bisect any object, by turning the box around horizontally. F is a mirror, made to slide on or off the sight-vane, E; and it may be reversed at pleasure, that is, turned face downwards; it can also be inclined at any angle, by means of its joint, *d*; and it will remain stationary on any part of the vane, by the friction of its slides. Its use is to reflect the image of an object to the eye of an observer when the object is much above or below the horizontal plane. The colored glasses represented at G, are intended for observing the sun. At *e*, is shown a spring, which being pressed by the finger at the time of observation, and then released, checks the vibrations of the card, and brings it more speedily to rest. A stop is likewise fixed to the other side of the box, by which the needle may be thrown off its centre.

The method of using this instrument is very simple. First raise the prism in its socket, *b*, until you obtain a distinct view of the divisions on the card. Then, standing over the point where the angles are to be taken, hold the instrument to the eye, and, looking through the slit, *C*, turn around till the thread in the sight-vane bisects one of the objects whose bearing is required; then by touching the spring, *e*, bring the needle to rest, and the division on the card which coincides with the thread on the vane, will be the bearing of the object from the north or south points of the magnetic meridian. Then turn to any other object, and repeat the operation; the difference between the bearing of this object and that of the former, will be the angular distance of the objects in question. Thus, suppose the former bearing to be 40° 30′, and the latter 10° 15′, both east, or both west, from the north or south, the angle will be 30° 15′. The divisions are generally numbered 5°, 10°, 15°, &c. around the circle to 360°.

Fig. 162.

The figures on the compass card are reversed, or written upside down, as in the figure (in which only every fifteenth degree is marked), because they are again reversed by the prism.

(233) The prismatic compass is generally held in the hand, the bearing being caught, as it were, in passing; but more accurate readings would of course be obtained if it rested on a support, such as a stake cut flat on its top.

In the former mode, the needle never comes completely to rest, particularly in the wind. In such cases, observe the extreme divisions between which the needle vibrates, and take their arithmetical mean.

(234) Defects of compass. The compass is deficient in both precision and correctness.*

The former defect arises from the indefiniteness of its mode of indicating the part of the circle to which it points. The point of the needle has considerable thickness; it cannot quite touch the divided circle; and these divisions are made only to whole or half degrees, though a fraction of a division may be estimated, or guessed at. The Vernier does not much better this, as we shall see when explaining its use. Now an inaccuracy of one quarter of a degree in an angle, i. e. in the difference of the directions of two lines, causes them to separate from each other $5\frac{1}{4}$ inches at the end of 100 feet; at the end of 1000 feet nearly $4\frac{1}{2}$ feet; and at the end of a mile, 23 feet. A difference of only one-tenth of a degree, or six minutes, would produce a difference of $1\frac{3}{4}$ feet at the end of 1000 feet; and $9\frac{1}{4}$ feet at the distance of a mile. Such are the differences which may result from the want of *precision* in the indications of the compass.

But a more serious defect is the want of *correctness* in the compass. Its not pointing exactly to the true north does not indeed affect the correctness of the angles measured by it. But it does not point in the same or in a parallel direction, during even the same day, but changes its direction between sunrise and noon nearly a quarter of a degree, as will be fully explained in Chapter VIII. The effect of such a difference we have just seen. This direction

* The student must not confound these two qualities. To say that the sun appears to rise in the eastern quarter of the heavens and to set in the western, is *correct*, but not *precise*. A watch with a second hand indicates the time of day *precisely*, but not always *correctly*. The statement that two and two make five, is *precise*, but is not usually regarded as *correct*.

may also be greatly altered in a moment, without the knowledge of the surveyor, by a piece of iron being brought near to the com pass, or by some other local attraction, as will be noticed hereafter. This is the weak point in the compass.

Notwithstanding these defects, the compass is a very valuable instrument, from its simplicity, rapidity and convenience in use; and though never precise, and seldom correct, it is generally not *very* wrong.

CHAPTER III.

THE FIELD WORK.

(235) Taking Bearings. The "Bearing" of a line is the angle which it makes with the direction of the needle. Thus, in Fig. 147, page 124, the angle NAB is the Bearing of the line AB, and NAC is the Bearing of AC. The Bearing and length of a line are named collectively the *Course.*

To take the Bearing of any line, set the compass exactly over any point of it by a plumb-line suspended from beneath the centre of the compass, or, approximately, by dropping a stone. Level the compass by bringing the air bubbles to the middle of the level tubes. Direct the sights to a rod held truly vertical, or "plumb," at another point of the line, the more distant the better. The two ends are usually taken. Sight to the lowest visible point of the rod. When the needle comes to rest, note what division on the circle it points to; taking the one indicated by the North end of the needle, if the North point on the circle is farthest from you, and *vice versa.*

In reading the division to which one end of the needle points, the eye should be placed over the other end, to avoid the error which might result from the "parallax," or apparent change of place, of the end read from, when looked at obliquely.

The bearing is read and recorded by noting between what letters the end of the needle comes, and to what number; naming, or writing down, *firstly*, that letter, N or S, which is at the 0° point nearest to that end of the needle from which you are reading; *secondly*, the number of degrees to which it points, and *thirdly*, the letter, E or W, of the 90° point which is nearest to the same end of the needle. Thus, in the figure, if when the sights were directed along a line, (the North point of the compass being most distant from the observer), the North end of the needle was at the point A, the bearing of the line sighted on, would be North 45° East; if the end of the needle was at B, the bearing would be *East;* if at C, S. 30° E; if at D, *South;* if at E, S. 60° W; if at F, West; if at G, N. 60° W; if at H, *North.*

Fig. 163.

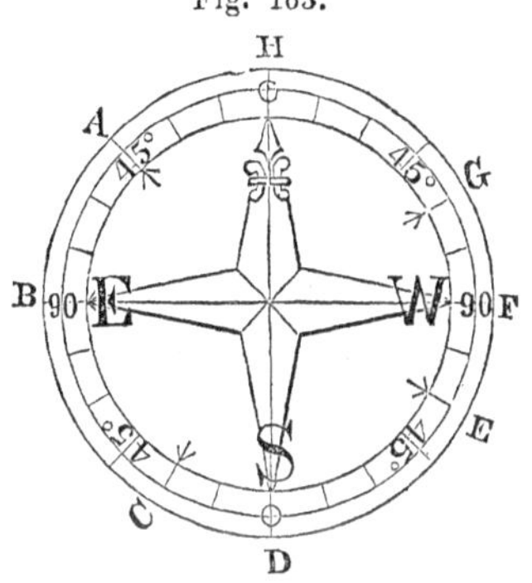

(236) We can now understand why W is on the right hand of the compass-box, and E on the left. Let the direction from the centre of the compass to the point B in the figure, be required, and suppose the sights in the first place to be pointing in the direction of the needle, S N, and the North sight to be ahead. When the sights (and the circle to which they are fastened) have been turned so as to point in the direction of B, the point of the circle marked E, will have come round to the North end of the needle, (*since the needle remains immovable,*) and the reading will therefore be "East," as it should be. The effect on the reading is the same as if the needle had moved to the left the same quantity which the sights have moved to the right, and the left side is therefore properly marked "East," and *vice versa.* So, too, if the bearing of the line to C be desired, half-way between North and

Fig. 164.

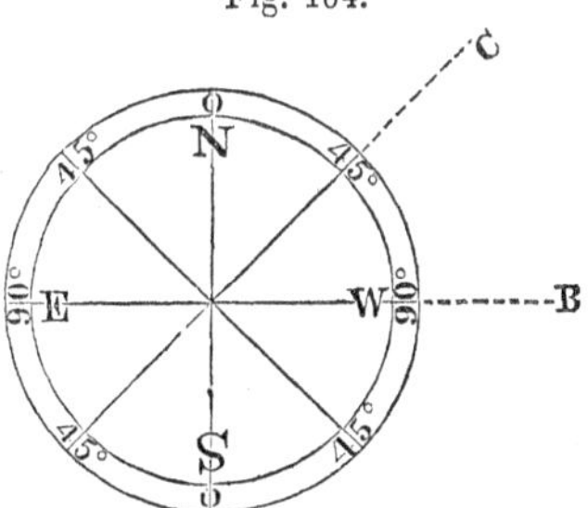

East, i. e. N. 45° E.; when the sights and the circle have turned 45 degrees to the right, the needle, really standing still, has apparently arrived at the point half-way between N. and E., i. e. N. 45° E.

Some surveyors' compasses are marked the reverse of this, the E on the right and the W cn the left. These letters must then be reversed in the mind before the bearing is noted down.

(237) **Reading with Vernier.** When the needle does not point precisely to one of the division marks on the circle, the fractional part of the smallest space is usually estimated by the eye, as has been explained. But this fractional part may be measured by the Vernier, described in Art. (**229**), as follows. Suppose the needle to point between N. 31° E. and N. 31½° E. Turn the tangent screw, which moves the compass-box, till the smaller division (in this case 31°) has come round to the needle. The Vernier will then indicate through what space the compass-box has moved, and therefore how much must be added to the reading of the needle. Suppose it indicates 10 minutes of a degree. Then the bearing is N. 31° 10′ E. It is, however, so difficult to move the Vernier without disturbing the whole instrument, that this is seldom resorted to in practice. The chief use of the Vernier is to set the instrument for running lines and making an allowance for the variation of the needle, as will be explained in the proper place. A Vernier-

A Vernier arc is sometimes attached to one end of the needle and carried around by it.

(238) **Practical Hints.** Mark every station, or spot, at which the compass is set, by driving a stake, or digging up a sod, or piling up stones, or otherwise, so that it can be found if any error, or other cause, makes it necessary to repeat the survey.

Very often when the line of which the bearing is required, is a fence, &c., the compass cannot be set upon it. In such cases, set the compass so that its centre is a foot or two from the line, and set the flag-staff at precisely the same distance from the line at the other end of it. The bearing of the flag-staff from the compass will be the same as that of the fence, the two lines being parallel

The distances should be measured on the real line. If more convenient the compass may be set at some point on the line prolonged, or at some intermediate point of the line, "in line" between its extremities.

In setting the compass level, it is more important to have it level crossways of the sights than in their direction; since if it be not so, on looking up or down hill through the upper part of one sight and the lower part of the other, the line of sight will not be parallel to the N and S, or zero line, on the compass, and an incorrect bearing will therefore be obtained.

The compass should *not* be levelled by the needle, as some books recommend, i. e. so levelled that the ends of the needle shall be at equal distances below the glass. The needle should be brought so originally by the maker, but if so adjusted in the morning, it will not be so at noon, owing to the daily variation in the *dip*. If then the compass be levelled by it, the lines of sight will generally be more or less oblique, and therefore erroneous. If the needle touches the glass, when the compass is levelled, balance it by sliding the coil of wire along it.

The same end of the compass should always go ahead. The North end is preferable. The South end will then be nearest to the observer. Attention to this and to the caution in the next paragraph, will prevent any confusion in the bearings.

Always take the readings from the same end of the needle; from the North end, if the North end of the compass goes ahead; and *vice versa*. This is necessary, because the two ends will not always cut opposite degrees. With this precaution, however, the angle of two meeting lines can be obtained correctly from either end, provided the same one is used in taking the bearings of both the lines.

Fig. 165.

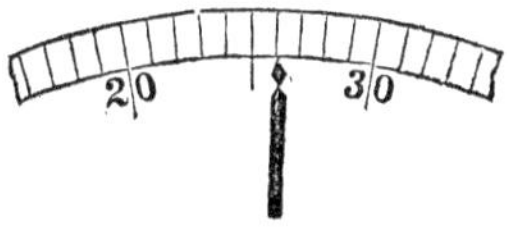

Guard against a very frequent source of error with beginners, in reading from the wrong number of the two between which the needle points, such as reading 34° for 26°, in a case like that in the figure.

Check the vibrations of the needle by gently raising it off the pivot so as to touch the glass, and letting it down again, by the screw on the under side of the box.

The compass should be smartly tapped after the needle has settled, to destroy the effect of any adhesion to the pivot, or friction of dust upon it.

All iron, such as the chain, &c., must be kept at a distance from the compass, or it will attract the needle, and cause it to deviate from its proper direction.

The surveyor is sometimes troubled by the needle refusing to traverse and adhering to the glass of the compass, after he has briskly wiped this off with a silk handkerchief, or it has been carried so as to rub against his clothes. The cause is the electricity excited by the friction. It is at once discharged by applying a wet finger to the glass.

A compass should be carried with its face resting against the side of the surveyor, and one of the sights hooked over his arm.

In distant surveys an extra centre pin should be carried, (as it is very liable to injury, and its perfection is most essential), and, also, an extra needle. When two such are carried, they should be placed so that the north pole of one rests against the south pole of the other.

(239) When the magnetism of the needle is lessened or destroyed by time, it may be renewed as follows. Obtain two bar magnets. Provide a board with a hole to admit of the axis, so that its collar may fit fairly, and that the needle may rest flat on it, without bearing at the centre. Place the board before you, with the north end of the needle to your right. Take a magnet in each hand, the left holding the North end of the bar, or that which has the mark across, downwards; and the right holding the same mark upwards. Bring the bars over the axis, about a foot above it, without approaching each other within two inches:—bring them down vertically on the needle, (the marks as directed) about an inch on each side of its axis; slide them outwards to its ends with slight pressure; raise them up; bring them to their former position, and repeat this a number of times.

(240) Back Sights. To test the accuracy of the bearing of a line, taken at one end of it, set up the compass at the other end, or point sighted to, and look back to a rod held at the first station, or point where the compass had been placed originally. The reading of the needle should now be the same as before.

If the position of the sights had been reversed, the reading would be the *Reverse Bearing;* a former bearing of N. 30° E. would then be S. 30° W., and so on.

(241) Local attraction. If the Back-sight does not agree with the first or forward sight, this latter must be taken over again. If the same difference is again found, this shows that there is *local attraction* at one of the stations; i. e. some influence, such as a mass of iron ore, ferruginous rocks, &c., under the surface, which attracts the needle, and makes it deviate from its usual direction. Any high object, such as a house, a tree, &c., has recently been found to produce a similar effect.

To discover at which station the attraction exists, set the compass at several intermediate points in the line which joins the two stations, and at points in the line prolonged, and take the bearing of the line at each of these points. The agreement of several of these bearings, taken at distant points, will prove their correctness. Otherwise, set the compass at a third station; sight to each of the two doubtful ones, and then from them back to this third station. This will show which is correct.

When the difference occurs in a series of lines, such as around a field, or along a road, proceed thus. Let C be the station at which the back-sight to B differs from the foresight from B to C. Since the back-sight from B to A is supposed to have agreed with the foresight from A to B, the local attraction must be at C, and the forward bearing must be corrected by the difference just found between the fore and back sights, adding or subtracting it, according to circumstances. An easy method is to draw a

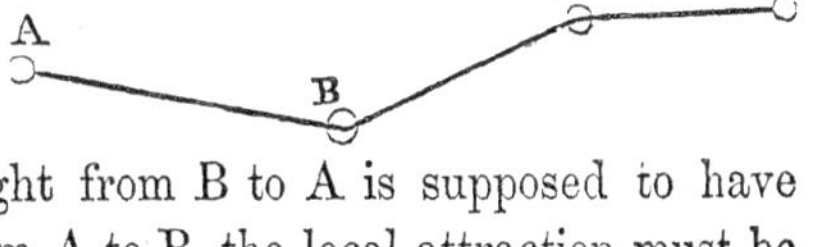

Fig. 166.

figure for the case, as in Fig. 167. In it, suppose the true bearing of BC, as given by a fore-sight from B to C, to be N. 40° E., but that there is local attraction at C, so that the needle is drawn aside 10°, and points in the direction S'N', instead of SN. The back-sight from C to B will then give a bearing of N. 50° E.; a difference, or correction for the next fore-sight, of 10°. If the next fore-sight, from C to D, be N. 70° E, this 10° must be subtracted from it, making the true fore-sight N. 60° E.

Fig. 167.

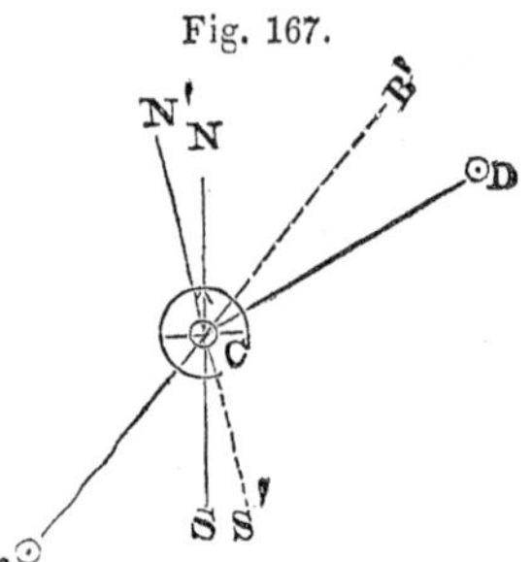

A general rule may also be given. *When the back-sight is greater than the fore-sight*, as in this case, subtract the difference from the next fore-sight, if that course and the preceding one have both their letters the same (as in this case, both being N. and E.), or both their letters different; or add the difference if either the first or last letters of the two courses are different. *When the back-sight is less than the fore-sight*, add the difference in the case in which it has just been directed to subtract it, and subtract it where it was before directed to add it.

(242) Angles of deflection. When the compass indicates much local attraction, the difference between the directions of two meeting lines, (or the "*angle of deflection*" of one from the other), can still be correctly measured, by taking the difference of the bearings of the two lines, as observed at the same point. For, the error caused by the local attraction, whatever it may be, affects both bearings equally, inasmuch as a "Bearing" is the angle which a line makes with the direction of the needle, and that here remains fixed in some one direction, no matter what, during the taking of the two bearings. Thus, in Fig. 167, let the true bearing of BC, i. e. the angle which it makes with the line SN, be, as before, N. 40° E., and that of CD N. 60° E. The true "angle of deflection" of these lines, or the angle B'CD, is therefore 20°. Now, if local attraction at C causes the needle to point in the direc- S'N', 10° to the left of its proper direction, BC will bear N. 50°

E., and CD N. 70° E., and the difference of these bearings, i. e. the angle of deflection, will be the same as before.

(243) Angles between Courses. To determine the angle of deflection of two courses meeting at any point, the following simple rules, the reasons of which will appear from the accompanying figures, are sufficient.

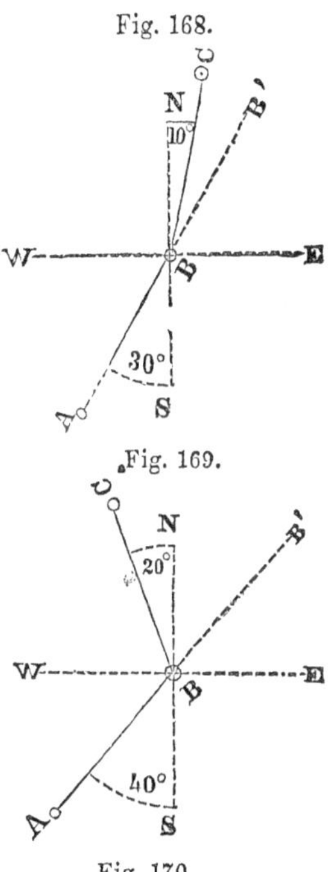

Fig. 168.

Fig. 169.

Case 1. When the first letters of the bearing are alike, (i. e. both N. or both S.), and the last letters also alike, (i. e. both E. or both W.), take the difference of the bearings. *Example.* If AB bears N. 30° E. and BC bears N. 10° E., the angle of deflection CBB′ is 20°.

Case 2. When the first letters are alike and the last letters different; take the sum of the bearings. *Ex.* If AB bears N. 40° E. and BC bears N. 20° W.; the angle CBB′ is 60°.

Fig. 170.

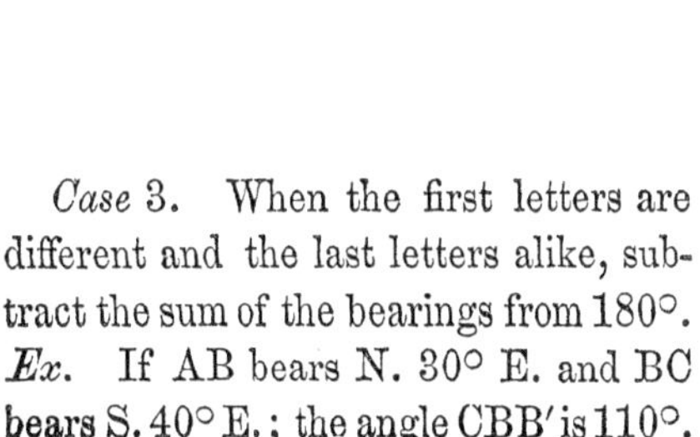
Case 3. When the first letters are different and the last letters alike, subtract the sum of the bearings from 180°. *Ex.* If AB bears N. 30° E. and BC bears S. 40° E.; the angle CBB′ is 110°.

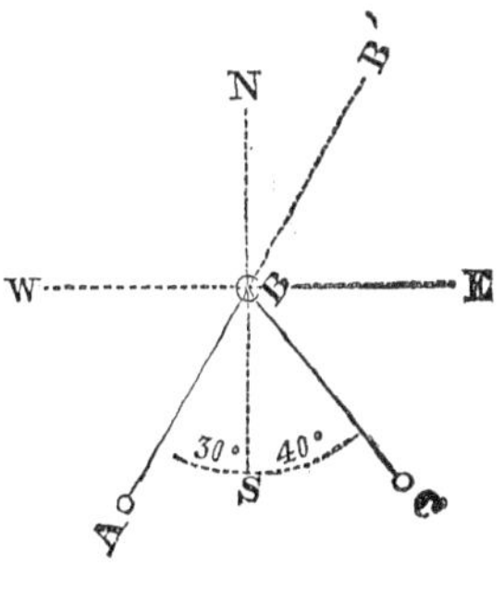

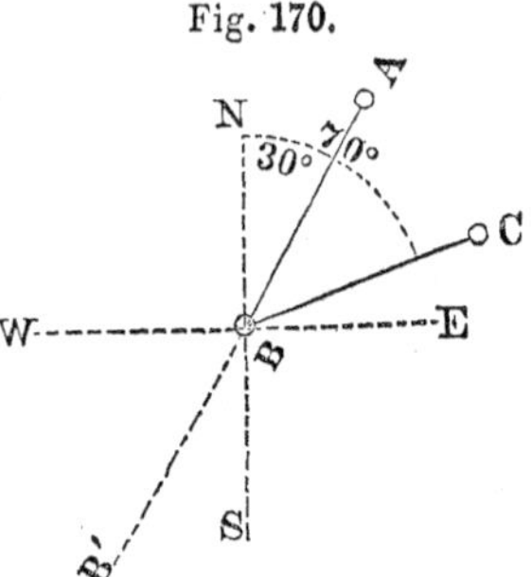

Fig. 170.

Case 4. When both the first and last letters are different, subtract the difference of the bearings from 180°. *Ex.* If AB bears S. 30° W. and BC bears N. 70° E.; the angle CBB′ is 140°.

If the angles included between the courses are desired, they will be at once found by reversing one bearing, and then applying the above rules; or by subtracting the results obtained as above from 180°; or an analogous set of rules could be formed for them.

(244) To change Bearings. It is convenient in certain calculations to suppose one of the lines of a survey to change its direction so as to become due North and South; that is, to become a new Meridian line. It is then necessary to determine what the bearings of the other lines will be, supposing them to change with it. The subject may be made plain by supposing the survey to be platted in the usual way, with the North uppermost, and the plat to be then turned around, till the line to be changed is in the desired direction. The effect of this on the other lines will be readily seen. A *General Rule* can also be formed.

Take the *difference* between the original bearing of the side which becomes a Meridian and each of those bearings which have both their letters the same as it, or both different from it. The changed bearings of these lines retain the same letters as before, if they were originally greater than the original bearing of the new Meridian line; but, if they were less, they are thrown on the other side of the N. and S. line, and their last letters are changed; E. being put for W. and W for E.

Take the *sum* of the original bearing of the new Meridian line, and each of those bearings which have one letter the same as one letter of the former bearing, and one different. If this sum exceeds

90°, this shews that the line is thrown on the other side of the East or West point, and the difference between this sum and 180° will be the new bearing and the first letter will be changed, N. being put for S. and S. for N.

Example. Let the Bearings of the sides of a field be as follows: N. 32° E.; N. 80° E.; S. 48° E.; S. 18° W.; N. 73½° W.; North. Suppose the first side to become due North; the changed bearings will then be as follows: North; N. 48° E.; S. 80° E.; S. 14° E.; S. 74½° W.; N. 32° W.

To apply the rule to the "North" course, as above, it must be called N. 0° W.; and then by the Rule, 32° must be added to it.

The true bearings can of course be obtained from the changed bearings, by reversing the operation, taking the sum instead of the difference, and *vice versa.*

(245) Line Surveying. This name may be given to surveys of lines, such as the windings of a brook, the curves of a road, &c., by way of distinction from *Farm Surveying*, in which the lines surveyed enclose a space.

To survey a *brook*, or any similar line, set the compass at, or near, one end of it, and take the bearing of an imaginary or visual line, running in the general average direction of the brook,

Fig. 172.

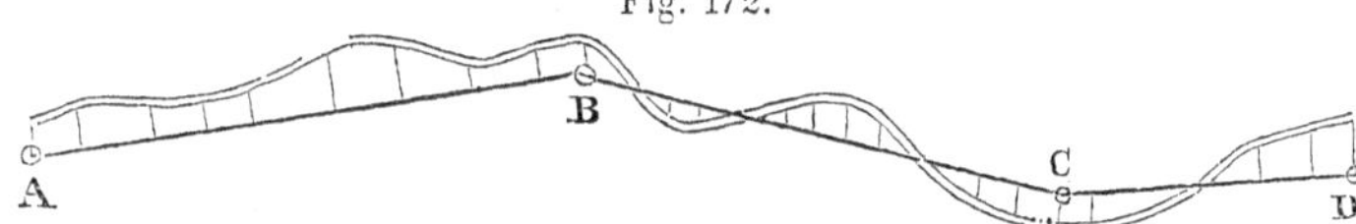

such as AB in the figure. Measure this line, taking offsets to the various bends of the brook, as to the fence explained in Art.(115). Then set the compass at B, and take a back-sight to A, and if they agree, take a fore-sight to C, and proceed as before, noting particularly the points where the line crosses the brook.

To survey a *road*, take the bearings and lengths of the lines

Fig. 173.

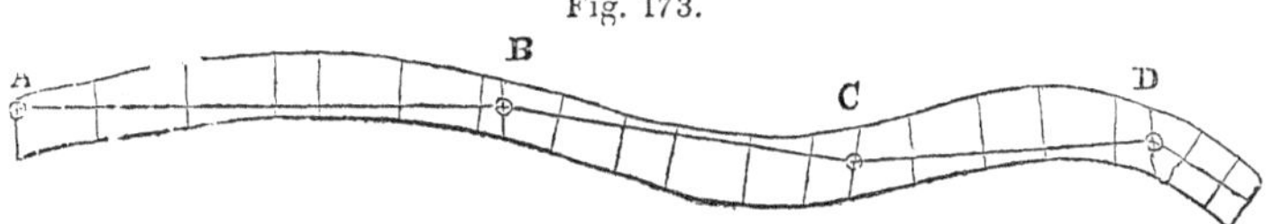

which can be most conveniently measured in the road, and measure offsets on each side, to the outside of the road.

When the line of a new road is surveyed, the bearings and lengths of the various portions of its intended centre line should be measured, and the distance which it runs through each man's land should be noted. Stones should be set in the ground at recorded distances from each angle of the line, or in each line prolonged a known distance, so as not to be disturbed in making the road.

In surveying a wide river, one bank may be surveyed by the method just given, and points on the opposite banks, as trees, &c., may be fixed by the method of intersections, founded on the Fourth Method of determining the position of a point; and fully explained in Part IV.

(246) Checks by intersecting bearings. At each station at which the compass is set, take bearings to some remarkable object, such as a church steeple, a distant house, a high tree, &c. At least three bearings should be taken to each object to make it of any use: since two are necessary to determine it, (by our Fourth Method), and, till thus determined, it can be no check. When the line is platted, by the methods to be explained in the next chapter, plat also the lines given by these bearings. If those taken to the same object from three different stations, intersect in the same point, this proves that there has been no mistake in the survey or platting of those stations.

If any bearing does not intersect a point fixed by previous bearings, it shows that there has been an error, either between the last station and one of those which fixed the point, or in the last bearing to the point. To discover which it was, plat the following line of the survey, and, at its extremity, set off the bearing from it to the point; and if the line thus platted passes through the point, it proves that there was no error in the line, but only in the bearing to the point. If otherwise, the error was somewhere in the line between the stations from which the bearings to that point were taken.

(247) Keeping the Field-notes. The simplest and easiest method for a beginner is to make a rough sketch of the survey by eye, and write down on the lines their bearings and lengths.

An improvement on this is to actually lay down the precise bear ings and lengths of the lines in the field-book in the manner to be explained in the chapter on Platting, Art. (**269**).

(248) A *second* method is to draw a straight line up the page of the field-book, and to write on it the bearings and lengths of the lines. The only advantage of this method is that the line will not run off the side of the page, as it is apt to do in the preceding method.

(249) A *third* method is to represent the line surveyed, by a double column, as in Part II, Chapter I, Art. (**95**), which should be now referred to. The bearings are written obliquely up the columns. At the end of each course, its length is written in the column, and a line drawn across it. Dotted lines are drawn across the column at any intermediate measurement. Offsets are noted as explained in Art. (**114**).

The intersection-bearings, described in Art. (**246**), should be entered in the field-book *before* the bearings of the line, in order to avoid mistakes of platting, in setting off the measured distances on the wrong line.

(250) A *fourth* method is to write the Stations, Bearings, and Distances in three columns. This is compact, and has the advantage, when applied to farm surveying, of presenting a form suitable for the subsequent calculations of Content, but does not give facilities for noting offsets.

Examples of these four methods are given in Art. (**254**) ; which contains the field-notes of the lines bounding a field.

(251) New-York Canal Maps. The following is a description of the original maps of the survey of the line of the New-York Erie Canal, as published by the Canal Commissioners. The figure represents a portion of such a map; but, necessarily, with all its lines black; red and blue lines being used on the real map.

Fig. 174.

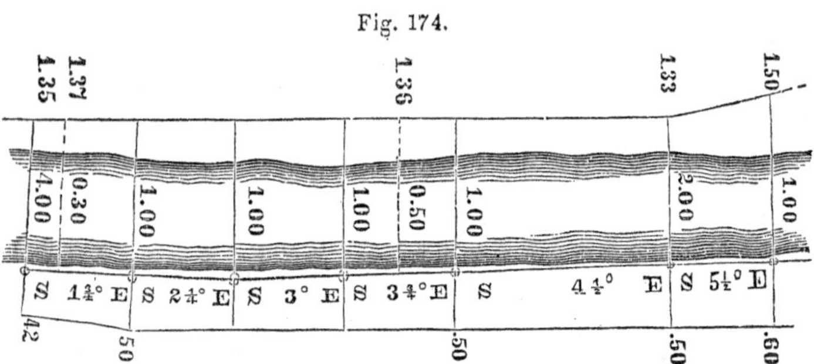

"The RED LINE described along the inner edge of the towing path is the *base line*, upon which all the measurements in the direction of the length of the canal were made. The *bearings* refer to the magnetic meridian at the time of the survey. The *lengths* of the several portions are inserted at the *end* of each, in chains and links. The *offsets* at each station are represented by red lines drawn across the canal in such a direction as to bisect the angles formed by the two contiguous portions of the red or base line, upon the towing path. The intermediate offsets are set off at right angles to the base line; and the distances on both are given from it in links. The *intermediate offsets* are represented by *red dotted lines*, and the distances to them upon the base line are reckoned, in each case, from the last preceding station. The same is likewise done with the other distances upon the base line; those to the *Bridges* being taken to the lines joining the nearest angles, or corner posts of their abutments; those to the *Locks* extending to the lines passing through the centres of the two nearest quoin posts; and those to the *Aqueducts*, to the faces of their abutments. The space enclosed by the BLUE LINES represents the portion embraced within the limits of the survey as belonging to the state; and the names of the adjoining proprietors are given as they stood at the time of executing the survey. The distances are projected upon a *scale* of two chains to the inch."

(252) Farm Surveying. A farm, or field, or other space included within known lines, is usually surveyed by the compass thus. Begin by walking around the boundary lines, and setting stakes at all the corners, which the flag-man should specially note, so that he may readily find them again. Then set the compass at any corner, and send the flag-man to the next corner. Take the bearing of the bounding line running from corner to corner, which is usually a fence. Measure its length, taking offsets if necessary. Note where any other fence, or road, or other line, crosses or meets it, and take their bearings. Take the compass to the end of this first bounding line; sight back, and if the back-sight agrees, take the bearing and distance of the next bounding line; and so proceed till you have got back to the point of starting.

(253) Where speed is more important than accuracy in a survey, whether of a line or a farm, the compass need be set only at every other station, taking a forward sight, from the 1st station to the 2d; then setting the compass at the 3d station, taking a back-sight to the 2d station (but with the north point of the compass always ahead), and a fore-sight to the 4th; then going to the 5th, and so on. This is, however, not to be recommended.

(254) Field-notes. The Field-notes of a Farm survey may be kept by any of the methods which have been described with reference to a Line survey. Below are given the Field-notes of the same field recorded by each of the methods.

First Method.

Fig. 175.

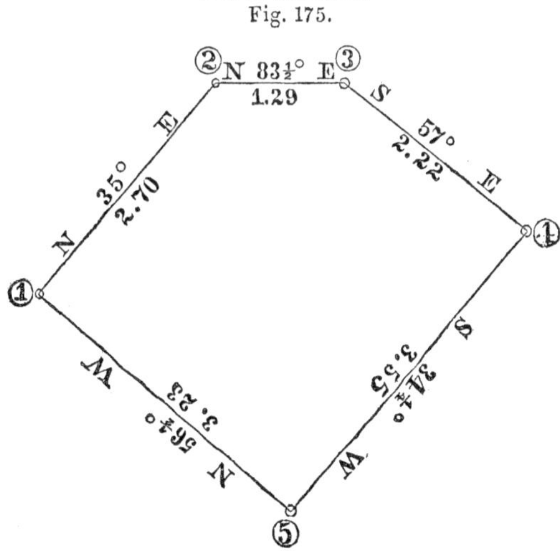

Second Method.

⊙ (1)
N. 56½° W. | 3.23
⊙ (5)
S. 34¼° W. | 3.55
⊙ (4)
S. 57° E. | 2.22
⊙ (3)
N. 83½° E. | 1.29
⊙ (2)
N. 35° E. | 2.70
⊙ (1)

*Third Method.**

-(1)-
3.23
N. 56½ W.
-(5)-
3.54
S. 34¼ W.
-(4)-
2.22
S. 57 E.
-(3)-
1.29
N. 83½ E.
-(2)-
2.70
N. 35 E.
-(1)-

Fourth Method.

STATIONS.	BEARINGS.	DISTANCES.
1	N. 35° E.	2.70
2	N. 83½° E.	1.29
3	S. 57° E.	2.22
4	S. 34¼° W.	3.55
5	N. 56½° W.	3.23

Fig. 176.

—3— 0
2.77
-0.90- 12
-0.25- 6
N. 79½ E.
—2— 0
1.34
-0.70- 8
S. 66° E.
—1— 0

(255) The Field-notes of a field, in which offsets occur, may be most easily recorded by the Third Method; as in Fig. 176.

When the Field-notes are recorded by the Fourth Method, the offsets may be kept in a separate Table; in which the 1st co.umn will contain the stations from which the measurements are made, the 2d column the distances at which they occur, the 3d

* In the "Third Method," the bearings should be written obliquely upward, as directed in Art, (249) but are not so printed here, from typographical difficulties,

column the lengths of the offsets, and the 4th column the side of the line, "Right," or "Left," on which they lie.

For calculation, four more columns may be added to the table, containing the intervals between the offsets; the sums of the adjoining pairs; and the products of the numbers in the two preceding columns, separated into Right and Left, one being additive to the field, and the other subtractive.

(256) Tests of accuracy. 1st. The check of intersections described in Art. (**246**), may be employed to great advantage, when some conspicuous object near the centre of the farm can be seen from most of its corners.

2nd. When the survey is platted, if the last course meets the starting point, it proves the work, and the survey is then said to "close."

3d. Diagonal lines, running from corner to corner of the farm, like the "Proof-lines" in Chain Surveying, may be measured and their bearings taken. When these are laid down on the plat, their meeting the points to which they had been measured, proves the work.

4th. The only certain and precise test is, however, that by "Latitudes and Departures." This is fully explained in Chapter V, of this Part.

(257) A very fallacious test is recommended by several writers on this subject. It is a well-known proposition of Geometry, that in any figure bounded by straight lines, the sum of all the interior angles is equal to twice as many right angles, as the figure has sides less two; since the figure can be divided into that number of triangles. Hence this common rule. "Calculate [by the last paragraph of Art. (**243**)] the *interior* angles of the field or farm surveyed; add them together, and if their sum equals twice as many right angles as the figure has sides less two, the angles have been correctly measured." This rule is *not* applicable to a compass survey; for, in Fig. 167, page 144, the interior angle BCD will contain the same number of degrees (in that case 160°) whether the bearings of the sides have been noted correctly, as being the angles which they make with NS—or incorrectly, as being the angles which they make with N′S′. This rule would therefore prove the work in either case.

(258) Method of Radiation. *A field may be surveyed from one station, either within it or without it,* by taking the bearings and the distances from that point to each of the corners of the field. These corners are then "determined," by the 3d method, Art. (7). This modification of that method, we named, in Art. (220), the *Method of Radiation.* All our preceding surveys with the compass have been by the *Method of Progression.*

The compass may be set at one corner of the field, or at a point in one of its sides, and the same method of Radiation employed.

This method is seldom used however, since, unlike the method of Progression, its operations are not checks upon each other.

(259) Method of Intersection. A field may also be surveyed by measuring a *base line*, either within it or without it, setting the compass at each end of the base line, and taking, from each end, the bearings of each corner of the field; which will then be fixed and determined, by the 4th method, Art. (8). This mode of surveying is the *Method of Intersections*, noticed in Art. (220). It will be fully treated of in Part V, under the title of **Triangular Surveying.**

(260) Running out old lines. The original surveys of lands in the older States of the American Union, were exceedingly deficient in precision. This arose from two principal causes; the small value of land at the period of these surveys, and the want of skill in the surveyors. The effect at the present day is frequent dissatisfaction and litigation. Lots sometimes contain more acres than they were sold for, and sometimes less. Lines which are straight in the deed, and on the map, are found to be crooked on the ground. The recorded surveys of two adjoining farms often make one overlap the other, or leave a gore between them. The most difficult and delicate duty of the land-surveyor, is to run out these old boundary lines. In such cases, his first business is to find monuments, stones, marked trees, stumps, or any other old "corners," or landmarks. These are his starting points. The owners whose lands join at these corners should agree on them. Old fences must generally be accepted by right of possession; though such questions belong rather to the lawyer than to the surveyor.* His business is to mark out on the ground the lines given in the deed. When the bounds are given by compass-bearings, the surveyor must be reminded that these bearings are very far from being the same now as originally, having been changing every year. The method of determining this important change, and of making the proper allowance, will be found in Chapter VIII, of this Part.

(261) Town Surveying. Begin at the meeting of two or more of the principal streets, through which you can have the longest prospects. Having fixed the instrument at that point, and taken the bearings of all the streets issuing from it, measure all these lines with the chain, taking offsets to all the corners of streets, lanes, bendings, or windings; and to all remarkable objects, as churches, markets, public buildings, &c. Then remove the instrument to the next street, take its bearings, and measure along the street as before, taking offsets as you go along, with the offset-staff. Proceed in this manner from street to street, measuring the distances and offsets as you proceed.

Fig. 177.

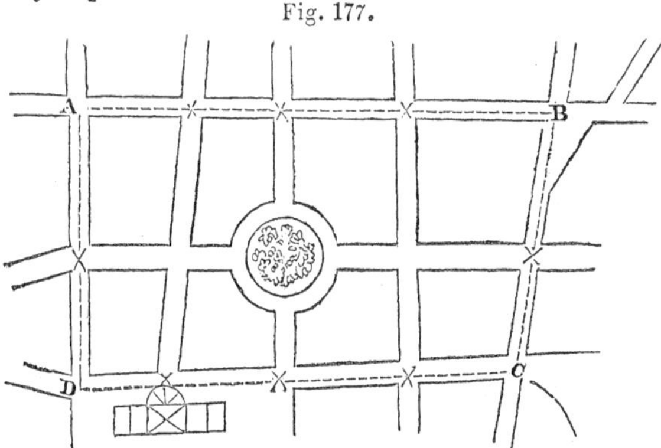

* "In the description of land conveyed, the rule is, that known and fixed monuments control courses and distances. So, the certainty of metes and bounds will include and pass all the lands within them, though they vary from the given quantity expressed in the deed. In New-York, to remove, deface or alter land marks maliciously, is an indictable offence."—*Kent's Commentaries*, IV, 515

Thus, in the figure, fix the instrument at A, and measure lines in the direction of all the streets meeting there, noting their bearings; then measure AB, noting the streets at X, X. At the second station, B, take the bearings of all the streets which meet there; and measure from B to C, noting the places and the bearings of all the cross-streets as you pass them. Proceed in like manner from C to D, and from D to A, "closing" there, as in a farm survey. Having thus surveyed all the principal streets in a particular neighborhood, proceed then to survey the smaller intermediate streets, and last of all, the lanes, alleys, courts, yards, and every other place which it may be thought proper to represent in the plan. The several cross-streets answer as good check lines, to prove the accuracy of the work. In this manner you continue till you take in all the town or city.

(262) Obstacles in Compass Surveying. The various obstacles which may be met with in Compass Surveying, such as woods, water, houses, &c., can be overcome much more easily than in Chain Surveying. But as some of the best methods for effecting this involve principles which have not yet been fully developed, it will be better to postpone giving any of them, till they can be all treated of together; which will be done in Part VII.

CHAPTER IV.

PLATTING THE SURVEY.

(263) The platting of a survey made with the compass, consists in drawing on paper the lines and the angles which have been measured on the ground. The lines are drawn "to scale," as has been fully explained in Part I, Chapter III. The manner of platting angles was referred to in Art. (**41**), but its explanation has been reserved for this place.

(264) With a Protractor. A Protractor is an instrument made for this object, and is usually a semicircle of brass, as in the figure, with its semi-circumference divided into 180 equal parts, or

Fig. 178.

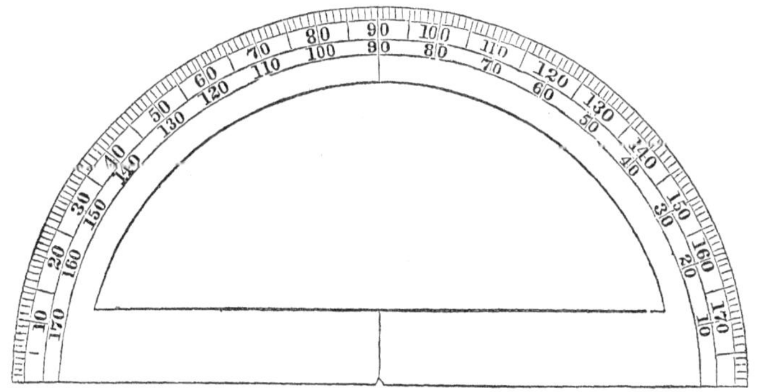

degrees, and numbered in both directions. It is, in fact, a miniature of the instrument, (or of half of it), with which the angles have been measured. To lay off any angle at any point of a straight line, place the Protractor so that its straight side, the diameter of the semi-circle, is on the given line, and the middle of this diameter, which is marked by a notch, is at the given point. With a needle, or sharp pencil, make a mark on the paper at the required number of degrees, and draw a line from the mark to the given point.

Sometimes the protractor has an arm turning on its centre, and extending beyond its circumference, so that a line can be at once drawn by it when it is set to the desired angle. A Vernier scale is sometimes added to it to increase its precision.

A Rectangular Protractor is sometimes used, the divisions of degrees being engraved along three edges of a plane scale. The semi-circular one is preferable. The objection to the rectangular protractor is that the division corresponding to a degree is very

Fig. 179.

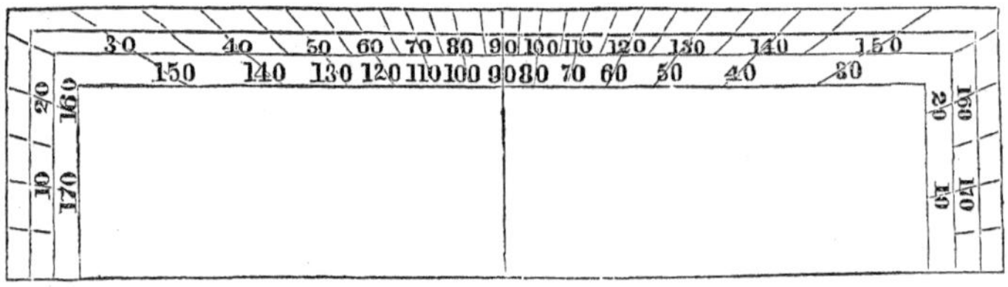

unequal on different parts of the scale, being usually two or three times as great at its ends as at its middle.

A Protractor embracing an entire circle, with arms carrying verniers, is also sometimes employed, for the sake of greater accuracy.

(265) Platting Bearings. Since "Bearings" taken with the Compass are the angles which the various lines make with the Magnetic Meridian, or the direction of the compass-needle, which, as we have seen, remains always (approximately) parallel to itself, it is necessary to draw these meridians through each station, before laying off the angles of the bearings.

The T square, shown in Fig. 14, is the most convenient instrument for this purpose. The paper on which the plat is to be made is fastened on the board so that the intended direction of the North and South line may be parallel to one of the sides of the board. The inner side of the stock of the T square being pressed against one of the other sides of the board and slid along, the edge of the long blade of the square will always be parallel to itself and to the first named side of the board, and will thus represent the meridian passing through any station.

If a straight-edged drawing board or table cannot be procured, nail down on a table of any shape a straight-edged ruler, and slide along against it the outside of the stock of a T square, one side of the stock being flush with the blade.

A parallel ruler may also be used, one part of it being screwed down to the board in the proper position.

Fig. 180.

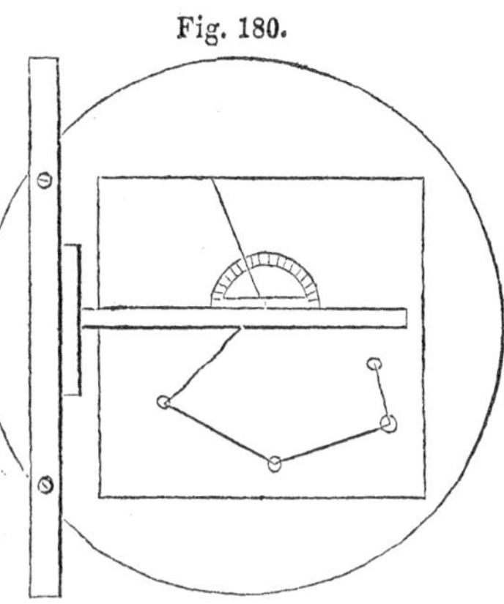

If none of these means are at hand, approximately parallel meridians may be drawn by the edges of a common ruler, at distances apart equal to its width, and the diameter of the protractor made parallel to them by measuring equal distances between it and them.

(266) To plat a survey with these instruments, mark, with a fine point enclosed in a circle, a convenient spot in the paper to represent the first station, 1 in the figure. Its place must be so chosen

Fig. 181.

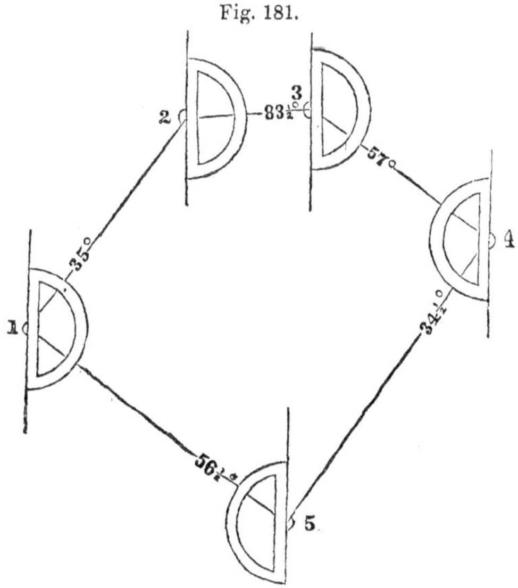

that the plat may not "run off" the paper. With the T square draw a meridian through it. The top of the paper is usually, though not necessarily, called North. With the protractor lay off the angle of the first bearing, as directed in Art. (264). Set off the length of the first line, to the desired scale, by Art. (42), from 1 to 2. The line 1----2 represents the first course.

Through 2, draw another meridian, lay off the angle of the second course, and set off the length of this course, from 2 to 3.

Proceed in like manner for each course. When the last course is platted, it should end precisely at the starting point, as the survey did, if it were a closed survey, as of a field. If the plat does not "close," or "come together," it shows some error or inaccuracy either in the original survey, if that have not been "tested" by Latitudes and Departures, or in the work of platting. A method of correction is explained in Art. (268). The plat here given is the same as that of Fig. 175, page 151.

This manner of laying down the directions of lines, by the angles which they make with a meridian line, has a great advantage, in both accuracy and rapidity, over the method of platting lines by the angles which each makes with the line which comes before it. In the latter method, any error in the direction of one line makes all that follow it also wrong in their directions. In the former, the *direction* of each line is independent of the preceding line, though its *position* would be changed by a previous error.

Instead of drawing a meridian through each station, sometimes only one is drawn, near the middle of the sheet, and all the bearings of the survey are laid off from some one point of it, as shown in the figure, and numbered to correspond with the stations from which these bearings were taken. The circular protractor is convenient for this. They are then transferred to the places where they are wanted, by a triangle or other parallel ruler, as explained on page 27. The figure at the top of the next page represents the same field platted by this method.

A semi-circular protractor is sometimes attached to the stock end of the T square, so that its blade may be set at any desired angle with the meridian, and any bearing be thus protracted without drawing a meridian. It has some inconveniences.

Fig. 182.

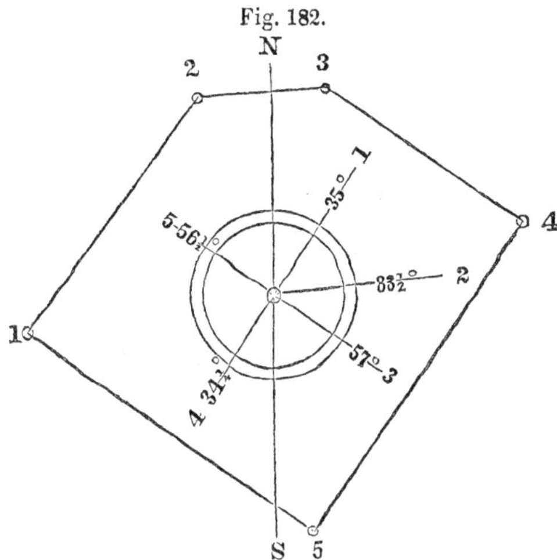

(267) The Compass itself may be used to plat bearings. For this purpose it must be attached to a square board so that the N and S line of the compass box may be parallel to two opposite edges of the board. This is placed on the paper, and the box is turned till the needle points as it did when the first bearing was taken. Then a line drawn by one edge of the board will be in a proper direction. Mark off its length, and plat the next and the succeeding bearings in the same manner.

(268) When the plat of a survey does not "close," it may be corrected as follows. Let ABCDE be the boundary lines platted according to the given bearings and distances, and suppose that the last course comes to E, instead of ending at A, as it should. Suppose also that there is no reason to suspect any single great error, and that no one of the lines was measured over very rough

Fig. 183.

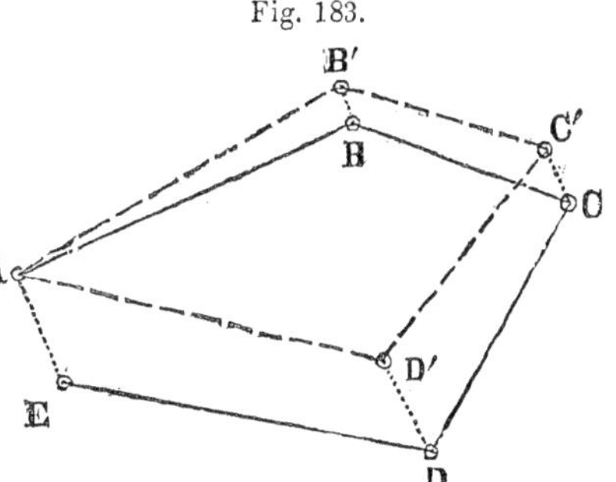

ground, or was specially uncertain in its direction when observed. The inaccuracy must then be distributed among all the lines *in proportion to their length*. Each point in the figure, B, C, D, E, must be moved in a direction parallel to EA, by a certain distance which is obtained thus. Multiply the distance EA by the distance AB, and divide by the sum of all the courses. The quotient will be the distance BB′. To get CC′, multiply EA by AB + BC, and divide the product by the same sum of all the courses. To get DD′, multiply EA by AB + BC + CD, and divide as before. So for any course, multiply by the sum of the lengths of that course and of all those preceding it, and divide as before. Join the points thus obtained, and the closed polygon AB′C′D′A will thus be formed, and will be the most *probable* plat of the given survey.*

The method of Latitudes and Departures, to be explained hereafter, is, however, the best for effecting this object.

(269) Field Platting. It is sometimes desirable to plat the courses of a survey in the field, as soon as they are taken, as was mentioned in Art. (247), under the head of "Keeping the field-notes." One method of doing this is to have the paper of the Field-book ruled with parallel lines, at *unequal* distances apart, and to use a rectangular protractor (which may be made of Bristol-board, or other stout drawing paper,) with lines ruled across it at equal distances of some fraction of an inch. A bearing having been taken and noted, the protractor is laid on the paper and its centre placed at the station where the bearing is to be laid off. It is then turned till one of its cross-lines coincides with some one of the lines on the paper, which represent East and West lines. The long side of the protractor will then be on a meridian and the proper angle (40° in the figure) can be at once marked off. The length of the course can also be set off by the equal spaces between the cross-lines, letting each space represent any convenient number of links.

Fig. 184.

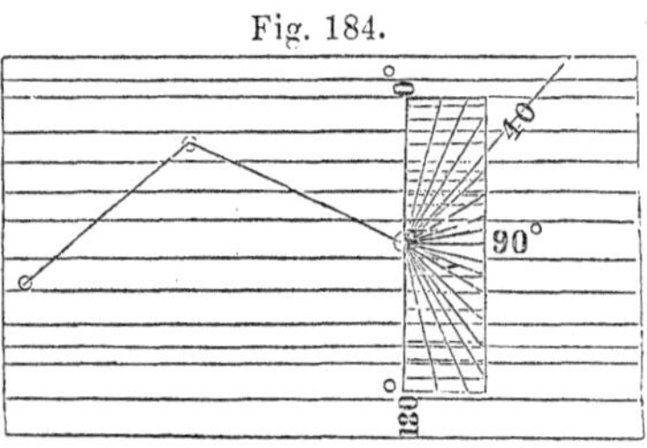

* This was demonstrated by Dr. Bowditch, in No. 4, of "The Analyst."

(270) A common rectangular protractor without any cross-lines, or a semi-circular one, can also be used for the same purpose. The parallel lines on the paper (which, in this method, may be equi-distant, as in common ruled writing paper) will now represent meridians. Place the centre of the protractor on the meridian nearest to the station at which the angle is to be laid off, and turn it till the given number of degrees is cut by the meridian. Slide the protractor up or down the meridian (which must continue to pass through the centre and the proper degree) till its edge passes through the station, and then draw by this edge a line, which will have the bearing required.

Fig. 185.

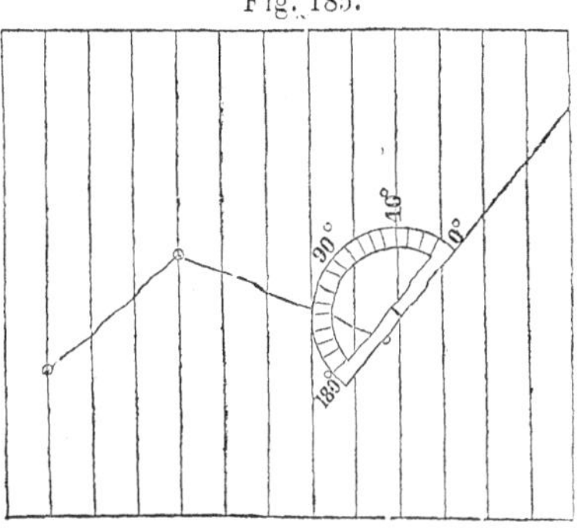

(271) *Paper ruled into squares*, (as are sometimes the right-hand pages of surveyors' field-books), may be used for platting bearings in the field. The lines running up the page may be called North and South lines, and those running across the page will then be East and West lines. Any course of the survey will be the hypothenuse of a right-angled triangle, and the ratio of its other two sides will determine the angle. Thus, if the ratio of the two sides of the right-angled triangle, of which the line AB in the figure is the hypothenuse, is 1, that line makes an angle of 45° with the meridian. If the ratio of the long to the short side of the right-angled triangle of which the line AC is the hypothenuse, is 4 to 1, the line AC makes an angle of 14° with the meridian. The line AD, the hypothenuse of an

Fig. 186.

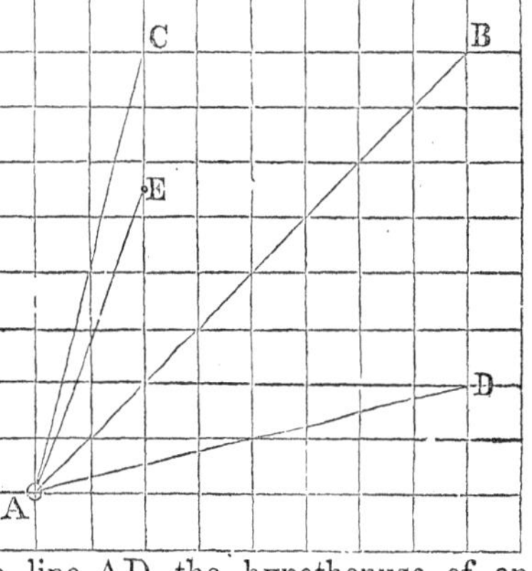

equal triangle, which has its long side lying East and West, makes likewise an angle of 14° with that side, and therefore makes an angle of 76° with the meridian.*

To facilitate the use of this method, the following table has been prepared.

TABLE FOR PLATTING BY SQUARES.

Angle opposite short side.	Ratio of long side to short side.	Angle opposite long side.	Angle opposite short side.	Ratio of long side to short side.	Angle opposite long side.	Angle opposite short side.	Ratio of long side to short side.	Angle opposite short side.
1°	57.3 to 1	89°	16°	3.49 to 1	74°	31°	1.664 to 1	59°
2°	28.6 to 1	88°	17°	3.27 to 1	73°	32°	1.600 to 1	58°
3°	19.1 to 1	87°	18°	3.08 to 1	72°	33°	1.540 to 1	57°
4°	14.3 to 1	86°	19°	2.90 to 1	71°	34°	1.483 to 1	56°
5°	11.4 to 1	85°	20°	2.75 to 1	70°	35°	1.428 to 1	55°
6°	9.5 to 1	84°	21°	2.61 to 1	69°	36°	1.376 to 1	54°
7°	8.1 to 1	83°	22°	2.48 to 1	68°	37°	1.327 to 1	53°
8°	7.1 to 1	82°	23°	2.36 to 1	67°	38°	1.280 to 1	52°
9°	6.3 to 1	81°	24°	2.25 to 1	66°	39°	1.235 to 1	51°
10°	5.7 to 1	80°	25°	2.14 to 1	65°	40°	1.192 to 1	50°
11°	5.1 to 1	79°	26°	2.05 to 1	64°	41°	1.150 to 1	49°
12°	4.9 to 1	78°	27°	1.96 to 1	63°	42°	1.111 to 1	48°
13°	4.3 to 1	77°	28°	1.88 to 1	62°	43°	1.072 to 1	47°
14°	4.0 to 1	76°	29°	1.80 to 1	61°	44°	1.036 to 1	46°
15°	3.7 to 1	75°	30°	1.73 to 1	60°	45°	1.000 to 1	45°

To use this table, find in it the ratio corresponding to the angle which you wish to plat. Then count, on the ruled paper, any number of squares to the right or to the left of the point which represents the station, according as your bearing was East or West; and count upward or downward according as your bearing was North or South, the number of squares given by multiplying the first number by the ratio of the Table. Thus; if the given bearing from A in the figure, was N. 20° E. and two squares were counted to the right, then $2 \times 2.75 = 5\frac{1}{2}$ squares, should be counted upward, to E, and AE would be the required course.

(272) With a paper protractor. Engraved paper protractors may be obtained from the instrument-makers, and are very conve-

* This and all the following ratios may be obtained directly from Trigonometrical Tables; for the ratio of the long side to the short side, the latter being taken as unity, is the natural cotangent of the angle.

nient. A circle of large size, divided into degrees and quarters, is engraved on copper, and impressions from it are taken on drawing paper. The divisions are not numbered. Draw a straight line to represent a meridian, through the centre of the circle, in any convenient direction. Number the degrees from 0 to 90°, each way from the ends of this meridian, as on the compass-plate. The protractor is now ready for use. Choose a convenient point for the first station. Suppose the first bearing to be N. 30° E. The line passing through the centre of the circle and through the opposite points N. 30° E. and S. 30° W. has the bearing required. But it does not pass through the station 1. Transfer it thither by drawing through station 1 a line parallel to it, which will be the course required, its proper length being set off on it from 1 to 2. Now suppose the bearing from 2 to be S. 60° E. Draw through 2 a line parallel to the line passing through the centre of the circle and through the opposite points S. 60° E., and N. 60° W., and it will be the line desired. On it set off the proper length from 2 to 3, and so proceed.

Fig. 187.

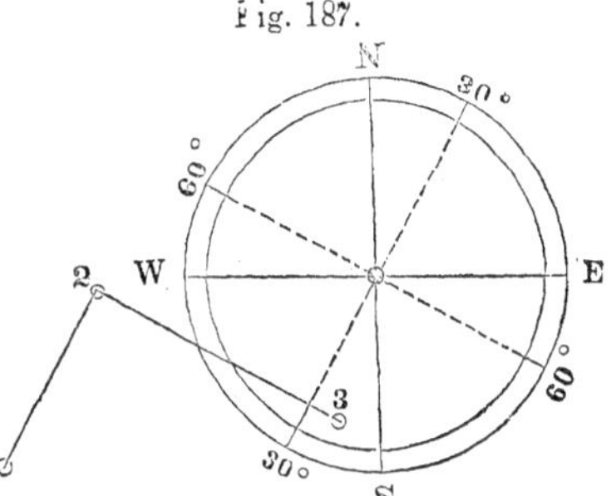

When the plat is completed, the engraved sheet is laid on a clean one, and the stations "pricked through," and the points thus obtained on the clean sheet are connected by straight lines. The pencilled plat is then rubbed off from the engraved sheet, which can be used for a great number of plats.

If the central circle be cut out, the plat, if not too large, can be made directly on the paper where it is to remain.

The surveyor can make such a paper protractor for himself, with great ease, by means of the *Table of Chords* at the end of this volume, the use of which is explained in Art. (275). The engraved ones may have shrunk after being printed.

Such a circle is sometimes drawn on the map itself. This will be particularly convenient if the bearings of any lines on the map, not taken on the ground, are likely to be required. If the map be very long, more than one may be needed.

(273) Drawing-Board Protractor. Such a divided circle, as has just been described, or a circular protractor, may be placed on a drawing board near its centre, and so that its 0° and 90° lines are parallel to the sides of the drawing board. Lines are then to be drawn, through the centre and opposite divisions, by a ruler long enough to reach the edges of the drawing board, on which they are to be cut in, and numbered. The drawing board thus becomes, in fact, a double rectangular protractor. A strip of white paper may have previously been pasted on the edges, or a narrow strip of white wood inlaid. When this is to be used for platting, a sheet of paper is put on the board as usual, and lines are drawn by a ruler laid across the 0° points and the 90° points, and the centre of the circle is at once found, and should be marked ⊙. The bearings are then platted as in the last method.

(274) With a scale of chords. On the plane scale contained in cases of mathematical drawing instruments will be found a series of divisions numbered from 0 to 90, and marked CH, or C. This is a scale of chords, and gives the lengths of the chords of any arc for a radius equal in length to the chord of 60° on the scale. To lay off an angle with this scale, as for example, to draw a line making at A an angle of 40° with AB, take, in the dividers, the distances from 0 to 60 on the scale of chords; with this for radius and A for centre, describe an indefinite arc CD. Take the distance from 0 to 40 on the same scale, and set it off on the arc as a chord, from C to some point D. Join AD, and prolong it. BAE is the angle required.

Fig. 188.

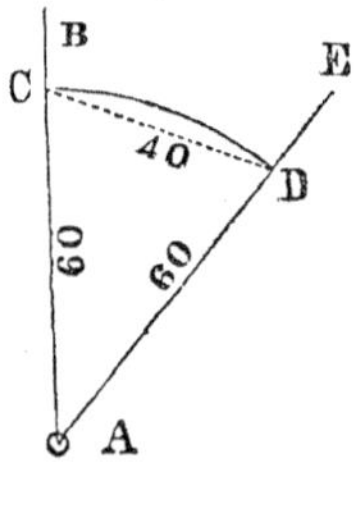

The Sector, represented on page 36, supplies a modification of this method, sometimes more convenient. On each of its legs is a scale marked C, or CH. Open it at pleasure; extend the compass from 60 to 60, one on each leg, and with this radius describe an arc. Then extend the compasses from 40 to 40, and the distance will be the chord of 40° to that radius. It can be set off as above.

The smallness of the scale renders the method with a scale of chords practically deficient in exactness; but it serves to illustrate the next and *best* method.

(275) **With a Table of chords.** At the end of this volume will be found a Table of the lengths of the chords of arcs for every degree and minute of the quadrant, calculated for a radius equal to 1.

To use it, take in the compasses one inch, one foot, or any other convenient distance (the longer the better) divided into tenths and hundredths, by a diagonal scale, or otherwise. With this as radius describe an arc as in the last case. Find in the table of chords the length of the chord of the desired angle. Take it from the scale just used, to the nearest decimal part which the scale will give. Set it off as a chord, as in the last figure, and join the point thus obtained to the starting point. This gives the angle desired.

The superiority of this method to that which employs a protractor, is due to the greater precision with which a straight line can be divided than can a circle.

A slight modification of this method is to take in the compasses 10 equal parts of any convenient length, inches, half inches, quarter inches, or any other at hand, and with this radius describe an arc as before, and set off a chord 10 times as great as the one found in the Table, i. e. imagine the decimal point moved one place to the right.

If the radius be 100 or 1000 equal parts, imagine the decimal point moved two, or three, places to the right.

Whatever radius may be taken or given, the product of that radius into a chord of the Table, will give the chord for that radius.

This gives an easy and exact method of getting a right angle; by describing an arc with a radius of 1, and setting off a chord equal to 1.4142.

If the angle to be constructed is more than 90°, construct on the other side of the given point, upon the given line prolonged, an angle equal to what the given angle wants of 180°; i. e. its *Supplement*, in the language of Trigonometry.

This same Table gives the means of measuring any angle. With the angular point for a centre, and 1, or 10, for a radius, describe an arc. Measure the length of the chord of the arc between the legs of the angle, find this length in the Table, and the angle corresponding to it is the one desired.*

(276) With a Table of natural sines. In the absence of a Table of chords, heretofore rare, a table of natural sines, which can be found anywhere, may be used as a less convenient substitute. Since the chord of any angle equals twice the sine of half the angle, divide the given angle by two; find in the table the natural sine of this half angle; double it, and the product is the chord of the whole angle. This can then be used precisely as was the chord in the preceding article.

An ingenious modification of this method has been much used. Describe an arc from the given point as centre, as in the last two articles, but with a radius of 5 equal parts. Take, from a Table, the length of the natural sine of half the given angle to a radius of 10. Set off this length as a chord on the arc just described, and join the point thus obtained to the given point.†

(277) By Latitudes and Departures. When the Latitudes and Departures of a survey have been obtained and corrected, (as explained in Chapter V), either to test its accuracy, or to obtain its content, they afford the easiest and best means of platting it. The description of this method will be given in Art. (285).

* This Table will also serve to find the *natural sine*, or *cosine*, of any angle. Multiply the given angle by two; find, in the Table, the chord of this double angle; and half of this chord will be the natural sine required For, the chord of any angle is equal to twice the sine of half the angle. To find the *cosine*, proceed as above, with the angle which added to the given angle would make 90°.

Another use of this Table is to inscribe regular polygons in a circle by setting off the chords of the arcs which their sides subtend.

Still another use is to divide an arc or angle into any number of equal parts by setting off the fractional arc or angle.

Fig. 189.

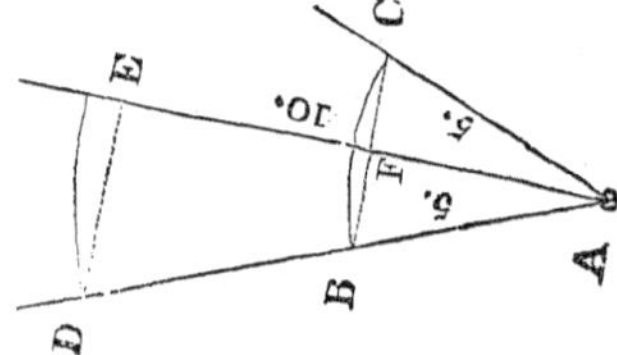

† The reason of this is apparent from the figure. DE is the sine of half the angle BAC, to a radius of 10 equal parts, and BC is the chord directed to be set off, to a radius of 5 equal parts. BC is equal to DE; for BC = 2.BF, by Trigonometry, and DE = 2.BF, by similar triangles; hence BC = DE.

CHAPTER V.

LATITUDES AND DEPARTURES.

(278) Definitions. The LATITUDE of a point is its distance North or South of some "*Parallel of Latitude*," or line running East or West. The LONGITUDE of a point is its distance East or West of some "*Meridian*," or line running North and South. In Compass-Surveying, the Magnetic Meridian, i. e. the direction in which the Magnetic Needle points, is the line from which the Longitudes of points are measured, or reckoned.

The distance which one end of a line is due North or South of the other end, is called the *Difference of Latitude* of the two ends of the line; or its *Northing* or *Southing;* or simply its *Latitude.*

The distance which one end of the line is due East or West of the other, is here called the *Difference of Longitude* of the two ends of the line; or its *Easting* or *Westing;* or its *Departure.*

Latitudes and *Departures* are the most usual terms, and will be generally used hereafter, for the sake of brevity.

This subject may be illustrated geographically, by noticing that a traveller in going from New-York to Buffalo in a straight line, would go about 150 miles due north, and 250 miles due west. These distances would be the differences of Latitude and of Longitude between the two places, or his Northing and Westing. Returning from Buffalo to New-York, the same distances would be his Southing and Easting.*

In mathematical language, the operation of finding the Latitude and Longitude of a line from its Bearing and Length, would be called the transformation of Polar Co-ordinates into Rectangular Co-ordinates. It consists in determining, by our *Second Principle*, the position of a point which had originally been determined by the *Third Principle*. Thus, in the figure, (which is the same as

* It should be remembered that the following discussions of the Latitudes and Longitudes of the points of a survey will not always be fully applicable to those of distant places, such as the cities just named, in consequence of the surface of the earth not being a plane.

that of Art. (9)), the point S is determined by the angle SAC and by the distance AS. It is also determined by the distances AC and CS, measured at right angles to each other; and then, supposing CS to run due North and South, CS will be the *Latitude*, and AC the *Departure* of the line AS.

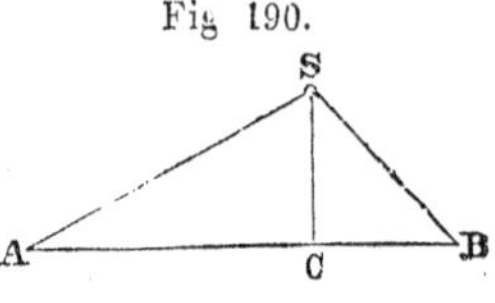

Fig. 190.

(279) Calculation of Latitudes and Departures. Let AB be a given line, of which the length AB, and the bearing (or angle, BAC, which it makes with the Magnetic Meridian), are known. It is required to find the differences of Latitude and of Longitude between its two extremities A and B: that is, to find AC and CB; or, what is the same thing, BD and DA.

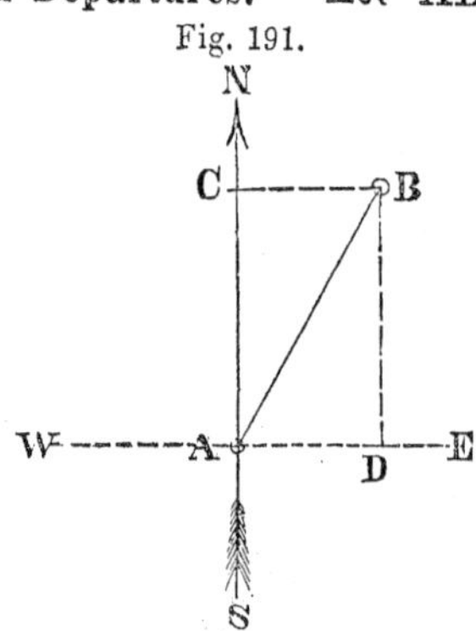

Fig. 191.

It will be at once seen that AB is the hypothenuse of a right-angled triangle, in which the "Latitude" and the "Departure" are the sides about the right angle. We therefore know, from the principles of trigonometry, that

$$AC = AB \,.\, \cos.\, BAC,$$
$$BC = AB \,.\, \sin.\, BAC.$$

Hence, to find the *Latitude* of any course, multiply the natural cosine of the bearing by the length of the course; and to find the *Departure* of any course, multiply the natural sine of the bearing by the length of the course.

If the course be Northerly, the *Latitude* will be North, and will be marked with the algebraic sign +, *plus*, or additive; if it be Southerly, the Latitude will be South, and will be marked with the algebraic sign —, *minus*, or subtractive.

If the course be Easterly, the *Departure* will be East, and marked +, or additive; if the course be Westerly, the Departure will be West, and marked —, or subtractive.

(280) Formulas. The rules of the preceding article may be expressed thus;

$$\text{Latitude} = \text{Distance} \times \text{cos. Bearing},$$
$$\text{Departure} = \text{Distance} \times \text{sin. Bearing.}^*$$

From these formulas may be obtained others, by which, when any two of the above four things are given, the remaining two can be found.

When the Bearing and Latitude are given;

$$\text{Distance} = \frac{\text{Latitude}}{\text{cos. Bearing}} = \text{Latitude} \times \text{ sec. Bearing},$$
$$\text{Departure} = \text{Latitude} \times \text{tang. Bearing.}$$

When the Bearing and Departure are given;

$$\text{Distance} = \frac{\text{Departure}}{\text{sin. Bearing}} = \text{Departure} \times \text{cosec. Bearing},$$
$$\text{Latitude} = \text{Departure} \times \text{cotang. Bearing.}$$

When the Distance and Latitude are given;

$$\text{Cos. Bearing} = \frac{\text{Latitude}}{\text{Distance}},$$
$$\text{Departure} = \text{Latitude} \times \text{tang. Bearing.}$$

When the Distance and Departure are given;

$$\text{Sin. Bearing} = \frac{\text{Departure}}{\text{Distance}},$$
$$\text{Latitude} = \text{Departure} \times \text{cotang. Bearing.}$$

When the Latitude and Departure are given;

$$\text{Tang. of Bearing} = \frac{\text{Departure}}{\text{Latitude}},$$
$$\text{Distance} = \text{Latitude} \times \text{sec. Bearing.}$$

Still more simply, any two of these three—Distance, Latitude and Departure—being given, we have

$$\text{Distance} = \sqrt{(\text{Latitude}^2 + \text{Departure}^2)}$$
$$\text{Latitude} = \sqrt{(\text{Distance}^2 - \text{Departure}^2)}$$
$$\text{Departure} = \sqrt{(\text{Distance}^2 - \text{Latitude}^2)}$$

(281) Traverse Tables. The Latitude and Departure of any distance, for any bearing, could be found by the method given in Art. (279), with the aid of a table of Natural Sines. But to

* Whenever sines, cosines, tangents, &c., are here named, they mean the natural sines &c., of an arc described with a radius equal to *one*, or to the unit by which the sines, &c., are measured.

facilitate these calculations, which are of so frequent occurrence and of so great use, *Traverse Tables* have been prepared, originally for navigators, (whence the name *Traverse*), and subsequently for surveyors.*

The Traverse Table at the end of this volume gives the Latitude and Departure for any bearing, to each quarter of a degree, and for distances from 1 to 9.

To use it, find in it the number of degrees in the bearing, on the left hand side of the page, if it be less than 45°, or on the right hand side if it be more. The numbers on the same line running across the page,† are the Latitudes and Departures for that bearing, and for the respective distances—1, 2, 3, 4, 5, 6, 7, 8, 9,—which are at the top and bottom of the page, and which may represent chains, links, rods, feet, or any other unit. Thus, if the bearing be 15°, and the distance 1, the Latitude would be 0.966 and the Departure 0.259. For the same bearing, but a distance of 8, the Latitude would be 7.727, and the Departure 2.071.

Any distance, however great, can have its Latitude and Departure readily obtained from this table; since, for the same bearing, they are directly proportional to the distance, because of the similar triangles which they form. Therefore, to find the Latitude or Departure for 60, multiply that for 6 by 10, which merely moves the decimal point one place to the right; for 500, multiply the numbers found in the Table for 5, by 100, i. e. move the decimal point two places to the right, and so on. Merely moving the decimal point to the right, one, two, or more places, will therefore enable this Table to give the Latitude and Departure for any decimal multiple of the numbers in the Table.

For compound numbers, such as 873, it is only necessary to find separately the Latitudes and Departures of 800, of 70, and of 3, and add them together. But this may be done, with scarcely any risk of error, by the following simple rule.

* The first Traverse Table for Surveyors seems to have been published in 1791, by John Gale. The most extensive table is that of Capt. Boileau, of the British army, being calculated for every minute of bearing, and to five decimal places, for distances from 1 to 10. The Table in this volume was calculated for it, and then compared with the one just mentioned.

† In using this or any similar Table, lay a ruler across the page, just above or below the line to be followed out. This is a very valuable mechanica. assistance

Write down the Latitude and Departure for the first figure of the given number, as found in the Table, neglecting the decimal point; write under them the Latitude and Departure of the second figure, setting them one place farther to the right; under them write the Latitude and Departure of the third figure, setting them one place farther to the right, and so proceed with all the figures of the given number. Add up these Latitudes and Departures, and cut off the three right hand figures. The remaining figures will be the Latitude and Departure of the given number in links, or chains, or feet, or whatever unit it was given in.

For example; let the Latitude and Departure of a course having a distance of 873 links, and a bearing of 20°, be required. In the Table find 20°, and then take out the Latitude and Departure for 8, 7 and 3, in turn, placing them as above directed, thus:

Distances.	*Latitudes.*	*Departures.*
800	7518	2736
70	6578	2394
3	2819	1026
873	820.399	298.566

Taking the nearest whole numbers and rejecting the decimals, we find the desired Latitude and Departure to be 820 and 299.*

When a 0 occurs in the given number, the next figure must be set *two* places to the right, the reason of which will appear from the following example, in which the 0 is treated like any other number.

Given a bearing of 35°, and a distance of 3048 links.

Distances.	*Latitudes.*	*Departures.*
3000	2457	1721
000	0000	0000
40	3277	2294
8	6553	4589
3048	2496.323	1748.529

Here the Latitudes and Departures are 2496 and 1749 links.

* It is frequently doubtful, in many calculations, when the final decimal is 5, whether to increase the preceding figure by one or not. Thus, 43.5 may be called 43 or 44 with equal correctness. It is better in such cases not to increase the whole number, so as to escape the trouble of changing the original figure, and the increased chance of error. If, however, more than one such a case occurs in the same column to be added up, the larger and smaller number should be taken alternately.

When the bearing is over 45°, the names of the columns must be read from the bottom of the page, the Latitude of any bearing, as 50°, being the Departure of the complement of this bearing, or 40°, and the Departure of 40° being the Latitude of 50°, &c. The reason of this will be at once seen on inspecting the last figure, (page 170), and imagining the East and West line to become a Meridian. For, if AC be the magnetic meridian, as before, and therefore BAC be the bearing of the course AB, then is AC the Latitude, and CB the Departure of that course. But if AE be the meridian and BAD (the complement of BAC) be the bearing, then is AD (which is equal to CB) the Latitude, and DB, (which is equal to AC), the Departure.

As an example of this, let the bearing be 63¼°, and the distance 3469 links. Proceeding as before, we have

Distances.	*Latitudes.*	*Departures.*
3000	1350	2679
400	1800	3572
60	2701	5358
9	4051	8037
3469.	1561.061	3097.817

The required Latitude and Departure are 1561 and 3098 links.

In the few cases occurring in Compass-Surveying, in which the bearing is recorded as somewhere between the fractions of a degree given in the Table, its Latitude and Departure may be found by interpolation. Thus, if the bearing be 10⅜°, take the half sum of the Latitudes and Departures for 10¼° and 10½°. If it be 10° 20′, add one-third of the difference between the Lats. and Deps. for 10¼ and for 10½°, to those opposite to 10¼°; and so in any similar case.

The uses of this table are very varied. The principal applications of it, which will now be explained, are to *Testing the accuracy of surveys;* to *Supplying omissions in them*; to *Platting them*, and to *Calculating their content.**

* The Traverse Table admits of many other minor uses. Thus, it may be used for solving, approximately, any right-angled triangle by mere inspection, the bearing being taken for one of the acute angles; the Latitude being the side adjacent, the Departure the side opposite, and the Distance the hypothenuse. Any two of these being given, the others are given by the Table. The Table will therefore serve to show the allowance to be made in chaining on slopes (see Art.

(282) Application to Testing a Survey. It is self-evident, that when the surveyor has gone completely around a field or farm, taking the bearings and distances of each boundary line, till he has got back to the starting point, that he has gone precisely as far South as North, and as far West as East. But the sum of the North Latitudes tells how far North he has gone, and the sum of the South Latitudes how far South he has gone. Hence these two sums will be equal to each other, if the survey has been correctly made. In like manner, the sums of the East and of the West Departures must also be equal to each other.

We will apply this principle to testing the accuracy of the survey of which Fig. 175, page 151, is a plat. Prepare seven columns, and head them as below. Find the Latitude and Departure of each course to the nearest link, and write them in their appropriate columns. Add up these columns. Then will the difference between the sums of the North and South Latitudes, and between the sums of the East and West Departures, indicate the degree of accuracy of the survey.

STATION.	BEARING.	DISTANCE.	LATITUDE.		DEPARTURE.	
			N.	S.	E.	W.
1	N. 35° E.	2.70	2.21		1.55	
2	N. 83½° E.	1.29	.15		1.28	
3	S. 57° E.	2.22		1.21	1.86	
4	S. 34¼° W.	3.55		2.93		2.00
5	N. 56½° W.	3.23	1.78			2.69
			4.14	4.14	4.69	4.69

The entire work of the above example is given below.

35°	1638	1147	34¼°	2480	1688
	57340	40150		4133	2814
				4133	2814
270.	221.140	154.850			
			355.	293.463	199.754

(26)); for, look in the column of bearings for the slope of the ground, i. e. the angle it makes with the horizon, find the given distance, and the Latitude corresponding will be the desired horizontal measurement, and the difference between it and the Distance will be the allowance to be made

83½°	113 226 1019	994 1987 8942	56½°	1656 1104 1656	2502 1668 2502
129.	14.579	128.212	323.	178.296	269.382
57°	1089 1089 1089	1677 1677 1677			
222.	120.879	186.147			

The nearest link is taken to be inserted in the Table, and the remaining Decimals are neglected.

In the preceding example the respective sums were found to be exactly equal. This, however, will rarely occur in an extensive survey. If the difference be great, it indicates some mistake, and the survey must be repeated with greater care; but if the difference be small it indicates, not absolute errors, but only inaccuracies, unavoidable in surveys with the compass, and the survey may be accepted.

How great a difference in the sums of the columns may be allowed, as not necessitating a new survey, is a dubious point. Some surveyors would admit a difference of 1 link for every 3 chains in the sum of the courses: others only 1 link for every 10 chains. One writer puts the limit at 5 links for each station; another at 25 links in a survey of 100 acres. But every practical surveyor soon learns how near to an equality his instrument and his skill will enable him to come in ordinary cases, and can therefore establish a standard for himself, by which he can judge whether the difference, in any survey of his own, is probably the result of an error, or only of his customary degree of inaccuracy, two things to be very carefully distinguished.*

(283) Application to supplying omissions. Any two omissions in the Field-notes can be supplied by a proper use of the method of Latitudes and Departures; as will be explained in Part VII, which treats of "Obstacles to Measurement," under which head this subject most appropriately belongs. But a knowledge of the fact that any two omissions can be supplied, should not lead

* A French writer fixes the allowable difference in chaining at 1-400 of level lines 1-200 of lines on moderate slopes; 1-100 of lines on steep slopes.

the young surveyor to be negligent in making every possible measurement, since an omission renders it necessary to assume all the notes taken to be correct, the means of testing them no longer existing.

(284) Balancing a Survey. The subsequent applications of this method require the survey to be previously *Balanced*. This operation consists in *correcting* the Latitudes and Departures of the courses, so that their sums *shall* be equal, and thus "balance." This is usually done by distributing the differences of the sums among the courses in proportion to their length; saying, *As* the sum of the lengths of all the courses *Is to* the whole difference of the Latitudes, *So is* the length of each course *To* the correction of its Latitude. A similar proportion corrects the Departures.*

It is not often necessary to make the exact proportion, as the correction can usually be made, with sufficient accuracy, by noting how much per chain it should be, and correcting accordingly.

In the example given below, the differences have purposely been made considerable. The corrected Latitudes and Departures have been here inserted in four additional columns, but in practice they should be written *in red ink* over the original Latitudes and Departures, and the latter crossed out with red ink.

STA.	BEARING.	DIST.	LATITUDES.		DEP'TURES.		CORRECTED LATITUDES.		CORRECTED DEPARTURES.	
			N.+	S.—	E.+	W.—	N.+	S.—	E.+	W.—
1	N. 52° E.	10.63	6.54		8.38		6.58		8.34	
2	S. 29¾° E.	4.10		3.56	2.03			3.55	2.01	
3	S. 31¾° W.	7.69		6.54		4.05		6.51		4.08
4	N. 61° W.	7.13	3.46			6.24	3.48			6.27
		29.55	10.00	10.10	10.41	10.29	10.06	10.06	10.35	10.35

The corrections are made by the following proportions; the nearest whole numbers being taken:

For the Latitudes.	*For the Departures.*
29.55 : 10.63 :: 10 : 4	29.55 : 10.63 :: 12 : 4
29.55 : 4.10 :: 10 : 1	29.55 : 4.10 :: 12 : 2
29.55 : 7.69 :: 10 : 3	29.55 : 7.69 :: 12 : 3
29.55 : 7.13 :: 10 : 2	29.55 : 7.13 :: 12 : 3
10	12

* A demonstration of this principle was given by Dr. Bowditch, in No. 4 of "The Analyst."

This rule is not always to be strictly followed. If one line of a survey has been measured over very uneven and rough ground, or if its bearing has been taken with an indistinct sight, while the other lines have been measured over level and clear ground, it is probable that most of the error has occurred on that line, and the correction should be chiefly made on its Latitude and Departure.

If a slight change of the bearing of a long course will favor the Balancing, it should be so changed, since the compass is much more subject to error than the chain. So, too, if shortening any doubtful line will favor the Balancing, it should be done, since distances are generally measured too long.

(285) Application to Platting. Rule three columns; one for Stations; the next for total Latitudes; and the third for total Departures. Fill the last two columns by beginning at any convenient station (the extreme East or West is best) and adding up (algebraically) the Latitudes of the following stations, noticing that the South Latitudes are subtractive. Do the same for the Departures, observing that the Westerly ones are also subtractive.

Taking the example given on page 175, Art. (282), and beginning with Station 1, the following will be the results:

STA.	TOTAL LATITUDES FROM STATION 1.	TOTAL DEPARTURES FROM STATION 1.
1	0.00	0.00
2	+2.21 N.	+1.55 E.
3	+2.36 N.	+2.83 E.
4	+1.15 N.	+4.69 E.
5	—1.78 S.	+2.69 E.
1	0.00	0.00

It will be seen that the work proves itself, by the total Latitudes and Departures for Station 1, again coming out equal to zero.

To use this table, draw a meridian through the point taken for Station 1, as in the figure on the following page. Set off, upward from this, along the meridian, the Latitude, 221 links, to A, and from A, to the right perpendicularly, set off the Departure, 155 links.* This gives the point 2. Join 1....2. From 1 again, set

* This is most easily done with the aid of a right-angled triangle, sliding one of the sides adjacent to the right angle along the blade of the square, to which the other side will then be perpendicular.

off, upward, 236 links, to B, and from B, to the right, perpendicularly, set off 283 links, which will fix the point 3. Join 2....3; and so proceed, setting off North Latitudes along the Meridian upwards, and South Latitudes along it downwards; East Departures perpendicularly to the right, and West Departures perpendicularly to the left.

Fig. 192.

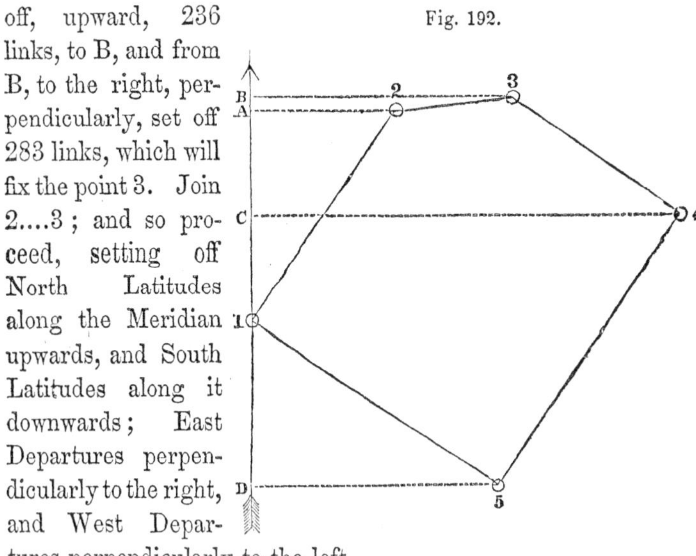

The advantages of this method are its rapidity, ease and accuracy; the impossibility of any error in platting any one course affecting the following points; and the certainty of the plat "coming together," if the Latitudes and Departures have been "Balanced."

CHAPTER VI.

CALCULATING THE CONTENT.

(286) Methods. WHEN a field has been platted, by what ever method it may have been surveyed, its content can be obtained from its plat by dividing it up into triangles, and measuring on the plat their bases and perpendiculars; or by any of the other means explained in Part I, Chapter IV.

But these are only approximate methods; their degree of accuracy depending on the largeness of scale of the plat, and the skill of the draftsman. The invaluable method of Latitudes and Departures gives another means, perfectly accurate, and not requiring the previous preparation of a plat. It is sometimes called the Rectangular, or the Pennsylvania, or Rittenhouse's, method of calculation.*

(287) Definitions. Imagine a Meridian line to pass through the extreme East or West corner of a field. According to the definitions established in Chapter V, Art. (278), (and here recapitulated for convenience of reference), the perpendicular distance of each Station from that Meridian, is the *Longitude* of that Station; additive, or *plus*, if East; subtractive, or *minus*, if West. The distance of the middle of any line, such as a side of the field, from the Meridian, is called the *Longitude* of that side.† The difference of the Longitudes of the two ends of a line is called the *Departure* of that line. The difference of the Latitudes of the two ends of a line is called the *Latitude* of the line.

* It is, however, substantially the same as Mr. Thomas Burgh's "Method to determine the areas of right lined figures universally," published nearly a century ago.

† The phrase "Meridian Distance," is generally used for what is here called 'Longitude"; but the analogy of "Differences of Longitude" with "Differences of Latitude," usually but anomalously united with the word "Departure," borrowed from Navigation, seems to put beyond all question the propriety of the innovation here introduced.

(288) **Longitudes.** To give more definiteness to the development of this subject, the figure in the margin will be referred to, and may be considered to represent any space enclosed by straight lines.

Let NS be the Meridian passing through the extreme Westerly Station of the field ABCDE. From the middle and ends of each side draw perpendiculars to the Meridian. These perpendiculars will be the *Longitudes* and Departures of the respective sides. The Longitude, FG, of the *first course*, AB, is evidently equal to half its Departure HB. The Longitude, JK, of the second course, BC, is equal to JL + LM + MK, or equal to the Longitude of the preceding course, plus half its Departure, plus half the Departure of the course itself. The Longitude, YZ, of some other course, as EA, taken anywhere, is equal to WX -- VX — UV, or equal to the Longitude of the preceding course, minus half its Departure, minus half the Departure of the course itself, i. e. equal to the *Algebraic* sum of these three parts, remembering that *Westerly* Departures are negative, and therefore to be subtracted when the directions are to make an *Algebraic* addition.

Fig. 193.

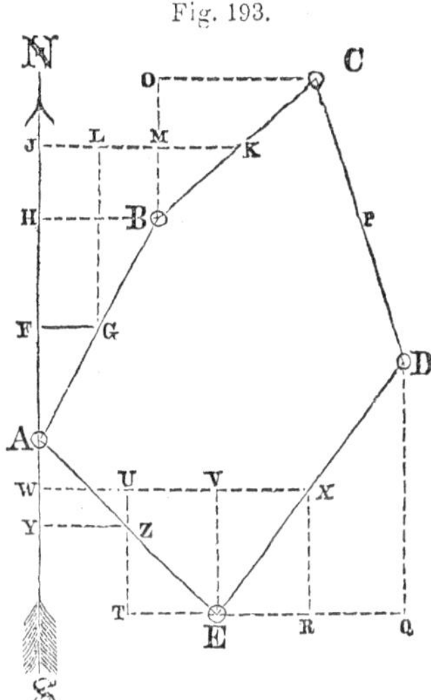

To avoid fractions, it will be better to double each of the preceding expressions. We shall then have a

GENERAL RULE FOR FINDING DOUBLE LONGITUDES.

The Double Longitude of the FIRST COURSE *is equal to its Departure.*

The Double Longitude of the SECOND COURSE *is equal to the Double Longitude of the first course, plus the Departure of that course, plus the Departure of the second course.*

The Double Longitude of the THIRD COURSE *is equal to the Double Longitude of the second course, plus the Departure of that course, plus the Departure of the course itself.*

The Double Longitude of ANY *course is equal to the Double Longitude of the preceding course, plus the Departure of that course, plus the Departure of the course itself.**

The Double Longitude of the *last* course (as well as of the first) is equal to its Departure. Its "coming out" so, when obtained by the above rule, proves the accuracy of the calculation of all the preceding Double Longitudes.

(289) Areas. We will now proceed to find the Area, or Content of a field, by means of the "Double Longitudes" of its sides, which can be readily obtained by the preceding rule, whatever their number.

(290) Beginning with a *three-sided field*, ABC in the figure, draw a Meridian through A, and draw perpendiculars to it as in the last figure. It is plain that its content is equal to the difference of the areas of the Trapezoid DBCE, and of the Triangles ABD and ACE.

Fig. 194.

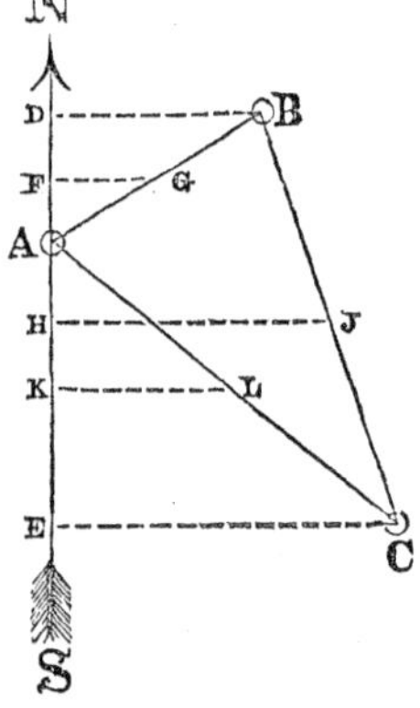

The area of the Triangle ABD is equal to the product of AD by half of DB, or to the product of AD by FG; i. e. equal to the product of the Latitude of the 1st course by its Longitude.

The area of the Trapezoid DBCE is equal to the product of DE by half the sum of DB and CE, or by HJ; i. e. to the product of the Latitude of the 2d course by its Longitude.

The area of the Triangle ACE is equal to the product of AE by half EC, or by KL; i. e. to the product of the Latitude of the 3d course by its Longitude.

Calling the products in which the Latitude was North, *North Products*, and the products in which the Latitude was South, *South Products*, we shall find the area of the Trapezoid to be a *South Product*, and the areas of the Triangles to be *North Pro-*

* The last course is a "preceding course" to the first course, as will appear on remembering that these two courses join each other on the ground

ducts. The Difference of the North Products and the South Products is therefore the desired area of the three-sided field ABC.

Using the *Double* Longitudes, (in order to avoid fractions), in each of the preceding products, their difference will be the *double* area of the Triangle ABC.

(291) Taking now a *four-sided field*, ABCD in the figure, and drawing a Meridian and Longitudes as before, it is seen, on inspection, that its area would be obtained by taking the two Triangles, ABE, ADG, from the figure EBCDGE, or from the sum of the two Trapezoids EBCF and FCDG.

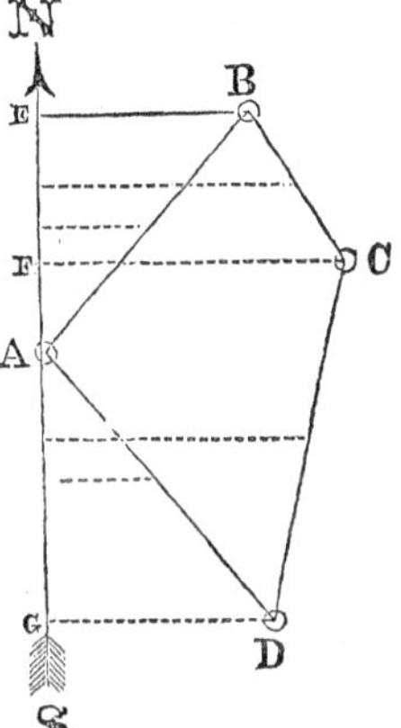

Fig. 155.

The area of the Triangle AEB will be found, as in the last article, to be equal to the product of the Latitude of the 1st course by its Longitude. The Product will be *North*.

The area of the Trapezoid EBCF will be found to equal the Latitude of the 2d course by its Longitude. The product will be *South*.

The area of the Trapezoid FCDG will be found to equal the product of the Latitude of the 3d course by its Longitude. The product will be *South*.

The area of the Triangle ADG will be found to equal the product of the Latitude of the 4th course by its Longitude. The product will be *North*.

The difference of the North and South products will therefore be the desired area of the four-sided field ABCD.

Using the *Double* Longitude as before, in each of the preceding products, their difference will be *double* the area of the field.

(292) Whatever the number or directions of the sides of a field, or of any space enclosed by straight lines, its area will always be equal to half of the difference of the North and South Products arising from multiplying together the Latitude and Double Longitude of each course or side.

We have therefore the following

GENERAL RULE FOR FINDING AREAS.

1. *Prepare ten columns, headed as in the example below, and in the first three write the Stations, Bearings and Distances.*

2. *Find the Latitudes and Departures of each course, by the Traverse Table, as directed in Art.* (281), *placing them in the four following columns.*

3. *Balance them, as in Art.* (284), *correcting them in red ink.*

4. *Find the Double Longitudes, as in Art.* (288), *with reference to a Meridian passing through the extreme East or West Station, and place them in the eighth column.*

5. *Multiply the Double Longitude of each course by the corrected Latitude of that course, placing the North Products in the ninth column, and the South Products in the tenth column.*

6. *Add up the last two columns, subtract the smaller sum from the larger, and divide the difference by two. The quotient will be the content desired.*

(293) To find the most Easterly or Westerly Station of a survey, without a plat, it is best to make a rough hand-sketch of the survey, drawing the lines in an approximation to their true directions, by drawing a North and South, and East and West lines, and considering the Bearings as fractional parts of a right angle, or 90°; a course N. 45° E. for example, being drawn about half way between a North and an East direction; a course N. 28° W. being not quite one-third of the way around from North to West; and so on, drawing them of approximately true proportional lengths.

(294) *Example* 1, given below, refers to the five-sided field, of which a plat is given in Fig. 175, page 151, and the Latitudes and Departures of which were calculated in Art. (282), page 175. Station 1 is the most Westerly Station, and the Meridian will be supposed to pass through it. The Double Longitudes are best found by a continual addition and subtraction, as in the margin, where they are marked D. L. The Double Longitude of the last course comes out equal to its Departure, thus proving the work.

STA.		
1	+ 1.55	D. L.
	+ 1.55	
	+ 1.28	
2	+ 4.38	D. L.
	+ 1.28	
	+ 1.86	
3	+ 7.52	D. L.
	+ 1.86	
	− 2.00	
4	+ 7.38	D. L.
	− 2.00	
	− 2.69	
5	+ 2.69	D. L.

The Double Longitudes being thus obtained, are multiplied by the corresponding Latitudes, and the content of the field obtained as directed in the General Rule.

This example may serve as a pattern for the most compact manner of arranging the work.

STATION.	BEARINGS.	DIS-TANCES.	LATITUDES. N. +	S. —	DEP'TURES. E. +	W. —	DOUBLE LONGITUDES.	DOUBLE AREAS. N. +	S. —
1	N. 35° E.	2.70	2.21		1.55		+ 1.55	3.4255	
2	N. 83½° E.	1.29	.15		1.28		+ 4.38	0.6570	
3	S. 57° E.	2.22		1.21	1.86		+ 7.52		9.0992
4	S. 34¼° W.	3.55		2.93		2.00	+ 7.38		21.6234
5	N. 56½° W.	3.23	1.78			2.69	+ 2.69	4.7882	
			4.14	4.14	4.69	4.69		8.8707	30.7226
									8.8707
									2)21.8519
								Square Chains,	10.9259

Content=1A. 0R. 15P.

(295) The Meridian might equally well have been supposed to pass through the most Easterly station, 4 in the figure. The Double Longitudes could then have been calculated as in the margin. They will of course be all West, or minus. The products being then calculated, the sum of the North products will be found to be 29.9625, and of the South products 8.1106, and their difference to be 21.8519, the same result as before.

STA.		
4	− 2.00	D. L.
	− 2.00	
	− 2.69	
5	− 6.69	D. L.
	− 2.69	
	+ 1.55	
1	− 7.83	D. L.
	+ 1.55	
	+ 1.28	
2	− 5.00	D. L.
	+ 1.28	
	+ 1.86	
3	− 1.86	

(296) A number of examples, with and without answers, will now be given as exercises for the student, who should plat them by some of the methods given in the preceding chapter, using each of them at least once. He should then calculate their content by the method just given, and *check* it, by also calculating the area of the plat by some of the Geometrical or Instrumental methods given in Part I, Chapter IV; for no single calculation is ever reliable.

All the examples (except the last) are from the author's actual surveys.

Example 2, given below, is also fully worked out, as another pattern for the student, who need have no difficulty with any possible case if he strictly follows the directions which have been given. The plat is on a scale of 2 chains to 1 inch, (= 1:1584).

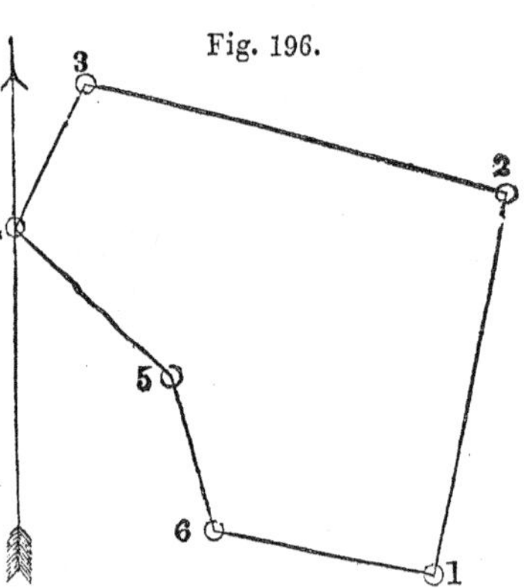

Fig. 196.

STATION.	BEARINGS.	DISTANCES.	LATITUDES. N. +	LATITUDES. S. —	DEP'TURES. E. +	DEP'TURES. W. —	DOUBLE LONGITUDES.	DOUBLE AREAS. N. +	DOUBLE AREAS. S. —
1	N. 12¼° E.	2.81	2.75		.60		+ 6.56	18.0400	
2	N. 76° W.	3.20	.77			3.11	+ 4.05	3.1185	
3	S. 24½° W.	1.14		1.04		.47	+ .47		.4888
4	S. 48° E.	1.53		1.02	1.14		+ 1.14		1.1628
5	S. 12½° E.	1.12		1.09	.24		+ 2.52		2.7468
6	S. 77° E.	1.64		.37	1.60		+ 4.36		1.6132
			3.52	3.52	3.58	3.58		21.1585	6.0116
								6.0116	
								2)15.1469	
							Square Chains,	7.5734	

Content = 0A. 3R. 1P.

Example 3.

STA.	BEARING.	DISTANCE.
1	N. 52° E.	10.64
2	S. 29¾° E.	4.09
3	S. 31¾° W.	7.68
4	N. 61° W.	7.24

Ans. 4A. 3R. 28P.

Example 4.

STA.	BEARING.	DISTANCE.
1	S. 21° W.	12.41
2	N. 83¼° E.	5.86
3	N. 12° E.	8.25
4	N. 47° W.	4.24

Ans. 4A. 2R. 37P.

Example 5.

STA.	BEARING.	DISTANCE.
1	N. 34¼° E.	2.73
2	N. 85° E.	1.28
3	S. 56¾° E.	2.20
4	S. 34¼° W.	3.53
5	N. 56½° W.	3.20

Ans. 1A. 0R. 14P.

Example 6.

STA.	BEARING.	DISTANCE.
1	N. 35° E.	6.49
2	S. 56¼° E.	14.15
3	S. 34° W.	5.10
4	N. 56° W.	5.84
5	S. 29½° W.	2.52
6	N. 48¼° W.	8.73

Example 7.

STA.	BEARING.	DISTANCE.
1	S. $21\frac{1}{4}$° W.	17.62
2	S. 34° W.	10.00
3	N. 56° W.	14.15
4	N. 34° E.	9.76
5	N. 67° E.	2.30
6	N. 23° E.	7.03
7	N. $18\frac{1}{2}$° E.	4.43
8	S. $76\frac{1}{2}$° E.	12.41

Example 8.

STA.	BEARING.	DISTANCE.
1	S. $65\frac{1}{2}$° E.	4.98
2	S. 58° E.	8.56
3	S. $14\frac{1}{4}$° W.	20.69
4	S. 47° W.	0.60
5	S. $57\frac{1}{4}$° W.	8.98
6	N. 56° W.	12.90
7	N. 34° E.	10.00
8	N. $21\frac{1}{4}$ E.	17.62

Example 9.

STA.	BEARING.	DISTANCE.
1	S. 57° E.	5.77
2	S. $36\frac{1}{4}$° W.	2.25
3	S. $39\frac{1}{4}$° W.	1.00
4	S. $70\frac{1}{4}$° W.	1.04
5	N. $68\frac{3}{4}$° W.	1.23
6	N. 56° W.	2.19
7	N. $33\frac{1}{4}$° E.	1.05
8	N. $56\frac{1}{2}$° W.	1.54
9	N. $33\frac{1}{2}$° E.	3.18

Ans. 2A. 0R. 32P.

Example 10.

STA.	BEARING.	DISTANCE.
1	N. 63° 51′ W.	6.91
2	N. 63° 44′ W	7.26
3	N. 69° 35′ W.	3.34
4	N. 77° 50′ W.	6.54
5	N. 31° 24′ E.	14.38
6	N. 31° 18′ E.	16.81
7	S. 68° 55′ E.	13.64
8	S. 68° 42′ E.	11.54
9	S. 33° 45′ W.	31.55

Ans. 74 Acres.

Example 11.

STA.	BEARING.	DISTANCE.
1	N. $18\frac{3}{4}$° E.	1.93
2	N. 9° W.	1.29
3	N. 14° W.	2.71
4	N. 74° E.	0.95
5	S. $48\frac{1}{2}$° E.	1.59
6	S $14\frac{1}{4}$° E.	1.14
7	S $19\frac{1}{2}$° E.	2.15
8	S. $23\frac{1}{2}$° W.	1.22
9	S. 5° W.	1.40
10	S. 30° W.	1.02
11	S. $81\frac{1}{2}$° W.	0.69
12	N. $32\frac{1}{2}$° W.	1.98

Example 12.

STA.	BEARING.	DISTANCE.
1	N. $72\frac{3}{4}$° E.	0.88
2	S. $20\frac{1}{2}$° E.	0.22
3	S. 63° E.	0.75
4	N. 51° E.	2.35
5	N. 44° E.	1.10
6	N. $25\frac{1}{2}$° W.	1.96
7	N. $8\frac{1}{2}$° W.	1.05
8	S. 29° W.	1.63
9	N. $71\frac{1}{2}$° W.	0.81
10	N. $13\frac{1}{2}$° W.	1.17
11	N. 63° W.	1.28
12	West.	1.68
13	N. 49° W.	0.80
14	S. $19\frac{1}{2}$ E.	6.20

Example 13. A farm is described in an old Deed, as bounded thus. Beginning at a pile of stones, and running thence twenty-seven chains and seventy links South-Easterly sixty-six and a half degrees to a white-oak stump; thence eleven chains and sixteen links North-Easterly twenty and a half degrees to a hickory tree; thence two chains and thirty-five links North-Easterly thirty-six degrees to the South-Easterly corner of the homestead; thence nineteen chains and thirty-two links North-Easterly twenty-six degrees to a stone set in the ground; thence twenty-eight chains and eighty links North-Westerly sixty-six degrees to a pine stump; thence thirty-three chains and nineteen links South-Westerly twenty-two degrees to the place of beginning, containing ninety-two acres, be the same more or less. Required the exact content.

Fig. 197.

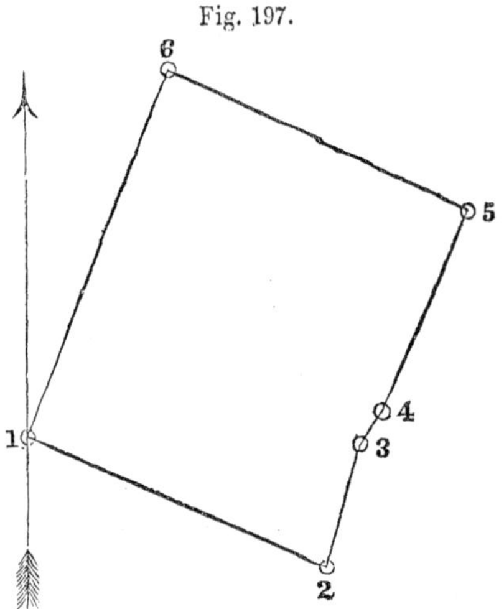

(297) **Mascheroni's Theorem.** *The surface of any polygon is equal to half the sum of the products of its sides (omitting any one side) taken two and two, into the sines of the angles which those sides make with each other.*

Fig. 198.

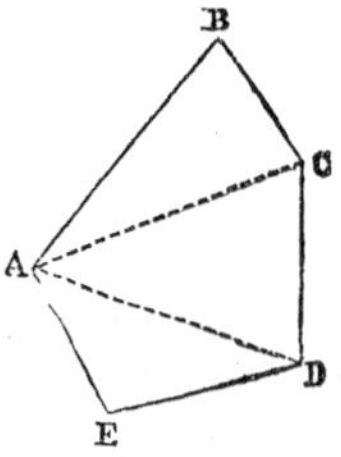

Thus, take any polygon, such as the five-sided one in the figure. Express the angle which the directions of any two sides, as AB, CD, make with each other, thus (AB $\wedge$ CD). Then will the content of that polygon be, as below;

$$= \tfrac{1}{2}[AB \,.\, BC \,.\, \sin(AB \wedge BC) + AB \,.\, CD \,.\, \sin(AB \wedge CD) + AB \,.\, DE \,.\, \sin(AB \wedge DE) + BC \,.\, CD \,.\, \sin(BC \wedge CD) + BC \,.\, DE \,.\, \sin(BC \wedge DE) + CD \,.\, DE \,.\, \sin(CD \wedge DE)]$$

The demonstration consists merely in dividing the polygon into triangles by lines drawn from any angle, (as A); then expressing the area of each triangle by half the product of its base and the perpendicular let fall upon it from the above named angle; and finally separating the perpendicular into parts which can each be expressed by the product of some one side into the sine of the angle made by it with another side. The sum of these triangles equals the polygon.

The expressions are simplified by dividing the proposed polygon into two parts by a diagonal, and computing the area of each part separately, making the diagonal the side omitted.*

CHAPTER VII.

THE VARIATION OF THE MAGNETIC NEEDLE.

(298) Definitions. The *Magnetic Meridian* is the direction indicated by the Magnetic Needle. The *True Meridian* is a true North and South line, which, if produced, would pass through the poles of the earth. The *Variation*, or *Declination*, of the needle is the angle which one of these lines makes with the other.†

In the figure, if NS represent the direction of the True Meridian, and N′S′ the direction of the Magnetic Meridian at any place, then is the angle NAN′ the *Variation of the Needle* at that place.

Fig. 199

N′ N A S S′

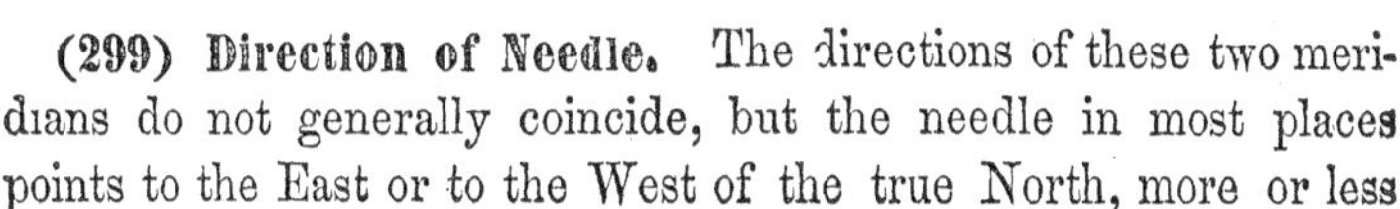

(299) Direction of Needle. The directions of these two meridians do not generally coincide, but the needle in most places points to the East or to the West of the true North, more or less

* The original Theorem is usually accredited to Lhuillier, of Geneva, who published it in 1789. But Mascheroni, the ingenious author of the "Geometry of the Compasses," had published it at Pavia, two years previously. The method is well developed in Prof. Whitlock's "Elements of Geometry."

† "Declination" is the more correct term, and "Variation" should be reserved for the *change* in the Declination which will be considered in the next chapter; but custom has established the use of Variation in the sense of Declination.

according to the locality. Observations of the amount and the direction of this variation have been made in nearly all parts of the world. In the United States the Variation in the Eastern States is Westerly, and in the Western States is Easterly, as will be given in detail, after the methods for determining the True Meridian, and consequently the Variation, at any place, have been explained.

TO DETERMINE THE TRUE MERIDIAN.

(300) By equal shadows of the Sun. On the South side of any level surface, erect an upright staff, shown, in horizontal projection, at S. Two or three hours before noon, mark the extremity, A, of its shadow. Describe an arc of a circle with S, the foot of the staff, for centre, and SA, the distance to the extremity of the shadow, for radius. About as many hours after noon as it had been before noon when the first mark was made, watch for the moment when the end of the shadow touches the arc at another point, B. Bisect the arc AB at N. Draw SN, and it will be the true meridian, or North and South line required.

Fig. 200.

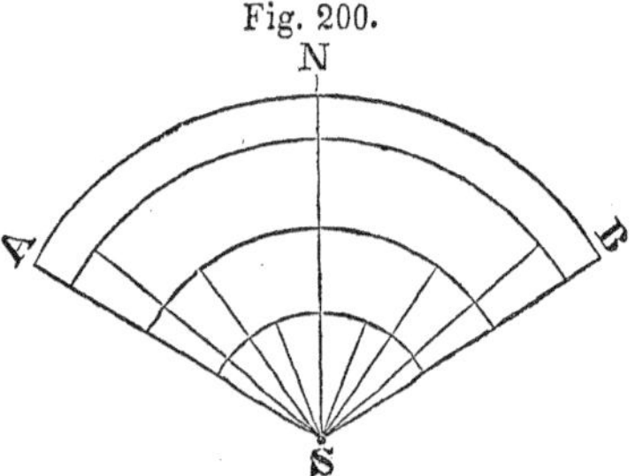

For greater accuracy, describe several arcs before hand, mark the points in which each of them is touched by the shadow, bisect each, and adopt the average of all. The shadow will be better defined, if a piece of tin with a hole through it be placed at the top of the staff, as a bright spot will thus be substituted for the less definite shadow. Nor need the staff be vertical, if from its summit a plumb-line be dropped to the ground, and the point which this strikes be adopted as the centre of the arcs.

This method is a very good approximation, though perfectly correct only at the time of the solstices; about June 21st and December 22d. It was employed by the Romans in laying out cities.

To get the Variation, set the compass at one end of the True Meridian line thus obtained, sight to the other end of it, and take the Bearing as of any ordinary line. The number of degrees in the reading will be the desired variation of the needle.

(301) By the North Star, when in the Meridian. The North Star, or Pole Star, (called by astronomers *Alpha Ursæ Minoris*, or *Polaris*), is not situated precisely at the North Pole of the heavens. If it were, the Meridian could be at once determined by sighting to it, or placing the eye at some distance behind a plumb-line so that this line should hide the star. But the North Star is about $1\frac{1}{2}°$ from the Pole. Twice in 24 hours, however, (more precisely 23h. 56m.), it is in the Meridian, being then exactly above or below the Pole, as at A and C in the figure. To know when it is so, is rendered easy by the aid of another star, easily identified, which at these times is almost exactly above or below the North Star, i. e. situated in the same vertical plane. If then we watch for the moment at which a suspended plumb-line will cover both these stars, they will then be in the Meridian.

Fig. 201.

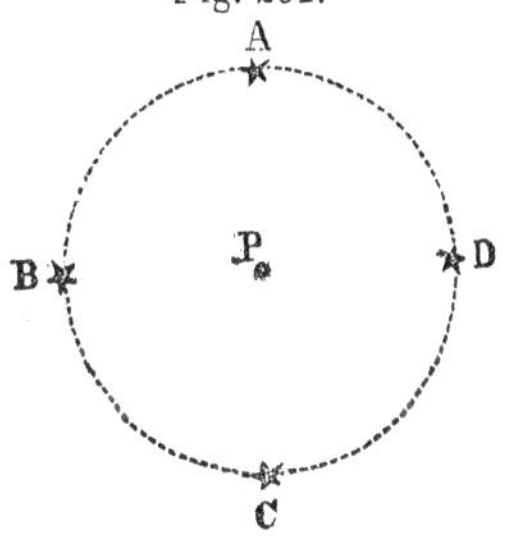

The other star is in the well known constellation of the Great Bear, called also the Plough, or the Dipper, or Charles's Wain.

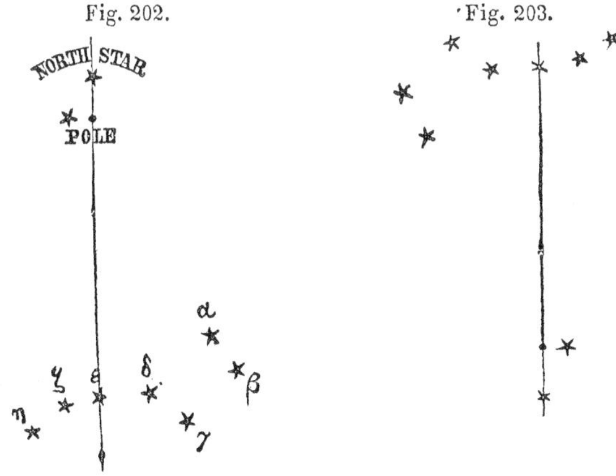

Fig. 202. Fig. 203.

Two of its five bright stars (the right-hand ones in Fig. 202) are known as the "Pointers," from their pointing near to the North

Star, thus assisting in finding it. The star in the tail or handle, nearest to the four which form a quadrilateral, is the star which comes to the Meridian at the same time with the North Star, twice in 24 hours, as in Fig. 202 or 203. It is known as *Alioth*, or *Epsilon Ursæ Majoris*.*

To determine the Meridian by this method, suspend a long plumb-line from some elevated point, such as a stick projecting from the highest window of a house suitably situated. The plumb-bob may pass into a pail of water to lessen its vibrations. South of this set up the compass, at such a distance from the plumb-line that neither of the stars will be seen above its highest point, i. e. in Latitudes of 40° or 50° not quite as far from the plumb-line as it is long. Or, instead of a compass, place a board on two stakes, so as to form a sort of bench, running East and West, and on it place one of the compass-sights, or anything having a small hole in it to look through. As the time approaches for the North Star to be on the Meridian (as taken from the table given below) place the compass, or the sight, so that, looking through it, the plumb-line shall seem to cover or hide the North Star. As the star moves one way, move the eye and sight the other way, so as to constantly keep the star behind the plumb-line. At last *Alioth*, too, will be covered by the plumb-line. At that moment the eye and the plumb-line are (approximately) in the Meridian. Fasten down the sight on the board till morning, or with the compass take the bear ing at once, and the reading is the variation.†

Instead of one plumb-line and a sight, two plumb-lines may be suspended at the end of a horizontal rod, turning on the top of a pole.

The line thus obtained points to the East of the true line when the North Star is above Alioth, and vice versa. The North Star is exactly in the Meridian about 17 minutes after it has been in the same vertical plane with Alioth, and may be sighted to after that interval of time, with perfect accuracy.

* The North Pole is very nearly at the intersection of the line from Polaris to Alioth, and a perpendicular to this line from the small star seen to the left of it in Fig. 202.

† If a Transit or Theodolite be used, the cross-hairs must be illuminated by throwing the light of a lamp into the telescope by its reflection from white paper

Another bright star, which is on the opposite side of the Pole, and is known to astronomers as *Gamma Cassiopeiæ*, also comes on the Meridian nearly at the same time as the North Star, and will thus assist in determining its direction.

(302) The time at which the North Star passes the Meridian above the Pole, for every 10th day in the year, is given in the following Table, in common clock time.* The upper transit is the most convenient, since at the other transit Alioth is too high to be conveniently observed.

Times of North Star passing the Meridian.

MONTH.	1st DAY.	11th DAY.	21st DAY.
	H. M.	H. M.	H. M.
January,	6 21 P. M.	5 41 P. M.	5 02 P. M.
February,	4 18 P. M.	3 39 P. M.	3 00 P. M.
March,	2 28 P. M.	1 49 P. M.	1 09 P. M.
April,	0 26 P. M.	11 47 A. M.	11 08 A. M.
May,	10 28 A. M.	9 49 A. M.	9 10 A. M.
June,	8 27 A. M.	7 48 A. M.	7 08 A. M.
July,	6 29 A. M.	5 50 A. M.	5 11 A. M.
August,	4 28 A. M.	3 49 A. M.	3 09 A. M.
September,	2 26 A. M.	1 47 A. M.	1 07 A. M.
October,	0 28 A. M.	11 45 P. M.	11 06 P. M.
November,	10 22 P. M.	9 43 P. M.	9 04 P. M.
December,	8 24 P. M.	7 45 P. M.	7 06 P. M.

* To calculate the time of the North Star passing the Meridian at its upper culmination: Find in the "American Almanac," (Boston), or the "Astronomical Ephemeris," (Washington), or the "Nautical Almanac," (London), or by interpolation from the data at the end of this note, the right ascension of the star, and from it (increased by twenty-four hours if necessary to render the subtraction possible) subtract the Right ascension of the Sun at mean noon, or the sidereal time at mean noon, for the given day, as found in the "Ephemeris of the Sun," in the same Almanacs. From the remainder subtract the acceleration of sidereal on mean time corresponding to this remainder, (3m. 56s. for 24 hours), and the new remainder is the required mean solar time of the upper passage of the star across the Meridian, in "Astronomical" reckoning, the astronomical day beginning at noon of the common civil day of the same date.

The right ascension of the North Star for Jan. 1, 1850, is 1h. 05m. 01.4s.; for 1860, 1h. 08m. 02.8s.; for 1870, 1h. 11m. 16.9s.; for 1880, 1h. 14m. 45.1s.; for 1890, 1h. 18m. 29.2s.; for 1900, 1h. 22m. 31s.

To find the time of the star's passage of the Meridian for other days than those given in the Table, take from it the time for the day most nearly preceding that desired, and subtract from this time 4 minutes for each day from the date of the day in the Table to that of the desired day; or, more accurately, interpolate, by saying: *As* the number of days between those given in the Table *is to* the number of days from the next preceding day in the Table to the desired day, *so is* the difference between the times given in the Table for the days next preceding and following the desired day *to* the time to be subtracted from that of the next preceding day. The first term of the preceding proportion is always *ten*, except at the end of months having more or less than 30 days. For example, let the time of the North Star's passing the Meridian on July 26th be required. From July 21st to August 1st being 11 days, we have this proportion: 11 days : 5 days :: 43 minutes : $19\frac{6}{11}$ minutes. Taking this from 5h. 11m. A. M., we get 4h. $51\frac{1}{2}$m. A. M. for the time of passage required.

The North Star passes the Meridian later every year. In 1860, it will pass the Meridian about two minutes later than in 1854; in 1870, five minutes, in 1880, eight minutes, in 1890, twelve minutes, and in 1900, sixteen minutes, later than in 1854: the year for which the preceding table has been calculated.

The times at which the North Star passes the Meridian *below* the Pole, in its lower Transit, can be found by adding 11h. 58m. to the time of the upper Transit, or by subtracting that interval from it.*

(303) By the North Star at its extreme elongation. When the North Star is at its greatest *apparent* angular distance East or West of the Pole, as at B or D in Fig. 201, it is said to be at its extreme Eastern, or extreme Western, Elongation. If it be observed at either of these times, the direction of the Meridian can be easily

* The North Star, which is now about 1° 28′ from the Pole, was 12° distant from it when its place was first recorded. Its distance is now diminishing at the rate of about a third of a minute in a year, and will continue to do so till it approaches to within half a degree, when it will again recede. The brightest star in the Northern hemisphere, *Alpha Lyræ*, will be the Pole Star in about 12,000 years, being then within about 5° of the Pole, though now more than 51° distant from it

obtained from the observation. The great advantage of this method over the preceding is that then the star's motion apparently ceases for a short time.

(304) The following Table gives the

TIMES OF EXTREME ELONGATIONS OF THE NORTH STAR.*

MONTH.	1ST DAY.		11TH DAY.		21ST DAY.	
	EASTERN.	WESTERN.	EASTERN.	WESTERN.	EASTERN.	WESTERN.
	H. M.	H. M.	H. M.	H. M.	H. M.	H. M.
Jan'y,	0 27 P.M.	0 19 A.M.	11 47 A.M.	11 35 P.M.	11 08 A.M.	10 56 P.M.
Feb'y,	10 24 A.M.	10 13 P.M.	9 45 A.M.	9 33 P.M.	9 06 A.M.	8 54 P.M.
March,	8 34 A.M.	8 22 P.M.	7 55 A.M.	7 43 P.M.	7 15 A.M.	7 04 P.M.
April,	6 32 A.M.	6 20 P.M.	5 53 A.M.	5 41 P.M.	5 14 A.M.	5 02 P.M.
May,	4 34 A.M.	4 22 P.M.	3 55 A.M.	3 43 P.M.	3 16 A.M.	3 04 P.M.
June,	2 33 A.M.	2 21 P.M.	1 53 A.M.	1 42 P.M.	1 14 A.M.	1 02 P.M.
July,	0 35 A.M.	0 23 P.M.	11 52 P.M.	11 44 A.M.	11 13 P.M.	11 05 A.M.
August,	10 30 P.M.	10 22 A.M.	9 51 P.M.	9 43 A.M.	9 11 P.M.	9 03 A.M.
Sept'r,	8 28 P.M.	8 20 A.M.	7 49 P.M.	7 41 A.M.	7 09 P.M.	7 01 A.M.
Oct'r,	6 30 P.M.	6 22 A.M.	5 51 P.M.	5 43 A.M.	5 12 P.M.	5 04 A.M.
Nov'r,	4 28 P.M.	4 21 A.M.	3 49 P.M.	3 41 A.M.	3 10 P.M.	3 02 A.M.
Dec'r,	2 30 P.M.	2 22 A.M.	1 51 P.M.	1 43 A.M.	1 12 P.M.	1 04 A.M.

The Eastern Elongations from October to March, and the Western Elongations from April to September, occurring in the day time, they will generally not be visible except with the aid of a powerful telescope.

* To calculate the times of the greatest elongation of the North Star: Find in one of the Almanacs before referred to, or from the data below, its Polar distance at the given time. Add the logarithm of its tangent to the logarithm of the tangent of the Latitude of the place, and the sum will be the logarithm of the cosine of the Hour angle before or after the culmination. Reduce the space to time; correct for sidereal acceleration (3m. 56s. for 24 hours) and subtract the result from the time of the star's passing the meridian on that day, to get the time of the Eastern elongation, or add it to get the Western.

The Polar distance of the North Star, for Jan. 1, 1850, is 1° 29′ 25″; for 1860, 1° 26′ 12″.7; for 1870, 1° 23° 01″; for 1880, 1° 19 50″.4; for 1890, 1° 16′ 40″.7; for 1900, 1° 13′ 32″.2.

The preceding Table was calculated for Latitude 40°. The Time at which the Elongations occur vary slightly for other Latitudes. In Latitude 50°, the Eastern Elongations occur about 2 minutes later and the Western Elongations about 2 minutes earlier than the times in the Table. In Latitude 26°, precisely the reverse takes place.

The Times of Elongation are continually, though slowly, becoming later. The preceding Table was calculated for July 1st, 1854. In 1860, the times will be nearly 2 minutes later; and in 1900, the Eastern Elongations will be about 15 minutes, and the Western Elongations 17 minutes later than in 1854.

(305) Observations. Knowing from the preceding Table the hour and minute of the extreme Elongation on any day, a little before that time suspend a plumb-line, precisely as in Art. **(301)**, and place yourself south of it as there directed. As the North Star moves one way, move your eye the other, so that the plumb-line shall continually seem to cover the star. At last the star will appear to stop moving for a time, and then begin to move backwards. Fix the sight on the board (or the compass, &c.) in the position in which it was when the star ceased moving; for the star was then at its extreme apparent Elongation, East or West, as the case may be.

(306) Azimuths. The angle which the line from the eye to the plumb-line, makes with the True Meridian (i. e. the angle between the meridian plane and the vertical plane passing through the eye and the star) is called the *Azimuth* of the Star. It is given in the following Table for different Latitudes, and for a number of years to come. For the intermediate Latitudes, it can be obtained by a simple proportion, similar to that explained in detail in Art. **(302)**.*

* To calculate this Azimuth: From the logarithm of the sine of the Polar distance of the star, subtract the logarithm of the cosine of the Latitude of the place; the remainder will be the logarithm of the sine of the angle required. The Polar distance can be obtained as directed in the last note.

AZIMUTHS OF THE NORTH STAR.

Latitudes.	1854	1855	1856	1857	1858	1859	1860	1870
50°	2° 16¾′	2° 16¼′	2° 16′	2° 15½′	2° 15′	2° 14½′	2° 14¼′	2° 09¼′
49°	2° 14′	2° 13½′	2° 13¼′	2° 12¾′	2° 12¼′	2° 12′	2° 11½′	2° 06½′
48°	2° 11½′	2° 11′	2° 10½′	2° 10¼′	2° 09¾′	2° 09¼′	2° 09′	2° 04′
47°	2° 09′	2° 08½′	2° 08′	2° 07¾′	2° 07¼′	2° 06¾′	2° 06½′	2° 01¾′
46°	2° 06¾′	2° 06¼′	2° 05¾′	2° 05½′	2° 05′	2° 04½′	2° 04¼′	1° 59½′
45°	2° 04½′	2° 04′	2° 03½′	2° 03¼′	2° 02¾′	2° 02¼′	2° 02′	1° 57½′
44°	2° 02½′	2° 02′	2° 01¾′	2° 01½′	2° 01′	2° 00½′	2° 00′	1° 55½′
43°	2° 00½′	2° 00′	1° 59½′	1° 59′	1° 58¾′	1° 58¼′	1° 58′	1° 53½′
42°	1° 58½′	1° 58′	1° 57½′	1° 57¼′	1° 56¾′	1° 56½′	1° 56′	1° 51¾′
41°	1° 56¾′	1° 56¼′	1° 55¾′	1° 55½′	1° 55′	1° 54½′	1° 54¼′	1° 50′
40°	1° 55′	1° 54½′	1° 54′	1° 53¾′	1° 53¼′	1° 53′	1° 52½′	1° 48¼′
39°	1° 53¼′	1° 52¾′	1° 52½′	1° 52′	1° 51¾′	1° 51¼′	1° 51′	1° 46¾′
38°	1° 51¾′	1° 51¼′	1° 51′	1° 50½′	1° 50′	1° 49¾′	1° 49½′	1° 45¼′
37°	1° 50¼′	1° 49¾′	1° 49½′	1° 49′	1° 48¾′	1° 48¼′	1° 48′	1° 44′
36°	1° 48¾′	1° 48¼′	1° 48′	1° 47¾′	1° 47¼′	1° 47′	1° 46½′	1° 42¾′
35°	1° 47½′	1° 47′	1° 46¾′	1° 46¼′	1° 46′	1° 45½′	1° 45¼′	1° 41½′
34°	1° 46¼′	1° 45¾′	1° 45½′	1° 45′	1° 44¾′	1° 44¼′	1° 44′	1° 40¼′
33°	1° 45′	1° 44½′	1° 44¼′	1° 43¾′	1° 43½′	1° 43′	1° 42¾′	1° 39′
32°	1° 44′	1° 13½′	1° 43′	1° 42¾′	1° 42¼′	1° 42′	1° 41½′	1° 38′
31°	1° 42¾′	1° 42¼′	1° 42′	1° 41½′	1° 41′	1° 40¾′	1° 40½′	1° 37′
30°	1° 41½′	1° 41¼′	1° 41′	1° 40½′	1° 40¼′	1° 40′	1° 39½′	1° 36′

(307) Setting out a Meridian. When two points in the direction of the North Star at its extreme elongation have been obtained, as in Art. (**305**), the True Meridian can be found thus. Let A and B be the two points. Multiply the natural tangent of the Azimuth given in the Table, by the distance AB. The product will be the length of a line which is to be set off from B, perpendicular to AB, to some point C. A and C will then be points in the True Meridian. This operation may be postponed till morning.

Fig. 204.

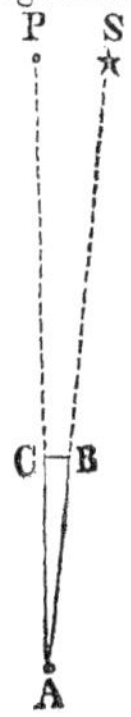

P S

C B

A

If the directions of both the extreme Eastern and extreme Western elongations be set out, the line lying midway between them will be the True Meridian.

(308) Determining the Variation. The variation would of course be given by taking the Bearing of the Meridian thus obtained, but it can also be determined by taking the Bearing of the star at the time of the extreme elongation, and applying the following rules.

When the Azimuth of the star and its magnetic bearing are one East and the other West, the sum of the two is the Magnetic Variation, which is of the same name as the Azimuth; i. e. East, if that be East, and West, if it be West.

When the Azimuth of the star and its Magnetic Bearing are both East, or both West, their difference is the Variation, which will be of the same name as the Azimuth and Bearing, if the Azimuth be the greater of the two, or of the contrary name if the Azimuth be the smaller.

Fig. 205.

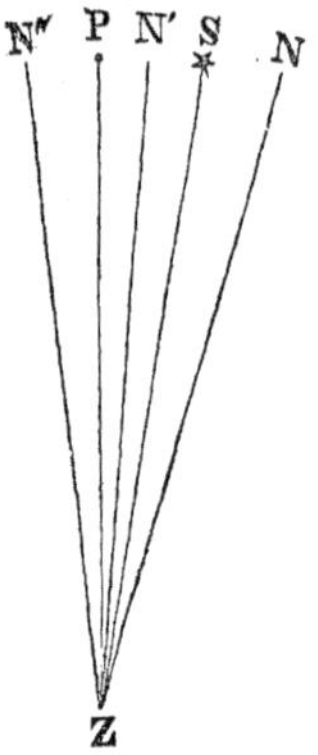

All these cases are presented together in the figure, in which P is the North Pole; Z the place of the observer; ZP the True Meridian; S the star at its greatest Eastern elongation; and ZN, ZN′, ZN″, various supposed directions of the needle.

Call the Azimuth of the star, i. e. the angle PZS, 2° East.

Suppose the needle to point to N, and the Bearing of the star, i. e. SZN, to be 5° West of Magnetic North. The variation PZN will evidently be 7° East of true North.

Suppose the needle to point to N′, and the bearing of the star, i. e. N′ZS, to be $1\frac{1}{4}$° East of Magnetic North. The Variation will be $\frac{3}{4}$° East of true North, and of the same name as the Azimuth, because that is greater than the bearing.

Suppose the needle to point to N″ and the bearing of the star, i. e. N″ZS, to be 10° East of Magnetic North. The Variation will be 8° West of true North, of the contrary name to the Azimuth, because that is the smaller of the two.*

* Algebraically, always subtract the Bearing from the Azimuth, and give the remainder its proper resulting algebraic sign. It will be the Variation; East if *plus*, and West, if minus. Thus in the first case above, the Variation $= +2° - (-5°) = +7° = 7°$ East. In the second case, the Variation $= +2° - (+1\frac{1}{4}°) = +\frac{3}{4}° = \frac{3}{4}°$ East. In the third case, the Variation $= +2° - (+10°) = -8° = 8°$ West.

If the star was on the other side of the Pole, the rules would apply likewise.

(309) Other Methods. Many other methods of determining the true Meridian are employed; such as by equal altitudes and azimuths of the sun, or of a star; by one azimuth, knowing the time; by observations of circumpolar stars at equal times before and after their culmination, or before and after their greatest elongation, &c

All these methods however require some degree of astronomical knowledge; and those which have been explained are abundantly sufficient for all the purposes of the ordinary Land-Surveyor.

"Burt's Solar Compass" is an instrument by which, "when adjusted for the Sun's declination, and the Latitude of the place, the azimuth of any line from the true North and South can be read off, and the difference between it and the Bearing by the compass will then be the variation."

(310) Magnetic variation in the United States. The variation of the Magnetic needle in any part of the United States, can be approximately obtained by mere inspection of the map at the beginning of this volume.* Through all the places at which the needle in 1850,† pointed to the true North, a line is drawn on the map, and called the *Line of no Variation*. It will be seen to be nearly straight, and to pass in a N.N.W. direction from a little west of Cape Hatteras, N. C. through the middle of Virginia, about midway between Cleveland, (Ohio), and Erie, (Pa.), and through the middle of Lake Erie and Lake Huron. If followed South-Easterly it would be found to touch the most Easterly point of South America. It is now slowly moving Westward.

At all places situated to the East of this line (including the New-England States, New-York, New-Jersey, Delaware, Maryland, nearly all of Pennsylvania, and the Eastern half of Virginia and North Carolina) the Variation is Westerly, i. e. the north end of the needle points to the west of the true North. At all places

* Copied (by permission) from one prepared in 1856, by Prof. A. D. Bache, Supt. U. S. Coast Survey, from the U. S. C. S. Observations. The dotted portions of the lines are interpolations due to the kindness of J. E. Hilgard, Assist. U. S. Coast Survey.

† A gradual change in the Variation is going on from year to year, as will be explained in the next Chapter.

situated to the West of this line (including the Western and Southern States) the Variation is easterly, i. e. the North end of the needle points to the East of the true North. This variation increases in proportion to the distance of the place on either side of the line of no variation, reaching 21° of Easterly Variation in Oregon, and 18° of Westerly Variation in Maine.

Lines of equal Variation are lines drawn through all the places which have the same variation. On the map they are drawn for each degree. All the places situated on the line marked 1°, East or West, have 1° Variation; those on the 2° line, have 2° Variation, &c. The variation at the intermediate places can be approximately estimated by the eye. These lines all refer to 1840.

The lines of equal Variation, if continued Northward, would all meet in a certain point called the *Magnetic Pole*, and situated in the neighborhood of 96° West Longitude from Greenwich, and 70° of North Latitude. Towards this pole the needle tends to point.

Another Magnetic pole is found in the Southern hemisphere; but the farther development of this subject belongs to a treatise on Natural Philosophy.

The Variation on the Pacific slope of this country has been very imperfectly ascertained. A few leading points are as below.

California;	Point Conception,	Sept. 1850,	13° 49½′ E.
	Point Penos, Monterey,	Feb. 1851,	14° 58′ E.
	Presidio, San Francisco,	Feb. 1852,	15° 27′ E.
	San Diego,	Mar. 1851,	12° 29′ E.
Oregon;	Cape Disappointment,	July, 1851,	20° 45′ E.
	Ewing Harbor,	Nov. 1851,	18° 29′ E.
Wash. Ter'y.	Scarboro' Harbor,	Aug. 1852,	21° 30′ E.

(311) To correct Magnetic Bearings. The Variation at any place and time being known, the Magnetic Bearings taken there and then, may be reduced to their true Bearings, by these Rules.

RULE 1. *When the Variation is West*, as it is in the North-Eastern States, the true Bearing will be the *sum* of the Variation and a Bearing which is North and West, or South and East; and the *difference* of the Variation and a Bearing which is North and East, or South and West. To apply this to the cardinal points, a

North Bearing must be called N. 0° West, an East Bearing N. 90° E., a South Bearing S. 0° E., and a West Bearing S. 90° W.; counting around from N′ to N, in the figure, and so onward, "with the Sun."

The reasons for these corrections are apparent from the Figure, in which the dotted lines and the accented letters represent the direction of the needle, and the full lines and the unaccented letters represent the true North and South and East and West lines.

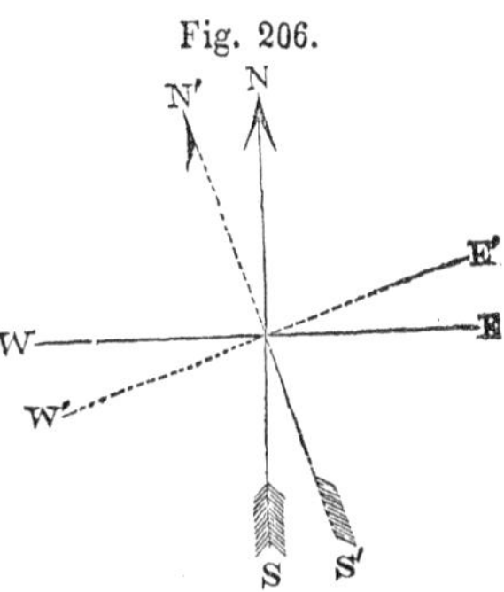

Fig. 206.

When the sum of the Variation and the Bearing is directed to be taken, and comes to more than 90°, the supplement of the sum is to be taken, and the first letter changed. When the difference is directed to be taken, and the Variation is greater than the Bearing, the last letter must be changed. A diagram of the case will remove all doubts. Examples of all these cases are given below for a Variation of 8° West.

MAGNETIC BEARING.	TRUE BEARING.	MAGNETIC BEARING.	TRUE BEARING.
North.	N. 8° W.	South.	S. 8° E.
N. 1° E.	N. 7° W.	S. 2° W.	S. 6° E.
N. 40° E.	N. 32° E.	S. 60° W.	S. 52° W.
East.	N. 82° E.	West.	S. 82° W.
S. 50° E.	S. 58° E.	N. 70° W.	N. 78° W.
S. 89° E.	N. 83° E.	N. 83° W.	S. 89° W.

RULE 2. *When the Variation is East*, as in the Western and Southern States, the preceding directions must be exactly reversed; i. e. the true Bearing will be the *difference* of the Variation and a Bearing which is North and West, or South and East; and the *sum* of the Variation and a Bearing which is North and East, or South and West. A North Bearing

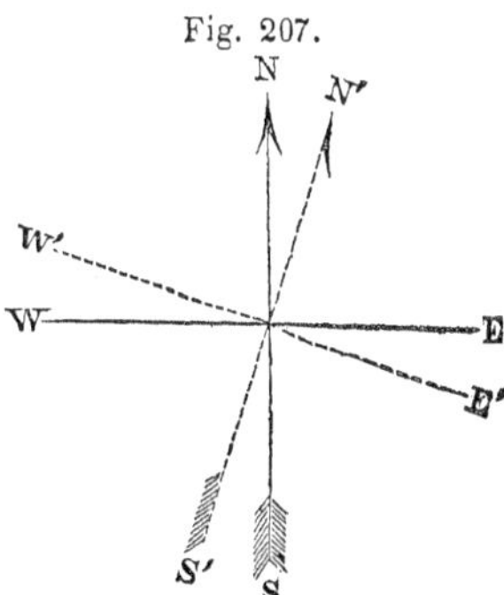

Fig. 207.

must be called N. 0° E., a West Bearing N. 90° W., a South Bearing S. 0° W., and an East Bearing S. 90° E., counting from N′ to N, and so onward, "against the sun." The reasons for these rules are seen in the Figure. Examples are given below, for a Variation of 5° E.

MAGNETIC BEARING.	TRUE BEARING.	MAGNETIC BEARING.	TRUE BEARING.
North.	N. 5° E.	South.	S. 5° W.
N. 40° E.	N. 45° E.	S. 60° W.	S. 65° W.
N. 89° E.	S. 86° E.	S. 87° W.	N. 88° W.
East.	S. 85° E.	West.	N. 85° W.
S. 1° E.	S. 4° W.	N. 70° W.	N. 65° W.
S. 50° E.	S. 45° E.	N. 2° W.	N. 3° E.

(312) To survey a line with true Bearings. The compass may be set, or adjusted, by means of the Vernier, (noticed in Arts. (**229**) and (**237**), and shown in Fig. 148, page 126) according to the Variation in any place, so that the Bearings of any lines then taken with it will be their true Bearings. To effect this, turn aside the compass plate, by means of the Tangent Screw which moves the Vernier, a number of degrees equal to the Variation, moving the S. end of the Compass-box to the *right*, (the North end being supposed to go ahead) if the Variation be Westerly, and *vice versa;* for that moves the North end of the Compass-box in the contrary direction, and thus makes a line which before was N. by the needle, now read, as it should truly, North, so many degrees, West if the Variation was West; and similarly in the reverse case.

CHAPTER VIII.

CHANGES IN THE VARIATION.

(313) The *Changes* in the Variation are of more practical importance than its absolute amount. They are of four kinds: Irregular, Diurnal, Annual and Secular.

(314) Irregular changes. The needle is subject to sudden and violent changes, which have no known law. They are sometimes coincident with a thunder storm, or an Aurora Borealis, (during which, changes of nearly 1° in one minute, $2\frac{1}{2}$° in eight minutes, and 10° in one night, have been observed), but often have no apparent cause, except an otherwise invisible "Magnetic Storm."

(315) The Diurnal change. On continuing observations of the direction of the needle throughout an entire day, it will be found, in the Northern Hemisphere, that the North end of the needle moves Westward from about 8 A. M. till about 2 P. M. over an arc of from 10′ to 15′, and then gradually returns to its former position.* In the Southern Hemisphere, the direction of this motion is reversed. The period of this change being a day, it is called the *Diurnal Variation.* Its effect on the permanent Variation is necessarily to cause it, in places where it is West, to attain its maximum at about 2 P. M., and its minimum at about 8 A. M.; and the reverse where the Variation is East.

This Diurnal change adds a new element to the inaccuracies of the compass; since the Bearings of any line taken on the same day, at a few hours interval, might vary a quarter of a degree, which would cause a deviation of the end of the line, amounting to nearly half a link at the end of a chain, and to 35 links, or 23 feet, at the end of a mile. The hour of the day at which any important Bearing is taken should therefore be noted.

* A similar but smaller movement takes place during the night.

(316) The Annual change. If the observations be continued throughout an entire year, it will be found that the Diurnal changes vary with the seasons, being about twice as great in Summer as in Winter. The period of this change being a year, it is called the Annual Variation.

(317) The Secular change. When accurate observations on the Variation of the needle in the same place are continued for several years, it is found that there is a continual and tolerably regular increase or decrease of the Variation, continuing to proceed in the same direction for so long a period, that it may be called the *Secular* change of Variation.*

The most ancient observations are those taken in Paris. In the year 1541 the needle pointed 7° East of North; in 1580 the Variation had increased to $11\frac{1}{2}$° East, being its maximum; the needle then began to move Westward, and in 1666, it had returned to the Meridian; the Variation then became West, and continued to increase till in 1814 it attained its maximum, being 22° 34′ West of North. It is now decreasing, and in 1853 was 20° 17′ W. In London, the Variation in 1576 was 11° 15′ E.; in 1662, 0°; in 1700, 9° 40′ W.; in 1778, 22° 11′ W.; in 1815, 24° 27′ W.; and in 1843, 23° 8′ W.

In this country the north end of the needle was moving Eastward at the earliest recorded observations, and continued to do so till about the year 1810 (variously recorded as from 1793 to 1819), when it began to move Westward which it has ever since continued to do. Thus, in Boston, from 1708 to 1807 the Variation changed from 9° W. to 6° 5′ W., and from 1807 to 1840, it changed from 6° 5′ W. to 9° 18′ W.

Valuable Tables of the Secular changes of the Variation in various parts of the United States have been published by Prof. Loomis in Silliman's "American Journal of Science," Vol. 34, July, 1838, p. 301; Vol. 39, Oct. 1840, p. 42; and Vol. 43, Oct. 1842, p. 107. An abstract of the most reliable of them is here given. Troy and Schenectady are from other sources.

* If the term "Declination of the Needle" could be restored to its proper use, this "Change of Variation" would be properly called the "Variation of the Declination."

PLACE.	LATITUDE.	LONGITUDE.	DATES.	ANNUAL MOTION.
Burlington, Vt.	44° 27′	73° 10′	1811...1834	4′.4
Chesterfield, N. H.	42° 53′	72° 20′	1820...1836	6′.4
Deerfield, Mass.	42° 34′	72° 29′	1811...1837	5′.7
Cambridge, Mass.	42° 22′	71° 7′	1810...1840	3′.4
New-Haven, Conn.	41° 18′	72° 58′	1819...1840	4′.6
Keeseville, N. Y.	44° 28′	73° 32′	1825...1838	5′.4
Albany, N. Y.	42° 39′	73° 45′	1818...1842	3′.6
"	"	"	1842...1854	4′.9
Troy, N. Y.	42° 44′	73° 40′	1821...1837	6′.2
Schenectady, N. Y.	42° 49′	73° 55′	1829...1841	7′.2
"	"	"	1841...1854	6′.0
New-York City.	40° 43′	74° 01′	1824...1837	3′.7
Philadelphia.	39° 57′	75° 11′	1813...1837	3′.6
Milledgeville, Ga.	33° 7′	83° 20′	1805...1835	1′.7
Mobile, Ala.	30° 40′	88° 11′	1809...1835	2′.2
Cleveland, O.	41° 30′	81° 46′	1825...1838	4′.5
Marietta, O.	39° 25′	81° 26′	1810...1838	2′.4
Cincinnati, O.	39° 6′	84° 27′	1825...1840	2′.0
Detroit, Mich.	42° 24′	82° 58	1822...1840	4′.3
Alton, Ill.	38° 52′	90° 12′	1835...1840	3′.0

From these and other observations it appears that at present the lines of equal variation are moving Westward, producing an annual change of variation (increasing the Westerly and lessening the Easterly) which is different in different parts of the country, and is about five or six minutes in the North-Eastern States, three or four minutes in the Middle States, and two minutes in the Southern States.

(318) Determination of the change, by Interpolation. To determine the change at any place and for any interval not found in the recorded observations, an approximation, sufficient for most purposes of the surveyor, may be obtained by interpolation (by a simple proportion) between the places given in the Tables, assuming the movements to have been uniform between the given dates; and also assuming the change at any place not found in the Tables, to have been intermediate between those of the lines of equal variation, which pass through the places of recorded observations on each side of it, and to have been in the ratio of its respective distances from those two lines; for example, taking their arithmetical mean, if the required place is midway between them; if it be twice as near one as the other, dividing the sum of twice the change of the nearest line, and once the change of the other, by three; and so in other cases; i. e. giving the change at each place, a "weight" inversely as its distance from the place at which the change is to be found.

(319) Determination of the change, by old lines. When the former Bearing of any old line, such as a farm-fence, &c. is recorded, the change in the Variation from the date of the original observation to the present time can be at once found by setting the compass at one end of the line and sighting to the other. The difference of the two Bearings is the required change.

If one end of the old line cannot be seen from the other, as is often the case when the line is fixed only by a "corner" at each end of it, proceed thus. Run a line from one corner with the old Bearing and with its distance. Measure the distance from the end of this line to the other corner, to which it will be opposite. Multiply this distance by 57.3, and divide by the length of the line. The quotient will be the change of variation in degrees.*

For example, a line 63 chains long, in 1827 had a Bearing of North 1° East. In 1847 a trial line was run from one end of the former line with the same Bearing and distance, and its other end was found to be 125 links to the West of the true corner. The change of Variation was therefore $\frac{1.25 \times 57.3}{63} = 1°.137 = 1° 8'$ Westerly.

Fig. 208.

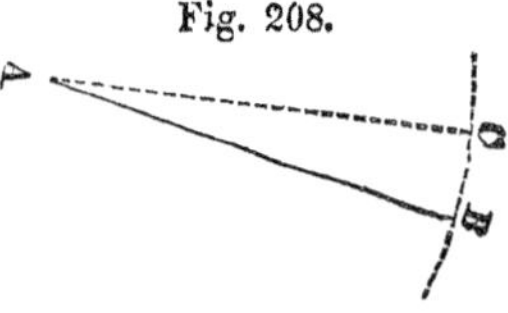

* Let AB be the original line; AC the trial line, and BC the distance between their extremities. AB and AC may be regarded as radii of a circle and BC as a chord of the arc which subtends their angle. Assuming the chord and arc to coincide (which they will, nearly, for small angles) we have this proportion; Whole circumference : arc BC :: 360° : BAC : or, 2 × AC × 3.1416 : BC : 360° : BAC, whence $BAC = \frac{BC}{AB} \times 57.3$; or more precisely 57.29578.

(320) Effects of the Secular change. These are exceedingly important in the re-survey of farms by the Bearings recorded in old deeds. Let SN denote the direction of the needle at the time of the original Survey, and S′N′ its direction at the time of the re-survey, a number of years later. Suppose the change to have been 3°, the needle pointing so much farther to the west of North. The line SN, which before was due North and South by the needle will now bear N. 3° E. and S. 3° W; the line AB, which before was N. 40° E. will now bear N. 43° E; the line DF which before was N. 40° W. will now bear N. 37° W; and the line WE, which before was due East and West, will now bear S. 87° E. and N. 87° W. Any line is similarly changed. The proof of this is apparent on inspecting the figure.

Fig. 209.

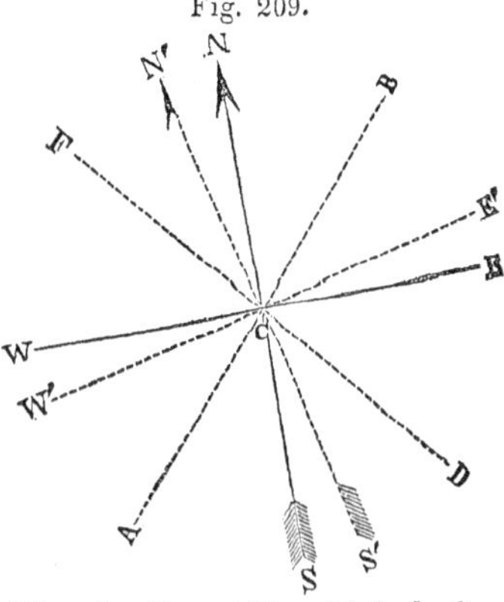

Suppose now that a surveyor, ignorant or neglectful of this change, should attempt to run out a farm by the old Bearings of the deed, none of the old fences or corners remaining. The full lines in the figure represent the original bounds of the farm, and the dotted lines those of the *new* piece of land which, starting from A, he would unwittingly run out. It would be of the same size and the same shape as the true one, but it would be in the wrong place. None of its lines would agree with the true ones, and in some places it would encroach on one neighbor, and in other places would leave a gore which belongs to it, between itself and another neighbor. Yet this is often done, and is the source of a great part of the litigation among farmers respecting their "lines."

Fig. 210.

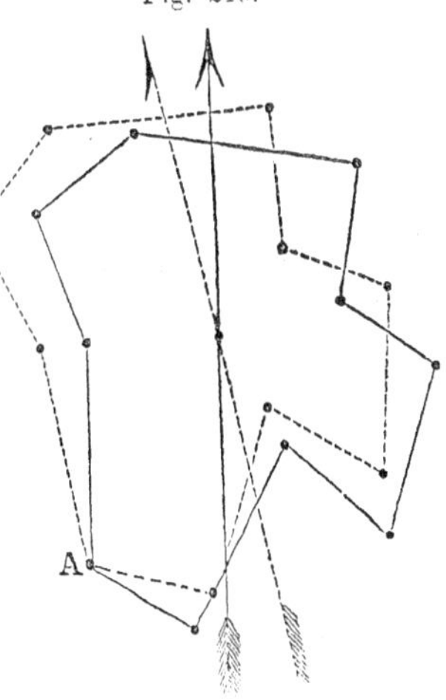

(321) To run out old lines. To succeed in retracing old lines, proper allowance must be made for the change in the variation since the date of the original survey. That date must first be accurately ascertained; for the survey may be much older than the deed, into which its bearings may have been copied from an older one. The amount and direction of the change is then to be ascertained by the methods of Arts. (**318**) or (**319**). The bearings may then be corrected by the following Rules.

When the North end of the needle has been moving Westerly, (as it has for about forty years), the present Bearings will be the *sums* of the change and the old Bearings which were North-Easterly or South-Westerly, and the *differences* of the change and the old Bearings which were North-Westerly or South-Easterly.

If the change have been *Easterly*, reverse the preceding rules, subtracting where it is directed to add, and adding where it is directed to subtract.

Run out the lines with the Bearings thus corrected.

It will be noticed that the process is precisely the reverse of that in Art. (**311**). The rules there given in more detail, may therefore be used; Rule 1, "when the Variation is West," being employed when the *change* has been a movement of the N. end of the needle to the East; and Rule 2, "when the Variation is East," being employed when the N. end of the needle has been moving to the West.

If the compass has a Vernier, it can be set for the change, once for all, precisely as directed in Art. (**312**), and then the courses can be run out as given in the deed, the correction being made by the instrument.

(322) Example. The following is a remarkable case which recently came before the Supreme Court of New-York. The North line of a large Estate was fixed by a royal grant, dated in 1704, as a due East and West line. It was run out in 1715, by a surveyor, whom we will call Mr. A. It was again surveyed in 1765, by Mr. B. who ran a course N. 87° 30′ E. It was run out for a third time in 1789, by Mr. C. who adopted the course N. 86° 18′ E. In 1845 it was surveyed for the fourth time by

Mr. D. with a course of N. 88° 30′ E. He found old "corners," and "blazes" of a former survey, on his line. They are also found on another line, South of his. Which of the preceding courses were correct, and where does the true line lie?

The question was investigated as follows. There were no old records of variation at the precise locality, but it lies between the lines of equal variation which pass through New-York and Boston, its distance from the Boston line being about twice its distance from the New-York line. The records of those two cities (referred to in Art. (317)) could therefore be used in the manner explained in Art. (318). For the later dates, observations at New-Haven could serve as a check. Combining all these, the author inferred the variation at the desired place to have been as follows:

In 1715, Variation 8° 02′ West.
In 1765, " 5° 32′ " Decrease since 1715, 2° 30′.
In 1789, " 5° 05′ " Decrease since 1765, 0° 27′.
In 1845, " 7° 23′ " Increase since 1789, 2° 18′.

We are now prepared to examine the correctness of the allowances made by the old surveyors.

The course run by Mr. B. in 1765, N. 87° 30′ E. made an allowance of 2° 30′ as the decrease of variation, agreeing precisely with our calculation. The course of Mr. C. in 1789, N. 86° 18′ E., allowed a change of 1° 12′, which was wrong by our calculation, which gives only about 27′, and was deduced from three different records. Mr. D. in 1845, ran a course of N. 88° 30′ E, calling the increase of variation since 1789, 2° 12′. Our estimate was 2° 18′, the difference being comparatively small. Our conclusion then is this: the second surveyor retraced correctly the line of the first: the third surveyor ran out a *new* and incorrect line: and the fourth surveyor correctly retraced the line of the third, and found his marks, but this line was wrong originally and therefore wrong now. All the surveyors ran their lines on the supposition that the original "due East and West line" meant East and West as the needle pointed at the time of the original survey.

The preponderance of the testimony as to old land marks agreed with the results of the above reasoning, and the decision of the court was in accordance therewith.

Fig. 211

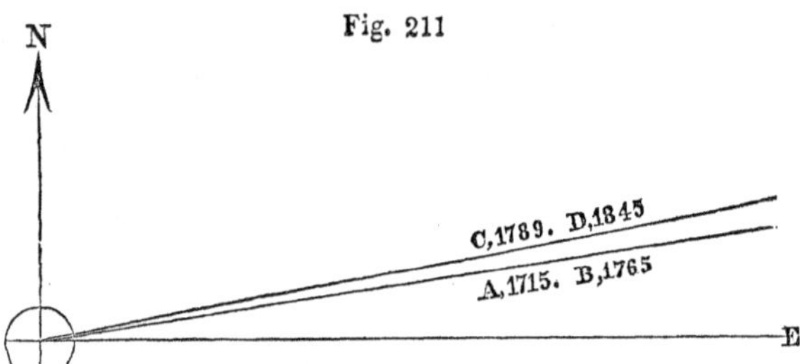

In the above figure the horizontal and vertical lines represent true East and North lines ; and the two upper lines running from left to right represent the two lines set out by the surveyors and in the years, there named.

(323) Remedy for the evils of the Secular change. The only complete remedy for the disputes, and the uncertainty of bounds, resulting from the continued change in the variation, is this. Let a Meridian, i. e. a true North and South line, be established in every town or county, by the authority of the State; monuments, such as stones set deep in the ground, being placed at each end of it. Let every surveyor be obliged by law to test his compass by this line, at least once in each year. This he could do as easily as in taking the Bearing of a fence, by setting his instrument on one monument, and sighting to a staff held on the other. Let the variation thus ascertained be inserted in the notes of the survey and recorded in the deed. Another surveyor, years or centuries afterwards, could test his compass by taking the Bearing of the same monuments, and the difference between this and the former Bearing would be the change of variation. He could thus determine with entire certainty the proper allowance to be made (as in Art. (**321**)) in order to retrace the original line, no matter how much, or how irregularly, the variation may have changed, or how badly adjusted was the compass of the original survey. Any permanent line employed in the same manner as the meridian line, would answer the same purpose, though less conveniently, and every surveyor should have such a line at least, for his own use.*

* This remedy seems to have been first suggested by Rittenhouse. It has since been recommended by T. Sopwith, in 1822; by E. F. Johnson, in 1831, and by W. Roberts, of Troy, in 1839. The errors of re-surveys, in which the change is neglected, were noticed in the "Philosophical Transactions," as long ago as 1679

PART IV.

TRANSIT AND THEODOLITE SURVEYING:

By the Third Method.

CHAPTER I.

THE INSTRUMENTS.

(324) THE TRANSIT and THE THEODOLITE (figures of which are given on the next two pages) are *Goniometers*, or Angle-Measurers. Each consists, essentially, of a circular plate of metal, supported in such a manner as to be horizontal, and divided on its outer circumference into degrees, and parts of degrees. Through the centre of this plate passes an upright axis, and on it is fixed a second circular plate, which nearly touches the first plate, and can turn freely around to the right and to the left. This second plate carries a Telescope, which rests on upright standards firmly fixed to the plate, and which can be pointed upwards and downwards. By the combination of this motion and that of the second plate around its axis, the Telescope can be directed to any object. The second plate has some mark on its edge, such as an arrow-head, which serves as a pointer or index for the divided circle, like the hand of a clock. When the Telescope is directed to one object, and then turned to the right or to the left, to some other object, this index, which moves with it and passes around the divided edge of the other plate, points out the arc passed over by this change of direction, and thus measures the angle made by the lines imagined to pass from the centre of the instrument to the two objects.

THE TRANSIT.

Fig 212

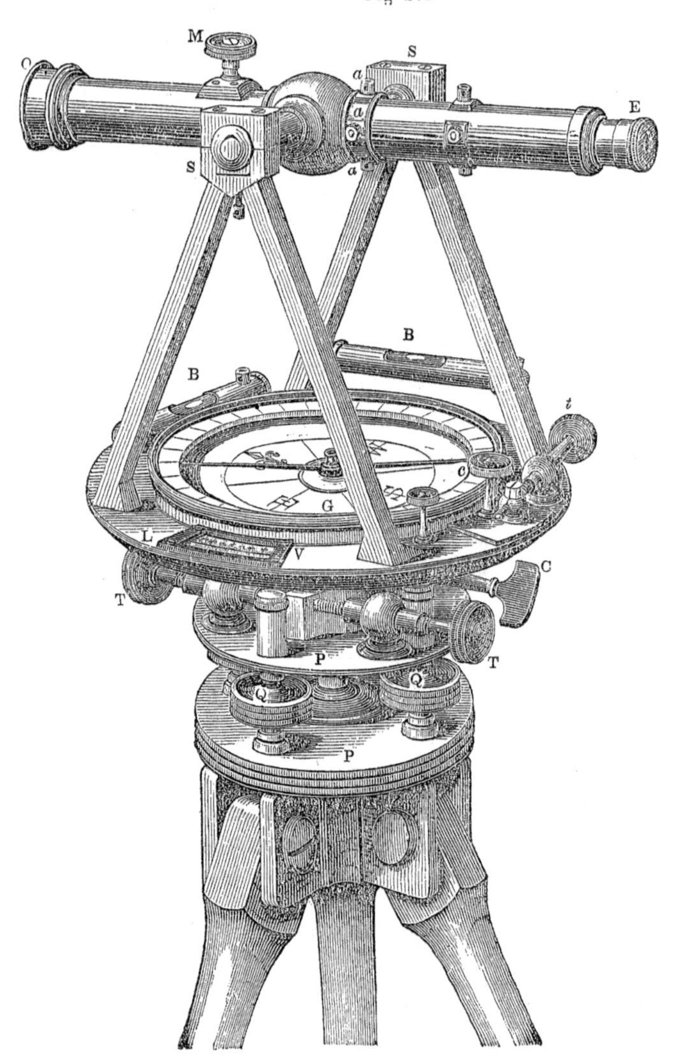

THE THEODOLITE.

Fig. 213

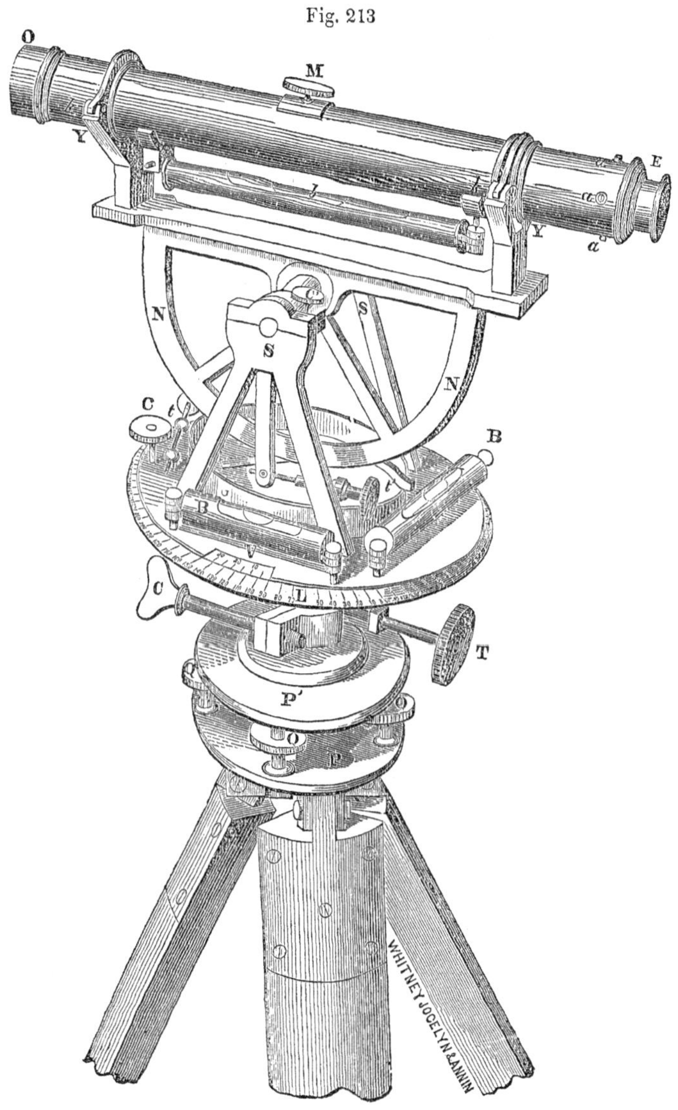

(325) Distinction. The preceding description applies to both the Transit and the Theodolite. But an essential difference between them is, that in the Transit the Telescope can turn completely over, so as to look both forward and backward, while in the Theodolite it cannot do so. Hence the name of the Transit.*

This capability of reversal enables a straight line to be prolonged from one end of it, or to be ranged out in both directions from any one point. The Telescope of the Theodolite can indeed be taken out of the Y shaped supports in which it rests, and be replaced end for end, but this operation is an imperfect substitute for the revolution of the Telescope of the Transit. So also is the turning half way around of the upper plate which carries the Telescope.

The Theodolite has a level attached to its Telescope, and a vertical circle for measuring vertical angles. The Transit does not usually have these, though they are sometimes added to it. The instrument may then be named a Transit-Theodolite. It then corresponds to the altitude and azimuth instrument of Astronomy. As the greater part of the points to be explained are common to both the Transit and the Theodolite, the descriptions to be given may be regarded as applicable to either of the instruments, except when the contrary is expressly stated, and some point peculiar to either is noticed.

(326) The great value of these instruments, and the accuracy of their measurements of angles are due chiefly to two things; to the *Telescope*, by which great precision in sighting to a point is obtained; and to the *Vernier Scale*, which enables minute portions of any arc to be read with ease and correctness. The former assists the eye in directing the line of sight, and the latter aids it in reading off the results. Arrangements for giving slow and steady motion to the movable parts of the instruments add to the value of the above. A contrivance for *Repeating* the observation of angles still farther lessens the unavoidable inaccuracies of these observations.

* It is sometimes called the "Engineers' Transit," or "Railroad Transit," to distinguish it from the Astronomical Transit-instrument. In this country it has almost entirely supplanted the Theodolite.

The inaccurate division of the limb of the instrument is also averaged and thus diminished by the last arrangement. Its want of true "centring," is remedied by reading off on opposite sides of the circle.

Imperfections in the parallelism and perpendicularity of the parts of the instrument in which those qualities are required, are corrected by various "adjustments," made by the various screws whose heads appear in the engravings.

The arrangements for attaining all these objects render necessary the numerous parts and apparent complication of the instrument. But this complication disappears when each part is examined in turn, and its uses and relations to the rest are distinctly indicated. This we now propose to do, after explaining the engravings.

(327) In the figures of the instruments, given on pages 212 and 213, the same letters refer to both figures, so far as the parts are common to both.* L is the limb or divided circle. V is the index, or "Vernier," which moves around it. In the Transit, only a small portion of the divided limb is seen, the upper circle (which in it is the movable one) covering it completely, so that only a short piece of the arc is visible through an opening in the upper plate. S, S, are standards, fastened to the upper plate and supporting the telescope, EO. G is a compass-box, also fastened to the upper plate. *c* is a clamp-screw, which presses together the two plates, and prevents one from moving over the other. *t* is a tangent-screw, or slow-motion screw, which gives a slow and gentle motion to one plate over the other. C is a clamp-screw which fastens the lower plate to the body of the instrument, and thus prevents it from moving on its own axis. T is the tangent-screw to give this part a slow-motion. P and P′ are parallel plates through which pass four screws, Q, Q, Q, Q, by which the circular plate L is made level,

* The arrangements of these instruments are differently made by almost every maker; but any form of them being thoroughly understood, any new one will cause no difficulty. The figure of the Transit was drawn from one made by W. & L. E. Gurley, of Troy, N. Y. to the latter of whom the Author is indebted for some valuable information respecting the details of the instrument. The Theodolite is of the favorite English form.

as determined by the bubbles in the small spirit levels, B, B, of which there are two at right angles to each other.

In the figure of the *Theodolite*, the large level *b*, and the semicircle NN are for the purposes of Levelling, and of measuring Vertical angles. They will therefore not be described in this place.

(328) As the value of either of these instruments depends greatly on the accurate fitting and bearings of the two concentric vertical axes, and as their connection ought to be thoroughly understood, a vertical section through the body of the instrument is given in Fig. 214, to half the real size. The tapering spindle or

Fig. 214.

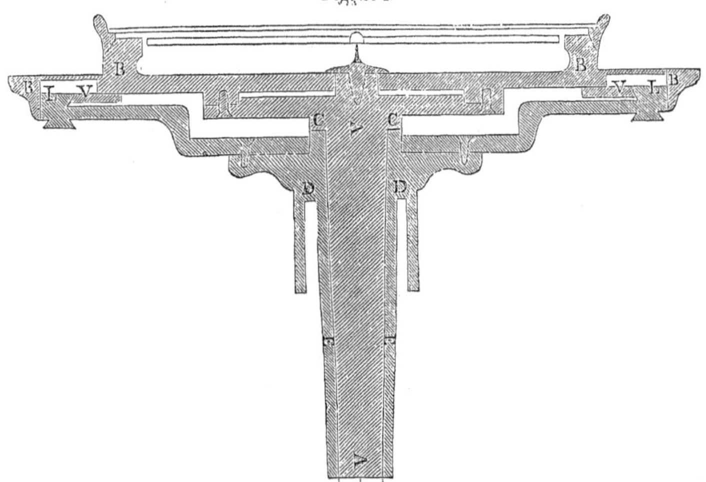

inverted frustum of a cone, marked AA, supports the upper plate BB, which carries the index, or Verniers, V, V, and the Telescope. The whole bearing of this plate is at C, C, on the top of the hollow inverted cone EE, in which the spindle turns freely, but steadily. This interior position of the bearings preserves them from dust and injury. This hollow cone carries the lower or graduated plate, and it can itself turn around on the bearings D, D, carrying with it the lower circle, and also the upper one and all above it.

The Vernier scales V, V, are attached to the upper plate, but lie in the same plane as the divisions L, L, of the lower plate, (so that the two can be viewed together, without parallax,) and are covered with glass, to exclude dust and moisture. In the figure the hatchings are drawn in different directions on the parts which move with the Vernier, and on those which move only with the limb.

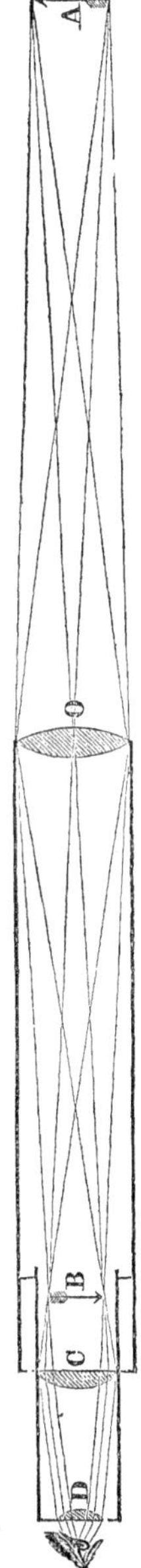

Fig. 215

(329) The Telescope. This is a combination of lenses, placed in a tube, and so arranged, in accordance with the laws of optical science, that an image of any object to which the Telescope may be directed, is formed within the tube, (by the rays of light coming from the object and bent in passing through the object-glass) and there magnified by an Eye-glass, or Eye-piece, composed of several lenses. The arrangement of these lenses are very various. Those two combinations which are preferred for surveying instruments, will be here explained.

Fig. 215 represents a Telescope which inverts objects. Any object is rendered visible by every point of it sending forth rays of light in every direction. In this figure, the highest and lowest points of the object, which here is an arrow, A, are alone considered. Those of the rays proceeding from them, which meet the object-glass, O, form a cone. The centre line of each cone, and its extreme upper and lower lines are alone shown in the figure. It will be seen that these rays, after passing through the object-glass, are refracted, or bent, by it, so as to cross one another, and thus to form at B an inverted image of the object. This would be rendered visible, if a piece of ground glass, or other semi-transparent substance, was placed at the point B, which is called the *focus* of the object-glass. The rays which form this image continue onward and pass through the two lenses C and D, which act like one magnifying glass, so that the rays, after being refracted by them, enter the eye at such angles as to form there a magnified and inverted image of the object. This combination of the two plano-convex lenses, C and D, is known as "Ramsden's Eye-piece."

Fig. 216

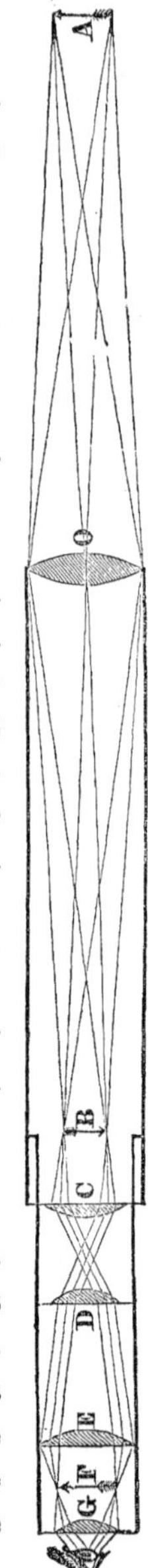

This Telescope, inverting objects, shows them upside down, and the right side on the left. They can be shown erect by adding one or two more lenses as in the marginal figure. But as these lenses absorb light and lessen the distinctness of vision, the former arrangement is preferable for the glasses of a Transit or a Theodolite. A little practice makes it equally convenient for the observer, who soon becomes accustomed to seeing his flagmen standing on their heads, and soon learns to motion them to the right when he wishes them to go to the left, and *vice versa.*

Figure 216 represents a Telescope which shows objects erect. Its eye-piece has four lenses. The eye-piece of the common terrestrial Telescope, or spy-glass, has three. Many other combinations may be used, all intended to show the object achromatically, or free from false coloring, but the one here shown is that most generally preferred at the present day. It will be seen that an inverted image of the object A, is formed at B, as before, but that the rays continuing onward are so refracted in passing through the lens C as to again cross, and thus, after farther refraction by the lenses D and E, to form, at F, an erect image, which is magnified by the lens G.

In both these figures, the limits of the page render it necessary to draw the angles of the rays very much out of proportion.

(330) Cross-hairs. Since a considerable field of view is seen in looking through the Telescope, it is necessary to provide means for directing the line of sight to the precise point which is to be observed. This could be effected by placing a very fine point, such as that of a needle, within the Telescope, at some place where it could be distinctly seen. In practice this fine point is obtained by the intersection of two very fine lines, placed in the common *focus* of the object-glass and of the eye-piece. These lines are called the *cross-hairs*, or *cross-wires*. Their intersection can be seen through the eye-piece, at the same time, and apparently at the same place, as the image of the distant object. The magnifying powers of the eye-piece will then detect the slightest deviation from perfect coincidence. "This application of the Telescope may be considered as completely annihilating that part of the error of observation which might otherwise arise from an erroneous estimation of the direction in which an object lies from the observer's eye, or from the centre of the instrument. It is, in fact, the grand source of all the precision of modern Astronomy, without which all other refinements in instrumental workmanship would be thrown away." What Sir John Herschel here says of its utility to Astronomy, is equally applicable to Surveying.

The imaginary line which passes through the intersection of the cross-hairs and the optical centre of the object-glass, is called the *line of collimation* of the Telescope.*

The cross-hairs are attached to a ring, or short thick tube of brass, placed within the Telescope tube, through holes in which pass loosely four screws, (their heads being seen at *a*, *a*, *a*, in Figs. 212 and 213), whose threads enter and take hold of the ring, behind or in front of the cross-hairs, as shown (in front view and in section) in the two figures in the margin. Their movements will be explained in Chapter III.

Fig. 217.

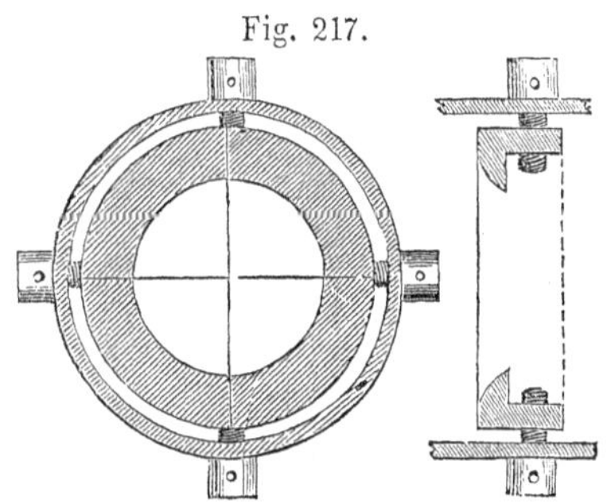

Usually, one cross-hair is horizontal, and the other vertical, as in Fig. 217, but sometimes they are arranged as in Fig. 218, which is thought to enable the object to be bisected with more precision. A horizontal hair is sometimes added.

Fig. 218.

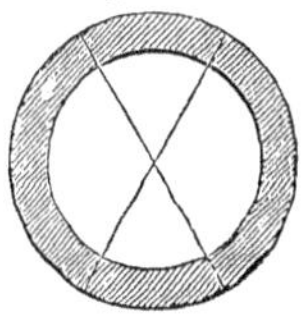

The cross-hairs are best made of platinum wire, drawn out very fine by being previously enclosed

* From the Latin word *Collimo*, or *Collineo*, meaning to direct one thing towards another in a straight line, or to aim at. The *line of aim* would express the meaning.

in a larger wire of silver, and the silver then removed by nitric acid. Silk threads from a cocoon are sometimes used. Spiders' threads are, however, the most usual. If a cross-hair is broken, the ring must be taken out by removing two opposite screws, and inserting a wire with a screw cut on its end, or a stick of suitable size, into one of the holes thus left open in the ring, it being turned sideways for that purpose, and then removing the other screws The spider's threads are then stretched across the notches seen in the end of the ring, and are fastened by gum, or varnish, or bees-wax. The operation is a very delicate one. The following plan has been employed. A piece of wire is bent, as in the figure, so as to leave an opening a little wider than the ring of the cross-hairs. A cobweb is chosen, at the end of which a spider is hanging, and it is wound around the bent wire, as in the figure, the weight of the insect keeping it tight and stretching it ready for use, each part being made fast by gum, &c. When a cross-hair is wanted, one of these is laid across the ring and there attached. Another method is to draw the thread out of the spider, persuading him to spin, if he sulks, by tossing him from hand to hand. A stock of such threads must be obtained in warm weather for the winter's wants. A piece of thin glass, with a horizontal and a vertical line etched on it, may be made a substitute.

Fig. 219.

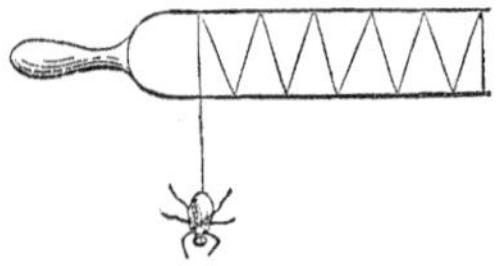

(331) Instrumental Parallax. This is an apparent movement of the cross-hairs about the object to which the line of sight is directed, taking place on any slight movement of the eye of the observer. It is caused by the image and the cross-hairs not being precisely in the common focus, or point of distinct vision of the eye-piece and the object glass. To correct it, move the eye-piece out or in till the cross-hairs are seen clearly and sharply defined against any white object. Then move the object glass in or out till the object is also distinctly seen. The cross-hairs will then seem to be fixed to the object, and no movement of the eye will cause them to appear to change their place.

(332) The milled-headed screw seen at M, passing into the tele scope has a pinion at its other end entering a toothed rack, and is used to move the object glass, O, out and in, according as the object looked at is nearer or farther than the one last observed. Short distances require a long tube: long distances a short tube.

Fig. 220.

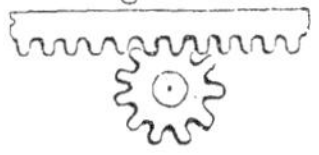

The eye-piece, E, is usually moved in and out by hand, but a similar arrangement to the preceding is a great improvement. This movement is necessary in order to obtain a distinct view of the cross-hairs. Short-sighted persons require the eye-piece to be pushed farther in than persons of ordinary sight, and old or long-sighted persons to have it drawn further out.

(333) Supports. The Telescope of the *Transit* is supported by a hollow axis at right angles to it, which itself rests at each end, on two upright pieces, or standards, spreading at their bases so as to increase their stability. In the *Theodolite*, the telescope rests at each end in forked supports, called Ys, from their shape. These Ys are themselves supported by a cross-bar, which is carried by an axis at right angles to it and to the telescope. This axis rests on standards similar to those of the Transit. The Telescope of the *Theodolite* can be taken out of the Ys, and turned "end for end." This is not usual in the Transit. Either of the above arrangements enables the Telescope to be raised or depressed so as to suit the height of the object to which it is directed. A telescope so disposed is called a "plunging telescope."

In some instruments there is an arrangement for raising or lowering one end of the axis. This is sometimes required for reasons to be given in connection with "Adjustments."

(334) The Indexes. The supports, or standards, of the telescope just described are attached to the upper, or index-carrying circle.* This, as has been stated, can turn freely on the lower or graduated circle, by means of its conical axis moving in the hollow conical axis of the latter circle. This upper circle carries the index, V,

* In some instruments this circle is the under one. In our figures it is the upper one, and we will therefore always speak of it as such.

which is an arrow-head or other mark on its edge, or the zero-point of a Vernier scale. There are usually two of these, situated exactly opposite to each other, or at the extremities of a diameter of the upper circle, so that the readings on the graduated circle pointed out by them differ, if both are correct, exactly 180°. The object of this arrangement is to correct any error of *eccentricity*, arising from the centre of the axis which carries the upper circle, (and with which it and its index pointers turn), not being precisely in the centre of the graduated circle. In the figure, let C be the true centre of the graduated circle, but C′ the centre on which the plate carrying the indexes turns. Let AC′B represent the direction of a sight taken to one object, and D′C′E′ the direction when turned to a second object. The angle subtended by the two objects at the centre of the instrument is required. Let DE be a line passing through C, and parallel to D′E′. The angle ACD equals the required angle, which is therefore truly measured by the arc AD or BE. But if the arc shown by the index is read, it will be AD′ on one side, and BE′ on the other; the first being too small by the arc DD′ and the other too large by the equal arc EE′. If however the half-sum of the two arcs AD′ and BE′ be taken, it will equal the true arc, and therefore correctly measure the angle. Thus if AD′ was 19°, and BE′ 21°, their half sum, 20°, would be the correct angle.

Fig. 221.

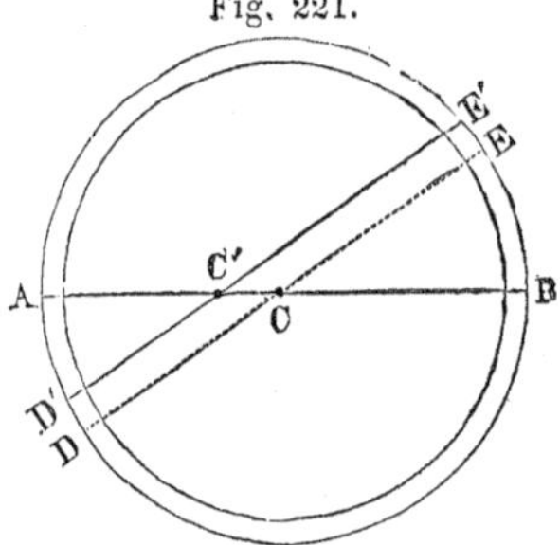

Three indexes, 120° apart, are sometimes used. They have the advantage of *averaging* the unavoidable inaccuracies and inequali ties of graduation on different parts of the limb, and thus diminish ing their effect on the resulting angle.

Fig. 222.

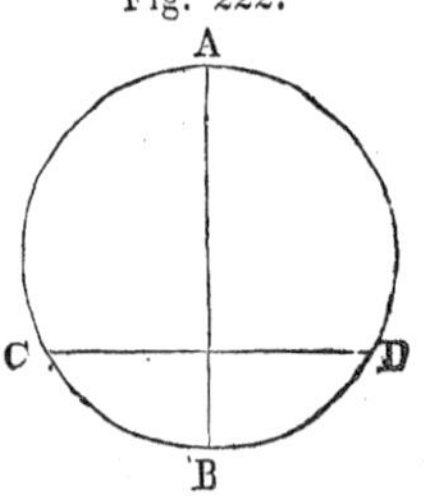

Four were used on the large Theodolite of the English Ordnance Survey, two, A and B, opposite to each other, and two, C and D, 120° from A and from each other. The half-sum or arithmetical mean, of A and B was taken, then the mean of A, C, and D, and then the mean of these two means. But this was wrong, for it gave too great value to the reading of A, and also to B, though in a less degree; since the share of each Vernier in the final mean was as follows: A = 5, B = 3, C = 2, D = 2. This results from the expression for that mean, $= \frac{1}{2}\left(\frac{A + B}{2} + \frac{A + C + D}{3}\right) = \frac{1}{12}$ (5 A + 3 B + 2 C + 2 D).

(335) The graduated circle. This is divided into three hundred and sixty equal parts, or Degrees, and each of these is subdivided into two or three parts or more, according to the size of the instrument. In the first case, the smallest division on the circle will of course be 30′; in the second case 20′. More precise reading, to single minutes or even less, is effected by means of the Vernier of the index, all the varieties of which will be fully explained in the next chapter. The numbers run from 0° around to 360°, which number is necessarily at the same point as the 0, or *zero-point.** Each tenth degree is usually numbered, each fifth degree is distinguished by a longer line of division, and each degree-division line is longer than those of the sub-divisions. A magnifying glass is needed for reading the divisions with ease. In the Theodolite engraving this is shown at *m*. It should be attached to each Vernier.

(336) Movements. When the line of sight of the telescope is directed to a distant well-defined point, the unaided hand of the observer cannot move it with sufficient delicacy and precision to make the intersection of the cross hairs exactly cover or "bisect" that point. To effect this, a clamp, and a Tangent, or slow-motion, screw are required. This arrangement, as applied to the movement of the upper, or Vernier plate, consists of a short piece of brass, D, which is attached to the Vernier plate, and through which passes a long and fine-threaded "Tangent-screw," *t*. The other end of this screw enters into and carries the *clamp*. This consists of two pieces of brass, which, by turning the clamp-screw *c*, which passes through them on the outside, can be made to take

* In some instruments there is another concentric circle on which the degrees are also numbered from 0° to 90° as on the compass circle.

hold of and pinch tightly the edge of the lower circle, which lies between them on the inside. The upper circle is now prevented from moving on the lower one; for, the tangent-screw, passing through hollow screws in both the clamp and the piece D, keeps them at a fixed distance apart, so that they cannot move to or from one another, nor consequently the two circles to which they are respectively made fast. But when this tangent-screw is turned by its milled-head, it gives the clamp and with it the upper plate a smooth and slow motion, backward or forward, whence it is called the "Slow motion screw," as well as "Tangent-screw," from the direction in which it acts. It is always placed at the south end of the compass-box.

A little different arrangement is employed to give a similar motion to the lower circle (which we have hitherto regarded as immovable) on the body of the instrument. Its axis is embraced by a brass ring, into which enters another tangent-screw, which also passes through a piece fastened to the plate P. The clamp-screw, C, causes the ring to pinch and hold immovably the axis of the lower circle, while a turn of the Tangent-screw, T, will slowly move the clamp ring itself, and therefore with it the lower circle. When the clamp is loosened, the lower circle, and with it every thing above it, has a perfectly free motion. A recent improvement is the employment for this purpose of *two* tangent screws, pressing against opposite sides of a piece projecting from the clamp-ring. One is tightened as the other is loosened, and a very steady motion is thus obtained.

(337) Levels. Since the object of the instrument is to measure *horizontal* angles, the circular plate on which they are measured must itself be made horizontal. Whether it is so or not is known by means of two small levels placed on the plate at right angles to each other. Each consists of a glass tube, slightly curved upward in its middle and so nearly filled with alcohol, that only a small bubble of air is left in the tube. This always rises to the highest part of the tubes. They are so "adjusted" (as will be explained in chapter III) that when this bubble of air is in the middle of the tubes, or its ends equidistant from the central mark, the plate on which they are fastened shall be level, which way soever it may be turned.

The levels are represented in the figure of the Transit, on page 212, as being under the plate. They are sometimes placed above it. In that case, the Verniers are moved to one side, between the feet of the standards, and one of the levels is fixed between the standards above one of the Verniers, and the other on the plate at the south end of the compass-box.

(338) Parallel Plates. To raise or lower either side of the circle, so as to bring the bubbles into the centres of the tubes, requires more gentle and steady movements than the unaided hands can give, and is attained by the Parallel Plates P, P′, (so called because they are never parallel except by accident), and their four screws Q, Q, Q, Q, which hold the plates firmly apart, and, by being turned in or out, raise or lower one side or the other of the upper plate P′, and thereby of the graduated circle. The two plates are held together by a ball and socket joint. To level the instrument, loosen the lower clamp and turn the circle till each level is parallel to the vertical plane passing through a pair of opposite screws. Then take hold of two opposite screws and turn them simultaneously and equally, but in contrary directions, screw-

Fig. 223.

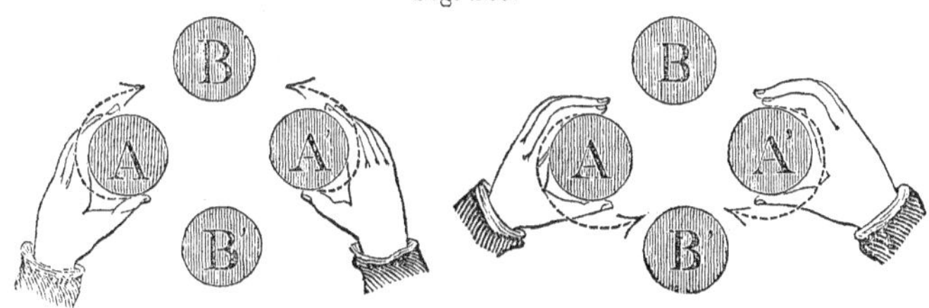

ing one in and the other out, as shown by the arrows in the figures. A rule easily remembered is that both thumbs must turn in, or both out. The movements represented in the first of these figures would raise the left-hand side of the circle and lower the right-hand side. The movements of the second figure would produce the reverse effect. Care is needed to turn the opposite screws equally, so that they shall not become so loose that the instrument will rock, or so tight as to be cramped. When this last occurs, one of the other pair should be loosened.

Sometimes one of each pair of the screws is replaced by a strong spring against which the remaining screws act.

The French and German instruments are usually supported by only three screws. In such cases, one level is brought parallel to one pair of screws and levelled by them, and the other level has its bubble brought to its centre by the third screw. If there is only one level on the instrument, it is first brought parallel to one pair of screws and levelled, and is then turned one quarter around so as to be perpendicular to them and over the third screw, and the operation is repeated.

(339) Watch Telescope. A second Telescope is sometimes attached to the lower part of the instrument. When a number of angles are to be observed from any one station, direct the upper and principal Telescope to the first object, and then direct the lower one to any other well-defined point. Then make all the desired observations with the upper Telescope, and when they are finished, look again through the lower one, to see that it and therefore the divided circle has not been moved by the movements of the Vernier plate. The French call this the *Witness Telescope*, (*Lunette temoin*).

(340) The Compass. Upon the upper plate is fixed a compass. Its use has been fully explained in Part III. It is little used in connection with the Transit or Theodolite, which are so incomparably more accurate, except as a "check," or rough test of the accuracy of the angles taken, which should about equal the difference of the magnetic bearings. Its use will be farther noticed in Chapter IV, on "Field Work."

(341) The Surveyor's Transit. In this instrument (so named by its introducers, Messrs. Gurley, and shown in Fig. 224), the Vernier-plate, which carries the standards and telescope, is *under* the plate which carries the graduated circle, and the compass is attached to the latter. By this arrangement, when the Vernier is set at any angle, the line of sight of the telescope will make that angle with the N. and S. lines of the compass. Consequently, this instrument can be used precisely like the Vernier compass

Fig. 224.

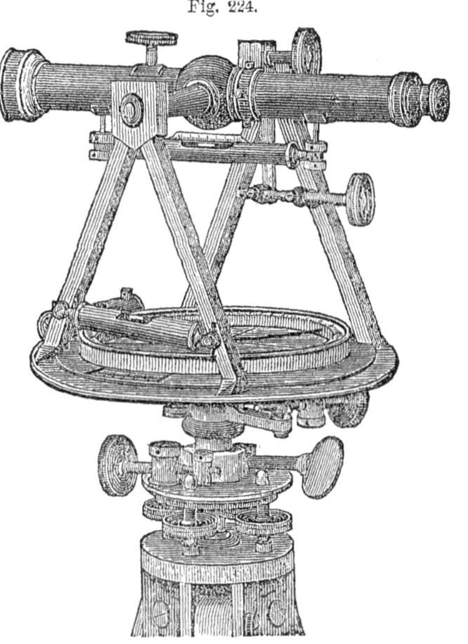

to allow for magnetic variation, and thus to run out a line with true bearings, as in Art. **(312)**, or to run out old lines, allowing for the secular variation, as in Art. **(321)**.

The instrument may also be used like the common Engineer's Transit. The compass, however, will then not give the bearings of the lines surveyed, but they can easily be deduced from that of any one line.

(342) Goniasmometre. A very compact instrument to which the above name has been given in France, where it is much used, is shown in the figure. The upper half of the cylinder is movable on its lower half. The observations may be taken through the slits, as in the Surveyor's Cross, or a Telescope may be added to it. Readings may be taken both from the compass, and from the divided edge of the lower half of the cylinder, by means of a Vernier on the upper half.*

Fig. 224'.

* The proper care of instruments must not be overlooked. If varnished, they should be wiped gently with fine and clean linen. If polished with oil, they should be rubbed more strongly. The parts neither varnished nor oiled, should be cleaned with Spanish white and alcohol. Varnished wood, when spotted, should be wiped with very soft linen, moistened with a little olive oil or alcohol. Unpainted wood is cleaned with sand-paper. Apply olive oil where steel rubs against brass; and wax softened by tallow where brass rubs against brass.—Clean the glasses with kid or buck skin. Wash them, if dirtied, with alcohol.

CHAPTER II.

VERNIERS.

(343) Definition. A Vernier is a contrivance for measuring smaller portions of space than those into which a line is actually divided. It consists of a second line or scale, movable by the side of the first, and divided into equal parts, which are a very little shorter or longer than the parts into which the first line is divided. This small difference is the space which we are thus enabled to measure.*

The Vernier scale is usually constructed by taking a length equal to any number of parts on the divided line, and then dividing this length into a number of equal parts, one more or one less than the number into which the same length on the original line is divided.

(344) Illustration. The figure represents (to twice the real size) a scale of inches divided into tenths, with a Vernier scale beside it, by which hundredths of an inch can be measured. The

Fig. 225.

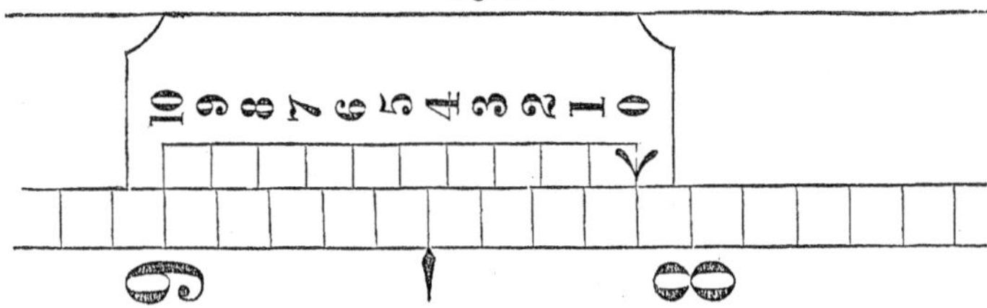

Vernier is made by setting off on it 9 tenths of an inch, and dividing that length into 10 equal parts. Each space on the Vernier is therefore equal to a tenth of nine-tenths of an inch, or to nine-hundredths of an inch, and is consequently one-hundredth of an inch shorter than one of the divisions of the original scale. The

* The Vernier is so named from its inventor, in 1631. The name "Nonius," often improperly given to it, belongs to an entirely different contrivance for a similar object.

first space of the Vernier will therefore fall short of, or be overlapped by, the first space on the scale by this one-hundredth of an inch; the second space of the Vernier will fall short by two-hundredths of an inch; and so on. If then the Vernier be moved up by the side of the original scale, so that the line marked 1 coincides, or forms one straight line, with the line of the scale which was just above it, we know that the Vernier has been moved one-hundredth of an inch. If the line marked 2 comes to coincide with a line of the scale, the Vernier has moved up two-hundredths of an inch; and so for other numbers. If the position of the

Fig. 226.

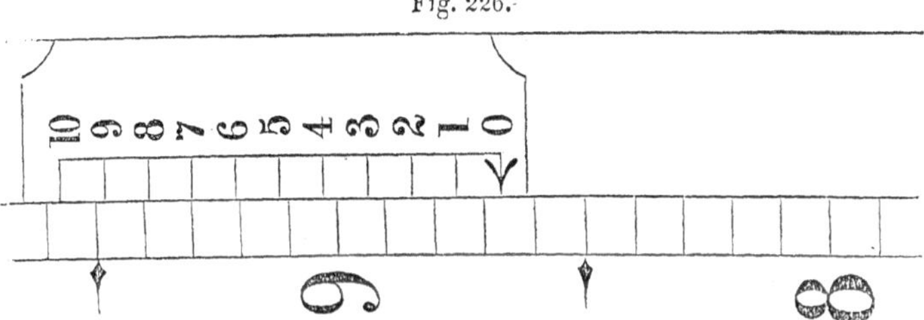

Vernier be as in this figure, the line marked 7 on the Vernier corresponding with some line on the scale, the zero line of the Vernier is 7 hundredths of an inch above the division of the scale next below this zero line. If this division be, as in the figure, 8 inches and 6 tenths, the reading will be 8.67 inches.*

A Vernier like this is used on some levelling rods, being engraved on the sides of the opening in the part of the target above its middle line. The rod being divided into hundredths of a foot, this Vernier reads to thousandths of a foot. It is also used on some French Mountain Barometers, which are divided to hundredths of a *metre*, and thus read to thousandths of that unit.

(345) General rules. *To find what any Vernier reads to*, i. e. to determine how small a distance it can measure, observe how many parts on the original line are equal to the same number increased or diminished by one on the Vernier, and divide the

* The student will do well to draw such a scale and Vernier on two slips of thick paper, and move one beside the other till he can read them in any possible position; and so with the following Verniers.

length of a part on the original line by this last number. It will give the required distance.*

To read any Vernier, firstly, look at the zero line of the Ver nier, (which is sometimes marked by an arrow-head), and if it coincides with any division of the scale, that will be the correct reading, and the Vernier divisions are not needed. But if, as usually happens, the zero line of the Vernier comes between any two divisions of the scale, note the nearest next less division on the scale, and then look along the Vernier till you come to some line on it which exactly coincides, or forms a straight line, with some line (no matter which) on the fixed scale. The number of this line *on the Vernier* (the 7th in the last figure) tells that so many of the sub-divisions which the Vernier indicates, are to be added to the reading of the entire divisions on the scale.

When several lines on the Vernier appear to coincide equally with lines of the scale, take the middle line.

When no line coincides, but one line on the Vernier is on one side of a line on the scale, and the next line on the Vernier is as far on the other side of it, the true reading is midway between those indicated by these two lines.

(346) Retrograde Verniers. The spaces of the Vernier in modern instruments, are usually each shorter than those on the scale, a certain number of parts on the scale being divided into a larger number of parts on the Vernier.† In the contrary case,‡ there is the inconvenience of being obliged to number the lines of the Vernier and to count their coincidences with the lines of the scale, in a retrograde or contrary direction to that in which the numbers on the scale run. We will call such arrangements *retrograde* Verniers.

* In Algebraic language, let s equal the length of one part on the original line, and v the unknown length of one part on the Vernier. Let m of the former $=$ $m+1$ of the latter. Then $ms = (m+1)\,v$. $v = \frac{m}{m+1}s$. $s - v = s - \frac{m}{m+1}s = \frac{s}{m+1}$. If $ms = (m-1)\,v$, then $v - s = \frac{s}{m-1}$.

† i. e. Algebraically, $v = \frac{m}{m+1}\,s$. ‡ i. e. When $v = \frac{m}{m-1}s$.

(347) Illustration. In this figure, the scale, as before, represents (to twice the real size) inches divided into tenths, but the Vernier is made by dividing 11 parts of the scale into 10 equal

Fig. 227.

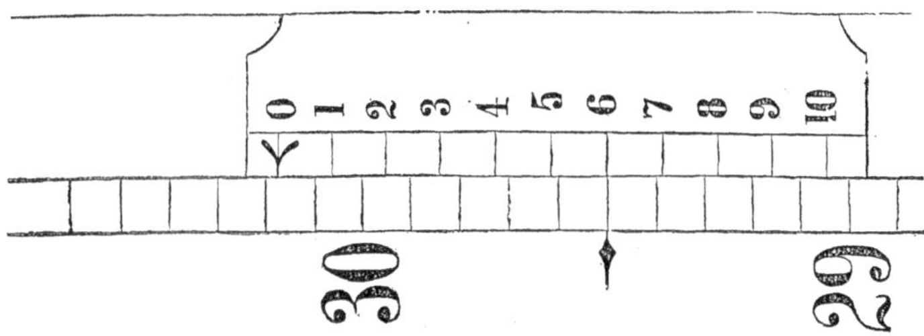

parts, each of which is therefore one-tenth of eleven-tenths of an inch, i. e. eleven-hundredths of an inch, or a tenth and a hundredth. Each space of the Vernier therefore overlaps a space on the scale by one-hundredth of an inch. The manner of reading this Vernier is the same as in the last one, except that the numbers run in a reverse direction. The reading of the figure is 30.16.

This Vernier is the one generally applied to the common Barometer, the zero point of the Vernier being brought to the level of the top of the mercury, whose height it then measures. It is also employed for levelling rods which read downwards from the middle of the target.

(348) The figure below represents (to double size) the usual scale of the English Mountain Barometer.* The scale is first divided into inches. These are subdivided into tenths by the

Fig. 228.

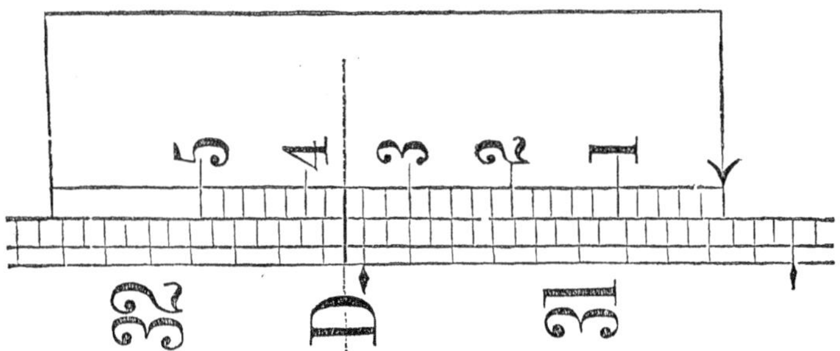

* This figure, and others in this chapter, are from Bree's "Present Practice."

longer lines, and the shorter lines again divide these into half tenths, or to 5 hundredths. 24 of these smaller parts are set off on the Vernier, and divided into 25 equal parts, each of which is therefore $= \frac{24 \times .05}{25} = .048$ inch, and is shorter than a division of the scale by $.050 - .048 = .002$, or two thousandths of an inch, a twenty-fifth part of a division on the scale, to which minuteness the Vernier can therefore read. The reading in the figure is 30.686, (30.65 by the scale and .036 by the Vernier), the dotted line marked D showing where the coincidence takes place.

(349) Circle divided into degrees. The following illustrations apply to the measurements of angles, the circle being variously divided. In this article, the circle is supposed to be divided into degrees.

If 6 spaces on the Vernier are found to be equal to 5 on the circle, the Vernier can read to one-sixth of a space on the circle, i. e. to 10′.

If 10 spaces on the Vernier are equal to 9 on the circle, the Vernier can read to one-tenth of a space on the circle, i. e. to 6′.

If 12 spaces on the Vernier are equal to 11 on the circle, the Vernier can read to one-twelfth of a space on the circle, i. e. to 5′.

Fig. 229.

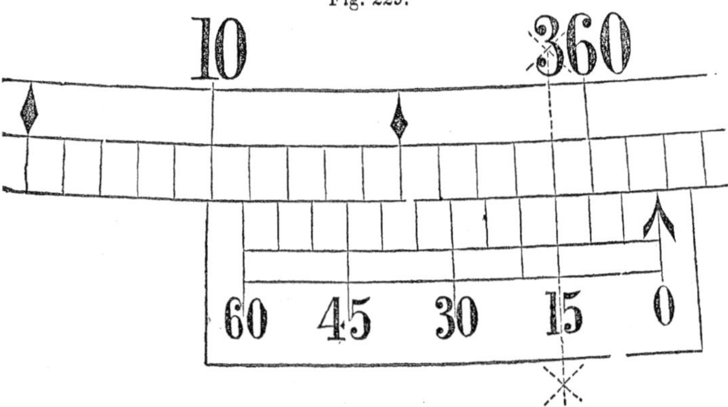

The above figure shows such an arrangement. The index, or zero, of the Vernier is at a point beyond 358°, a certain distance, which the coincidence of the third line of the Vernier (as indicated by the dotted and crossed line) shows to be 15′. The whole reading is therefore 358° 15′.

If 20 spaces on the Vernier are equal to 19 on the circle, the Vernier can read to one-twentieth of a division on the circle, i. e. to 3′. English compasses, or "Circumferentors," are sometimes thus arranged.

If 60 spaces on the Vernier are equal to 59 on the circle, the Vernier can read to one-sixtieth of a division on the circle, i. e. to 1′.

(350) Circle divided to 30′. Such a graduation is a very common one. The Vernier may be variously constructed.

Suppose 30 spaces on the Vernier to be equal to 29 on the circle. Each space on the Vernier will be $= \frac{29 \times 30'}{30} = 29'$, and will therefore be less than a space of the circle by 1′, to which the Vernier will then read.

Fig. 230.

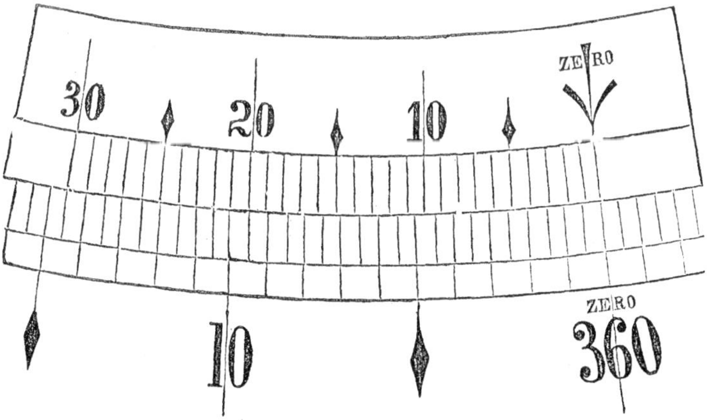

The above figure shows this arrangement. The reading is 0°, or 360°.

In the following figure, the dotted and crossed line shows what divisions coincide, and the reading is 20° 10′; the Vernier being the same as in the preceding figure, and its zero being at a point of the circle 10′ beyond 20°.

Fig. 231.

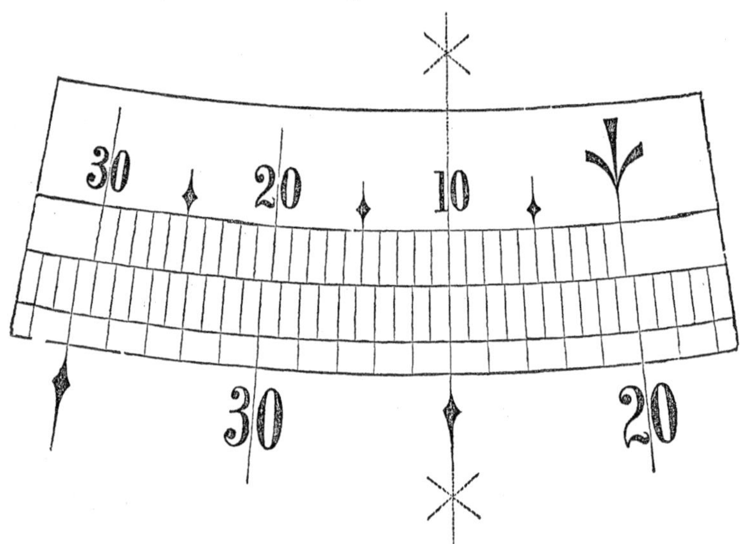

In the following figure, the reading is 20° 40′, the index being at a point beyond 20° 30′, and the additional space being shown by the Vernier to be 10′.

Fig. 232.

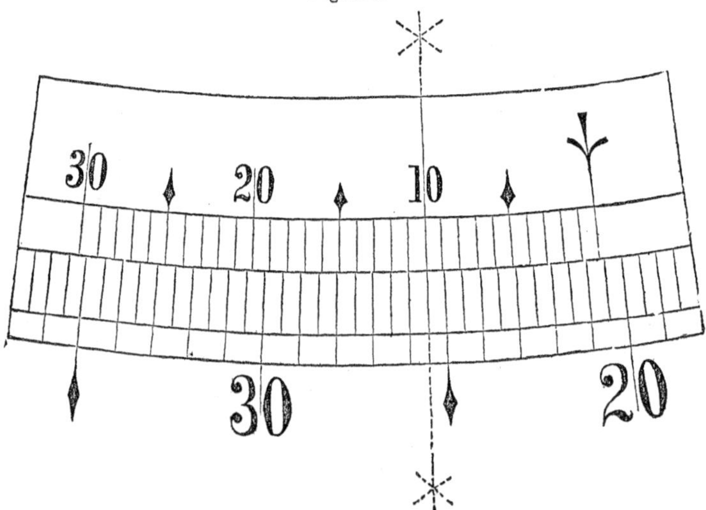

Sometimes 30 spaces on the Vernier are equal to 31 on the circle. Each space on the Vernier will therefore be $= \frac{31 \times 30'}{30} = 31'$, and will be longer than a space on the circle by 1′, to which it will therefore read, as in the last case, but the Vernier will be "retrograde." This is the Vernier of the compass, Fig. 148. The peculiar manner in which it is there applied is shown in Fig. 239.

If 15 spaces on the Vernier are equal to 16 on the circle, each space on the Vernier will be $= \frac{16 \times 30'}{15} = 32'$, and the Vernier will therefore read to 2′.

(351) Circle divided to 20′. If 20 spaces on the Vernier are equal to 19 on the circle, each space of the latter will be $= \frac{19 \times 20'}{20} = 19'$, and the Vernier will read to $20' - 19' = 1'$.

If 40 spaces on the Vernier are equal to 41 on the circle, each space on the Vernier will be $= \frac{41 \times 20'}{40} = 20\frac{1}{2}'$; and the Vernier will therefore read to $20\frac{1}{2}' - 20' = 30''$. It will be retrograde. In the following figure the reading is 360°, or 0°; and it will be seen that the 40 spaces on the Vernier (numbered to whole minutes) are equal to 13° 40′ on the limb, i. e. to 41 spaces, each of 20′.

Fig.233.

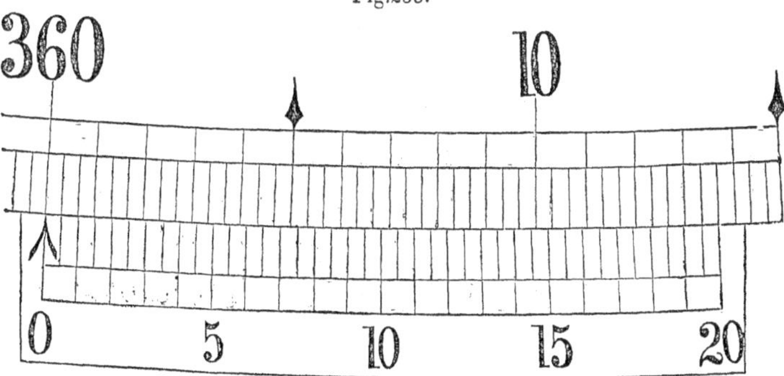

If 60 spaces on the Vernier are equal to 59 on the circle, each of the former will be $= \frac{59 \times 20'}{60} = 19'\ 40''$, and the Vernier will therefore read to 20′ — 19′ 40″ = 20″. The following figure shows such an arrangement. The reading in that position would be 40° 46′ 20″.

Fig. 234.

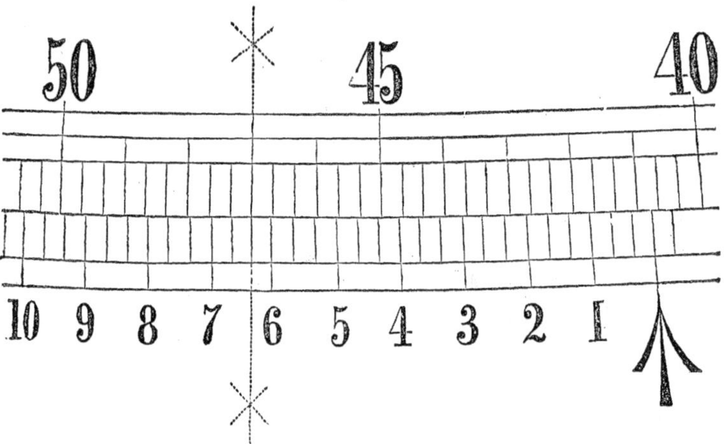

(352) Circle divided to 15′. If 60 spaces on the Vernier are equal to 59 on the circle, each space on the Vernier will be = $\frac{59 \times 15'}{60}$ = 14′ 45″, and the Vernier will read to 15″. In the following figure the reading is 10° 20′ 45″, the index pointing to 10° 15′, and something more, which the Vernier shows to be 5′ 45′

Fig. 235.

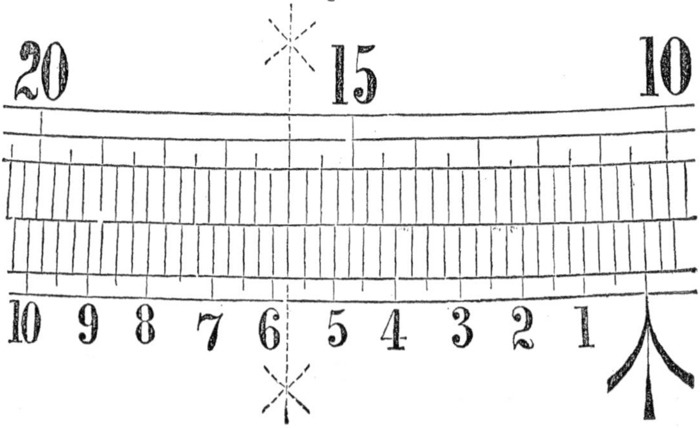

(353) Circle divided to 10′. If 60 spaces on the Vernier be equal to 59 on the limb, the Vernier will read to 10″. In the following figure, the reading is 7° 25′ 40″, the reading on the circle being 7° 20′, and the Vernier showing the remaining space to be 5′ 40″.

Fig. 236.

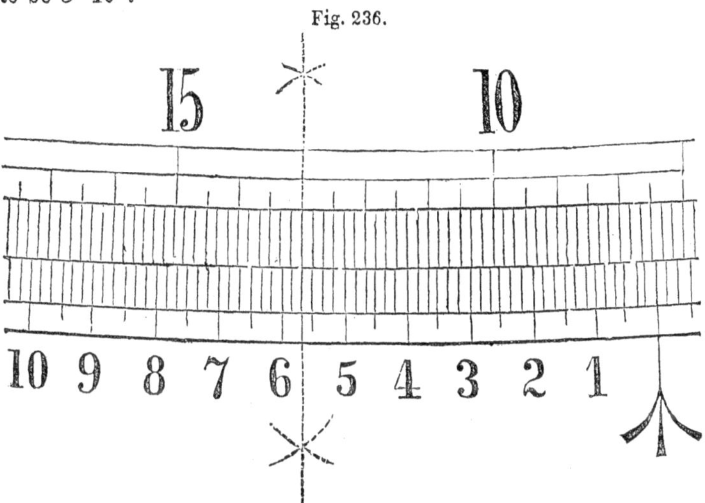

(354) Reading backwards. When an index carrying a Vernier is moved backwards, or in a contrary direction to that in which the numbers on the circle run, if we wish to read the space which it has passed over in this direction from the zero point, the Vernier must be read backwards, (i. e. the highest number be called 0), or its actual reading must be subtracted from the value of the smallest space on the circle. The reason is plain; for, since the Vernier shows how far the index, moving in one direction, has gone past one division line, the distance which it is from the next division line (which it may be supposed to have passed, moving in a contrary direction), will be the difference between the reading and the value of one space.

Thus, in Fig. 229, page 232, the reading is 358° 15′. But, counting backwards from the 360°, or zero point, it is 1° 45′.

Caution on this point is particularly necessary in using small angles of deflection for railroad curves.

(355) Arc of excess. On the sextant and similar instruments, the divisions of the limb are carried onward a short distance beyond the zero point. This portion of the limb is called the "Arc of excess." When the index of the Vernier points to this arc, the reading must be made as explained in the last article. Thus, in the figure, the reading on the arc from the zero of the limb to the

Fig. 237

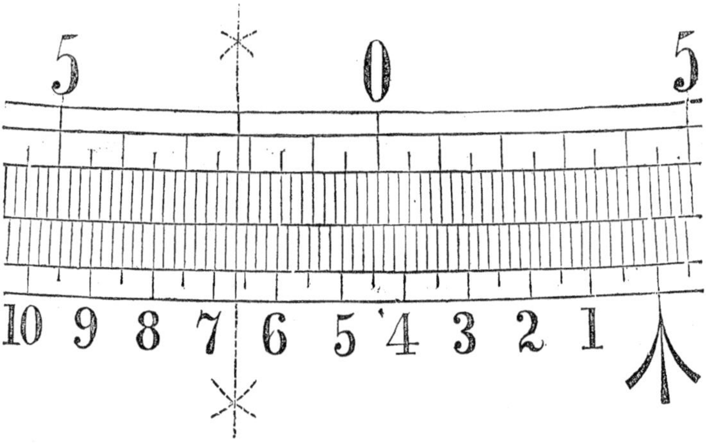

zero of the Vernier is 4° 20′, and something more, and the reading of the Vernier from 10 towards to the right, where the lines coincide, is 3′ 20″, (or it is 10′ — 6′ 40″ = 3′ 20″), and the entire reading is therefore 4° 23′ 20″.

(356) Double Verniers. To avoid the inconveniences of reading backwards, double Verniers are sometimes used. The figure below shows one applied to a Transit. Each of the Verniers is

Fig. 238.

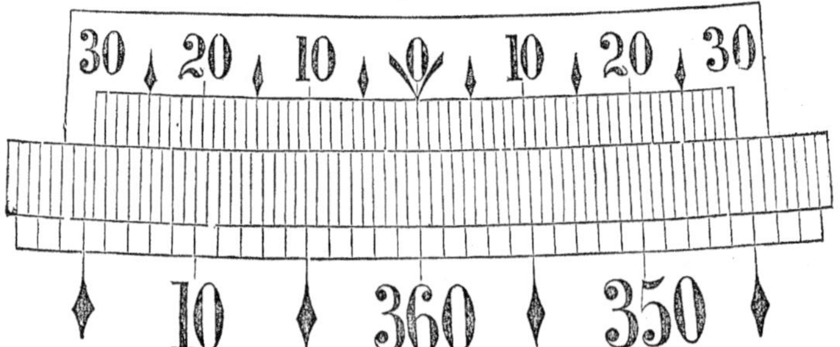

like the one described in Art. (350), Figs. 230, 231, and 232. When the degrees are counted to the left, or as the numbers run, as is usual, the left-hand Vernier is to be read, as in Art. (350); but when the degrees are counted to the right, from the 360° line, the right-hand Vernier is to be used.

(357) Compass-Vernier. Another form of double Vernier, often applied to the compass, is shown in the following figure. The

Fig. 239.

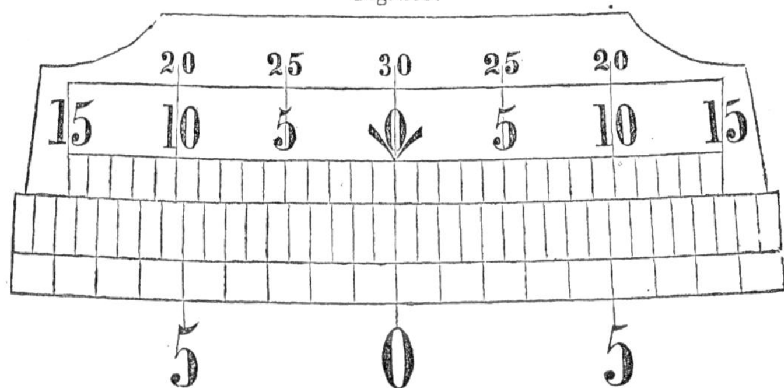

limb is divided to half degrees, and the Vernier reads to minutes, 30 parts on it being equal to 31 on the limb. But the Vernier is only half as long as in the previous case, going only to 15′, the upper figures on one half being a sort of continuation of the lower figures on the other half. Thus in moving the index to the right, read the *lower* figures on the left hand Vernier (it being retrograde) at any coincidence, when the space passed over is less than 15′; but if it be more, read the *upper* figures on the right hand Vernier: and *vice versa*.

CHAPTER III.

ADJUSTMENTS.

(358) THE purposes for which the Transit and Theodolite (as well as most surveying and astronomical instruments) are to be used, require and presuppose certain parts and lines of the instrument to be placed in certain directions with respect to others; these respective directions being usually parallel or perpendicular. Such arrangements of their parts are called their *Adjustments.* The same word is also applied to placing these lines in these directions. In the following explanations the operations which determine whether these adjustments are correct, will be called their *Verifications;* and the making them right, if they are not so, their *Rectifications.**

(359) In observations of horizontal angles with the Transit or the Theodolite,† it is required,

1° That the circular plates shall be horizontal in whatever way they may be turned around.

2° That the Telescope, when pointed forward, shall look in precisely the reverse of its direction when pointed backward, i. e. that its two lines of sight (or lines of collimation) forward and backward shall lie in the same plane.

3° That the Telescope in turning upward or downward, shall move in a truly vertical plane, in order that the angle measured between a low object and a high one, may be precisely the same as would be the angle measured between the low object and a point exactly under the high object, and in the same horizontal plane as the low one.

* It has been well said, that "in the present state of science it may be laid down as a maxim, that every instrument should be so contrived, that the observer may easily examine and rectify the principal parts; for, however careful the instrument-maker may be, however perfect the execution thereof, it is not possible that any instrument should long remain accurately fixed in the position in which it came out of the maker's hands."—*Adams'* "*Geometrical and Graphical Essays,*" 1791.

† The Theodolite adjustments which relate only to levelling, or to measuring vertical angles, will not be here discussed.

We shall see that all these adjustments are finally resolvable into these; 1st. Making the vertical axis of the instrument perpendicular to the plane of the levels; 2d. Making the line of collimation perpendicular to its axis; and 3d. Making this axis parallel to the plane of the levels. They are all best tested by the invaluable principle of " Reversion."

We have now, firstly, to examine whether these things *are* so, that is, to "verify" the adjustments; and, secondly, if we find that they are not so, to *make* them so, i. e. to "rectify," or "adjust" them correctly. The above three requirements produce as many corresponding adjustments.

(360) First adjustment. *To cause the circle to be horizontal in every position.**

Verification.—Turn the Vernier plate which carries the levels, till one of them is parallel to one pair of the parallel plate screws. The other will then be parallel to the other pair. Bring each bubble to the middle of its tube, by that pair of screws to which it is parallel. Then turn the vernier plate half way around, i. e. till the index has passed over 180°. If the bubbles remain in the centres of the tubes, they are in adjustment. If either of them runs to one end of the tube, it requires rectification.

Rectification.—The fault which is to be rectified is that the plane of the level (i. e. the plane tangent to the highest point of the level tube) is not perpendicular to the vertical axis, AA in figure 214, on which the plate turns. For, let AB represent this

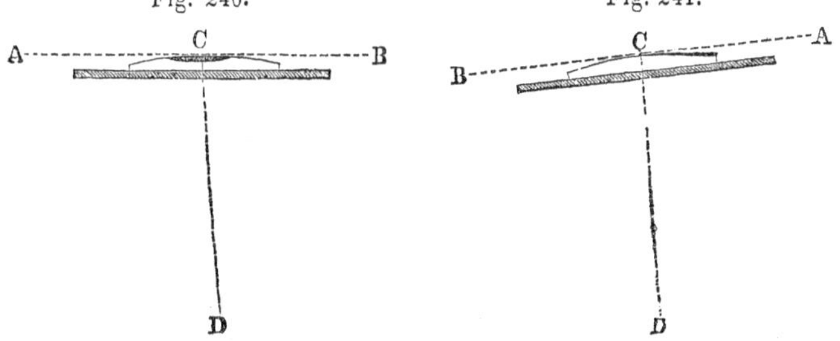

Fig. 240. Fig. 241.

plane, seen edgeways, and CD the centre line of the vertical axis,

* This applies equally to the Transit and the Theodolite.

which is here drawn as making an acute angle with this plane on the right hand side. The first figure represents the bubble brought to the centre of the tube. The second figure represents the plate turned half around. The centre line of the axis is supposed to remain unmoved. The acute angle will now be on the left hand side, and the plate will no longer be horizontal. Consequently the bubble will run to the higher end of the tube. The rectification necessary is evidently to raise one end of the tube and lower the other. The real error has been doubled to the eye by the reversion. Half of the motion of the bubble was caused by the tangent plane not being perpendicular to the axis, and half by this axis not being vertical. Therefore raise or lower one end of the level by the screws which fasten it to the plate, till the bubble comes about *half way* back to the centre, and then bring it quite back by turning its pair of parallel plate screws. Then again reverse the vernier plate 180°. The bubble should now remain in the centre. If not, the operation should be repeated. The same must be done with the other level if required. Then the bubbles will remain in the centre during a complete revolution. This proves that the axis of the vernier plate is then vertical; and as it has been fixed by the maker perpendicular to the plate, the latter must then be horizontal.

It is also necessary to examine whether the bubbles remain in the centre, when the divided circle is turned round on its axis. If not, the axes of the two plates are not parallel to each other. The defect can be remedied only by the maker; for if the bubbles be altered so as to be right for this reversal, they will be wrong for the vernier plate reversal

(361) Second adjustment. *To cause the line of collimation to revolve in a plane.**

Verification. Set up the Transit in the middle of a level piece of ground, as at A in the figure. Level it carefully. Set a stake, with a nail driven into its head, or a chain pin, as far from the instrument as it is distinctly visible, as at B. Direct the telescope

* This adjustment is not the same in the Transit and in the Theodolite. That for the Transit will be first given, and that for the Theodolite in the next article.

Fig. 242

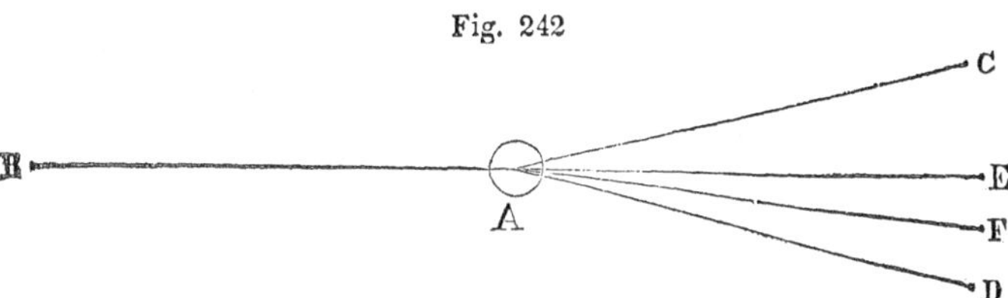

to it, and fix the intersection of the cross-hairs very precisely upon it. Clamp the instrument. Measure from A to B. Then turn over the telescope, and set another stake at an equal distance from the Transit, and also precisely in the line of sight. If the line of collimation has *not* continued in the same plane during its half-revolution, this stake will not be at E, but to one side, as at C. To discover the truth, loosen the clamp and turn the vernier plate half around without touching the telescope. Sight to B, as at first, and again clamp it. Then turn over the telescope, and the line of sight will strike, as at D in the figure, as far to the right of the point, as it did before to its left.

Rectification. The fault which is to be rectified, is that the line of collimation of the telescope is not perpendicular to the horizontal axis on which the telescope revolves. This will be seen by the figures, which represent the position of the lines in each of the four

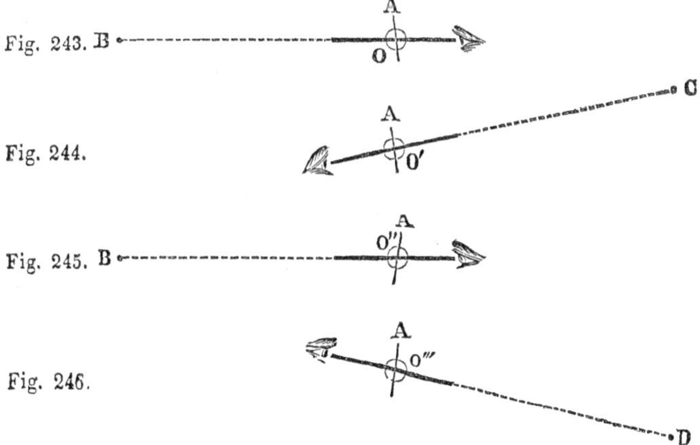

observations which have been made. In each of the figures the long thick line represents the telescope, and the short one the axis on which it turns. In Fig. 243 the line of sight is directed to B.

In Fig. 244 the telescope has been turned over, and with it the axis, so that the obtuse angle, marked O in the first figure, has taken the place, O′, of the acute angle, and the telescope points to C instead of to E. In Fig. 245 the vernier plate has been turned half around so as to point to B again, and the same obtuse angle has got around to O″. In Fig. 246 the telescope has been turned over, the obtuse angle is at O‴, and the telescope now points to D.

To make the line of collimation perpendicular to the axis, the former must have its direction changed. This is effected by moving the vertical hair the proper distance to one side. As was explained in Art. (**330**), and represented in Fig. 217, the cross-hairs are on a ring held by four screws. By loosening the left-hand screw and tightening the right-hand one, the ring, and with it the cross-hairs, will be drawn to the right; and *vice versa.* Two holes at right angles to each other pass through the outer heads of the screws. Into these holes a stout steel wire is inserted, and the screws can thus be turned around. Screws so made are called "capstan-headed." One of the other pair of screws may need to be loosened to avoid straining the threads. In some French instruments, one of each pair of screws is replaced by a spring.

To find how much to move this vertical hair, measure from C to D, Fig. 242, page 243. Set a stake at the middle point E, and set another at the point F, midway between D and E. Move the vertical hair till the line of sight strikes F. Then the instrument is adjusted; and if the line of sight be now directed to E, it will strike B, when the telescope is turned over; since the hair is moved half of the doubled error, DE. The operation will generally require to be repeated, not being quite perfected at first.

It should be remembered, that if the Telescope used does not invert objects, its eye-piece will do so. Consequently, with such a telescope, if it seems that the vertical hair should be moved to the left, it must be moved to the right, and *vice versa.* An inverting telescope does not invert the cross-hairs.

If the young surveyor has any doubts as to the perfection of his rectification, he may set another stake exactly under the instrument by means of a plumb-line suspended from its centre; and then, in like manner, set his Transit over B or E. He will find that the other two stakes, A and the extreme one, *are* in the same straight line with his instrument.

In some instruments, the horizontal axis of the telescope can be taken out of its supports, and turned over, end for end. In such a case, the line of sight may be directed to any well defined point, and the axis then taken out and turned over. If the line of sight again strikes the same point, this line is perpendicular to the axis. If not, the apparent error is double the real error, as appears from the figures, the obtuse angle O coming to O′, and the desired per-

Fig. 247.

Fig. 248.

pendicular line falling at C midway between B and B′. The rectification may be made as before; or, in some large instruments, in which the telescope is supported on Ys, by moving one of the Ys laterally.

(362) The Theodolite must be treated differently, since its telescope does not reverse. One substitute for this reversal, when it is desired to range out a line forward and backward from one station, is, after sighting in one direction, to take the telescope out of the Ys and turn it end for end, to sight in the reverse direction. This it can be made to do by adjusting its line of collimation as explained in the last article. Another substitute is, after sighting in one direction, and noting the reading, to turn the vernier plate around exactly 180°. But this supposes not only that the graduation is perfectly accurate, but also that the line of collimation is exactly over the centre of the circle. To test this, after sighting to a point, and noting the reading, take the telescope out of the Ys and turn it end for end, and then turn the vernier plate around exactly 180°. If the line of sight again strikes the same point, the latter condition exists. If not, the maker must remedy the defect. This error of eccentricity is similar to that explained with respect to the compass, in the latter part of Art. (**226**).

(363) Third adjustment. *To cause the line of collimation to revolve in a vertical plane.**

Verification. Suspend a long plumb-line from some high point. Set the instrument near this line, and level it carefully. Direct the telescope to the plumb-line, and see if the intersection of the cross-hairs follows and remains upon this line, when the telescope is turned up and down. If it does, it moves in a vertical plane.

The angle of a new and well-built house will form an imperfect substitute for the plumb-line.

Otherwise; the instrument being set up and levelled as above, place a basin of some reflecting liquid (quicksilver being the best, though molasses, or oil, or even water, will answer, though less perfectly,) so that the top of a steeple, or other point of a high object, can be seen in it through the telescope by reflection. Make the intersection of the cross-hairs cover it. Then turn up the telescope, and if the intersection of the cross-hairs bisects also the object seen directly, the line of sight has moved in a vertical plane. If a star be taken as the object, the star and its reflection will be equivalent (if it be nearly over head) to a plumb-line at least fifty million million miles long.

Otherwise; set the instrument as close as possible to the base of a steeple, or other high object; level it, and direct it to the top of the steeple, or to some other elevated and well defined point. Clamp the plates. Turn down the telescope, and set up a pin in the ground precisely "in line." Then loosen the clamp, turn over the telescope, and turn it half-way around, or so far as to again sight to the high point. Clamp the plates, and again turn down the telescope. If the line of sight again strikes the pin, the telescope has moved in a vertical plane. If not, the apparent error is double the real error. For, let S be the top of the steeple,

Fig. 249

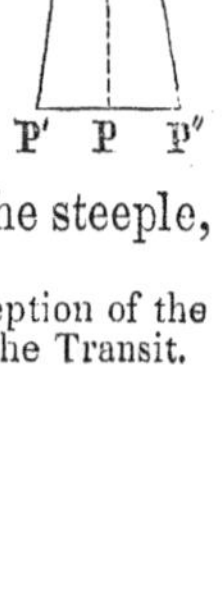

S

P′ P P″

* This applies to both the Transit and the Theodolite, with the exception of the method of verification by the steeple and pin, which applies only to the Transit.

(Fig. 249) and P′ the pin; then the plane in which the telescope moves, seen edgewise, is SP′; and, after being turned around, the line of sight moves in the plane SP″, as far to one side of the vertical plane SP, as SP′ was on the other side of it.

Rectification. Since the second adjustment causes the line of sight to move in a plane perpendicular to the axis on which it turns, it will move in a vertical plane if that axis be horizontal. It may be made so by filing off the feet of the standards which support the higher end of the axis. This will be best done by the maker. In some instruments one end of the axis can be raised or lowered.

Fig. 250.

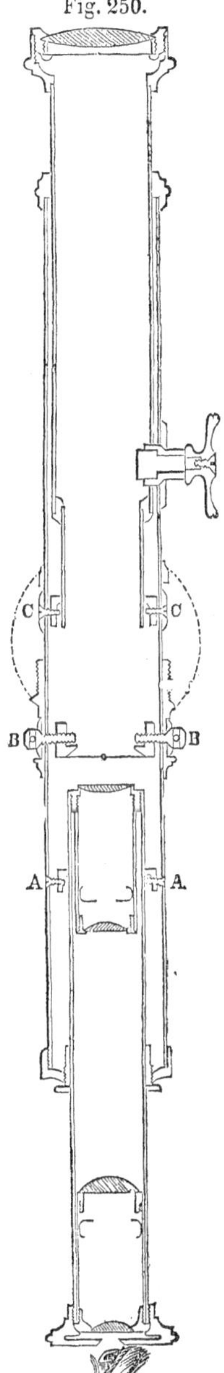

(364) Centring eye-piece. In some instruments, such as that of which a longitudinal section is shown in the margin, the inner end of the eye-piece may be moved so that the cross-hairs shall be seen precisely in the centre of its field of view. This is done by means of four screws, arranged in pairs, like those of the cross-hair-ring screws, and capable of moving the eye-piece up and down, and to right or left, by loosening one and tightening the opposite one. Two of them are shown at A, A, in the figure; in which B, B, are two of the cross-hair screws.

(365) Centring object-glass. In some instruments four screws, similarly arranged, two of which are shown at C, C, can move, in any direction, the inner end of the slide which carries the object-glass. The necessity for such an arrangement arises from the impossibility of drawing a tube perfectly straight. Consequently, the line of collimation, when the tube is drawn in, will not coincide with the same line when the tube is pushed out. If adjusted for one position, it will therefore be wrong for the other. These screws, however, can make it right in both positions. They are used as follows.

Sight to some well defined point as far off as it can be distinctly seen. Then revolve the telescope half around in its supports; i. e. turn it upside down. If the line of collimation was not in the imaginary axis of the rings or collars on which the telescope rests, it will now no longer bisect the object sighted to. Thus, if the horizontal hair was too high, as in Fig. 251, this line of

Fig. 251.

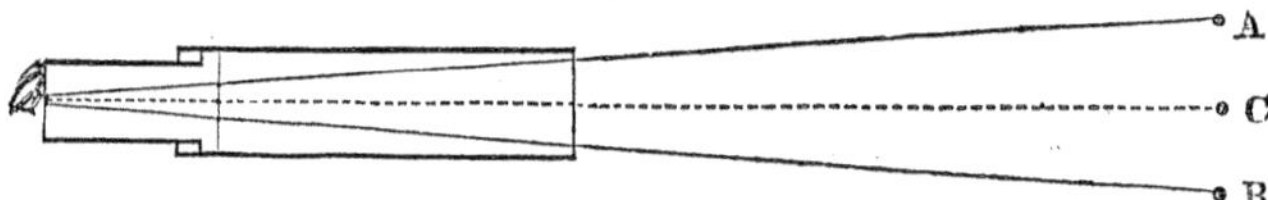

collimation would point at first to A, and after being turned over, it would point to B. The error is doubled by the reversion, and it should point to C, midway between A and B. Make it do so, by un screwing the upper capstan-headed screw, and screwing in the lower one, till the horizontal hair is brought half way back to the point. Remember that in an erecting telescope, the cross-hairs are reversed, and *vice versa*. Bring it the rest of the way by means of the parallel plate screws. Then revolve it in the Ys back to its original position, and see if the intersection of the cross-hairs now bisects the point, as it should. If not, again revolve, and repeat the operation till it is perfected. If the vertical hair passes to the right or to the left of the point when the telescope is turned half around, it must be adjusted in the same manner by the other pair of cross-hairs screws. One of these adjustments may disturb the other, and they should be repeated alternately. When they are perfected, the intersection of the cross-hairs, when once fixed on a point, will not move from it when the telescope is revolved in its

In Theodolites, the Telescope is revolved in the Ys. In Transits, the maker, by whom this adjustment is usually performed, revolves the Telescope, in the same manner, before it is fixed in its cross-bar.

supports. This double operation is called *adjusting the line of collimation.**

This line is now adjusted for distant objects. It would be so for near ones also, if the tube were perfectly straight. To test this, sight to some point, as near as is distinctly visible. Then turn the telescope half over. If the intersection does not now bisect the point, bring it half way there by the screws C, C, of Fig. 250, moving only one of the hairs at a time, as before. Then repeat the former adjustment on the distant object. If this is not quite perfect, repeat the operation.

This adjustment, in instruments thus arranged, should precede the first one which we have explained. It is usually performed by the maker, and its screws are not visible in the Transit, being enclosed in the ball seen where the telescope is connected with the cross-bar.†

All the adjustments should be meddled with as little as possible, lest the screws should get loose; and when once made right they should be kept so by careful usage.

* This "adjustment of the line of collimation" has merely brought the intersection of the cross-hairs (which fixes the line of sight) into the line joining the centres of the collars on which the telescope turns in the Ys; but the maker is supposed to have originally fixed the optical axis of the telescope (i. e. the line joining the optical centres of the glasses), in the same line.

† The adjustment of " Centring the object-glass is the invention of Messrs. Gurley, of Troy.

CHAPTER IV.

THE FIELD-WORK.

(366) To measure a horizontal angle. Set up the instrument so that its centre shall be exactly over the angular point, or in the intersection of the two lines whose difference of direction is to be measured; as at B in the figure. A plumb line must be suspended from under the centre. Dropping a stone is an imperfect substitute for this. Set the instrument so that its *lower* parallel plate may be as nearly horizontal as possible. The levels will serve as guides, if the four parallel-plate screws be first so screwed up or down that equal lengths of them shall be above the upper plate. Then level the instrument carefully, as in Art. (338). Direct the telescope to a rod, stake, or other object, A in the figure, on one of the lines which form the angle. Tighten the clamps, and by the tangent-screw, (see Art. (336)), move the telescope so that the intersection of the cross-hairs shall very precisely bisect this object. Note the reading of the vernier, as explained in the preceding chapter. Then loosen the clamp of the vernier, and direct the telescope on the other line (as to C) precisely as before, and again read. The difference of the two readings will be the desired angle, ABC. Thus, if the first reading had been 40° and the last 190°, the angle would be 150°. If the vernier had passed 360° in turning to the second object, 360° should be added to the last reading before subtracting. Thus, if the first reading had been 300°, and the last reading 90°, the angle would be found by calling the last reading, as it really is, 360° + 90° = 450°, and then subtracting 300°.

Fig. 252.

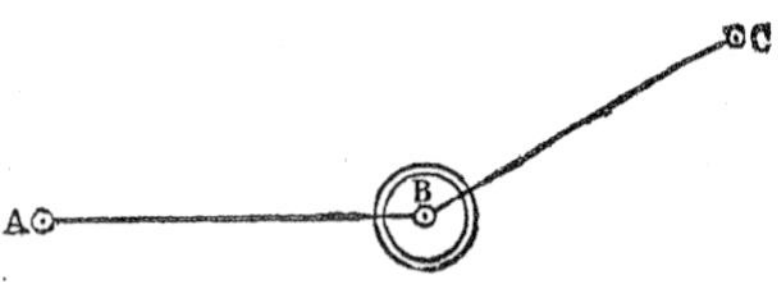

It is best to sight first to the left hand object and then to the right hand one, turning "with the sun," or like the hands of a watch, since the numbering of the degrees usually runs in that direction.

It is convenient, though not necessary, to begin by setting the vernier at zero, by the upper movement (that of the vernier plate on the circle) and then, by means of the lower motion, (that of the whole instrument on its axis), to direct the telescope to the first object. Then fasten the lower clamp, and sight to the second object as before. The reading will then be the angle desired. An objection to this is that the two verniers seldom read alike.*

After one or more angles have been observed from one point, the telescope must be directed back to the first object, and the reading to it noted, so as to make sure that it has not slipped. A watch-telescope (see Art. 339) renders this unnecessary.

The error arising from the instrument not being set precisely over the centre of the station, will be greater the nearer the object sighted to. Thus a difference of one inch would cause an error of only 3″ in the apparent direction of an object a mile distant, but one of nearly 3′ at a distance of a hundred feet.

(367) Reduction of high and low objects. When one of the objects sighted to is higher than the other, the "plunging telescope" of these instruments causes the angle measured to be the true horizontal angle desired; i. e. the same angle as if a point exactly under the high object and on a level with the low object (or *vice versa*) had been sighted to. For, the telescope has been caused to move in a vertical plane by the 3d adjustment of Chapter II, and the angle measured is therefore the angle between the vertical planes which pass through the two objects, and which "project" the two lines of sight on the same horizontal plane.

This constitutes the great practical advantage of these instruments over those which are held in the planes of the two objects observed, such as the sextant, and the "circle" much used by the French.

* The learner will do well to gauge his own precision and that of the instrument (and he may rest assured that his own will be the one chiefly in fault) by measuring, from any station, the angles between successive points all around him, till he gets back to the first point, beginning at different parts of the circle for each angle. The sum of all these angles *should* exactly equal 360°. He will probably find quite a difference from that.

(368) Notation of angles. The angles observed may be noted in various ways. Thus, the observation of the angle ABC, in Fig. 252, may be noted "At B, from A to C, 150°," or better, "At B, between A and C, 150°." In column form, this becomes

Between A	150°	and C.
At	B	

When the vernier had been set at zero before sighting to the first object, and other objects were then sighted to, those objects, the readings to which were less than 180°, will be on the left of the first line, and those to which the readings were more than 180°, will be on its right, looking in the direction in which the survey is proceeding, from A to B, and so on.*

(369) Probable error. When a number of separate observations of an angle have been made, the mean or average of them all, (obtained by dividing the sum of the readings by their number,) is taken as the true reading. The "Probable error" of this mean, is the quantity, (minutes or seconds) which is such that there is an even chance of the real error being more or less than it. Thus, if ten measurements of an angle gave a mean of 35° 18′, and it was an equal wager that the error of this result, too much or too little, was half a minute, then half a minute would be the "Probable error" of this determination. This probable error is equal to the square root of the sum of the squares of the errors (i. e. the differences of each observation from the mean) divided by the number of observations, and multiplied by the decimal 0.674489.

The same result would be obtained by using what is called "*The weight*" of the observation. It is equal to the square of the number of observations divided by twice the sum of the squares of the errors. The "Probable error" is equal to 0.476936 divided by the square root of the weight. These rules are proved by the "Theory of Probabilities."

(370) To repeat an angle. Begin as in Art. (366), an measure the angle as there directed. Then unclamp below, and turn the circle around till the telescope is again directed to the first object, and made to bisect it precisely by the lower tan-

* This is very useful in preventing any ambiguity in the field-notes

gent screw. Then unclamp above and turn the vernier plate till the telescope again points to the second object, the first reading remaining unchanged. The angle will now have been measured a second time, but on a part of the circle adjoining that on which it was first measured, the second arc beginning where the first ended. The difference between the first and last readings will therefore be twice the angle.

This operation may be repeated a third, a fourth, or any number of times, always turning the telescope back to the first object by the lower movement, (so as to start with the reading at which the preceding observation left off) and turning it to the second object by the upper movement. Take the difference of the first and last readings and divide by the number of observations.

The advantage of this method is that the errors of *observation* (i. e. sighting sometimes to the right and sometimes to the left of the true point) balance each other in a number of repetitions; while the constant error of *graduation* is reduced in proportion to this number. This beautiful principle has some imperfections in practice, probably arising from the slipping and straining of the clamps.

(371) Angles of deflection. The angle of deflection of one line from another, is the angle which one line makes with the other line produced. Thus, in the figure, the angle of deflection of BC from AB, is B′BC. It is evidently the supplement of the angle ABC.

Fig. 253.

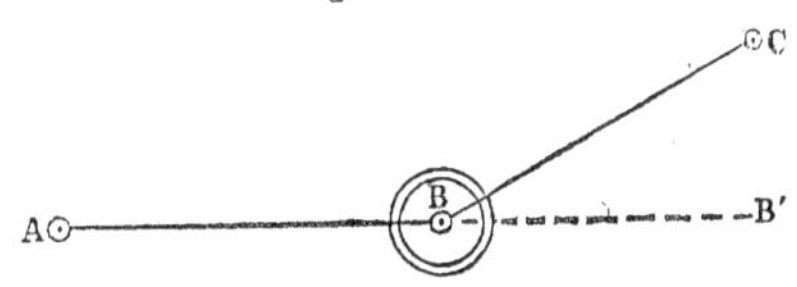

To measure it with the *Transit*, set the instrument at B, direct the telescope to A, and then turn it over. It will now point in the direction of AB produced, or to B′, if the 2d adjustment of Chapter II, has been performed. Note the reading. Then direct the telescope to C. Note the new reading, and their difference will be the required angle of deflection, B′BC.

If the vernier be set at zero, before taking the first observation, the readings for objects on the right of the first line will be less than

180°, and more than 180° for objects on the left; conversely to Art. (368).

(372) Line surveying. The survey of a line, such as a road, &c., can be made by the Theodolite or Transit, with great precision; measuring the angle which each line makes with the preceding line, and noting their lengths, and the necessary offsets on each side.

Short lines of sight should be avoided, since a slight inaccuracy in setting the centre of the instrument exactly over or under the point previously sighted to, would then much affect the angle, as noticed at close of Art. (366). Very great accuracy can be obtained by using three tripods. One would be set at the first station and sighted back to from the instrument placed at the second station, and a forward sight be then taken to the third tripod placed at the third station. The instrument would then be set on this third tripod, a back sight taken to the tripod remaining on the second station, and a foresight taken to the tripod brought from the first station to the fourth station; to which the instrument is next taken: and so on. This is especially valuable in surveys of mines.

The field-notes may be taken as directed in Chapter III of Compass Surveying, pages 149, &c., the angles taking the place of the Bearings. The "Checks by intersecting Bearings," explained in Art. (246), should also be employed. The angles made on each side of the stations may both be measured, and the equality of their sum to 360°, would at once prove the accuracy of the work.

If the magnetic Bearing of any one of the lines be given, and that of any of the other lines of the series be required, it can be deduced by constructing a diagram, or by modifications of the rules given for the reverse object, in Art. (243).

(373) Traversing: Or Surveying by the back-angle. This is a method of observing and recording the different directions of successive portions of a line, (such as a road, the boundaries of a farm, &c.,) so as to read off on the instrument, at each station, the angle which each line makes—not with the preceding line, but—with the first line observed. This line is, therefore, called the *meridian* of that survey.

Fig. 254.

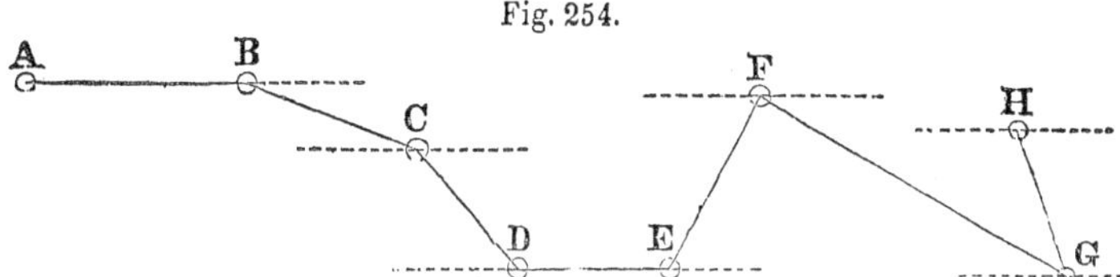

Set up the instrument at the first angle, or second station, (B, in the figure), of the line to be surveyed. Sight to A and then to C. Clamp the vernier, and take the instrument to C. Loosen the lower clamp, and direct the telescope to B, the reading remaining as it was at B. Clamp below, loosen above, and sight to D. The reading of the instrument will be the angle which the line CD makes with the first line, or Meridian, AB.

Take the instrument to D. Sight back to C, and then forward to E, as before directed, and the reading of the instrument will be the angle which DE makes with AB.

So proceed for any number of lines.

When the Transit is used, the angles of deflection of each line from the first, obtained by reversing the telescope, may be used in "Traversing," and with much advantage when the successive lines do not differ greatly in their directions.

A	0°
B	200°
C	50°
D	180°
E	300°
F	210°
G	250°

The survey represented in the figure, is recorded in the first of the accompanying Tables, as observed with the Theodolite; and in the second Table, as observed with the Transit.

A	0°
B	20°
C	50°
D	0°
E	300°
F	30°
G	250°

The chief advantage of this method is its greater rapidity in the field and in platting, the angles being all laid down from one meridian, as in Compass-surveying. This also increases the accuracy of the plat, since any error in the direction of one line does not affect the directions of the following lines.*

(374) Use of the Compass. The chief use of the Compass attached to a Transit or Theodolite, is as a check on the observations; for the difference between the magnetic Bearings of any

* If there are two verniers; take care always to read the degrees from the same vernier. Mark it A.

two lines should be the same, approximately, as the angle between them, measured by the more accurate instruments. The Bearing also prevents any ambiguity, as to whether an angle was taken to the right or to the left.

The instrument may also be used like a simple compass, the telescope taking the place of the sights, and requiring similar tests of accuracy. A more precise way of taking a Bearing is to turn the plate to which the compass box is attached, till the needle points to zero, and note the reading of the vernier; then sight to the object, and again read the vernier. The Bearing will thus be obtained more minutely than the divisions on the compass box could give it.

(375) Measuring distances with a telescope and rod. On the cross-hair ring, described in Art. **(330)**, stretch two more horizontal spider-threads at equal distances above and below the original one; or all may be replaced by a plate of thin glass, placed precisely in the focus, with the necessary lines, as in the figure, etched by fluoric acid. Let a rod, 10 or 15 feet long, be held up at 1000 feet off, and let there be marked on it precisely the length which the distance between two of these lines covers. Let this be subdivided as minutely as the spaces, painted alternately white and red and numbered, can be seen. If ten subdivisions are made, each will represent a distance of 100 feet off, and so on. Continue these divisions over the whole length of the rod. It is now ready for use. The French call it a *stadia*. When it is held up at any unknown distance, the number of divisions on it intercepted between the two lines, will indicate the distance with considerable precision. It should be tested at various distances.

Fig. 255.

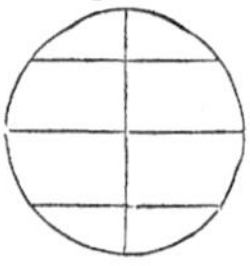

A "Levelling-rod," divided into feet, tenths and hundredths, may be used as a *stadia*, with less convenience but more precision. Experiments must previously determine at what distances the space between the lines in the telescope covers one foot, &c. Then, at any unknown distance, let the sliding "target" of the rod be moved till one line bisects it, and its place on the rod be read off; let the target be then moved so that the other line bisects it and let its place be again noted. Then the required distance will be equal to the difference of the readings on the rod, in feet, multiplied by the distance at which a foot was intercepted between the lines.

One of the horizontal hairs may be made movable, and its distance from the other, when the space between them exactly covers an object of known height, can be very precisely measured by counting the number of turns and fractions of a turn, of a screw by which this movable hair is raised or lowered. A simple proportion will then give the distance.

On sloping ground a double correction is necessary to reduce the slope to the horizon and to correct the oblique view of the rod. The horizontal distance is, in consequence, approximately equal to the observed distance multiplied by the *square* of the cosine of the slope of the ground.

The latter of the above two corrections will be dispensed with by holding the rod perpendicular to the line of sight, with the aid of a right angled triangle, one side of which coincides with the rod at the height of the telescope, and the other side of which adjoining the right angle, is caused, by leaning the rod, to point to the telescope.

Other contrivances have been used for the same object, such as a Binocular Telescope with two eye-pieces inclined at a certain angle; a Telescope with an object-glass cut into two movable parts; &c.

(376) Ranging out lines. This is the converse of Surveying lines. The instrument is fixed over the first station with great precision, its telescope being very carefully adjusted to move in a vertical plane. A series of stakes, with nails driven in their tops, or otherwise well defined, are then set in the desired line as far as the power of the instrument extends. It is then taken forward to a stake three or four from the last one set, and is fixed over it, first by the plumb and then by sighting backward and forward to the first and last stake. The line is then continued as before. A good object for a long sight is a board painted like a target, with black and white concentric rings, and made to slide in grooves cut in the tops of two stakes set in the ground about in the line. It is moved till the vertical hair bisects the circles (which the eye can determine with great precision) and a plumb-line dropped from their centre, gives the place of the stake. "Mason & Dixon's Line" was thus ranged.

If a Transit be used for ranging, its "Second Adjustment" is most important to ensure the accuracy of the reversal of its Telescope. If a Theodolite be used, the line is continued by turning the vernier 180°, or by reversing the telescope in its Ys, as noticed in Arts. (325) and (362).

(377) Farm Surveying, &c. A large farm can be most easily and accurately surveyed, by measuring the angles of its main boundaries (and a few main diagonals, if it be very large,) with a Theodolite or Transit, as in Arts. (366) or (371), and filling up the interior details, as fences, &c., with the Compass and Chain.

If the *Theodolite* be used, keep the field on the left hand, as in following the order of the letters in this figure, and turn the telescope around "with the sun," and the angles measured as in Art. (366), will be the interior angles of the field, as noted in the figure.

Fig. 256.

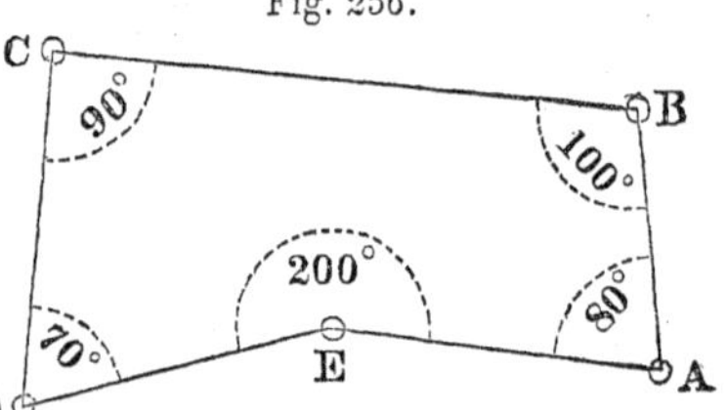

The accuracy of the work will be proved, as alluded to in Art. (257), if the sum of all the interior angles be equal to the product of 180° by the number of sides of the figure less two. Thus in the figure, the sum of all the interior angles $= 540° = 180° \times (5 - 2)$. The sum of the exterior angles would of course equal $180° \times (5 + 2) = 1260°$.

If the *Transit* be used, the farm should be kept on the right hand, and then the angles measured will be the supplements of the interior angles. If the angles to the right be called *positive*, and those to the left *negative*, their algebraic sum should equal 360°.

If the boundary lines be surveyed by "Traversing," as in Art. (373), the reading, on getting back to the last station and looking back to the first line, should be 360°, or 0°.

The content of any surface surveyed by "Traversing" with the Transit can be calculated by the Traverse Table, as in Chapter VI, of Part III, by the following modification. When the angle of deflection of any side from the first side, or Meridian, is less than 90°, call this angle the Bearing, find its Latitude and Departure, and call them both *plus*. When the angle is between 90° and 180°, call the difference between the angle and 180° the Bearing, and call its Latitude *minus* and its Departure *plus*. When the angle is between 180° and 270°, call its difference from 180° the Bearing, and call its Latitude *minus* and its Departure *minus*. When the angle is more than 270°, call its difference from 360° the Bearing, and call its Latitude *plus* and its Departure *minus*. Then use these as in getting the content of a Compass-survey. The signs of the Latitudes and Departures follow those of the cosines and sines in the successive quadrants.

Town-Surveying would be performed as directed in Art. (**261**), substituting "angles" for "Bearings." "Traversing" is the best method in all these cases.

Inaccessible areas would be surveyed nearly as in Art. (**134**), except that the angles of the lines enclosing the space would be measured with the instrument, instead of with the chain.

(**378**) **Platting.** Any of these surveys can be platted by any of the methods explained and characterized in Chapter IV, of the preceding Part. A circular Protractor, Art. (**264**), may be regarded as a Theodolite placed on the paper. "Platting Bearings," Art. (**265**), can be employed when the survey has been made by "Traversing." But the method of "Latitudes and Departures," Art. (**285**), is by far the most accurate.

PART V.

TRIANGULAR SURVEYING;

OR

By the Fourth Method.

(379) TRIANGULAR SURVEYING is founded on the *Fourth Method* of determining the position of a point, by the intersection of two known lines, as given in Art. (8). By an extension of the principle, a field, a farm, or a country, can be surveyed by measuring only one line, and calculating all the other desired distances, which are made sides of a connected series of imaginary *Triangles*, whose angles are carefully measured. The district surveyed is covered with a sort of net-work of such triangles, whence the name given to this kind of Surveying. It is more commonly called "Trigonometrical Surveying;" and sometimes "Geodesic Surveying," but improperly, since it does not necessarily take into account the curvature of the earth, though always adopted in the great surveys in which that is considered.

(380) Outline of operations. A *base line*, as long as possible, (5 or 10 miles in surveys of countries), is measured with extreme accuracy.

From its extremities, angles are taken to the most distant objects visible, such as steeples, signals on mountain tops, &c.

The distances to these and between these are then calculated by the rules of Trigonometry.

The instrument is then placed at each of these new stations, and angles are taken from them to still more distant stations, the calculated lines being used as new base lines.

This process is repeated and extended till the whole district is embraced by these "primary triangles" of as large sides as possible.

One side of the last triangle is so located that its length can be obtained by measurement as well as by calculation, and the agreement of the two proves the accuracy of the whole work.

Within these primary triangles, *secondary* or smaller triangles are formed, to fix the position of the minor local details, and to serve as starting points for common surveys with chain and compass, &c. Tertiary triangles may also be required.

The larger triangles are first formed, and the smaller ones based on them, in accordance with the important principle in all surveying operations, always to work from the whole to the parts, and from greater to less.

Each of these steps will now be considered in turn, in the following order:

1. The Base; articles **(381)**, **(382)**.
2. The Triangulation; articles **(383)** to **(390)**.
3. Modifications of the method; articles **(391)** to **(395)**.

(381) Measuring a Base. Extreme accuracy in this is necessary, because any error in it will be *multiplied* in the subsequent work. The ground on which it is located must be smooth and nearly level, and its extremities must be in sight of the chief points in the neighborhood. Its point of beginning must be marked by a stone set in the ground with a bolt let into it. Over this a Theodolite or Transit is to be set, and the line "ranged out" as directed in Art. **(376)**. The measurement may be made with chains, (which should be formed like that of a watch,) &c. but best with rods. We will notice in turn their *Materials*, *Supports*, *Alinement*, *Levelling*, and *Contact*.

As to *Materials*, iron, brass and other metals have been used, but are greatly lengthened and shortened by changes of temperature. Wood is affected by moisture. Glass rods and tubes are preferable on both these accounts. But wood is the most convenient. Wooden rods should be straight-grained white pine, &c.; well seasoned, baked, soaked in boiling oil, painted and varnished. They may be trussed, or framed like a mason's plumb-line level, to prevent their bending. Ten or fifteen feet is a convenient length. Three are required, which may be of different colors, to prevent mistakes in recording. They must be very carefully compared with a standard measure.

Supports must be provided for the rods, in accurate work. Posts set in line at distances equal to the length of the rods, may be driven or sawed to a uniform line, and the rods laid on them, either directly, or on beams a little shorter. Tripods, or trestles, with screws in their tops to raise or lower the ends of the rods resting on them, or blocks with three long screws passing through them and serving as legs, may also be used. Staves, or legs, for the rods have been used; these legs bearing pieces which can slide up and down them and on which the rods themselves rest.

The *Alinement* of the rods can be effected, if they are laid on the ground, by strings, two or three hundred feet long, stretched between the stakes set in the line, a notched peg being driven when the measurement has reached the end of one string, which is then taken on to the next pair of stakes; or, if the rods rest on supports, by projecting points on the rods being alined by the instrument.

The *Levelling* of the rods can be performed with a common mason's level; or their angle measured, if not horizontal, by a "slope-level."

The *Contacts* of the rods may be effected by bringing them end to end. The third rod must be applied to the second before the first has been removed, to detect any movement. The ends must be protected by metal, and should be rounded (with radius equal to length of rod) so as to touch in only one point. Round-headed nails will answer tolerably. Better are small steel cylinders, horizontal on one end and vertical on the other. Sliding ends, with verniers, have been used. If one rod be higher than the next one, one must be brought to touch a plumb-line which touches the other, and its thickness be added. To prevent a shock from contact, the rods may be brought not quite in contact, and a wedge be let down between them till it touches both at known points on its graduated edges. The rods may be laid side by side, and lines drawn across the end of each be made to coincide or form one line. This is more accurate. Still better is a "visual contact," a double microscope with cross-hairs being used, so placed that one tube bisects a dot at the end of one rod, and the other tube bisects a dot at the end of the next rod. The rods thus never touch. The distance between the two sets of cross-hairs is of course to be added.

A Base could be measured over very uneven ground, or even water, by suspending a series of rods from a stretched rope by rings in which they can move, and levelling them and bringing them into contact as above.

(382) Corrections of Base. If the rods were not level, their length must be reduced to its horizontal projection. This would be the square root of the difference of the squares of the length of the rod (or of the base) and of the height of one end above the other; or the product of the same length by the cosine of the angle which it makes with the horizon.*

If the rods were metallic, they would need to be corrected for temperature. Thus, if an iron bar expands $\frac{7}{1000000}$ of its length for 1° Fahrenheit, and had been tested at 32°, and a Base had been measured at 72° with such a bar 10 feet long, and found to contain 3000 of them, its apparent length would be 30,000 feet, but its real length would be 8.4 feet more. An iron and a brass bar can be so combined that the difference of their expansion causes two points attached to their ends to remain at the same distance at all temperatures. Such a combination is used on the U. S. Coast Survey.

(383) Choice of Stations. The stations, or "Trigonometrical points," which are to form the vertices of the triangles, and to be observed to and from, must be so selected that the resulting triangles may be "well-conditioned," i. e. may have such sides and angles that a small error in any of the measured quantities will cause the least possible errors in the quantities calculated from them. The higher Calculus shows that the triangles should be as nearly equilateral as possible. This is seldom attainable, but no angle should be admitted less than 30°, or more than 120°.†

* More precisely, A being this angle, and not more than 2° or 3°, the difference between the inclined and horizontal lengths, equals the inclined or real length multiplied by the square of the minutes in A, and that by the decimal 0.00000004231; as shewn in Appendix B. In a Geodesic survey, the base would also be required to be reduced to the level of the sea.

† When two angles only are observed, as is often the case in the secondary triangulation, the unobserved angle ought to be nearly a right angle.

To extend the triangulation, by continually increasing the sides of the triangles, without introducing "ill-conditioned" triangles, may be effected as in the figure. AB is the measured base.

Fig. 257.

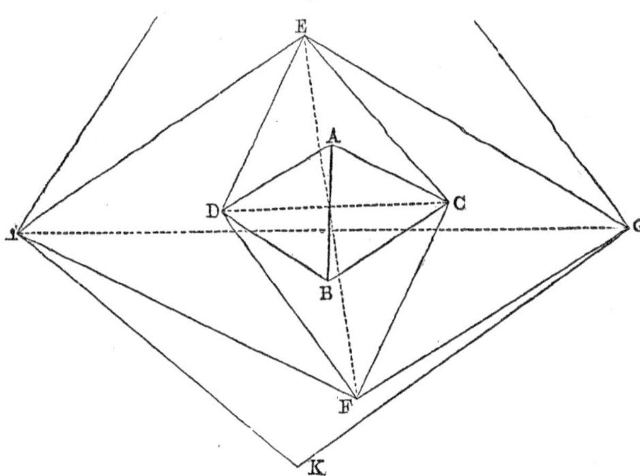

C and D are the nearest stations. In the triangles ABC and ABD, all the angles being observed and the side AB known, the other sides can be readily calculated. Then in each of the triangles DAC and DBC, two sides and the contained angles are given to find DC, one calculation checking the other. DC then becomes a base to calculate EF; which is then used to find GH; and so on.

The fewer primary stations used, the better; both to prevent confusion and because the smaller number of triangles makes the correctness of the results more "probable."

The United States Coast Survey, under the superintendence of Prof. A. D. Bache, displays some fine illustrations of these principles, and of the modifications they may undergo to suit various localities. The figure on the opposite page represents part of the scheme of the primary triangulation resting on the Massachusetts base and including some remarkably well-conditioned triangles, as well as the system of quadrilaterals which is a valuable feature of the scheme when the sides of the triangles are extended to considerable lengths, and quadrilaterals, with both diagonals determined, take the place of simple triangles.

The engraving is on a scale of 1:1200,000.

Fig. 258.

NEW HAMPSHIRE.
MASSACHUSETTS.
RHODE ISLAND.
ATLANTIC OCEAN
Boston.
BASE

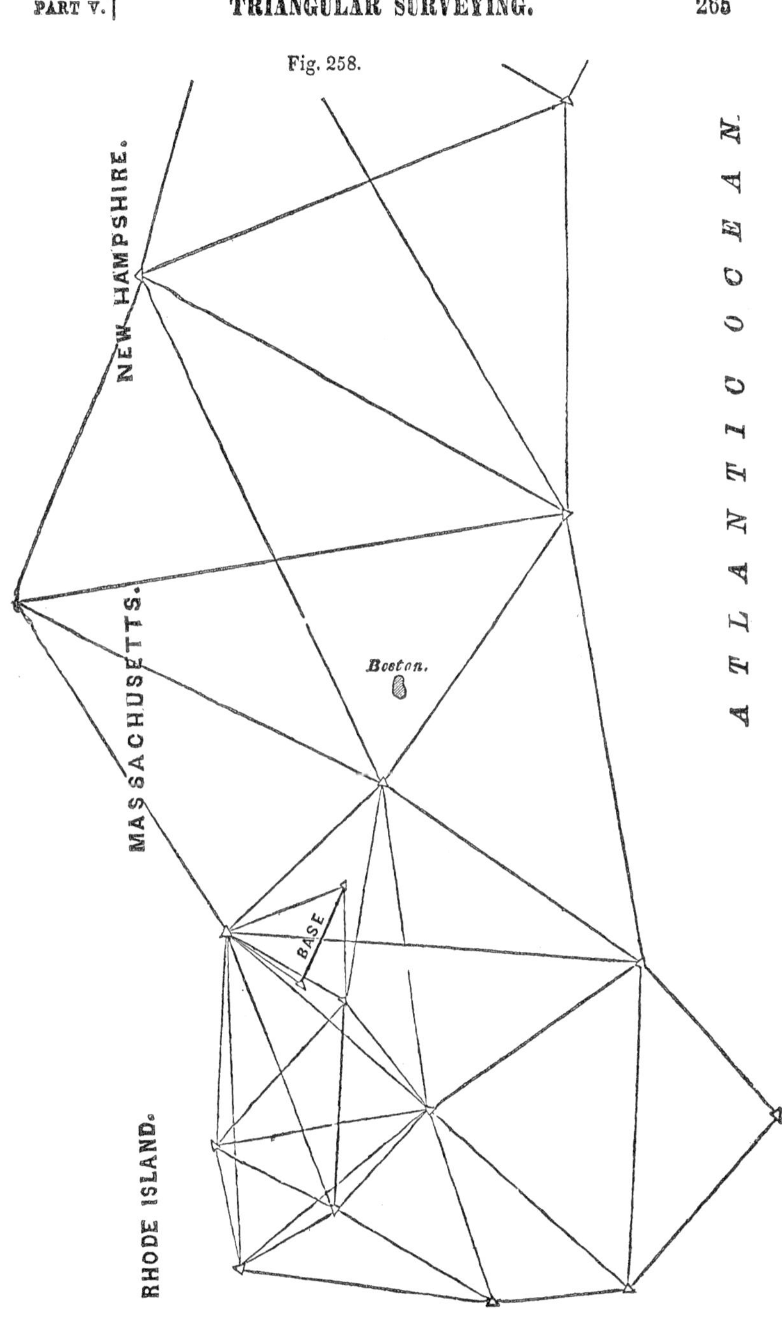

(384) Signals. They must be high, conspicuous, and so made that the instrument can be placed precisely under them.

Three or four timbers framed into a pyramid, as in the figure, with a long mast projecting above, fulfil the first and last conditions. The mast may be made vertical by directing two theodolites to it and adjusting it so that their telescopes follow it up and down, their lines of sight being at right angles to each other. Guy ropes may be used to keep it vertical.

Fig. 259.

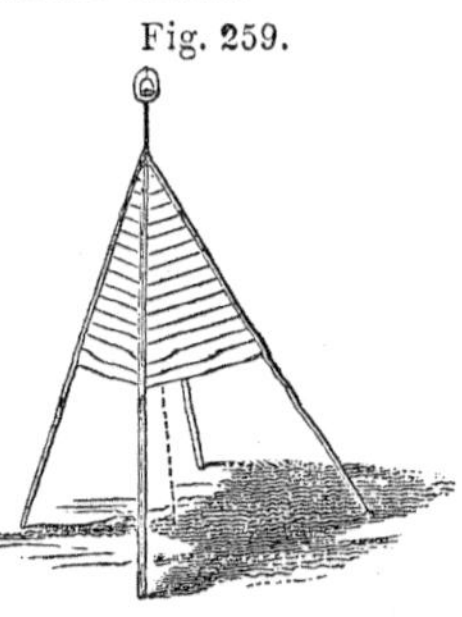

A very excellent signal, used on the Massachusetts State Survey, by Mr. Borden, is represented in the three following figures. It

Fig. 260.

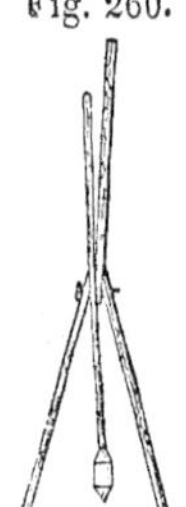

Fig. 261.

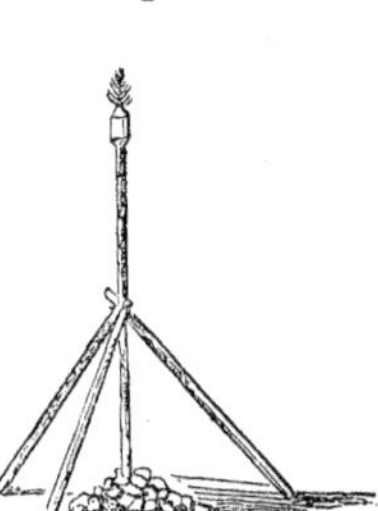

Fig. 262

consists merely of three stout sticks, which form a tripod, framed with the signal staff, by a bolt passing through their ends and its middle. Fig. 260 represents the signal as framed on the ground; Fig. 261 shews it erected and ready for observation, its base being steadied with stones; and Fig. 262 shews it with the staff turned aside, to make room for the Theodolite and its protecting tent. The heights of these signals varied between 15 and 80 feet.

Fig. 263

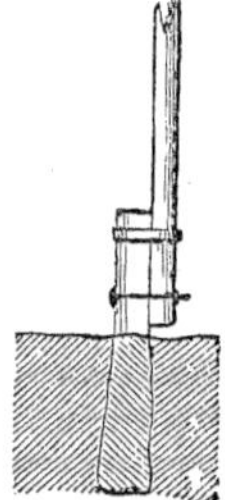

Another good signal consists of a stout post let into the ground, with a mast fastened to it by a bolt below and a collar above. By opening the collar, the mast can be turned down and the Theodolite set exactly under the former summit of the signal, i. e. in its vertical axis.

Signals should have a height equal to at least $\frac{1}{7000}$ of their distance, so as to subtend an angle of half a minute, which experience has shown to be the least allowable.

To make the tops of the signal-masts conspicuous, flags may be attached to them; white and red, if to be seen against the ground, and red and green if to be seen against the sky.* The motion of flags renders them visible, when much larger motionless objects are not. But they are useless in calm weather. A disc of sheet-iron, with a hole in it, is very conspicuous. It should be arranged so as to be turned to face each station. A barrel, formed of muslin sewn together four or five feet long, with two hoops in it two feet apart, and its loose ends sewn to the signal-staff, which passes through it, is a cheap and good arrangement. A tuft of pine boughs fastened to the top of the staff, will be well seen against the sky.

In sunshine, a number of pieces of tin nailed to the staff at different angles, will be very conspicuous. A truncated cone of burnished tin will reflect the sun's rays to the eye in almost every situation. But a "heliotrope," which is a piece of looking-glass, so adjusted as to reflect the sun directly to any desired point, is the most perfect arrangement.

For night signals, an Argand lamp is used; or, best of all, Drummond's light, produced by a stream of oxygen gas directed through a flame of alcohol upon a ball of lime. Its distinctness is exceedingly increased by a parabolic reflector behind it, or a lens in front of it. Such a light was brilliantly visible at 66 miles distance.

(385) Observations of the Angles. These should be repeated as often as possible. In extended surveys, three sets, of ten each, are recommended. They should be taken on different parts of the circle. In ordinary surveys, it is well to employ the method of "Traversing," Art. (373). In long sights, the state of the atmos-

Fig. 264.

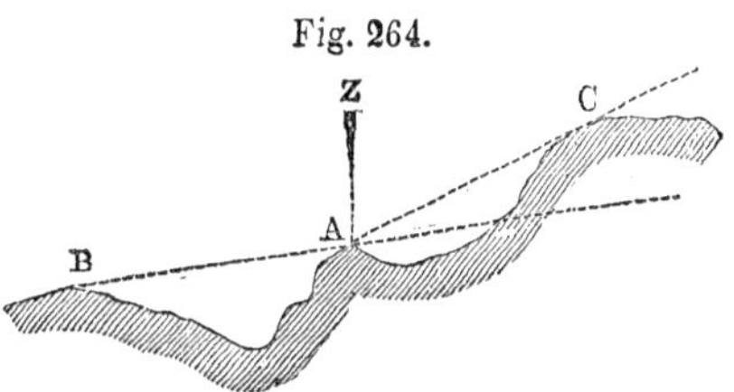

* To determine at a station A, whether its signal can be seen from B, projected against the sky or not, measure the vertical angles BAZ and ZAC. If their sum equals or exceeds 180°, A will be thus seen from B. If not, the signal at A must be raised till this sum equals 180°.

phere has a very remarkable effect on both the visibility of the signals, and on the correctness of the observations.

When many angles are taken from one station, it is important to record them by some uniform system. The form given below is convenient. It will be noticed that only the minutes and seconds of the second vernier are employed, the degrees being all taken from the first.

Observations at ————————.

STATION	READINGS.		MEAN	RIGHT OR LEFT OF	REMARKS.
OBSERVED TO	VERNIER A.	VERNIER B.	READING.	PRECED'G OBJ'T.	
A	70° 19′ 0″	18′ 40″	70° 18′ 50″		
B	103° 32′ 20″	32′ 40″	103° 32′ 30″	R.	
C	115° 14′ 20″	14′ 50″	115° 14′ 35″	R.	

When the angles are "repeated," Art. **(370)**, the multiple arcs will be registered under each other, and the mean of the seconds shewn by all the verniers at the first and last readings be adopted.

(386) Reduction to the centre. It is often impossible to set the instrument precisely at or under the signal which has been observed. In such cases proceed thus. Let C be the centre of the signal, and RCL the desired angle, R being the right hand object and L the left hand one. Set the instrument at D,

Fig. 265.

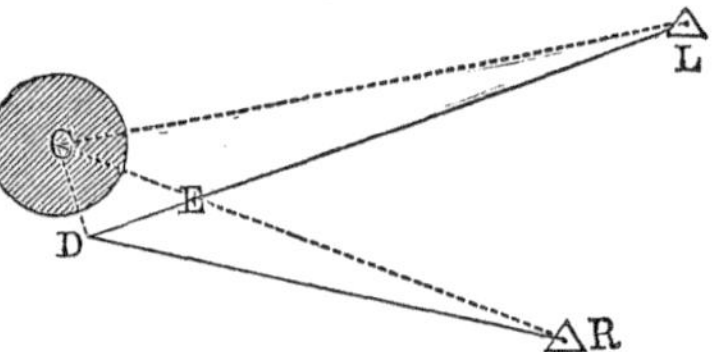

as near as possible to C, and measure the angle RDL. It may be less than RCL, or greater than it, or equal to it, according as D lies without the circle passing through C, L and R, or within it, or in its circumference. The instrument should be set as nearly as possible in this last position. To find the proper correction for the observed angle, observe also the angle LDC, (called the angle of direction), counting it from 0° to 360°, going from the left-hand object toward the left; and measure the distance DC. Calculate the distances CR and CL with the angle RDL instead of RCL, since they are sufficiently nearly equal. Then

$$RCL = RDL + \frac{CD \cdot \sin.\ (RDL + LDC)}{CR \cdot \sin.\ 1''} - \frac{CD \cdot \sin.\ LDC}{CL \cdot \sin. 1''}.\text{*}$$

The last two terms will be the number of seconds to be added or subtracted. The Trigonometrical signs of the sines must be attended to. The log. sin. 1″ =4. 6855749. Instead of dividing by sin. 1″, the correction without it, which will be a very small fraction, may be reduced to seconds by multiplying it by 206265.

Example. Let RDL = 32° 20′18″.06; LDC = 101° 15′ 32″.4; CD = 0.9; CR = 35845.12; CL = 29783.1.

The first term of the correction will be + 3″.750, and the second term — 6″.113. Therefore, the observed angle RDL must be diminished by 2″.363, to reduce it to the desired angle RCL.

Much calculation may be saved by taking the station D so that all the signals to be observed can be seen from it. Then only a single distance and angle of direction need be measured.

It may also happen that the centre, C, of the signal cannot be seen from D. Thus, if the signal be a solid circular tower, set the Theodolite at D, and turn its telescope so that its line of sight becomes tangent to the tower at T, T′; measure on these tangents equal distances DE, DF, and direct the telescope to the middle, G, of the line EF. It will then point to the centre, C; and the distance DC will equal the distance from D to the tower plus the radius obtained by measuring the circumference.

Fig. 266

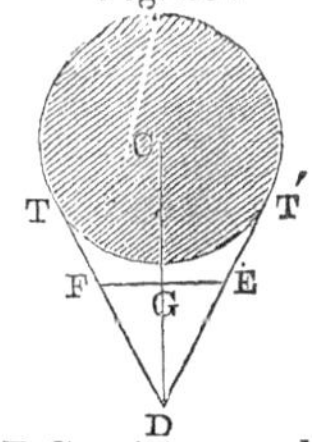

If the signal be rectangular, measure DE, DF. Take any point G on DE, and on DF set off DH $= DG \frac{DF}{DE}$. Then is GH parallel to EF, (since DG : DH :: DE : DF) and the telescope directed to its middle, K, will point to the middle of the diagonal EF. We shall also have $DC = DK \frac{DE}{DG}$. Any such case may be solved by similar methods.

Fig. 267.

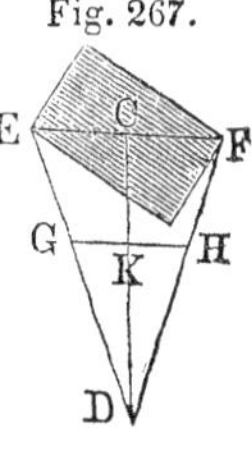

* For the investigation, see Appendix B.

The "*Phase*" of objects is the effect produced by the sun shining on only one side of them, so that the telescope will be directed from a distant station to the middle of that bright side instead of to the true centre. It is a source of error to be guarded against. Its effect may however be calculated.

(387) Correction of the angles. When all the angles of any triangle can be observed, their sum should equal 180.* If not they must be corrected. If all the observations are considered equally accurate, one-third of the difference of their sum from 180°, is to be added to, or subtracted from, each of them. But if the angles are the means of unequal numbers of observations, their errors may be considered to be inversely as those numbers, and they may be corrected by this proportion; *As* the sum of the reciprocals of each of the three numbers of observations *Is to* the whole error, *So is* the reciprocal of the number of observations of one of the angles *To* its correction. Thus if one angle was the mean of three observations, another of four, and the third of ten, and the sum of all the angles was 180° 3′, the first named angle must be diminished by the fourth term of this proportion; $\frac{1}{3} + \frac{1}{4} + \frac{1}{10} : 3' :: \frac{1}{3} : 1' \, 27''.8$. The second angle must in like manner be diminished by 1′ 5″.9; and the third by 26″.3. Their corrected sum will then be 180°.

It is still more accurate but laborious, to apportion the total error, or difference from 180°, among the angles inversely as the "*Weights*," explained in Art. (**369**). On the U. S. Coast Survey, in six triangles measured in 1844 by Prof. Bache, the *greatest* error was six-tenths of a second.

(388) Calculation and platting. The lengths of the sides of the triangles should be calculated with extreme accuracy, in two ways if possible, and by at least two persons. Plane Trigonometry may be used for even large surveys; for, though these sides are really arcs and not straight lines, the difference will be only one-

* If the triangles were very large, they would have to be regarded as spherical, and the sum of their angles would be more than 180°; but this "spherical excess" would be only 1″ for a triangle containing 76 square miles, 1′ for 4500 square miles, &c.; and may therefore be neglected in all ordinary surveying operations.

twentieth of a foot in a distance of $11\frac{1}{2}$ miles; half a foot in 23 miles; a foot in $34\frac{1}{2}$ miles, &c.

The platting is most correctly done by constructing the triangles, as in Art. (90), by means of the calculated lengths of their sides. If the measured angles are platted, the best method is that of chords, Art. (275). If many triangles are successively based on one another, they will be platted most accurately, by referring all their sides to some one meridian line by means of "Rectangular Co-ordinates," the Method of Art. (6), and platting as in Art. (277.) In the survey of a country, this Meridian would be the true North and South line passing through some well determined point.

(389) Base of Verification. As mentioned in Art. (380), a side of the last triangle is so located that it can be measured, as was the first base. If the measured and calculated lengths agree, this proves the accuracy of all the previous work of measurement and calculation, since the whole is a chain of which this is the last link, and any error in any previous part would affect the very last line, except by some improbable compensation. How near the agreement should be, will depend on the nicety desired and attained in the previous operations. Two bases 60 miles distant differed on one great English survey 28 inches; on another one inch; and on a French triangulation extending over 500 miles, the difference was less than two feet. Results of equal or greater accuracy are obtained on the U. S. Coast Survey.

(390) Interior filling up. The stations whose positions have been determined by the triangulation are so many fixed points, from which more minute surveys may start and interpolate any other points. The Trigonometrical points are like the observed Latitudes and Longitudes which the mariner obtains at every opportunity, so as to take a new departure from them and determine his course in the intervals by the less precise methods of his compass and log. The chief interior points may be obtained by "Secondary Triangulation," and the minor details be then filled in by any of the methods of surveying, with Chain, Compass, or Transit, already explained, or by the Plane Table, described in Part VIII.

With the Transit, or Theodolite, "Traversing" is the best mode of surveying, the instrument being set at zero, and being then directed from one of the Trigonometrical points to another, which line therefore becomes the "Meridian" of that survey. On reaching this second point, in the course of the survey, and sighting back to the first, the reading should of course be 0°, as explained in Art. (377).

(391) Radiating Triangulation. This name may be given to a method shown in the figure. Choose a conspicuous point, O, nearly in the centre of the field or farm to be surveyed. Find other points, A, B, C, D, &c. such that the signal at O can be seen from all of them, and that the triangles ABO, BCO, &c, shall be as nearly equilateral as possible. Measure one side, AB for example. At A measure the angles OAB, and OAG; at B measure the angles OBA and OBC; and so on, around the polygon. The correctness of these measurements may be tested by the sum of the angles, as in Art. (377). It may also be tested by the Trigonometrical principle that the product of the sines of every alternate angle, or the odd numbers in the figure, should equal the product of the sines of the remaining angles, the even numbers in the figure.*

Fig. 268.

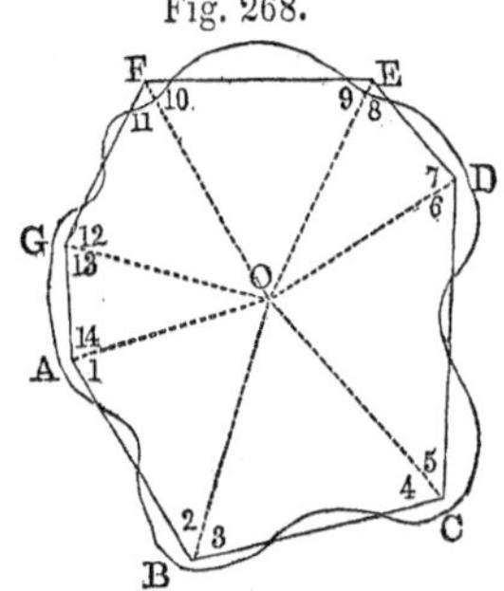

The calculations of the unknown sides are readily made. In the triangle ABO, one side and all the angles are given to find AO and BO. In the triangle BCO, BO and all the angles are given to find BC and CO; and so with the rest. Another proof of the accuracy of the work will be given by the calculation of the length of the side AO in the last triangle, agreeing with its length as obtained in the first triangle.

(392) Farm Triangulation. A Farm or Field may be surveyed by the previous methods, but the following plan will often be more

* For the demonstration, see Appendix B.

convenient. Choose a base, as XY, within the field, and from its ends measure the angles between it and the direction of each corner of the field, if the Theodolite or Transit be used, or take the bearing of each, if the Compass be used. Consider first the triangles which have XY for a base, and the corners of the field, A, B, C, &c., for vertices. In each of them one side and the angles will be known to find the other sides, XA, XB, &c. Then consider the field as made up of triangles which have their vertices at X. In each of them two sides and the included angle will be given to find its content, as in Art. (65). If Y be then taken for the common vertex, a test of the former work will be obtained.

Fig. 269.

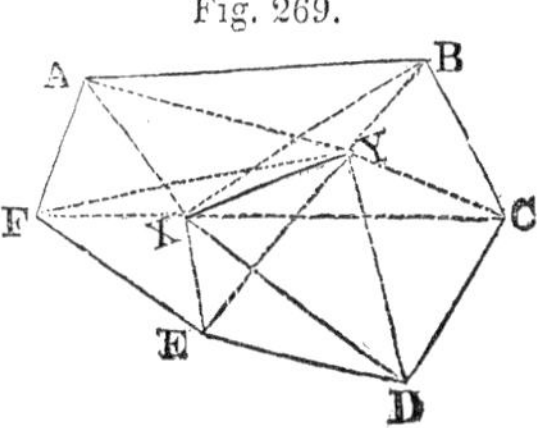

The operation will be somewhat simplified by taking for the base line a diagonal of the field, or one of its sides.

(393) Inaccessible Areas. A field or farm may be surveyed, by this "Fourth Method," without entering it. Choose a base line XY, from which all the corners of the field can be seen. Take their Bearings, or the angles between the Base line and their directions. The distances from X and Y to each of them can be calculated as in the last article. The figure will then shew in what manner the content of the field is the difference between the contents of the triangles, having X (or Y) for a vertex, which lie outside of it, and those which lie partly within the field and partly outside of it. Their contents can be calculated as in the last article, and their difference will be the desired content. If the figure be regarded as generated by the revolution of a line one end of which is at X, while its other end passes along the boundaries of the field, shortening and lengthening accordingly, and if those triangles generated by its movement in one direction be called *plus* and those generated by the contrary movement be called *minus*, their algebraic sum will be the content.

Fig, 270.

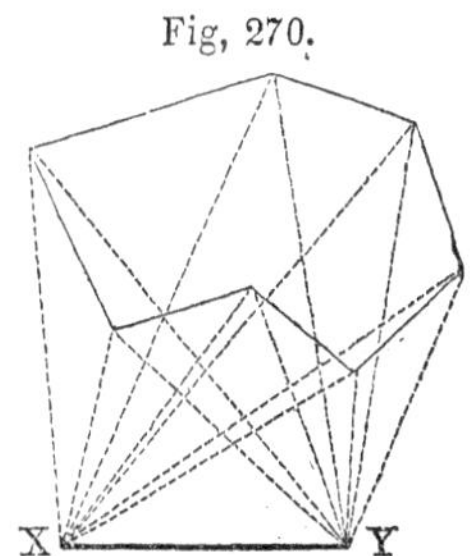

(394) Inversion of the Fourth Method. In all the operations which have been explained, the position of a point has been determined, as in Art. (8), by taking the angles, or bearings, of two lines passing from the two ends of a Base line to the unknown point. But the same determination may be effected inversely, by taking from the point the bearings, by compass, of the two ends of the Base line, or of any two known points. The unknown point will then be fixed by platting from the two known points the *opposite* bearings, for it will be at the intersection of the lines thus determined.

(395) Defects of the Method of Intersection. The determination of a point by the Fourth Method (enunciated in Art. (8), and developed in this Part) founded on the intersection of lines, has the serious defect that the point sighted to will be very indefinitely determined if the lines which fix it meet at a very acute or a very obtuse angle, which the relative positions of the points observed from and to, often render unavoidable. Intersections at right angles should therefore be sought for, so far as other considerations will permit.

PART VI.

TRILINEAR SURVEYING;

By the Fifth Method.

(396) Trilinear Surveying is founded on the Fifth Method of determining the position of a point, by measuring the angles betwen three lines conceived to pass from the required point to three known points, as illustrated in Art. (**10**).

To fix the place of the point from these data is much more difficult than in the preceding methods, and is known as the "Problem of the three points." It will be here solved Geometrically, Instrumentally and Analytically.

(397) Geometrical Solution. Let A, B and C be the known

Fig. 271.

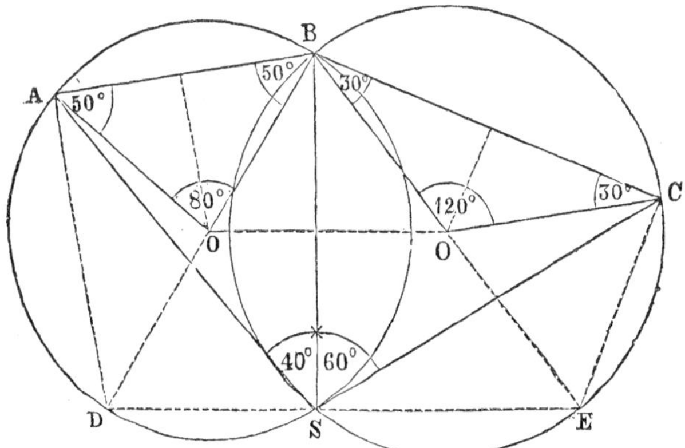

objects observed from S, the angles ASB and BSC being there measured. To fix this point, S, on the plat containing A, B and C, draw lines from A and B, making angles with AB each equal to 90°—ASB. The intersection of these lines at O will be the centre of a circle passing through A and B, in the circumference of which the point S will be situated.* Describe this circle. Also, draw lines from B and C, making angles with BC, each equal to 90°—BSC. Their intersection, O′, will be the centre of a circle passing through B and C. The point S will lie somewhere in its circumference, and therefore in its intersection with the former circumference. The point is thus determined.

In the figure the observed angles, ASB and BSC, are supposed to have been respectively 40° and 60°. The angles set off are therefore 50° and 30°. The central angles are consequently 80° and 120°, twice the observed angles.

The dotted lines refer to the checks explained in the latter part of this article.

When one of the angles is obtuse, set off its difference from 90° on the opposite side of the line joining the two objects to that on which the point of observation lies.

When the angle ABC is equal to the supplement of the sum of the observed angles, the position of the point will be indeterminate; for the two centres obtained will coincide, and the circle described from this common centre will pass through the three points, and any point of the circumference will fulfil the conditions of the problem.

A third angle, between one of the three points and a fourth point, should always be observed if possible, and used like the others, to serve as a check.

Many tests of the correctness of the position of the point determined may be employed. The simplest one is that the centres of the circles, O and O′, should lie in the perpendiculars drawn through the middle points of the lines AB and BC.

Another is that the line BS should be bisected perpendicularly by the line OO′.

A third check is obtained by drawing at A and C perpendiculars to AB and CB, and producing them to meet BO and BO′ produced,

* For, the arc AB measures the angle AOB at the centre, which angle = 180° —2 (90° — ASB) = 2 ASB. Therefore, any angle inscribed in the circumference and measured by the same arc is equal to ASB

in D and E. The line DE should pass through S; for, the angles BSD and BSE being right angles, the lines DS and SE form one straight line.

The figure shews these three checks by its dotted lines.

(398) Instrumental Solution. The preceding process is tedious where many stations are to be determined. They can be more readily found by an instrument called a *Station-pointer*, or *Chorograph*. It consists of three arms, or straight-edges, turning about a common centre, and capable of being set so as to make with each other any angles desired. This is effected by means of graduated arcs carried on their ends, or by taking off with their points (as with a pair of dividers) the proper distance from a scale of chords (see Art. (274)) constructed to a radius of their length. Being thus set so as to make the two observed angles, the instrument is laid on a map containing the three given points, and is turned about till the three edges pass through these points. Then their centre is at the place of the station, for the three points there subtend on the paper the angles observed in the field.

A simple and useful substitute is a piece of transparent paper, or ground glass, on which three lines may be drawn at the proper angles and moved about on the paper as before.

(399) Analytical Solution. The distances of the required point from each of the known points may be obtained analytically. Let AB $= c$; BC $= a$; ABC = B; ASB = S; BSC = S′. Also, make T = 360° — S — S′ — B. Let BAS = U; BCS = V. Then we shall have (as will be shewn in Appendix B)

$$\text{Cot. U} = \text{cot. T} \left(\frac{c \,.\, \text{sin. S}'}{a \,.\, \text{sin. S} \,.\, \text{cos. T}} + 1 \right)$$

$$\text{V} = \text{T} - \text{U}$$

$$\text{SB} = \frac{c \,.\, \text{sin. U}}{\text{sin. S}}; \text{ or, } = \frac{a \,.\, \text{sin. V}}{\text{sin. S}'}$$

$$\text{SA} = \frac{c \,.\, \text{sin. ABS}}{\text{sin. S}}. \qquad \text{SC} = \frac{a \,.\, \text{sin. CBS}}{\text{sin. S}'}$$

Attention must be given to the algebraic signs of the trigonometrical functions.

Example. ASB = 33° 45′; BSC = 22° 30′; AB = 600 feet; BC = 400 feet; AC = 800 feet. Required the distances and directions of the point S from each of the stations.

In the triangle ABC, the three sides being known, the angle ABC is found to be 104° 28′ 39″. The formula then gives the angle BAS = U = 105° 8′ 10″; whence BCS is found to be 94° 8′ 11″; and SB = 1042.51; SA = 710.193; and SC = 934.291.

(400) Maritime Surveying. The chief application of the Trilinear Method is to *Maritime* or *Hydrographical* Surveying, the object of which is to fix the positions of the deep and shallow points in harbors, rivers, &c., and thus to discover and record the shoals, rocks, channels and other important features of the locality. To effect this, a series of signals are established on the neighboring shore, any three of which may be represented by our points A, B, C. They are observed to from a boat, by means of a sextant, and the position of the boat is thus fixed as just shewn. The boat is then rowed in any desired direction, and soundings are taken at regular intervals, till it is found convenient to fix the new position of the boat as before. The precise point where each sounding was taken can now be platted on the map or chart. A repetition of this process will determine the depths and the places of each point of the bottom.

PART VII

OBSTACLES IN ANGULAR SURVEYING.

(401) THE obstacles, such as trees, houses, hills, vallies, rivers, &c., which prevent the direct alinement or measurement of any desired course, can be overcome much more easily and precisely with any angular instrument than with the chain, methods for using which were explained in Part II, Chapter V. They will however be taken up in the same order.* As before, the given and measured lines are drawn with fine full lines; the visual lines with broken lines; and the lines of the result with heavy full lines.

CHAPTER I.

PERPENDICULARS AND PARALLELS.

(402) Erecting Perpendiculars. *To erect a perpendicular to a line at a given point*, set the instrument at the given point, and, if it be a *Compass*, direct its sights on the line, and then turn them till the new Bearing differs 90° from the original one, as explained in Art. (**243**). A convenient approximation is to file notches in the Compass-plate, at the 90° points, and stretch over them a thread, sighting across which will give a perpendicular to the direction of the sights.

The *Transit* or *Theodolite* being set as above, note the reading of the vernier and then turn it till the new reading is 90° more or less than the former one.

* The Demonstrations of the Problems which require them, and from which they can conveniently be separated, will be found in Appendix B.

(403) *To erect a perpendicular to an inaccessible line, at a given point of it.* Let AB be the line and A the point. Calculate the distance from A to any point C, and the angle CAB, by the method of Art. (**430**). Set the instrument at C, sight to A, turn an angle = CAB, and measure in the direction thus obtained a distance CP = CA . cos. CAB. PA will be the required perpendicular.

Fig. 272.

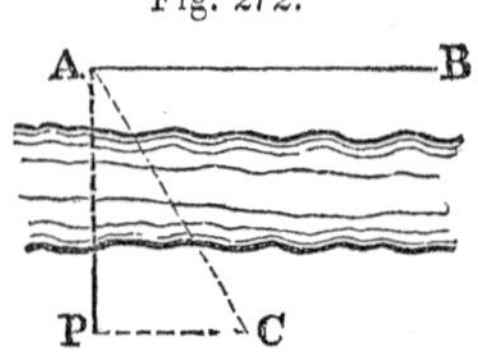

(404) Letting fall perpendiculars. *To let fall a perpendicular to a line from a given point.* With the *Compass*, take the Bearing of the given line and then from the given point run a line, with a Bearing differing 90° from the original Bearing, till it reaches the given line.

With the *Transit* or *Theodolite*, set it at any point of the given line, as A, and observe the angle between this line and a line thence to the given point, P. Then set at P, sight to the former position of the instrument, and turn a number of degrees equal to what the observed angle at A wanted of 90°. The instrument will then point in the direction of the required perpendicular PB.

Fig. 273.

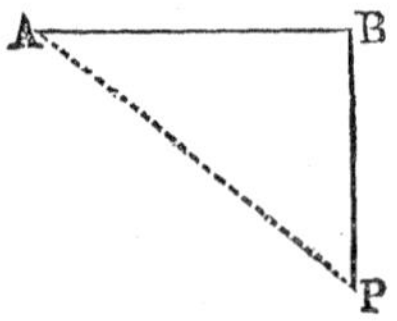

(405) *To let fall a perpendicular to a line from an inaccessible point.* Let AB be the line and P the point. Measure the angles PAB, and PBA. Measure AB. The angles APC and BPC are known, being the complements of the angles measured. Then is

Fig. 274.

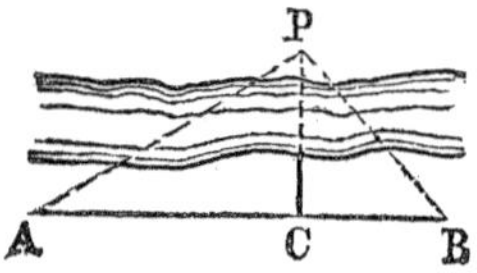

$$AC = AB \cdot \frac{\text{tan. APC}}{\text{tan. APC} + \text{tan. BPC}}.$$

(406) *To let fall a perpendicular to an inaccessible line from a given point.* Let C be the point and AB the line. Calculate the angle CAB by the method of Art. **(430)**. Set the instrument at C, sight to A, and turn an angle = 90 — CAB. It will then point in the direction of the required perpendicular CE.

Fig. 275.

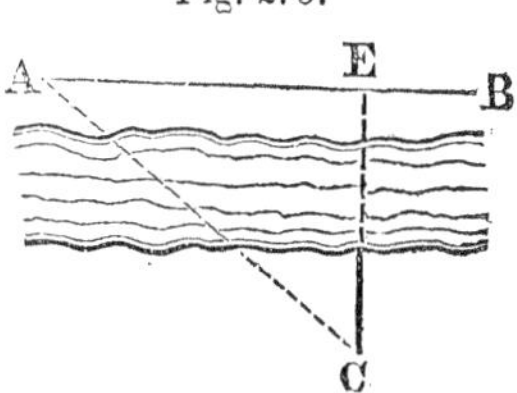

(407) Running Parallels. *To trace a line through a given point parallel to a given line.* With the *Compass*, take the Bearing of the given line, and then, from the given point, run a line with the same Bearing.

With the *Transit* or *Theodolite*, set it at any convenient point of the given line, as A, direct it on this line, and note the reading. Then turn the vernier till the cross-hairs bisect the given point, P. Take the instrument to this point and sight back to the former station, by the lower motion, without changing the reading. Then move the vernier till the reading is either the same as it was when the telescope was directed on the given line, or is 180° different. It will then be directed (forward or backward) on PQ, a parallel to AB, since equal angles have been measured at A and P. The manner of reading them is similar to the method of "Traversing," Art. **(373)**.

Fig. 276.

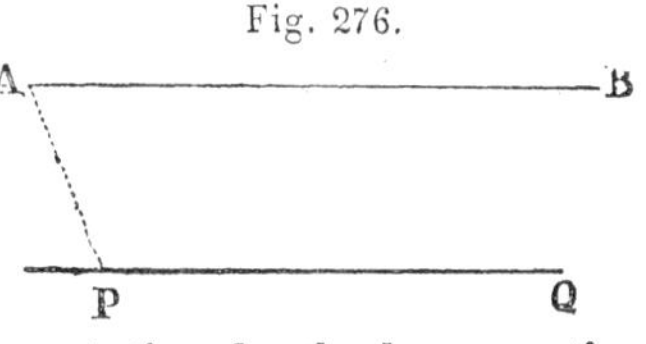

(408) *To trace a line through a given point parallel to an inaccessible line.* Let C be the given point, and AB the inaccessible line. Find the angle CAB, as in Art. **(430)**. Set the instrument at C, direct it to A, and then turn it so as to make an angle with CA equal to the supplement of the angle CAB. It will then point in a direction, CE, parallel to AB.

Fig. 277.

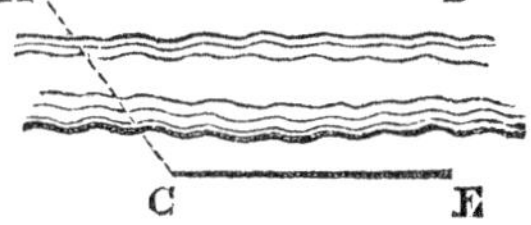

A B C E

CHAPTER II.

OBSTACLES TO ALINEMENT.

A. To prolong a line.

(409) The instrument being set at the farther end of a line, and directed back to its beginning, the sights of the *Compass*, if that be used, will at once give the forward direction of the line. They serve the purpose of the rods described in Art. **(169)**. A distant point being thus obtained, the Compass is taken to it and the process repeated. The use of the *Transit* or *Theodolite*, for this purpose, was fully explained in Art. **(376)**.

(410) By perpendiculars. When a tree, or house, obstructing the line, is met with, place the instrument at a point B of the line, and set off there a perpendicular, to C; set off another at C to D, a third at D to E, making DE = BC, and a fourth at E, which last will be in the direction of AB prolonged. If perpendiculars cannot be conveniently used, let BC and DE make any equal angles with the line AB, so as to make CD parallel to it.

Fig. 278.

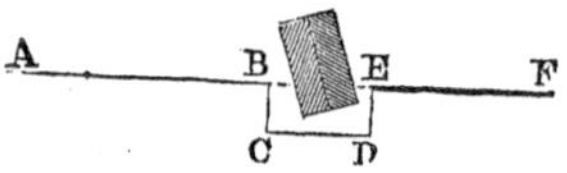

(411) By an equilateral triangle. At B, turn aside from the line at an angle of 60°, and measure some convenient distance BC. At C, turn 60° in the contrary direction, and measure a distance CD = BC. Then will D be a point in the line AB prolonged. At D, turn 60° from CD prolonged, and the new direction will be in the line of AB prolonged. This method requires the measurement of one angle less than the preceding.

Fig. 279.

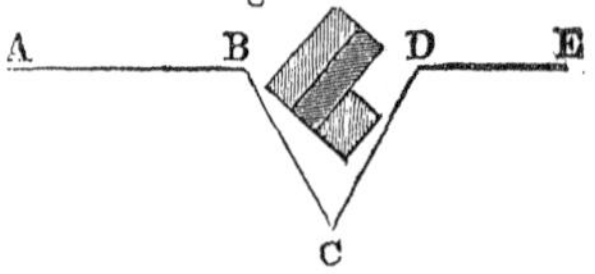

(412) By triangulation. Let AB be the line to be prolonged. Choose some station C, whence can be seen A, B, and a point beyond the obstacle. Measure AB and the angles A and B, of the triangle ABC, and thence calculate the side AC. Set the instrument at C, and measure the angle ACD, CD being any line which will clear the obstacle. Let E be the desired point in the lines AB and CD prolonged. Then in the triangle ACE, will be known the side AC and its including angles, whence CE can be calculated. Measure the resulting distance on the ground, and its extremity will be the desired point E. Set the instrument at E, sight to C, and turn an angle equal to the supplement of the angle AEC, and you will have the direction, EF, of AB prolonged

Fig. 280.

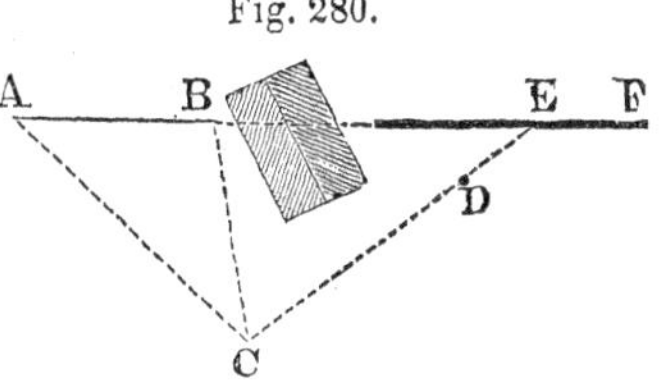

(413) When the line to be prolonged is inaccessible. In this case, before the preceding method can be applied, it will be necessary to determine the lengths of the lines AB and AC, and the angle A, by the method given in Art. (430).

(414) To prolong a line with only an angular instrument. This may be done when no means of measuring any distance can be obtained. Let AB be the line to be prolonged. Set the instrument at B and deflect angles of 45° in the directions C and D. Set at some point, C, on one of these lines and deflect from CB 45°, and mark the point D where this direction intersects the direction BD. Also, at C, deflect 90° from CB. Then, at D, deflect 90° from DB. The intersections of these last directions will fix a point E. At E deflect 135° from EC or ED, and a line EF, in the direction of AB will be obtained and may be continued.*

Fig. 281.

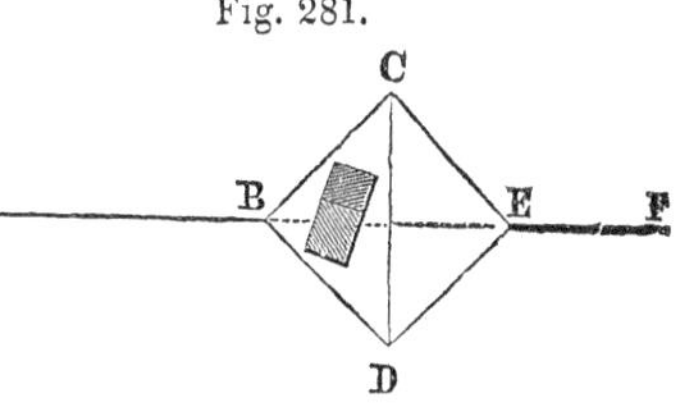

* This ingenious contrivance is due to a former student, Mr. R. Hood, in whose practice, while running an air line for a railroad, the necessity occurred.

B. TO INTERPOLATE POINTS IN A LINE.

(415) The instrument being set at one end of a line and directed to the other, intermediate points can be found as in Art. (**177**), &c. If a valley intervenes, the sights of the Compass, (if the Compass-plate be very carefully kept level cross-ways), or the telescope of the Transit or Theodolite, answer as substitutes for the plumb-line of Art. (**179**).

(416) By a random line. When a wood, hill, or other obstacle, prevents one end of the line, Z, from being seen from the other, A, run a random line AB with the Compass or Transit, &c., as nearly in the desired direction as can be guessed, till you arrive opposite the point Z. Measure the error, BZ, at right angles to AB, as an offset. Multiply this error by $57\frac{3}{10}$, and divide the product by the distance AB. The quotient will be the degrees and decimal parts of a degree, contained in the angle BAZ. Add or subtract this angle to or from the Bearing or reading with which AB was run, according to the side on which the error was, and start from A, with this corrected Bearing or reading, to run another line, which will come out at Z, if no error has been committed.*

Fig. 282.

Example. A random line was run, by compass, with a Bearing of S. 80° E. At 20 chains' distance a point was reached opposite to the desired point, and 10 links distant from it on its right. Required the correct Bearing.

Ans. By the rule, $\frac{10 \times 57^\circ.3}{2000} = 0^\circ.2865 = 17'$. The correct Bearing is therefore S. 80° 17′ E. If the Transit had been used, its reading would have been changed for the new line by the same 17′. A simple diagram of the case will at once shew whether the correction is to be added to the original Bearing or angle, or subtracted from it.

* This rule is substantially identical with that of Art. (319), where its reason is given.

If Trigonometrical Tables are at hand, the correction will be more precisely obtained from this equation; Tan. BAZ $= \frac{BZ}{AB}$.

In this example, $\frac{BZ}{AB} = \frac{10}{2000} = .005 = \text{tan. } 17'$.

The 57°.3 rule, as it is sometimes called, may be variously modified. Thus, multiply the error by 86°, and divide by one and a half times the distance; or, to get the correction in minutes, multiply by 3438 and divide by the distance; or, if the error is given in feet and the distance in four-rod chains, multiply the former by 52 and divide by the distance, to get the correction in minutes.

The correct line may be run with the Bearing of the random line, by turning the vernier for the correction, as in Art. (**312**).

(417) By Latitudes and Departures. When a single line, such as AB, cannot be run so as to come opposite to the given point Z, proceed thus, with the *Compass*. Run any number of zig-zag courses, AB, BC, CD, DZ, in any convenient direction, so as at last to arrive at the desired point. Calculate the Latitude and Departure of each of these courses and take their *algebraic* sums. The sum of the Latitudes will be equal to AX, and that of the Departures to XZ. Then is Tan. ZAX $= \frac{XZ}{XA}$; i. e. the algebraic sum of the Departures divided by the algebraic sum of the Latitudes is equal to the tangent of the Bearing.*

Fig. 283.

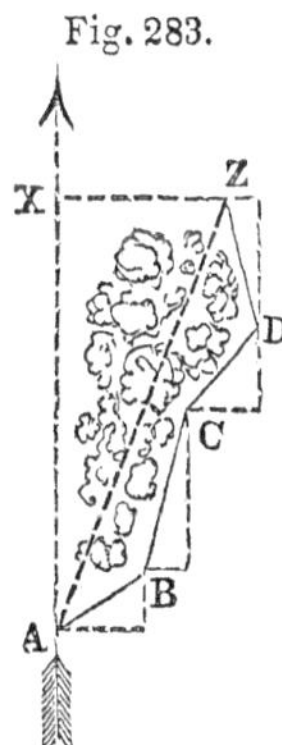

(418) When the *Transit* or *Theodolite* is used, any line may be taken as a Meridian, i. e. as the line to which the following lines are referred; as in "Traversing," Art. (**373**), page 254, all the successive lines were referred to the first line. In the figure, on the next page, the same lines as in the preceding figure are repre-

* The length of the line AZ can also be at once obtained since it is equal to the square root of the sum of the squares of AX and XZ; or to the Latitude divided by the cosine of the Bearing.

Fig. 284.

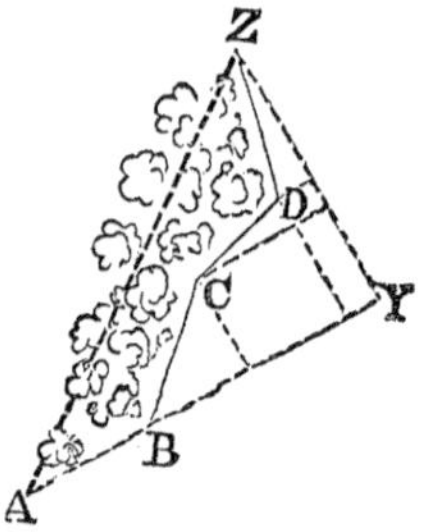

sented, but they are referred to the first course, AB, instead of to the Magnetic Meridian as before, and their Latitudes are measured along its produced line, and its Departures perpendicular to it. As before, a right-angled triangle will be formed, and the angle ZAY will be the angle at A between the first line AB and the desired line AZ.

This method of operation has many useful applications, such as in obtaining data for running Railroad Curves, &c., and the student should master it thoroughly.

The desired angle (and at the same time the distance) can be obtained, approximately, in this and the preceding case, by finding in a Traverse Table, the final Latitude and Departure of the desired line (or a Latitude and Departure having the same ratio) and the Bearing and Distance corresponding to these will be the angle and distance desired.

(419) By similar triangles. Through A measure any line CD. Take a point E, on the line CB, beyond the obstacle, and from it set off a parallel to CD, to some point, F, in the line DB. Measure EF, CD, and CA. Then this proportion, CD : CA :: EF : EG, will give the distance EG, from E to a point in the line AB. So for other points.

Fig 285.

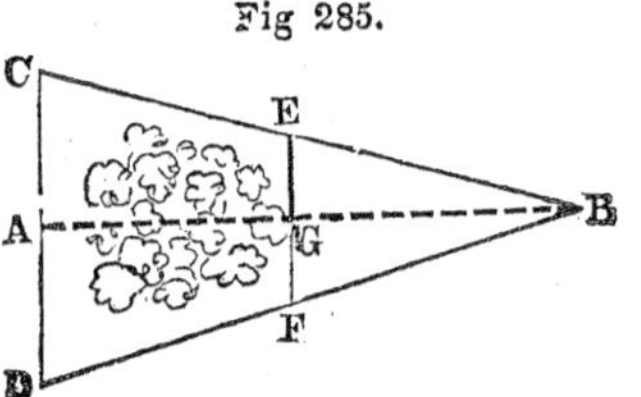

(420) By triangulation. When obstacles prevent the preceding methods being used, if a point, C, can be found, from which A and B are accessible, measure the distances CA, CB, and the angle ACB, and thence calculate the angle CAB. Then observe any angle ACD, beyond the obstacle. In the triangle ACD, a side and its including angles are known, to find CD. Measure it, and a point, D, in the desired line, will be obtained.

Fig. 286.

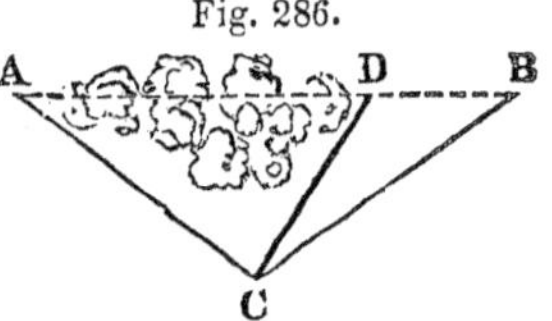

CHAPTER III.

OBSTACLES TO MEASUREMENT.

A. WHEN BOTH ENDS OF THE LINE ARE ACCESSIBLE.

(421) The methods given in the preceding Chapter for prolonging a line and for interpolating points in it, will generally give the length of the line by the same operation. Thus, in Fig. 278, the inaccessible distance BE is equal to CD; in Fig. 279, BD = BC = CD; in Fig. 280, the distance BE can be calculated from the same data as CE; in Fig. 282, $AZ = \sqrt{(AB^2 + BZ^2)}$; in Fig. 283, $AZ = \sqrt{(AX^2 + XZ^2)}$; in Fig. 284, $AZ = \sqrt{(AY^2 + YZ^2)}$; in Fig. 285, $AG = \frac{GB\ (CA - EG)}{EG}$; in Fig. 286, the triangle ACD will give the distance AD. The method of Latitudes and Departures, Arts. **(417)** and **(418)**, is very generally applicable. So is the following.

(422) By triangulation. Let AB be the inaccessible distance. From any point, C, from which both A and B are accessible, measure CA, CB, and the angle ACB. Then in the triangle ABC two sides and the included angle are known to find the side AB. If all the angles can be measured, they may be corrected, as in Art. **(387)**.*

Fig. 287.

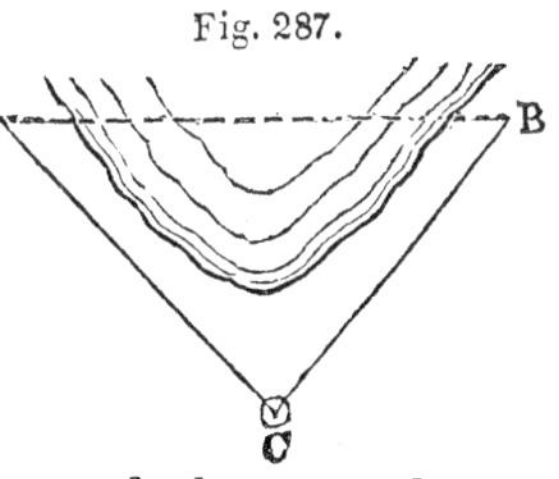

(423) A broken Base. When the angle C is very obtuse, the preceding problem may be modified as follows. Naming the lines as is usual in Trigonometry, by small letters corresponding to the

* In this figure, and the following ones, the angular point enclosed in a circle indicates the place at which the instrument is set.

capital letters at the angles to which they are opposite, and letting K = the number of minutes in the supplement of the angle C, we

Fig. 288.

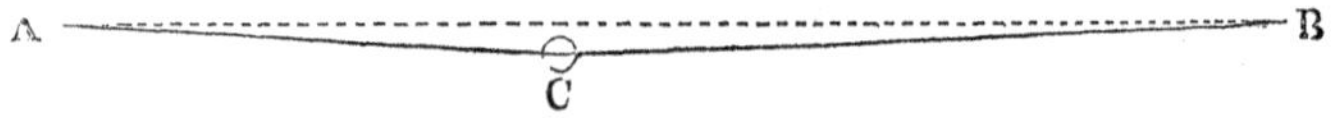

shall have

$$AB = c = a + b - 0.000000042308 \times \frac{abK^2}{a+b}.$$

This formula is chiefly used in the case of what is called in Triangular Surveying "A broken Base;" such as above; AC and CB being measured and forming very nearly a straight line, and the length of AB being required.

Log. 0.000000042308 = 2.6264222 — 10.

(424) By angles to known points. The length of a line, both ends of which are accessible, may also be determined by angles measured at its extremities between it and the directions of two or more known points. But as the methods of calculation involve subsequent problems, they will be postponed to Articles **(435)**, **(436)** and **(437)**.

B. When one end of the line is inaccessible.

(425) By perpendiculars. Many of the methods given for the chain, in Part II, Chapter V, may be still more advantageously employed with angular instruments, which can so much more easily and precisely set off the Perpendiculars required in Articles **(191)**, **(192)**, **(193)**, &c.

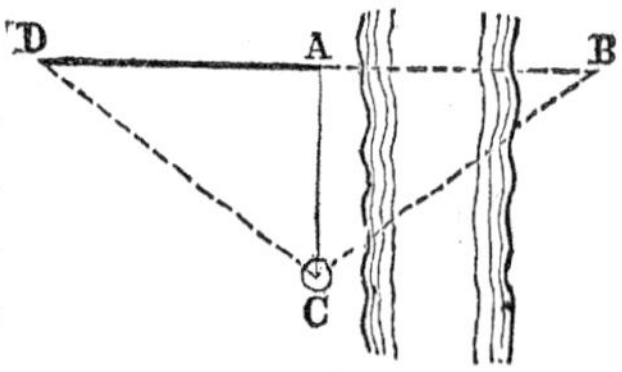

(426) By equal angles. Let AB be the inaccessible line. At A set off AC, perpendicular to AB, and as nearly equal to it, by estimation, as the ground will permit. At C, measure the angle ACB, and turn the sights, or vernier, till ACD = ACB. Find the point, D, at the intersections of the lines CD and BA produced. Then is AD = AB.

Fig. 289.

(427) By triangulation. Measure a distance AC, about equal to AB. Measure the angles at A and C. Then in the triangle ABC, two angles and the included side are known, to find another side, $AB = \frac{AC \sin. ACB}{\sin. ABC}$.

Fig. 290.

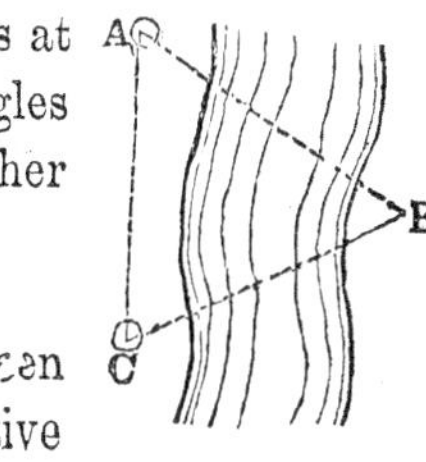

When the compass is used, the angles between the lines will be deduced from their respective Bearings, by the principles of Art. (243).

If the angle at A is 90°, $AB = AC \,.\, \text{tang.}\, ACB$.

If $A = 90°$, and $C = 45°$, then $AC = AB$; but this position could not easily be obtained, except by the use of the Sextant, a reflecting instrument, not described in this volume.

(428) When one point cannot be seen from the other.—Choose two points, C and D, in the line of A, and such that from C, A and B can be seen, and from D, A and B. Measure AC, AD, and the angles C and D. Then, in the triangle BCD, are known two angles and the included side, to find CB. Then, in the triangle ABC, are known two sides and the included angle, to find the third side, AB.

Fig. 291.

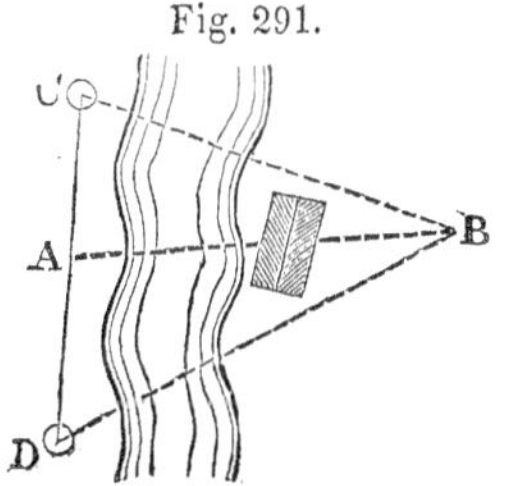

(429) To find the distance from a given point to an inaccessible line. In Fig. 275, Art. (406), the required distance is CE. The operations therein directed give the line CA and the angle CAB, or CAE. The required distance $CE = CA \,.\, \sin.\, CAE$.

C. When both ends of the line are inaccessible.

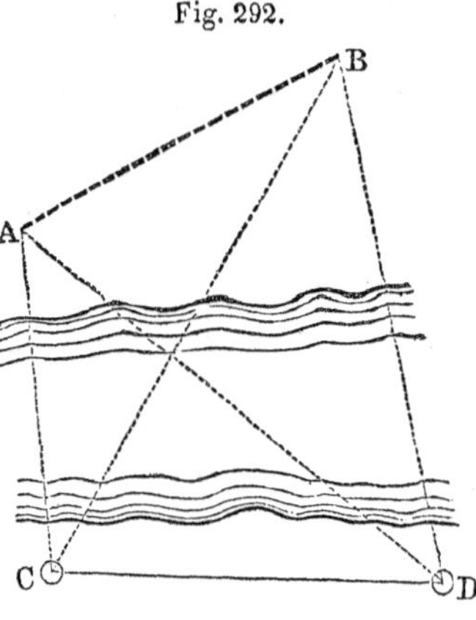

Fig. 292.

(430) General Method. Let AB be the inaccessible line. Measure any convenient distance CD, and the angles ACD, BCD, ADC, BDC.

Then, in the triangle CDA, two angles and the included side are given, to find CA. In the triangle CDB, two angles and the included side are given, to find CB. Then, in the triangle ABC, two sides and the included angle are given, to find AB.

The work may be verified by taking another set of triangles, and finding AB from the triangle ABD instead of ABC.

The following formulas will however give the desired distance with less labor.

Find an angle K, such that $\text{tang. K} = \dfrac{\text{sin. ADC . sin. CBD}}{\text{sin. CAD . sin. BDC}}$.

Then find the difference of the unknown angles in the triangle CAB from the formula

$\text{Tang. } \frac{1}{2}\,(\text{CAB} - \text{ABC}) = \text{tang. } (45° - \text{K}) \text{ . cot. } \frac{1}{2}\,\text{ACB}.$

Then is $\text{CAB} = \frac{1}{2}\,(\text{CAB} - \text{ABC}) + \frac{1}{2}\,(\text{CAB} + \text{ABC})$.

Finally, $\text{AB} = \text{CD}\,\dfrac{\text{sin. BDC . sin. ACB}}{\text{sin. CBD . sin. CAB}}$.

Example. Let CD = 7106.25 feet; ACD = 95° 17′ 20″; BCD = 61° 41′ 50″; ADC = 39° 38′ 40″; BDC = 78° 35′ 10″; required AB.

The figure is constructed with these data on a scale of 5000 feet to 1 inch = 1 : 60000.

By the above formulas, K is found to be 30° 26′ 5″; CAB = 113° 55′ 37″; and lastly AB = 6598.32.

Both the methods may be used as mutual checks in any important case.

If the lines AB and CD crossed each other, as in Fig. 293, instead of being situated as in the preceding figure, the same method of calculation would apply.

Fig. 293.

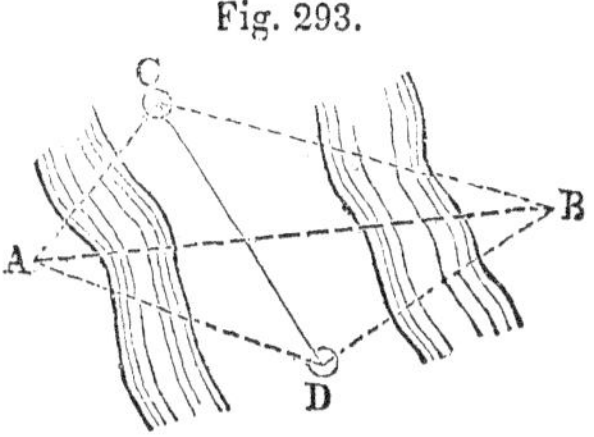

(431) **Problem.** *To measure an inaccessible distance*, AB, *when a point*, C, *in its line can be obtained.* Set the instrument at a point, D, from which A, B and C can be seen, and measure the angles CDA and ADB. Measure also the line DC and the angle C. Then in the triangle ACD two angles and the included side are given to find AD. In the triangle DAB, the angle DAB is known, (being equal to ACD + CDA), and AD having been found, we again have two angles and the included side to find AB.

Fig. 294.

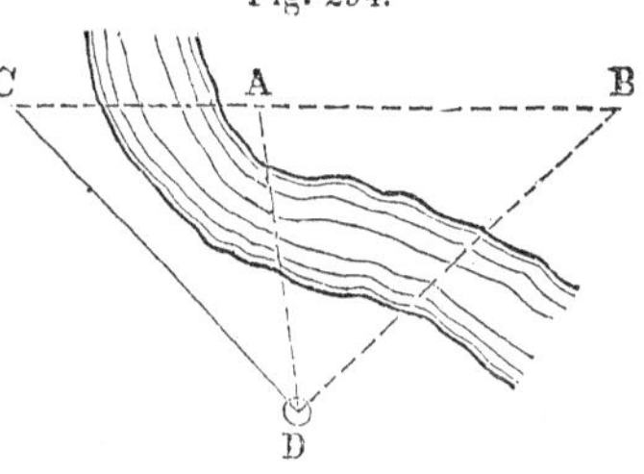

(432) **Problem.** *To measure an inaccessible distance*, AB, *when only one point*, C, *can be found from which both ends of the line can be seen.* Consider CA and CB as distances to be determined, having one end accessible. Determine them, as in Art. (427), by choosing a point D, from which C and A are visble, and a point E from which C and B are visible. At C observe the angles DCA, ACB and BCE. Measure the distances CD and CE. Observe the angles ADC and BEC. Then in the triangle ADC, two angles and the included side are given, to find CA; and the same in the triangle CBE, to find CB. Lastly, in the triangle ACB two sides and the included angle are known, to find AB.

Fig. 295.

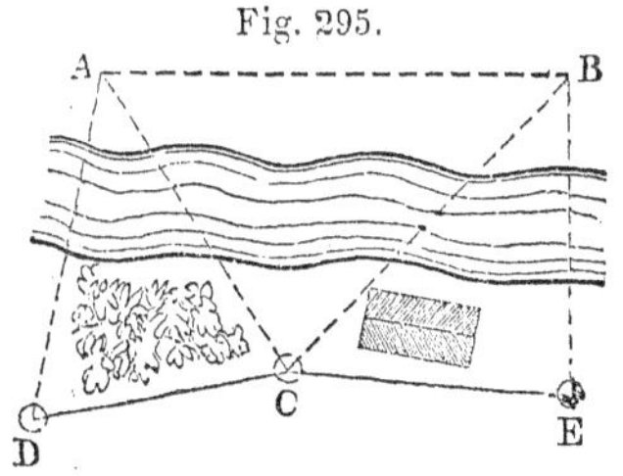

(433) Problem. *To measure an inaccessible distance,* AB, *when no point can be found from which the two ends can be seen.* Let C be a point from which A is visible, and D a point from which B is visible, and also C. Measure CD. Find the distances CA and DB, as in the preceding problem; i. e. choose a point E, from which A and C are visible, and another point, F, from which D and B are visible. Measure EC and DF. Observe the angles AEC, ECA, BDF and DFB; and at the same time the angles ACD and CDB, for the subsequent work. Then CA and DB will be found, as were CA and CB in the last problem. Then in the triangle CDB, two sides and the included angle are known to find CB and the angle DCB; and, lastly, in the triangle ACB, two sides and the included angle (the difference of ACD and DCB) to find AB.

Fig. 296.

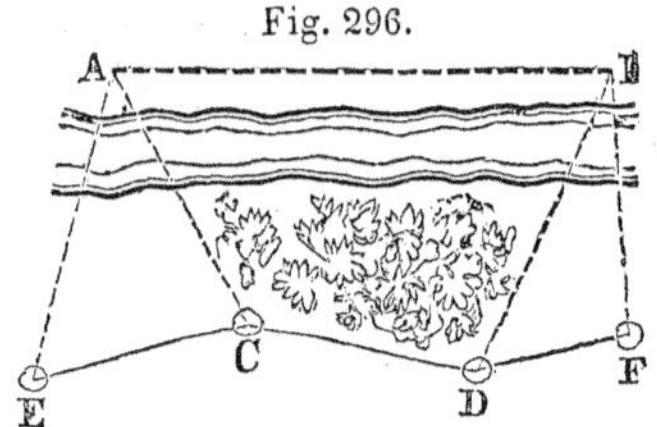

(434) Problem. To interpolate a Base. *Four inaccessible objects,* A, B, C, D, *being in a right line, and visible from only one point,* E, *it is required to determine the distance between the middle points,* B *and* C, *the exterior distances,* AB *and* CD, *being known.*

Fig. 297.

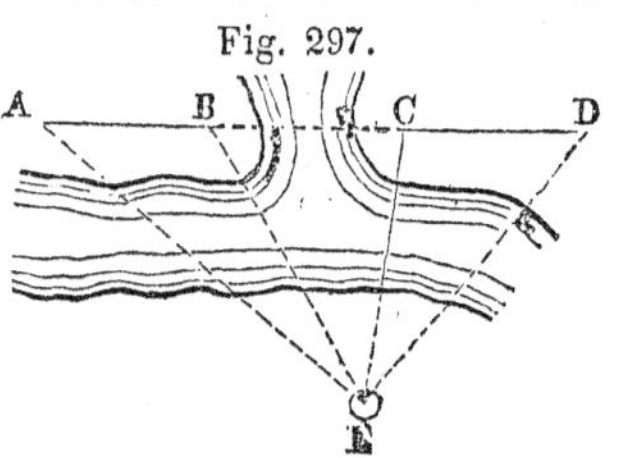

Let AB $= a$, CD $= b$, BC $= x$; AEB $=$ P, AEC $=$ Q, AED $=$ R.

Calculate an auxiliary angle, K, such that

$$\text{tang.}^2\,\text{K} = \frac{4ab}{(a-b)^2} \cdot \frac{\text{sin. Q . sin. (R — P)}}{\text{sin. P . sin. (R — Q)}}.$$

Then is $x = -\frac{a+b}{2} \pm \frac{a-b}{2\,.\,\cos.\,\text{K}}.$

Of the two values of x, the positive one is alone to be taken.

This problem is used in Triangular Surveying when a portion of a Base line passes over water, &c.

(435) Problem. *Given the angles observed, at the ends of a line which cannot be measured, between it and the ends of a line of known length but inaccessible, required the length of the former line.* This Problem is the converse of that given in Art. (**430**). Its figure, 292, may represent the case, if the distance AB be regarded as known and CD as that to be found. Use the first and second formulas as before, and invert the last formula, obtaining $CD = AB \frac{\sin. CBD \cdot \sin. CAB}{\sin. BDC \cdot \sin. ACB}$.

This problem may also be solved, indirectly, by assuming any length for CD, and thence calculating as in the first part of Art. (**430**), the length of AB on this hypothesis. The imaginary figure thus calculated is *similar* to the true one; and the true length of CD will be given by this proportion; calculated length of AB : true length of AB :: assumed length of CD : true length of CD.

The length of CD can also be obtained graphically. Take a line of any length, as C′D′, and from C′ and D′ lay off angles equal to those observed at C and D, and thus fix points A, B′. Produce AB′ till it equals the given distance AB, on any desired scale. From B draw a parallel to B′D′, meeting AD′ produced in D; and from D draw a parallel to D′C′ meeting AC′ produced in C. Then CD will be the required distance to the same scale as AB.*

Fig. 298.

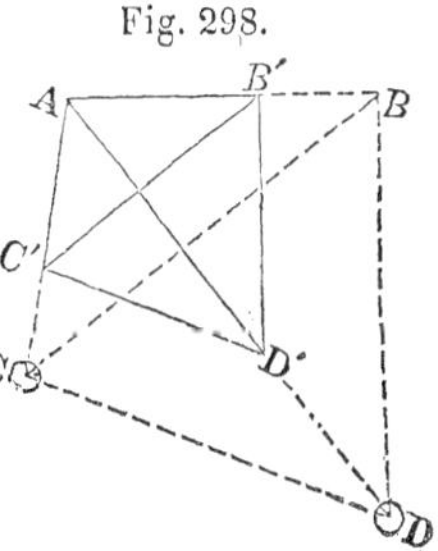

(436) Problem. *Three points,* A, B, C, *being given by their distances from each other, and two other points,* P *and* Q, *being so situated that from each of them two of the three points can be seen and the angles* APQ, BPQ, CQP, BQP, *be measured, it is required to determine the positions of* P *and* Q.

* See Article (458) for a solution of this problem by the Plane-Table.

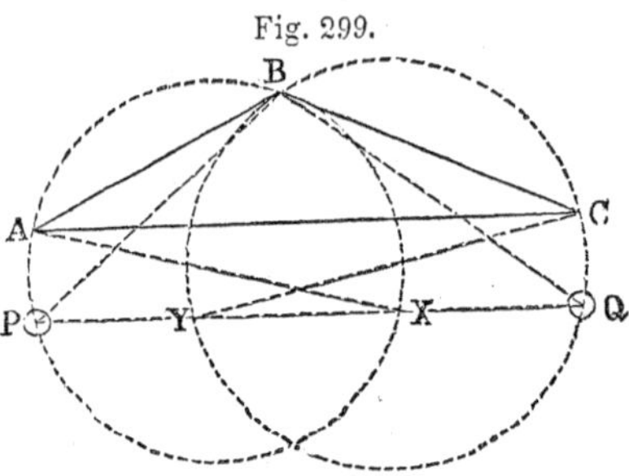

Fig. 299.

CONSTRUCTION. Begin, as in Art. (397), by describing a circle passing through A and B, and having the central angle subtended by AB, equal to twice the given angle APB, and thus containing that angle. The point P will lie somewhere in its circumference. Describe another circle passing through B and C, and having a central angle subtended by BC equal to twice the given angle BQC. The point Q will lie somewhere in its circumference. From A draw a line making with AB an angle = BPQ, and meeting at X the circle first drawn. From C draw a line making with CB an angle = BQP, and meeting the second circle in Y. Join XY and produce it till it cuts the circles in points P and Q, which will be those required; since BPX = BAX = BPQ; and BQY = BCY = BQP.

CALCULATION. In the triangle ABC, the sides being given, the angle ABC is known. In the triangle ABX, a side and all the angles are known, to find BX. In the triangle CBY, BY is similarly found. By subtracting the angle ABC from the sum of the angles ABX and CBY, the angle XBY can be obtained. Then in the triangle XBY, the sides BX, BY, and the included angle are given to find the other angles. Then in the triangle BPX are known all the angles and the side BX to find BP. In the triangle BQY, BQ is found in like manner. Finally, in the triangle BPQ, PQ can then be found.

If desired, we can also obtain AP in the triangle APB; and CQ in the triangle CBQ.

(437) Problem. *Four points,* A, B, C, D, *being given in position, by their mutual distances and directions, and two other points,* P *and* Q, *being so situated that from each of them two of the four points can be seen and the angles* APB, APQ, PQC *and* PQD *measured, it is required to determine the position of* P *and* Q.

Fig. 300.

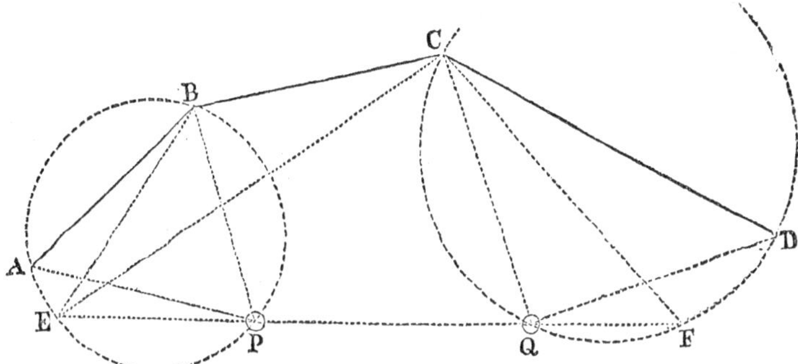

Construction. Begin as in the last article, by describing on AB the segment of a circle to contain an angle equal to APB. From B draw a chord BE, making an angle with BA equal to the supplement of the angle APQ. On CD describe another segment to contain an angle equal to CQD. From C draw a chord CF, making an angle with CD equal to the supplement of the angle DQP. Draw the line EF, and it will cut the two circles in the required points P and Q.*

Calculation. To obtain PQ = EF — EP — QF, we proceed to find those three lines thus. In the triangle ABE, we know the side AB, the angle ABE, and the angle AEB = APB; whence to find EB. In the same way, the triangle CFD gives FC. In the triangle EBC are known EB and BC, and the angle EBC = ABC — ABE; whence EC and the angle ECB are found. In the triangle ECF are known EC, FC, and the angle ECF = BCD — ECB — FCD; whence we find EF, and the angles CEF and CFE.

In the triangle BEP, we have EB, the angle BEP = BEC + CEP, and the angle BPE = BPA + APE; to find EP and PB. In the triangle QCF, we have CF, and the angles CQF and CFQ, to find QC and QF. Then we know PQ = EF — EP — QF.

* For, the angle APQ in the figure equals the measured angle APQ, because the supplement of the former, EPA, equals the supplement of the latter, since it is measured by the same arc as the angle ABE, equal to that supplement by construction. So too with the angle DQP.

The other distances, if desired, can be easily found from the above data, some of the calculations, not needed for PQ, being made with reference to them. In the triangle ABP, we know AB, BP, and the angle BAP, to find the angle ABP and AP. In the triangle QDC we know QC, CD, and the angle CQD, to find the angle QCD and QD. In the triangle PBC, we know PB, BC, and the angle PBC = ABC — ABP, to find PC. Lastly, in the triangle QCB, we know QC, CB, and the angle QCB = DCB — DCQ, to find QB.

The solution of this problem includes the two preceding; for, let the line BC be reduced to a point so that its two ends come together and the three lines become two, and we have the problem of Art. (436); and let the line AB be reduced to a point, B, and CD to a point, C, and we have but one line, and the problem becomes that of Art. (435).

In these three problems, if the two stations lie in a right line with one of the given points, the problem is indeterminate.

(438) Problem of the eight points. *Four points*, A, B, C, D, *are inaccessible, but visible from four other points*, E, F, G, H; *it is required to find the respective distances of these eight points; the only data being the observation, from each of the points of the second system, of the angles under which are seen the points of the first system.*

Fig. 301.

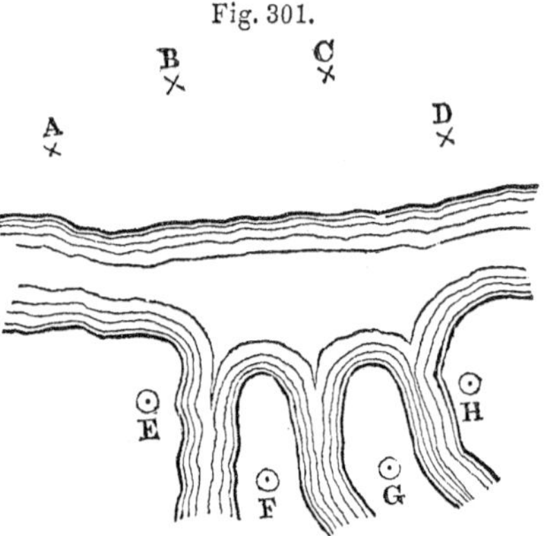

This problem can be solved, but the great length and complication of the investigation and resulting formulas render it more a matter of curiosity than of utility. It may be found in Puissant's "*Topographie*," page 55; Lefevre's "*Trigonometrie*," p. 90, and Lefevre's "*Arpentage*," No. 387.

CHAPTER IV.

TO SUPPLY OMISSIONS.

(439) Any two omissions in a closed survey, whether of the direction or of the length, or of both, of one or more of the sides bounding the area surveyed, can always be supplied by a suitable application of the principle of Latitudes and Departures, as was stated in Art. (**283**); although this means should be resorted to only in cases of absolute necessity, since any omission renders it impossible to "Test the survey," as directed in Art. (**282**). In the following articles the survey will be considered to have been made with the Compass. All the rules will however apply to a Transit or Theodolite survey, the angles being referred to any line as a meridian, as in "Traversing."

To save unnecessary labor, the examples in the various cases now to be examined, will all be taken from the same survey, a plat of which is given in the margin on the scale of 40 chains to 1 inch (1:31,680), and the Field-notes of which, with the Latitudes and Departures carried out to five decimal places, are given on the following page.*

Fig. 302.

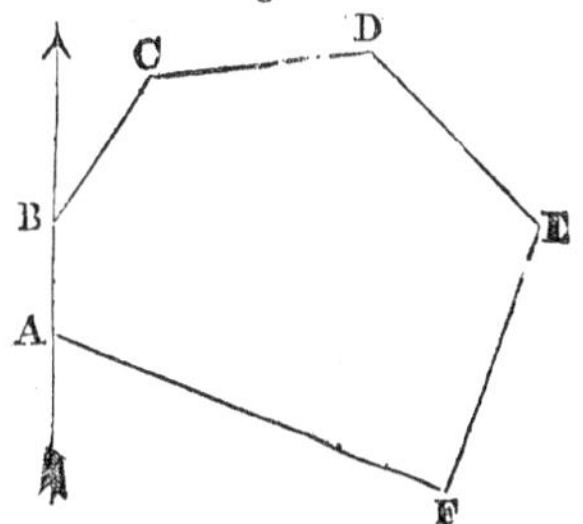

* The teacher can make any number of examples for his own use by taking a tolerably accurate survey, striking out the bearing and distance of any one course, and calculating it precisely as in Case 1, given below. He can then omit any two quantities at will, to be supplied by the student by means of the rules now to be given.

STA.	BEARING.	DIST. IN LINKS.	LATITUDES.		DEPARTURES.	
			N.	S.	E.	W.
A	North.	1284	1284.00000		0	0
B	N. 32° E.	1782	1511.22171		944.31619	
C	N. 80° E.	2400	416.75568		2363.53872	
D	S. 48° E.	2700		1806.65262	2006.49096	
E	S. 18° W.	2860		2720.02159		883.78862
F	N. 73° 28′ 21″ W.	4621½	1314.69682			4430.55725
			4526.67421	4526.67421	5314.34587	5314.34587

CASE 1. *When the length and the Bearing of any one side are wanting.*

(440) Find the Latitudes and the Departures of the remaining sides. The difference of the North and South Latitudes of these lines, is the Latitude of the omitted line, and the difference of their Departures is its Departure. This Latitude and Departure are two sides of a right angled triangle of which the omitted line is the hypothenuse. Its length is therefore equal to the square root of the sum of their squares, and the quotient of the Departure divided by the Latitude is the tangent of its Bearing; as in Art. (**417**).

In the above survey, suppose the course from F to A to have been omitted or lost. The difference of the Latitudes of the remaining courses will be found to be 1314.69682, and the difference of the Departures to be 4430.55725. The square root of the sum of their squares is 4621.5; and the quotient of the Departure divided by the Latitude is the tangent of 73° 28′ 21″. The deficiencies were in North Latitude and West Departure; and the omitted course is therefore N. 73° 28′ 21″ W., 4621.5

CASE 2. *When the length of one side and the Bearing of another are wanting.*

(441) When the deficient sides adjoin each other. Find, as in Case 1, the length and Bearing of the line joining the ends of the remaining courses. This line and the deficient lines will form a triangle, in which two sides will be known, and the angle between the calculated side and the side whose Bearing is given can be found by Art. (**243**). The parts wanting can then be obtained by the common rules of Trigonometry.

Fig. 303.

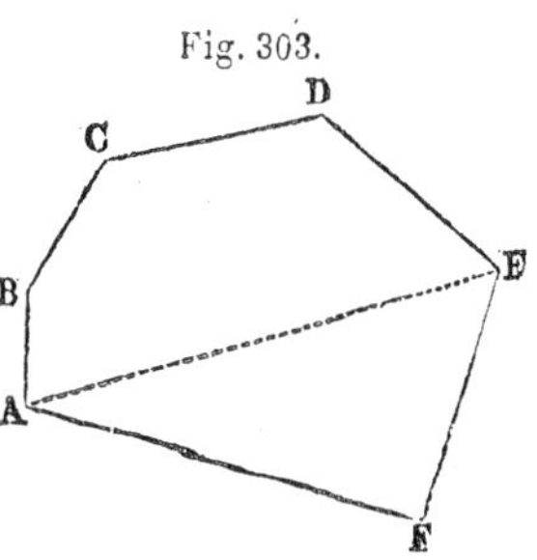

In the figure, let the length of EF, and the Bearing of FA be the omitted parts. The difference of the sums of the N. and S. Latitudes, and the E. and W. Departures of the complete courses from A to E, are respectively 1405.32477 North Latitude, and 5314.34587 East Departure. The course, EA, corresponding to this deficiency we find, by proceeding as in case 1, to be S. 75° 11′ 15 W., 5497.026. The angle AEF is therefore = 75° 11′ 15″ 18° = 57° 11′ 15″. Then in the triangle AEF are given the sides AE, AF, and the angle AEF to find the remaining parts; viz. the angle AFE = 91° 28′ 21″, whence the Bearing of FA = 91° 28′ 21″ — 18° = N. 73° 28′ 21″ W.; and the side EF = 2860.

(442) **When the deficient sides are separated from each other.** A modification of the preceding method will still apply. In this figure let the omissions be the Bearing of FA and the length of CD. Imagine the courses to change places without changing Bearings or lengths, so as to bring the deficient lines next to each other, by transferring CD to AG, AB to GH, and BC to HD. This will not affect their Latitudes or Departures. Join GF. Then in the figure DEFGH, the Latitudes and Departures of all the sides but FG are known, whence its length and Bearing can be found as in Case 1. Then the triangle AGF may be treated like the triangle AEF in the last article, to obtain the length of AG = CD, and the Bearing of FA.

Fig. 304.

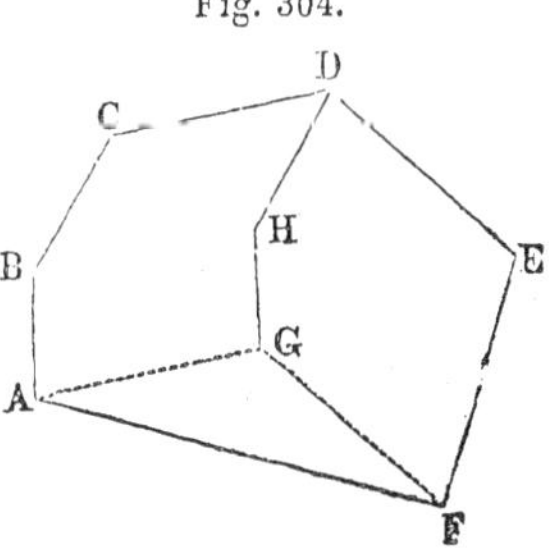

(443) *Otherwise, by changing the Meridian.* Imagine the field to turn around, till the side of which the distance is unknown, becomes the Meridian, i. e. comes to be due North and South

all the other sides retaining their *relative* positions, and continuing to make the same angles with each other. Change their Bearings, accordingly, as directed in Art. (**244**). Find the Latitudes and Departures of the sides in their new positions. Since the side whose length was unknown has been made the Meridian, it has no Departure, whatever may be its unknown length; and the difference of the columns of Departure will therefore be the Departure of the side whose Bearing is unknown. The length of this side is given. It is the hypothenuse of a right angled triangle, of which the Departure is one side. Hence the other side, which is the Latitude, can be at once found; and also the unknown Bearing.

Put this Latitude in the Table in the blank where it belongs. Then add up the columns of Latitude, and the difference of their sums will be the unknown length of the side which had been made a Meridian.*

Let the omitted quantities be, as in the last article, the length of CD and the Bearing of FA. Make CD the Meridian. The changed Bearings will then be found by Art. (**244**) to be as in the margin. To aid the imagination, turn the book around till CD points up and down, as North lines are usually placed on a map. Then obtain the Latitudes of the courses with their new Bearings and old distances, and proceed as has been directed.

STA.	OLD BEARING.	NEW BEARING.
A	North.	N. 80° W.
B	N. 32° E.	N. 48° W.
C	N. 80° E.	*North.*
D	S. 48° E.	N. 52° E.
E	S. 18° W.	S. 62° E.
F		

CASE 3. *When the lengths of two sides are wanting.*

(444) When the deficient sides adjoin each other. Find the Latitudes and Departures of the other courses, and then, by Case 1, find the length and Bearing of the line joining the extremities of the deficient courses. Then, in the triangle thus formed, are known one side and all the angles (deduced from the Bearings) to find the lengths of the other two sides.

* This conception of thus changing the Bearings is stated to be due to Prof. Robert Patterson, of Philadelphia, by whom it was communicated to Mr. John Gummere, and published by him, in 1814, in his "Treatise on Surveying."

Thus, in Fig. 303, page 299, let EF and FA be the sides whose lengths are unknown. EA is then to be calculated, and its length will be found, as in Art. (441), to be 5497.026, and its bearing S. 75° 11′ 15″ W., whence the angle AEF = 75° 11′ 15″ — 18° = 57° 11′ 15″; AFE = 18° + 73° 28′ 21″ = 91° 28′ 21″; and EAF = 31° 20′ 24″; whence can be obtained EF = 2860 and FA = 4621.5.

(445) When the deficient sides are separated from each other. Let the lengths of BC and DE be those omitted. Again imagine the courses to change places, so as to bring the deficient lines together, DE being transferred to CG, and CD to GE. Join BG. Then in the figure ABGEFA, are known the Latitudes and Departures of all the courses except BG, whence its length and Bearing can be found as in Case 1. Then in the triangle BCG, the angle CBG can be found from the Bearings of CB and BG, and the angle CGB from the Bearings of BG and GC. Then all the angles of the triangle are known and one side, BG, whence to find the required sides, BC = 1782, and CG = DE = 2700.

Fig. 305.

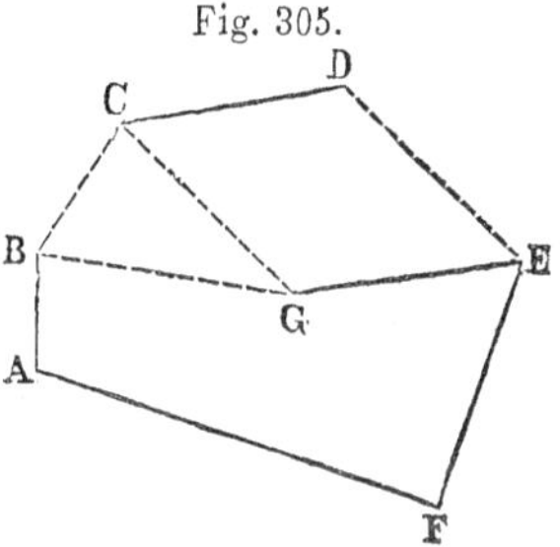

(446) *Otherwise, by changing the Meridian.* As in Art. (443), imagine the field to turn around, till one of the sides whose length is wanting, becomes a Meridian or due North and South. Change all the Bearings correspondingly. Find the Latitudes and Departures of the changed courses. The difference of the columns of Departure will be the Departure of the second course of unknown length, since the course made Meridian has now no Departure. The new Bearing of this second course being given, in the right angled triangle formed by this course (as an hypothenuse) and its Departure and Latitude, we know one side, the Departure, and the acute angles, which are the Bearing and its complement. The length of the course is then readily calculated; and also its Latitude. This Latitude being inserted in its proper place, the difference of the columns of Latitude will be the length of that wanting side which had been made a Meridian.

Thus, let the lengths of BC and DE be wanting, as in the preceding example. Make BC a Meridian. The other Bearings are then changed as in the margin. Calculate new Latitudes and Departures. The difference of the Departures will be the Departure of DE, since BC, being a Meridian, has no Departure. Hence the length and Latitude of DE are readily obtained. This Latitude being put in the table, and the columns of Latitude then added up, their difference will be the length of BC.

STA.	OLD BEARING.	NEW BEARING.
A	North.	N. 32° W.
B	N. 32° E.	*North.*
C	N. 80° E.	N. 48° E.
D	S 48° E.	S. 80° E.
E	S. 18° W.	S. 14° E.
F	N. 73° 28′ 21″ W.	S. 74° 31′ 39″ W.

CASE 4. *When the Bearings of two sides are wanting.*

(447) When the deficient sides adjoin each other. Find the Latitudes and Departures of the other sides, and then, as in Case 1, find the length and bearing of the line joining the extremities of the deficient sides. Then in the triangle thus formed we have the three sides to find the angles and thence the Bearings.

(448) When the deficient sides are separated from each other Change the places of the sides so as to bring the deficient ones next to each other. Thus, in the figure, supposing the Bearings of CD, and EF to be wanting, transfer EF to DG, and DE to GF. Then calculate, as in Case 1, the length and Bearing of the line joining the extremities of the deficient sides, CG in the figure. This line and the deficient sides form a triangle in which the three sides are given to determine the angles and thence the required Bearings.

Fig. 306.

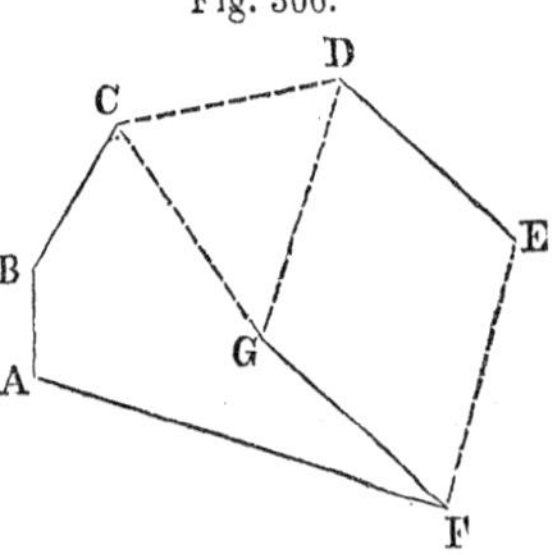

* The fullest investigation of this subject, developing many curious points, will be found in Mascheroni's "*Problèmes de Géométrie pour les Arpenteurs,*" and Lhuillier's "*Polygonométrie.*" The method of Arts. (442), (445), and (448) is new.

PART VIII.

PLANE TABLE SURVEYING.

(449) The Plane Table is in substance merely a drawing board fixed on a tripod, so that lines may be drawn on it by a ruler placed so as to point to any object in sight. All its parts are mere additions to render this operation more convenient and precise.*

Such an arrangement may be applied to any kind of "Angular Surveying"; such as the Third Method, "Polar Surveying," in its two modifications of *Radiation* and *Progression*, (characterized in Art. (**220**)), and the Fourth Method, by *Intersections*. Each of these will be successively explained. The instrument is very convenient for filling in the details of a survey, when the principal points have been determined by the more precise method of "Triangular Surveying," and can then be platted on the paper in advance. It has the great advantage of dispensing with all notes and records of the measurements, since they are platted as they are made. It thus saves time and lessens mistakes, but is wanting in precision.

(450) The Table. It is usually a rectangular board of well seasoned pine, about 20 inches wide and 30 long. The paper to be drawn upon may be attached to it by drawing-pins, or by clamping plates fixed on its sides for that purpose, or by springs pressed upon it, or it may be held between rollers at opposite sides of the table. Tinted paper is less dazzling in the sun. Cugnot's joint, described on page 134, is the best for connecting it with its tripod, though a pair of parallel plates, like those of the Theodolite, are often used. A detached level is placed on the board to test its horizontality; though a smooth ball, as a marble, will answer the same purpose approximately.

* The Plane Table is not a *Goniometer*, or *Angle-measure*, like the Compass, Transit, &c.; but a *Gonigraph*, or *Angle-drawer*.

A pair of sights, like those of the compass, are sometimes placed under the board, serving, like a "Watch Telescope," (Art. (339), to detect any movement of the instrument. To find what point on the lower side of the board is exactly under a point on the upper side, so that by suspending a plumb-line from the former the latter may be exactly over any desired point of ground, a large pair of "callipers," or dividers with curved legs, may be used, one of their points being placed on the upper point of the board, and their other point then determining the corresponding under point; or a frame forming three sides of a rectangle, like a slate frame, may be placed so that one end of one side of it touches the upper point, and the end of the corresponding side is under the table precisely below the given point, so that from this end a plumb-line can be dropped. A compass is sometimes attached to the table, or a detached compass, consisting of a needle in a narrow box, (called a Declinator), is placed upon it, as desired. The edges of the table are sometimes divided into degrees, like the "Drawing board Protractor," Art. (273). It then becomes a sort of Goniometer, like that of Art. (213).

(451) The Alidade. The ruler has a fiducial or feather edge, which may be divided into inches, tenths, &c. At each end it carries a sight like those of the compass. Two needles would be tolerable substitutes. The sights project beyond its edge so that their centre lines shall be precisely in the same vertical plane as this edge, in order that the lines drawn by it may correspond to the lines sighted on by them. To test this, fix a needle in the board, place the ruler against it, sight to some near point, draw a line by the ruler, turn it end for end, again place it against the needle, again sight to the same point, and draw a new line. If it coincides with the former line, the above condition is satisfied. The ruler and sights together take the name of *Alidade*. If a point should be too high or too low to be seen with the alidade, a plumb-line, held between the eye and the object, will remove the difficulty.

A telescope is sometimes substituted for the sights, being supported above the ruler by a standard, and capable of pointing upward or downward. It admits of adjustments similar in principle to the 2d and 3d adjustments of the Transit, Part IV, Chapter 3, pages 242 and 246.

But even without these adjustments, whether of the sights or of the telescope, a survey could be made which would be perfectly correct as to the relative position of its parts, however far the line of sight might be from lying in the same vertical plane as the edge of the ruler, or even from being parallel to it; just as in the Transit or Theodolite the index or vernier need not to be exactly under the vertical hair of the telescope, since the angular deviation affects all the observed directions equally.

(452) Method of Radiation. This is the simplest, though not the best, method of surveying with the Plane-table. It is especially applicable to surveying a field, as in the figure. In it and the following figures, the size of the Table is much exaggerated. Set the instrument at any convenient point, as O; level it, and fix a needle (having a head of sealing-wax) in the board to represent the station. Direct the alidade to any corner of the field, as A, the fiducial edge of the ruler touching the needle, and draw an indefinite line by it. Measure OA, and set off the distance, to any desired scale, from the needle point, along the line just drawn, to *a*. The line OA is thus platted on the paper of the table as soon as determined in the field. Determine and plat in the same way, OB, OC, &c., to *b*, *c*, &c. Join *ab*, *bc*, &c., and a complete plat of the field is obtained. Trees, houses, hills, bends of rivers, &c., may be determnied in the same manner. The corresponding method with the Compass or Transit, was described in Articles (258) and (391). The table may be set at one of the angles of the field, if more convenient. If the alidade has a telescope, the method of measuring distances with a stadia, described in Art. (375), may be here applied with great advantage.

Fig. 307.

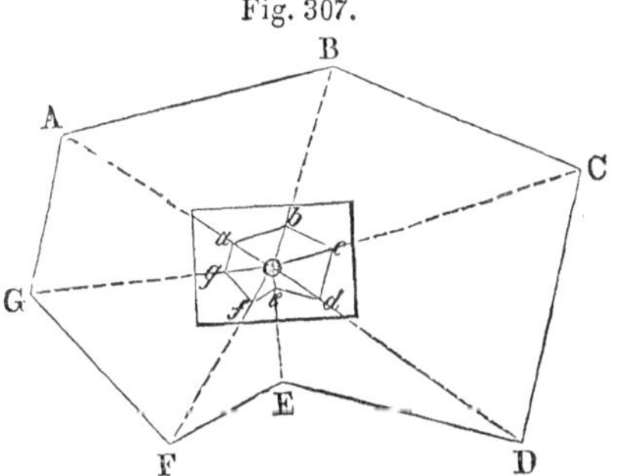

(453) Method of Progression. Let ABCD, &c., be the line to be surveyed. Fix a needle at a convenient point of the Plane-table, near a corner so as to leave room for the plat, and set up the table at B, the second angle of the line, so that the needle, whose point represents B, and which should be named *b*, shall be exactly over that station. Sight to A, pressing the fiducial edge of the ruler against the needle, and draw a line by it. Measure BA, and set off its length, to the desired scale, on the line just drawn, from *b* to a point *a*, representing A. Then sight to C, draw an indefinite line by the ruler, and on it set off the length of BC from *b* to *c*. Fix the needle at *c*. Set up at C, the point *c* being over this station, and make the line *cb* of the plat coincide in direction with CB on the ground, by placing the edge of the ruler on *cb*, and turning the table till the sights point to B. The compass, if the table have one, will facilitate this. Then sight forward from C to D, and fix CD, *cd* on the plat, as *bc* was fixed. Set up at D, make *dc* coincide with DC, and proceed as before. The figure shews the lines drawn at each successive station. The Table drawn at A shews how the survey might be commenced there.

Fig. 308.

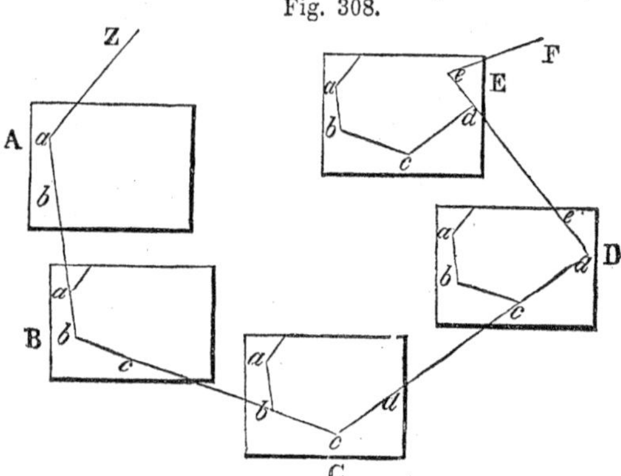

In going around a field, the work would be proved by the last line "closing" at the starting point; and, during the progress of the survey, by any direction, as from C to A on the ground, coinciding with the corresponding line, *ca*, on the plat.

This method is substantially the same as the method of surveying a line with the Transit, explained in Art. (**372**). It requires all the points to be accessible. It is especially suited to the survey of a road, a brook, a winding path through woods, &c. The offsets required may often be sketched in by eye with sufficient precision.

When the paper is filled, put on a new sheet, and begin by fixing on it two points, such as C and D, which were on the former sheet, and from them proceed as before. The sheets can then be afterwards united, so that all the points on both shall be in their true relative positions.

(454) Method of Intersection. This is the most usual and the most rapid method of using the Plane-table. The principle was referred to in Articles (**259**) and (**392**). Set up the instrument at any convenient point, as X in the figure, and sight to all

Fig. 309.

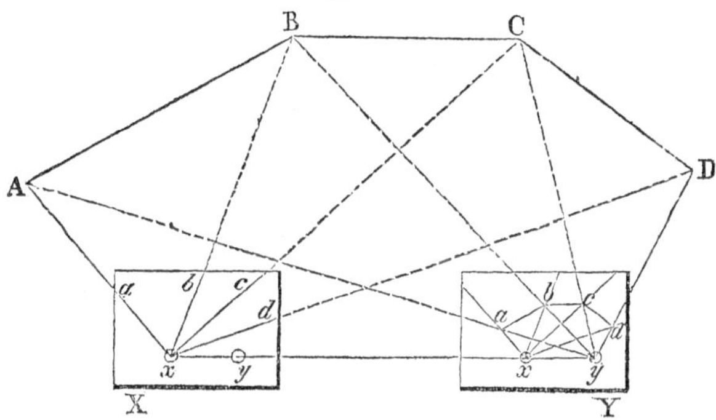

the desired points A, B, C, &c., which are visible, and draw indefinite lines in their directions. Measure any line XY, Y being one of the points sighted to, and set off this line on the paper to any scale. Set up at Y, and turn the table till the line XY on the paper lies in the direction of XY, on the ground, as at C in the last method. Sight to all the former points and draw lines in their directions, and the intersections of the two lines of sight to each point will determine them, by the Fourth Method, Art. (8). Points on the other side of the line XY could be determined at the same time. In surveying a field, one side of it may be taken for the base XY. Very acute or obtuse intersections should be avoided. 30° and 150° should be the *extreme* limits. The impossibility of always doing this, renders this method often deficient in precision. When the paper is filled, put on a new sheet, by fixing on it two known points, as in the preceding method.

(455) Method of Resection. This method (called by the French *Recoupement*) is a modification of the preceding method of Inter

Fig. 310.

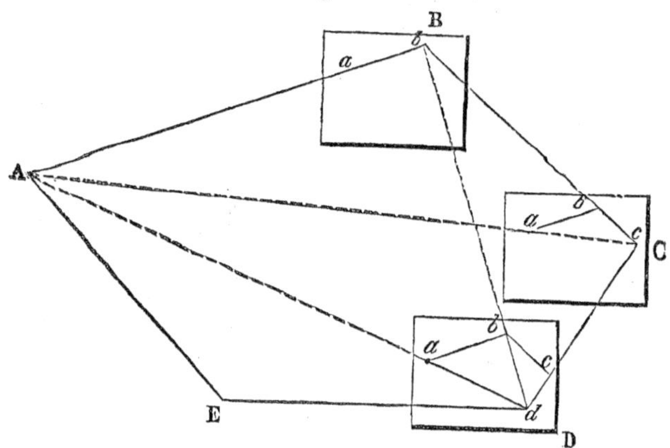

section. It requires the measurement of only one distance, but all the points must be accessible. Let AB be the measured distance. Lay it off on the paper as *ab*. Set the table up at B, and turn it till the line *ba* on the paper coincides with BA on the ground, as in the Method of Progression. Then sight to C, and draw an indefinite line by the ruler. Set up at C, and turn the line last drawn so as to point to B. Fix a needle at *a* on the table, place the alidade against the needle and turn it till it sights to A. Then the point in which the edge of the ruler cuts the line drawn from B will be the point *c* on the table. Next sight to D, and draw an indefinite line. Set up at D, and make the line last drawn point to C. Then fix the needle at *a* or *b*, and by the alidade, as at the last station, get a new line back from either of them, to cut the last drawn line at a point which will be *d*. So proceed as far as desired.

(456) To orient the table.* The operation of orientation consists in placing the table at any point so that its lines shall have the same directions as when it was at previous stations in the same survey.

* The French phrase, To *orient* one's self, meaning to determine one's position, usually with respect to the four quarters of the heavens, of which the Orient is the leading one, well deserves naturalization in our language.

With a compass, this is very easily effected by turning the table till the needle of the attached compass, or that of the Declinator, placed in a fixed position, points to the same degree as when at the previous station.

Without a compass the table is oriented, when set at one end of a line previously determined, by sighting back on this line, as at C in the Method of Progression, Art. (453).

To orient the table, when at a station unconnected with others, is more difficult. It may be effected thus. Let *ab* on the table represent a line AB on the ground. Set up at A, make *ab* coincide with AB, and draw a line from *a* directed towards a steeple, or other conspicuous object, as S. Do the same at B. Draw a line *cd*, parallel to *ab*, and intercepted between *a*S, and *b*S. Divide *ab* and *cd* into the same number of equal parts. The table is then prepared. Now let there be a station, P, *p* on the table, at which the table is to be oriented. Set the table, so that *p* is over P, apply the edge of the ruler to *p*, and turn it till this edge cuts *cd* in the division corresponding to that in which it cuts *ab*. Then turn the table till the sights point to S, and the table will be oriented.

Fig. 311.

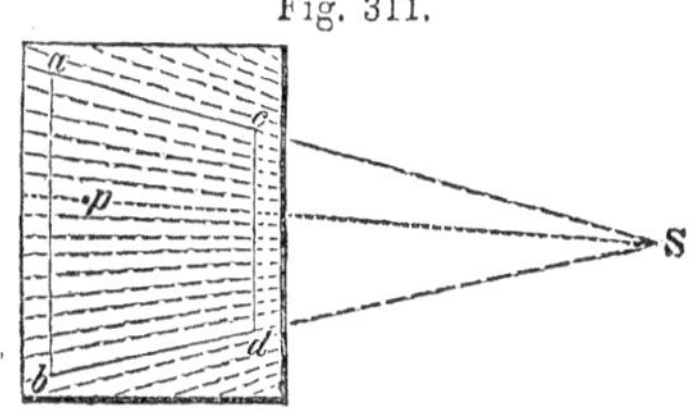

(457) To find one's place on the ground. This problem may be otherwise expressed as Interpolating a point in a plat. It is most easily performed by reversing the Method of Intersection. Set up the table over the station, O in the figure, whose place on the plat already on the table is desired, and *orient* it, by one of the means described in the last article. Make the edge of the ruler pass through some point, *a* on the table, and turn it till the sights point to the corresponding station, A on the ground. Draw a line by the ruler. The desired

Fig. 312.

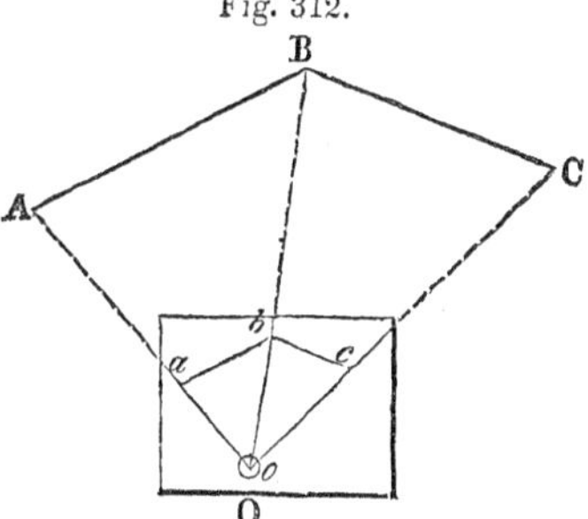

point is somewhere in this line. Make the ruler pass through another point, *b* on the table, and make the sights point to B on the ground Draw a second line, and its intersection with the first will be the point desired. Using C in the same way would give a third line to prove the work. This operation may be used as a new method of surveying with the plane-table, since any number of points can have their places fixed in the same manner.

This problem may also be executed on the principle of Trilinear Surveying. Three points being given on the table, lay on it a piece of transparent paper, fix a needle any where on this, and with the alidade sight and draw lines towards each of these three points on the ground. Then use this paper to find the desired point, precisely as directed in the last sentence of Art. (**398**), page 277.

(**458**) **Inaccessible distances.** Many of the problems in Part VII. can be at once solved on the ground by the plane-table, since it is at the same time a Goniometer and a. Protractor. Thus, the Problem of Art. (**435**) may be solved as follows, on the principle of the construction in the last paragraph of that article. Set the table at C. Mark on it a point, c', to represent C, placing c' vertically over C. Sight to A, B and D, and draw corresponding lines from c'. Set up at D, mark any point on the line drawn from c' towards D, and call it d'. Let d' be exactly over D, and direct $d'c'$ toward C. Then sight to A and B, and draw corresponding lines, and their intersections with the lines before drawn towards A and B will fix points a' and b'. Then on the line joining a and b, given on the paper to represent A and B, ab being equal to AB on any scale, construct a figure, $abcd$, *similar* to $a'b'c'd'$, and the line cd thus determined will represent CD on the same scale as AB

PART IX.

SURVEYING WITHOUT INSTRUMENTS.

(459) THE Principles which were established in Part I, and subsequently applied to surveying with various instruments, may also be employed, with tolerable correctness, for determining and representing the relative positions of larger or smaller portions of the earth's surface without any Instruments but such as can be extemporized.

The prominent objects on the ground, such as houses, trees, the summits of hills, the bends of rivers, the crossings of roads, &c., are regarded as "points" to be "determined." Distances and angles are consequently required. Approximate methods of obtaining these will therefore be first given.

(460) Distances by pacing. Quite an accurate measurement of a line of ground may be made by walking over it at a uniform pace, and counting the steps taken. But the art of walking in a straight line must first be acquired. To do this, fix the eye on two objects in the desired line, such as two trees, or bushes, or stones, or tufts of grass. Walk forward, keeping the nearest of these objects steadily covering the other. Before getting up to the nearest object, choose a new one in line farther ahead, and then proceed as before, and so on. It is better not to attempt to make each of the paces three feet, but to take steps of the natural length, and to ascertain the value of each by walking over a known distance, and dividing it by the number of paces required to traverse it. Every person should thus determine the usual length of his own steps, repeating the experiment sufficiently often. The French "Geographical Engineers" accustom themselves to take regular steps of eight-tenths of a *metre*, equal to two feet seven and a half inches. The English military pace is two feet and six inches. This is regarded as a usual average. 108 such paces per minute give 3.07 English miles per hour. Quick pacing of 120 such paces per minute gives 3.41 miles per hour. Slow paces, of three feet each and 60 per minute, give 2.04 miles per hour.*

An instrument, called a Pedometer, has been contrived, which counts the steps taken by one wearing it, without any attention on his part. It is attached to the body, and a cord, passing from it to the foot, at each step moves a toothed wheel one division, and some intermediate wheelwork records the whole number upon a dial.

(461) Distances by visual angles. Prepare *a scale*, by marking off on a pencil what length of it, when it is held off at arm's length, a man's height appears to cover at different distances (previously measured with accuracy) of 100, 500, 1000 feet, &c. To apply this, when a man is seen at any unknown distance, hold up the pencil at arm's length, making the top of it come in the line from the eye to his head, and placing the thumb nail in the line from

Fig. 313.

the eye to his feet, as in Fig. 313. The pencil having been previously graduated by the method above explained, the portion of it now intercepted between these two lines will indicate the corresponding distance.

If no previous scale have been prepared, and the distance of a man be required, take a foot-rule, or any measure minutely divided, hold it off at arm's length as before, and see how much a man's height covers. Then knowing the distance from the eye to the rule, a statement by the Rule of Three (on the principle of similar triangles) will give the distance required. Suppose a man's height, of 70 inches, covers 1 inch of the rule. He is then 70 times as far

* A horse, on a walk, averages 330 feet per minute, on a trot 650, and on a common gallop 1040. For longer times, the difference in horses is more apparent.

from the eye as the rule; and if its distance be 2 feet, that of the man is 140 feet. Instead of a man's height, that of an ordinary house, of an apple-tree, the length of a fence-rail, &c., may be be taken as the standard of comparison.

To keep the arm immovable, tie a string of known length to the pencil, and hold between the teeth a knot tied at the other end of the string.

(462) Distances by visibility. The degree of visibility of various well-known objects will indicate approximately how far distant they are. Thus, by ordinary eyes, the windows of a large house can be counted at a distance of about 13000 feet, or $2\frac{1}{2}$ miles; men and horses will be perceived as points at about half that distance, or $1\frac{1}{4}$ miles; a horse can be clearly distinguished at about 4000 feet; the movements of men at 2600 feet, or half a mile; and the head of a man, occasionally, at 2300 feet, and very plainly at 1300 feet, or a quarter of a mile. The Arabs of Algeria define a mile as "the distance at which you can no longer distinguish a man from a woman." These distances of visibility will of course vary somewhat with the state of the atmosphere, and still more with individual acuteness of sight, but each person should make a corresponding scale for himself.

(463) Distances by sound. Sound passes through the air with a moderate and known velocity; light passes almost instantaneously. If, then, two distant points be visible from each other, and a gun be fired at night from one of them, an observer at the other, noting by a stop-watch the time at which the flash is seen, and then that at which the report is heard, can tell by the intervening number of seconds how far apart the points are, knowing how far sound travels in a second. Sound moves about 1090 feet per second in dry air, with the temperature at the freezing point, 32° Fahrenheit. For higher or lower temperatures add or subtract $1\frac{1}{7}$ foot for each degree of Fahrenheit. If a wind blows with or against the movement of the sound, its velocity must be added or subtracted. If it blows obliquely, the correction will evidently equal its velocity multiplied by the cosine of the angle which the direction of the wind makes with the direction of the sound.* If the gun be fired at each end of the base in turn, and the means of the times taken, the effect of the wind will be eliminated.

If a watch is not at hand, suspend a pebble to a string (such as a thread drawn from a handkerchief) and count its vibrations. If it be $39\frac{1}{8}$ inches long, it will vibrate in one second; if $9\frac{3}{4}$ inches long, in half a second, &c. If its length is unknown at the time, still count its vibrations; measure it subsequently; and then will the time of its vibration, in seconds, $= \sqrt{\left(\frac{\text{length of string}}{39\frac{1}{8}}\right)}$.

(464) Angles. Right angles are those most frequently required in this kind of survey, and they can be estimated by the eye with much accuracy. If other angles are desired, they will be determined by measuring equal distances along the lines which make the angle, and then the line, or chord, joining the ends of these distances, thus forming chain angles, explained in Art. (**100**).

(465) Methods of operation. The "First Method" of determining the position of a point, Art. (**5**), is the one most generally applicable. Some line, as AB in Fig. 1, is paced, or otherwise measured, and then the lines AS and BS; the point S is thus determined.

The "Second Method," Art. (**6**), is also much employed, the right angles being obtained by eye, or by the easy methods given in Part II, Chapter V, Arts. (**140**), &c. It is used for offsets, as in Part II, Chapter III, Arts. (**114**), &c.

The "Third Method," Art. (**7**), may also be used, the angles being determined as in Art. (**464**).

The "Fourth Method," Art. (**8**), may also be employed, the angles being similarly determined.

The "Fifth Method," Art. (**10**), would seldom be used, unless by making an extempore plane-table, and proceeding as directed in the last paragraph of Art. (**457**).

* A gentle, pleasant wind has a velocity of 10 feet per second; a brisk gale 20 feet per second; a very brisk gale 30 feet; a high wind 50 feet; a very high wind 70 feet; a storm or tempest 80 feet; a great storm 100 feet; a hurricane 120 feet; and a violent hurricane, that tears up trees, &c., 150 feet per second

The method referred to in Art. (11) may also be employed. When a sketch has made some progress, new points may be fixed on it by their being in line with others already determined.

All these methods of operation are shown in the following figure AB is a line paced, or otherwise measured approximately.

Fig. 314.

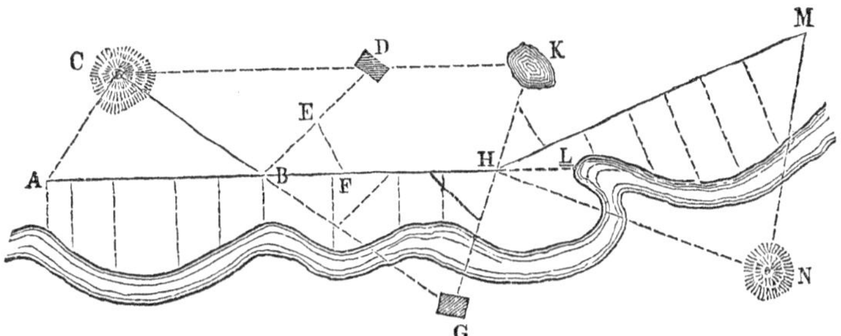

The hill C is determined by the first method. The river on the other side of AB is determined by offsets according to the Second Method. The house D is determined by the Third Method, EBF being a chain angle. The house G is determined by the Fourth Method, chain angles being measured at B and H, a point in AB prolonged. The pond K is determined, as in Art. (11), by the intersection of the alinements CD and GH prolonged. The bend of the river at L is determined by its distance from H in the line of AH prolonged. A new base line, HM, is fixed by a chain angle at H, and employed like the former one so as to fix the hill at N, &c. All these methods may thus be used collectively and successively. The necessary lines may always be ranged with rods, as directed in Art. (169), and very many of the instrumental methods already explained, may be practiced with extempore contrivances. The use of the Plane-table is an admirable preparation for this style of surveying or sketching, which is most frequently employed by Military Engineers, though they generally use a prismatic Compass, or pocket Sextant, and a sketching case, which may serve as a Plane-table.

PART X.

MAPPING.

CHAPTER I.

COPYING PLATS.

(466) The Plat of a survey necessarily has many lines of construction drawn upon it, which are not needed in the finished map These lines, and the marks of instruments, so disfigure the paper that a fair copy of the plat is usually made before the map is finished. The various methods of copying plats, &c., whether on the same scale, or reduced or enlarged, will therefore now be described.

(467) Stretching the paper. If the map is to be colored, the paper must first be wetted and stretched, or the application of the wet colors will cause its surface to swell or blister and become uneven. Therefore, with a soft sponge and clean water wet the back of the paper, working from the centre outward in all directions. The "water-mark" reads correctly only when looked at from the front side, which it thus distinguishes. When the paper is thoroughly wet and thus greatly expanded, glue its edges to the drawing board, for half an inch in width, turning them up against a ruler, passing the glue along them, and then turning them down and pressing them with the ruler. Some prefer gluing down opposite edges in succession, and others adjoining edges. The paper must be moderately stretched smooth during the process. Hot glue is best. Paste or gum may be used, if the paper be kept wet by a damp cloth, so that the edges may dry first. "Mouth-glue" may be used by rubbing it (moistened in the mouth or in boiling water) along the turned up edges, and then rubbing them dry by an ivory folder, a piece of dry paper being interposed. As this is a slower process, the middle of each side should first be fastened down, then the four angles, and lastly the intermediate portions. When the paper becomes dry, the creases and puckerings will have disappeared, and it will be as smooth and tight as a drum-head.

(468) Copying by tracing. Fix a large pane of clear glass in a frame, so that it can be supported at any angle before a window, or, at night, in front of a lamp. Place the plat to be copied on this glass, and the clean paper upon it. Connect them by pins, &c. Trace all the desired lines of the original with a sharp pencil, as lightly as they can be easily seen. Take care that the paper does not slip. If the plat is larger than the glass, copy its parts successively, being very careful to fix each part in its true relative position. Ink the lines with India ink, making them very fine and pale, if the map is to be afterwards colored.

(469) Copying on tracing paper. A thin transparent paper is prepared expressly for the purpose of making copies of maps and drawings, but it is too delicate for much handling. It may be prepared by soaking tissue paper in a mixture of turpentine and Canada balsam or balsam of fir (two parts of the former to one of the latter), and drying very slowly. Cold drawn linseed oil will answer tolerably, the sheets being hung up for some weeks to dry. Linen is also similarly prepared, and sold under the name of "Vellum tracing paper." It is less transparent than the tracing paper, but is very strong and durable. Both of these are used rather for preserving duplicates than for finished maps.

(470) Copying by transfer paper. This is thin paper, one side of which is rubbed with blacklead, &c., smoothly spread by cotton. It is laid on the clean paper, the blackened side downward, and the plat is placed upon it. All the lines of the plat are then gone over with moderate pressure by a blunt point, such as the eye-end of a small needle. A faint tracing of these lines will then be found on the clean paper, and can be inked at leisure. If the original cannot be thus treated, it may first be copied on tracing paper, and this copy be thus transferred. If the transfer paper be prepared by rubbing it with lampblack ground up with hard soap, its lines will be ineffaceable. It is then called "Camp-paper."

(471) Copying by punctures. Fix the clean paper on a drawing board and the plat over it. Prepare a fine needle with a sealing-wax head. Hold it very truly perpendicular to the board, and prick through every angle of the plat, and every corner and intersection of its other lines, such as houses, fences, &c., or at least the two ends of every line. For circles, the centre and one point of the circumference are sufficient. For irregular curves, such as rivers, &c., enough points must be pricked to indicate all their sinuosities. Work with system, finishing up one strip at a time, so as not to omit any necessary points nor to prick through any twice, though the latter is safer. When completed, remove the plat. The copy will present a wilderness of fine points. Select those which determine the leading lines, and then the rest will be easily recognized. A beginner should first pencil the lines lightly, and then ink them. An experienced draftsman will omit the pencilling. Two or three copies may be thus pricked through at once. The holes in the original plat may be made nearly invisible by rubbing them on the back of the sheet with a paper-folder, or the thumb nail.

(472) Copying by intersections. Draw a line on the clean paper equal in length to some important line of the original. Two starting points are thus obtained. Take in the dividers the distance from one end of the line on the original to a third point. From the corresponding end on the copy, describe an arc with this distance for radius and about where the point will come. Take the distance on the original from the other end of the line to the point, and describe a corresponding arc on the copy to intersect the former arc in a point which will be that desired. The principle of the operation is that of our "First Method," Art. (**5**). Two pairs of dividers may be used as explained in Art. (**90**). "Triangular compasses," having three legs, are used by fixing two of their legs on the two given points of the original, and the third leg on the point to be copied, and then transferring them to the copy. All the points of the original can thus be accurately reproduced. The operation is however very slow. Only the chief points of a plat may be thus transferred, and the details filled in by the following method.

(473) Copying by squares. On the original plat draw a series of parallel and equidistant lines. The T square does this most readily. Draw a similar series at right angles to these. The plat will then be covered with squares, as in Fig. 38, page 48. On the clean paper draw a similar series of squares. The important points may now be fixed as in the last article, and the rest copied by eye, all the points in each square of the original being properly placed in the corresponding square of the copy, noticing whether they are near the top or bottom of each square, on its right or left side, &c. This method is rapid, and in skilful hands quite accurate.

Instead of drawing lines on the original, a sheet of transparent paper containing them may be placed over it; or an open frame with threads stretched across it at equal distances and at right angles.

This method supplies a transition to the *Reduction* and *Enlargement* of plats in any desired ratio; under which head *Copying* by the Pantagraph and Camera Lucida will be noticed.

(474) Reducing by squares. Begin, as in the preceding article, by drawing squares on the original, or placing them over it. Then on the clean paper draw a similar set of squares, but with their sides one-half, one third, &c., (according to the desired reduction), of those of the original plat. Then proceed as before to copy into each small square all the points and lines found in the large square of the plat in their true positions relative to the sides and corners of the square, observing to reduce each distance, by eye or as directed in the following article, in the given ratio.

(475) Reducing by proportional scales. Many graphical methods of finding the proportionate length on the copy, of any line of the original, may be used. The "Angle of reduction" is con structed thus. Draw any line AB. With it for radius and A for centre, describe an indefinite arc. With B for centre and a radius equal to one-half, one-third, &c., of AB according to the desired reduction describe another arc intersecting the former arc in C. Join AC. From A as centre describe a series of arcs. Now to reduce any distance, take it in the dividers, and set it off from A on AB, as to D. Then the distance from D to E, the other end of the arc passing through D, will be the proportionate length to be set off on the copy, in the manner directed in Art. (472).

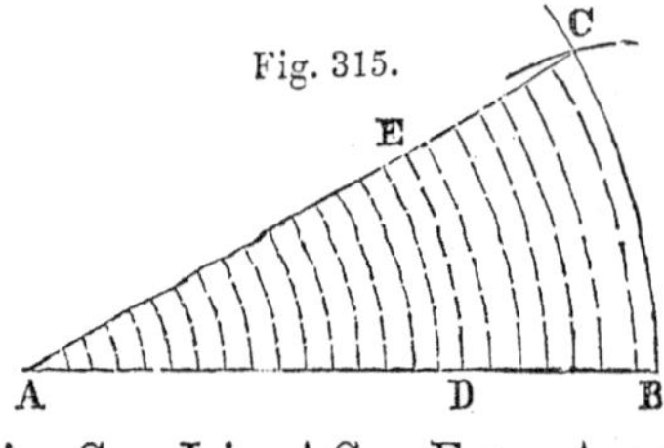

Fig. 315.

The Sector, or "Compass of proportion," described in Art. (52), presents such an "Angle of reduction," always ready to be used in this manner.

The "Angle of reduction" may be simplified thus. Draw a line, AB, parallel to one side of the drawing board, and another, BC, at right angles to it, and one-half, &c., of it, as desired. Join AC. Then let AD be the distance required to be reduced. Apply a T square so as to pass through D. It will meet AC in some point E, and DE will be the reduced length required.

Fig. 316.

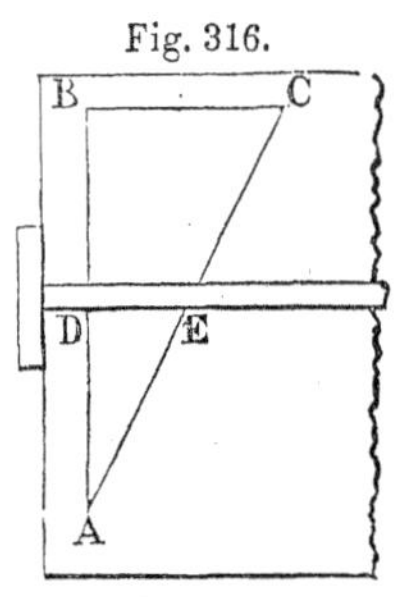

Another arrangement for the same object is shown in Fig. 317. Draw two lines, AB, AC, at any angle, and describe a series of arcs from their intersection, A, as in the figure. Suppose the reduced scale is to be half the original scale. Divide the outermost arc into three equal parts, and draw a line from A to one of the points of division, as D. Then *each* arc will be divided into parts, one of which is twice the other. Take any distance on the original scale, and find by trial which of the arcs on

Fig. 317.

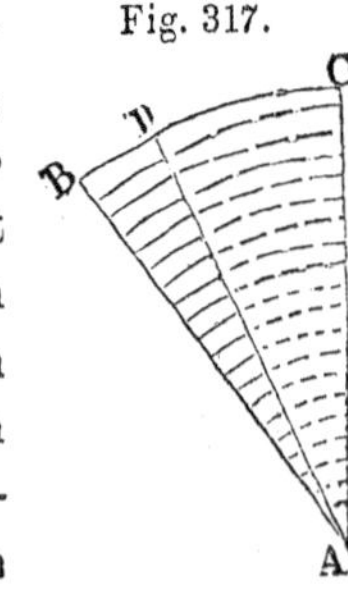

the right hand side of the figure it corresponds to. The other part of that arc will be half of it, as desired.

"Proportional compasses," being properly set, reduce lines in any desired ratio. A simple form of them, known as "Wholes and halves," is often useful. It consists of two slender bars, pointed at each end, and united by a pivot which is twice as far from one pair of the points as from the other pair. The long ends being set to any distance, the short ends will give precisely half that distance.

(476) Reducing by a pantagraph. This instrument consists of two long and two short rulers, connected so as to form a parallelogram, and capable of being so adjusted that when a tracing point attached to it is moved over the lines of a map, &c., a pencil attached to another part of it will mark on paper a precise copy, reduced on any scale desired. It is made in various forms. It is troublesome to use, though rapid in its work.

(477) Reducing by a camera lucida. This is used in the Coast Survey Office. It cannot reduce smaller than one-fourth, without losing distinctness, and is very trying to the eyes. Squares drawn on the original are brought to apparently coincide with squares on the reduction, and the details are then filled in with the pencil, as seen through the prism of the instrument.

(478) Enlarging plats. Plats may be enlarged by the principal methods which have been given for reducing them, but this should be done as seldom as possible, since every inaccuracy in the original becomes magnified in the copy. It is better to make a new plat from the original data.

CHAPTER II.

CONVENTIONAL SIGNS.

(479) Various conventional signs or marks have been adopted, more or less generally, to represent on maps the inequalities of the surface of the ground, its different kinds of culture or natural products, and the objects upon it, so as not to encumber and disfigure it with much writing or many descriptive legends. This is the purpose of what is called *Topographical Mapping.*

(480) The relief of ground. The inequalities of the surface of the earth, its elevations and depressions, its hills and hollows, constitute its "Relief." The representation of this is sometimes called "Hill drawing." Its difficulty arises from our being accustomed to see hills sideways, or "in elevation," while they must be represented as they would be seen from above, or "in plan." Various modes of thus drawing them are used; their positions being laid down in pencil as previously sketched by eye or measured.

If light be supposed to fall *vertically*, the slopes of the ground will receive less light in proportion to their steepness. The relief of ground will be indicated on this principle by making the steep slopes very dark, the gentler inclinations less so, and leaving the level surfaces white. The shades may be produced by tints of India ink applied with a brush, their edges, at the top and bottom of a hill or ridge, being softened off with a clean brush.

If light be supposed to fall *obliquely*, the slopes facing it will be light, and those turned from it dark. This mode is effective, but not precise. In it the light is usually supposed to come from the upper left hand corner of the map.

Horizontal contour lines are however the best convention for this purpose. Imagine a hill to be sliced off by a number of equidistant horizontal planes, and their intersections with it to be drawn as they would be seen from above, or horizontally projected on the map. These are "Contour lines." They are the same lines as would be formed by water surrounding the hill, and rising one foot at a time (or any other height) till it reached the top of the hill. The edge of the water, or its shore, at each successive rise, would be one of these horizontal contour lines. It is plain that their nearness or distance on the map would indicate the steepness or gentleness of the slopes. A right cone would thus be represented by a series of concentric circles, as in Fig. 318; an oblique cone by circles not concentric, but nearer to each other on the steep side than on the other, as in Fig. 319; and a half-egg, somewhat as in Fig. 320.

Fig. 318. Fig. 319. Fig. 320.

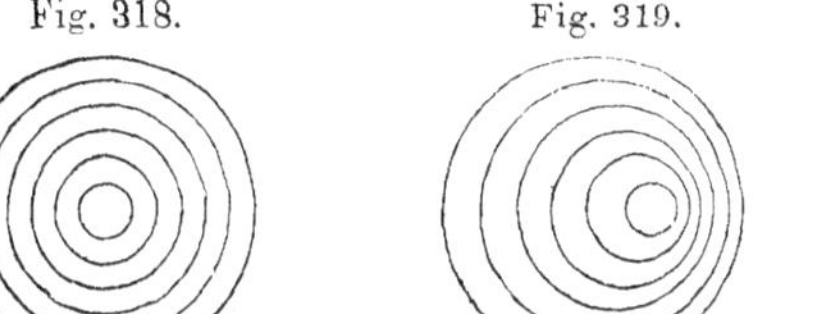

Vertical sections, perpendicular to these contour lines, are usually combined with them. They are the "Lines of greatest slope," and may be supposed to represent water running down the sides of the hill. They are also made thicker and nearer together on the steeper slopes, to produce the effect required by the convention of vertical light already referred to. The marginal figure shews an elongated half-egg, or oval hill, thus represented.

Fig. 321.

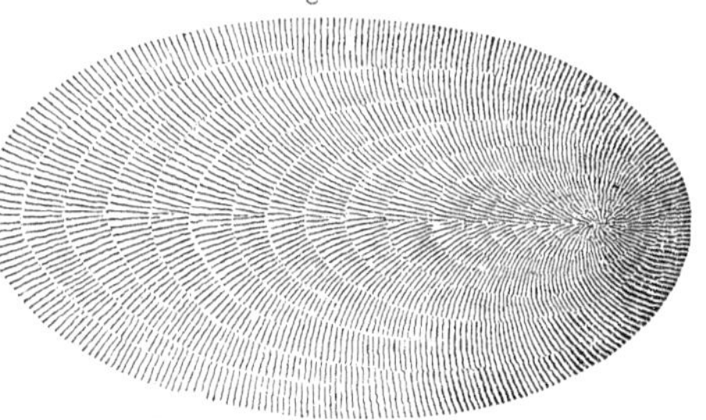

The spaces between the rows of vertical "Hatchings" indicate the contour lines, which are not actually drawn. The beauty of the graphical execution of this work depends on the uniformity of the strokes representing uniform slopes, on their perfectly regular gradation in thickness and nearness for varying slopes, and on their being made precisely at right angles to the contour lines between which they are situated.

The methods of determining the contour lines are applications of Levelling, and will therefore be postponed, together with the farther details of "Hill-drawing," to the volume treating of that subject, which is announced in the Preface.

(481) Signs for natural surface. *Sand* is represented by fine dots made with the point of the pen; *gravel* by coarser dots. *Rocks* are drawn in their proper places in irregular angular forms, imitating their true appearance as seen from above. The nature of the rocks, or the *Geology* of the country, may be shown by applying the proper colors, as agreed on by geologists, to the back of the map, so that they may be seen by holding it up against the light, while they will thus not confuse the usual details.

(482) Signs for vegetation. *Woods* are represented by scolloped circles, irregularly disposed, imitating trees seen "in plan," and closer or farther apart according to the thickness of the forest. It is usual to shade their lower and right hand sides and to represent their shadows, as in the figure, though, in strictness, this is inconsistent with the hypothesis of vertical light, adopted for "hill-drawing." For pine and similar forests, the signs may have a star-like form, as on the right hand side of the figure. Trees are sometimes drawn "in elevation," or sideways, as usually seen. This makes them more easily recognized, but is in utter violation of the principles of mapping in horizontal projection, though it may be defended as a pure convention. *Orchards* are represented by trees arranged in rows. *Bushes* may be drawn like trees, but smaller.

Fig. 322.

Grass-land is drawn with irregularly scattered groups of short lines, as in the figure, the lines being arranged in odd numbers, and so that the top of each group is convex and its bottom horizontal or parallel to the base of the drawing. *Meadows* are sometimes represented by pairs of diverging lines, (as on the right

Fig. 323.

of the figure), which may be regarded as tall blades of grass. *Uncultivated* land is indicated by appropriately intermingling the signs for grass land, bushes, sand and rocks. *Cultivated* land is shown by parallel rows of broken and dotted lines, as in the figure, representing furrows. *Crops* are so temporary that signs for them are unnecessary, though often used. They are usually imitative, as for cotton, sugar, tobacco, rice, vines, hops, &c. *Gardens* are drawn with circular and other beds and walks.

Fig. 324.

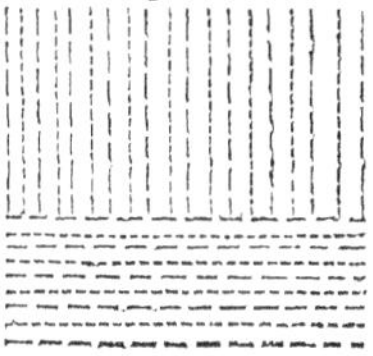

(483) Signs for water. The *Sea-coast* is represented by drawing a line parallel to the shore, following all its windings and indentations, and as close to it as possible, then another parallel line a little more distant, then a third still more distant, and so on. Examples are seen in figures 287, &c. If these lines are drawn from the low tide mark, a similar set may be drawn between that and the high tide mark, and dots, for sand, be made over the included space. *Rivers* have each shore treated like the sea shore, as in the figures of Part VII.* *Brooks* would be shown by only two lines, or one, according to their magnitude. *Ponds* may be drawn like sea shores, or represented by parallel horizontal lines ruled across them. *Marshes* and *Swamps* are represented by an irregular intermingling of the preceding sign with that for grass and bushes, as in the figure.

Fig. 325.

(484) Colored Topography. The conventional signs which have been described, as made with the pen, require much time and labor. Colors are generally used by the French as substitutes for them, and combine the advantages of great rapidity and effectiveness. Only three colors (besides India ink) are required; viz. *Gamboge* (yellow), *Indigo* (blue), and *Lake* (pink). Sepia, Burnt Sienna, Yellow ochre, Red lead, and Vermillion, are also sometimes used. The last three are difficult to work with. To

* Those in Part II, Chapter V, have the lines too close together in the middle.

use these paints, moisten the end of a cake and rub it up with a drop of water, afterwards diluting this to the proper tint, which should always be light and delicate. To cover any surface with a uniform flat tint, use a large camel's hair or sable brush, keep it always moderately full, incline the board towards you, previously moisten the paper with clean water if the outline is very irregular, begin at the top of the surface, apply a tint across the upper part, and continue it downwards, *never letting the edge dry.* This last is the secret of a smooth tint. It requires rapidity in returning to the beginning of a tint to continue it, and dexterity in following the outline. *Marbling*, or variegation, is produced by having a brush at each end of a stick, one for each color, and applying first one, and then the other beside it before it dries, so that they may blend but not mix, and produce an irregularly clouded appearance. Scratched parts of the paper may be painted over by first applying strong alum water to the place.

The conventions for colored Topography, adopted by the French Military Engineers, are as follows. WOODS, *yellow;* using gamboge and a very little indigo. GRASS-LAND, *green;* made of gamboge and indigo. CULTIVATED LAND, *brown;* lake, gamboge, and a little India ink. "Burnt Sienna" will answer. Adjoining fields should be slightly varied in tint. Sometimes furrows are indicated by strips of various colors. GARDENS are represented by small rectangular patches of brighter *green* and *brown.* UNCULTIVATED LAND, marbled *green* and light *brown.* BRUSH, BRAMBLES, &c., marbled *green* and *yellow.* HEATH, FURZE, &c., marbled *green* and *pink.* VINEYARDS, *purple;* lake and indigo. SANDS, a light *brown;* gamboge and lake. "Yellow ochre" will do. LAKES and RIVERS, light *blue*, with a darker tint on their upper and left hand sides. SEAS, dark *blue*, with a little yellow added. MARSHES, the *blue* of water, with spots of grass *green*, the touches all lying horizontally. ROADS, *brown;* between the tints for sand and cultivated ground, with more India ink. HILLS, *greenish brown;* gamboge, indigo, lake and India ink, instead of the pure India ink, directed in Art. (480). WOODS may be finished up by drawing the trees as in Art. (482) and coloring them green, with touches of gamboge towards the light (the upper and left hand side) and of indigo on the opposite side.

(485) Signs for detached objects. Too great a number of these will cause confusion. A few leading ones will be given, the meanings of which are apparent.

	Figs.		Figs.
Court house,	326.	*Wind mill,*	334.
Post office,	327.	*Steam mill,*	335.
Tavern,	328.	*Furnace,*	336.
Blacksmith's shop,	329.	*Woollen factory,*	337.
Guide board,	330.	*Cotton factory,*	338.
Quarry,	331.	*Glass works,*	339
Grist mill,	332.	*Church,*	340.
Saw mill,	333.	*Grave yard,*	341.

An ordinary house is drawn in its true position and size, and the ridge of its roof shown if the scale of the map is large enough. On a very small scale, a small shaded rectangle represents it. If colors are used, buildings of masonry are tinted a deep crimson, (with lake), and those of wood with India ink. Their lower and right hand sides are drawn with heavier lines. Fences of stone or wood, and hedges, may be drawn in imitation of the realities; and, if desired, colored appropriately.

Mines may be represented by the signs of the planets which were anciently associated with the various metals. The signs here given represent respectively,

Gold,	Silver,	Iron,	Copper,	Tin,	Lead,	Quicksilver.
☉	☽	♂	♀	♃	♄	☿

A large black circle, ●, may be used for Coal.

Boundary lines, of private properties, of townships, of counties, and of states, may be indicated by lines formed of various combinations of short lines, dots and crosses, as below.*

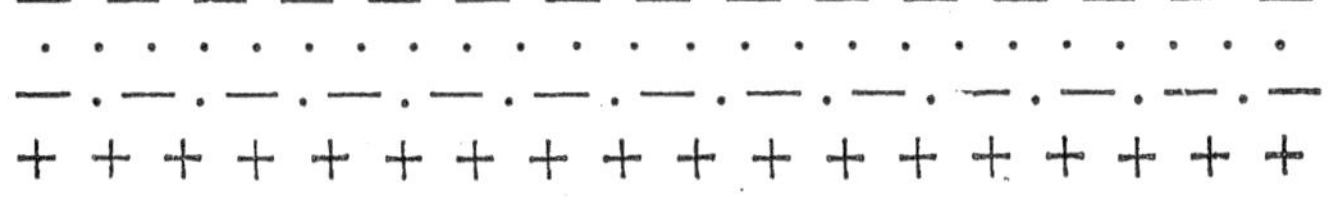

* Very minute directions for the execution of the details described in this chapter, are given in Lieut. R. S. Smith's "Topographical Drawing." Wiley, N. Y.

CHAPTER III.

FINISHING THE MAP.

(486) Orientation. The map is usually so drawn that the top of the paper may represent the North. A Meridian line should also be drawn, both True and Magnetic, as in Fig. 199, page 189. The number of degrees and minutes in the Variation, if known, should also be placed between the two North points. Sometimes a compass-star is drawn and made very ornamental.

(487) Lettering. The style in which this is done very much affects the general appearance of the map. The young surveyor should give it much attention and careful practice. It must all be in imitation of the best printed models. No writing, however beautiful, is admissible. The usual letters are the ordinary ROMAN CAPITALS, Small Roman, *ITALIC CAPITALS*, *Small Italic*, and GOTHIC OR EGYPTIAN. This last, when well done, is very effective. For the Titles of maps, various fancy letters may be used. For very large letters, those formed only of the shades of the letters regarded as blocks (the body being rubbed out after being pencilled as a guide to the placing of the shades) are most easily made to look well. The simplest lettering is generally the best. The sizes of the names of places, &c., should be proportional to their importance. Elaborate tables for various scales have been published. It is better to make the letters too small than too large. They should not be crowded. Pencil lines should always be ruled as guides. The lettering should be in lines parallel to the bottom of the map, except the names of rivers, roads, &c., whose general course should be followed.

(488) Borders. The *Border* may be a single heavy line, enclosing the map in a rectangle, or such a line may be relieved by a finer line drawn parallel and near to it. Time should not be wasted in ornamenting the border. The simplest is the best.

(489) Joining paper. If the map is larger than the sheets of paper at hand, they should be joined with a feather-edge, by proceeding thus. Cut, with a knife guided by a ruler, about one-third through the thickness of the paper, and tear off on the under side, a strip of the remaining thickness, so as to leave a thin sharp edge. Treat the other sheet in the same way on the other side of it. When these two feather edges are then put together, (with paste, glue or varnish), they will make a neat and strong joint. The sheet which rests upon the other must be on the right hand side, if the sheets are joined lengthways, or below if they are joined in that direction, so that the thickness of the edge may not cast a shadow, when properly placed as to the light. The sheets must be joined before lines are drawn across them, or the lines will become distorted. Drawing paper is now made in rolls of great length, so as to render this operation unnecessary.

(490) Mounting maps. A map is sometimes required to be mounted, i. e. backed with canvas or muslin. To do this, wet the muslin and stretch it strongly on a board by tacks driven very near together. Cover it with strong paste, beating this in with a brush to fill up the pores of the muslin. Then spread paste over the back of the paper, and when it has soaked into it, apply it to the muslin, inclining the board, and pasting first a strip, about two inches wide, along the upper side of the paper, pressing it down with clean linen in order to drive out all air bubbles. Press down another strip in like manner, and so proceed till all is pasted. Let it dry very gradually and thoroughly before cutting the muslin from the board.

Maps may be varnished with picture varnish; or by applying four or five coats of isinglass size, letting each dry well before applying the next, and giving a full flowing coat of Canada balsam diluted with the best oil of turpentine.

PART XI.

LAYING OUT, PARTING OFF, AND DIVIDING UP LAND.*

CHAPTER I.

LAYING OUT LAND.

(491) Its nature. This operation is precisely the reverse of those of Surveying properly so called. The latter measures certain lines as they are; the former marks them out in the ground where they are required to be, in order to satisfy certain conditions. The same instruments, however, are used as in Surveying.

Perpendiculars and parallels are the lines most often employed. The *Perpendiculars* may be set out either with the chain alone, Arts. (**140**) to (**159**); still more easily with the Cross-staff, Art. (**104**), or the Optical-square, Art. (**107**); and most precisely with a Transit or Theodolite, Arts. (**402**) to (**406**). *Parallels* may also be set out with the chain alone, Arts. (**160**) to (**166**); or with Transit, &c., Arts. (**407**) and (**408**). The ranging out of lines by rods is described in Arts. (**169**) and (**178**), and with an Angular instrument, in Arts. (**376**), (**409**) and (**415**).

(492) To lay out squares. Reduce the desired content to square chains, and extract its square root. This will be the length of the required side, which is to be set out by one of the methods indicated in the preceding article.

An *Acre*, laid out in the form of a square, is frequently desired by farmers. Its side must be made $316\frac{1}{4}$ links of a Gunter's

* The Demonstrations of the Problems in this part, when required, will be found in Appendix B.

chain; or $208\frac{71}{100}$ feet; or $69\frac{57}{100}$ yards. It is often taken at 70 paces.

The number of plants, hills of corn, loads of manure, &c., which an acre will contain at any uniform distance apart, can be at once found by dividing 209 by this distance in feet, and multiplying the quotient by itself; or by dividing 43560 by the square of the distance in feet. Thus, at 3 feet apart, an acre would contain 4840 plants, &c.; at 10 feet apart, 436; at a rod apart, 160; and so on. If the distances apart be unequal, divide 43560 by the product of these distances in feet; thus, if the plants were in rows 6 feet apart, and the plants in the rows were 3 feet apart, 2420 of them would grow on one acre.

(493) To lay out rectangles. *The content and length being given*, both as measured by the same unit, divide the former by the latter, and the quotient will be the required breadth. Thus, 1 acre or 10 square chains, if 5 chains long, must be 2 chains wide.

The content being given and the length to be a certain number of times the breadth. Divide the content in square chains, &c., by the ratio of the length to the breadth, and the square root of the quotient will be the shorter side desired, whence the longer side is also known. Thus, let it be required to lay out 30 acres in the form of a rectangle 3 times as long as broad. 30 acres = 300 square chains. The desired rectangle will contain 3 squares, each of 100 sq. chs., having sides of 10 chs. The rectangle will therefore be 10 chs. wide and 30 long.

An *Acre* laid out in a rectangle twice as long as broad, will be 224 links by 448 links, nearly; or $147\frac{1}{2}$ feet by 295 feet; or $49\frac{1}{5}$ yards by $98\frac{2}{5}$ yards. 50 paces by 100 is often used as an approximation, easy to be remembered.

The content being given, and the difference between the length and breadth. Let c represent this content, and d this difference. Then the longer side $= \frac{1}{2} d + \frac{1}{2} \sqrt{(d^2 + 4c)}$.

Example. Let the content be 6.4 acres, and the difference 12 chains. Then the sides of the rectangle will be respectively 16 chains and 4 chains.

The content being given, and the sum of the length and breadth. Let c represent this content, and s this sum. Then the longer side $= \frac{1}{2} s + \frac{1}{2} \sqrt{(s^2 - 4c)}$.

Example. Let the content be 6.4 acres, and the sum 20 chains. The above formula gives the sides of the rectangle 16 chains and 4 chains as before.

(494) To lay out triangles. The content and the base being given, divide the former by half the latter to get the height. At any point of the base erect a perpendicular of the length thus obtained, and it will be the vertex of the required triangle.

The content being given and the base having to be m times the height, the height will equal the square root of the quotient obtained by dividing twice the given area by m.

The content being given and the triangle to be equilateral, take the square root of the content and multiply it by 1.520. The product will be the length of the side required. This rule makes the sides of an equilateral triangle containing *one acre* to be $480\frac{1}{2}$ links. A quarter of an acre laid out in the same form would have each side 240 links long. An equilateral triangle is very easily set out on the ground, as directed in Art. (**90**), under "Platting," using a rope or chain for compasses.

(495) The content and base being given, and one side having to make a given angle, as B, with the base AB, the length of the side $BC = \frac{2 \times ABC}{AB \cdot \sin. B}$.

Fig. 342.

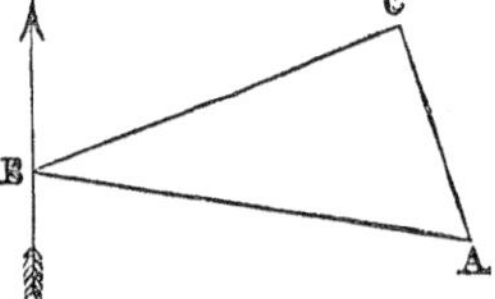

Example. Eighty acres are to be laid out in the form of a triangle, on a base, AB, of sixty chains, bearing N. 80° W. the bearing of the side BC being N. 70° E. Here the angle B is found from the Bearings (by Art. (**243**), reversing one of them) to be 30°. Hence BC = 53.33. The figure is on a scale of 50 chains to 1 inch = 1:39600.

Any right-line figure may be laid out by analogous methods.

(496) To lay out circles. Multiply the given content by 7, divide the product by 22, and take the square root of the quotient.

This will give the radius, with which the circle can be described on the ground with a rope or chain. A circle containing one acre has a radius of 178¼ links. A circle containing a quarter of an acre will have a radius of 89 links.

(497) Town lots. House lots in cities are usually laid off as rectangles of 25 feet front and 100 feet depth, variously combined in blocks. Part of New-York is laid out in blocks 200 feet by 800, each containing 64 lots, and separated by streets, 60 feet wide, running along their long sides, and avenues, 100 feet wide, on their short sides. The eight lots on each short side of the block, front on the avenues, and the remaining forty-eight lots front on the streets. Such a block covers almost precisely 3⅔ acres, and 17½ such lots about make an acre. But, allowing for the streets, land laid out into lots, 25 by 100, arranged as above, would contain only 11.9, or not quite 12 lots per acre.

Lots in small towns and villages are laid out of greater size and less uniformity. 50 feet by 100 is a frequent size for new villages, the blocks being 200 feet by 500, each therefore containing 20 lots.

(498) Land sold for taxes. A case occurring in the State of New-York will serve as an application of the modes of laying out squares and rectangles. Land on which taxes are unpaid is sold at auction to the *lowest* bidder; i. e. to him who will accept the smallest portion of it in return for paying the taxes on the whole. The lot in question was originally the east half of the square lot ABCD, containing 500 acres. At a sale for taxes in 1830, 70 acres were bid off, and this area was set off to the purchaser in a square lot, from the north-east corner. Required the side of the square in links. Again, in 1834, 29 acres more were thus sold, to be set off in a strip of equal width

Fig. 343.

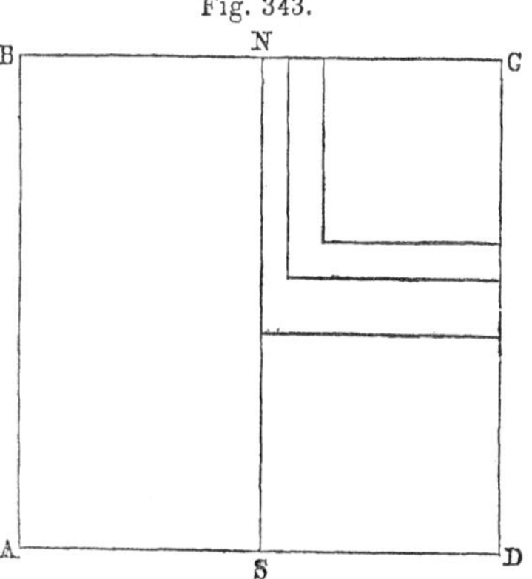

around the square previously sold. Required the width of this strip. Once more, in 1839, 42 acres more were sold, to be set off around the preceding piece. Required the dimensions of this third portion. The answer can be proved by calculating if the dimensions of the remaining rectangle will give the content which it should have, viz. 250 — (70 + 29 + 42) = 109 Acres.

The figure is on a scale of 40 chains to 1 inch = 1:31680.

(499) New countries. The operations of laying out land for the purposes of settlers, are required on a large scale in new countries, in combination with their survey. There is great difficulty in uniting the necessary precision, rapidity and cheapness. "Triangular Surveying" will ensure the first of these qualities, but is deficient in the last two, and leaves the laying out of lots to be subsequently executed. "Compass Surveying" possesses the last two qualities, but not the first. The United States system for surveying and laying out the Public Lands admirably combines an accurate determination of standard lines (Meridians and Parallels) with a cheap and rapid subdivision by compass. The subject is so important and extensive that it will be explained by itself in Part XII.

CHAPTER II.

PARTING OFF LAND.

(500) It is often required to part off from a field, or from an indefinite space, a certain number of acres by a fence or other boundary line, which is also required to run in a particular direction, to start from a certain point, or to fulfil some other condition. The various cases most likely to occur will be here arranged according to these conditions. Both graphical and numerical methods will generally be given.*

* The given lines will be represented by fine full lines; the lines of construction by broken lines, and the lines of the result by heavy full lines.

The given content is always supposed to be reduced to square chains and decimal parts, and the lines to be in chains and decimals.

A. By a line parallel to a side.

(501) To part off a rectangle. If the sides of the field adjacent to the given side make right angles with it, the figure parted off by a parallel to the given side will be a rectangle, and its breadth will equal the required content divided by that side, as in Art. (**493**).

If the field be bounded by a curved or zigzag line outside of the given side, find the content between these irregular lines and the given straight side, by the method of offsets, subtract it from the content required to be parted off, and proceed with the remainder as above. The same directions apply to the subsequent problems.

(502) To part off a parallelogram. If the sides adjacent to the given side be parallel, the figure parted off will be a parallelogram, and its perpendicular width, CE, will be obtained as above. The length of one of the parallel sides, as

$AC = \frac{CE}{\sin. A} = \frac{ABDC}{AB \,.\, \sin. A}$.

Fig. 344.

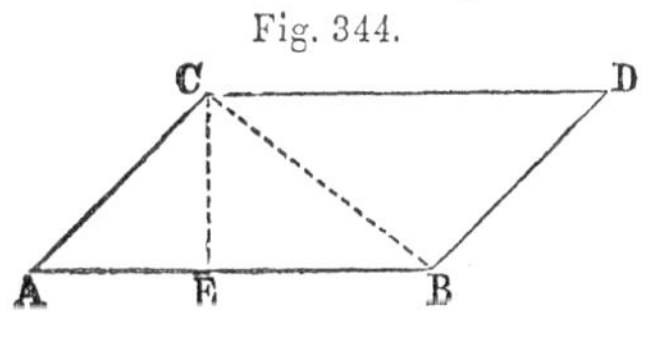

(503) To part off a trapezoid. When the sides of the field adjacent to the given side are not parallel, the figure parted off will be a trapezoid.

When the field or figure is given on the ground, or on a plat, begin as if the sides were parallel, dividing the given content by the base AB. The quotient will be an *approximate* breadth, CE, or DF; too small if the sides converge, as in the figure, and *vice versa*. Measure CD. Calculate the content of ABDC. Divide the difference of it and the required

Fig. 345.

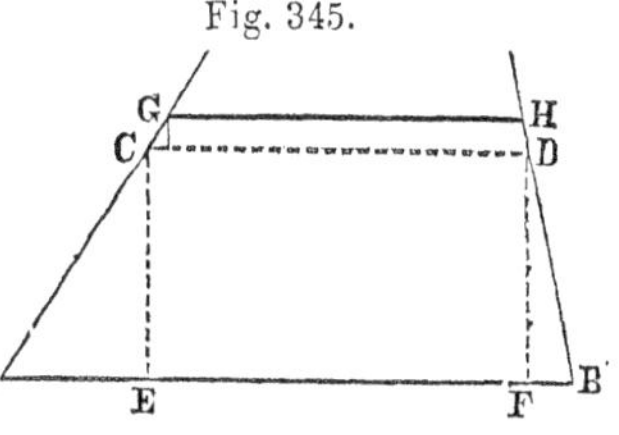

content by CD. Set off the quotient perpendicular to CD, (in this figure, outside of it,) and it will give a new line, GH, a still nearer approximation to that desired. The operation may be repeated, if found necessary.

(504) When the field is given by Bearings, deduce from them, as in Art. (**243**), the angles at A and B. The required sides will then be given by these formulas :

Fig. 346.

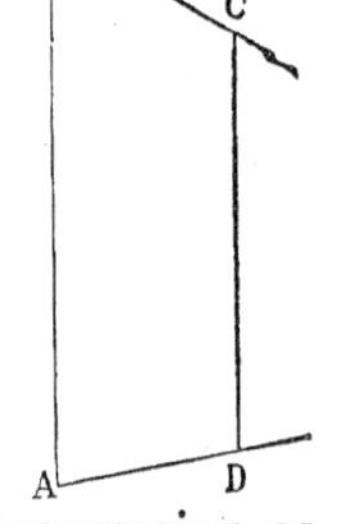

$$CD = \sqrt{\left(AB^2 - \frac{2 \times ABCD \,.\, \sin.\ (A + B)}{\sin.\ A \,.\, \sin.\ B}\right)}.$$

$$AD = (AB - CD)\frac{\sin.\ B}{\sin.\ (A + B)}.$$

$$BC = (AB - CD)\frac{\sin.\ A}{\sin.\ (A + B)}.$$

When the sides AD and BC diverge, instead of converging, as in the figure, the negative term, in the expression for CD, becomes positive; and in the expressions for both AD and BC, the first factor becomes (CD — AB).

The perpendicular breadth of the trapezoid = AD . sin. A; or = BC . sin. B.

Example. Let AB run North, six chains; AD, N. 80° E.; BC, S. 60° E. Let it be required to part off one acre by a fence parallel to AB. Here AB = 6.00, ABCD = 10 square chains, A = 80°, B = 60°. *Ans.* CD = 4.57, AD = 1.92, BC = 2.18, and the breadth = 1.89.

The figure is on a scale of 4 chains to 1 inch = 1 : 3168.

B. By a line perpendicular to a side.

(505) To part off a triangle. Let FG be the required line. When the field is given on the ground, or on a plat, at any point, as D, of the given side AB, set out a "guess line," DE, perpendicular to AB, and calculate the content of DEB. Then the required distance BF, from the angular point to the foot of the desired perpendicular, $= BD\sqrt{\left(\frac{BFG}{BDE}\right)}$.

Fig. 347.

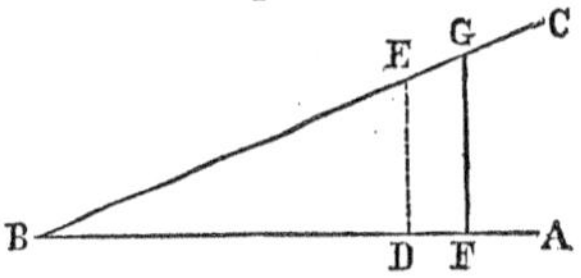

Example. Let BD = 30 chains; ED = 12 chains; and the desired area = 24.8 acres. Then BF = 35.22 chains.

The scale of the figure is 30 chains to 1 inch = 1:23760.

(506) When the field is given by Bearings, find the angle B from the Bearings; then is $BF = \sqrt{\left(\frac{2 \times BFG}{\text{tang. } B}\right)}$.

Fig. 348.

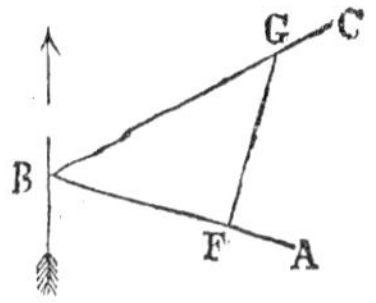

Example. Let BA bear S. 75° E., and BC N. 60° E., and let five acres be required to be parted off from the field by a perpendicular to BA. Here the angle B = 45°, and BF = 10.00 chains.

The scale of the figure is 20 chains to 1 inch = 1:15840.

(507) To part off a quadrilateral. Produce the converging sides to meet at B. Calculate the content of the triangle HKB, whether on the ground or plat, or from Bearings. Add it to the content of the quadrilateral required to be parted off, and it will give that of the triangle FGB, and the method of the preceding case can then be applied.

Fig. 369.

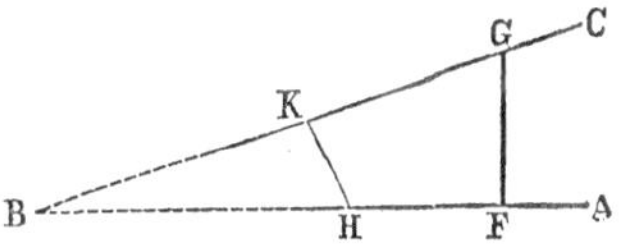

(508) To part off any figure. If the field be very irregularly shaped, find by trial any line which will part off a little less than the required area. This trial line will represent HK in the preceding figure, and the problem is reduced to parting off, according to the required condition, a *quadrilateral*, comprised between the trial line, two sides of the field, and the required line, and containing the difference between the required content and that parted off by the trial-line.

C. By a line running in any given direction.

(509) To part off a triangle. By construction, on the ground or the plat, proceed nearly as in Art. (505), setting out a line in the required direction, calculating the triangle thus formed, and obtaining BF by the same formula as in that Article.

22

(510) If the field be given by Bearings, find from them the angles CBA and GFB; then is $BF = \sqrt{\left(\frac{2 \times BFG \sin (B + F)}{\sin. B . \sin. F}\right)}$.

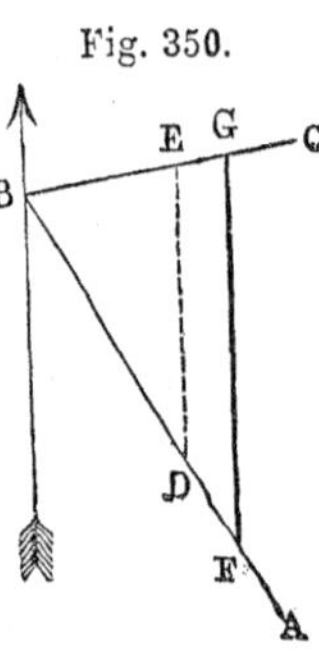

Fig. 350.

Example. Let BA bear S. 30° E.; BC, N. 80° E.; and a fence be required to run, from some point in BA, a due North course, and to part off one acre. Required the distance from B to the point F, whence it must start. *Ans.* The angle B = 70°, and F = 30°. Then BF = 6.47.

The scale of Fig. 350 is 6 chains to 1 inch = 1:4752.

(511) To part off a quadrilateral. Let it be required to part off, by a line running in a given direction, a quadrilateral from a field in which are given the side AB, and the directions of the two other sides running from A and from B.

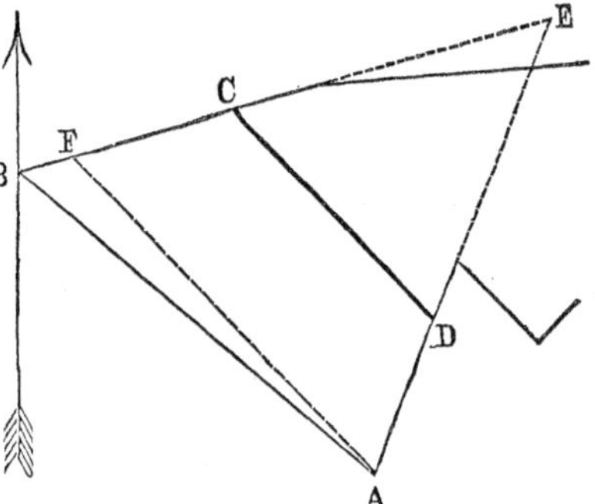

Fig. 351.

On the ground or plat produce the two converging sides to meet at some point E. Calculate the content of the triangle ABE. Measure the side AE. From ABE subtract the area to be cut off, and the remainder will be the content of the triangle CDE. From A set out a line AF parallel to the given direction. Find the content of ABF. Take it from ABE, and thus obtain AFE. Then this formula, $ED = AE\sqrt{\frac{CDE}{FAE}}$, will fix the point D, since AD = AE — ED.

(512) When the field and the dividing line are given by Bearings, produce the sides as in the last article. Find all the angles from the Bearings. Calculate the content of the triangle ABE, by the formula for one side and its including angles. Take the desired content from this to obtain CDE. Calculate the side $AE = AB \frac{\sin. B}{\sin. E}$. Then is $AD = AE - \sqrt{\left(\frac{2 \times CDE . \sin. DCE}{\sin. E . \sin. CDE}\right)}$.*

Example. Let DA bear S. $20\frac{1}{4}°$ W.; AB, N. $51\frac{1}{2}°$ W., 8.19; BC, N. $73\frac{1}{2}°$ E.; and let it be required to part off two acres by a fence, DC, running N. 45° W. *Ans.* ABE = 32.50 sq. chains; whence CDE = 12.50 sq. chs. Also, AE = 8.37; and finally AD = 8.37 — 5.49 = 2.88 chains.

The scale of Fig. 351 is 5 chains to 1 inch = 1:3960.

If the sum of the angles at A and B was more than two right angles, the point E would lie on the other side of AB. The necessary modifications are apparent.

(513) To part off any figure. Proceed in a similar manner to that described in Art. (**508**), by getting a suitable trial-line, producing the sides it intersects, and then applying the method just given.

D. BY A LINE STARTING FROM A GIVEN POINT IN A SIDE.

(514) To part off a triangle. Let it be required to cut off from a corner of a field a triangular space of given content, by a line starting from a given point on one of the sides, A in the figure, the base, AB, of the desired triangle being thus given. If the field be given on the ground or on a plat, divide the given content by half the base, and the quotient will be the height of the triangle. Set off this distance from any point of AB, perpendicular to it, as from A to C; from C set out a parallel to AB, and its intersection with the second side, as at D, will be the vertex of the required triangle.

Fig. 352.

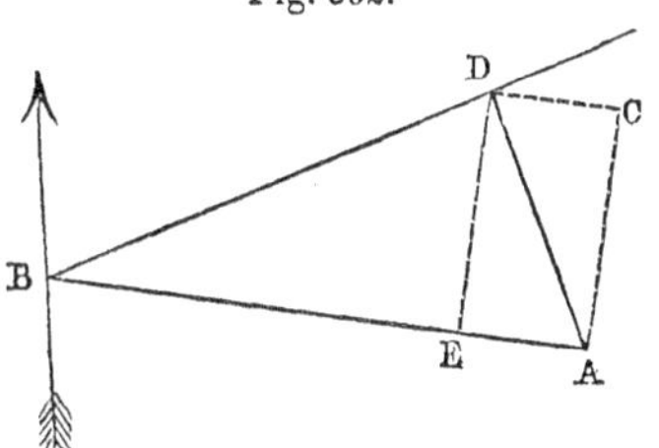

Otherwise, divide the required content by half of the perpendicular distance from A to BD, and the quotient will be BD.

* This original formula is very convenient for logarithmic computation.

(515) If the field be given by the Bearings of two sides and the length of one of them, deduce the angle B (Fig. 352) from the Bearings, as in Art. (**243**). Then is $BD = \frac{2 \times ABD}{AB \,.\, \text{sin. } B}$.

If it is more convenient to fix the point D, by the Second Method, Art. (**6**), that of rectangular co-ordinates, we shall have $BE = BD \,.\, \text{cos. } B$; and $ED = BD \,.\, \text{sin. } B$.

The Bearing of AD is obtained from the angle BAD; which is known, since $\frac{ED}{EA} = \frac{ED}{AB - BE} = \text{tang. } BAD$.

Example. Eighty acres are to be set off from a corner of a field, the course AB being N. 80° W., sixty chains; and the Bearing of BD being N. 70° E. *Ans.* BD = 53.33; BE = 46.19; ED = 26.67; and the Bearing of AD, N. 17° 23′ W.

The scale of Fig. 352 is 40 chains to 1 inch = 1 : 31680.

If the field were right angled at B, of course $BD = \frac{2\ ABD}{AB}$.

(516) To part off a quadrilateral. Imagine the two converging sides of the field produced to meet, as in Art. (**511**). Calculate the content of the triangle thus formed, and the question will then be reduced to the one explained in the last two articles.

(517) To part off any figure. Proceed as directed in Art. (**513**). Otherwise, proceed as follows.

The field being given on the ground or on a plat, find on which side of it the required line will end, by drawing or running "guess lines" from the given point to various angles, and roughly measuring the content thus parted off. If, as in the figure, A being the given point, the guess line AD parts off less than the required content, and AE parts off more, then the desired division line AZ will end in the side DE. Subtract the area parted off by AD from the required content, and the difference will be the content of the tri-

Fig. 353.

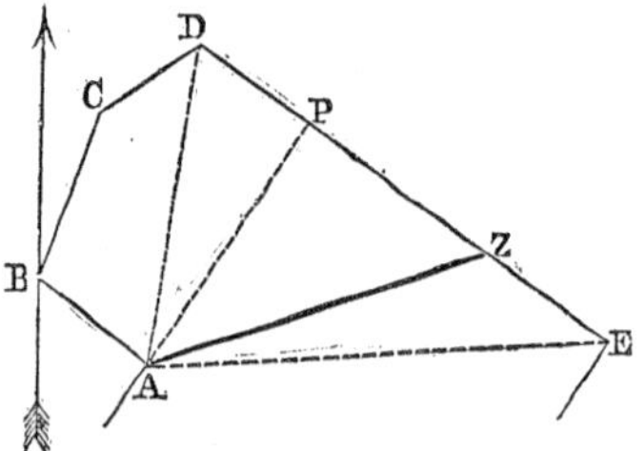

angle ADZ. Divide this by half the perpendicular let fall from the given point A to the side DE, and the quotient will be the base, or distance from D to Z.

Or, find the content of ADE and make this proportion ; ADE : ADZ :: DE : DZ.

(518) The field being given by Bearings and distances, find as before, by approximate trials on the plat, or otherwise, which side the desired line of division will terminate in, as DE in the last figure. Draw AD. Find the Latitude and Departure of this line, and thence its length and Bearing, as in Art. (**440**). Then calculate the area of the space this line parts off, ABCD in the figure, by the usual method, explained in Part III, Chapter VI. Subtract this area from that required to be cut off, and the remainder will be the area of the triangle ADZ. Then, as in Art. (**515**), $DZ = \frac{2\ ADZ}{AD \cdot \sin.\ ADZ}$.

This problem may be executed without any other Table than that of Latitudes and Departures, thus. Find the Latitude and Departure of DA, as before, the area of the space ABCD, and thence the content of ADZ. Then find the Latitude and Departure of EA, and the content of ADE. Lastly, make this proportion: ADE : ADZ :: DE : DZ.*

Example. In the field ABCDE, &c., part of which is shown in Fig. 353, (on a scale of 4 chains to 1 inch = 1 : 3168), one acre is to be parted off on the west side, by a line starting from the angle A. Required the distance from D to Z, the other end of this dividing line.†

The only courses needed are these. AB, N. 53° W., 1.55, BC, N. 20° E., 2.00 ; CD, N. 53½° E., 1.32 ; DE, S. 57° E., 5.79. A rough measurement will at once shew that ABCD is less than an acre, and that ABCDE is more ; hence the desired line will fall

* The problem may also be performed by making the side on which the division line is to fall, a Meridian, and changing the Bearings as in Art. (244). The difference of the new Departures will be the Departure of the Division line. Its position can then be easily determined, by calculations resembling those in Part VII, Chapter IV, Arts. (443), &c.

† If the whole field has been surveyed and balanced, the balanced Latitudes and Departures should be used. We will here suppose the survey to have proved perfectly correct.

on DE. The Latitudes and Departures of AB, BC and CD are then found. From them the course AD is found to be N. 8° E., 3.63. The content of ABCD will be 3.19 square chains. Subtracting this from one acre, the remainder, 6.81 sq. chs., is the content of ADZ. AP = 3.63 × sin. 65° = 3.29. Dividing ADZ by half of this, we obtain DZ = 4.14 chains.

By the Second Method, the Latitude and Departure of DA, the area of ABCD, and of ADZ, being found as before, we next find the Latitude and Departure of EA, from those of AD and DE, and thence the area of ADE = 9.53. Lastly, we have the proportion 9.53 : 6.81 :: 5.79 : DZ = 4.14, as before.

E. By a line passing through a given point within the field.

(519) To part off a triangle. Let P be a point within a field through which it is required to run a line so as to part off from the field, a given area in the form of a triangle.

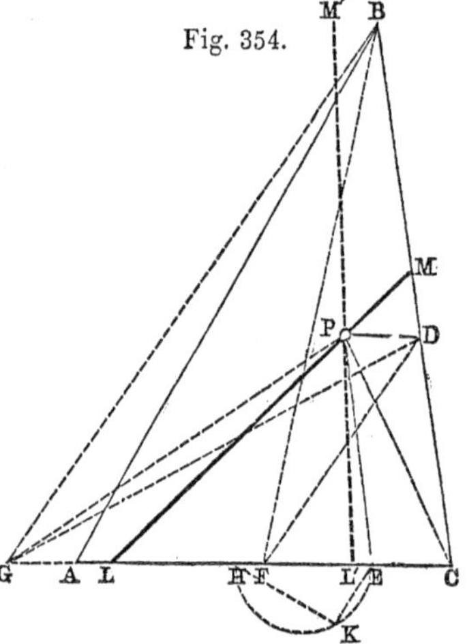

Fig. 354.

When the field is given on the ground or on a plat, the division can be made by construction, thus. From P draw PE, parallel to the side BC. Divide the given area by half of the perpendicular distance from P to AC, and set off the quotient from C to G. Bisect GC in H. On HE describe a semi-circle. On it set off EK = EC. Join KH. Set off HL = HK. The line LM, drawn from L through P, will be the division line required.* If HK be set off in the contrary direction, it will fix another line L′PM′, meeting CB produced, and thus parting off another triangle of the required content.

Example. Let it be required to part off 31.175 acres by a fence passing through a point P, the distance PD of P from the

* As some lines in the figure are not used in the construction, though needed for the Demonstration, the student should draw it himself to a large scale.

side BC, measured parallel to AC, being 6 chains, and DC 18 chains. The angle at C is fixed by a "tie-line" AB = 48.00, BC being 42.00, and CA being 30.00. *Ans.* CL = 27.31 chains, or CL′ = 7.69 chains.

The figure is on a scale of 20 chains to 1 inch = 1 : 15840.

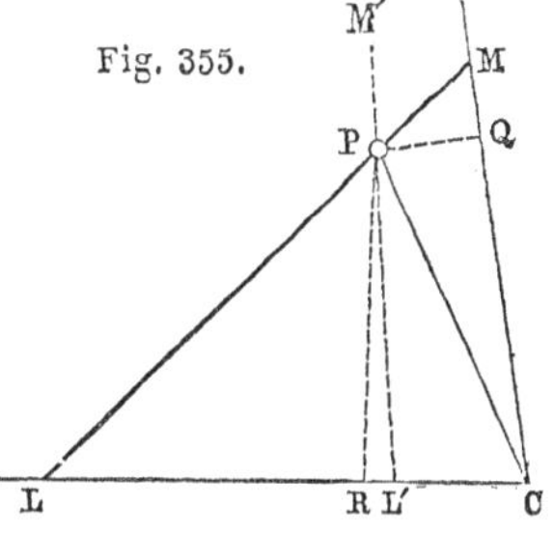

Fig. 355.

(520) If the angle of the field and the position of the point P are given by Bearings or angles, proceed thus. Find the perpendicular distances, PQ and PR, from the given point to the sides, by the formulas PQ = PC . sin. PCQ; and PR = PC . sin. PCR. Let PQ = q, PR = p, and the required content = c. Then $CL = \frac{c}{p} \pm \sqrt{\left(\frac{c^2}{p^2} - \frac{2\,qc}{\sin.\ LCM}\right)}$.

Example. Let the angle LCM = 82°. Let it be required to part off the same area as in the preceding example. Let PC = 19.75, PCQ = 17° 30½′, PCR = 64° 29½′. Required CL. *Ans.* PQ = 5.94, PR = 17.82, and therefore, by the formula, CL = 27.31, or CL′ = 7.69; corresponding to the graphical solution. The figure is on the same scale.

If the given point were *without* the field, the division line could be determined in a similar manner.

(521) To part off a quadrilateral. Conceive the two sides of the field which the division line will intersect, DA and CB, produced till they meet at a point G, not shown in the figure. Calculate the triangle thus formed outside of the field. Its area increased by the required area, will be that of the triangle EFG. Then the problem is identical with that in the last article. The following example is that given in Gummere's Surveying. The figure represents it on a scale of 20 chains to 1 inch = 1 : 15840.

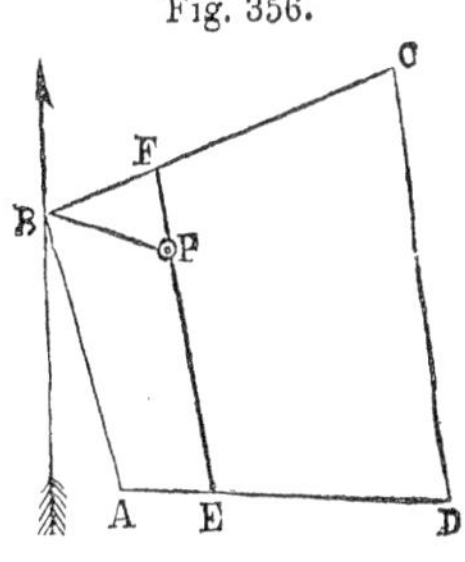

Fig. 356.

Example. A field is bounded thus: N. 14° W., 15.20; N. 70½° E., 20.43; S. 6° E., 22.79; N. 86½° W., 18.00. A spring within it bears from the second corner S. 75° E., 7.90. It is required to cut off 10 acres from the West side of the field by a straight fence through the spring. How far will it be from the first corner to the point at which the division fence meets the fourth side? *Ans.* 4.6357 chains.

(522) To part off any figure. Let it be required to part off from a field a certain area by a line passing through a given point P within the field. Run a guess-line AB through P. Calculate the area which it parts off. Call the difference between it and the required area $= d$. Let CD be the desired line of division, and let P represent the angle, APC or BPD, which it makes with the given line. Obtain the angles PAC = A, and PBD = B, either by measurement, or by deduction from Bearings. Measure PA and PB. Then the desired angle P will be given by the following formula.

Fig. 357.

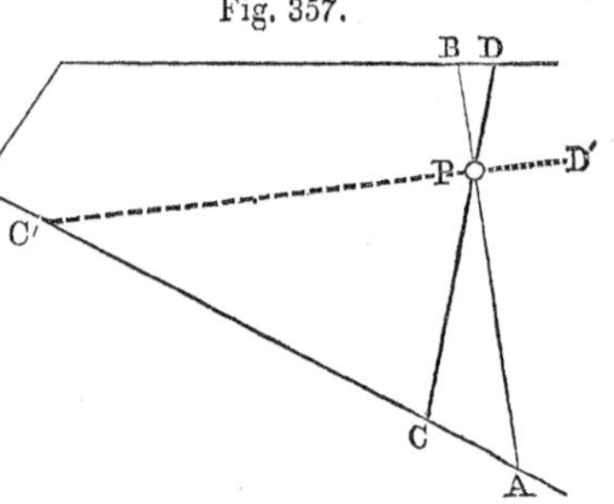

$$\text{Cot. } P = -\tfrac{1}{2}\left(\text{cot. } A + \text{cot. } B - \frac{AP^2 - BP^2}{2d}\right) \pm$$

$$\sqrt{\left[\frac{AP^2 \,.\, \text{cot. } B - BP^2 \,.\, \text{cot. } A}{2d} - \text{cot. } A \,.\, \text{cot. } B + \tfrac{1}{4}\left(\text{cot. } A + \text{cot. } B - \frac{AP^2 - BP^2}{2d}\right)^2\right]}.$$

If the guess line be run so as to be perpendicular to one of the sides of the field, at A, for example, the preceding expression reduces to the following simpler form.

$$\text{Cot. } P = -\tfrac{1}{2}\left(\text{cot. } B - \frac{AP^2 - BP^2}{2d}\right) \pm$$

$$\sqrt{\left[\frac{AP^2 \,.\, \text{cot. } B}{2d} + \tfrac{1}{4}\left(\text{cot. } B - \frac{AP^2 - BP^2}{2d}\right)^2\right]}.$$

Example. It was required to cut off from a field twelve acres by a line passing through a spring, P. A guess-line, AB, was run making an angle with one side of the field, at A, of 55°, and with the opposite side, at B, of 81°. The area thus cut off was found to be 13.10 acres. From the spring to A was 9.30 chains, and to B 3.30 chains. Required the angle which the required line, CD, must make with the guess line, AB, at P. *Ans.* 20° 45′; or — 86° 25′. The heavy broken line, C′D′, shows the latter.

The scale of the figure is 10 chains to 1 inch = 1 : 7920.

If the given point were outside of the field, the calculations would be similar

F. By the shortest possible line.

(523) To part off a triangle. Let it be required to part off a triangular space, BDE, of given content, from the corner of a field, ABC, by the shortest possible line, DE.

Fig. 358.

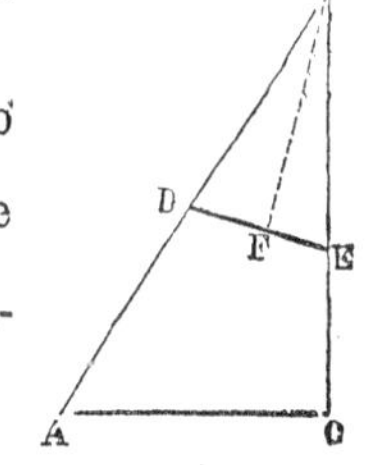

From B set off BD and BE each equal to $\sqrt{\left(\frac{2\ \text{BDE}}{\sin.\ \text{B}}\right)}$. The line DE thus obtained will be perpendicular to the line, BF, which bisects the angle B. The length of DE $= \frac{\sqrt{(2\ .\ \text{DBE}\ .\ \sin.\ \text{B})}}{\cos.\ \frac{1}{2}\ \text{B}}$.

Example. Let it be required to part off 1.3 acre from the corner of a field, the angle, B, being 30°. *Ans.* BD = BE = 7.21; and DE = 3.73.

The scale of the figure is 10 chains to 1 inch =1 : 7920.

G. Land of variable value.

(524) Let the figure represent a field in which the land is of two qualities and values, divided by the "quality line" EF. It is required to part off from it a quantity of land worth a certain sum, by a straight fence parallel to AB.

Fig. 359.

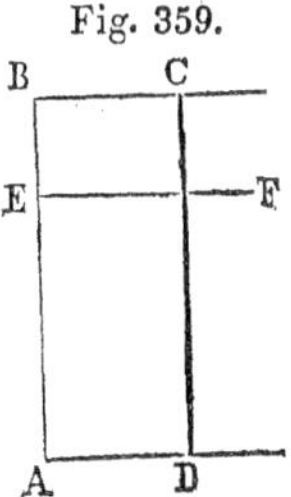

Multiply the value per acre of each part by its length (in chains) on the line AB, add the products, multiply the value to be set off by 10, divide by the above sum, and the quotient will be the desired breadth, BC or AD, in chains.

Example. Let the land on one side of EF be worth $200 per acre, and on the other side $100. Let the length of the former, BE, be 10 chains, and EA be 30 chains. It is required to part off a quantity of land worth $7500. *Ans.* The width of the desired strip will be 15 chains.

The scale of the figure is 40 chains to 1 inch = 1 : 31680.

If the "quality line" be not perpendicular to AB, it may be made so by "giving and taking," as in Art. (**124**), or as in the article following this one.

The same method may be applied to land of any number of different qualities; and a combination of this method with the preceding problems will solve any case which may occur.

H. STRAIGHTENING CROOKED FENCES.

(**525**) It is often required to substitute a straight fence for a crooked one, so that the former shall part off precisely the same quantity of land as did the latter. This can be done on a plat by the method given in Art. (**83**), by which the irregular figure

Fig. 360.

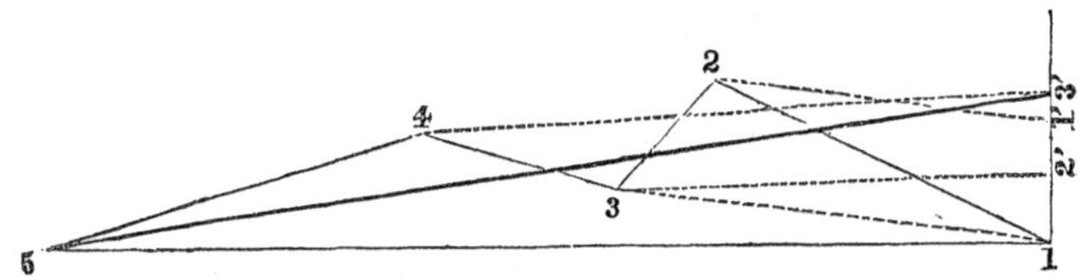

1...2...3...4...5 is reduced to the equivalent triangle 1...5...3′, and the straight line 5...3′ therefore parts off the same quantity of land on either side as did the crooked one. The distance from 1 to 3′, as found on the plat, can then be set out on the ground and the straight fence be then ranged from 3′ to 5

The work may be done on the ground more accurately by running a guess line, AC, Fig. 361, across the bends of the fence which crooks from A to B, measuring offsets to the bends on each side of the guess line, and calculating their content. If the sums of these areas on each side of AC chanced to be equal, that would be the line desired; but if, as in the figure, it passes too far on one

Fig. 361.

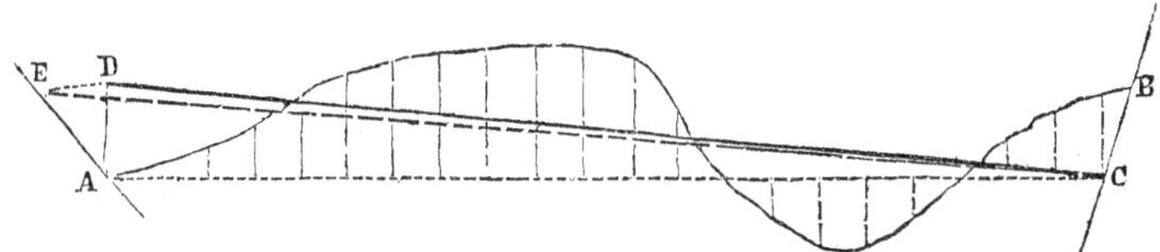

side, divide the difference of the areas by half of AC, and set it off at right angles to AC, from A to D. DC will then be a line parting off the same quantity of land as did the crooked fence. If the fence at A was not perpendicular to AC, but oblique, as AE, then from D run a parallel to AC, meeting the fence at E, and EC will be the required line.

CHAPTER III.

DIVIDING UP LAND.

(526) Most of the problems for "Dividing up" land may be brought under the cases in the preceding chapter, by regarding one of the portions into which the figure is to be divided, as an area to be "Parted off" from it. Many of them, however, can be most neatly executed by considering them as independent problems, and this will be here done. They will be arranged, firstly, according to the simplicity of the figure to be divided up, and then sub-arranged, as in the leading arrangement of Chapter II, according to the manner of the division.

DIVISION OF TRIANGLES.

Fig. 362.

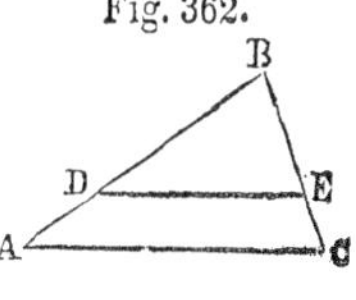

(527) By lines parallel to a side. Suppose that the triangle ABC is to be divided into two equivalent parts by a line parallel to AC. The desired point, D, from which this line is to start, will be obtained by measuring $BD = AB\ \sqrt{\frac{1}{2}}$. So, too, E is fixed by $BE = BC\ \sqrt{\frac{1}{2}}$.

Generally, to divide the triangle into two parts, BDE and ACED which shall have to each other a ratio $= m : n$, we have $BD = AB \sqrt{\frac{m}{m+n}}$.

Fig. 363.

This may be constructed thus. Describe a semicircle on AB as a diameter. From B set off $BF = \frac{m}{m+n} \cdot BA$. At F erect a perpendicular meeting the semicircle at G. Set off BG from B to D. D is the starting point of the division line required. In the figure, the two parts are as 2 to 3, and BF is therefore $= \frac{2}{5}$ BA.

Fig. 364.

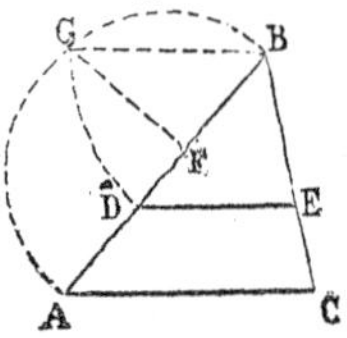

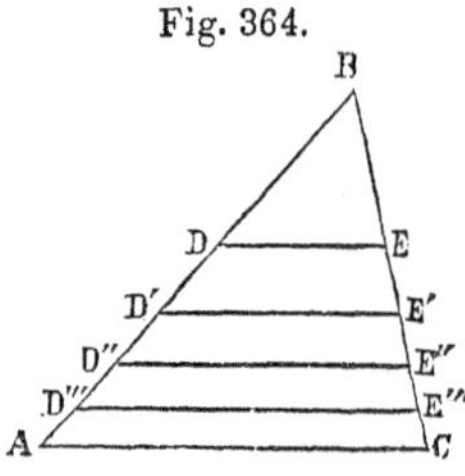

To divide the triangle ABC into five equivalent parts, we should have, similarly, $BD = AB \sqrt{\frac{1}{5}}$; $BD' = AB \sqrt{\frac{2}{5}}$; $BD'' = AB \sqrt{\frac{3}{5}}$; $BD''' = AB \sqrt{\frac{4}{5}}$.

The same method will divide the triangle into any desired number of parts having any ratios to each other.

(528) By lines perpendicular to a side. Suppose that ABC is to be divided into two parts having a ratio $= m : n$, by a line perpendicular to AC. Let EF be the dividing line whose position is required. Let BD be a perpendicular let fall from B to AC. Then is $AE = \sqrt{\left(AC \times AD \times \frac{m}{m+n}\right)}$. In this figure, AFE : EFBC :: $m : n$ :: 1 : 2.

Fig. 365.

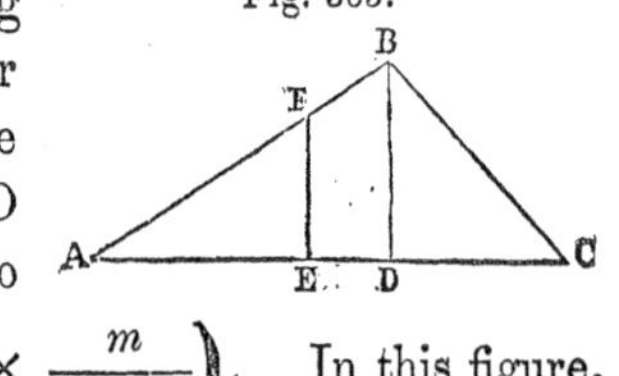

If the triangle had to be divided into two equivalent parts, the above expression would become $AE = \sqrt{(\frac{1}{2} AC \times AD)}$.

(529) By lines running in any given direction. Let a triangle, ABC, be given to be divided into two parts, having a ratio $= m : n$, by a line making a given angle with a side. Part off, as in Art (**509**) or (**510**), Fig. 350, an area $BFG = \frac{m}{m+n} \cdot ABC$.

(530) By lines starting from an angle. Divide the side opposite to the given angle into the required number of parts, and draw lines from the angle to the points of division. In the figure the triangle is represented as being thus divided into two equivalent parts.

Fig. 366.

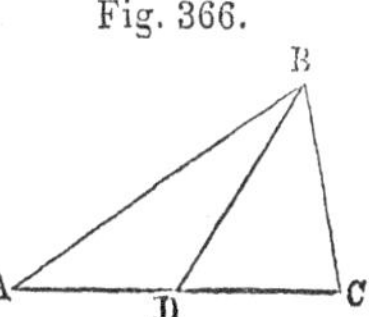

If the triangle were required to be divided into two parts, having to each other a ratio $= m : n$, we should have $AD = AC \frac{m}{m+n}$, and $DC = AC \frac{n}{m+n}$.

If the triangle had to be divided into three parts which should be to each other $:: m : n : p$, we should have $AD = AC \frac{m}{m+n+p}$, $DE = AC \frac{n}{m+n+p}$, and $EC = AC \frac{p}{m+n+p}$.

Fig. 367.

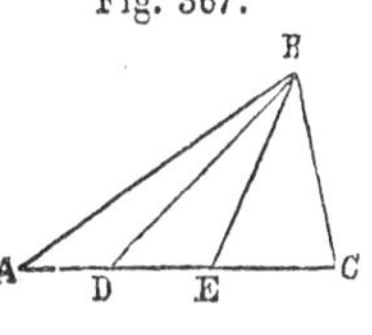

Suppose that a triangular field ABC, had to be divided among five men, two of them to have a quarter each, and three of them each a sixth. Divide AC into two equal parts, one of these again into two equal parts, and the other one into three equal parts. Run the lines from the four points thus obtained to the angle B.

(531) By lines starting from a point in a side. Suppose that the triangle ABC is to be divided into *two* equivalent parts by a line starting from a point D in the side AC. Take a point E in the middle of AC. Join BD, and from E draw a parallel to it, meeting AB in F. DF will be the dividing line required.

Fig. 368

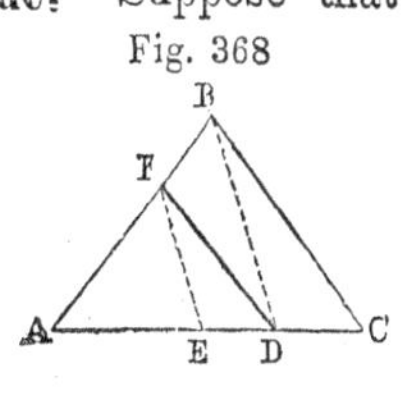

The point F will be most easily obtained on the ground by the proportion $AD : AB :: AE = \frac{1}{2} AC : AF$.

The altitude of AFD of course equals $\frac{1}{2} ABC \div \frac{1}{2} AD$.

If the triangle is to be divided into two parts having any other ratio to each other, divide AC in that ratio, and then proceed as before. Let this ratio $= m : n$, then $AF = \frac{AB \times AC}{AD} \cdot \frac{m}{m+n}$.

(532) Next suppose that the triangle ABC is to be divided into *three* equivalent parts, meeting at D. The altitudes, EF and GH, of the parts ADE and DCG, will be obtained by dividing $\frac{1}{3}$ ABC, by half of the respective bases AD and DC.

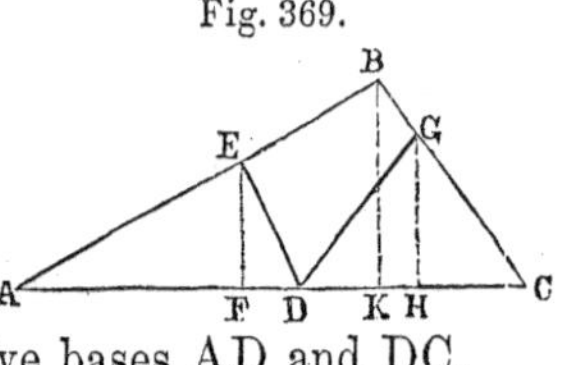

Fig. 369.

If one of these quotients gives an altitude greater than that of the triangle ABC, it will shew that the two lines DE and DG would both cut the same side, as in Fig. 370, in which EF is obtained as above, and GH = $\frac{2}{3}$ ABC ÷ $\frac{1}{2}$ AD.

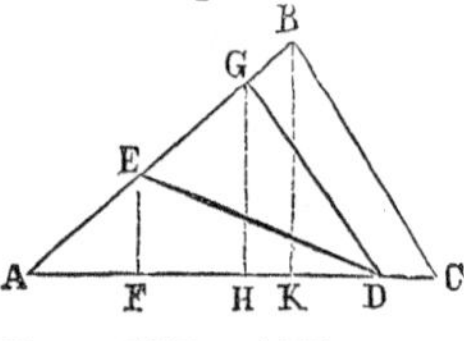

Fig. 370.

In practice it is more convenient to determine the points F and G, by these proportions;

BK : AK : : EF : AF; and BK : AK : : GH : AH.

The division of a triangle into a greater number of parts, having any ratios, may be effected in a similar manner.

(533) This problem admits of a more elegant solution, analogous to that given for the division into two parts, graphically. Divide AC into three equal parts at L and M. Join BD, and from L and M draw parallels to it, meeting AB and BC in E and G. Draw ED and GD, which will be the desired lines of division. The figure is the same triangle as Fig. 369.

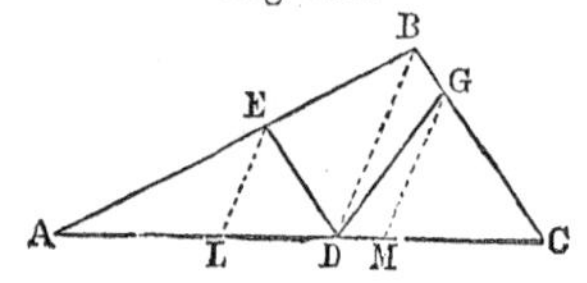

Fig. 371.

The points E and G can be obtained on the ground by measuring AD and AB, and making the proportion AD : AB : : $\frac{1}{3}$ AC : AE. The point G is similarly obtained.

The same method will divide a triangle into a greater number of parts.

(534) To divide a triangle into *four* equivalent triangles by lines terminating in the sides, is very easy. From D, the middle point of AB, draw DE parallel to AC, and from F, the middle of AC, draw FD and FE. The problem is now solved.

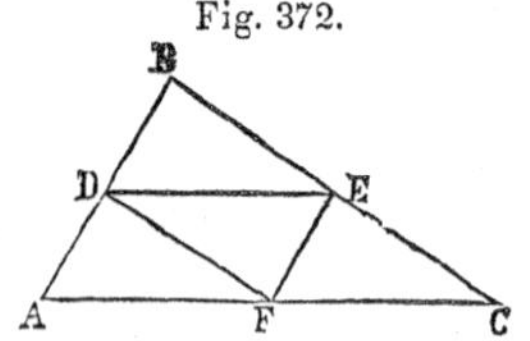

Fig. 372.

(535) By lines passing through a point within the triangle. Let D be a given point (such as a well, &c.) within a triangular field ABC, from which fences are to run so as to divide the triangle into *two* equivalent parts. Join AD. Take E in the middle of BC, and from it draw a parallel to DA, meeting AC in F. EDF is the fence required.

Fig. 373.

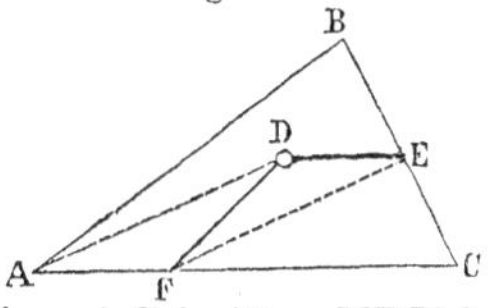

(536) If it be required to divide a triangle into two equivalent parts by a straight line passing through a point within it, proceed thus. Let P be the given point. From P draw PD parallel to AC, and PE parallel to BC. Bisect AC at F. Join FB. From B draw BG parallel to DF. Then bisect GC in H. On HE describe a semicircle. On it set off EK = EC. Join KH. Set off HL = HK. The line LM drawn from L, through P, will be the division line required.

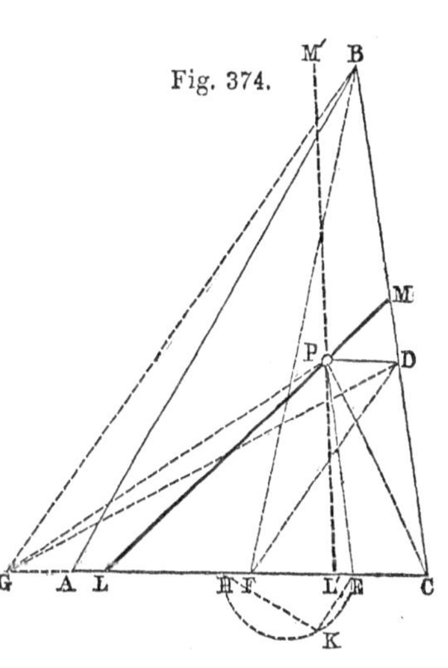

Fig. 374.

This figure is the same as that of Art. (519). The triangle ABC contains 62.35 acres, and the distance CL = 27.31 chains, as in the example in that article.

(537) Next suppose that the triangle ABC is to be divided into *three* equivalent parts by lines starting from a point D, within the triangle, given by the rectangular co-ordinates AE and and ED. Let ED be one of the lines of division, and F and G the other points required. The point F will be determined if AH is known; AH and HF being its rectangular co-ordinates. From B let fall the perpendicular BK on AC.

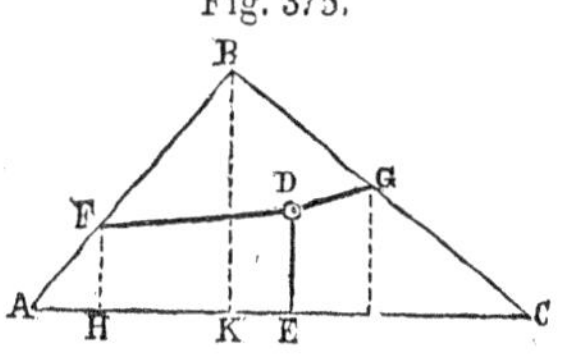

Fig. 375.

Then is $AH = \frac{AK\ (\frac{2}{3}\ ABC - AE \times ED)}{AE \times BK - ED \times AK}$. The position of the other point, G, is determined in a similar manner.

Fig. 376

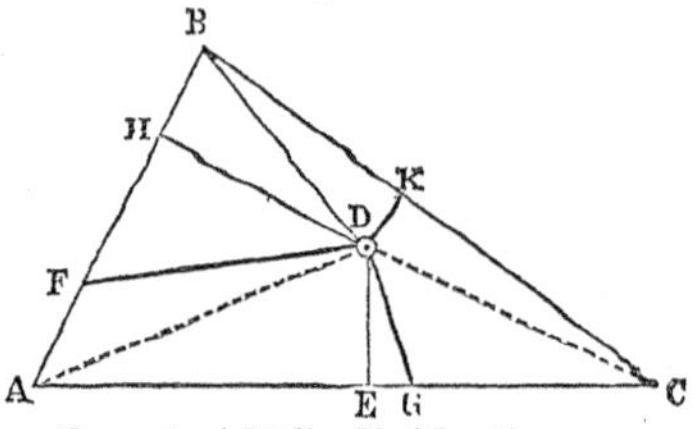

(538) Let DB, instead of DE, be one of the required lines of division. Divide $\frac{1}{3}$ ABC by half of the perpendicular DH, let fall from D to AB, and the quotient will be the distance BF. To find G, if, as in this figure, the triangle BDC ($= BC \times \frac{1}{2} DK$) is less than $\frac{1}{3}$ ABC, divide the excess of the latter (which will be CDG) by $\frac{1}{2}$ DE, and the quotient will be CG.

Example. Let AB = 30.00; BC = 45.00; CA = 50.00. Let the perpendiculars from D to the sides be these; DE = 10.00; DH = 20.00; DK = $5.17\frac{1}{3}$. The content of the triangle ABC will be 666.6 square chains. Each of the small triangles must therefore contain 222.2 sq. chs., BD being one division line. We shall therefore have $BF = 222.2 \div \frac{1}{2} DH = 22.2$ chains. BDC $= 45 \times \frac{1}{2} \times 5.17\frac{1}{3} = 116.4$ sq. chs., not enough for a second portion, but leaving 105.8 sq. chs. for CDG; whence CG = 21.16 chs. To prove the work, calculate the content of the remaining portion, GDFA. We shall find DGA = 144.2 sq. chs., and ADF = 78.0 sq. chs., making together 222.2 sq. chs., as required.

The scale of Fig. 376 is 30 chains to 1 inch = 1 : 23760.

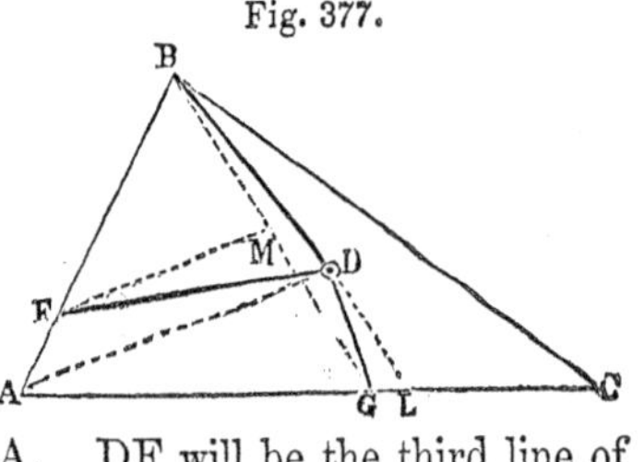

Fig. 377.

(539) The preceding case may be also solved graphically, thus. Take CL = $\frac{1}{3}$ AC. Join DL, and from B draw BG parallel to DL. Join DG. It will be a second line of division. Then take a point, M, in the middle of BG, and from it draw a line, MF, parallel to DA. DF will be the third line of division. This method is neater on paper than the preceding; but less convenient on the ground.

(540) Let it be required to divide the triangle ABC into three equivalent triangles, by lines drawn from the three angular points to some *unknown* point within the triangle. This point is now to be found. On any side, as AB, take AD = $\frac{1}{3}$ AB. From D draw DE parallel to AC. The middle, F, of DE, is the point required.

Fig. 378.

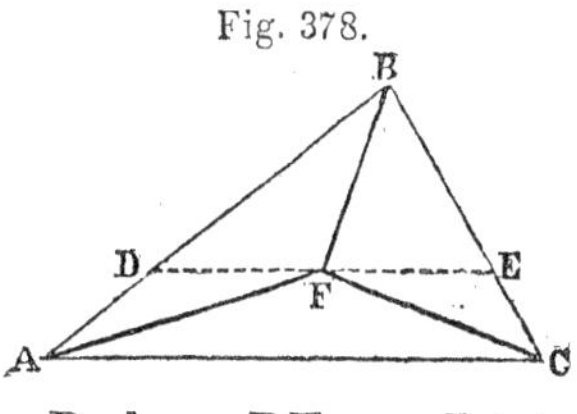

If the three small triangles are not to be equivalent, but are to have to each other the ratios :: $m : n : p$, divide a side, AB, into parts having these ratios, and through each point of division, D, E, draw a parallel to the side nearest to it. The intersection of these parallels, in F, is the point required. In the figure the parts ACF, ABF, BCF, are as 2 : 3 : 4.

Fig. 379.

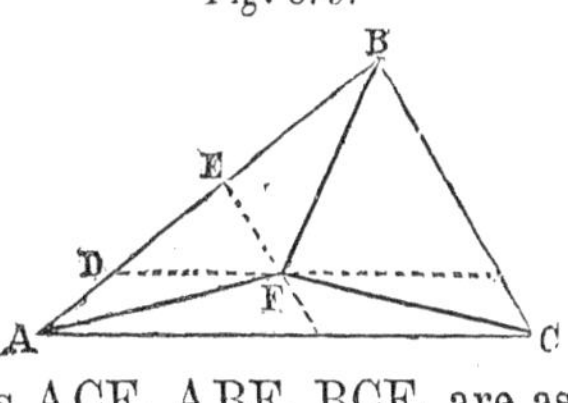

(541) Let it be required to find the position of a point, D, situated within a given triangle, ABC, and equally distant from the points A, B, C; and to determine the ratios to each other of the three triangles into which the given triangle is divided.

Fig. 380.

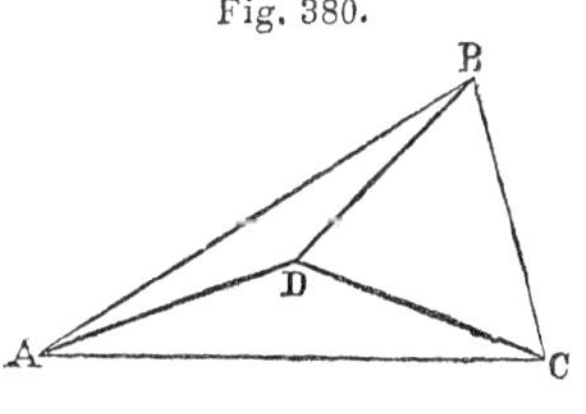

By construction, find the centre of the circle passing through A, B, C. This will be the required point.

By calculation, the distance $DA = DB = DC = \frac{AB \times BC \times CA}{4 \times \text{area } ABC}$.

The three small triangles will be to each other as the sines of their angles at D; i. e. ADB : ADC : BDC :: sin. ADB : sin. ADC : sin. BDC. These angles are readily found, since the sine of half of each of them equals the opposite side divided by twice one of the equal distances.

Fig. 381.

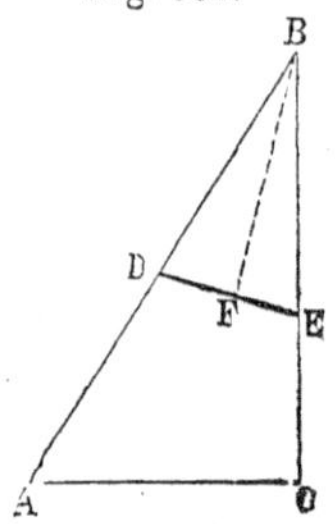

(542) By the shortest possible line. Let it be required to divide the triangle ABC by the shortest possible line, DE, into two parts, which shall be to each other : : $m : n$; or DBE : ABC : : $m : m + n$.

From the smallest angle, B, of the triangle, measure along the sides, BA and BC, a distance $\mathrm{BD} = \mathrm{BE} = \sqrt{\left(\frac{m}{m+n} \times \mathrm{AB} \times \mathrm{BC}\right)}$. DE is the line required. It is perpendicular to the line BF which bisects the angle ABC; and it is $= \frac{\sin. \mathrm{B}}{\cos. \frac{1}{2}\mathrm{B}} \sqrt{\left(\frac{m}{m+n} \times \mathrm{AB} \times \mathrm{BC}\right)}$.

DIVISION OF RECTANGLES.

(543) By lines parallel to a side. Divide two opposite sides into the required number of parts, either equal or in any given ratio to each other, and the lines joining the points of division will be the lines desired.

The same method is applicable to any parallelogram.

Fig. 382.

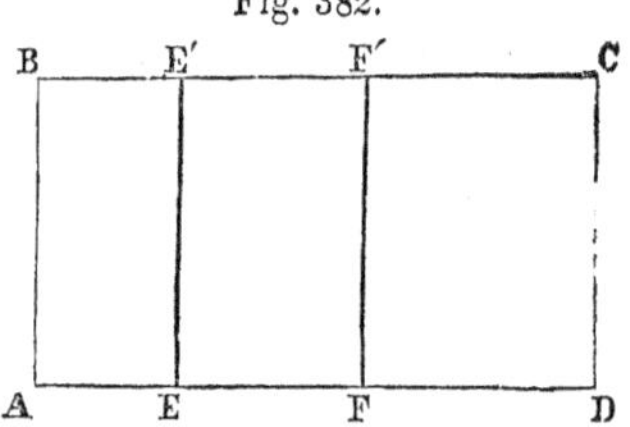

Example. A rectangular field ABCD, measuring 15.00 chains by 8.00, is bought by three men, who pay respectively $300, $400 and $500. It is to be divided among them in that proportion. *Ans.* The portion of the first, AEE′B, is obtained by making the proportion 300 + 400 + 500 : 300 : : 15.00 : AE = 3.75. EF is in like manner found to be 5.00; and FD = 6.25. BE′ is made equal to AE; E′F′ to EF; and F′C to FD. Fences from E to E′, and from F to F′, will divide the land as required.

The scale of the figure is 10 chains to 1 inch = 1 : 7920.

The other modes of dividing up rectangles will be given under the head of "Quadrilaterals," Art. (**548**), &c.

DIVISION OF TRAPEZOIDS.

(544) By lines parallel to the bases. Given the bases and a third side of the trapezoid, ABCD, to be divided into two parts, such that BCFE : EFDA : : m : n.

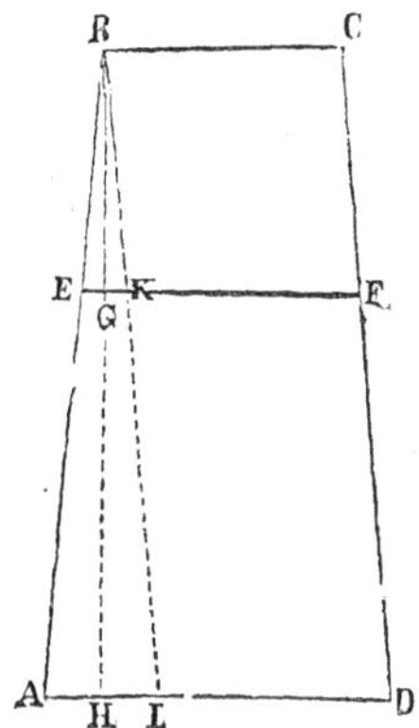

Fig. 383.

The length of the desired dividing line, $EF = \sqrt{\left(\frac{m \times AD^2 + n \times BC^2}{m + n}\right)}$.

The distance $BE = \frac{AB\ (EF - BC)}{AD - BC}$.

Example. Let AD = 30 chains; BC = 20 chs.; and AB = $54\frac{1}{3}$ chs.; and the parts to be as 1 to 2; required EF and BE. *Ans.* EF = 23.80; and BE = 20.65.

The figure is on a scale of 30 chains to 1 inch = 1 : 23760.

(545) Given the bases of a trapezoid, and the perpendicular distance, BH, between them; it is required to divide it as before, and to find EF, and the altitude, BG, of one of the parts. Let BCFE : EFDA : : m : n. Then $BG = -\frac{BC \times BH}{AD - BC} +$

$$\sqrt{\left[\frac{m}{m+n} \times \frac{2 \times ABCD \times BH}{AD - BC} + \left(\frac{BC \times BH}{AD - BC}\right)^2\right]}.$$

$$EF = BC + BG \times \frac{AD - BC}{BH}.$$

Example. Let AD = 30.00; BC = 20.00; BH = 54.00; and the two parts to be to each other : : 46 : 89.

The above data give the content of ABCD = 1350 square chains. Substituting these numbers in the above formula, we obtain BG = 20.96, and EF = 23.88.

(546) By lines starting from points in a side. To divide a trapezoid into parts equivalent, or having any ratios, divide its parallel sides in the same ratios, and join the corresponding points.

If it be also required that the division lines shall start from *given* points on a side, proceed thus. Let it be required to divide the trapezoid ABCD into three equivalent parts by fences starting from P and Q Divide the trapezoid, as above directed, into three equivalent trapezoids by the lines EF and GH. These three trapezoids mu now be transformed, thus. Join EP, and from F draw FR paral lel to it. Join PR, and it will be one of the division lines required.

Fig. 384.

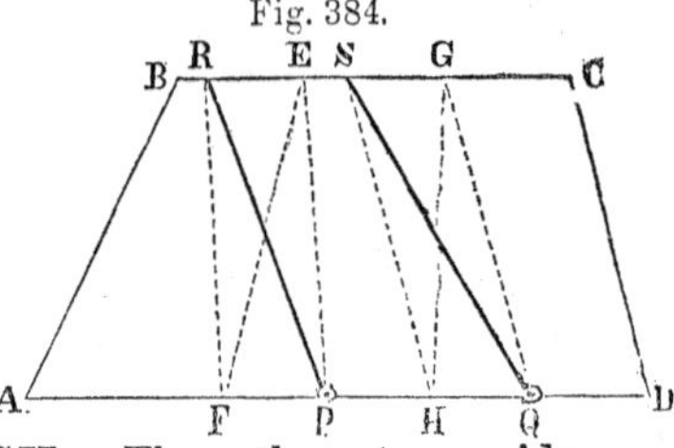

The other division line, QS, is obtained similarly.

(547) Other cases. For other cases of dividing trapezoids, apply those for quadrilaterals in general, given in the following articles.*

DIVISION OF QUADRILATERALS.

(548) By lines parallel to a side. Let ABCD be a quadrilateral which it is required to divide, by a line EF, parallel to AD, into two parts, BEFC and EFDA, which shall be to each other as $m : n$. Prolong AB and CD to intersect in G. Let a be the area of the triangle ADG, obtained by any method, graphical or trigonometrical, and a' = the area of the triangle BCG, obtained by subtracting the area of the given quadrilateral from that of the triangle ADG. Then GK = GH $\sqrt{\left(\frac{ma + na'}{(m+n)\,a}\right)}$. Having measured this length of GK from G on GH, set off at K a perpendicular to GK, and it will be the required line of division.

Fig. 385.

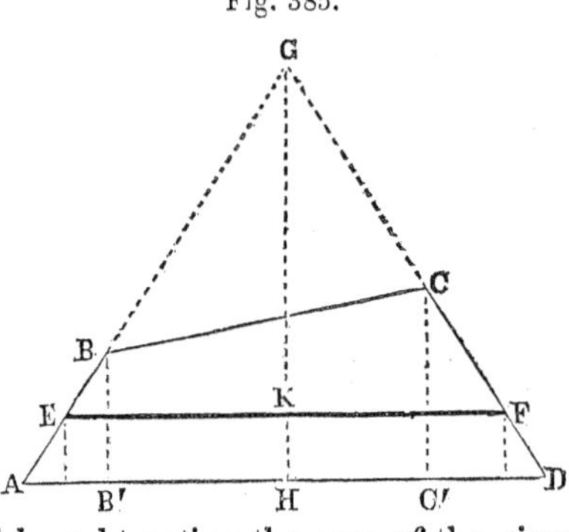

* If a line be drawn joining the middle points of the parallel bases of a trapezoid, *any line* drawn through the middle of the first line, and meeting the parallel bases, will divide the trapezoid into two equivalent parts.

Otherwise, take $GE = GA\sqrt{\left(\frac{ma + na'}{(m + n)\,a}\right)}$; and from E run a parallel to AD.

If the two parts of the quadrilateral were to be equivalent, $m = n$, and we have $GK = GH\,\sqrt{\left(\frac{a + a'}{2\,a}\right)}$; and consequently GE to GA in the same ratio.

Example. Let a quadrilateral, ABCD, be required to be thus divided, and let its angles, B and C, be given by rectangular co-ordinates, viz: AB′ = 6.00; B′B = 9.00; DC′ = 8.00; C′C = 13.00; B′C′ = 24.00. Here GH is readily found to be 29.64; ADG = 563.16 square chains; and BGC = 220.16 square chains. Hence, by the formula, GK = 24.72; whence KH = GH — GK = 4.92; and the abscissas for the points E and F can be obtained by a simple proportion.

The scale of the figure is 20 chains to 1 inch = 1:15840.

If the quadrilateral be given by Bearings, part off the desired area $= \frac{n}{m + n}$. ABCD, by the formulas of Art. (**504**).

Suppose now that a quadrilateral, ABCD, is to be divided into p equivalent parts, by lines parallel to AD. Measure, or calculate by Trigonometry, AG. Let Q be the quadrilateral ABCD, and, as before, $a' = $ BCG. Then

Fig. 386.

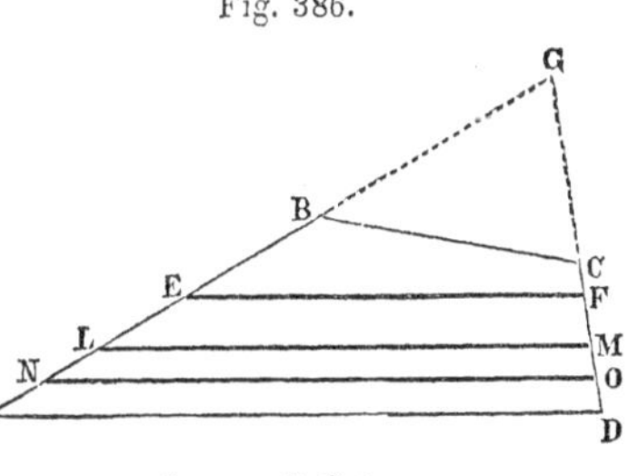

$$GE = AG\sqrt{\left\{\frac{a' + \frac{Q}{p}}{a' + Q}\right\}};\quad GL = AG\,\sqrt{\left\{\frac{a' + \frac{2\,Q}{p}}{a' + Q}\right\}};$$

$$GN = AG\sqrt{\left\{\frac{a' + \frac{3\,Q}{p}}{a' + Q}\right\}};\ \&c.$$

If the quadrilateral be given by Bearings, part off, by Art. (**504**), $\frac{1}{p}$. ABCD, then part off $\frac{2}{p}$. ABCD; &c.; so in any similar case.

(549) By lines perpendicular to a side. Let ABCD be a quadrilateral which is to be divided, by a line perpendicular to AD, into two parts having a ratio $= m : n$. By hypothesis, $\text{ABEF} = \frac{m}{m+n} \cdot \text{ABCD}$.

Fig. 387.

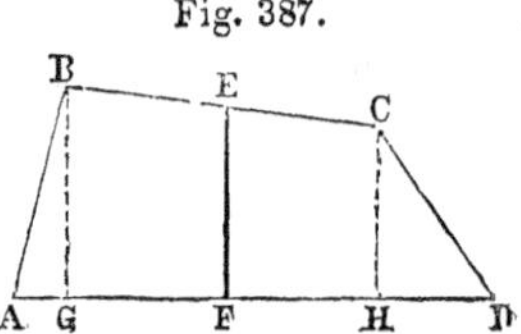

Taking away the triangle ABG, the remainder, GBEF, will be to the rest of the figure in a known ratio, and the position of EF, parallel to BG, will be found as in the last article.

(550) By lines running in any given direction. To divide a quadrilateral ABCD into two parts $:: m : n$, part off from it an area $= \frac{m}{m+n} \cdot \text{ABCD}$, by the methods of Arts. (**509**) or (**510**), if the area parted off is to be a triangle, or Arts. (**511**) or (**512**), if the area parted off is to be a quadrilateral.

(551) By lines starting from an angle. ABCD is to be divided, by the line CE, into two parts having the ratio $m : n$. Since the area of the triangle $\text{CDE} = \frac{m}{m+n} \cdot \text{ABCD}$, DE will be obtained by dividing this area by half of the altitude CF.

Fig. 388.

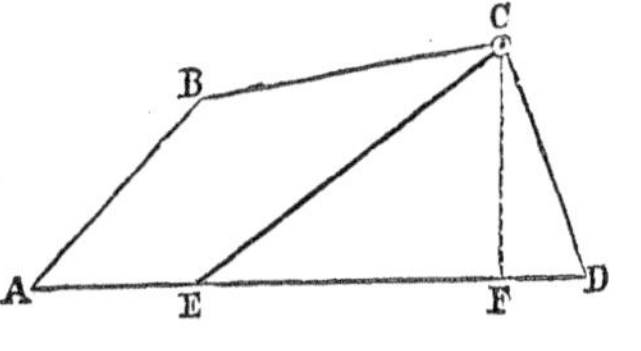

(552) By lines starting from points in a side. Let it be required to divide ABCD into two parts $:: m : n$, by a line starting from the point E. The area ABFE is known, (being $= \frac{m}{m+n} \cdot \text{ABCD}$) as also ABE; AB, BE, and EA being given on the ground. BEF will then be known $=$ ABFE $-$ ABE. Then $\text{GF} = \frac{\text{BEF}}{\frac{1}{2}\text{BE}}$, and the point F is obtained by running a parallel to BE, at a perpendicular distance from it $=$ GF.

Fig. 389.

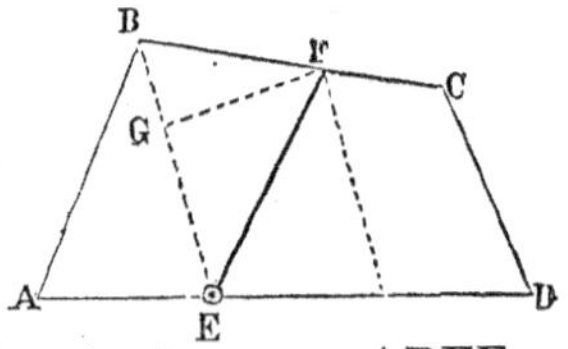

To divide a quadrilateral, ABCD, graphically, into *two equivalent* parts by a line from a point, E, on a side, proceed thus. Draw the diagonal CA, and from B draw a parallel to it, meeting DA prolonged in F. Mark the middle point, G, of FD. Join GE. From C draw a parallel to EG, meeting DA in H. EH is the required line. The quadrilateral could also be divided in any ratio $= m : n$, by dividing FD in that ratio.

Fig. 390.

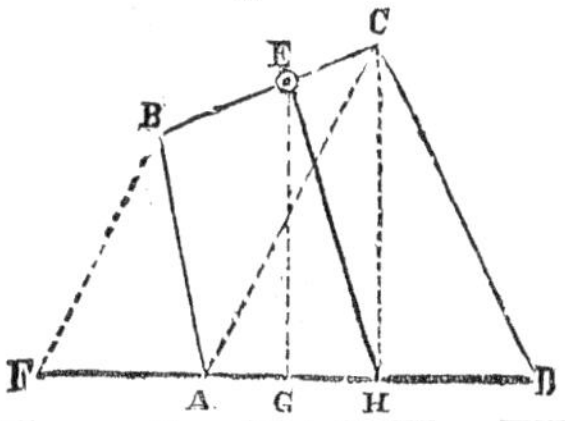

If the quadrilateral be given by Bearings, proceed to part off the desired area, as in Art. (**515**) or (**516**).

(**553**) Let it be required to divide a quadrilateral, ABCD, into *three equivalent* parts. From any angle, as C, draw CE, parallel to DA. Divide AD and EC, each into three equal parts, at F, F′, and G, G′. Draw BF, BF′. From G draw GH, parallel to FB, and from G′ draw G′H′, parallel to F′B. FH and F′H′ are the required lines of division.

Fig. 391.

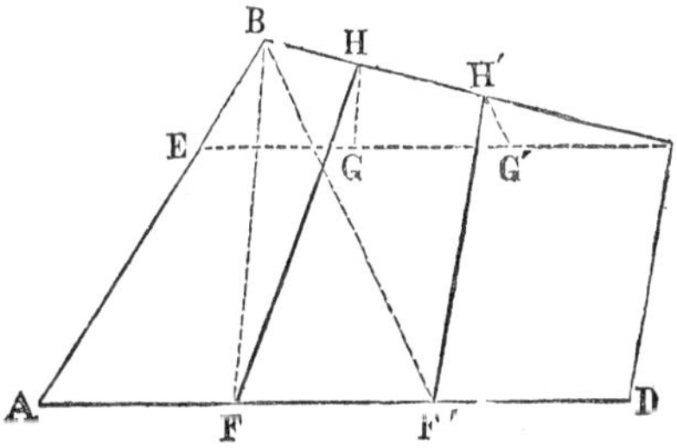

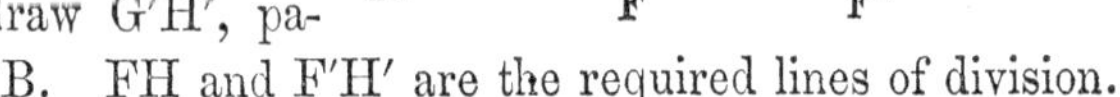

Let it be required to make the above division by *lines starting from two given points*, P and Q. Reduce the quadrilateral to an equivalent triangle CBE, as in Art. (87). Divide EB into three equal parts at F and G. Join CQ, and, from G, draw GK parallel to it. Join CP, and from F draw FL parallel to it. Join PL and QK, and they will be the division lines required.

Fig. 392.

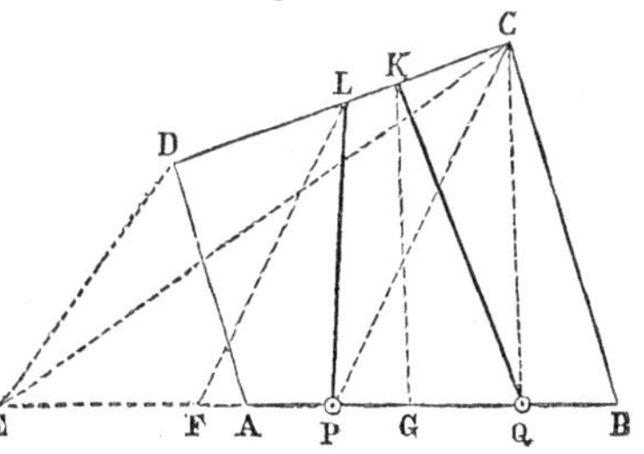

(**554**) **By lines passing through a point within the figure.** Proceed to part off the desired area as in Arts. (**519**), (**520**), or (**521**), according to the circumstances of the case.

DIVISION OF POLYGONS.

(555) By lines running in any direction. Let ABCDEFG be a given polygon, and BH the direction parallel to which is to be drawn a line PQ, dividing the polygon into two parts in any desired ratio $= m : n$. The area

Fig. 393.

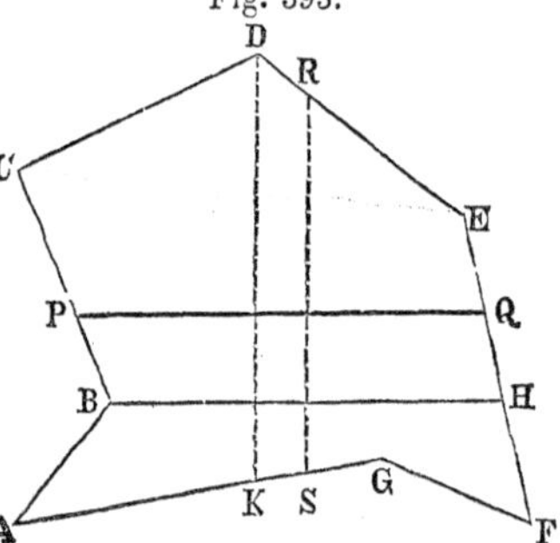

$$PCDEQ = \frac{m}{m+n} \,.\, ABCDEFG.$$

Taking it from the area BCDEH, the remainder will be the area BPQH. The quadrilateral BCEH, CE being supposed to be drawn, can then be divided by the method of Art. (**548**), into two parts, BPQH and PQEC, having to each other a known relation.

If DK were the given direction, at right angles to the former, the position of a dividing line RS could be similarly obtained.

(556) By lines starting from an angle. Produce one side, AB,

Fig. 394.

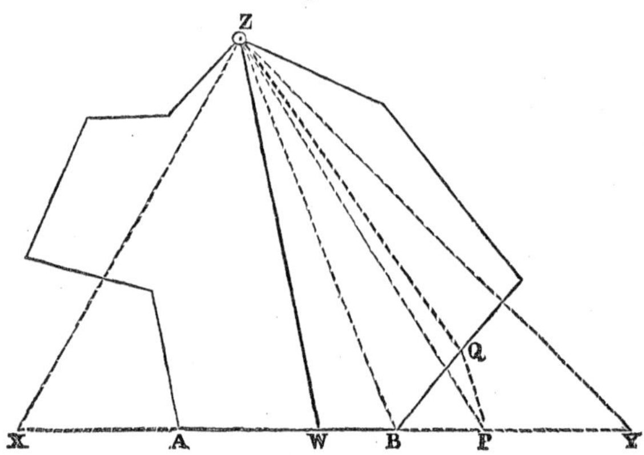

of the given polygon, both ways, and reduce the polygon to a single equivalent triangle, XYZ, by the method of Art. (82). Then divide the base, XY, in the required ratio, as at W, and draw ZW, which will be the division line desired. In this figure the polygon is divided into two equivalent parts.

If the division line should pass outside of the polygon, as does ZP, through P draw a parallel to BZ, meeting the adjacent side of the polygon in Q, and ZQ will be the division line desired.

(557) By lines starting from a point on a side. See Articles (517) and (518) in the preceding chapter.

(558) By lines passing through a point within the figure. Part off, as in Arts. (519) or (522) in the preceding chapter, if a straight line be required; or by guess lines and the addition of triangles, as in Art. (538) of this chapter, if the lines have merely to start from the point, such as a spring or well.

(559) Other problems. The following is from Gummere's Surveying. *Question.* A tract of land is bounded thus: N. 35¼° E., 23.00; N. 75½° E., 30.50; S. 3¼° E., 46.49; N. 66¼° W., 49.64. It is to be divided into four equivalent parts by two straight lines, one of which is to run parallel to the third side; required the distance of the parallel division line from the first corner, measured on the fourth side; also the Bearing of the other division line, and its distance from the same corner measured on the first side. *Ans.* Distance of the parallel division line from the first corner, 32.50; the Bearing of the other, S. 88° 22′ E.; and its distance from the same corner 5.99.

Fig. 395.

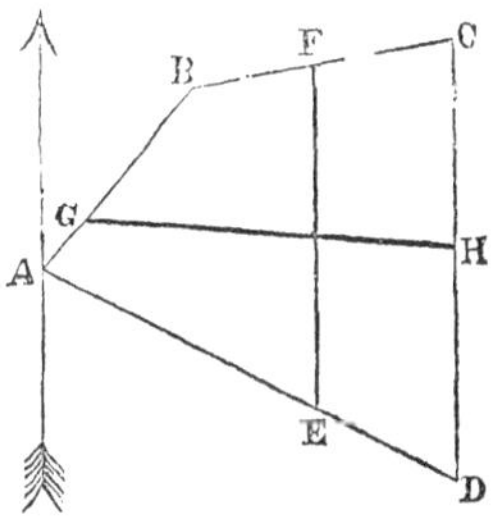

The scale of the figure is 40 chains to 1 inch = 1 : 31680.

An indefinite number of problems on this subject might be proposed, but they would be matters of curiosity rather than of utility, and exercises in Geometry and Trigonometry rather than in Surveying; and the youngest student will find his life too short for even the hastiest survey of merely the most fruitful parts of the boundless field of Mathematics.

Fig. 396.

1st Standard Parallel North
COLUMBIA
MERIDIAN
Ft Vancouver
BASE LINE
III
II
I
I
II
III
WILLAMETTE
Tualatin R.
Clackamas R.
Oregon City
WILLAMETTE RIVER
Butte
1st Standard Parallel South.
WHITNEY & JOCELYN, SC.

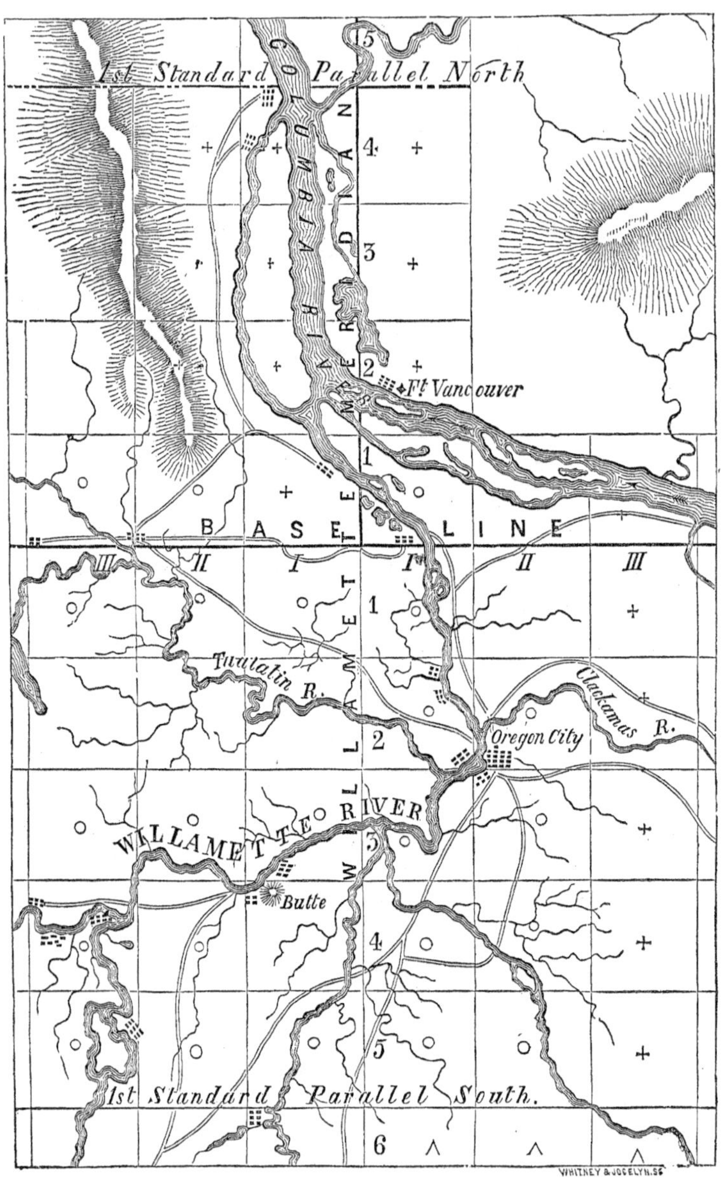

PART XII.

THE PUBLIC LANDS OF THE UNITED STATES.*

(560) **General system.** The Public Lands of the United States of America are generally divided and laid out into squares, the sides of which run truly North and South, or East and West.

This is effected by means of Meridian lines and Parallels of Latitude, established six miles apart. The principal meridians and base lines are established astronomically, and the intermediate ones are run with chain and compass. The squares thus formed are called TOWNSHIPS. They contain 36 square miles, or 23040 acres, "as nearly as may be." The map on the opposite page represents a portion of the Territory of Oregon thus laid out. The scale is 10 miles to 1 inch = 1 : 633600. On it will be seen the "Willamette Meridian," running truly North and South, and a "Base line," which is a "Parallel of Latitude," running truly East and West. Parallel to these, and six miles from them, are other lines, forming Townships. All the Townships, situated North or South of each other, form a RANGE. The Ranges are named by their number East or West of the principal Meridian. In the figure are seen three Ranges East and West of the Willamette Meridian. They are noted as R. I. E., R. I. W., &c. The Townships in each Range are named by their number North or South of the Base line. In

* The substance of this Part is mainly taken from "Instructions to the Surveyor General of Oregon, being a Manual for Field Operations," prepared, in March, 1851, by John M. Moore, "Principal Clerk of Surveys," by direction of Hon. J. Butterfield, "Commissioner of the General Land Office," and communicated to the author by Hon. John Wilson, the present Commissioner. The aim of the "Instructions" is stated to be "simplicity, uniformity and permanency." They seem admirably adapted for these objects, and the lasting importance of the subject in this country has led the author to reproduce about half of them in this place. They were subsequently directed to be adopted for the Surveying service in Minnesota and California.

the figure along the principal Meridian are seen four North and five South of the Base line. They are noted as T. 1 N., T. 2 N., T. 1 S., &c.*

Each Township is divided into 36 SECTIONS, each 1 mile square, and therefore containing, "as nearly as may be," 640 acres. The sections in each Township are numbered, as in the margin, from 1 to 36, beginning at the North-east angle of the Township, and going West from 1 to 6, then East from 7 to 12, and so on alternately to Section 36, which will be in the South-east angle of the Township. The Sections are sub-divided into Quarter-sections, half-a-mile square, and containing 160 acres, and sometimes into half-quarter-sections of 80 acres, and quarter-quarter-sections of 40 acres.

N

6	5	4	3	2	1
7	8	9	10	11	12
18	17	16	15	14	13
19	20	21	22	23	24
30	29	28	27	26	25
31	32	33	34	35	36

W E

S

By this beautiful system, the smallest subdivision of land can be at once designated; such as the North-east quarter of Section 31, in Township *two* South, in range *two* East of Willamette Meridian.

(561) Difficulty. "The law requires that the lines of the public surveys shall be governed by the true meridian, and that the townships shall be *six miles square*,—two things involving in connection a mathematical impossibility—for, strictly to conform to the meridian, necessarily throws the township out of square, by reason of *the convergency of meridians;* hence, adhering to the true meridian renders it necessary to depart from the strict requirements of law as respects the precise area of townships, and the subdivisional parts thereof, the township assuming something of a trapezoidal form, which inequality developes itself, more and more as such, the higher the latitude of the surveys. In view of these circumstances, the law provides that the sections of a mile square shall contain the quantity of 640 acres, *as nearly as may be;* and, moreover, provides that 'In all cases where the exterior lines of the townships, thus to be subdivided into sections or half-sections, shall exceed, or shall not extend, six miles, the excess or deficiency

* The marks O, + and ∧, merely refer to the dates of the surveys. They are sometimes used to point out lands offered for sale, or reserved, &c.

shall be specially noted, and added to or deducted from the *western* or *northern* ranges of sections or half-sections in such township, according as the error may be in running the lines from east to west, or from south to north.' "

" In order to throw the excesses or deficiencies, as the case may be, on the *north* and on the *west* sides of a township, according to law, it is necessary to survey the *section* lines from *south* to north on a true meridian, leaving the result in the northern line of the township to be governed by the convexity of the earth and the convergency of meridians."

Thus, suppose the land to be surveyed lies between 46° and 47° of North Latitude. The length of a degree of Longitude in Lat. 46° N. is taken as 48.0705 statute miles, and in Lat. 47° N. as 47.1944. The difference, or convergency per square degree = 0.8761 = 70.08 chains. The convergency per Range (8 per degree of Longitude) equals one-eighth of this, or 8.76 chains; and per Township ($11\frac{1}{2}$ per degree of Latitude) equals the above divided by $11\frac{1}{2}$, i. e. 0.76 chain. We therefore know that the width of the Townships along their Northern line is 76 links less than on their Southern line. The townships North of the base line therefore become narrower and narrower than the six mile width with which they start, by that amount; and those South of it as much wider than six miles.

" STANDARD PARALLELS (usually called *correction lines*), are established at stated intervals (24 or 30 miles) to provide for or counteract the error that otherwise would result from the convergency of meridians; and, because the public surveys have to be governed by the true meridian, such lines serve also to arrest error arising from inaccuracies in measurements. Such lines, when lying north of the principal base, themselves constitute a *base* to the surveys on the north of them; and where lying south of the principal base, they constitute the base for the surveys south of them."

The convergency or divergency above noticed is taken up on these Correction lines, from which the townships start again with their proper widths. On these therefore there are found *Double Corners*, both for Townships and Sections, one set being the *Closing Corners* of the surveys ending there, and the other set being the *Standard Corners* for the surveys starting there.

(562) Running Township lines. "The principal meridian, the base line, and the standard parallels having been first astronomically run, measured, and marked, according to instructions, on true meridians, and true parallels of latitude, the process of running, measuring, and marking the exterior lines of townships will be as follows.

Townships situated NORTH *of the base line, and* WEST *of the principal meridian.** Commence at No. 1, being the southwest corner of T. 1 N.—R. 1 W., as established on the base line; thence run *north*, on a true meridian line, four hundred and eighty chains, establishing the mile and half-mile corners thereon, as per instructions, to No. 2, (the northwest corner of the same township), whereat establish the corner of Tps. 1 and 2 N.—Rs. 1 and 2 W.; thence *east*, on a random or trial line, setting *temporary* mile and half-mile stakes to No. 3, (the northeast corner of the same township), where measure and note the distance at which the line intersects the eastern boundary, north or south of the *true* or established corner. Run and measure *westward*, on the true line, (taking care to note all the land and water crossings, &c., as per instructions), to No. 4, which is identical with No. 2, establishing the mile and half-mile PERMANENT CORNERS on said line, the last half-mile of which will fall short of being forty chains, by about the amount of the calculated convergency per township, 76 links in the case above supposed. Should it ever happen, however, that such random line materially falls short, or overruns in length, or intersects the eastern boundary of the township at any considerable distance from the *true* corner thereon, (either of which would indicate an important error in the surveying), the lines must be *retraced*, even if found necessary to remeasure the meridional boundaries of the township (especially the western boundary), so as to discover and correct the error; in doing which, the *true corners* must be established and marked, and the *false ones* destroyed and obliterated, to prevent confusion in future; and *all the facts* must be distinctly set forth in the notes. Thence proceed in a similar manner north, from No. 4 to No. 5, (the N. W. corner of T. 2 N. —R. 1 W.), east from No. 5 to No. 6, (the N. E. corner of the same township), west from No. 6 to No. 7, (the same as No. 5), north from No. 7 to No. 8, (the N. W. corner of T. 3 N., R. 1 W.), east from No. 8 to No. 9, (the N. E. corner of same township), and thence west to No. 10, (the same as No. 8), or the southwest corner T. 4 N.—R. 1 W. Thence north, still on a true meridian line, establishing the mile and half-mile corners, until reaching the STANDARD PARALLEL or correction line, (which is here four town-

* The Surveyor should prepare a diagram of the townships, with the numbers here referred to, in their proper places, as here indicated

ships north of the base line); throwing the *excess* over, or *deficiency* under, *four hundred and eighty chains*, on the *last* half-mile, according to law, and at the intersection establishing the "CLOSING CORNER," the distance of which *from* the standard corner must be measured and noted as required by the instructions. But should it ever so happen that some impassable barrier will have prevented or delayed the extension of the standard parallel along and above the field of present survey, then the surveyor will plant, in place, the corner for the township, subject to correction thereafter, should such parallel be extended.

Townships situated NORTH *of the base line, and* EAST *of the principal meridian.* Commence at No. 1, being the *southeast* corner of T. 1 N.—R. 1 E., and proceed as with townships situated "north and west," except that the *random* or trial lines will be run and measured *west*, and the *true* lines, east, throwing the excess over or deficiency under four hundred and eighty chains on the *west end* of the line, as required by law; wherefore, the surveyor will commence his measurement with the length of the deficient or excessive half-section boundary on the west of the township, and thus the remaining measurements will all be *even* miles and half-miles.

Townships situated SOUTH *of the base line, and* WEST *of the principal meridian.* Commence at No. 1, the *northwest* corner of township 1 S., range 1 W., and proceed *due south* in running and measuring line, establishing and marking the mile, half-mile, and township corners thereon, precisely in the method prescribed for running NORTH and WEST, with the exception that, in order to throw the excess or deficiency (over or under four hundred and eighty chains) of the *western* boundaries of such of those townships as *close on the standard parallel* on the *south*, upon the most *northern half-mile* of the townships, according to law, the proceeding will be as follows.

The western (meridional) boundary line of every township, *closing on the standard parallel*, (being every *fifth* one in this case), will be carefully run *south*, on a true meridian, until it intersects the standard, planting stakes and making distinctive marks on line trees, in sufficient number to serve as *guides* in afterwards retracing the line *north* with ease and certainty. At the point of the line's intersection of the standard, the surveyor will establish the "*closing*" (southwest) corner of the township, noting in his field-book its distance and direction from the "standard corner." Then starting from such "closing corner," he will proceed *north* on the line identified by the guide stakes and marks, measuring such line, and establishing thereon the *mile* and *half-mile* stations, and noting, as he goes, all the land and water crossings, &c.

Townships situated SOUTH *of the base line, and* EAST *of the principal meridian.* Commence at No. 1, at the northeast corner of township 1 S., range 1 E., and proceed precisely as with the townships situated "south and west," except that the *random* lines will be run and measured *west*, and the *true* lines *east;* the deficiency or excess of the measurements being, as in all other cases, thrown upon the most western half-mile of line."

(563) Running Section lines. The interior or sectional lines of all townships, however situated in reference to the BASE and MERIDIAN lines, are laid off and surveyed as below.

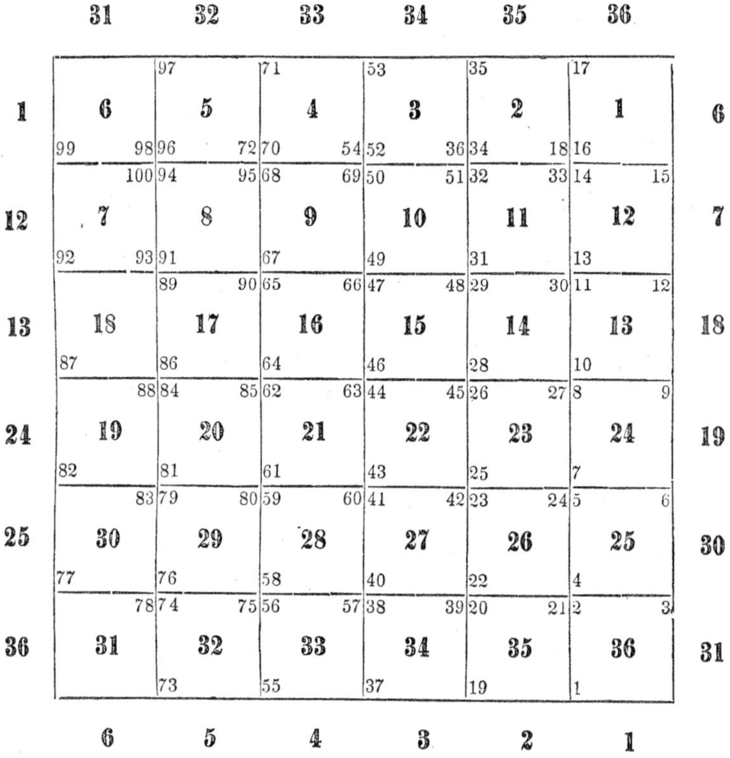

	31	32	33	34	35	36	
1	**6** 99 98	97 **5** 96 72	71 **4** 70 54	53 **3** 52 36	35 **2** 34 18	17 **1** 16	6
12	100 **7** 92 93	94 95 **8** 91	68 69 **9** 67	50 51 **10** 49	32 33 **11** 31	14 15 **12** 13	7
13	**18** 87	89 90 **17** 86	65 66 **16** 64	47 48 **15** 46	29 30 **14** 28	11 12 **13** 10	18
24	88 **19** 82	84 85 **20** 81	62 63 **21** 61	44 45 **22** 43	26 27 **23** 25	8 9 **24** 7	19
25	83 **30** 77	79 80 **29** 76	59 60 **28** 58	41 42 **27** 40	23 24 **26** 22	5 6 **25** 4	30
36	78 **31**	74 75 **32** 73	56 57 **33** 55	38 39 **34** 37	20 21 **35** 19	2 3 **36** 1	31
	6	5	4	3	2	1	

In the above Diagram, the squares and large figures represent sections, and the small figures at their corners are those referred to in the following directions.

"Commence at No. 1, (see *small* figures on diagram), the corner established on the township boundary for sections 1, 2, 35, and

36; thence run *north* on a true meridian; at 40 chains setting the half-mile or quarter-section post, and at 80 chains (No. 2) establishing and marking the corner of sections 25, 26, 35, and 36. Thence *east*, on a *random* line, to No. 3, setting the temporary quarter-section post at 40 chains, noting the measurement to No. 3, and the measured distance of the random's intersection *north* or *south* of the true or established corner of sections 25, 36, 30, and 31, on the township boundary. Thence *correct*, *west*, on the *true* line to No. 4, setting the quarter-section post on this line exactly at the *equidistant point*, now known, between the section corners indicated by the small figures Nos. 3 and 4. Proceed, in like manner, from No. 4 to No. 5, 5 to 6, 6 to 7, and so on to No. 16, the corner to sections 1, 2, 11, and 12. Thence *north*, on a random line, to No. 17, setting a temporary quarter-section post at 40 chains, noting the length of the whole line, and the measured distance of the random's intersection *east* or *west* of the true corner of sections 1, 2, 35, and 36, established on the township boundary, thence *southwardly* from the latter, on a true line, noting the course and distance to No. 18, the established corner to sections 1, 2, 11, and 12, taking care to establish the quarter-section corner on the true line, at the distance of 40 chains from said section corner, so as to throw the *excess* or *deficiency* on the northern half-mile, according to law. Proceed in like manner through all the intervening tiers of sections to No. 73, the corner to sections 31, 32, 5, and 6; thence *north*, on a true meridian line, to No. 74, establishing the quarter-section corner at 40 chains, and at 80 chains the corner to sections 29, 30, 31, and 32; thence *east*, on a random line to No. 75, setting a temporary quarter-section post at 40 chains, noting the measurement to No. 75, and the distance of the random's intersection *north* or *south* of the established corner of sections 28, 29, 32, and 33; thence *west* from said corner, on the true line, setting the quarter-section post at the equidistant point, to No. 76, which is identical with 74; thence *west*, on a random line, to No. 77, setting a temporary quarter-section post at 40 chains, noting the measurement to No. 77, and the distance of the random's intersection with the western boundary, *north* or *south* of the established corner of sections 25, 36, 30, and 31; and from No. 77, correct, *eastward*, on the true line, *giving its course*, but establishing the quarter-section post, on this line, so as to retain the distance of 40 chains from the corner of sections 29, 30, 31, and 32; thereby throwing the *excess* or *deficiency* of measurement on the most *western* half-mile. Proceed *north*, in a similar manner, from No. 78 to 79, 79 to 80, 80 to 81, and so on to 96, the south-east corner of section 6, where having established the corner for sections, 5, 6, 7, and 8, run thence, successively, on random line *east* to 95, *north* to 97, and *west* to 99; and by reverse courses *correct on true lines back* to said *south-east* corner of section 6, establishing the quarter-section corners, and noting the courses, distances, &c., as before described.

In townships contiguous to standard parallels, the above method will be varied as follows. In every township SOUTH of the principal base line, which *closes* on a standard parallel, the surveyor will begin at the *south-east* corner of the township, and measure *west* on the standard, establishing thereon the *mile* and *half-mile* corners, and noting their distances from the pre-established corners. He then will proceed to subdivide, as directed under the above head.

In the townships NORTH of the principal base line, which *close* on the standard parallel, the sectional lines must be closed on the standard by true meridians, instead of by course lines, as directed under the above head for townships otherwise situated; and the connexions of the closing corners with the pre-established standard corners are to be ascertained and noted. Such procedure does away with any necessity for running the randoms. But in case he is unable to close the lines on account of the standard not having been run, from some inevitable necessity, as heretofore mentiond, he will plant a *temporary* stake, or mound, at the end of the *sixth* mile, thus leaving the lines and their connexions to be finished, and the *permanent* corners to be planted, at such time as the standard shall be extended."

(564) Exceptional methods. Departures from the general system of subdividing public lands have been authorized by law in certain cases, particularly on water-fronts.

Thus, an act of Congress, March 3, 1811, authorized the surveyors of Lousiana, "in surveying and dividing such of the public lands in the said territory, which are or may be authorized to be surveyed and divided, as are adjacent to any river, lake, creek, bayou, or water course, to lay out the same into tracts, as far as practicable, of fifty-eight poles in front, and four hundred and sixty-five poles in depth, of such shape, and bounded by such lines, as the nature of the country will render practicable and most convenient." Another act, of May 24, 1824, authorizes lands similarly situated "to be surveyed in tracts of two acres in width, fronting on any river, bayou, lake, or water course, and running back the depth of forty acres; which tracts of land, so surveyed, shall be offered for sale entire, instead of in half-quarter-sections."

The "Instructions" from which we have quoted say, "In those localities where it would best subserve the interests of the people to have fronts on the navigable streams, and to run back into the uplands for quantity and timber, the principles of the act of May 24th, 1824, may be adopted, and you are authorized to enlarge the quantity, so as to embrace four acres front by forty in depth, forming tracts of one hundred and sixty acres. But in so doing it is designed only to survey the lines *between every four lots*, (or 640 acres), but to establish the boundary posts, or mounds, *in front* and *in rear*, at the distances requisite to secure the quantity of 160 acres to each lot, either rectangularly, when practicable, or at oblique angles, when otherwise. The angle is not important, so that the principle be maintained, as far as practicable, of making the work to square in the rear with the regular sectioning.

The numbering of all anomalous lots will commence with No. 37, to avoid the possibility of conflict with the numbering of the regular sections."

The act of Sept. 27, 1850, authorized the Department, should it deem expedient, to cause the Oregon surveys to be executed according to the principles of what is called the "Geodetic Method."

The complete adoption of this has not been thought to be expedient; but "it was deemed useful to institute on the principal base and meridian lines of the public surveys in Oregon, ordered to be established by the act referred to, a system of triangulations from the recognized legal stations, to all prominent objects within the range of the theodolite; by means of which the relative distances of such objects, in respect to those main lines, and also to each other, might be observed, calculated, and protracted, with the view of contributing to the knowledge of the topography of the country in advance of the progressing linear surveys, and to obtain the elements for estimating areas of valleys intervening between the spurs of the mountains."

"Meandering" is a name given to the usual mode of surveying with the compass, particularly as applied to navigable streams. The "Instructions" for this are, in part, as follows.

"Both banks of *navigable* rivers are to be meandered by taking the courses and distances of their sinuosities, and the same are to be entered in the '*Meander* field-book.' At those points where either the township or section lines intersect the banks of a navigable stream, POSTS, or, where necessary, MOUNDS of *earth* or *stone*, (as noted in Art. (**566**,)) are to be established at the time of running these lines. These are called "meander corners;" and in meandering you are to commence at one of those corners on the township line, coursing the banks, and measuring the distance of each course from your commencing corner to the next 'meander corner,' upon the same or another boundary of the same township; carefully noting your intersection with all intermediate meander corners. By the same method you are to meander the opposite bank of the same river.

The crossing distance *between* the MEANDER CORNERS, on same line, is to be ascertained by triangulation, in order that the river may be protracted with entire accuracy. The particulars to be given in the field-notes.

The courses and distances on meandered navigable streams, govern the calculations wherefrom are ascertained the true areas of the tracts of land (sections, quarter sections, &c.) known to the law as *fractional*, and bounding on such streams."

You are also to meander, in manner aforesaid, all *lakes* and deep ponds of the area of twenty-five acres and upwards; also navigable bayous.

The precise relative position of islands, in a township made fractional by the river in which the same are situated, is to be determined trigonometrically. Sighting to a flag or other fixed object on the island, from a special and carefully measured base line, connected with the surveyed lines, on or near the river bank, you are to form connexion between the meander corners on the river to points corresponding thereto, in direct line, on the bank of the island, and there establish the proper meander corners, and calculate the distance across."

(565) Marking Lines. "All lines on which are to be established the legal corner boundaries, are to be marked after this method, viz: Those trees which may intercept your line, must have two chops or notches cut on each side of them without any other marks whatever. These are called '*sight trees*,' or '*line trees*.'

A sufficient number of other trees standing nearest to your line, on either side of it, are to be *blazed* on two sides, diagonally or quartering towards the line, in order to render the line conspicuous, and readily to be traced, the blazes to be opposite each other, coinciding in direction with the line where the trees stand very near it, and to approach nearer each other, the further the line passes from the blazed trees. Due care must ever be taken to have the lines so well marked as to be readily followed."

(566) Marking Corners. "After a true coursing, and most exact measurements, the corner boundary is the consummation of the work, for which all the previous pains and expenditure have been incurred. A boundary corner, in a timbered country, is to be a *tree*, if one be found at the precise spot; and if not, a *post* is to be planted thereat; and the position of the corner post is to be indicated by trees adjacent, (called Bearing trees) the angular bearings and distances of which from the corner are facts to be ascertained and registered in your field book.

In a region where stone abounds, the corner boundary will be a small *monument of stones* along side of a single marked stone, for a township corner—and *a single stone* for all other corners.

In a region where timber is not near, nor stone, the corner will be a *mound of earth*, of prescribed size, varying to suit the case.

Corners are to be fixed, for township boundaries at intervals of every six miles; for section boundaries at intervals of every mile, or 80 chains; and, for quarter section boundaries at intervals of every half mile, or 40 chains.

Meander Corner Posts are to be planted at all those points where the township or section lines intersect the banks of such rivers, lakes, or islands, as are by law directed to be meandered," as explained in Art. (**564**).

When *posts* are used, their length and size must be proportioned to the importance of the corner, whether township, section, or quarter-section, the first being at least 24 inches above ground, and 3 inches square.

Where a township post is a corner common to *four* townships, it is to be set in the earth *diagonally*, thus: N W◇E S, and the cardinal points of the compass are to be indicated thereon by a cross line, or wedge, (one-eighth of an inch deep at least), cut or sawed out of its top, as in the figure. On each surface of the post is to be marked the number of the particular township, and its range, which it *faces*. Thus, if the post be a common boundary to four townships, say *one* and *two*, south of the base line, of range *one*, west of the meridian; also to townships *one* and *two*, south of the base line, of range *two*, west of the meridian, it is to be marked thus:

From N. to E.	R. 1 W. T. 1 S. S. 31
from N. to W.	2 W. 1 S. 36
from E. to S.	1 W. 2 S. 6
from W. to S.	2 W. 2 S. 1

The position of the post which is here taken as an example, is shewn in the following diagram.

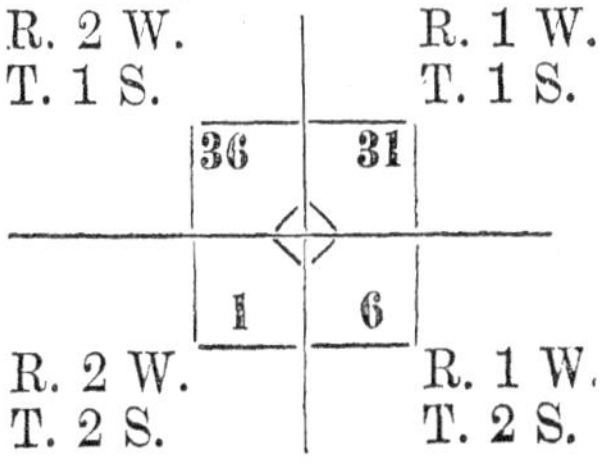

R. 2 W. T. 1 S. | R. 1 W. T. 1 S.
36 | 31
1 | 6
R. 2 W. T. 2 S. | R. 1 W. T. 2 S.

These marks are to be distinctly and neatly chiselled into the wood, at least the eighth of an inch deep; and to be also marked with *red chalk*. The *number* of the *sections* which they respectively *face*, will *also be marked* on the township post.

Section or mile posts, being corners of sections, when they are common to *four* sections, are to be set *diagonally* in the earth, (in the manner provided for township corner posts), and with a similar cross cut in the top, to indicate the cardinal points of the compass; and on each side of the squared surfaces is to be marked the appropriate *number* of the particular one of the *four sections*, respectively, which such side *faces;* also on one side thereof are to be marked the numbers of its *township* and *range;* and to make such marks yet more conspicuous, (in manner aforesaid), a streak of red chalk is to be applied.

In the case of an *isolated* township, subdivided into thirty-six sections, there are twenty-five interior sections, the south-west corner boundary of each of which will be *common* to *four* sections. On all the extreme sides of an isolated township, the outer tiers of sections have corners *common* only to *two* sections then surveyed. The posts, however, must be planted precisely like the former, but presenting two *vacant* surfaces to receive the appropriate marks when the adjacent survey may be made.

A quarter-section or half-mile post is to have no other mark on it than $\frac{1}{4}$ S., to indicate what it stands for.

Township corner posts are to be NOTCHED with *six* notches on each of the four angles of the squared part set to the cardinal points.

All mile posts *on township lines* must have as many notches on them, on two opposite *angles* thereof, as they are miles distant from the township corners, respectively. Each of the posts at the corners of sections in the *interior* of a township must indicate, by a number of notches on each of its four corners directed to the cardinal points, the corresponding number of miles that it stands from the *outlines* of the township. The four sides of the post will indicate the number of the section they respectively *face*. Should a tree be found at the place of any corner, it will be marked and notched, as aforesaid, and answer for the corner in lieu of a post; the kind of tree and its diameter being given in the field-notes.

The position of all corner posts, or corner trees of whatever description, which may be established, is to be perpetuated in the following manner, viz: From such post or tree the courses shall be taken, and the distances measured, to two or more adjacent trees, in opposite directions, as nearly as may be, which are called '*Bearing trees*,' and are to be blazed near the ground, with a large blaze facing the post, and having one notch in it, neatly and plainly made with an axe, square across, and a little below the middle of the blaze. The kind of tree and the diameter of each are facts to be distinctly set forth in the field-book.

On each bearing tree the letters, B. T., must be distinctly cut into the wood, in the blaze, a little above the notch, or on the bark, with the number of the range, township, and section.

At all township corners, and at all section corners, on range or township lines, *four* bearing trees are to be marked in this manner, one in each of the adjoining sections.

At interior section corners *four* trees, one to stand within each of the four sections to which such corner is common, are to be marked in manner aforesaid, if such be found.

From quarter section and meander corners two bearing trees are to be marked, one within each of the adjoining sections.

Stones at township corners (a small monument of stones being alongside thereof) must have *six* notches cut with a pick or chisel on each edge or side towards the cardinal points; and where used as section corners on the range and township lines, or as section corners in the interior of a township, they will also be notched by a pick or chisel, to correspond with the directions given for notching posts similarly situated.

Stones, when used as quarter-section corners, will have ¼ cut on them; on the west side on north and south lines, and on the north side on east and west lines.

Whenever bearing trees are not found, MOUNDS of earth, or stone, are to be raised *around posts* on which the corners are to be marked in the manner aforesaid. Wherever a mound of earth is adopted, the same will present a conical shape; but at its base, on the earth's surface, a *quadrangular trench* will be dug; a *spade deep* of earth being thrown up from the four sides of the line, *outside* the trench, so as to form a *continuous elevation along its outer edge*. In mounds of earth, common to *four* townships or to *four* sections, they will present the *angles* of the quadrangular trench (*diagonally*) towards the cardinal points. In mounds common only to *two* townships or *two* sections, the *sides* of the quadrangular trench will *face* the cardinal points.

Prior to piling up the earth to construct a mound, in a *cavity* formed at the corner boundary point is to be deposited a *stone*, or a portion of *charcoal*, or a *charred stake* is to be driven twelve inches down into such centre point, to be a *witness* for the future.

The surveyor is farther specially enjoined to plant *midway* between each pit and the trench, seeds of some tree, those of fruit trees adapted to the climate being always to be preferred.

DOUBLE CORNERS are to be found nowhere except on the Standard Parallels or Correction lines, whereon are to appear both the cor ners which mark the intersections of the lines which close thereon, and those from which the surveys start in the opposite direction.

The corners which are established on the standard parallel, at the time of running it, are to be known as '*Standard Corners*,' and, in addition to all the *ordinary* marks, (as herein prescribed), they will be marked with the letters S. C. The '*closing corners*' will be marked C. C."

(567) Field Books. There should be several distinct and separate field-books; viz.:

"1. Field-notes of the MERIDIAN and BASE lines, showing the establishment of the *township*, *section* or mile, and *quarter-section* or half-mile, boundary corners thereon; with the crossings of streams, ravines, hills, and mountains; character of soil, timber, minerals, &c. These notes will be arranged, in series, by *mile stations*, from number *one* to number ——.

2. Field-notes of the 'STANDARD PARALLELS, or correction lines,' showing the establishment of the township, section, and quarter-section corners, besides exhibiting the topography of the country on line, as required on the base and meridian lines.

3. Field-notes of the EXTERIOR lines of TOWNSHIPS, showing the establishment of the corners on line, and the topography, as aforesaid.

4. Field notes of the SUBDIVISIONS of TOWNSHIPS into sections and quarter-sections; at the close whereof will follow the notes of the MEANDERS of navigable streams. These notes will also show, by *ocular* observation, the estimated rise and fall of the land on the line. A description of the timber, undergrowth, surface, soil, and minerals, upon each section line, is to follow the notes thereof, and not to be mixed up with them."

5. The "Geodetic Field-book," comprising all triangulations, angles of elevation and depression, levelling, &c.

The examples on the next two pages, taken from the "Instructions" which we have followed throughout, will shew what is required.

The ascents and descents are recorded in the right-hand columns.

FIELD NOTES OF

THE EXTERIOR LINES

OF AN ISOLATED TOWNSHIP.

Field notes of the Survey of township 25 *north, of range* 2 *west, of the Willamette meridian, in the Territory of* OREGON, *by Robert Acres, deputy surveyor, under his contract No.* 1, *bearing date the* 2*d day of January*, 1851.

	Chs. lks.		Feet.
Random tp. S. boundary.		TOWNSHIP LINES commenced January 20, 1851.	
		Southern boundary variation 18° 41′ E.	
	East.	On a *random* line on the south boundaries of sections 31, 32, 33, 34, 35, and 36. Set temporary mile and half-mile posts, and intersected the eastern boundary 2 chains 20 links north of the true corner 5 miles 74 chains 53 links.	
		Therefore the correction will be 5 chains 47 links W. 37.1 links S. per mile.	
Timbered corners.		TRUE SOUTHERN BOUNDARY variation 18° 41′ E.	
	West	On the southern boundary of sec. 36, Jan. 24, 1851.	
	40.00	Set qr. sec. post from which	*a* 10
		a beech 24 in. dia. bears N. 11 E. 38 lks. dist.	
		a do 9 do . do S. 9 E. 17 do	
	62.50	a brook 8 l. wide, course NW.	*d* 10
	80.00	Set post cor. of secs. 35 & 36, 1 & 2, from which	*a* 5
		a beech 9 in. dia. bears S. 46 E. 8 l. dist.	
		a do 8 do do S. 62 W. 7 do	
		a W. oak 10 do do N. 19 W. 14 do	
		a B. oak 14 do do N. 29 E. 16 do	
		Land level, part wet and swampy; timber beech, oak, ash, hickory, &c.	
Deficient timbered corners.	West.	On the S. boundary of sec. 35—	
	40.00	Set qr. sec. post, with trench, from which	*a* 10
		a beech 6 in. dia. bears N. 80 E. 8 l. dist.	
		planted SW. a yellow locust seed.	
	65.00	To beginning of hill	*a* 5
	80.00	Set post, with trench, cor. of secs. 34 & 35, 2 & 3, from which	*a* 20.
		a beech 10 in. dia. bears S. 51 E. 13 l. dist.	
		do 10 do do N. 56 W. 9 do	
		planted SW. a white oak acorn,	
		NE. a beech nut.	
		Land level, rich, and good for farming; timber same.	
Mound section corner.	West.	On the S. boundary of sec. 34—	
	40.00	Set qr. sec. post, with trench, from which	*a* 5
		a B. oak 10 in. dia. bears N. 2 E. 635 l. dist.	
		Planted SW. a beech nut.	
	80.00	To corner of sections 33, 34, 3 and 4, drove charred stakes raised mound with trench as per instructions, and	*a* 10
		Planted NE. a W. oak ac'n; NW. a yel. locust seed.	
		SE. a butternut; SW. a beech nut	
		Land level, rich and good for farming, some scattering oak and walnut.	

&c., &c., &c.

FIELD NOTES OF THE

SUBDIVISIONAL OR SECTIONAL LINES,

AND MEANDERS.

Township 25 *N.*, *Range* 2 *W.*, *Willamette Mer.*

	Chs. lks.		Feet.
		SUBDIVISIONS. Commenced February 1, 1851.	
True line.	North.	Between secs. 35 and 36—	
	9.19	A beech 30 in. dia	d 10
	29.97	A beech 30 in. dia	d 5
	40.00	Set qr. sec. post, from which a beech 15 in. dia. bears S. 48 E. 12 l. dist. a do 8 do do N. 23 W. 45 do	d 5
	51.90	A beech 18 in. dia	d 5
	76.73	A sugar 30 in. dia	d 8
	80.00	Set a post cor. of secs. 25, 26, 35, 36, from which a beech 24 in. dia. bears N. 62 W. 17 l. dist. a poplar 36 do do S. 66 E. 34 do. a do 20 do do S. 70 W. 50 do. a beech 28 do do N. 60 E. 45 do.	d 2
		Land level, second rate; timber beech, poplar, sugar, and und'gr. spice, &c.	
Random.	East.	On random line between secs. 25 and 36—	
	9.00	A brook 30 l. wide, course N	d 10
	15.00	To foot of hill	d 10
	40.00	Set temporary qr. sec. post	a 60
	55.00	To opposite foot of hill	d 40
	72.00	A brook 15 l. wide, course N	d 20
	80.00	Intersect E. boundary at post	a 10
		Land level, second rate; timber, beech, oak, ash, &c.	
		&c., &c., &c.	

MEANDERS OF CHICKEELES RIVER.

Beginning at a meander post in the northern township boundary, and thence on the left bank down stream. *Commenced February* 11, 1851.

Courses.	Dist. Chs. lks.	REMARKS.
S. 76 W.	18.46	In section 4 bearing to corner sec. 4 on right bank N. 70° W
S. 61 W.	10.00	Bearing to cor. sec. 4 and 5, right bank N. 52° W.
S. 61 W.	8.18	To post in line between sections 4 and 5, breadth of river by triangulation 9 chains 51 links.
S. 54 W.	10.69	In section 5.
S. 40 W.	5.59	
S. 50 W.	8.46	
S. 37 W.	16.50	To upper corner of John Smith's claim, course E.
S. 44 W.	21.96	
S. 36 W.	27.53	To post in line between sections 5 and 8, breadth of river by triangulation 8 chains 78 links.
		&c., &c., &c.

APPENDIX.

APPENDIX A.

SYNOPSIS OF PLANE TRIGONOMETRY.*

(1) Definition. Plane Trigonometry is that branch of Mathematical Science which treats of the relations between the sides and angles of plane triangles. It teaches how to find any three of these six parts, when the other three are given and one of them, at least, is a side.

(2) Angles and Arcs. The *angles* of a triangle are measured by the *arcs* described, with any radius, from the angular points as centres, and intercepted between the legs of the angles. These arcs are measured by comparing them with an entire circumference, described with the same radius. Every circumference is regarded as being divided into 360 equal parts, called *degrees*. Each degree is divided into 60 equal parts, called *minutes*, and each minute into 60 *seconds*. These divisions are indicated by the marks $^\circ\ '\ ''$. Thus 28 degrees, 17 minutes, and 49 seconds, are written $28^\circ\ 17'\ 49''$. Fractions of a second are best expressed decimally. An arc, including a quarter of a circumference and measuring a right angle, is therefore 90°. A semicircumference comprises 180°. It is often represented by π, which equals 3.14159, &c., or $3\frac{1}{7}$ approximately, the radius being unity.

The length of 1° in parts of radius $= 0.01745329$; that of $1' = 0.00029089$; and that of $1'' = 0.00000485$.

The length of the radius of a circle in degrees, or 360ths of the circumference $= 57^\circ.29578 = 57^\circ\ 17'\ 24''.8 = 3437'.747 = 206264''.8.$†

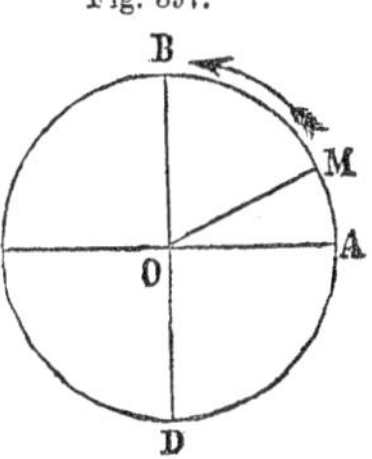

Fig. 397.

An arc may be regarded as generated by a point, M, moving from an origin, A, around a circle, in the direction of the arrow. The point may thus describe arcs of any lengths, such as AM; $AB = 90^\circ = \frac{1}{2}\pi$; $ABC = 180^\circ = \pi$; $ABCD = 270^\circ = \frac{3}{2}\pi$; $ABCDA = 360^\circ = 2\pi$.

The point may still continue its motion, and generate arcs greater than a circumference, or than two circumferences, or than three; or even infinite in length.

While the point, M, describes these arcs, the radius, OM, indefinitely produced, generates corresponding angles.

---

* For merely solving triangles, only Articles (1), (2), (3), (5), (6), (10), (11), and (12), are needed.

† The number of seconds in any arc which is given in parts of radius, radius being unity, equals the length of the arc so given divided by the length of the arc of one second; or multiplied by the number of seconds in radius.

If the point, M, should move from the origin, A, in the contrary direction to its former movement, the arcs generated by it are regarded as *negative*, or *minus;* and so too, of necessity, the angles measured by the arcs.

Arcs and angles may therefore vary in length from 0 to $+\infty$ in one direction, and from 0 to $-\infty$ in the contrary direction.

The *Complement* of an arc is the arc which would remain after subtracting the arc from a quarter of the circumference, or from 90°. If the arc be more than 90°, its complement is necessarily negative.

The *Supplement* of an arc is what would remain after subtracting it from half the circumference, or from 180°. If the arc be more than 180°, its supplement is necessarily negative.

(3) Trigonometrical Lines. The relations of the sides of a triangle to its angles are what is required; but it is more convenient to replace the angles by arcs; and, once more, to replace the arcs by certain straight lines depending upon them, and increasing and decreasing with them, or conversely, in such a way that the length of the lines can be found from that of the arcs, and vice versâ. It is with these lines that the sides of a triangle are compared.* These lines are called *Trigonometrical Lines;* or *Circular Functions,* because their length is a function of that of the circular arcs. The principal Trigonometrical lines are *Sines, Tangents,* and *Secants.* Chords and versed sines are also used.

The SINE of an arc, AM, is the perpendicular, MP, let fall, from one extremity of the arc, upon the diameter which passes through the other extremity.

Fig. 398.

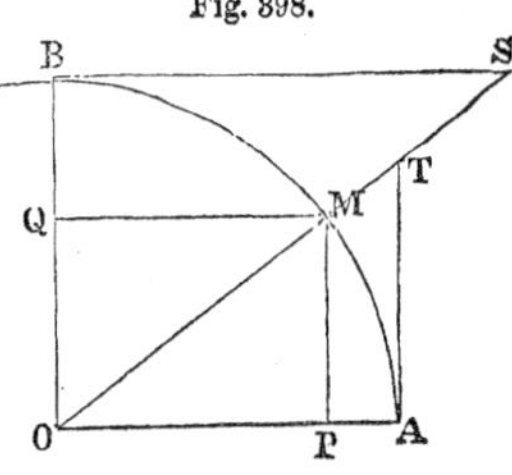

The TANGENT of an arc, AM, is the distance, AT, intercepted, on the tangent drawn at one extremity of the arc, between that extremity and the prolongation of the radius which passes through the other extremity.

The SECANT of an arc, AM, is the part, OT, of the prolonged radius, comprised between the centre and the tangent.

The sine, tangent, and secant of the complement of an arc are called the Co-sine, Co-tangent, and Co-secant of that arc. Thus, MQ is the cosine of AM, BS its cotangent, and OS its cosecant. The cosine MQ is equal to OP, the part of the radius comprised between the centre and the foot of the sine.

The *chord* of an arc is equal to twice the sine of half that arc.

The *versed-sine* of an arc, AM, is the distance, AP, comprised between the origin of the arc and the foot of the sine. It is consequently equal to the difference between the radius and the sine.

The Trigonometrical lines are usually written in an abbreviated form. Calling the arc $\text{AM} = a$, we write,

$$\text{MP} = \sin.\ a. \qquad \text{AT} = \tan.\ a. \qquad \text{OT} = \sec.\ a.$$
$$\text{MQ} = \cos.\ a. \qquad \text{BS} = \cot.\ a. \qquad \text{OS} = \text{cosec.}\ a.$$

The period after sin., tan., &c., indicating abbreviation, is frequently omitted.

The arcs whose sines, tangents, &c., are equal to a line $=a$, are written,

$$\sin.^{-1} a, \text{ or arc } (\sin. = a);$$
$$\tan.^{-1} a, \text{ or arc } (\tan. = a);\ \&c.$$

* For the great value of this indirect mode of comparing the sides and angles of triangles, see Comte's "Philosophy of Mathematics," (Harpers', 1851,) page 225.

Fig. 399.

(4) The lines as ratios. The ratios between the trigonometrical lines and the radius are the same for the same angles, or number of degrees in an arc, whatever the length of the radius or arc. Consequently, radius being unity, these lines may be expressed as simple ratios. Thus, in the right-angled triangle A B C, we would have

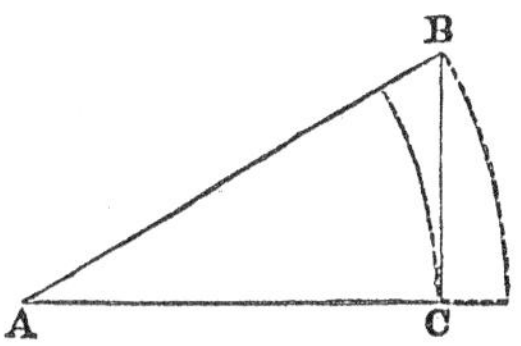

$$\sin. A = \frac{BC}{AB} = \frac{\text{opposite side}}{\text{hypothenuse}}, \qquad \cos. A = \frac{AC}{AB} = \frac{\text{adjacent side}}{\text{hypothenuse}},$$

$$\tan. A = \frac{BC}{AC} = \frac{\text{opposite side}}{\text{adjacent side}}, \qquad \cot. A = \frac{AC}{BC} = \frac{\text{adjacent side}}{\text{opposite side}},$$

$$\sec. A = \frac{AB}{AC} = \frac{\text{hypothenuse}}{\text{adjacent side}}, \qquad \text{cosec. } A = \frac{AB}{BC} = \frac{\text{hypothenuse}}{\text{opposite side}}.$$

When the radius of the arcs which measure the angles is unity, these ratios may be used for the lines. If the radius be any other length, the results which have been obtained by the above supposition, must be modified by dividing each of the trigonometrical lines in the result by radius, and thus rendering the equations of the results "homogeneous." The same effect would be produced by multiplying each term in the expression by such a power of radius as would make it contain a number of *linear* factors equal to the greatest number in any term. The radius is usually represented by r, or R.

(5) Their variations in length. As the point M moves around the circle, and the arc thus increases, the sines, tangents, and secants, starting from zero, also increase; till, when the point M has arrived at B, and the arc has become 90°, the sine has become equal to radius, or unity, and the tangent and secant have become infinite. The complementary lines have decreased; the cosine being equal to radius or unity at starting and becoming zero, and the cotangent and cosecant passing from infinity to zero. When the point M has passed the first quadrant at B and is proceeding towards C, the sines, tangents, and secants begin to decrease, till, when the point has reached C, they have the same values as at A. They then begin to increase again, and so on. The Table on page 382 indicates these variations.

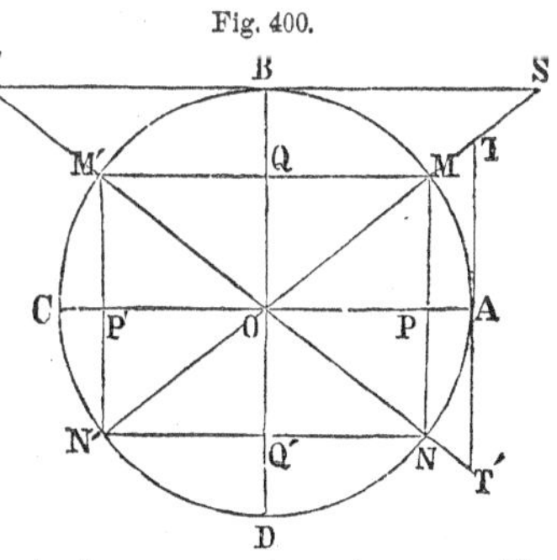

Fig. 400.

The sines and tangents of very small arcs may be regarded as sensibly proportional to the arcs themselves; so that for sin. a'', we may write a . sin. $1''$; and similarly, though less accurately, for sin. a', we may write a . sin. $1'$.

The sines and tangents of very small arcs may similarly be regarded as sensibly of the same length as the arcs themselves.*

* Consequently, the note on page 379 may read thus: The number of seconds in any very small arc given in parts of radius, radius being unity, is equal to the length of the arc so given divided by sin. $1''$.

a being the length of any arc expressed in parts of radius, the lengths of its sine and cosine may be obtained by the following series:

$$\sin. a = a - \frac{a^3}{2.3} + \frac{a^5}{2.3.4.5} - \frac{a^7}{2.3....7} +, \text{etc.}$$

$$\cos. a = 1 - \frac{a^2}{2} + \frac{a^4}{2.3.4} - \frac{a^6}{2....6} +, \text{etc.}$$

Let it be required to find cos. 30°, by the above series.

$$30° = \frac{30}{180}\pi = \tfrac{1}{6} \times 3.1416 = .5236.$$

Substituting this number for a, the series becomes, taking only three terms of it,

$$1 - \frac{(.5236)^2}{2} + \frac{(.5236)^4}{24} -, \text{etc.} = 1 - 0.137078 + 0.003130 = .866052;$$

which is the correct value of cos. 30° for the first four places of decimals.

The lengths of the other lines can be obtained from the mutual relations given in Art. (7.) Some particular values are given below.

sin. $30° = \frac{1}{2}$.	sin. $45° = \frac{1}{2}\sqrt{2}$.	sin. $60° = \frac{1}{2}\sqrt{3}$.
tan. $30° = \frac{1}{3}\sqrt{3}$.	tan. $45° = 1$.	tan. $60° = \sqrt{3}$.
sec. $30° = \frac{2}{3}\sqrt{3}$.	sec. $45° = \sqrt{2}$.	sec. $60° = 2$.

(6) **Their changes of sign.** Lines measured in contrary directions from a common origin, usually receive contrary algebraic signs. If then all the lines in the first quadrant are called positive, their signs will change in some of the other quadrants. Thus the *sines* in the first quadrant being all measured upward, when they are measured downward, as they are in the third and fourth quadrants, they will be negative. The *cosines* in the first quadrant are measured from left to right, and when they are measured from right to left, as in the second and third quadrants, they will be negative. The *tangents* and *secants* follow similar rules.

The variations in length and the changes of sign are all indicated in the following table, radius being unity. The terms "increasing" and "decreasing" apply to the lengths of the lines without any reference to their signs.

Lengths and Signs of the Trigonometrical Lines for Arcs from 0° *to* 360°

Arcs.	0°	Between 0° and 90°.	90°	Between 90° and 180°.	180°
Sine . . .	0	+, and increasing,	+1	+, and decreasing,	0
Tangent . .	0	+, and increasing,	±∞	−, and decreasing,	0
Secant . .	+1	+, and increasing,	±∞	−, and decreasing,	−1
Cosine . .	+1	+, and decreasing,	0	−, and increasing,	−1
Cotangent .	±∞	+, and decreasing,	0	−, and increasing,	∓∞
Cosecant . .	±∞	+, and decreasing,	+1	+, and increasing,	±∞

Arcs.	180°	Between 180° and 270°.	270°	Between 270° and 360°.	360°
Sine . . .	0	−, and increasing,	−1	−, and decreasing,	0
Tangent . .	0	+, and increasing,	±∞	−, and decreasing,	0
Secant . .	−1	−, and increasing,	∓∞	+, and decreasing,	+1
Cosine . . .	−1	−, and decreasing,	0	+, and increasing,	+1
Cotangent .	∓∞	+, and decreasing,	0	−, and increasing,	∓∞
Cosecant .	±∞	−, and decreasing,	−1	−, and increasing,	∓∞

From this table, and Fig. 400, we see that *an arc and its supplement* have the same sine; and that their tangents, secants, cosines, and cotangents are of equal length but of contrary signs; while the cosecants are the same in both length and sign.

We also deduce from the figure the following consequences:

$$\sin.\ (a^\circ + 180^\circ) = -\sin.\ a^\circ. \qquad \cos.\ (a^\circ + 180^\circ) = -\cos.\ a^\circ.$$
$$\tan.\ (a^\circ + 180^\circ) = \tan.\ a^\circ. \qquad \cot.\ (a^\circ + 180^\circ) = \cot.\ a^\circ.$$
$$\sec.\ (a^\circ + 180^\circ) = -\sec.\ a^\circ. \qquad \text{cosec.}\ (a^\circ + 180^\circ) = -\text{cosec.}\ a^\circ.$$

$$\sin.\ (-a^\circ) = -\sin.\ a^\circ. \qquad \cos.\ (-a^\circ) = \cos.\ a^\circ.$$
$$\tan.\ (-a^\circ) = -\tan.\ a^\circ. \qquad \cot.\ (-a^\circ) = -\cot.\ a^\circ.$$
$$\sec.\ (-a^\circ) = \sec.\ a^\circ. \qquad \text{cosec.}\ (-a^\circ) = -\text{cosec.}\ a^\circ.$$

An infinite number of arcs have the same trigonometrical lines; for, an arc a, the same arc plus a circumference, the same arc plus two circumferences, and so on, would have the same sine, &c.

"To bring back to the first quadrant" the trigonometrical lines of any large arc, proceed thus: Let 1029° be an arc the sine of which is desired. Take from it as many times 360° as possible. The remainder will be 309°. Then we shall have

$$\sin.309^\circ = \sin.(180^\circ - 309^\circ) = \sin. -129^\circ = -\sin.129^\circ = -\sin.(180^\circ - 129^\circ) = -\sin.51^\circ$$

(7) Their mutual relations. Radius being unity,

$$\tan.\ a^\circ = \frac{\sin.\ a^\circ}{\cos.\ a^\circ}. \qquad \cot.\ a^\circ = \frac{\cos.\ a^\circ}{\sin.\ a^\circ}.$$

$$\sec.\ a^\circ = \frac{1}{\cos.\ a^\circ} \qquad \text{cosec.}\ a^\circ = \frac{1}{\sin.\ a^\circ}.$$

$$\tan.\ a^\circ \times \cot.\ a^\circ = 1. \qquad (\sin.\ a^\circ)^2 + (\cos.\ a^\circ)^2 = 1.^*$$
$$1 + (\tan.\ a^\circ)^2 = (\sec.\ a^\circ)^2. \qquad 1 + (\cot.\ a^\circ)^2 = (\text{cosec.}\ a^\circ)^2.$$

Hence, any one of the trigonometrical lines being given, the rest can be found from some of these equations.

(8) Two arcs. Let a and b represent any two arcs, a being the greater Then the following formulas apply:

$$\sin.\ (a + b) = \sin.\ a \,.\, \cos.\ b + \cos.\ a \,.\, \sin.\ b.$$
$$\sin.\ (a - b) = \sin.\ a \,.\, \cos.\ b - \cos.\ a \,.\, \sin.\ b.$$
$$\cos.\ (a + b) = \cos.\ a \,.\, \cos.\ b - \sin.\ a \,.\, \sin.\ b.$$
$$\cos.\ (a - b) = \cos.\ a \,.\, \cos.\ b + \sin.\ a \,.\, \sin.\ b.$$

$$\tan.\ (a + b) = \frac{\tan.\ a + \tan.\ b}{1 - \tan.\ a \,.\, \tan.\ b}$$

$$\tan.\ (a - b) = \frac{\tan.\ a - \tan.\ b}{1 + \tan.\ a \,.\, \tan.\ b}.$$

$$\cot.\ (a + b) = \frac{\cot.\ a \,.\, \cot.\ b - 1}{\cot.\ b + \cot.\ a}.$$

$$\cot.\ (a - b) = \frac{\cot.\ a \,.\, \cot.\ b + 1}{\cot.\ b - \cot.\ a}.$$

* The square, &c., of the sine, &c., of an arc, is often expressed by placing the exponent between the abbreviation of the name of the trigonometrical line and the number of the degrees in the arc; thus, $\sin.^2 a^\circ$, $\tan.^2 a^\circ$, &c. But the notation given above, places the index as used by Gauss, Delambre, Arbogast, &c., though the first two omit the parentheses.

$$\sin. a . \sin. b = \tfrac{1}{2} . \cos. (a - b) - \tfrac{1}{2} \cos. (a + b).$$
$$\cos. a . \cos. b = \tfrac{1}{2} . \cos. (a + b) + \tfrac{1}{2} \cos. (a - b).$$
$$\sin. a . \cos. b = \tfrac{1}{2} . \sin. (a + b) + \tfrac{1}{2} \sin. (a - b).$$
$$\cos. a . \sin. b = \tfrac{1}{2} . \sin. (a + b) - \tfrac{1}{2} \sin. (a - b).$$
$$\sin. a + \sin. b = 2 \sin. \tfrac{1}{2} (a + b) \cos. \tfrac{1}{2} (a - b).$$
$$\cos. a + \cos. b = 2 \cos. \tfrac{1}{2} (a + b) \cos. \tfrac{1}{2} (a - b).$$
$$\sin. a - \sin. b = 2 \sin. \tfrac{1}{2} (a - b) \cos. \tfrac{1}{2} (a + b).$$
$$\cos. b - \cos. a = 2 \sin. \tfrac{1}{2} (a - b) \sin. \tfrac{1}{2} (a + b).$$
$$\tan. a + \tan. b = \frac{\sin. (a + b)}{\cos. a . \cos. b}.$$
$$\tan. a - \tan. b = \frac{\sin. (a - b)}{\cos. a . \cos. b}.$$
$$\cot. b + \cot. a = \frac{\sin. (a + b)}{\sin. a . \sin. b}.$$
$$\cot. b - \cot. a = \frac{\sin. (a - b)}{\sin. a . \sin. b}.$$

(9) Double and half arcs. Letting a represent any arc, as before, we have the following formulas:

$$\sin. 2a = 2 \sin. a . \cos. a.$$
$$\cos. 2a = (\cos. a)^2 - (\sin. a)^2 = 2 (\cos. a)^2 - 1 = 1 - 2 (\sin. a)^2.$$
$$\tan. 2a = \frac{2 \tan. a}{1 - (\tan. a)^2} = \frac{2 \cot. a}{(\cot. a)^2 - 1} = \frac{2}{\cot. a - \tan. a}.$$
$$\cot. 2a = \frac{(\cot. a)^2 - 1}{2 \cot. a} = \tfrac{1}{2} (\cot. a - \tan. a).$$
$$\sin. \tfrac{1}{2} a = \sqrt{\left[\tfrac{1}{2} (1 - \cos a) \right]}.$$
$$\cos. \tfrac{1}{2} a = \sqrt{\left[\tfrac{1}{2} (1 + \cos. a) \right]}.$$
$$\tan. \tfrac{1}{2} a = \frac{\sin. a}{1 + \cos. a} = \frac{1 - \cos. a}{\sin. a} = \sqrt{\left(\frac{1 - \cos. a}{1 + \cos. a} \right)}.$$
$$\cot. \tfrac{1}{2} a = \frac{1 + \cos. a}{\sin. a} = \frac{\sin. a}{1 - \cos. a} = \sqrt{\left(\frac{1 + \cos. a}{1 - \cos. a} \right)}.$$

(10) Trigonometrical Tables. In the usual tables of the natural Trigonometrical lines, the degrees from 0° to 45° are found at the top of the table, and those from 45° to 90° at the bottom; the latter being complements of the former. Consequently, the columns which have *Sine* and *Tangent* at top have *Cosine* and *Cotangent* at bottom, since the cosine or cotangent of any arc is the same thing as the sine or tangent of its complement. The minutes to be added to the degrees are found in the left-hand column, when the number of degrees at the top of the page are used, and in the right-hand column for the degrees when at the bottom of the page. The lines for arcs intermediate between those in the tables are found by proportion. The lines are calculated for a radius equal unity. Hence, the values of the sines and cosines are decimal fractions, though the point is usually omitted. So too are the tangents from 0° to 45°, and the cotangents from 90° to 45°. Beyond those points they are integers and decimals.

The calculations, like all others involving large numbers, are shortened by the use of logarithms, which substitute addition and subtraction for multiplication and division; but the young student should avoid the frequent error of regarding logarithms as a necessary part of trigonometry.

SOLUTION OF TRIANGLES.

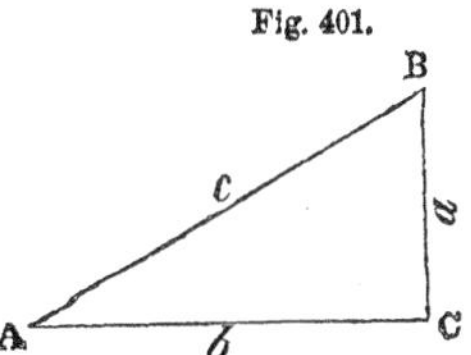

Fig. 401.

(11) Right-angled Triangles. Let ABC be any right-angled triangle. Denote the sides opposite the angles by the corresponding small letters. Then any one side and one acute angle, or any two sides being given, the other parts can be obtained by one of the following equations:

Given.	Required.	Formulas.
$a,\ b$	$c,\ \text{A},\ \text{B}$	$c=\sqrt{(a^2+b^2)}$; tan. $\text{A}=\frac{a}{b}$; cot. $\text{B}=\frac{a}{b}$.
$a,\ c$	$b,\ \text{A},\ \text{B}$	$b=\sqrt{(c^2-a^2)}$; sin. $\text{A}=\frac{a}{c}$; cos. $\text{B}=\frac{a}{c}$.
$a,\ \text{A}$	$b,\ c,\ \text{B}$	$b=a\,.\,\text{cot. A}$; $c=\frac{a}{\text{sin. A}}$; $\text{B}=90°-\text{A}$.
$b,\ \text{A}$	$a,\ c,\ \text{B}$	$a=b\,.\,\text{tan. A}$; $c=\frac{b}{\text{cos. A}}$; $\text{B}=90°-\text{A}$.
$c,\ \text{A}$	$a,\ b,\ \text{B}$	$a=c\,.\,\text{sin. A}$; $b=c\ \text{cos. A}$; $\text{B}=90°-\text{A}$.

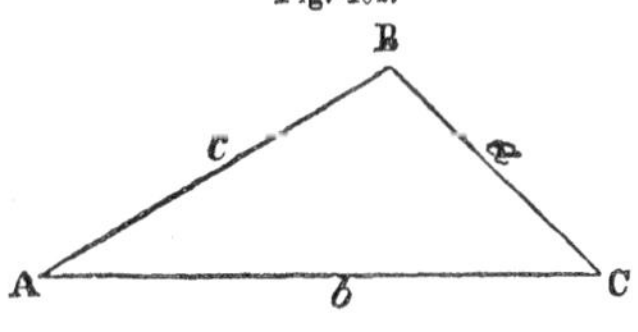

Fig. 402.

(12) Oblique-angled Triangles. Let ABC be any oblique-angled triangle, the angles and sides being noted as in the figure. Then any three of its six parts being given, and one of them being a side, the other parts can be obtained by one of the following methods, which are founded on these three theorems.

THEOREM I.—*In every plane triangle, the sines of the angles are to each other as the opposite sides.*

THEOREM II.—*In every plane triangle, the sum of two sides is to their difference as the tangent of half the sum of the angles opposite those sides is to the tangent of half their difference.*

THEOREM III.—*In every plane triangle, the cosine of any angle is equal to a fraction whose numerator is the sum of the squares of the sides adjacent to the angle,* minus *the square of the side opposite to the angle, and whose denominator is twice the product of the sides adjacent to the angle.*

All the cases for solution which can occur, may be reduced to four.

CASE 1.—*Given a side and two angles.* The third angle is obtained by subtracting the sum of the two given angles from 180°. Then either unknown side can be obtained by Theorem I.

Calling the given side a, we have $b=a\,.\,\frac{\text{sin. B}}{\text{sin. A}}$; and $c=a\,\frac{\text{sin. C}}{\text{sin. A}}$.

CASE 2.—*Given two sides and an angle opposite one of them.* The angle opposite the other given side is found by Theorem I. The third angle is obtained by subtracting the sum of the other two from 180°. The remaining side is then obtained by Theorem I.

Calling the given sides a and b, and the given angle A, we have $\sin. B = \sin. A . \frac{b}{a}$

Since an angle and its supplement have the same sine, the result is ambiguous; for the angle B may have either of the two supplementary values indicated by the sine, if $b > a$, and A is an acute angle.

$$C = 180^\circ - (A + B). \qquad c = \sin. C \frac{a}{\sin. A}.$$

CASE 3.—*Given two sides and their included angle.* Applying Theorem II. (obtaining the sum of the angles opposite the given sides by subtracting the given included angle from 180°), we obtain the difference of the unknown angles. Adding this to their sum we obtain the greater angle, and subtracting it from their sum we get the less. Then Theorem I. will give the remaining side.

Calling the given sides a and b, and the included angle C, we have $A + B = 180^\circ - C$. Then

$$\tan. \tfrac{1}{2}(A - B) = \tan. \tfrac{1}{2}(A + B) . \frac{a - b}{a + b}.$$

$$\tfrac{1}{2}(A + B) + \tfrac{1}{2}(A - B) = A. \qquad \tfrac{1}{2}(A + B) - \tfrac{1}{2}(A - B) = B. \qquad c = a \frac{\sin. C}{\sin. A}.$$

In the first equation $\cot. \frac{1}{2} C$ may be used in the place of $\tan. \frac{1}{2}(A + B)$.

CASE 4.—*Given the three sides.* Let s represent half the sum of the three sides $= \frac{1}{2}(a + b + c)$. Then any angle, as A, may be obtained from either of the following formulas, founded on Theorem III.:

$$\sin. \tfrac{1}{2} A = \sqrt{\left[\frac{(s - b)(s - c)}{bc}\right]}.$$

$$\cos. \tfrac{1}{2} A = \sqrt{\left[\frac{s(s - a)}{bc}\right]}.$$

$$\tan. \tfrac{1}{2} A = \sqrt{\left[\frac{(s - b)(s - c)}{s(s - a)}\right]}.$$

$$\sin. A = \frac{2\sqrt{[s(s - a)(s - b)(s - c)]}}{bc}$$

$$\cos. A = \frac{b^2 + c^2 - a^2}{2bc}.$$

The first formula should be used when $A < 90^\circ$, and the second when $A > 90^\circ$. The third should not be used when A is nearly 180°; nor the fourth when A is nearly 90°; nor the fifth when A is very small. The third is the most convenient when all the angles are required.

APPENDIX B.

DEMONSTRATIONS OF PROBLEMS, ETC.

MANY of the problems, &c., contained in the preceding pages, require Demonstrations. These will be given here, and will be designated by the same numbers as those of the Articles to which they refer.

As many of these Demonstrations involve the beautiful Theory of Transversals, &c., which has not yet found its way into our Geometries, a condensed summary of its principal Theorems will first be given.

TRANSVERSALS.

THEOREM I.—*If a straight line be drawn so as to cut any two sides of a triangle, and the third side prolonged, thus dividing them into six parts (the prolonged side and its prolongation being two of the parts), then will the product of any three of those parts, whose extremities are not contiguous, equal the product of the other three parts.*

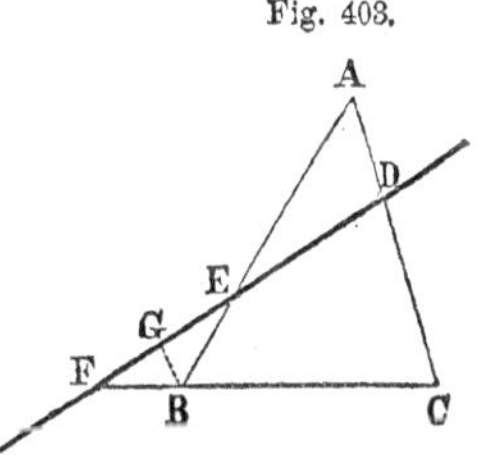

Fig. 403.

That is, in Fig. 403, ABC being the triangle, and DF the Transversal, BE×AD×CF=EA×DC×BF.

To prove this, from B draw BG, parallel to CA. From the similar triangles BEG and AED, we have BG : BE :: AD : AE. From the similar triangles BFG and CFD, we have CD : CF :: BG : BF. Multiplying these proportions together, we have BG×CD : BE×CF :: AD×BG : AE×BF. Multiplying extremes and means, and suppressing the common factor BG, we have BE×AD×CF=EA×DC×BF.

These six parts are sometimes said to be *in involution.*

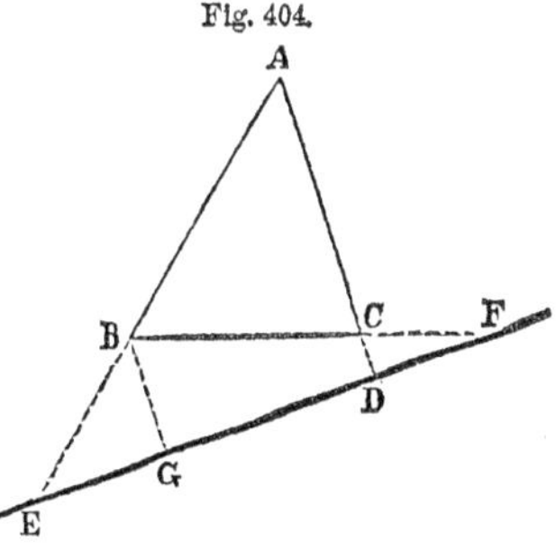

Fig. 404.

If the Transversal passes entirely outside of the triangle, and cuts the prolongations of all three sides, as in Fig. 404, the theorem still holds good. The same demonstration applies without any change.*

THEOREM II.—Conversely: *If three points be taken on two sides of a triangle, and on the third side prolonged, or on the prolongations of the three sides, dividing them into six parts, such that the product of three non-consecutive parts equals the product of the other three parts; then will these three points lie in the same straight line.*

This Theorem is proved by a *Reductio ad absurdum.*

---

* This Theorem may be extended to polygons.

Fig. 405.

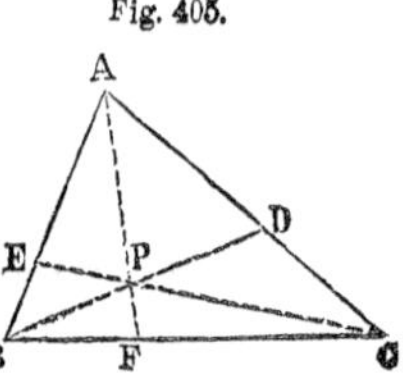

THEOREM III.—*If from the summits of a triangle, lines be drawn, to a point situated either within or without the triangle, and prolonged to meet the sides of the triangle, or their prolongations, thus dividing them into six parts; then will the product of any three non-consecutive parts be equal to the product of the other three parts.*

That is, in Fig. 405, or Fig. 406,

$$AE \times BF \times CD = EB \times FC \times DA.$$

Fig. 406.

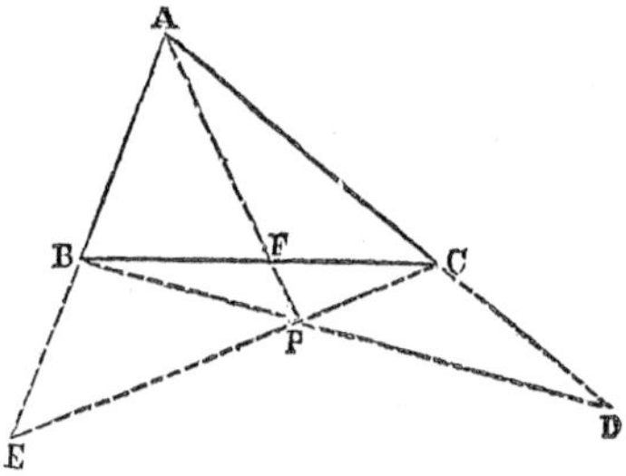

For, the triangle ABF being cut by the transversal EC, gives the relation (Theorem I.),

$$AE \times BC \times FP = EB \times FC \times PA.$$

The triangle ACF, being cut by the transversal DB, gives

$$DC \times FB \times PA = AD \times CB \times FP.$$

Multiplying these equations together, and suppressing the common factors PA, CB, and FP, we have $AE \times BF \times CD = EB \times FC \times DA$.

THEOREM IV.—Conversely: *If three points are situated on the three sides of a triangle, or on their prolongations (either one, or three, of these points being on the sides), so that they divide these lines in such a way that the product of any three non-consecutive parts equals the product of the other three parts, then will lines drawn from these points to the opposite angles meet in the same point.*

This Theorem can be demonstrated by a *Reductio ad absurdum.*

COROLLARIES OF THE PRECEDING THEOREMS.

COR. 1.—*The* MEDIANS *of a triangle* (i. e., the lines drawn from its summits to the middles of the opposite sides) *meet in the same point.*

For, supposing, in Fig. 405, the points D, E, and F to be the middles of the sides, the products of the non-consecutive parts will be equal, i. e., $AE \times BF \times CD = DA \times EB \times FC$; since $AE = EB$, $BF = FC$, $CD = DA$. Then Theorem IV. applies.

COR. 2.—*The* BISSECTRICES *of a triangle* (i. e., the lines bisecting its angles) *meet in the same point.*

For, in Fig. 405, supposing the lines AF, BD, CE to be Bissectrices, we have (Legendre IV. 17):

$$\left.\begin{array}{l} BF : FC :: AB : AC, \\ CD : DA :: BC : BA, \\ AE : EB :: CA : CB, \end{array}\right\} \text{ whence } \left\{\begin{array}{l} BF \times AC = FC \times AB, \\ CD \times BA = DA \times BC, \\ AE \times CB = EB \times CA. \end{array}\right.$$

Multiplying these equations together, and omitting the common factors, we have $BF \times CD \times AE = FC \times DA \times EB$. Then Theorem IV. applies.

COR. 3.—*The* ALTITUDES *of a triangle* (i. e., the lines drawn from its summits perpendicular to the opposite sides) *meet in the same point.*

For, in Fig. 405, supposing the lines AF, BD, and CE, to be Altitudes, we have three pairs of similar triangles, BCD and FCA, CAE and DAB, ABF and EBC, by comparing which we obtain relations from which it is easy to deduce BF×CD×AE = EB×FC×DA; and then Theorem IV. again applies.

COR. 4.—*If, in Fig.* 405, *or Fig.* 406, *the point* F *be taken in the middle of* BC, *then will the line* ED *be parallel to* BC.

For, since BF = FC, the equation of Theorem III. reduces to AE×CD=EB×DA; whence AE : EB :: AD : DC; consequently ED is parallel to BC.

COR. 5.—Conversely: *If* ED *be parallel to* BC, *then is* BF = FC.

For, since AE : EB :: AD : DC, we have AE × DC = EB × AD; whence, in the equation of Theorem III., we must have BF = FC.

COR. 6.—From the preceding Corollary, we derive the following:

If two sides of a triangle are divided proportionally, starting from the same summit, as A, *and lines are drawn from the extremities of the third side to the points of division, the intersections of the corresponding lines will all lie in the same straight line joining the summit* A, *and the middle of the base.*

Fig. 407.

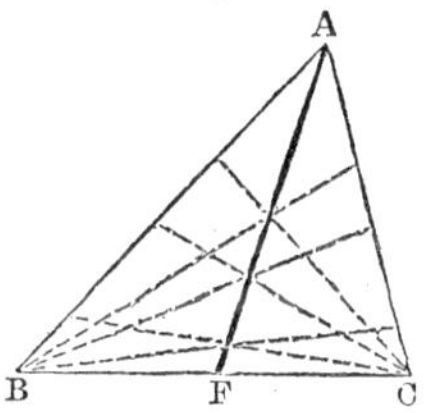

A
B F C

COR. 7.—A particular case of the preceding corollary is this:

In any trapezoid, the straight line which joins the intersection of the diagonals and the point of meeting of the non-parallel sides produced, passes through the middle of the two parallel bases.

COR. 8.—*If the three lines drawn through the corresponding summits of two triangles cut each other in the same point, then the three points in which the corresponding sides, produced if necessary, will meet, are situated in the same straight line.*

This corollary may be otherwise enunciated, thus:

If two triangles have their summits situated, two and two, on three lines which meet in the same point, then, &c.

This is proved by obtaining by Theorem I. three equations, which, being multiplied together, and the six common factors cancelled, give an equation to which Theorem II. applies.

Triangles thus situated are called *homologic;* the common point of meeting of the lines passing through their summits is called the *centre of homology;* and the line on which the sides meet, the *axis of homology.*

HARMONIC DIVISION.

Fig. 408.

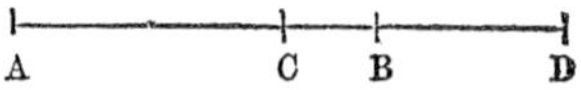

A C B D

DEFINITIONS.—A straight line, AB, is said to be *harmonically divided* at the points C and D, when these points determine two additive segments, AC, BC, and two subtractive segments, AD, BD, proportional to one another; so that AC : BC : : AD : BD. It will be seen that AC must be more than BC, since AD is more than BD.*

This relation may be otherwise expressed, thus: the product of the whole line by the middle part equals the product of the extreme parts.

Reciprocally, the line DC is harmonically divided at the points B and A; since the preceding proportion may be written DB : CB : : DA : CA.

The four points, A, B, C, D, are called *harmonics.* The points C and D are called *harmonic conjugates.* So are the points A and B.

When a straight line, as AB, is divided harmonically, its half is a mean proportional between the distance from the middle of the line to the two points, C and D, which divide it harmonically.

If, from any point, O, lines be drawn so as to divide a line harmonically, these lines are called an *harmonic pencil.* The four lines which compose it, OA, OC, OB, OD, in the figure, are called its *radii,* and the pairs which pass through the conjugate points are called *conjugate radii.*

Fig. 409.

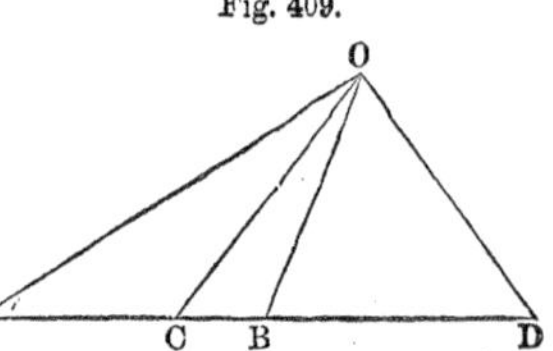

THEOREM V.—*In any harmonic pencil, a line drawn parallel to any one of the radii, is divided by the three other radii into two equal parts.*

Let EF be the line, drawn parallel to OA. Through B draw GH, also parallel to OA. We have,

GB : OA : : BD : AD; and
BH : OA : : BC : AC.

But, by hypothesis, AC : BC : : AD : BD. Hence, the first two proportions reduce to GB = BH; and consequently, EK = KF.

Fig. 410.

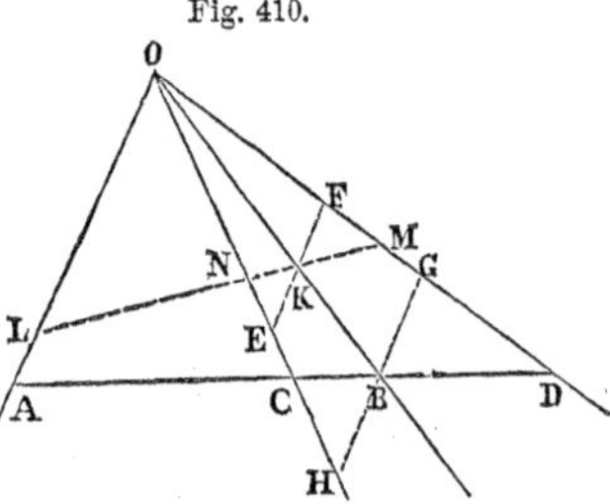

The *Reciprocal* is also true; i. e.,

If four lines radiating from a point are such that a line drawn parallel to one of them is divided into two equal parts by the other three, the four lines form an harmonic pencil.

---

* Three numbers, *m*, *n*, *p*, arranged in decreasing order of size, form an *harmonic proportion*, when the difference of the first and the second is to the difference of the second and the third, as the first is to the third. Such are the numbers 6, 4, and 3; or 6, 3, and 2; or 15, 12, and 10; &c. So, in Fig. 408, are the lines AD, AB, and AC, which thus give BD : CB : : AD : AC; or AC : CB : : AD : BD. The series of fractions, $\frac{1}{1}$, $\frac{1}{2}$, $\frac{1}{3}$, $\frac{1}{4}$, $\frac{1}{5}$, &c., is called an *harmonic progression,* because any consecutive three of its terms form an *harmonic proportion.*

THEOREM VI.—*If any transversal to an harmonic pencil be drawn, it will be divided harmonically.*

Let LM be the transversal. Through K, where LM intersects OB, draw EF parallel to OA. It is bisected at K by the preceding theorem; and the similar triangles, FMK and LMO, EKN and LNO, give the proportions

LM : KM : : OL : FK, and LN : NK : : OL : EK; whence,
since FK = EK, we have LN : NK : : LM : KM.

COROLLARY.—*The two sides of any angle, together with the bissectrices of the angle and of its supplement, form an harmonic pencil.*

THEOREM VII.—*If, from the summits of any triangle,* ABC, *through any point,* P, *there be drawn the transversals* AD, BE, CF, *and the transversal* ED *be drawn to meet* AB *prolonged, in* F′, *the points* F *and* F′ *will divide the base* AB *harmonically.*

Fig. 411.

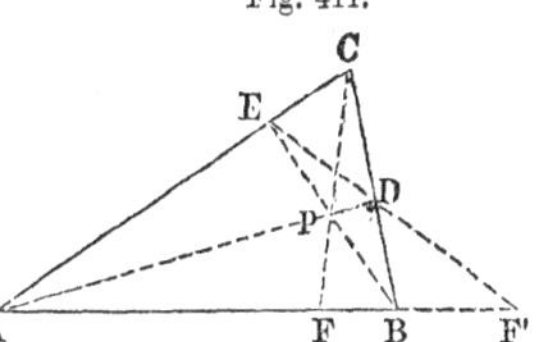

This may be otherwise expressed, thus:

The line, CP, *which joins the intersection of the diagonals of any quadrilateral,* ABDE, *with the point of meeting,* C, *of two opposite sides prolonged, cuts the side* AB *in a point* F, *which is the harmonic conjugate of the point of meeting,* F′, *of the other two sides,* ED *and* AB, *prolonged.*

For, by Theorem I., AF′ × BD × CE = F′B × DC × EA; and
by Theorem III., AF × BD × CE = FB × DC × EA;
whence AF : FB : : AF′ : F′B.

THE COMPLETE QUADRILATERAL.

A *Complete Quadrilateral* is formed by drawing any four straight lines, so that each of them shall cut each of the other three, so as to give six different points of intersection. It is so called because in the figure thus formed are found three quadrilaterals; viz., in Fig. 412, ABCD, a common *convex* quadrilateral; EAFC, a *uni-concave* quadrilateral; and EBAFD, a *bi-concave* quadrilateral, composed of two opposite triangles.

The complete quadrilateral, AEBCDF, has three diagonals; viz., two interior, AC, BD; and one exterior, EF.

Fig. 412.

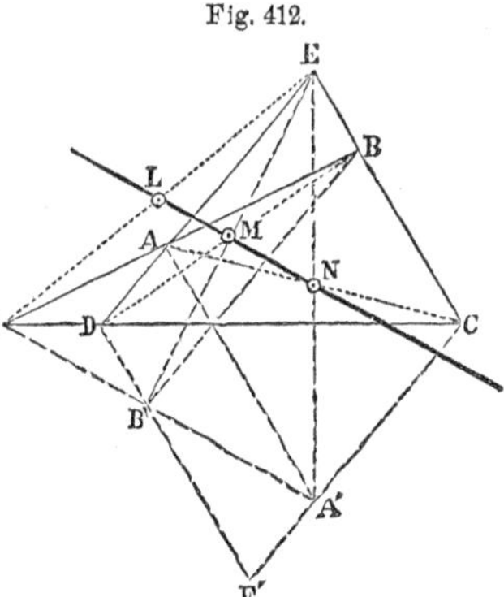

THEOREM VIII.—*In every* COMPLETE QUADRILATERAL *the middle points of its three diagonals lie in the same straight line.*

AEBCDF is the quadrilateral, and LMN the middle points of its three diagonals. From A and D draw parallels to BC, and from B and C draw parallels to

AD. The triangle EDC being cut by the transversal BF, we have (Theorem I.), DF × CB × EA = CF × EB × DA. From the equality of parallels between parallels, we have CB = E′B′, EA = CA′, EB = DB′, DA = E′A′. Hence, the above equation becomes DF × E′B′ × CA′ = CF × DB′ × E′A′; therefore, by Theorem II., the points, F, B′, A′, lie in the same straight line. Now, since the diagonals of the parallelogram ECA′A bisect each other at N, and those of the parallelogram EBB′D at M, we have EN : NA′ : : EM : MB′. Then MN is parallel to FA′; and we have EN : NA′ : : EL : LF, or EL = LF, so that L is the middle of EF, and the same straight line passes through L, M, and N.

Theorem IX.—*In every complete quadrilateral each of the three diagonals is divided harmonically by the two others.*

Fig. 413.

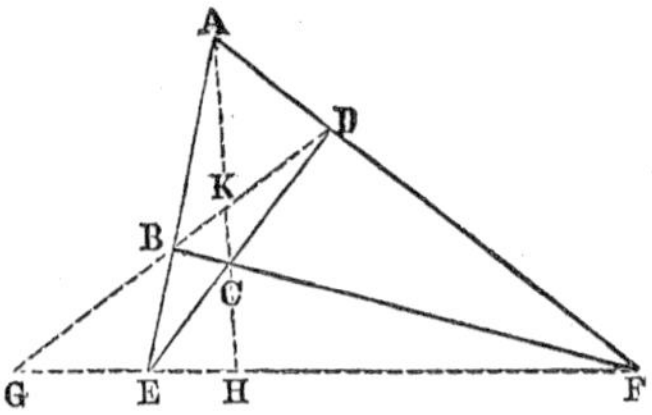

CEBADF is the complete quadrilateral. The diagonal EF is divided harmonically at G and H, by DB and AC produced; since AH, DE, and FB are three transversals drawn from the summits of the triangle AEF through the same point C; and therefore, by Theorem VII., DBG and ACH divide EF harmonically.

So too, in the triangle ABD, CB, CA, CD, are the three transversals passing through C; and G and K therefore divide the diagonal BD harmonically.

So too, in the triangle, ABC, DA, DB, DC are the transversals, and H and K the points which divide the diagonal AC harmonically.

Fig. 414.

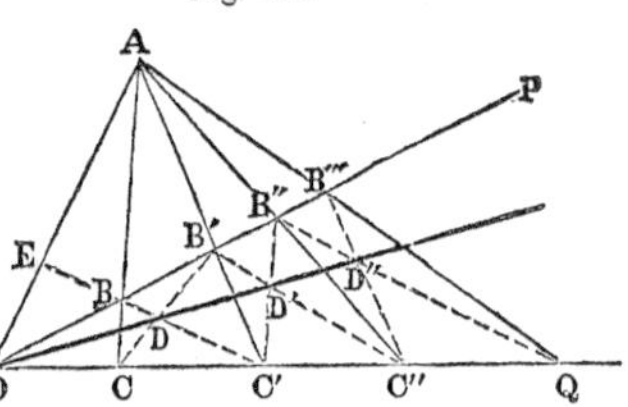

Theorem X.—*If from a point,* A, *any number of lines be drawn, cutting the sides of an angle* POQ, *the intersections of the diagonals of the quadrilaterals thus formed will all lie in the same straight line passing through the summit of the angle.*

By the preceding Theorem, the diagonal BC′ of the complete quadrilateral, BAB′C′CO, is divided harmonically at D and E. Hence, OA, OP, OD, and OQ, form an harmonic pencil. So do OA, OP, OD′, and OQ. Therefore, the lines OD, OD′ coincide. So for the other intersections.

If the point A moves on OA, the line OD is not displaced. If, on the contrary, OA is displaced, OD turns around the point O. Hence, the point A is said to be a *pole* with respect to the line OD, which is itself called the *polar* of the point A. Similarly, D is a pole of OA, which is the polar of D. OD is likewise the polar of any other point on the line OA; and this property is necessarily reciprocal for the two conjugate radii OA, OD, with respect to the lines OP, OQ, which are also conjugate radii. Hence; In every harmonic pencil, each of the radii is a *polar* with respect to each point of its conjugate; and each point of this latter line is a *pole* with respect to the former.

DEMONSTRATIONS.*

PART II.; CHAPTER V.

(140), **(141)** The equality of the triangles formed in these methods proves their correctness.

(143), **(144)** These methods depend on the principle of the square of the hypothenuse.

(145) CAD is an angle inscribed in a semicircle.

(146) Let fall a perpendicular from B to AC, meeting it at a point E, not marked in Fig. 91. Then (Legendre, IV. 12),

$$AB^2 = AC^2 + BC^2 - 2\ AC \cdot CE;\ \text{whence}\ CE = \frac{AC^2 + BC^2 - AB^2}{2\ AC}.$$

When AC = AB, this becomes $CE = \frac{BC^2}{2\ AC}$. The similar triangles, BCE and DCA, give EC CB :: AC : CD; whence

$$CD = \frac{CB \times AC}{CE} = CB \times AC \div \frac{BC^2}{2\ AC} = \frac{2\ AC^2}{BC}.$$

(147) Mark a point, G, in the middle of DF, and join GA. The triangle AGD will then be isosceles, since it is equal to the isosceles triangle ABC, having two sides and the included angle equal. Then AG = GD = AB = GF. The triangle AGF is then also isosceles. Now the angle FAG = ½ AGD; and GAD = ½ FGA. Therefore

$$FAG + GAD = FAD = \tfrac{1}{2}(AGD + FGA) = \tfrac{1}{2}(180°) = 90°.$$

(149) See Part VII., Art. (403).

(150) The proof follows from the equal triangles formed.

(151) The proof is found in the first half of the proof of Art. (146).

(153) ACP is an angle inscribed in a semicircle.

(154) Draw from C a perpendicular to the given line, meeting it at a point E. As in the proof of Art. (146), changing the letters suitably, we have $AE = \frac{AC^2}{2\ AB}$. The similar triangles AEC and ADP give

$$AC : AE :: AP : AD = \frac{AP}{AC} \times AE = \frac{AP}{AC} \times \frac{AC^2}{2\ AB} = \frac{AP \times AC}{2\ AB}.$$

(155) Similar triangles prove this.

(156) The equal triangles which are formed give BP = CF. Hence FP is parallel to BC, and consequently perpendicular to the given line DG.

(157) The proof of this is found in the "Theory of Transversals," corollary 3.

(158) The proof of this is the same as the last.

(161) The lines are parallel because of the equal angles formed.

---

* Additional lines to the figures in the text will sometimes be employed. The student should draw them on the figures, as directed.

(**162**) The equal triangles give equal angles, and therefore parallels.

(**163**) AB is parallel to PF, since it cuts the sides of the triangle proportionally.

(**164**) The proof is found in corollary 4 of "Transversals."

(**165**) From the similar triangles, CAD and CEP, we have CE : CD :: CP : CA. From the similar triangles, CEF and CBD, we have CE : CD :: CF : CB. These two proportions give the following; CP : CA :: CF : CB. Therefore PF is parallel to AB.

(**166**) Draw PE. The similar triangles PCE and ACD give PE : CE :: AD : CD. The similar triangles CEF and CDB give EF : CE :: DB : CD. These proportions produce PE : EF :: AD : DB. Hence PEF is similar to ADB, and PF is parallel to AB.

(**173**) The equality of the symmetrical triangles which are formed, proves this method.

(**174**) ABP is a transversal to the triangle CDE. Then, by Theorem I. of "Transversals," $CA \times EB \times DP = AE \times BD \times CP$; whence we have

$$CP : DP :: CA \times EB : AE \times BD.$$

By "division," $CP - DP : DP :: CA \times EB - AE \times BD : AE \times BD$.

Hence, since $CP - DP = CD$, we obtain $DP = \frac{DC \times AE \times BD}{CA \times EB - AE \times BD}$.

The other formulas are simplified by the common factors obtained by making $AE = AC$, or $BE = BD$.

(**175**) By Theorem VII. "Harmonic Division," in the quadrilateral ABED, the line CF cuts DE in a point, L, which is the harmonic conjugate of the point at which AB and DE, produced, would meet. So too, in the quadrilateral DEHK, this same line, CG, produced, cuts DE in a point, L, which is the harmonic conjugate of the point at which DE and KH, produced, would meet. Consequently, AB, DE, and KH must meet in the same point. *Otherwise;* this problem may be regarded as the converse of Theorem X. of "Transversals," BCA being the angle, and P the point from which the radiating lines are drawn.

(**176**) EGCFDH is the "Complete Quadrilateral." Its three diagonals are FE, DC, and HG; and their middle points A, B, and P lie in the same straight line, by our Theorem VIII.

(**182**) This instrument depends on the optical principle of the equality of the angles of incidence and reflection.

(**184**) The first method given, Fig. 120, is another application of the Theory of Transversals. The second method in the article is proved by supposing the figure to be constructed, in which case we should have a triangle QZR, whose base, QR, and a parallel to it, BD, would be cut proportionally by the required line PSZ; so that $QR : BD :: QP : BS = \frac{BD \times QP}{QR}$.

(**189**) By "Transversals," Theorem I., we obtain, regarding CD as the transversal of the triangle ABE, $CB \times AF \times ED = AC \times FE \times DB$; and since $ED = DB$, this becomes $CB \times AF = AC \times FE$; whence the proportion $CB : AC :: FE : AF$. By "division," we have $CB - AC : AC :: FE - AF : AF$. Observing that $CB - AC = AB$, we obtain $AB = \frac{AC}{AF} \cdot (FE - AF)$.

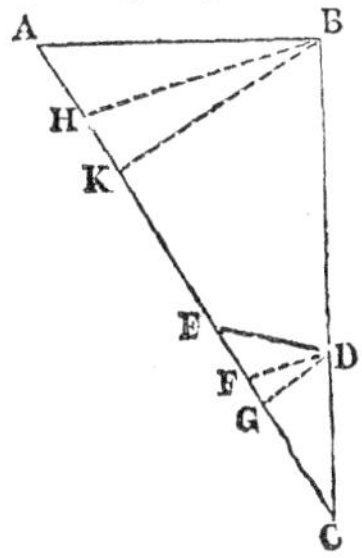

Fig. 124, bis.

(**190**) Take $CH = CB$; and from B let fall a perpendicular, BK, to AC. Then, in the triangle CBH, we have (Legendre IV. 12),

$$HK = \frac{CH^2 + BH^2 - BC^2}{2\,CH} = \frac{BH^2}{2\,BC}; \qquad [1]$$

since $CH = BC$.

In the triangle ABH, we have (Leg. IV. 13)

$$AB^2 = AH^2 + BH^2 + 2\,AH \,.\, HK.$$

Substituting for HK, its value from [1], we get

$$AB^2 = AH^2 + BH^2\left(1 + \frac{AH}{BC}\right).$$

But $\qquad AH = AC - CH = AC - BC$

$$\therefore\ AB^2 = AH^2 + BH^2\left(1 + \frac{AC - BC}{BC}\right) = AH^2 + BH^2 \,.\, \frac{AC}{BC}. \qquad [2]$$

In the above expression for AB, BH is unknown. To find it, proceed thus. Take $CF = CD$. Then DF is parallel to BH; and we have $CD : CB :: DF : BH$; whence

$$BH^2 = DF^2 \,.\, \frac{CB^2}{CD^2}. \qquad [3]$$

In this equation DF^2 is unknown; but by proceeding as at the beginning of this investigation, we get an equation analogous to [2], giving $ED^2 = EF^2 + DF^2 \,.\, \frac{CE}{CD}$; whence $DF^2 = (DE^2 - EF^2) \,.\, \frac{CD}{CE}$.

Substituting this value of DF^2 in [3], we have

$$BH^2 = (DE^2 - EF^2)\frac{CB^2}{CD \times CE}.$$

Substituting this value of BH^2 in [2], we have

$$AB^2 = AH^2 + (DE^2 - EF^2) \,.\, \frac{AC \times BC}{CD \times CE} = (AC - BC)^2 + [DE^2 - (CE - CD)^2] \times \frac{AC \times BC}{CD \times CE}.$$

(**191**) Since BCD is a right angle, AC is a mean proportional between AB and AD.

(**192**) The proof follows from the similar triangles constructed.

(**193**) The similar triangles give $DE : AC :: DB : AB$; whence, by "division," $DE - AC : AC :: DB - AB : AB$; whence, since $DB - AB = AD$, we have $AB = \frac{AC \times AD}{DE - AC}$.

(**194**) From the similar triangles, we have $DE : CA :: EB : AB$; whence $DE - CA : CA :: EB - AB : AB$; whence, since $EB - AB = AE$, we get $AB = \frac{AC \times AE}{DE - AC}$.

(**195**) The triangles DEF and BAF, similar because of the parallelogram which is constructed, give $FE : ED :: AF : AB = \frac{ED \times AF}{FE} = \frac{AC \times AF}{FE}$.

The triangles DEF and BCD give similarly $FE : ED :: DC : CB = \frac{AC \times DC}{FE}$.

(196) The equality of the triangles formed proves this problem.

(197) The proof of this problem also depends on the equality of the triangles constructed. The details of the proof require attention.

(198) EB is the transversal of the triangle ACD. Consequently, $CB \times AF \times DE = AB \times FD \times CE$; or, since $CB = AB + AC$, $(AB + AC) \times AF \times DE = AB \times FD \times CE$; whence $AB = \frac{AC \times AF \times DE}{FD \times CE - AF \times DE}$.

Taking E, in the middle of CD, $CE = DE$, and those lines are cancelled. Taking F in the middle of AD, $AF = FD$, and those lines are cancelled.

(199) The line BE is harmonically divided at the points H and A, from Theorem IX., ECFBGD being a "Complete Quadrilateral." Consequently, $AE : EH :: AB : HB$. Hence, by "division," $AE - EH : AE :: AB - HB : AB$. We therefore have, since $AB - HB = AH$, $AB = \frac{AE \times AH}{AE - EH}$.

(200) For the same reasons as in the last article, CF is harmonically divided at H and D; and we have $CH : HF :: CD : DF$; whence $CH - HF : CH :: CD - DF : CD$. Hence, since $CD - DF = CF$, $CD = \frac{CH \times CF}{CH - HF}$.

The other two expressions come from writing CF as $CH + HF$, and HF as $CF - CH$.

(201) The equality of the triangles formed proves the equality of the corresponding sides KD and DE, &c.

(202) The similar triangles (made so by the measurement of CE) give $CD : DE :: CA : AB = \frac{AC \times DE}{CD}$.

(203) The similar triangles (made so by the parallel) give $CE : EA :: CD : AB = \frac{CD \times EA}{CE} = \frac{CD \times (AC - CE)}{CE}$.

(204) The similar triangles DFH and BCD give $HF : FD :: DC : BC = \frac{DF \times CD}{FH}$

The similar triangles FGH and ABC give $FG : GH :: BC : AB = BC \frac{GH}{FG}$.

Substituting for BC, its above value, we have $AB = \frac{DF \times CD \times GH}{FH \times FG}$.

When $CD = CE$, $DF = CD$, whence the second formula.

(205) The equality of the symmetrical triangles which are formed, proves the equality of A'B' to AB.

(206) The proof of this is similar to the preceding.

(207) Because the two triangles ABC and ADE have a common angle at A, we have $ADE : ABC :: AD \times AE : AB \times AC$; whence the expression for ABC.

(208) From B let fall a perpendicular to AC, meeting it at a point B'. Call this perpendicular $BB' = p$. From D let fall a perpendicular to AC, meeting it at a point D'. Call this perpendicular $DD' = q$.

The quadrilateral $ABCD = AC \times \frac{1}{2}(p+q)$.

The triangle $BCE = CE \times \frac{1}{2} p$; whence $p = \frac{2 . BCE}{CE}$.

The similar triangles EDD′ and BEB′ give $p : q :: BE : DE$, whence $q = p \frac{DE}{BE} = \frac{2 . BCE \times DE}{CE \times BE}$.

Then $\frac{1}{2}(p+q) = \frac{BCE}{CE} + \frac{BCE \times DE}{CE \times BE} = BCE \times \frac{BE + DE}{CE \times BE} = BCE \times \frac{BD}{CE \times BE}$.

Lastly, $ABCD = AC \times BCE \times \frac{BD}{CE \times BE} = BCE \times \frac{AC \times BD}{CE \times BE}$.

DEMONSTRATIONS FOR PART V.

(382) Let B = the measured inclined length, b = this length reduced to a horizontal plane, and A = the angle which the measured base makes with the horizon. Then $b = B . \cos. A$ and the excess of B over b, i. e., $B - b = B (1 - \cos. A)$. Since $1 - \cos. A = 2 (\sin. \frac{1}{2} A)^2$ [Trigonometry, Art. (9)], we have $B - b = 2 B (\sin. \frac{1}{2} A)^2$. Substituting for $\sin. \frac{1}{2} . A$, its approximate equivalent, $\frac{1}{2} A \times \sin. 1'$ [Trigonometry, Art. (5)], we obtain $B - b = 2 B (\frac{1}{2} A \times \sin. 1')^2 = \frac{1}{2} (\sin. 1')^2 . A^2 . B, = 0.00000004231 A^2 B$. By logarithms, $\log. (B - b) = 2.626422 + 2 \log. A + \log. B$. The greater precision of this calculation than that of $b = B . \cos. A$, arises from the slowness with which the cosines of very small angles increase or decrease in length.

(386) The exterior angle $LER = LCR + CLD$. Also, $LER = LDR + CRD$.

$\therefore LCR + CLD = LDR + CRD$, and $LCR = LDR + CRD - CLD$.

From the triangle CRD we get $\sin. CRD = \sin. CDR \times \frac{CD}{CR}$.

From the triangle CLD we get $\sin. CLD = \sin. LDC \times \frac{CD}{CL}$.

As the angles CRD and CLD are very small, these values of the sines may be called the values of the arcs which measure the angles, and we shall have

$$LCR = LDR + \sin. CDR \times \frac{CD}{CR} - \sin. LDC \times \frac{CD}{CL}.$$

The last two terms are expressed in parts of radius, and to have them in seconds, they must be divided by sin. 1″ [Trigonometry, Art. (5), Note], which gives the formula in the text. Otherwise, the correction being in parts of radius, may be brought into seconds by multiplying it by the length of the radius in seconds; i. e., $\frac{180° \times 60 \times 60}{3.14159, \&c} = 206264''.80625$ [Trigonometry, Art. (2)].

(391) The triangles AOB, BOC, COD, &c., give the following proportions [Trigonometry, Art. (12), Theorem I.]; AO : OB :: sin. (2) : sin. (1); OB : OC :: sin. (4) : sin. (3); OC : OD :: sin. (6) : sin. (5); and so on around the polygon. Multiplying together the corresponding terms of all the proportions, the sides will all be cancelled, and there will result

1 : 1 :: sin. (2) × sin. (4) × sin. (6) × sin. (8) × sin. (10) × sin. (12) × sin. (14) :
sin. (1) × sin. (3) × sin. (5) × sin. (7) × sin. (9) × sin. (11) × sin. (13).

Hence the equality of the last two terms of the proportion.

DEMONSTRATION FOR PART VI.

(399) In the triangle ABS, we have

$$\text{sin. ASB} : \text{sin. BAS} :: \text{AB} : \text{SB} = \frac{\text{AB} . \text{sin. BAS}}{\text{sin. ASB}} = \frac{c . \text{sin. U}}{\text{sin. S}}. \qquad [1]$$

In the triangle CBS, we have

$$\text{sin. BSC} : \text{sin. BCS} :: \text{BC} : \text{SB} = \frac{\text{BC} . \text{sin. BCS}}{\text{sin. BSC}} = \frac{a . \text{sin. V}}{\text{sin. S}'}. \qquad [2]$$

Hence, $\frac{c . \text{sin. U}}{\text{sin. S}} = \frac{a . \text{sin. V}}{\text{sin. S}'}$; whence, $c . \text{sin. S}' . \text{sin. U} - a . \text{sin. S} . \text{sin. V} = 0.$ [3]

In the quadrilateral ABCS, we have

BCS = 360° — ASB — BSC — ABC — BAS; or V = 360° — S — S′ — B — U.

Let T = 360° — S — S′ — B, and we have V = T — U. [4]

Substituting this value of V, in equation [3], we get [Trig., Art. (8)],

$$c . \text{sin S}' \text{ sin. U} - a . \text{sin. S } (\text{sin. T} . \text{cos. U} - \text{cos. T} . \text{sin. U}) = 0.$$

Dividing by sin. U, we get

$$c . \text{sin. S}' - a . \text{sin. S} \left(\text{sin. T} . \frac{\text{cos. U}}{\text{sin. U}} - \text{cos. T}\right) = 0.$$

Whence we have

$$\frac{\text{cos. U}}{\text{sin. U}} = \text{cot. U} = \frac{c . \text{sin. S}' + a . \text{sin. S} . \text{cos. T}}{a . \text{sin. S} . \text{sin. T}}.$$

Separating this expression into two parts, and cancelling, we get

$$\text{cot. U} = \frac{c . \text{sin. S}'}{a . \text{sin. S} . \text{sin. T}} + \frac{\text{cos. T}}{\text{sin. T}}.$$

Separating the second member into factors, we get

$$\text{cot. U} = \frac{\text{cos. T}}{\text{sin. T}} \left(\frac{c . \text{sin. S}'}{a . \text{sin. S} . \text{cos. T}} + 1\right); \text{ or}$$

$$\text{cot. U} = \text{cot. T} \left(\frac{c . \text{sin. S}'}{a . \text{sin. S} . \text{cos. T}} + 1\right).$$

Having found U, equation [4] gives V; and either [1] or [2] gives **SB**; and **SA** and SC are then given by the familiar "Sine proportion" [Trig., Art. (12)].

DEMONSTRATIONS FOR PART VII.

(403) If APC be a right angle, $\frac{\text{CP}}{\text{CA}} = \cos. \text{CAB}$ [Trigonometry, Art. (4)].

(405) AC = PC . tan. APC; and CB = PC . tan. BPC [Trigonometry, Art. (4)]. Hence

$$\text{AC} : \text{CB} :: \tan. \text{APC} : \tan. \text{BPC}; \text{ and}$$
$$\text{AC} : \text{AC} + \text{CB} :: \tan. \text{APC} : \tan. \text{APC} + \tan. \text{BPC}.$$

Consequently, since AC + CB = AB, $\text{AC} = \text{AB} \cdot \frac{\tan. \text{APC}}{\tan. \text{APC} + \tan. \text{BPC}}$.

(414) The equal and supplementary angles formed prove the operation.

(421) In Fig. 285, CA : EG :: AB : GB. By "division," CA — EG : EG :: AB — GB : GB. Hence, observing that AB — GB = AG, we shall have $\text{AG} = \frac{\text{GB}(\text{CA} - \text{EG})}{\text{EG}}$.

(423) Art. (12), Theorem III., [Trigonometry, Appendix A,] gives $\cos. \text{C} = \frac{a^2 + b^2 - c^2}{2ab}$; or $c^2 = a^2 + b^2 - 2ab . \cos. \text{C}$. This becomes [Trig., Art (6)], K being the supplement of C, $c^2 = a^2 + b^2 + 2ab . \cos. \text{K}$. The series [Trig. Art. (5)] for the length of a cosine, gives, taking only its first two terms, since K is very small, $\cos. \text{K} = 1 - \frac{1}{2}\text{K}^2$. Hence,

$$c^2 = a^2 + b^2 + 2ab - ab\text{K}^2 = (a+b)^2 - ab\text{K}^2 = (a+b)^2\left(1 - \frac{ab\text{K}^2}{(a+b)^2}\right);$$

whence,
$$c = (a+b)\sqrt{\left(1 - \frac{ab\text{K}^2}{(a+b)^2}\right)}.$$

Developing the quantity under the radical sign by the binomial theorem, and neglecting the terms after the second, it becomes

$$1 - \frac{1}{2} \cdot \frac{ab\text{K}^2}{(a+b)^2} +, \&c.$$

Substituting for K minutes, K . sin. 1′ [Trig., Art. (5)], and performing the multiplication by $a + b$, we obtain

$$c = a + b - \frac{ab\text{K}^2 . (\sin. 1')^2}{2(a+b)}. \quad \text{Now } \frac{(\sin. 1')^2}{2} = 0.0000000423079;$$

whence the formula in the text, $c = a + b - 0.000000042308 \times \frac{ab\text{K}^2}{a+b}$.

(430) In the triangle ABC, designate the angles as A, B, C; and the sides opposite to them as a, b, c. Let CD = d. The triangle BCD gives [Trig., Art. (12), Theorem I], $a = d\frac{\sin. \text{BDC}}{\sin. \text{CBD}}$. The triangle ACD similarly gives $b = d \cdot \frac{\sin. \text{ADC}}{\sin. \text{CAD}}$.

In the triangle ABC, we have [Trig., Art. (12), Theorem II.],

$$\tan. \tfrac{1}{2}(\text{A} - \text{B}) : \cot. \tfrac{1}{2}\text{C} :: a - b : a + b;$$

whence
$$\tan. \tfrac{1}{2}(\text{A} - \text{B}) = \frac{a-b}{a+b} \cdot \cot. \tfrac{1}{2}\text{C}. \qquad [1]$$

Let K be an auxiliary angle, such that $b = a . \tan. \text{K}$; whence $\tan. \text{K} = \frac{b}{a}$.

Dividing the second member of equation [1], above and below, by a, and substituting tan. K for $\frac{b}{a}$, we get $\tan. \frac{1}{2} (A - B) = \frac{1 - \tan. K}{1 + \tan. K} \cdot \cot. \frac{1}{2} C.$

Since tan. $45° = 1$, we may substitute it for 1 in the preceding equation, and we get $\tan. \frac{1}{2} (A - B) = \frac{\tan. 45° - \tan. K}{\tan. 45° + \tan. K} \cdot \cot. \frac{1}{2} C.$

From the expression for the tangent of the difference of two arcs [Trig., Art. (8)], the preceding fraction reduces to tan. $(45° - K)$; and the equation becomes

$$\tan. \tfrac{1}{2} (A - B) = \tan. (45° - K) . \cot. \tfrac{1}{2} C. \qquad [2]$$

In the equation $\tan. K = \frac{b}{a}$, substitute the values of b and a from the formulas at the beginning of this investigation. This gives

$$\tan. K = d \cdot \frac{\sin. ADC}{\sin. CAD} \div d \cdot \frac{\sin. BDC}{\sin. CBD} = \frac{\sin. ADC . \sin. CBD}{\sin. CAD . \sin. BDC}.$$

$(A - B)$ is then obtained by equation [2]; $(A + B)$ is the supplement of C therefore the angle A is known.

Then $$c = AB = \frac{a . \sin. C}{\sin. A} = \frac{d . \sin. BDC . \sin. ACB}{\sin. CBD . \sin. CAB}.$$

The use of the auxiliary angle K, avoids the calculation of the sides a and b.

(**434**) In the figure on page 292, produce AD to some point F. The exterior angles, $EBC = A + P$; $ECD = A + Q$; $EDF = A + R$. The triangle ABE gives $\frac{BE}{a} = \frac{\sin. A}{\sin. P}$. The triangle ACE gives $\frac{CE}{a + x} = \frac{\sin. A}{\sin. Q}$. Dividing member by member, we get $\frac{BE}{CE} = \frac{a . \sin. Q}{(a + x) \sin. P}$.

In the same way the triangles BED and CED give $\frac{BE}{b + x} = \frac{\sin. (A + R)}{\sin. (R - P)}$; and $\frac{CE}{b} = \frac{\sin. (A + R)}{\sin. (R - Q)}$. Whence as before, $\frac{BE}{CE} = \frac{(b + x) \sin. (R - Q)}{b . \sin. (R - P)}$.

Equating these two values of the same ratio, we get

$$\frac{a . \sin. Q}{(a + x) \sin. P} = \frac{(b + x) \sin. (R - Q)}{b . \sin. (R - P)}; \text{ and thence}$$

$$\frac{ab . \sin. Q . \sin. (R - P)}{\sin. P . \sin. (R - Q)} = (a + x)(b + x) = ab + (a + b) x + x^2.$$

To solve this equation of the 2d degree, with reference to x, make

$$\tan.^2 K = \frac{4 ab}{(a - b)^2} \cdot \frac{\sin. Q (\sin. R - P)}{\sin. P (\sin. R - Q)}.$$

Then the first member of the preceding equation $= \frac{1}{4} \cdot (a - b)^2 \times \tan.^2 K \cdot$ and we get $$x^2 + (a + b) x = \tfrac{1}{4} (a - b)^2 \cdot \tan.^2 K - ab,$$

and
$$x = -\tfrac{1}{2} (a + b) \pm \sqrt{[\tfrac{1}{4} (a - b)^2 \cdot \tan.^2 K - ab + \tfrac{1}{4} (a + b)^2]}$$
$$= -\tfrac{1}{2} (a + b) \pm \sqrt{[\tfrac{1}{4} (a - b)^2 \cdot \tan.^2 K + \tfrac{1}{4} (a - b)^2]}$$
$$= -\tfrac{1}{2} (a + b) \pm \tfrac{1}{2} (a - b) \sqrt{(\tan.^2 K + 1)}.$$

Or, since $\sqrt{(\tan.^2 K + 1)} = \text{secant } K = \frac{1}{\cos. K}$, we have $x = -\frac{a + b}{2} \pm \frac{a - b}{2 . \cos. K}$.

DEMONSTRATIONS FOR PART XI.

(**493**) The content being given, and the length to be n times the breadth Breadth $\times$ n times breadth $=$ content; whence, Breadth $= \sqrt{\left(\frac{\text{content}}{n}\right)}$.

Given the content $= c$, and the difference of the length and breadth $= d$; to find the length l, and the breadth b. We have $l \times b = c$; and $l - b = d$. From these two equations we get $l = \frac{1}{2} d + \frac{1}{2} \sqrt{(d^2 + 4c)}$.

Given the content $= c$, and the sum of the length and breadth $= s$; to find l and b. We have $l \times b = c$; and $l + b = s$; whence we get $l = \frac{1}{2} s + \frac{1}{2} \sqrt{(s^2 - 4c)}$.

(**494**) The first rule is a consequence of the area of a triangle being the product of its height by half its base.

To get the second rule, call the height h; then the base $= mh$; and the area $= \frac{1}{2} h \times mh$; whence $h = \sqrt{\left(\frac{2 \times \text{area}}{m}\right)}$.

For the equilateral triangle, calling its side e, the formula for the area of a triangle $\sqrt{[(\frac{1}{2} s)(\frac{1}{2} s - a)(\frac{1}{2} s - b)(\frac{1}{2} s - c)]}$ reduces to $\frac{1}{4} e^2 \sqrt{3}$. Hence $e = 2\sqrt{\left(\frac{\text{area}}{\sqrt{3}}\right)}$ $= 1.5197 \sqrt{\text{area}}$.

(**495**) By Art. (65), Note, $\frac{1}{2}$. AB $\times$ BC $\times$ sin. B $=$ content of ABC; whence, $\text{BC} = \frac{2 \times \text{ABC}}{\text{AB} \cdot \text{sin. B}}$.

(**496**) The area of a circle $=$ radius$^2 \times \frac{22}{7}$; whence radius $= \sqrt{\left(\frac{7 \times \text{area}}{22}\right)}$

(**497**) The blocks, including half of the streets and avenues around them, are $900 \times 260 = 234000$ square feet. This area gives 64 lots; then an acre, or 43560 feet, would give not quite 12 lots.

(**502**) The parallelogram ABDC being double the triangle ABC, the proof for Art. (495), slightly modified, applies here.

(**504**) Produce BC and AD to meet in E. By similar triangles,

$$\text{ABE} : \text{DCE} :: \text{AB}^2 : \text{DC}^2.$$
$$\text{ABE} - \text{DCE} : \text{ABE} :: \text{AB}^2 - \text{DC}^2 : \text{AB}^2$$

Now ABE $-$ DCE $=$ ABCD; also, by Art. (65), Note,

$$\text{ABE} = \text{AB}^2 . \frac{\text{sin. A . sin. B}}{2 . \text{sin. (A+B)}}.$$

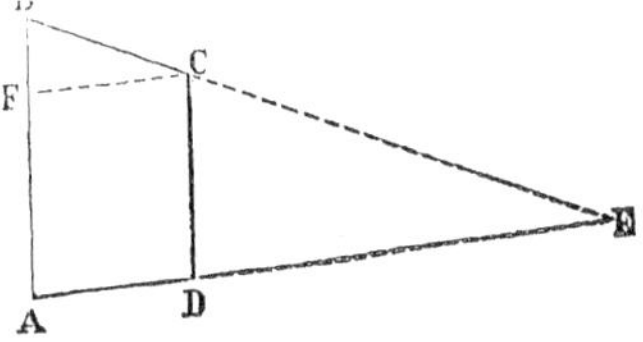

Fig. 346, bis.

The above proportion therefore becomes

$$\text{ABCD} : \text{AB}^2 . \frac{\text{sin. A . sin. B}}{2 . \text{sin. (A + B)}} :: \text{AB}^2 - \text{CD}^2 : \text{AB}^2.$$

Multiplying extremes and means, cancelling, transposing, and extracting the square root, we get $\text{CD} = \sqrt{\left[\text{AB}^2 - \frac{2 . \text{ABCD . sin. (A + B)}}{\text{sin. A . sin. B}}\right]}$.

When $A + B > 180°$, sin. $(A + B)$ is negative, and therefore the fraction in which it occurs becomes positive.

CF being drawn parallel to DA, we have

$$AD = FC = FB \,.\, \frac{\sin. B}{\sin. BCF} = FB \,.\, \frac{\sin. B}{\sin. (180° - A - B)} = (AB - CD)\frac{\sin. B}{\sin. (A + B)}$$

$$BC = (AB - CD)\frac{\sin. A}{\sin. (A + B)}.$$

(**505**) Since similar triangles are as the squares of their homologous sides, $BDE : BFG :: BD^2 : BF^2$; whence $BF = BD\sqrt{\left(\frac{BFG}{BDE}\right)}$.

(**506**) $BFG = \frac{1}{2} . BF \times FG = \frac{1}{2} . BF \times BF . \tan. B$;

whence, $$BF = \sqrt{\left(\frac{2 . BFG}{\tan. B}\right)}.$$

(**510**) By Art. (65), Note, $BFG = BF^2 . \frac{\sin. B . \sin. F}{2 . \sin. (B + F)}$;

whence, $$BF = \sqrt{\left(\frac{2 . \sin. (B + F) . BFG}{\sin. B . \sin. F}\right)}.$$

(**511**) The final formula results from the proportion

$$FAE : CDE :: AE^2 : ED^2.$$

(**512**) Since triangles which have an angle in each equal, are as the products of the sides about the equal angles, we have

$$ABE : CDE :: AE \times BE : CE \times DE.$$

$$ABE = \frac{1}{2} . AB^2 . \frac{\sin. A . \sin. B}{\sin. (A + B)}. \qquad AE = AB . \frac{\sin. B}{\sin. E}.$$

$$BE = AB . \frac{\sin. A}{\sin. E}. \qquad CE = DE . \frac{\sin. CDE}{\sin. DCE}.$$

Substituting these values in the preceding proportion, cancelling the common factors, observing that $\sin. (A + B) = \sin. E$, multiplying extremes and means, and dividing, we get $$DE = \sqrt{\left(\frac{2 . CDE . \sin. DCE}{\sin. E . \sin. CDE}\right)}.$$

(**515**) The first formula is a consequence of the expression for the area of a triangle, given in the first paragraph of the Note to Art. (65).

(**517**) The reasons for the operations in this article (which are of very frequent occurrence), are self-evident.

(**518**) The expression for DZ follows from Art. (65), Note. The proportion in the next paragraph exists because triangles having the same altitude are as their bases.

(**519**) By construction, GPC = the required content. Now, GPC = GDC, since they have the same base and equal altitudes. We have now to prove that LMC = GDC. These two triangles have a common angle at C. Hence, they are to each other as the rectangles of the adjacent sides; i. e.,

$$GDC : LMC :: GC \times CD :: LC \times CM.$$

Here CM is unknown, and must be eliminated. We obtain an expression for it by means of the similar triangles LCM and LEP, which give

$$LE : LC :: EP = CD : CM.$$

Hence, $CM = \frac{CD \times LC}{LE}$. Substituting this value of CM in the first proportion, and cancelling CD in the last two terms, we get

$$GDC : LMC :: GC : \frac{LC^2}{LE}; \text{ or } GDC : LMC :: GC \times LE : LC^2.$$

$$LC^2 = (LH + HC)^2 = LH^2 + 2\ LH \times HC + HC^2.$$

But, by construction,

$$LH^2 = HK^2 = HE^2 - EK^2 = HE^2 - EC^2 = (HE + EC)(HE - EC) = HC\ (HE - EC).$$

Also, $GC = 2\ HC$; and $LE = LH + HE$.

Substituting these values in the last proportion, it becomes

$$\begin{aligned} GDC : LMC &:: 2 . HC\ (LH + HE) : HC\ (HE - EC) + 2\ LH \times HC + HC^2. \\ &:: 2\ LH + 2\ HE \quad : HE - EC + 2\ LH + HC. \\ &\qquad\qquad\qquad\qquad : HE - EC + 2\ LH + HE + EC. \\ &\qquad\qquad\qquad\qquad : 2\ HE + 2\ LH. \end{aligned}$$

The last two terms of this proportion are thus proved to be equal. Therefore, the first two terms are also equal; i. e., LMC = GDC = the required content.

Since $HK = \sqrt{(HE^2 - EK^2)}$, it will have a negative as well as a positive value. It may therefore be set off in the contrary direction from L, i. e., to L′. The line drawn from L′ through P, and meeting CB produced beyond B, will part off *another* triangle of the required content.

(**520**) Suppose the line LM drawn. Then, by Art. (65), Note, the required content, $c = \frac{1}{2} \cdot CL \times CM . \sin. LCM$. This content will also equal the sum of the two triangles LCP and MCP; i. e., $c = \frac{1}{2} \cdot CL \times p + \frac{1}{2} \cdot CM \times q$. The first of these equations gives $CM = \frac{2\ c}{CL . \sin. LCM}$. Substituting this in the second equation, we have

$$c = \tfrac{1}{2} . CL \times p + \frac{cq}{CL . \sin. LCM}.$$

Whence, $\frac{1}{2}\ p . CL^2 . \sin. LCM + cq = c . CL . \sin. LCM.$

Transposing and dividing by the coefficient of CL^2, we get

$$CL^2 - \frac{2\ c}{p} \cdot CL = -\frac{2\ cq}{p . \sin. CLM}.$$

$$CL = \frac{c}{p} \pm \sqrt{\left(\frac{c^2}{p^2} - \frac{2\ cq}{p . \sin. LCM}\right)}.$$

If the given point is *outside* of the lines CL and CM, conceive the desired line to be drawn from it, and another line to join the given point to the corner of the field. Then, as above, get expressions for the two triangles thus formed, and put their sum equal to the expression for the triangle which comprehends them both, and thence deduce the desired distance, nearly as above.

(**522**) The difference *d*, between the areas parted off by the guess line AB, and the required line CD, is equal to the difference between the triangles APC and BPD

By Art. (65), Note, the triangle $APC = \frac{1}{2} \cdot AP^2 . \frac{\sin. A . \sin. P}{\sin. (A + P)}$.

Similarly the triangle $BPD = \frac{1}{2} \cdot BP^2 \frac{\sin. B . \sin. P}{\sin. (B + P)}$.

$$\therefore d = \tfrac{1}{2} \cdot AP^2 \frac{\sin. A . \sin. P}{\sin. (A + P)} - \tfrac{1}{2} BP^2 \cdot \frac{\sin. B . \sin. P}{\sin. (B + P)}$$

By the expression for sin. $(a+b)$ [Trigonometry, Art. (8)], we have

$$d=\frac{1}{2}\,AP^2\,.\,\frac{\sin. A\,.\,\sin. P}{\sin. A\,.\,\cos. P+\sin. P\,.\,\cos. A}-\frac{1}{2}\,BP^2\,.\,\frac{\sin. B\,.\,\sin. P}{\sin. B\,.\,\cos. P+\sin. P\,.\,\cos. B}.$$

Dividing each fraction by its numerator, and remembering that $\frac{\cos. a}{\sin. a}=\cot. a$, we have

$$d=\frac{\frac{1}{2}\,AP^2}{\cot. P+\cot. A}-\frac{\frac{1}{2}\,BP^2}{\cot. P+\cot. B}.$$

For convenience, let $p=\cot. P$; $a=\cot. A$; and $b=\cot. B$. The above equation will then read, multiplying both sides by 2,

$$2\,d=\frac{AP^2}{p+a}-\frac{BP^2}{p+b}.$$

Clearing of fractions, we have

$$2\,dp^2+2\,dap+2\,dbp+2\,dab=p\,.\,AP^2+b\,.\,AP^2-p\,.\,BP^2-a\,.\,BP^2.$$

Transposing, dividing through by $2\,d$, and separating into factors, we get

$$p^2+\left(a+b-\frac{AP^2-BP^2}{2\,d}\right)p=\frac{b\,.\,AP^2-a\,.\,BP^2}{2\,d}-ab.$$

$$\therefore p=-\frac{1}{2}\left(a+b-\frac{AP^2-BP^2}{2\,d}\right)\pm\sqrt{\left[\frac{b\,.\,AP^2-a\,.\,BP^2}{2\,d}-ab+\frac{1}{4}\left(a+b-\frac{AP^2-BP^2}{2d}\right)^2\right]}.$$

If $A=90°$, $\cot. A=a=0$; and the expression reduces to the simpler form given in the article.

(**523**) Conceive a perpendicular, BF, to be let fall from B to the required line DE. Let B represent the angle DBE, and β the unknown angle DBF. The angle $BDF=90°-\beta$; and the angle $BEF=90°-(B-\beta)=90°-B+\beta$. By Art. (65), Note, the area of the triangle $DBE=\frac{1}{2}\,DE^2\,.\,\frac{\sin. BDE\,.\,\sin. BED}{\sin. (BDE+BED)}=\frac{1}{2}\,.\,DE^2\,.\,\frac{\sin. (90°-\beta)\,\sin. (90°-B+\beta)}{\sin. B}$.

Hence, $$DE^2=\frac{2\times DBE\times \sin. B}{\sin. (90°-\beta)\,.\,\sin. (90°-B+\beta)}=\frac{2\times DBE\times \sin. B}{\cos. \beta\,.\,\cos. (B-\beta)}.$$

Now in order that DE may be the least possible, the denominator of the last fraction must be the greatest possible. It may be transformed, by the formula, $\cos. a\,.\,\cos. b=\frac{1}{2}\cos. (a+b)+\frac{1}{2}\,.\,\cos. (a-b)$ [Trigonometry, Art. (8)], into $\frac{1}{2}\cos. B+\frac{1}{2}\,.\,\cos. (B-2\,\beta)$. Since B is constant, the value of this expression depends on its second term, and that will be the greatest possible when $B-2\,\beta=0$, in which case $\beta=\frac{1}{2}\,B$.

It hence appears that the required line DE is perpendicular to the line, BF, which bisects the given angle B. This gives the *direction* in which DE is to be run. Its starting point, D or E, is found thus. The area of the triangle $DBE=\frac{1}{2}\,BD\,.\,BE\,.\,\sin. B$. Since the triangle is isosceles, this becomes

$$DBE=\frac{1}{2}\,BD^2\,.\,\sin. B;\text{ whence } BD=\sqrt{\left(\frac{2\,DBE}{\sin. B}\right)}.$$

DE is obtained from the expression for DE^2, which becomes, making $\beta=\frac{1}{2}B$,

$$DE^2=\frac{2\times DBE\times \sin. B}{\cos. \frac{1}{2}\,B\,.\,\cos. \frac{1}{2}\,B};\text{ whence, } DE=\frac{\sqrt{(2\,.\,DBE\,.\,\sin. B)}}{\cos. \frac{1}{2}\,B}$$

(**524**) Let a = value per acre of one portion of the land, and b that of the other portion. Let x = the width required, BC or AD. Then the value of $BCFE = a \times \frac{x \times BE}{10}$, and the value of $ADFE = b \times \frac{x \times AE}{10}$.

Putting the sum of these equal to the value required to be parted off, we obtain $x = \frac{\text{value required} \times 10}{a \times BE + b \times AE}$.

(**525**) All the constructions of this article depend on the equivalency of triangles which have equal bases, and lie between parallels. The length of AD is derived from the area of a triangle being equal to its base by half its altitude.

(**527**) Since similar triangles are to each other as the squares of their homologous sides,

$$ABC : DBE :: AB^2 : BD^2;\ \text{whence } BD = AB \sqrt{\frac{DBE}{ABC}} = AB \sqrt{\frac{m}{m+n}}.$$

The construction of Fig. 363 is founded on the proportion

$$BF : BG :: BG : BA;\ \text{when } BD = BG = \sqrt{(BA \times BF)} = BA \sqrt{\frac{m}{m+n}}.$$

(**528**) By hypothesis, $AEF : EFBC :: m : n$; whence $AEF : ABC :: m : m+n$ and $AEF = ABC \frac{m}{m+n} = \frac{AC \times DB}{2} \cdot \frac{m}{m+n}$. Also, $AEF = \frac{1}{2} \cdot AE \times EF$. The similar triangles AEF and ABD give $AD : DB :: AE : EF = \frac{DB \times AE}{AD}$. The second expression for AEF then becomes $AEF = \frac{1}{2} AE \cdot \frac{DB \times AE}{AD}$. Equating this with the other value of AEF, we have

$$\frac{AC \times DB}{2} \cdot \frac{m}{m+n} = \frac{AE^2 \times DB}{2 \cdot AD};\ \text{whence } AE = \sqrt{\left(AC \times AD \times \frac{m}{m+n}\right)}.$$

(**530**) In Fig. 366, the triangles ABD, DBC, having the same altitude, are to each other as their bases.

In the next paragraph, we have $ABD : DBC :: AD : DC :: m : n$; whence $AD : AC :: m : m+n$; and $AC : DC :: m+n : n$; whence the expressions for AD and DC.

In Fig. 367, the expression for AD is given by the proportion $AD : AC :: m : m+n$. Similarly for DE, and EC.

(**531**) In Fig. 368, conceive the line EB to be drawn. The triangle $AEB = \frac{1}{2} ABC$, having the same altitude and half the base; and AFD = AEB, because of the equivalency of the triangles EFD and EFB, which, with AEF, make up AFD and AEB.

The point F is fixed by the similar triangles ADB and AEF

The expression for AF, in the last paragraph, is given by the proportion,

$$ABC : ADF :: AB \times AC : AD \times AF;$$

whence,

$$AF = \frac{AB \times AC}{AD} \cdot \frac{ADF}{ABC} = \frac{AB \times AC}{AD} \cdot \frac{m}{m+n}.$$

(**532**) The areas of triangles being equal to the product of their altitudes by half their bases, the constructions in Fig. 369 and Fig. 370 follow therefrom.

(**533**) In Fig. 371, conceive the line BL to be drawn. The triangle ABL will be a third of ABC, having the same altitude and one-third the base; and AED is equivalent to ABL, because ELB = ELD, and AEL is common to both. A similar proof applies to DCG.

(**534**) In Fig. 372, the four smaller triangles are mutually equivalent, because of their equal bases and altitudes, two pairs of them lying between parallels.

(**535**) In Fig. 373, conceive AE to be drawn. The triangle AEC $= \frac{1}{2}$. ABC, having the same altitude and half the base; and EDFC = AEC, because of the common part FEC and the equivalency of FED and FEA.

(**536**) In Fig. 374, in addition to the lines used in the problem, draw BF and DG. The triangle BFC $= \frac{1}{2}$ ABC, having the same altitude and half the base. Also, the triangle DFG = DFB, because of the parallels DF and BG. Adding DFC to each of these triangles, we have DCG = BFC $= \frac{1}{2}$ ABC. We have then to prove LMC = DCG. This is done precisely as in the demonstration of Art. (519), page 402.

(**537**) Let AE $= x$, ED $= y$, AH $= x'$, HF $= y'$, AK $= a$, KB $= b$.

The quadrilateral AFDE, equivalent to $\frac{1}{3}$ ABC, but which we will represent, generally, by m^2, is made up of the triangle AFH and the trapezoid FHED.

$$\text{AFH} = \tfrac{1}{2} \,.\, x'y'. \qquad \text{FHED} = \tfrac{1}{2}(x - x')(y + y').$$

$$\therefore \text{AFDE} = m^2 = \tfrac{1}{2} \,.\, x'y' + \tfrac{1}{2}(x - x')(y + y') = \tfrac{1}{2}\, x\,(y + y') - \tfrac{1}{2}\, x'y.$$

The similar triangles, AHF and AKB, give

$$a : b :: x' : y' = \frac{bx'}{a}.$$

Substituting this value of y' in the expression for m^2, we have

$$m^2 = \tfrac{1}{2}\, x \left(y + \frac{bx'}{a}\right) - \tfrac{1}{2}\, x'y;$$

whence,

$$x' = \frac{a\,(2\,m^2 - xy)}{bx - ay} = \frac{\text{AK}\,(\frac{2}{3}\,\text{ABC} - \text{AE} \times \text{ED})}{\text{KB} \times \text{AE} - \text{AK} \times \text{ED}}.$$

The formula is general, whatever may be the ratio of the area m^2 to that of the triangle ABC.

(**538**) In Fig. 376, FD is a line of division, because BF = the triangle BDF divided by half its altitude, which gives its base. So for the other triangles.

(**539**) In Fig. 377, DG is a second line of division, because, drawing BL, the triangle BLC $= \frac{1}{3}$ ABC; and BDGC is equivalent to BLC, because of the common part BCLD, and the equivalency of the triangles DLG and DLB.

To prove that DF is a third line of division, join MD and MA. Then BMA $= \frac{1}{2}$ BGA. From BMA take MFA and add its equivalent MFD, and we have

$$\text{MDFB} = \tfrac{1}{2}\,\text{BGA} = \tfrac{1}{2}\,(\text{ABDG} - \text{BDG}) = \tfrac{1}{2}\,(\tfrac{2}{3}\,\text{ABC} - \text{BDG}) = \tfrac{1}{3}\,\text{ABC} - \tfrac{1}{2}\,\text{BDG}.$$

To MDFB add MDB, and add its equivalent, $\frac{1}{2}$ BDG, to the other side of the equation, and we have

$$\text{MDFB} + \text{MDB} = \tfrac{1}{3}\,\text{ABC} - \tfrac{1}{2}\,\text{BDG} + \tfrac{1}{2}\,\text{BDG}; \text{ or, BDF} = \tfrac{1}{3}\,\text{ABC}.$$

(**540**) In Fig. 378, the triangle AFC $= \frac{1}{3}$ ABC, having the same base and one-third the altitude. The triangles AFB and BFC are equivalent to each other, each being composed of two triangles of equal bases and altitudes; and each is therefore one-third of ABC.

In Fig. 379, AFC : ABC :: AD : AB; since these two triangles have the common base AC, and their altitudes are in the above ratio. So too, BFC : ABC :: BE : BA Hence, the remaining triangle AFB : ABC :: DE : AB.

(**541**) By Art. (65), Note, ABC $= \frac{1}{2}$ AC $\times$ CB $\times$ sin. ACB. But the angle ACB $=$ ACD $+$ DCB $= \frac{1}{2}(180° - \text{ADC}) + \frac{1}{2}(180° - \text{CDB}) = 180° - \frac{1}{2}(\text{ADC} + \text{CDB})$. Hence, ABC $= \frac{1}{2}$ AC $\times$ CB $\times$ sin. $\frac{1}{2}$ (ADC $+$ CDB) $= \frac{1}{2}$ AC $\times$ CB $\times$ sin. $\frac{1}{2}$ ADB.

Let $r =$ DA $=$ DB $=$ DC. Since AB is the chord of ADB to the radius r, and therefore equal to twice the sine of half that angle, we have

$$\text{sin. } \tfrac{1}{2} \text{. ADB} = \frac{\text{AB}}{2\,r}; \text{ whence, ABC} = \tfrac{1}{2}\,\text{AC} \times \text{CB} \times \frac{\text{AB}}{2\,r}; \text{ and } r = \frac{\text{AB} \times \text{BC} \times \text{CA}}{4\,.\,\text{ABC}}$$

Also, since the area of each of the three small triangles equals half the product of the two equal sides into the sine of the included angle at D, these triangles will be to each other as the sines of those angles. These angles are found thus:

$$\text{sin. } \tfrac{1}{2} \text{ ADB} = \frac{\text{AB}}{2\,r};\ \text{sin. } \tfrac{1}{2} \text{ BDC} = \frac{\text{BC}}{2\,r};\ \text{sin. } \tfrac{1}{2} \text{ ADC} = \frac{\text{AC}}{2\,r}.$$

(**542**) The formulas in this article are obtained by substituting, in those of Art. (523), for the triangle DBE, its equivalent $\frac{m}{m+n} \times \frac{1}{2}$ AB $\times$ BC $\times$ sin. B.

$$\text{BD thus becomes} = \sqrt{\left(\frac{m}{m+n} \cdot \frac{\text{AB} \times \text{BC} \times \text{sin. B}}{\text{sin. B}}\right)} = \sqrt{\left(\frac{m}{m+n} \times \text{AB} \times \text{BC}\right)};$$

$$\text{and DE} = \frac{\sqrt{\left(\frac{m}{m+n} \times \text{AB} \times \text{BC} \times \text{sin.}^2\,\text{B}\right)}}{\text{cos. } \frac{1}{2}\,\text{B}} = \frac{\text{sin. B}}{\text{cos. } \frac{1}{2}\,\text{B}} \cdot \sqrt{\left(\frac{m}{m+n} \times \text{AB} \times \text{BC}\right)}.$$

(**543**) The rule and example prove themselves.

(**544**) In Fig. 383, conceive the sides AB and DC, produced, to meet in some point P. Then, by reason of the similar triangles, ADP : BCP :: $\text{AD}^2 : \text{BC}^2$, whence, by "division," ADP — BCP $=$ ABCD : BCP :: $\text{AD}^2 - \text{BC}^2 : \text{BC}^2$.

In like manner, comparing EFP and BCP, we get EBCF : BCP :: $\text{EF}^2 - \text{BC}^2 : \text{BC}^2$. Combining these two proportions, we have

$$\text{ABCD : EBCF} :: \text{AD}^2 - \text{BC}^2 : \text{EF}^2 - \text{BC}^2;$$

or, $$m + n : m :: \text{AD}^2 - \text{BC}^2 : \text{EF}^2 - \text{BC}^2.$$

Whence, $$(m + n)\,\text{EF}^2 - m\,.\,\text{BC}^2 - n\,\text{BC}^2 = m\,.\,\text{AD}^2 - m\,.\,\text{BC}^2;$$

$$\therefore \text{EF} = \sqrt{\left(\frac{m \times \text{AD}^2 + n \times \text{BC}^2}{m+n}\right)}.$$

Also, from the similar triangles formed by drawing BL parallel to CD, we have

$$\text{AL : EK :: BA : BE} = \frac{\text{BA} \times \text{EK}}{\text{AL}} = \frac{\text{AB (EF} - \text{BC)}}{\text{AD} - \text{BC}}.$$

(**545**) Let BEFC $= \frac{m}{m+n} \cdot$ ABCD $= a$; let BC $= b$; BH $= h$; and AD — BC $= c$. Also let BG $= x$; and EF $= y$. Draw BL parallel to CD. By similar triangles, AL : EK :: BA : BE :: BH : BG; or, AD−BC : EF−BC :: BH : BG; i. e., $c : y - b :: h : x$; whence $x = \frac{h\,(y - b)}{c}$.

Also, the area BEFC $= a = \frac{1}{2}$. BG (EF $+$ BC) $= \frac{1}{2}\,x\,(y + b)$; whence $y = \frac{2\,a}{x} - b$

Substituting this value of y in the expression for x, and reducing, we obtain

$$x^2 + \frac{2\,bh}{c}\,x = \frac{2\,ah}{c};\ \text{whence we have } x = -\frac{bh}{c} \pm \sqrt{\left(\frac{2\,ah}{c} + \frac{b^2h^2}{c^2}\right)}.$$

The second proportion above gives $y - b = \frac{cx}{h}$; whence $y = b + \frac{c}{h} \cdot x$.

Replacing the symbols by their lines, we get the formulas in the text.

(546) ABEF $= \frac{1}{3}$ ABCD. But ABRP $=$ ABEF, because of the common part ABRF, and the triangles FRP and FRE, which make up the two figures, and which are equivalent because of the parallels FR and PE. So for the other parts.

(547) The truth of the foot-note is evident, since the first line bisects the trapezoid, and any other line drawn through its middle, and meeting the parallel sides, adds one triangle to each half, and takes away an equal triangle; and thus does not disturb the equivalency.

(548) In Fig. 385, since EF is parallel to AD, we have ADG : EGF :: $\text{GH}^2 : \text{GK}^2$. EGF is made up of the triangle BCG $= a'$, and the quadrilateral BEFC $=$ $\frac{m}{m+n} \cdot$ ABCD $= \frac{m}{m+n} \cdot (a - a')$. Hence the above proportion becomes

$$a : a' + \frac{m}{m+n}\,(a - a') :: \text{GH}^2 : \text{GK}^2;\ \text{or,}$$

$$(m+n)\,a : ma + na' :: \text{GH}^2 : \text{GK}^2;\ \text{whence GK} = \text{GH}\sqrt{\left(\frac{ma + na'}{(m+n)\,a}\right)}.$$

GE is given by the proportion GH : GK :: GA : GE $=$ GA $\cdot \frac{\text{GK}}{\text{GH}}$.

In Fig. 386, the division into p parts is founded on the same principle. The triangle EFG $=$ GBC $+$ EFCB $= a' + \frac{\text{Q}}{p}$. Now ADG : EFG :: $\text{AG}^2 : \text{EG}^2$;

or, $$a' + \text{Q} : a' + \frac{\text{Q}}{p} :: \text{AG}^2 : \text{EG}^2;\ \text{whence GE} = \text{AG}\sqrt{\left(\frac{a' + \frac{\text{Q}}{p}}{a' + \text{Q}}\right)}.$$

GL is obtained by taking the triangle LMG $= a' + \frac{2\,\text{Q}}{p}$; and so for the rest.

(552) In Fig. 390, join FC and GC. Because of the parallels CA and BF, the triangle FCD will be equivalent to the quadrilateral ABCD, of which GCD will therefore be one half; and because of the parallels GE and CH, EHDC will be equivalent to GCD.

(553) In Fig. 391, by drawing certain lines, the quadrilateral can be divided into three equivalent parts, each composed of an equivalent trapezoid and an equivalent triangle. These three equivalent parts can then be transformed, by means of the parallels, into the three equivalent quadrilaterals shown in the figure. The full development of the proof is left as an exercise for the student.

In Fig. 392, draw CG. Then CBG $= \frac{1}{3}$ ABCD. But CKQ $=$ CGQ. Therefore CKQB $= \frac{1}{3}$ ABCD. So for the other division line.

(556) The division of the base of the equivalent triangle, divides the polygon similarly. The point Q results from the equivalency of the triangles ZBP and ZBQ, PQ being parallel to BZ.

APPENDIX C.

INTRODUCTION TO LEVELLING.

(1) The Principles. LEVELLING is the art of finding how much one point is higher or lower than another; i. e., how much one of the points is above or below a level line or surface which passes through the other point.

A *level or horizontal line* is one which is perpendicular to the direction of gravity, as indicated by a plumb-line or similar means. It is therefore parallel to the surface of standing water.

A *level or horizontal surface* is defined in the same way. It will be determined by two level lines which intersect each other.*

Levelling may be named VERTICAL SURVEYING, or *Up-and-down Surveying;* the subject of the preceding pages being *Horizontal Surveying,* or *Right-and-left* and *Fore-and-aft Surveying.*

All the methods of Horizontal Surveying may be used in Vertical Surveying. The one which will be briefly sketched here corresponds precisely to the method of "Surveying by offsets," founded on the Second Method, Art. (6), "Rectangular Co-ordinates," and fully explained in Arts. (114), &c.

The operations of levelling by this method consist, firstly, in obtaining a level line or plane; and, secondly, in measuring how far below it or above it (usually the former) are the two points whose relative heights are required.

(2) The Instruments. A level line may be obtained by the following simple instrument, called a "*Plumb-line level.*" Fasten together two pieces of wood at right angles to each other, so as to make a **T**, and draw a line on the upright one so as to be exactly perpendicular to the top edge of the other. Suspend a plumb-line as in the figure. Fix the **T** against a staff stuck in the ground, by a screw through the middle of the cross-piece. Turn the **T** till the plumb-line exactly covers the line which was drawn.

Fig. 415.

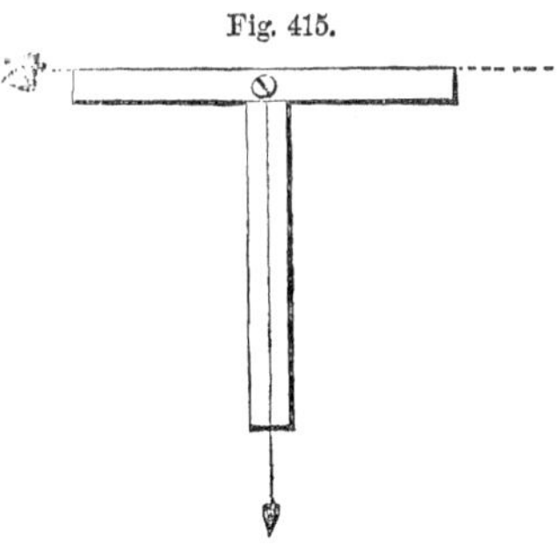

Then will the upper edge of the cross-piece be a level line, and the eye can sight across it, and note how far above or below any other point this level line, prolonged, would strike. It will be easier to look across sights fixed on each end of the cross-piece, making them of horsehair stretched across a piece of wire, bent into three sides of a square, and stuck into each end of the cross-piece; taking care that the hairs are at exactly equal heights above the upper edge of the cross-piece.

* Certain small corrections, to be hereafter explained, will be ignored for the present, and we will consider level lines as straight lines, and level surfaces as planes.

A modification of this is to fasten a common carpenter's square in a slit in the top of a staff, by means of a screw, and then tie a plumb-line at the angle so that it may hang beside one arm. When it has been brought to do so, by turning the square, then the other arm will be level.

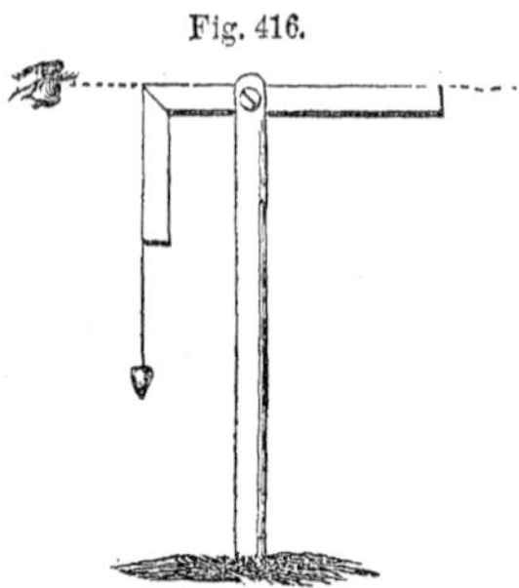
Fig. 416.

Another simple instrument depends upon the principle that "water always finds its level," corresponding to the second part of our definition of a level line. If a tube be bent up at each end, and nearly filled with water, the surface of the water in one end will always be at the same height as that in the other, however the position of the tube may vary. On this truth depends the "*Water-level.*" It may be easily constructed with a tube of tin, lead, copper, &c., by bending up, at right angles, an inch or two of each end, and supporting the tube, if too flexible, on a wooden bar. In these ends cement (with putty, twine dipped in white-lead, &c.), thin phials, with their bottoms broken off, so as to leave a free communication between them. Fill the tube and the phials, nearly to their top, with colored water. Blue vitriol, or cochineal, may be used for coloring it. Cork their mouths, and fit the instrument, by a steady but flexible joint, to a tripod. Figures of joints are given on page 134, and of tripods on page 133.

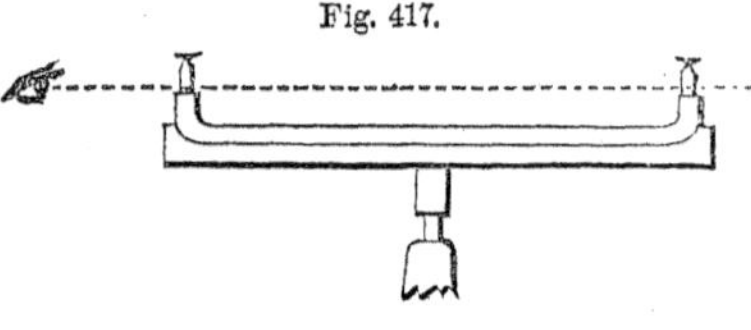
Fig. 417.

To use it, set it in the desired spot, place the tube by eye nearly level, remove the corks, and the surfaces of the water in the two phials will come to the same level. Stand about a yard behind the nearest phial, and let one eye, the other being closed, glance along the right-hand side of one phial and the left-hand side of the other. Raise or lower the head till the two surfaces seem to coincide, and this line of sight, prolonged, will give the level line desired. Sights of equal height, floating on the water, and rising above the tops of the phials, would give a better-defined line.

The "*Spirit-level*" consists essentially of a curved glass tube nearly filled with alcohol, but with a bubble of air left within, which always seeks the highest spot in the tube, and will therefore by its movements indicate any change in the position of the tube. Whenever the bubble, by raising or lowering one end, has been brought to stand between two marks on the tube, or, in case of expansion or contraction, to extend an equal distance on either side of them, the bottom of the block (if the tube be in one), or sights at each end of the tube, previously properly adjusted, will be on the same level line. It may be placed on a board fixed to the top of a staff or tripod.

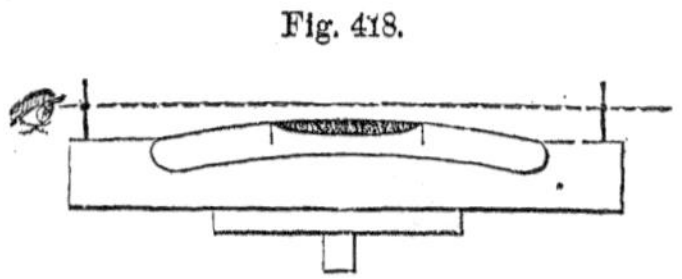
Fig. 418.

When, instead of the sights, a telescope is made parallel to the level, and various contrivances to increase its delicacy and accuracy are added, the instrument becomes the Engineer's spirit-level.

(3) The Practice. By whichever of these various means a level line has been obtained, the subsequent operations in making use of it are identical. Since the "water-level" is easily made and tolerably accurate, we will suppose it to be employed. Let A and B, Fig. 419, represent the two points, the difference of the heights of which is required. Set the instrument on any spot from which both the points can be seen, and at such a height that the level line will pass above the highest one. At A let an assistant hold a rod graduated into feet, tenths, &c. Turn the instrument towards the staff, sight along the level line, and note what division on the staff it strikes. Then send the staff to B, direct the instrument to it, and note the height observed at that point. If the level line, prolonged by the eye, passes 2 feet above A and 6 feet above B, the difference of their heights is 4 feet. The *absolute* height of the level line itself is a matter of indifference. The rod may carry a target or plate of iron, clasped to it so as to slide up and down, and be fixed, at will. This target may be variously painted, most simply with its upper half red and its lower half white. The horizontal line dividing the colors is the line sighted to, the target being moved up or down till the line of sight strikes it. A hole in the middle of the target shows what division on the rod coincides with the horizontal line, when it has been brought to the right height.

Fig. 419.

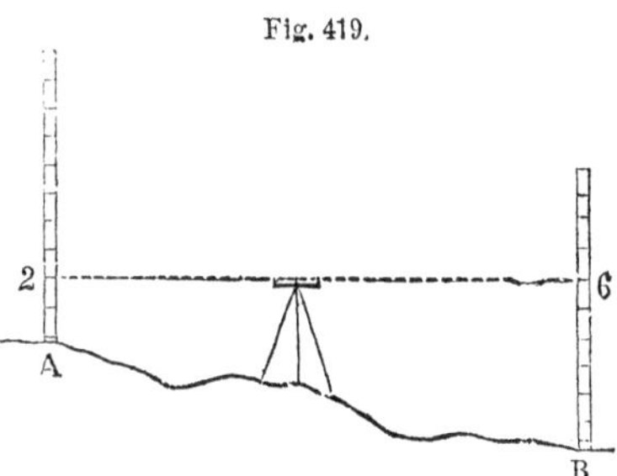

If the height of another point, C, Fig. 420, not visible from the first station, be required, set the instrument so as to see B and C, and proceed exactly as with A and B. If C be 1 foot below B, as in the figure, it will be 5 feet below A. If it were found to be 7 feet above B, it would be 3 feet above A. The comparative height of a series of any number of points, can thus be found in reference to any one of them.

Fig. 420.

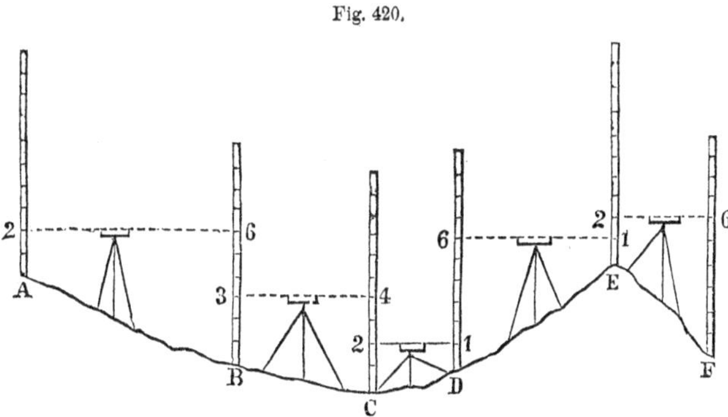

The beginner in the practice of levelling may advantageously make in his note-book a sketch of the heights noted, and of the distances, putting down each as it is observed, and imitating, as nearly as his accuracy of eye will permit, their proportional dimensions.* But when the observations are numerous, they should be kept in a tabular form, such as that which is given below. The names of the points, or "Stations," whose heights are demanded, are placed in the first column; and their heights, as finally ascertained, in reference to the first point, in the last column. The heights above the starting point are marked +, and those below it are marked —. The back-sight to any station is placed on the line below the point to which it refers. When a back-sight exceeds a fore-sight, their difference is placed in the column of "Rise;" when it is less, their difference is a "Fall." The following table represents the same observations as the last figure, and their careful comparison will explain any obscurities in either.

Stations.	Distances.	Back-sights.	Fore-sights.	Rise.	Fall.	Total Heights.
A						0.00
B	100	2.00	6.00		– 4.00	– 4.00
C	60	3.00	4.00		– 1.00	– 5.00
D	40	2.00	1.00	+ 1.[illegible]		– 4.00
E	70	6.00	1.00	+ 5.00		+ 1.00
F	50	2.00	6.00		– 4.00	– 3.00
		15.00	18.00		– 3.00	

The above table shows that B is 4 feet below A; that C is 5 feet below A; that E is 1 foot above A; and so on. To test the calculations, add up the back-sights and fore-sights. The difference of the sums should equal the last "total height."

Another form of the levelling field-book is presented below. It refers to the same stations and levels, noted in the previous form, and shown in Fig. 420.

Stations.	Distances.	Back-sights.	Ht. Inst. above Datum.	Fore-sights.	Total Heights.
A					0.00
B	100	2.00	+ 2.00	6.00	– 4.00
C	60	3.00	– 1.00	4.00	– 5.00
D	40	2.00	– 3.00	1.00	– 4.00
E	70	6.00	+ 2.00	1.00	+ 1.00
F	50	2.00	+ 3.00	6.00	– 3.00
		15.00		18.00	– 3.00

In the above form it will be seen that a new column is introduced, containing the Height of the Instrument (i. e., of its line of sight), not above the ground where it stands, but above the *Datum*, or starting-point, of the levels. The former columns of "Rise" and "Fall" are omitted. The above notes are taken thus: The height of the starting-point or "Datum," at A, is 0.00. The instrument being set up and levelled, the rod is held at A. The back-sight upon it is 2.00; therefore the height of the instrument is also 2.00. The rod is next held at B. The fore-sight to it is 6.00. That point is therefore 6.00 below the instrument, or 2.00 — 6.00 = — 4.00 below the datum. The instrument is now moved, and again set up, and the back-sight to B, being 3.00, the Ht. Inst. is — 4.00 + 3.00 = — 1.00

* In the figure, the limits of the page have made it necessary to contract the horizontal distances to one-tenth of their proper proportional size.

and so on: the Ht. Inst. being always obtained by adding the back-sight to the height of the peg on which the rod is held, and the height of the next peg being obtained by subtracting the fore-sight to the rod held on that peg, from the Ht. Inst.

The level lines given by these instruments are all lines of *apparent* level, and not of *true* level, which should curve with the surface of the earth. These level lines strike too high; but the difference is very small in sights of ordinary length, being only one-eighth of an inch for a sight of one-eighth of a mile, and diminishing as the square of the distance; and it may be completely compensated by setting the instrument midway between the points whose difference of level is desired; a precaution which should always be taken, when possible.

It may be required to show on paper the ups and downs of the line which has been levelled; and to represent, to any desired scale, the heights and distances of the various points of a line, its ascents and descents, as seen in a side-view. This is called a "*Profile.*" It is made thus. Any point on the paper being assumed for the first station, a horizontal line is drawn through it; the distance to the next station is measured along it, to the required scale; at the termination of this distance a vertical line is drawn; and the given height of the second station above or below the first is set off on this vertical line. The point thus fixed determines the second station, and a line joining it to the first station represents the slope of the ground between the two. The process is repeated for the next station, &c.

But the rises and falls of a line are always very small in proportion to the distances passed over; even mountains being merely as the roughnesses of the rind of an orange. If the distances and the heights were represented on a profile to the same scale, the latter would be hardly visible. To make them more apparent it is usual to "exaggerate the vertical scale" ten-fold, or more; i. e., to make the representation of a foot of height ten times as great as that of a foot of length, as in Fig. 420, in which one inch represents one hundred feet for the distances, and ten feet for the heights.

The preceding Introduction to Levelling has been made as brief as possible; but by any of the simple instruments described in it, and either of its tabular forms, any person can determine with sufficient precision whether a distant spring is higher or lower than his house, and how much; as well as how deep it would be necessary to cut into any intervening hill to bring the water. He may in like manner ascertain whether a swamp can be drained into a neighboring brook; and can cut the necessary ditches at any given slope of so many inches to the rod, &c., having thus found a level line; or he can obtain any other desired information which depends on the relative heights of two points.

To explain the peculiarities of the more elaborate levelling instruments, the precautions necessary in their use, the prevention and correction of errors, the overcoming of difficulties, and the various complicated details of their applications, would require a great number of pages. This will therefore be reserved for another volume, as announced in the Preface.

MAGNETIC VARIATIONS

IN THE UNITED STATES.

[From a Report by C. A. SCHOTT, Assistant U. S Coast Survey]. See Silliman's Journal, May, 1860, p. 335; and U. S. Coast Survey Report for 1859, App. 24, p. 296.

W. and E. indicate West and East Declinations. They are given below in Degrees and tenths.

	Portland, Me.	Boston, Mass.	Burlington, Vt.	Rutland, Vt.	Providence, R. I.	Hartford, Conn.	New Haven, Conn.	Albany, N. Y.	New York City.	Oxford, N. Y.	Philadelphia, Pa.	Washington, D. C.	Williamsburg, Va.
	W.	W.	W.	W.	W.	W.	W.	W.	W.	W.	W.	W.	
1680									8.8				4.8 W.
1690									8.7				4.8 W.
1700		9.7							8.5		8.8		
1710		9.0			10.4				8.0		8.4		
1720		8.3			9.5				7.6		7.9		
1730		7.8			8.9				7.0		7.1		
1740		7.4			8.3				6.4		6.3		
1750		7.2			7.7				5.8		5.3		
1760	8.1	7.0			6.9		6.1		5.2		4.4		
1770	8.1	6.8			6.3		5.5		4.7		3.5		1.2 W.
1780	8.3	6.8			6.1	5.2	5.0		4.4		2.8		0.7 W.
1790	8.5	6.8	7.8	6.3	6.3	5.0	4.8		4.2	3.0	2.2		0.2 W.
1800	8.9	7.0	7.5	6.2	6.4	5.0	4.6		4.2	3.0	2.0	0.4	0.2 E.
1810	9.4	7.3	7.3	6.3	6.5	5.2	4.7	5.4	4.3	3.1	1.9	0.5	0.4 E.
1820	10.0	7.8	7.6	6.7	6.8	5.6	5.0	5.8	4.7	3.4	2.2	0.8	0.4 E.
1830	10.6	8.4	8.3	7.3	7.5	6.1	5.4	6.3	5.2	3.8	2.7	1.1	0.2 E.
1840	11.2	9.1	9.1	8.1	8.4	6.7	6.0	7.0	5.7	4.4	3.4	1.5	0.1 W.
1850	11.8	9.9	9.7	8.9	9 1	7.4	6.7	7.7	6.4	5.2	4.3	2.0	0.6 W.
1860	12.3	10.6	10.3	9.9	9.7	8.1	7.5	8.3	7.0	6.0	5.2	2.6	1.2 W.
1870	12.7	11.1	11.2	10.9	10.2	8.9	8.3	9.0	7.6	6.8	6.1	3.1	1.9 W.
Minimum	1765	1782	1813	1800	1779	1794	1801	1787	1795	1799	1805	1798	1815

	Charleston, S. C.	Savannah, Ga.	Mobile, Ala.	San Diego, Cal.	Monterey, Cal.	San Francisco, Cal.	Cape Mendocino, Cal.	Cape Disappointment, Wash'n Territory.
	E.	E.	E.	E.	E.	E.	E.	E.
1770	3.7							
1780	4.0							
1790	4.1			11.1	11.4	13.6	15.1	18.9
1800	4.1	4.1	7.1	11.4	12.3	14.1	15.4	19.1
1810	4.0	4.2	7.2	11.7	13.0	14.5	15.7	19.3
1820	3.6	4.2	7.3	12.0	13.6	14.8	16.0	19.5
1830	3.2	4.1	7.2	12.2	14.2	15.1	16.3	19.7
1840	2.8	4.0	7.1	12.3	14.6	15.4	16.6	19.8
1850	2.2	3.7	7.0	12.5	15.0	15.6	16.9	20.0
1860	1.7	3.5	6.8	12.6	15.3	15.8	17.2	20.2
1870	1.2	3.2	6.6	12.6	15.4	15.9	17.2	20.4
Maximum.	1794	1817	1820	Not yet attained.				

ANALYTICAL TABLE OF CONTENTS.

PART I.

GENERAL PRINCIPLES AND FUNDAMENTAL METHODS.

CHAPTER I. Definitions and Methods.

CHAPTER II. Making the Measurements.

CHAPTER III. Drawing the Map.

CHAPTER IV. Calculating the Content.

PART II.

CHAIN SURVEYING.

CHAPTER I. Surveying by Diagonals.

CHAPTER II. Surveying by Tie-lines.

CHAPTER III. Surveying by Perpendiculars.

CHAPTER IV. Surveying by the methods combined.

CHAPTER V. Obstacles to Measurement in Chain Surveying.

OBSTACLES TO ALINEMENT.

PART III.

COMPASS SURVEYING.

CHAPTER I. Angular Surveying in general.

CHAPTER II. The Compass.

CHAPTER III. The Field-work.

CHAPTER IV. Platting the Survey.

CHAPTER V. Latitudes and Departures.

CHAPTER VI. Calculating the Content.

CHAPTER VII. The Variation of the Magnetic Needle.

CHAPTER VIII. Changes in the Variation.

PART IV.

TRANSIT AND THEODOLITE SURVEYING.

(BY THE 3d METHOD.)

CHAPTER I. The Instruments.

CHAPTER II. Verniers.

CHAPTER III. Adjustments.

CHAPTER IV. The Field-work.

PART V.

TRIANGULAR SURVEYING.

(BY THE 4th METHOD.)

PART VI.

TRILINEAR SURVEYING.

(BY THE 5th METHOD.)

PART VII.

OBSTACLES IN ANGULAR SURVEYING.

CHAPTER I. Perpendiculars and Parallels.

CHAPTER II. Obstacles to Alinement.

CHAPTER III. Obstacles to Measurement.

CHAPTER IV. To Supply Omissions.

PART VIII.

PLANE TABLE SURVEYING.

PART IX.

SURVEYING WITHOUT INSTRUMENTS.

PART X.

MAPPING.

CHAPTER I. Copying Plats.

CHAPTER II. Conventional Signs.

CHAPTER III. Finishing the Map.

PART XI.

LAYING OUT, PARTING OFF, AND DIVIDING UP LAND.

CHAPTER I. Laying out Land.

CHAPTER II. Parting off Land.

CHAPTER III. Dividing up Land.

PART XII.

UNITED STATES' PUBLIC LANDS.

APPENDIX.

APPENDIX A. Synopsis of Plane Trigonometry.

APPENDIX B. Demonstrations of Problems, &c.

APPENDIX C. Introduction to Levelling.

Levelling Rods.

Yankee or Boston	$18 00
New York, with improved mountings	18 00

Levelling Instruments.

Sixteen inch telescope, with adjusting tripod	$135 00
Eighteen " "	135 00
Twenty " "	135 00
Twenty-two " "	135 00
Builders' level, with adjusting tripod	50 00
" " leveling screws, and clamp and tangent movements	60 00

Chains.

100 feet, with oval rings, No. 5 refined iron wire	$12 00
" " " 6 " "	9 00
50 feet, " " 5 " "	6 50
50 feet, " " 6 " "	5 00
66 feet, " " 8 " "	4 75
33 feet, " " 8 " "	2 75
66 feet, " " 10 " "	4 00
33 feet, " " 10 " "	2 50
100 feet, " " 8 best steel wire	12 00
100 feet, " " 10 " "	10 50
50 feet, " " 8 " "	6 50
50 feet, " " 10 " "	5 75
66 feet, " " 8 " "	10 50
66 feet, " " 10 " "	8 00
33 feet, " " 8 " "	5 75
33 feet, " " 10 " "	4 50
100 feet, brazed links and rings, No. 12 best steel wire	15 00
50 feet, " " 12 "	8 00
66 feet, " " 12 "	14 00
33 feet, " " 12 "	7 00

Marking Pins.

Set of 11 pins, iron wire, No. 4	$1 50
" " steel wire, No. 6	2 00
" " brass wire, No. 4	3 00

Imported Measuring Tapes.

	Gold price.
Chesterman's steel, 33 feet	$10 50
" 50 feet	14 25
" 66 feet	18 00
" 100 feet	25 00
" metallic 33 feet	3 00
" " 50 feet	3 75
" " 66 feet	4 25
" " 70 feet	4 50
" " 80 feet	5 25
" " 100 feet	6 25

Pocket Compasses.

With folding sights, 2½ inch needle, very serviceable for tracing lines once surveyed	$ 9 00
With folding sights, 2½ inch needle, with Jacob Staff mountings	11 50
" 3½ " "	13 50
" 3½ " without "	11 00
Without sights, 1 to 2 inch needle ... from 25 cents to	5 00
Miners' compass, or Dipping needle, for tracing iron ore, a new and beautiful article, glass on both sides	10 00

INFORMATION TO PURCHASERS.

Manual.—To those who may wish to purchase any of the Instruments mentioned in the previous pages of this Advertisement, we will send our Manual—a Book of 125 pages, containing a full description of the same, with the adjustments, &c., free of charge, (postage included,) on application to us at Troy, N. Y.

Instruments Wanted.—In regard to the best kind of Instruments for particular purposes, we would here say, that where only common surveying, or the bearing of lines in the surveys for County Maps is required, a Plain Compass is all that is necessary. In cases where the variation of the needle is to be allowed, as in retracing the lines of an old survey, &c., the Vernier Compass, or the Vernier Transit, is required,

Where, in addition to the variation of the needle, horizontal angles are to be taken, and in cases of local attraction, the Rail Road Compass is preferable; and for a mixed practice of Surveying and Engineering, we consider the Surveyor's Transit superior to any instrument made by us or any other manufacturers.

In the surveys of U. S. public lands, the county and township lines are required to be run by such instruments as the Solar Compass.

Where Engineering is the exclusive design, the Engineers' Transit and the Leveling Instruments are of course indispensable.

Warranty.—All our instruments are examined and tested by us in person, and are sent to the purchaser adjusted and ready for immediate use.

They are warranted correct in all their parts—we agreeing in the event of any defect appearing after reasonable use, to repair, or replace with a new and perfect instrument, promptly and at our own cost, express charges included, or we will refund the money, and the express charges paid by the purchaser.

Instances may sometimes occur, in a business as large and widely extended as ours, where, owing to careless transportation, or to defects escaping the closest scrutiny of the maker, instruments may reach our customers in bad condition. We consider the retention of such instruments in all cases an injury very much greater to us than to the purchaser himself.

Trial of Instruments.—It may often happen that this statement of the prices and quality of our instruments, may come into the hands of those who are entirely unacquainted with us, or with the quality of our work, and who therefore feel unwilling to make a final purchase of an article, of the excellence of which they are not perfectly assured.

To such we make the following proposition: We will send the instrument to the express station nearest the person giving the order, and direct the Express Agent, on delivery of the same, to collect our bill, together with charges of transportation, and hold the money on deposit until the purchaser shall have had—say two weeks actual trial of its quality.

If not found as represented he may return the Instrument before the expiration of that time, and receive the money paid, in full, including express charges, and direct the Instrument to be returned to us.

Low Prices of our Instruments.—It is often urged by other makers, and persons prejudiced in their favor, that it is impossible to make first rate instruments, at the prices charged by us, and which are so very far below those of other skillful manufacturers.

We have only to reply, in addition to what we have stated in our Warranty, that a visit to our works, and a comparison of our facilities, with those of our competitors, would dispel all questions as to our ability to surpass them, not only in the cheapness, but also in the superior quality of our work.

Packing, &c.—Each instrument is packed in a well finished mahogany case, furnished with lock and key and brass hooks, the larger ones having besides these, a leather strap for convenience in carrying. Each case is provided with screw drivers, adjusting pin, and wrench for centre-pin, and, if accompanied by a tripod, with a brass plumb-bob; with all instruments for taking angles, without the needle, a reading microscope is also furnished.

Unless the purchaser is already supplied, each instrument is accompanied by our "Manual," giving full instructions for such adjustments and repairs as are possible to one not provided with the ordinary facilities of an instrument maker.

When sent to the purchaser, the mahogany cases are carefully enclosed in outside packing boxes, of pine, made a little larger on all sides to allow the introduction of elastic material, and so effectually are our instruments protected by these precautions that of several thousand sent out by us during the last thirteen years, in all seasons, by every mode of transportation, and to all parts of the Union and the Canadas, not more than three or four have sustained serious injury.

Means of Transportation.—Instruments can be sent by Express to almost every town in the United States and Canadas, regular agents being located at all the more important points, by whom they are forwarded to smaller places by stage. The charges of transportation from Troy to the purchaser are in all cases to be borne by him, we guarranteeing the safe arrival of our instruments to the extent of Express transportation, and holding the Express Companies responsible to us for all losses or damages on the way.

Terms of Payment are uniformly cash, and we have but one price. Our prices for instruments are nearly one-third less than those of other makers of established reputation. They are as low as we think instruments of equal quality can be made, and will not be varied from the list given on the previous pages.

Remittances may be made by a draft, payable to our order at Troy, Albany, New York, Boston or Philadelphia, which can be procured from Banks or Bankers in almost all of the larger villages.

These may be sent by mail with the order for the instrument, and if lost or stolen on the route, can be replaced by a duplicate draft, obtained as before, and without additional cost.

Or the customer may pay the bill on receipt of the instrument to the express agent taking care to send funds bankable in New York or Boston. The cost of returning bills collected by express of amounts under $15,00 will be charged to the customer.

W. & L. E. GURLEY,

Mathematical Instrument Makers

Fulton-st., opposite North End of Union R. R. Depot, Troy, N. Y.

TRAVERSE TABLES:

OR,

LATITUDES AND DEPARTURES OF COURSES,

CALCULATED TO

THREE DECIMAL PLACES:

FOR

EACH QUARTER DEGREE OF BEARING.

LATITUDES AND DEPARTURES.

Bearing.	1 Lat.	1 Dep.	2 Lat.	2 Dep.	3 Lat.	3 Dep.	4 Lat.	4 Dep.	5 Lat.	Bearing.
0°	1·000	0·000	2·000	0·000	3·000	0·000	4·000	0·000	5·000	**90°**
0¼	1·000	0·004	2·000	0·009	3·000	0·013	4·000	0·017	5·000	89¾
0½	1·000	0·009	2·000	0·017	3·000	0·026	4·000	0·035	5·000	89½
0¾	1·000	0·013	2·000	0·026	3·000	0·039	4·000	0·052	5·000	89¼
1°	1·000	0·017	2·000	0·035	3·000	0·052	3·999	0·070	4·999	**89°**
1¼	1·000	0·022	2·000	0·044	2·999	0·065	3·999	0·087	4·999	88¾
1½	1·000	0·026	1·999	0·052	2·999	0·079	3·999	0·105	4·998	88½
1¾	1·000	0·031	1·999	0·061	2·999	0·092	3·998	0·122	4·998	88¼
2°	0·999	0·035	1·999	0·070	2·998	0·105	3·998	0·140	4·997	**88°**
2¼	0·999	0·039	1·998	0·079	2·998	0·118	3·997	0·157	4·996	87¾
2½	0·999	0·044	1·998	0·087	2·997	0·131	3·996	0·174	4·995	87½
2¾	0·999	0·048	1·998	0·096	2·997	0·144	3·995	0·192	4·994	87¼
3°	0·999	0·052	1·997	0·105	2·996	0·157	3·995	0·209	4·993	**87°**
3¼	0·998	0·057	1·997	0·113	2·995	0·170	3·994	0·227	4·992	86¾
3½	0·998	0·061	1·996	0·122	2·994	0·183	3·993	0·244	4·991	86½
3¾	0·998	0·065	1·996	0·131	2·994	0·196	3·991	0·262	4·989	86¼
4°	0·998	0·070	1·995	0·140	2·993	0·209	3·990	0·279	4·988	**86°**
4¼	0·997	0·074	1·995	0·148	2·992	0·222	3·989	0·296	4·986	85¾
4½	0·997	0·078	1·994	0·157	2·991	0·235	3·988	0·314	4·985	85½
4¾	0·997	0·083	1·993	0·166	2·990	0·248	3·986	0·331	4·983	85¼
5°	0·996	0·087	1·992	0·174	2·989	0·261	3·985	0·349	4·981	**85°**
5¼	0·996	0·092	1·992	0·183	2·987	0·275	3·983	0·366	4·979	84¾
5½	0·995	0·096	1·991	0·192	2·986	0·288	3·982	0·383	4·977	84½
5¾	0·995	0·100	1·990	0·200	2·985	0·301	3·980	0·401	4·975	84¼
6°	0·995	0·105	1·989	0·209	2·984	0·314	3·978	0·418	4·973	**84°**
6¼	0·994	0·109	1·988	0·218	2·982	0·327	3·976	0·435	4·970	83¾
6½	0·994	0·113	1·987	0·226	2·981	0·340	3·974	0·453	4·968	83½
6¾	0·993	0·118	1·986	0·235	2·979	0·353	3·972	0·470	4·965	83¼
7°	0·993	0·122	1·985	0·244	2·978	0·366	3·970	0·487	4·963	**83°**
7¼	0·992	0·126	1·984	0·252	2·976	0·379	3·968	0·505	4·960	82¾
7½	0·991	0·131	1·983	0·261	2·974	0·392	3·966	0·522	4·957	82½
7¾	0·991	0·135	1·982	0·270	2·973	0·405	3·963	0·539	4·954	82¼
8°	0·990	0·139	1·981	0·278	2·971	0·418	3·961	0·557	4·951	**82°**
8¼	0·990	0·143	1·979	0·287	2·969	0·430	3·959	0·574	4·948	81¾
8½	0·989	0·148	1·978	0·296	2·967	0·443	3·956	0·591	4·945	81½
8¾	0·988	0·152	1·977	0·304	2·965	0·456	3·953	0·608	4·942	81¼
9°	0·988	0·156	1·975	0·313	2·963	0·469	3·951	0·626	4·938	**81°**
9¼	0·987	0·161	1·974	0·321	2·961	0·482	3·948	0·643	4·935	80¾
9½	0·986	0·165	1·973	0·330	2·959	0·495	3·945	0·660	4·931	80½
9¾	0·986	0·169	1·971	0·339	2·957	0·508	3·942	0·677	4·928	80¼
10°	0·985	0·174	1·970	0·347	2·954	0·521	3·939	0·695	4·924	**80°**
10¼	0·984	0·178	1·968	0·356	2·952	0·534	3·936	0·712	4·920	79¾
10½	0·983	0·182	1·967	0·364	2·950	0·547	3·933	0·729	4·916	79½
10¾	0·982	0·187	1·965	0·373	2·947	0·560	3·930	0·746	4·912	79¼
11°	0·982	0·191	1·963	0·382	2·945	0·572	3·927	0·763	4·908	**79°**
11¼	0·981	0·195	1·962	0·390	2·942	0·585	3·923	0·780	4·904	78¾
11½	0·980	0·199	1·960	0·399	2·940	0·598	3·920	0·797	4·900	78½
11¾	0·979	0·204	1·958	0·407	2·937	0·611	3·916	0·815	4·895	78¼
12°	0·978	0·208	1·956	0·416	2·934	0·624	3·913	0·832	4·891	**78°**
12¼	0·977	0·212	1·954	0·424	2·932	0·637	3·909	0·849	4·886	77¾
12½	0·976	0·216	1·953	0·433	2·929	0·649	3·905	0·866	4·881	77½
12¾	0·975	0·221	1·951	0·441	2·926	0·662	3·901	0·883	4·877	77¼
13°	0·974	0·225	1·949	0·450	2·923	0·675	3·897	0·900	4·872	**77°**
13¼	0·973	0·229	1·947	0·458	2·920	0·688	3·894	0·917	4·867	76¾
13½	0·972	6·233	1·945	0·467	2·917	0·700	3·889	0·934	4·862	76½
13¾	0·971	0·238	1·943	0·475	2·914	0·713	3·885	0·951	4·857	76¼
14°	0·970	0·242	1·941	0·484	2·911	0·726	3·881	0·968	4·851	**76°**
14¼	0·969	0·246	1·938	0·492	2·908	0·738	3·877	0·985	4·846	75¾
14½	0·968	0·250	1·936	0·501	2·904	0·751	3·873	1·002	4·841	75½
14¾	0·967	0·255	1·934	0·509	2·901	0·764	3·868	1·018	4·835	75¼
15°	0·966	0·259	1·932	0·518	2·898	0·776	3·864	1·035	4·830	**75°**
Bearing.	1 Dep.	1 Lat.	2 Dep.	2 Lat.	3 Dep.	3 Lat.	4 Dep.	4 Lat.	5 Dep.	Bearing.

Bearing.	5	6		7		8		9		Bearing.
	Dep.	Lat.	Dep.	Lat.	Dep.	Lat.	Dep.	Lat.	Dep.	
0°	0·000	6·000	0·000	7·000	0·000	8·000	0·000	9·000	0·000	**90°**
0¼	0·022	6·000	0·026	7·000	0·031	8·000	0·035	9·000	0·039	89¾
0½	0·044	6·000	0·052	7·000	0·061	8·000	0·070	9·000	0·079	89½
0¾	0·065	5·999	0·079	6·999	0·092	7·999	0·105	8·999	0·118	89¼
1°	0·087	5·999	0·105	6·999	0·122	7·999	0·140	8·999	0·157	**89°**
1¼	0·109	5·999	0·131	6·998	0·153	7·998	0·175	8·998	0·196	88¾
1½	0·131	5·998	0·157	6·998	0·183	7·997	0·209	8·997	0·236	88½
1¾	0·153	5·997	0·183	6·997	0·214	7·996	0·244	8·996	0·275	88¼
2°	0·174	5·996	0·209	6·996	0·244	7·995	0·279	8·995	0·314	**88°**
2¼	0·196	5·995	0·236	6·995	0·275	7·994	0·314	8·993	0·353	87¾
2½	0·218	5·994	0·262	6·993	0·305	7·992	0·349	8·991	0·393	87½
2¾	0·240	5·993	0·288	6·992	0·336	7·991	0·384	8·990	0·432	87¼
3°	0·262	5·992	0·314	6·990	0·366	7·989	0·419	8·988	0·471	**87°**
3¼	0·283	5·990	0·340	6·989	0·397	7·987	0·454	8·986	0·510	86¾
3½	0·305	5·989	0·366	6·987	0·427	7·985	0·488	8·983	0·549	86½
3¾	0·327	5·987	0·392	6·985	0·458	7·983	0·523	8·981	0·589	86¼
4°	0·349	5·985	0·419	6·983	0·488	7·981	0·558	8·978	0·628	**86°**
4¼	0·371	5·984	0·445	6·981	0·519	7·978	0·593	8·975	0·667	85¾
4½	0·392	5·982	0·471	6·978	0·549	7·975	0·628	8·972	0·706	85½
4¾	0·414	5·979	0·497	6·976	0·580	7·973	0·662	8·969	0·745	85¼
5°	0·436	5·977	0·523	6·973	0·610	7·970	0·697	8·966	0·784	**85°**
5¼	0·458	5·975	0·549	6·971	0·641	7·966	0·732	8·962	0·824	84¾
5½	0·479	5·972	0·575	6·968	0·671	7·963	0·767	8·959	0·863	84½
5¾	0·501	5·970	0·601	6·965	0·701	7·960	0·802	8·955	0·902	84¼
6°	0·523	5·967	0·627	6·962	0·732	7·956	0·836	8·951	0·941	**84°**
6¼	0·544	5·964	0·653	6·958	0·762	7·952	0·871	8·947	0·980	83¾
6½	0·566	5·961	0·679	6·955	0·792	7·949	0·906	8·942	1·019	83½
6¾	0·588	5·958	0·705	6·951	0·823	7·945	0·940	8·938	1·058	83¼
7°	0·609	5·955	0·731	6·948	0·853	7·940	0·975	8·933	1·097	**83°**
7¼	0·631	5·952	0·757	6·944	0·883	7·936	1·010	8·928	1·136	82¾
7½	0·653	5·949	0·783	6·940	0·914	7·932	1·044	8·923	1·175	82½
7¾	0·674	5·945	0·809	6·936	0·944	7·927	1·079	8·918	1·214	82¼
8°	0·696	5·942	0·835	6·932	0·974	7·922	1·113	8·912	1·253	**82°**
8¼	0·717	5·938	0·861	6·928	1·004	7·917	1·148	8·907	1·291	81¾
8½	0·739	5·934	0·887	6·923	1·035	7·912	1·182	8·901	1·330	81½
8¾	0·761	5·930	0·913	6·919	1·065	7·907	1·217	8·895	1·369	81¼
9°	0·782	5·926	0·939	6·914	1·095	7·902	1·251	8·889	1·408	**81°**
9¼	0·804	5·922	0·964	6·909	1·125	7·896	1·286	8·883	1·447	80¾
9½	0·825	5·918	0·990	6·904	1·155	7·890	1·320	8·877	1·485	80½
9¾	0·847	5·913	1·016	6·899	1·185	7·884	1·355	8·870	1·524	80¼
10°	0·868	5·909	1·042	6·894	1·216	7·878	1·389	8·863	1·563	**80°**
10¼	0·890	5·904	1·068	6·888	1·246	7·872	1·424	8·856	1·601	79¾
10½	0·911	5·900	1·093	6·883	1·276	7·866	1·458	8·849	1·640	79½
10¾	0·933	5·895	1·119	6·877	1·306	7·860	1·492	8·842	1·679	79¼
11°	0·954	5·890	1·145	6·871	1·336	7·853	1·526	8·835	1·717	**79°**
11¼	0·975	5·885	1·171	6·866	1·366	7·846	1·561	8·827	1·756	78¾
11½	0·997	5·880	1·196	6·859	1·396	7·839	1·595	8·819	1·794	78½
11¾	1·018	5·874	1·222	6·853	1·425	7·832	1·629	8·811	1·833	78¼
12°	1·040	5·869	1·247	6·847	1·455	7·825	1·663	8·803	1·871	**78°**
12¼	1·061	5·863	1·273	6·841	1·485	7·818	1·697	8·795	1·910	77¾
12½	1·082	5·858	1·299	6·834	1·515	7·810	1·732	8·787	1·948	77½
12¾	1·103	5·852	1·324	6·827	1·545	7·803	1·766	8·778	1·986	77¼
13°	1·125	5·846	1·350	6·821	1·575	7·795	1·800	8·769	2·025	**77°**
13¼	1·146	5·840	1·375	6·814	1·604	7·787	1·834	8·760	2·063	76¾
13½	1·167	5·834	1·401	6·807	1·634	7·779	1·868	8·751	2·101	76½
13¾	1·188	5·828	1·426	6·799	1·664	7·771	1·902	8·742	2·139	76¼
14°	1·210	5·822	1·452	6·792	1·693	7·762	1·935	8·733	2·177	**76°**
14¼	1·231	5·815	1·477	6·785	1·723	7·754	1·969	8·723	2·215	75¾
14½	1·252	5·809	1·502	6·777	1·753	7·745	2·003	8·713	2·253	75½
14¾	1·273	5·802	1·528	6·769	1·782	7·736	2·037	8·703	2·291	75¼
15°	1·294	5·796	1·553	6·761	1·812	7·727	2·071	8·693	2·329	**75°**
Bearing.	Lat.	Dep.	Lat.	Dep.	Lat.	Dep.	Lat.	Dep.	Lat.	Bearing.
	5	6		7		8		9		

LATITUDES AND DEPARTURES.

Bearing.	1		2		3		4		5	Bearing.
	Lat.	Dep.	Lat.	Dep.	Lat.	Dep.	Lat.	Dep.	Lat.	
15°	0·966	0·259	1·932	0·518	2·898	0·776	3·864	1·035	4·830	**75°**
15¼	0·965	0·263	1·930	0·526	2·894	0·789	3·859	1·052	4·824	74¾
15½	0·964	0·267	1·927	0·534	2·891	0·802	3·855	1·069	4·818	74½
15¾	0·962	0·271	1·925	0·543	2·887	0·814	3·850	1·086	4·812	74¼
16°	0·961	0·276	1·923	0·551	2·884	0·827	3·845	1·103	4·806	**74°**
16¼	0·960	0·280	1·920	0·560	2·880	0·839	3·840	1·119	4·800	73¾
16½	0·959	0·284	1·918	0·568	2·876	0·852	3·835	1·136	4·794	73½
16¾	0·958	0·288	1·915	0·576	2·873	0·865	3·830	1·153	4·788	73¼
17°	0·956	0·292	1·913	0·585	2·869	0·877	3·825	1·169	4·782	**73°**
17¼	0·955	0·297	1·910	0·593	2·865	0·890	3·820	1·186	4·775	72¾
17½	0·954	0·301	1·907	0·601	2·861	0·902	3·815	1·203	4·769	72½
17¾	0·952	0·305	1·905	0·610	2·857	0·915	3·810	1·220	4·762	72¼
18°	0·951	0·309	1·902	0·618	2·853	0·927	3·804	1·236	4·755	**72°**
18¼	0·950	0·313	1·899	0·626	2·849	0·939	3·799	1·253	4·748	71¾
18½	0·948	0·317	1·897	0·635	2·845	0·952	3·793	1·269	4·742	71½
18¾	0·947	0·321	1·894	0·643	2·841	0·964	3·788	1·286	4·735	71¼
19°	0·946	0·326	1·891	0·651	2·837	0·977	3·782	1·302	4·728	**71°**
19¼	0·944	0·330	1·888	0·659	2·832	0·989	3·776	1·319	4·720	70¾
19½	0·943	0·334	1·885	0·668	2·828	1·001	3·771	1·335	4·713	70½
19¾	0·941	0·338	1·882	0·676	2·824	1·014	3·765	1·352	4·706	70¼
20°	0·940	0·342	1·879	0·684	2·819	1·026	3·759	1·368	4·698	**70°**
20¼	0·938	0·346	1·876	0·692	2·815	1·038	3·753	1·384	4·691	69¾
20½	0·937	0·350	1·873	0·700	2·810	1·051	3·747	1·401	4·683	69½
20¾	0·935	0·354	1·870	0·709	2·805	1·063	3·741	1·417	4·676	69¼
21°	0·934	0·358	1·867	0·717	2·801	1·075	3·734	1·433	4·668	**69°**
21¼	0·932	0·362	1·864	0·725	2·796	1·087	3·728	1·450	4·660	68¾
21½	0·930	0·367	1·861	0·733	2·791	1·100	3·722	1·466	4·652	68½
21¾	0·929	0·371	1·858	0·741	2·786	1·112	3·715	1·482	4·644	68¼
22°	0·927	0·375	1·854	0·749	2·782	1·124	3·709	1·498	4·636	**68°**
22¼	0·926	0·379	1·851	0·757	2·777	1·136	3·702	1·515	4·628	67¾
22½	0·924	0·383	1·848	0·765	2·772	1·148	3·696	1·531	4·619	67½
22¾	0·922	0·387	1·844	0·773	2·767	1·160	3·689	1·547	4·611	67¼
23°	0·921	0·391	1·841	0·781	2·762	1·172	3·682	1·563	4·603	**67°**
23¼	0·919	0·395	1·838	0·789	2·756	1·184	3·675	1·579	4·594	66¾
23½	0·917	0·399	1·834	0·797	2·751	1·196	3·668	1·595	4·585	66½
23¾	0·915	0·403	1·831	0·805	2·746	1·208	3·661	1·611	4·577	66¼
24°	0·914	0·407	1·827	0·813	2·741	1·220	3·654	1·627	4·568	**66°**
24¼	0·912	0·411	1·824	0·821	2·735	1·232	3·647	1·643	4·559	65¾
24½	0·910	0·415	1·820	0·829	2·730	1·244	3·640	1·659	4·550	65½
24¾	0·908	0·419	1·816	0·837	2·724	1·256	3·633	1·675	4·541	65¼
25°	0·906	0·423	1·813	0·845	2·719	1·268	3·625	1·690	4·532	**65°**
25¼	0·904	0·427	1·809	0·853	2·713	1·280	3·618	1·706	4·522	64¾
25½	0·903	0·431	1·805	0·861	2·708	1·292	3·610	1·722	4·513	64½
25¾	0·901	0·434	1·801	0·869	2·702	1·303	3·603	1·738	4·503	64¼
26°	0·899	0·438	1·798	0·877	2·696	1·315	3·595	1·753	4·494	**64°**
26¼	0·897	0·442	1·794	0·885	2·691	1·327	3·587	1·769	4·484	63¾
26½	0·895	0·446	1·790	0·892	2·685	1·339	3·580	1·785	4·475	63½
26¾	0·893	0·450	1·786	0·900	2·679	1·350	3·572	1·800	4·465	63¼
27°	0·891	0·454	1·782	0·908	2·673	1·362	3·564	1·816	4·455	**63°**
27¼	0·889	0·458	1·778	0·916	2·667	1·374	3·556	1·831	4·445	62¾
27½	0·887	0·462	1·774	0·923	2·661	1·385	3·548	1·847	4·435	62½
27¾	0·885	0·466	1·770	0·931	2·655	1·397	3·540	1·862	4·425	62¼
28°	0·883	0·469	1·766	0·939	2·649	1·408	3·532	1·878	4·415	**62°**
28¼	0·881	0·473	1·762	0·947	2·643	1·420	3·524	1·893	4·404	61¾
28½	0·879	0·477	1·758	0·954	2·636	1·431	3·515	1·909	4·394	61½
28¾	0·877	0·481	1·753	0·962	2·630	1·443	3·507	1·924	4·384	61¼
29°	0·875	0·485	1·749	0·970	2·624	1·454	3·498	1·939	4·373	**61°**
29¼	0·872	0·489	1·745	0·977	2·617	1·466	3·490	1·954	4·362	60¾
29½	0·870	0·492	1·741	0·985	2·611	1·477	3·481	1·970	4·352	60½
29¾	0·868	0·496	1·736	0·992	2·605	1·489	3·473	1·985	4·341	60¼
30°	0·866	0·500	1·732	1·000	2·598	1·500	3·464	2·000	4·330	**60°**
	Dep.	Lat.	Dep.	Lat.	Dep.	Lat.	Dep.	Lat.	Dep.	
Bearing.	1		2		3		4		5	Bearing.

Bearing.	5	6		7		8		9		Bearing.
	Dep.	Lat.	Dep.	Lat.	Dep.	Lat.	Dep.	Lat.	Dep.	
15°	1·294	5·796	1·553	6·761	1·812	7·727	2·071	8·693	2·329	**75°**
15¼	1·315	5·789	1·578	6·754	1·841	7·718	2·104	8·683	2·367	74¾
15½	1·336	5·782	1·603	6·745	1·871	7·709	2·138	8·673	2·405	74½
15¾	1·357	5·775	1·629	6·737	1·900	7·700	2·172	8·662	2·443	74¼
16°	1·378	5·768	1·654	6·729	1·929	7·690	2·205	8·651	2·481	**74°**
16¼	1·399	5·760	1·679	6·720	1·959	7·680	2·239	8 640	2·518	73¾
16½	1·420	5·753	1·704	6·712	1·988	7·671	2·272	8·629	2·556	73½
16¾	1·441	5·745	1·729	6·703	2·017	7·661	2·306	8·618	2·594	73¼
17°	1·462	5·738	1·754	6·694	2·047	7·650	2·339	8·607	2·631	**73°**
17¼	1·483	5·730	1·779	6·685	2·076	7·640	2·372	8·595	2·669	72¾
17½	1·504	5·722	1·804	6·676	2·105	7·630	2·406	8·583	2·706	72½
17¾	1·524	5·714	1·829	6·667	2·134	7·619	2·439	8·572	2·744	72¼
18°	1·545	5·706	1·854	6·657	2·163	7·608	2·472	8·560	2·781	**72°**
18¼	1·566	5·698	1·879	6·648	2·192	7·598	2·505	8·547	2·818	71¾
18½	1·587	5·690	1·904	6·638	2·221	7·587	2·538	8·535	2·856	71½
18¾	1·607	5·682	1·929	6·629	2·250	7·575	2·572	8·522	2·893	71¼
19°	1·628	5·673	1·953	6·619	2·279	7·564	2·605	8·510	2·930	**71°**
19¼	1·648	5·665	1·978	6·609	2·308	7·553	2·638	8·497	2·967	70¾
19½	1·669	5·656	2·003	6·598	2·337	7·541	2·670	8·484	3·004	70½
19¾	1·690	5·647	2·028	6·588	2·365	7·529	2·703	8·471	3·041	70¼
20°	1·710	5·638	2·052	6·578	2·394	7·518	2·736	8·457	3·078	**70°**
20¼	1·731	5·629	2·077	6·567	2·423	7·506	2·769	8·444	3·115	69¾
20½	1·751	5·620	2·101	6·557	2·451	7·493	2·802	8·430	3·152	69½
20¾	1·771	5·611	2·126	6·546	2·480	7·481	2·834	8·416	3·189	69¼
21°	1·792	5·601	2·150	6·535	2·509	7·469	2·867	8·402	3·225	**69°**
21¼	1·812	5·592	2·175	6·524	2·537	7·456	2·900	8·388	3·262	68¾
21½	1·833	5·582	2·199	6·513	2·566	7·443	2·932	8·374	3·299	68½
21¾	1·853	5·573	2·223	6·502	2·594	7·430	2·964	8·359	3·335	68¼
22°	1·873	5·563	2·248	6·490	2·622	7·417	2·997	8·345	3·371	**68°**
22¼	1·893	5·553	2·272	6·479	2·651	7·404	3·029	8·330	3·408	67¾
22½	1·913	5·543	2·296	6·467	2·679	7·391	3·061	8·315	3·444	67½
22¾	1·934	5·533	2·320	6·455	2·707	7·378	3·094	8·300	3·480	67¼
23°	1·954	5·523	2·344	6·444	2·735	7·364	3·126	8·285	3·517	**67°**
23¼	1·974	5·513	2·368	6·432	2·763	7·350	3·158	8·269	3·553	66¾
23½	1·994	5·502	2·392	6·419	2·791	7·336	3·190	8·254	3·589	66½
23¾	2·014	5·492	2·416	6·407	2·819	7·322	3·222	8·238	3·625	66¼
24°	2·034	5·481	2·440	6·395	2·847	7·308	3·254	8·222	3·661	**66°**
24¼	2·054	5·471	2·464	6·382	2·875	7·294	3·286	8·206	3·696	65¾
24½	2·073	5·460	2·488	6·370	2·903	7·280	3·318	8·190	3·732	65½
24¾	2·093	5·449	2·512	6·357	2·931	7·265	3·349	8·173	3·768	65¼
25°	2·113	5·438	2·536	6·344	2·958	7·250	3·381	8·157	3·804	**65°**
25¼	2·133	5·427	2·559	6·331	2·986	7·236	3·413	8·140	3·839	64¾
25½	2·153	5·416	2·583	6·318	3·014	7·221	3·444	8·123	3·875	64½
25¾	2·172	5·404	2·607	6·305	3·041	7·206	3·476	8·106	3·910	64¼
26°	2·192	5·393	2·630	6·292	3·069	7·190	3·507	8·089	3·945	**64°**
26¼	2·211	5·381	2·654	6·278	3·096	7·175	3·538	8·072	3·981	63¾
26½	2·231	5·370	2·677	6·265	3·123	7·160	3·570	8·054	4·016	63½
26¾	2·250	5·358	2·701	6·251	3·151	7·144	3·601	8·037	4·051	63¼
27°	2·270	5·346	2·724	6·237	3·178	7·128	3·632	8·019	4·086	**63°**
27¼	2·289	5·334	2·747	6·223	3·205	7·112	3·663	8·001	4·121	62¾
27½	2·309	5·322	2·770	6·209	3·232	7·096	3·694	7·983	4·156	62½
27¾	2·328	5·310	2·794	6·195	3·259	7·080	3·725	7·965	4·190	62¼
28°	2·347	5·298	2·817	6·181	3·286	7·064	3·756	7·947	4·225	**62°**
28¼	2·367	5·285	2·840	6·166	3·313	7·047	3·787	7·928	4·260	61¾
28½	2·386	5·273	2·863	6·152	3·340	7·031	3·817	7·909	4·294	61½
28¾	2·405	5·260	2·886	6·137	3·367	7·014	3·848	7·891	4·329	61¼
29°	2·424	5·248	2·909	6·122	3·394	6·997	3·878	7·872	4·363	**61°**
29¼	2·443	5·235	2·932	6·107	3·420	6·980	3·909	7·852	4·398	60¾
29½	2·462	5·222	2·955	6·093	3·447	6·963	3·939	7·833	4·432	60½
29¾	2·481	5·209	2·977	6·077	3·474	6·946	3·970	7·814	4·466	60¼
30°	2·500	5·196	3·000	6·062	3·500	6·928	4·000	7·794	4·500	**60°**
Bearing.	Lat.	Dep.	Lat.	Dep.	Lat.	Dep.	Lat.	Dep.	Lat.	Bearing.
	5	6		7		8		9		

LATITUDES AND DEPARTURES.

Bearing.	1		2		3		4		5	Bearing.
	Lat.	Dep.	Lat.	Dep.	Lat.	Dep.	Lat.	Dep.	Lat.	
30°	0·866	0·500	1·732	1·000	2·598	1·500	3·464	2·000	4·330	**60°**
30¼	0·864	0·504	1·728	1·008	2·592	1·511	3·455	2·015	4·319	59¾
30½	0·862	0·508	1·723	1·015	2·585	1·523	3·447	2·030	4·308	59½
30¾	0·859	0·511	1·719	1·023	2·578	1·534	3·438	2·045	4·297	59¼
31°	0·857	0·515	1·714	1·030	2·572	1·545	3·429	2·060	4·286	**59°**
31¼	0·855	0·519	1·710	1·038	2·565	1·556	3·420	2·075	4·275	58¾
31½	0·853	0·522	1·705	1·045	2·558	1·567	3·411	2·090	4·263	58½
31¾	0·850	0·526	1·701	1·052	2·551	1·579	3·401	2·105	4·252	58¼
32°	0·848	0·530	1·696	1·060	2·544	1·590	3·392	2·120	4·240	**58°**
32¼	0·846	0·534	1·691	1·067	2·537	1·601	3·383	2·134	4·229	57¾
32½	0·843	0·537	1·687	1·075	2·530	1·612	3·374	2·149	4·217	57½
32¾	0·841	0·541	1·682	1·082	2·523	1·623	3·364	2·164	4·205	57¼
33°	0·839	0·545	1·677	1·089	2·516	1·634	3·355	2·179	4·193	**57°**
33¼	0·836	0·548	1·673	1·097	2·509	1·645	3·345	2·193	4·181	56¾
33½	0·834	0·552	1·668	1·104	2·502	1·656	3·336	2·208	4·169	56½
33¾	0·831	0·556	1·663	1·111	2·494	1·667	3·326	2·222	4·157	56¼
34°	0·829	0·559	1·658	1·118	2·487	1·678	3·316	2·237	4·145	**56°**
34¼	0·827	0·563	1·653	1·126	2·480	1·688	3·306	2·251	4·133	55¾
34½	0·824	0·566	1·648	1·133	2·472	1·699	3·297	2·266	4·121	55½
34¾	0·822	0·570	1·643	1·140	2·465	1·710	3·287	2·280	4·108	55¼
35°	0·819	0·574	1·638	1·147	2·457	1·721	3·277	2·294	4·096	**55°**
35¼	0·817	0·577	1·633	1·154	2·450	1·731	3·267	2·309	4·083	54¾
35½	0·814	0·581	1·628	1·161	2·442	1·742	3·257	2·323	4·071	54½
35¾	0·812	0·584	1·623	1·168	2·435	1·753	3·246	2·337	4·058	54¼
36°	0·809	0·588	1·618	1·176	2·427	1·763	3·236	2·351	4·045	**54°**
36¼	0·806	0·591	1·613	1·183	2·419	1·774	3·226	2·365	4·032	53¾
36½	0·804	0·595	1·608	1·190	2·412	1·784	3·215	2·379	4·019	53½
36¾	0·801	0·598	1·603	1·197	2·404	1·795	3·205	2·393	4·006	53¼
37°	0·799	0·602	1·597	1·204	2·396	1·805	3·195	2·407	3·993	**53°**
37¼	0·796	0·605	1·592	1·211	2·388	1·816	3·184	2·421	3·980	52¾
37½	0·793	0·609	1·587	1·218	2·380	1·826	3·173	2·435	3·967	52½
37¾	0·791	0·612	1·581	1·224	2·372	1·837	3·163	2·449	3·953	52¼
38°	0·788	0·616	1·576	1·231	2·364	1·847	3·152	2·463	3·940	**52°**
38¼	0·785	0·619	1·571	1·238	2·356	1·857	3·141	2·476	3·927	51¾
38½	0·783	0·623	1·565	1·245	2·348	1·868	3·130	2·490	3·913	51½
38¾	0·780	0·626	1·560	1·252	2·340	1·878	3·120	2·504	3·899	51¼
39°	0·777	0·629	1·554	1·259	2·331	1·888	3·109	2·517	3·886	**51°**
39¼	0·774	0·633	1·549	1·265	2·323	1·898	3·098	2·531	3·872	50¾
39½	0·772	0·636	1·543	1·272	2·315	1·908	3·086	2·544	3·858	50½
39¾	0·769	0·639	1·538	1·279	2·307	1·918	3·075	2·558	3·844	50¼
40°	0·766	0·643	1·532	1·286	2·298	1·928	3·064	2·571	3·830	**50°**
40¼	0·763	0·646	1·526	1·292	2·290	1·938	3·053	2·584	3·816	49¾
40½	0·760	0·649	1·521	1·299	2·281	1·948	3·042	2·598	3·802	49½
40¾	0·758	0·653	1·515	1·306	2·273	1·958	3·030	2·611	3·788	49¼
41°	0·755	0·656	1·509	1·312	2·264	1·968	3·019	2·624	3·774	**49°**
41¼	0·752	0·659	1·504	1·319	2·256	1·978	3·007	2·637	3·759	48¾
41½	0·749	0·663	1·498	1·325	2·247	1·988	2·996	2·650	3·745	48½
41¾	0·746	0·666	1·492	1·332	2·238	1·998	2·984	2·664	3·730	48¼
42°	0·743	0·669	1·486	1·338	2·229	2·007	2·973	2·677	3·716	**48°**
42¼	0·740	0·672	1·480	1·345	2·221	2·017	2·961	2·689	3·701	47¾
42½	0·737	0·676	1·475	1·351	2·212	2·027	2·949	2·702	3·686	47½
42¾	0·734	0·679	1·469	1·358	2·203	2·036	2·937	2·715	3·672	47¼
43°	0·731	0·682	1·463	1·364	2·194	2·046	2·925	2·728	3·657	**47°**
43¼	0·728	0·685	1·457	1·370	2·185	2·056	2·913	2·741	3·642	46¾
43½	0·725	0·688	1·451	1·377	2·176	2·065	2·901	2·753	3·627	46½
43¾	0·722	0·692	1·445	1·383	2·167	2·075	2·889	2·766	3·612	46¼
44°	0·719	0·695	1·439	1·389	2·158	2·084	2·877	2·779	3·597	**46°**
44¼	0·716	0·698	1·433	1·396	2·149	2·093	2·865	2·791	3·582	45¾
44½	0·713	0·701	1·427	1·402	2·140	2·103	2·853	2·804	3·566	45½
44¾	0·710	0·704	1·420	1·408	2·131	2·112	2·841	2·816	3·551	45¼
45°	0·707	0·707	1·414	1·414	2·121	2·121	2·828	2·828	3·536	**45°**
	Dep.	Lat.	Dep.	Lat.	Dep.	Lat.	Dep.	Lat.	Dep.	
Bearing.	1		2		3		4		5	Bearing.

Bearing.	5	6		7		8		9		Bearing.
	Dep.	Lat.	Dep.	Lat.	Dep.	Lat.	Dep.	Lat.	Dep.	
30°	2·500	5·196	3·000	6·062	3·500	6·928	4·000	7·794	4·500	**60°**
30¼	2·519	5·183	3·023	6·047	3·526	6·911	4·030	7·775	4·534	59¾
30½	2·538	5·170	3·045	6·031	3·553	6·893	4·060	7·755	4·568	59½
30¾	2·556	5·156	3·068	6·016	3·579	6·875	4·090	7·735	4·602	59¼
31°	2·575	5·143	3·090	6·000	3·605	6·857	4·120	7·715	4·635	**59°**
31¼	2·594	5·129	3·113	5·984	3·631	6·839	4·150	7·694	4·669	58¾
31½	2·612	5·116	3·135	5·968	3·657	6·821	4·180	7·674	4·702	58½
31¾	2·631	5·102	3·157	5·952	3·683	6·803	4·210	7·653	4·736	58¼
32°	2·650	5·088	3·180	5·936	3·709	6·784	4·239	7·632	4·769	**58°**
32¼	2·668	5·074	3·202	5·920	3·735	6·766	4·269	7·612	4·802	57¾
32½	2·686	5·060	3·224	5·904	3·761	6·747	4·298	7·591	4·836	57½
32¾	2·705	5·046	3·246	5·887	3·787	6·728	4·328	7·569	4·869	57¼
33°	2·723	5·032	3·268	5·871	3·812	6·709	4·357	7·548	4·902	**57°**
33¼	2·741	5·018	3·290	5·854	3·838	6·690	4·386	7·527	4·935	56¾
33½	2·760	5·003	3·312	5·837	3·864	6·671	4·416	7·505	4·967	56½
33¾	2·778	4·989	3·333	5·820	3·889	6·652	4·445	7·483	5·000	56¼
34°	2·796	4·974	3·355	5·803	3·914	6·632	4·474	7·461	5·033	**56°**
34¼	2·814	4·960	3·377	5·786	3·940	6·613	4·502	7·439	5·065	55¾
34½	2·832	4·945	3·398	5·769	3·965	6·593	4·531	7·417	5·098	55½
34¾	2·850	4·930	3·420	5·752	3·990	6·573	4·560	7·395	5·130	55¼
35°	2·868	4·915	3·441	5·734	4·015	6·553	4·589	7·372	5·162	**55°**
35¼	2·886	4·900	3·463	5·716	4·040	6·533	4·617	7·350	5·194	54¾
35½	2·904	4·885	3·484	5·699	4·065	6·513	4·646	7·327	5·226	54½
35¾	2·921	4·869	3·505	5·681	4·090	6·493	4·674	7·304	5·258	54¼
36°	2·939	4·854	3·527	5·663	4·115	6·472	4·702	7·281	5·290	**54°**
36¼	2·957	4·839	3·548	5·645	4·139	6·452	4·730	7·258	5·322	53¾
36½	2·974	4·823	3·569	5·627	4·164	6·431	4·759	7·235	5·353	53½
36¾	2·992	4·808	3·590	5·609	4·188	6·410	4·787	7·211	5·385	53¼
37°	3·009	4·792	3·611	5·590	4·213	6·389	4·815	7·188	5·416	**53°**
37¼	3·026	4·776	3·632	5·572	4·237	6·368	4·842	7·164	5·448	52¾
37½	3·044	4·760	3·653	5·554	4·261	6·347	4·870	7·140	5·479	52½
37¾	3·061	4·744	3·673	5·535	4·286	6·326	4·898	7·116	5·510	52¼
38°	3·078	4·728	3·694	5·516	4·310	6·304	4·925	7·092	5·541	**52°**
38¼	3·095	4·712	3·715	5·497	4·334	6·283	4·953	7·068	5·572	51¾
38½	3·113	4·696	3·735	5·478	4·358	6·261	4·980	7·043	5·603	51½
38¾	3·130	4·679	3·756	5·459	4·381	6·239	5·007	7·019	5·633	51¼
39°	3·147	4·663	3·776	5·440	4·405	6·217	5·035	6·994	5·664	**51°**
39¼	3·164	4·646	3·796	5·421	4·429	6·195	5·062	6·970	5·694	50¾
39½	3·180	4·630	3·816	5·401	4·453	6·173	5·089	6·945	5·725	50½
39¾	3·197	4·613	3·837	5·382	4·476	6·151	5·116	6·920	5·755	50¼
40°	3·214	4·596	3·857	5·362	4·500	6·128	5·142	6·894	5·785	**50°**
40¼	3·231	4·579	3·877	5·343	4·523	6·106	5·169	6·869	5·815	49¾
40½	3·247	4·562	3·897	5·323	4·546	6·083	5·196	6·844	5·845	49½
40¾	3·264	4·545	3·917	5·303	4·569	6·061	5·222	6·818	5·875	49¼
41°	3·280	4·528	3·936	5·283	4·592	6·038	5·248	6·792	5·905	**49°**
41¼	3·297	4·511	3·956	5·263	4·615	6·015	5·275	6·767	5·934	48¾
41½	3·313	4·494	3·976	5·243	4·638	5·992	5·301	6·741	5·964	48½
41¾	3·329	4·476	3·995	5·222	4·661	5·968	5·327	6·715	5·993	48¼
42°	3·346	4·459	4·015	5·202	4·684	5·945	5·353	6·688	6·022	**48°**
42¼	3·362	4·441	4·034	5·182	4·707	5·922	5·379	6·662	6·051	47¾
42½	3·378	4·424	4·054	5·161	4·729	5·898	5·405	6·635	6·080	47½
42¾	3·394	4·406	4·073	5·140	4·752	5·875	5·430	6·609	6·109	47¼
43°	3·410	4·388	4·092	5·119	4·774	5·851	5·456	6·582	6·138	**47°**
43¼	3·426	4·370	4·111	5·099	4·796	5·827	5·481	6·555	6·167	46¾
43½	3·442	4·352	4·130	5·078	4·818	5·803	5·507	6·528	6·195	46½
43¾	3·458	4·334	4·149	5·057	4·841	5·779	5·532	6·501	6·224	46¼
44°	3·473	4·316	4·168	5·035	4·863	5·755	5·557	6·474	6·252	**46°**
44¼	3·489	4·298	4·187	5·014	4·885	5·730	5·582	6·447	6·280	45¾
44½	3·505	4·280	4·206	4·993	4·906	5·706	5·607	6·419	6·308	45½
44¾	3·520	4·261	4·224	4·971	4·928	5·681	5·632	6·392	6·336	45¼
45°	3·536	4·243	4·243	4·950	4·950	5·657	5·657	6·364	6·364	**45°**
Bearing.	Lat.	Dep.	Lat.	Dep.	Lat.	Dep.	Lat.	Dep.	Lat.	Bearing.
	5	6		7		8		9		

TABLE OF CHORDS: [Radius = 1.0000].

M.	0°	1°	2°	3°	4°	5°	6°	7°	8°	9°	10°	M.
0'	·0000	·0175	·0349	·0524	·0698	·0872	·1047	·1221	·1395	·1569	·1743	0'
1	·0003	·0177	·0352	·0526	·0701	·0875	·1050	·1224	·1398	·1572	·1746	1
2	·0006	·0180	·0355	·0529	·0704	·0878	·1053	·1227	·1401	·1575	·1749	2
3	·0009	·0183	·0358	·0532	·0707	·0881	·1055	·1230	·1404	·1578	·1752	3
4	·0012	·0186	·0361	·0535	·0710	·0884	·1058	·1233	·1407	·1581	·1755	4
5	·0015	·0189	·0364	·0538	·0713	·0887	·1061	·1235	·1410	·1584	·1758	5
6	·0017	·0192	·0366	·0541	·0715	·0890	·1064	·1238	·1413	·1587	·1761	6
7	·0020	·0195	·0369	·0544	·0718	·0893	·1067	·1241	·1415	·1589	·1763	7
8	·0023	·0198	·0372	·0547	·0721	·0896	·1070	·1244	·1418	·1592	·1766	8
9	·0026	·0201	·0375	·0550	·0724	·0899	·1073	·1247	·1421	·1595	·1769	9
10	·0029	·0204	·0378	·0553	·0727	·0901	·1076	·1250	·1424	·1598	·1772	10
11	·0032	·0207	·0381	·0556	·0730	·0904	·1079	·1253	·1427	·1601	·1775	11
12	·0035	·0209	·0384	·0558	·0733	·0907	·1082	·1256	·1430	·1604	·1778	12
13	·0038	·0212	·0387	·0561	·0736	·0910	·1084	·1259	·1433	·1607	·1781	13
14	·0041	·0215	·0390	·0564	·0739	·0913	·1087	·1262	·1436	·1610	·1784	14
15	·0044	·0218	·0393	·0567	·0742	·0916	·1090	·1265	·1439	·1613	·1787	15
16	·0047	·0221	·0396	·0570	·0745	·0919	·1093	·1267	·1442	·1616	·1789	16
17	·0049	·0224	·0398	·0573	·0747	·0922	·1096	·1270	·1444	·1618	·1792	17
18	·0052	·0227	·0401	·0576	·0750	·0925	·1099	·1273	·1447	·1621	·1795	18
19	·0055	·0230	·0404	·0579	·0753	·0928	·1102	·1276	·1450	·1624	·1798	19
20	·0058	·0233	·0407	·0582	·0756	·0931	·1105	·1279	·1453	·1627	·1801	20
21	·0061	·0236	·0410	·0585	·0759	·0933	·1108	·1282	·1456	·1630	·1804	21
22	·0064	·0239	·0413	·0588	·0762	·0936	·1111	·1285	·1459	·1633	·1807	22
23	·0067	·0241	·0416	·0590	·0765	·0939	·1114	·1288	·1462	·1636	·1810	23
24	·0070	·0244	·0419	·0593	·0768	·0942	·1116	·1291	·1465	·1639	·1813	24
25	·0073	·0247	·0422	·0596	·0771	·0945	·1119	·1294	·1468	·1642	·1816	25
26	·0076	·0250	·0425	·0599	·0774	·0948	·1122	·1296	·1471	·1645	·1818	26
27	·0079	·0253	·0428	·0602	·0776	·0951	·1125	·1299	·1473	·1647	·1821	27
28	·0081	·0256	·0430	·0605	·0779	·0954	·1128	·1302	·1476	·1650	·1824	28
29	·0084	·0259	·0433	·0608	·0782	·0957	·1131	1305	·1479	·1653	·1827	29
30	·0087	·0262	·0436	·0611	·0785	·0960	·1134	·1308	·1482	·1656	·1830	30
31	·0090	·0265	·0439	·0614	·0788	·0962	·1137	·1311	·1485	·1659	·1833	31
32	·0093	·0268	·0442	·0617	·0791	·0965	·1140	·1314	·1488	·1662	·1836	32
33	·0096	·0271	·0445	·0619	·0794	·0968	·1143	·1317	·1491	·1665	·1839	33
34	·0099	·0273	·0448	·0622	·0797	·0971	·1145	·1320	·1494	·1668	·1842	34
35	·0102	·0276	·0451	·0625	·0800	·0974	·1148	·1323	·1497	·1671	·1845	35
36	·0105	·0279	·0454	·0628	·0803	·0977	·1151	·1325	·1500	·1674	·1847	36
37	·0108	·0282	·0457	·0631	·0806	·0980	·1154	·1328	·1502	·1676	·1850	37
38	·0111	·0285	·0460	·0634	·0808	·0983	·1157	·1331	·1505	·1679	·1853	38
39	·0113	·0288	·0462	·0637	·0811	·0986	·1160	·1334	·1508	·1682	·1856	39
40	·0116	·0291	·0465	·0640	·0814	·0989	·1163	·1337	·1511	·1685	·1859	40
41	·0119	·0294	·0468	·0643	·0817	·0992	·1166	·1340	·1514	·1688	·1862	41
42	·0122	·0297	·0471	·0646	·0820	·0994	·1169	·1343	·1517	·1691	·1865	42
43	·0125	·0300	·0474	·0649	·0823	·0997	·1172	·1346	·1520	·1694	·1868	43
44	·0128	·0303	·0477	·0651	·0826	·1000	·1175	·1349	·1523	·1697	·1871	44
45	·0131	·0305	·0480	·0654	·0829	·1003	·1177	·1352	·1526	·1700	·1873	45
46	·0134	·0308	·0483	·0657	·0832	·1006	·1180	·1355	·1529	·1703	·1876	46
47	·0137	·0311	·0486	·0660	·0835	·1009	·1183	·1357	·1531	·1705	·1879	47
48	·0140	·0314	·0489	·0663	·0838	·1012	·1186	·1360	·1534	·1708	·1882	48
49	·0143	·0317	·0492	·0666	·0840	·1015	·1189	·1363	·1537	·1711	·1885	49
50	·0145	·0320	·0494	·0669	·0843	·1018	·1192	·1366	·1540	·1714	·1888	50
51	·0148	·0323	·0497	·0672	·0846	·1021	·1195	·1369	·1543	·1717	·1891	51
52	·0151	·0326	·0500	·0675	·0849	·1023	·1198	·1372	·1546	·1720	·1894	52
53	·0154	·0329	·0503	·0678	·0852	·1026	·1201	·1375	·1549	·1723	·1897	53
54	·0157	·0332	·0506	·0681	·0855	·1029	·1204	·1378	·1552	·1726	·1900	54
55	·0160	·0335	·0509	·0683	·0858	·1032	·1206	·1381	·1555	·1729	·1902	55
56	·0163	·0337	·0512	·0686	·0861	·1035	·1209	·1384	·1558	·1732	·1905	56
57	·0166	·0340	·0515	·0689	·0864	·1038	·1212	·1386	·1560	·1734	·1908	57
58	·0169	·0343	·0518	·0692	·0867	·1041	·1215	·1389	·1563	·1737	·1911	58
59	·0172	0346	·0521	·0695	·0869	·1044	·1218	·1392	·1566	·1740	·1914	59
60	·0175	·0349	·0524	·0698	·0872	·1047	·1221	·1395	·1569	·1743	·1917	60

TABLE OF CHORDS: [Radius = 1.0000].

M.	11°	12°	13°	14°	15°	16°	17°	18°	19°	20°	21°	M.
0′	·1917	·2091	·2264	·2437	·2611	·2783	·2956	·3129	·3301	·3473	·3645	0′
1	·1920	·2093	·2267	·2440	·2613	·2786	·2959	·3132	·3304	·3476	·3648	1
2	·1923	·2096	·2270	·2443	·2616	·2789	·2962	·3134	·3307	·3479	·3650	2
3	·1926	·2099	·2273	·2446	·2619	·2792	·2965	·3137	·3310	·3482	·3653	3
4	·1928	·2102	·2276	·2449	·2622	·2795	·2968	·3140	·3312	·3484	·3656	4
5	·1931	·2105	·2279	·2452	·2625	·2798	·2971	·3143	·3315	·3487	·3659	5
6	·1934	·2108	·2281	·2455	·2628	·2801	·2973	·3146	·3318	·3490	·3662	6
7	·1937	·2111	·2284	·2458	·2631	·2804	·2976	·3149	·3321	·3493	·3665	7
8	·1940	·2114	·2287	·2460	·2634	·2807	·2979	·3152	·3324	·3496	·3668	8
9	·1943	·2117	·2290	·2463	·2636	·2809	·2982	·3155	·3327	·3499	·3670	9
10	·1946	·2119	·2293	·2466	·2639	·2812	·2985	·3157	·3330	·3502	·3673	10
11	·1949	·2122	·2296	·2469	·2642	·2815	·2988	·3160	·3333	·3504	·3676	11
12	·1952	·2125	·2299	·2472	·2645	·2818	2991	·3163	·3335	·3507	·3679	12
13	·1955	·2128	·2302	·2475	·2648	·2821	·2994	·3166	·3338	·3510	·3682	13
14	·1957	·2131	·2305	·2478	·2651	·2824	·2996	·3169	·3341	·3513	·3685	14
15	·1960	·2134	·2307	·2481	·2654	·2827	·2999	·3172	·3344	·3516	·3688	15
16	·1963	·2137	·2310	·2484	·2657	·2830	·3002	·3175	·3347	·3519	·3690	16
17	·1966	·2140	·2313	·2486	·2660	·2832	·3005	·3178	·3350	·3522	·3693	17
18	·1969	·2143	·2316	·2489	·2662	·2835	·3008	·3180	·3353	·3525	·3696	18
19	·1972	·2146	·2319	·2492	·2665	·2838	·3011	3183	·3355	·3527	·3699	19
20	·1975	·2148	·2322	·2495	·2668	·2841	·3014	·3186	·3358	·3530	·3702	20
21	·1978	·2151	·2325	·2498	·2671	·2844	·3017	·3189	·3361	·3533	·3705	21
22	·1981	·2154	·2328	·2501	·2674	·2847	·3019	·3192	·3364	·3536	·3708	22
23	·1983	·2157	·2331	·2504	·2677	·2850	·3022	·3195	·3367	·3539	·3710	23
24	·1986	·2160	·2333	·2507	·2680	·2853	·3025	·3198	·3370	·3542	·3713	24
25	·1989	·2163	·2336	·2510	·2683	·2855	·3028	·3200	·3373	·3545	·3716	25
26	·1992	·2166	·2339	·2512	·2685	·2858	·3031	·3203	·3376	·3547	·3719	26
27	·1995	·2169	·2342	·2515	·2688	·2861	·3034	·3206	·3378	·3550	·3722	27
28	·1998	·2172	·2345	·2518	·2691	·2864	·3037	·3209	·3381	·3553	·3725	28
29	·2001	·2174	·2348	·2521	·2694	·2867	·3040	·3212	·3384	·3556	·3728	29
30	·2004	·2177	·2351	·2524	·2697	·2870	·3042	·3215	·3387	·3559	·3730	30
31	·2007	·2180	·2354	·2527	·2700	·2873	·3045	·3218	·3390	·3562	·3733	31
32	·2010	·2183	·2357	·2530	·2703	·2876	·3048	·3221	·3393	·3565	·3736	32
33	·2012	·2186	·2359	·2533	·2706	·2878	·3051	·3223	·3396	·3567	·3739	33
34	·2015	·2189	·2362	·2536	·2709	·2881	·3054	·3226	·3398	·3570	·3742	34
35	·2018	·2192	·2365	·2538	·2711	·2884	·3057	·3229	·3401	·3573	·3745	35
36	·2021	·2195	·2368	·2541	·2714	·2887	·3060	·3232	·3404	·3576	·3748	36
37	·2024	·2198	·2371	·2544	·2717	·2890	·3063	·3235	·3407	·3579	·3750	37
38	·2027	·2200	·2374	·2547	·2720	·2893	·3065	·3238	·3410	·3582	·3753	38
39	·2030	·2203	·2377	·2550	·2723	·2896	·3068	·3241	·3413	·3585	·3756	39
40	·2033	·2206	·2380	·2553	·2726	·2899	·3071	·3244	·3416	·3587	·3759	40
41	·2036	·2209	·2383	·2556	·2729	·2902	·3074	·3246	·3419	·3590	·3762	41
42	·2038	·2212	·2385	·2559	·2732	·2904	·3077	·3249	·3421	·3593	·3765	42
43	·2041	·2215	·2388	·2561	·2734	·2907	·3080	·3252	·3424	·3596	·3768	43
44	·2044	·2218	·2391	·2564	·2737	·2910	·3083	·3255	·3427	·3599	·3770	44
45	·2047	·2221	·2394	·2567	·2740	·2913	·3086	·3258	·3430	·3602	·3773	45
46	·2050	·2224	·2397	·2570	·2743	·2916	·3088	·3261	·3433	·3605	·3776	46
47	·2053	·2226	·2400	·2573	·2746	·2919	·3091	·3264	·3436	·3608	·3779	47
48	·2056	·2229	·2403	·2576	·2749	·2922	·3094	·3267	·3439	·3610	·3782	48
49	·2059	·2232	·2406	·2579	·2752	·2925	·3097	·3269	·3441	·3613	·3785	49
50	·2062	·2235	·2409	·2582	·2755	·2927	·3100	·3272	·3444	·3616	·3788	50
51	·2065	·2238	·2411	·2585	·2758	·2930	·3103	·3275	·3447	·3619	·3790	51
52	·2067	·2241	·2414	·2587	2760	·2933	·3106	·3278	·3450	·3622	·3793	52
53	·2070	·2244	·2417	·2590	·2763	·2936	·3109	·3281	·3453	·3625	·3796	53
54	·2073	·2247	·2420	·2593	·2766	·2939	·3111	·3284	·3456	·3628	·3799	54
55	·2076	·2250	·2423	·2596	·2769	·2942	·3114	·3287	·3459	·3630	·3802	55
56	·2079	·2253	·2426	·2599	·2772	·2945	·3117	·3289	·3462	·3633	·3805	56
57	·2082	·2255	·2429	·2602	·2775	·2948	·3120	·3292	·3464	·3636	·3808	57
58	·2085	·2258	·2432	·2605	·2778	·2950	·3123	·3295	·3467	·3639	·3810	58
59	·2088	·2261	·2434	·2608	·2781	·2953	·3126	·3298	·3470	·3642	·3813	59
60	·2091	·2264	·2437	·2611	·2783	·2956	·3129	·3301	·3473	3645	·3816	60

TABLE OF CHORDS: [Radius = 1.0000].

M.	22°	23°	24°	25°	26°	27°	28°	29°	30°	31°	32°	M.
0'	.3816	.3987	.4158	.4329	.4499	.4669	.4838	.5008	.5176	.5345	.5513	0'
1	.3819	.3990	.4161	.4332	.4502	.4672	.4841	.5010	.5179	.5348	.5516	1
2	.3822	.3993	.4164	.4334	.4505	.4675	.4844	.5013	.5182	.5350	.5518	2
3	.3825	.3996	.4167	.4337	.4508	.4677	.4847	.5016	.5185	.5353	.5521	3
4	.3828	.3999	.4170	.4340	.4510	.4680	.4850	.5019	.5188	.5356	.5524	4
5	.3830	.4002	.4172	.4343	.4513	.4683	.4853	.5022	.5190	.5359	.5527	5
6	.3833	.4004	.4175	.4346	.4516	.4686	.4855	.5024	.5193	.5362	.5530	6
7	.3836	.4007	.4178	.4349	.4519	.4689	.4858	.5027	.5196	.5364	.5532	7
8	.3839	.4010	.4181	.4352	.4522	.4692	.4861	.5030	.5199	.5367	.5535	8
9	.3842	.4013	.4184	.4354	.4525	.4694	.4864	.5033	.5202	.5370	.5538	9
10	.3845	.4016	.4187	.4357	.4527	.4697	.4867	.5036	.5204	.5373	.5541	10
11	.3848	.4019	.4190	.4360	.4530	.4700	.4869	.5039	.5207	.5376	.5543	11
12	.3850	.4022	.4192	.4363	.4533	.4703	.4872	.5041	.5210	.5378	.5546	12
13	.3853	.4024	.4195	.4366	.4536	.4706	.4875	.5044	.5213	.5381	.5549	13
14	.3856	.4027	.4198	.4369	.4539	.4708	.4878	.5047	.5216	.5384	.5552	14
15	.3859	.4030	.4201	.4371	.4542	.4711	.4881	.5050	.5219	.5387	.5555	15
16	.3862	.4033	.4204	.4374	.4544	.4714	.4884	.5053	.5221	.5390	.5557	16
17	.3865	.4036	.4207	.4377	.4547	.4717	.4886	.5055	.5224	.5392	.5560	17
18	.3868	.4039	.4209	.4380	.4550	.4720	.4889	.5058	.5227	.5395	.5563	18
19	.3870	.4042	.4212	.4383	.4553	.4723	.4892	.5061	.5230	.5398	.5566	19
20	.3873	.4044	.4215	.4386	.4556	.4725	.4895	.5064	.5233	.5401	.5569	20
21	.3876	.4047	.4218	.4388	.4559	.4728	.4898	.5067	.5235	.5404	.5571	21
22	.3879	.4050	.4221	.4391	.4561	.4731	.4901	.5070	.5238	.5406	.5574	22
23	.3882	.4053	.4224	.4394	.4564	.4734	.4903	.5072	.5241	.5409	.5577	23
24	.3885	.4056	.4226	.4397	.4567	.4737	.4906	.5075	.5244	.5412	.5580	24
25	.3888	.4059	.4229	.4400	.4570	.4740	.4909	.5078	.5247	.5415	.5583	25
26	.3890	.4061	.4232	.4403	.4573	.4742	.4912	.5081	.5249	.5418	.5585	26
27	.3893	.4064	.4235	.4405	.4576	.4745	.4915	.5084	.5252	.5420	.5588	27
28	.3896	.4067	.4238	.4408	.4578	.4748	.4917	.5086	.5255	.5423	.5591	28
29	.3899	.4070	.4241	.4411	.4581	.4751	.4920	.5089	.5258	.5426	.5594	29
30	.3902	.4073	.4244	.4414	.4584	.4754	.4923	.5092	.5261	.5429	.5597	30
31	.3905	.4076	.4246	.4417	.4587	.4757	.4926	.5095	.5263	.5432	.5599	31
32	.3908	.4079	.4249	.4420	.4590	.4759	.4929	.5098	.5266	.5434	.5602	32
33	.3910	.4081	.4252	.4422	.4593	.4762	.4932	.5100	.5269	.5437	.5605	33
34	.3913	.4084	.4255	.4425	.4595	.4765	.4934	.5103	.5272	.5440	.5608	34
35	.3916	.4087	.4258	.4428	.4598	.4768	.4937	.5106	.5275	.5443	.5611	35
36	.3919	.4090	.4261	.4431	.4601	.4771	.4940	.5109	.5277	.5446	.5613	36
37	.3922	.4093	.4263	.4434	.4604	.4773	.4943	.5112	.5280	.5448	.5616	37
38	.3925	.4096	.4266	.4437	.4607	.4776	.4946	.5115	.5283	.5451	.5619	38
39	.3927	.4098	.4269	.4439	.4609	.4779	.4948	.5117	.5286	.5454	.5622	39
40	.3930	.4101	.4272	.4442	.4612	.4782	.4951	.5120	.5289	.5457	.5625	40
41	.3933	.4104	.4275	.4445	.4615	.4785	.4954	.5123	.5291	.5460	.5627	41
42	.3936	.4107	.4278	.4448	.4618	.4788	.4957	.5126	.5294	.5462	.5630	42
43	.3939	.4110	.4280	.4451	.4621	.4790	.4960	.5129	.5297	.5465	.5633	43
44	.3942	.4113	.4283	.4454	.4624	.4793	.4963	.5131	.5300	.5468	.5636	44
45	.3945	.4116	.4286	.4456	.4626	.4796	.4965	.5134	.5303	.5471	.5638	45
46	.3947	.4118	.4289	.4459	.4629	.4799	.4968	.5137	.5306	.5474	5641	46
47	.3950	.4121	.4292	.4462	.4632	.4802	.4971	.5140	.5308	.5476	.5644	47
48	.3953	.4124	.4295	.4465	.4635	.4805	.4974	.5143	.5311	.5479	.5647	48
49	.3956	.4127	.4298	.4468	.4638	.4807	.4977	.5145	.5314	.5482	.5650	49
50	.3959	.4130	.4300	.4471	.4641	.4810	.4979	.5148	.5317	.5485	.5652	50
51	.3962	.4133	.4303	.4474	.4643	.4813	.4982	.5151	.5320	.5488	.5655	51
52	.3965	.4135	.4306	.4476	.4646	.4816	.4985	.5154	.5322	.5490	.5658	52
53	.3967	.4138	.4309	.4479	.4649	.4819	.4988	.5157	.5325	.5493	.5661	53
54	.3970	.4141	.4312	.4482	.4652	.4822	.4991	.5160	.5328	.5496	.5664	54
55	.3973	.4144	.4315	.4485	.4655	.4824	.4994	.5162	.5331	.5499	.5666	55
56	.3976	.4147	.4317	.4488	.4658	.4827	.4996	.5165	.5334	.5502	.5669	56
57	.3979	.4150	.4320	.4491	.4660	.4830	.4999	.5168	.5336	.5504	.5672	57
58	.3982	.4153	.4323	.4493	.4663	.4833	.5002	.5171	.5339	.5507	.5675	58
59	.3985	.4155	.4326	.4496	.4666	.4836	.5005	.5174	.5342	.5510	.5678	59
60	.3987	.4158	.4329	.4499	.4669	.4838	.5008	.5176	.5345	.5513	.5680	60

TABLE OF CHORDS: [Radius = 1.0000].

M.	33°	34°	35°	36°	37°	38°	39°	40°	41°	42°	43°	M.
0'	.5680	.5847	.6014	.6180	.6346	.6511	.6676	.6840	.7004	.7167	.7330	0
1	.5683	.5850	.6017	.6183	.6349	.6514	.6679	.6843	.7007	.7170	.7333	1
2	.5686	.5853	.6020	.6186	.6352	.6517	.6682	.6846	.7010	.7173	.7335	2
3	.5689	.5856	.6022	.6189	.6354	.6520	.6684	.6849	.7012	.7176	.7338	3
4	.5691	.5859	.6025	.6191	.6357	.6522	.6687	.6851	.7015	.7178	.7341	4
5	.5694	.5861	.6028	.6194	.6360	.6525	.6690	.6854	.7018	.7181	.7344	5
6	.5697	.5864	.6031	.6197	.6363	.6528	.6693	.6857	.7020	.7184	.7346	6
7	.5700	.5867	.6034	.6200	.6365	.6531	.6695	.6860	.7023	.7186	.7349	7
8	.5703	.5870	.6036	.6202	.6368	.6533	.6698	.6862	.7026	.7189	.7352	8
9	.5705	.5872	.6039	.6205	.6371	.6536	.6701	.6865	.7029	.7192	.7354	9
10	.5708	.5875	.6042	.6208	.6374	.6539	.6704	.6868	.7031	.7195	.7357	10
11	.5711	.5878	.6045	.6211	.6376	.6542	.6706	.6870	.7034	.7197	.7360	11
12	.5714	.5881	.6047	.6214	.6379	.6544	.6709	.6873	.7037	.7200	.7362	12
13	.5717	.5884	.6050	.6216	.6382	.6547	.6712	.6876	.7040	.7203	.7365	13
14	.5719	.5886	.6053	.6219	.6385	.6550	.6715	.6879	.7042	.7205	.7368	14
15	.5722	.5889	.6056	.6222	.6387	.6553	.6717	.6881	.7045	.7208	.7371	15
16	.5725	.5892	.6058	.6225	.6390	.6555	.6720	.6884	.7048	.7211	.7373	16
17	.5728	.5895	.6061	.6227	.6393	.6558	.6723	.6887	.7050	.7214	.7376	17
18	.5730	.5897	.6064	.6230	.6396	.6561	.6725	.6890	.7053	.7216	.7379	18
19	.5733	.5900	.6067	.6233	.6398	.6564	.6728	.6892	.7056	.7219	.7381	19
20	.5736	.5903	.6070	.6236	.6401	.6566	.6731	.6895	.7059	.7222	.7384	20
21	.5739	.5906	.6072	.6238	.6404	.6569	.6734	.6898	.7061	.7224	.7387	21
22	.5742	.5909	.6075	.6241	.6407	.6572	.6736	.6901	.7064	.7227	.7390	22
23	.5744	.5911	.6078	.6244	.6410	.6575	.6739	.6903	.7067	.7230	.7392	23
24	.5747	.5914	.6081	.6247	.6412	.6577	.6742	.6906	.7069	.7232	.7395	24
25	.5750	.5917	.6083	.6249	.6415	.6580	.6745	.6909	.7072	.7235	.7398	25
26	.5753	.5920	.6086	.6252	.6418	.6583	.6747	.6911	.7075	.7238	.7400	26
27	.5756	.5922	.6089	.6255	.6421	.6586	.6750	.6914	.7078	.7241	.7403	27
28	.5758	.5925	.6092	.6258	.6423	.6588	.6753	.6917	.7080	.7243	.7406	28
29	.5761	.5928	.6095	.6260	.6426	.6591	.6756	.6920	.7083	.7246	.7408	29
30	.5764	.5931	.6097	.6263	.6429	.6594	.6758	.6922	.7086	.7249	.7411	30
31	.5767	.5934	.6100	.6266	.6432	.6597	.6761	.6925	.7089	.7251	.7414	31
32	.5769	.5936	.6103	.6269	.6434	.6599	.6764	.6928	.7091	.7254	.7417	32
33	.5772	.5939	.6106	.6272	.6437	.6602	.6767	.6931	.7094	.7257	.7419	33
34	.5775	.5942	.6108	.6274	.6440	.6605	.6769	.6933	.7097	.7260	.7422	34
35	.5778	.5945	.6111	.6277	.6443	.6608	.6772	.6936	.7099	.7262	.7425	35
36	.5781	.5947	.6114	.6280	.6445	.6610	.6775	.6939	.7102	.7265	.7427	36
37	.5783	.5950	.6117	.6283	.6448	.6613	.6777	.6941	.7105	.7268	.7430	37
38	.5786	.5953	.6119	.6285	.6451	.6616	.6780	.6944	.7108	.7270	.7433	38
39	.5789	.5956	.6122	.6288	.6454	.6619	.6783	.6947	.7110	.7273	.7435	39
40	.5792	.5959	.6125	.6291	.6456	.6621	.6786	.6950	.7113	.7276	.7438	40
41	.5795	.5961	.6128	.6294	.6459	.6624	.6788	.6952	.7116	.7279	.7441	41
42	.5797	.5964	.6130	.6296	.6462	.6627	.6791	.6955	.7118	.7281	.7443	42
43	.5800	.5967	.6133	.6299	.6465	.6630	.6794	.6958	.7121	.7284	.7446	43
44	.5803	.5970	.6136	.6302	.6467	.6632	.6797	.6961	.7124	.7287	.7449	44
45	.5806	.5972	.6139	.6305	.6470	.6635	.6799	.6963	.7127	.7289	.7452	45
46	.5808	.5975	.6142	.6307	.6473	.6638	.6802	.6966	.7129	.7292	.7454	46
47	.5811	.5978	.6144	.6310	.6476	.6640	.6805	.6969	.7132	.7295	.7457	47
48	.5814	.5981	.6147	.6313	.6478	.6643	.6808	.6971	.7135	.7298	.7460	48
49	.5817	.5984	.6150	.6316	.6481	.6646	.6810	.6974	.7137	.7300	.7462	49
50	.5820	.5986	.6153	.6318	.6484	.6649	.6813	.6977	.7140	.7303	.7465	50
51	.5822	.5989	.6155	.6321	.6487	.6651	.6816	.6980	.7143	.7306	.7468	51
52	.5825	.5992	.6158	.6324	.6489	.6654	.6819	.6982	.7146	.7308	.7471	52
53	.5828	.5995	.6161	.6327	.6492	.6657	.6821	.6985	.7148	.7311	.7473	53
54	.5831	.5997	.6164	.6330	.6495	.6660	.6824	.6988	.7151	.7314	.7476	54
55	.5834	.6000	.6166	.6332	.6498	.6662	.6827	.6991	.7154	.7316	.7479	55
56	.5836	.6003	.6169	.6335	.6500	.6665	.6829	.6993	.7156	.7319	.7481	56
57	.5839	.6006	.6172	.6338	.6503	.6668	.6832	.6996	.7159	.7322	.7484	57
58	.5842	.6009	.6175	.6341	.6506	.6671	.6835	.6999	.7162	.7325	.7487	58
59	.5845	.6011	.6178	.6343	.6509	.6673	.6838	.7001	.7165	.7327	.7489	59
60	.5847	.6014	.6180	.6346	.6511	.6676	.6840	.7004	.7167	.7330	.7492	60

TABLE OF CHORDS: [Radius = 1.0000].

M.	44°	45°	46°	47°	48°	49°	50°	51°	52°	53°	54°	M.
0′	.7492	.7654	.7815	.7975	.8135	.8294	.8452	.8610	.8767	.8924	.9080	0′
1	.7495	.7656	.7817	.7978	.8137	.8297	.8455	.8613	.8770	.8927	.9082	1
2	.7498	.7659	.7820	.7980	.8140	.8299	.8458	.8615	.8773	.8929	.9085	2
3	.7500	.7662	.7823	.7983	.8143	.8302	.8460	.8618	.8775	.8932	.9088	3
4	.7503	.7664	.7825	.7986	.8145	.8304	.8463	.8621	.8778	.8934	.9090	4
5	.7506	.7667	.7828	.7988	.8148	.8307	.8466	.8623	.8780	.8937	.9093	5
6	.7508	.7670	.7831	.7991	.8151	.8310	.8468	.8626	.8783	.8940	.9095	6
7	.7511	.7672	.7833	.7994	.8153	.8312	.8471	.8629	.8786	.8942	.9098	7
8	.7514	.7675	.7836	.7996	.8156	.8315	.8473	.8631	.8788	.8945	.9101	8
9	.7516	.7678	.7839	.7999	.8159	.8318	.8476	.8634	.8791	.8947	.9103	9
10	.7519	.7681	.7841	.8002	.8161	.8320	.8479	.8636	.8794	.8950	.9106	10
11	.7522	.7683	.7844	.8004	.8164	.8323	.8481	.8639	.8796	.8953	.9108	11
12	.7524	.7686	.7847	.8007	.8167	.8326	.8484	.8642	.8799	.8955	.9111	12
13	.7527	.7689	.7849	.8010	.8169	.8328	.8487	.8644	.8801	.8958	.9113	13
14	.7530	.7691	.7852	.8012	.8172	.8331	.8489	.8647	.8804	.8960	.9116	14
15	.7533	.7694	.7855	.8015	.8175	.8334	.8492	.8650	.8807	.8963	.9119	15
16	.7535	.7697	.7857	.8018	.8177	.8336	.8495	.8652	.8809	.8966	.9121	16
17	.7538	.7699	.7860	.8020	.8180	.8339	.8497	.8655	.8812	.8968	.9124	17
18	.7541	.7702	.7863	.8023	.8183	.8341	.8500	.8657	.8814	.8971	.9126	18
19	.7543	.7705	.7865	.8026	.8185	.8344	.8502	.8660	.8817	.8973	.9129	19
20	.7546	.7707	.7868	.8028	.8188	.8347	.8505	.8663	.8820	.8976	.9132	20
21	.7549	.7710	.7871	.8031	.8190	.8349	.8508	.8665	.8822	.8979	.9134	21
22	.7551	.7713	.7873	.8034	.8193	.8352	.8510	.8668	.8825	.8981	.9137	22
23	.7554	.7715	.7876	.8036	.8196	.8355	.8513	.8671	.8828	.8984	.9139	23
24	.7557	.7718	.7879	.8039	.8198	.8357	.8516	.8673	.8830	.8986	.9142	24
25	.7560	.7721	.7882	.8042	.8201	.8360	.8518	.8676	.8833	.8989	.9145	25
26	.7562	.7723	.7884	.8044	.8204	.8363	.8521	.8678	.8835	.8992	.9147	26
27	.7565	.7726	.7887	.8047	.8206	.8365	.8523	.8681	.8838	.8994	.9150	27
28	.7568	.7729	.7890	.8050	.8209	.8368	.8526	.8684	.8841	.8997	.9152	28
29	.7570	.7731	.7892	.8052	.8212	.8371	.8529	.8686	.8843	.8999	.9155	29
30	.7573	.7734	.7895	.8055	.8214	.8373	.8531	.8689	.8846	.9002	.9157	30
31	.7576	.7737	.7898	.8058	.8217	.8376	.8534	.8692	.8848	.9005	.9160	31
32	.7578	.7740	.7900	.8060	.8220	.8378	.8537	.8694	.8851	.9007	.9163	32
33	.7581	.7742	.7903	.8063	.8222	.8381	.8539	.8697	.8854	.9010	.9165	33
34	.7584	.7745	.7906	.8066	.8225	.8384	.8542	.8699	.8856	.9012	.9168	34
35	.7586	.7748	.7908	.8068	.8228	.8386	.8545	.8702	.8859	.9015	.9170	35
36	.7589	.7750	.7911	.8071	.8230	.8389	.8547	.8705	.8861	.9018	.9173	36
37	.7592	.7753	.7914	.8074	.8233	.8392	.8550	.8707	.8864	.9020	.9176	37
38	.7595	.7756	.7916	.8076	.8236	.8394	.8552	.8710	.8867	.9023	.9178	38
39	.7597	.7758	.7919	.8079	.8238	.8397	.8555	.8712	.8869	.9025	.9181	39
40	.7600	.7761	.7922	.8082	.8241	.8400	.8558	.8715	.8872	.9028	.9183	40
41	.7603	.7764	.7924	.8084	.8244	.8402	.8560	.8718	.8874	.9031	.9186	41
42	.7605	.7766	.7927	.8087	.8246	.8405	.8563	.8720	.8877	.9033	.9188	42
43	.7608	.7769	.7930	.8090	.8249	.8408	.8566	.8723	.8880	.9036	.9191	43
44	.7611	.7772	.7932	.8092	.8251	.8410	.8568	.8726	.8882	.9038	.9194	44
45	.7613	.7774	.7935	.8095	.8254	.8413	.8571	.8728	.8885	.9041	.9196	45
46	.7616	.7777	.7938	.8098	.8257	.8415	.8573	.8731	.8887	.9044	.9199	46
47	.7619	.7780	.7940	.8100	.8259	.8418	.8576	.8734	.8890	.9046	.9201	47
48	.7621	.7782	.7943	.8103	.8262	.8421	.8579	.8736	.8893	.9049	.9204	48
49	.7624	.7785	.7946	.8105	.8265	.8423	.8581	.8739	.8895	.9051	.9207	49
50	.7627	.7788	.7948	.8108	.8267	.8426	.8584	.8741	.8898	.9054	.9209	50
51	.7629	.7791	.7951	.8111	.8270	.8429	.8587	.8744	.8900	.9056	.9212	51
52	.7632	.7793	.7954	.8113	.8273	.8431	.8589	.8747	.8903	.9059	.9214	52
53	.7635	.7796	.7956	.8116	.8275	.8434	.8592	.8749	.8906	.9062	.9217	53
54	.7638	.7799	.7959	8119	.8278	.8437	.8594	.8752	.8908	.9064	.9219	54
55	.7640	.7801	.7962	.8121	.8281	.8439	.8597	.8754	.8911	.9067	.9222	55
56	.7643	.7804	.7964	.8124	.8283	.8442	.8600	.8757	.8914	.9069	.9225	56
57	.7646	.7807	.7967	.8127	.8286	.8444	.8602	.8760	.8916	.9072	.9227	57
58	.7648	.7809	.7970	.8129	.8289	.8447	.8605	.8762	.8919	.9075	.9230	58
59	.7651	.7812	.7972	.8132	.8291	.8450	.8608	.8765	.8921	.9077	.9232	59
60	.7654	.7815	.7975	.8135	.8294	.8452	.8610	.8767	.8924	.9080	.9235	60

TABLE OF CHORDS: [Radius = 1.0000].

M.	55°	56°	57°	58°	59°	60°	61°	62°	63°	64°	M.
0′	·9235	·9389	·9543	·9696	·9848	1·0000	1·0151	1·0301	1·0450	1·0598	0′
1	·9238	·9392	·9546	·9699	·9851	1·0003	1·0153	1·0303	1·0452	1·0601	1
2	·9240	·9395	·9548	·9701	·9854	1·0005	1·0156	1·0306	1·0455	1·0603	2
3	·9243	·9397	·9551	·9704	·9856	1·0008	1·0158	1·0308	1·0457	1·0606	3
4	·9245	·9400	·9553	·9706	·9859	1·0010	1·0161	1·0311	1·0460	1·0608	4
5	·9248	·9402	·9556	·9709	·9861	1·0013	1·0163	1·0313	1·0462	1·0611	5
6	·9250	·9405	·9559	·9711	·9864	1·0015	1·0166	1·0316	1·0465	1·0613	6
7	·9253	·9407	·9561	·9714	·9866	1·0018	1·0168	1·0318	1·0467	1·0616	7
8	·9256	·9410	·9564	·9717	·9869	1·0020	1·0171	1·0321	1·0470	1·0618	8
9	·9258	·9413	·9566	·9719	·9871	1·0023	1·0173	1·0323	1·0472	1·0621	9
10	·9261	·9415	·9569	·9722	·9874	1·0025	1·0176	1·0326	1·0475	1·0623	10
11	·9263	·9418	·9571	·9724	·9876	1·0028	1·0178	1·0328	1·0477	1·0626	11
12	·9266	·9420	·9574	·9727	·9879	1·0030	1·0181	1·0331	1·0480	1·0628	12
13	·9268	·9423	·9576	·9729	·9881	1·0033	1·0183	1·0333	1·0482	1·0630	13
14	·9271	·9425	·9579	·9732	·9884	1·0035	1·0186	1·0336	1·0485	1·0633	14
15	·9274	·9428	·9581	·9734	·9886	1·0038	1·0188	1·0338	1·0487	1·0635	15
16	·9276	·9430	·9584	·9737	·9889	1·0040	1·0191	1·0341	1·0490	1·0638	16
17	·9279	·9433	·9587	·9739	·9891	1·0043	1·0193	1·0343	1·0492	1·0640	17
18	·9281	·9436	·9589	·9742	·9894	1·0045	1·0196	1·0346	1·0495	1·0643	18
19	·9284	·9438	·9592	·9744	·9897	1·0048	1·0198	1·0348	1·0497	1·0645	19
20	·9287	·9441	·9594	·9747	·9899	1·0050	1·0201	1·0351	1·0500	1·0648	20
21	·9289	·9443	·9597	·9750	·9902	1·0053	1·0203	1·0353	1·0502	1·0650	21
22	·9292	·9446	·9599	·9752	·9904	1·0055	1·0206	1·0356	1·0504	1·0653	22
23	·9294	·9448	·9602	·9755	·9907	1·0058	1·0208	1·0358	1·0507	1·0655	23
24	·9297	·9451	·9604	·9757	·9909	1·0060	1·0211	1·0361	1·0509	1·0658	24
25	·9299	·9454	·9607	·9760	·9912	1·0063	1·0213	1·0363	1·0512	1·0660	25
26	·9302	·9456	·9610	·9762	·9914	1·0065	1·0216	1·0366	1·0514	1·0662	26
27	·9305	·9459	·9612	·9765	·9917	1·0068	1·0218	1·0368	1·0517	1·0665	27
28	·9307	·9461	·9615	·9767	·9919	1·0070	1·0221	1·0370	1·0519	1·0667	28
29	·9310	·9464	·9617	·9770	·9922	1·0073	1·0223	1·0373	1·0522	1·0670	29
30	·9312	·9466	·9620	·9772	·9924	1·0075	1·0226	1·0375	1·0524	1·0672	30
31	·9315	·9469	·9622	·9775	·9927	1·0078	1·0228	1·0378	1·0527	1·0675	31
32	·9317	·9472	·9625	·9778	·9929	1·0080	1·0231	1·0380	1·0529	1·0677	32
33	·9320	·9474	·9627	·9780	·9932	1·0083	1·0233	1·0383	1·0532	1·0680	33
34	·9323	·9477	·9630	·9783	·9934	1·0086	1·0236	1·0385	1·0534	1·0682	34
35	·9325	·9479	·9633	·9785	·9937	1·0088	1·0238	1·0388	1·0537	1·0685	35
36	·9328	·9482	·9635	·9788	·9939	1·0091	1·0241	1·0390	1·0539	1·0687	36
37	·9330	·9484	·9638	·9790	·9942	1·0093	1·0243	1·0393	1·0542	1·0690	37
38	·9333	·9487	·9640	·9793	·9945	1·0096	1·0246	1·0395	1·0544	1·0692	38
39	·9335	·9489	·9643	·9795	·9947	1·0098	1·0248	1·0398	1·0547	1·0694	39
40	·9338	·9492	·9645	·9798	·9950	1·0101	1·0251	1·0400	1·0549	1·0697	40
41	·9341	·9495	·9648	·9800	·9952	1·0103	1·0253	1·0403	1·0551	1·0699	41
42	·9343	·9497	·9650	·9803	·9955	1·0106	1·0256	1·0405	1·0554	1·0702	42
43	·9346	·9500	·9653	·9805	·9957	1·0108	1·0258	1·0408	1·0556	1·0704	43
44	·9348	·9502	·9655	·9808	·9960	1·0111	1·0261	1·0410	1·0559	1·0707	44
45	·9351	·9505	·9658	·0810	·9962	1·0113	1·0263	1·0413	1·0561	1·0709	45
46	·9353	·9507	·9661	·9813	·9965	1·0116	1·0266	1·0415	1·0564	1·0712	46
47	·9356	·9510	·9663	·9816	·9967	1·0118	1·0268	1·0418	1·0566	1·0714	47
48	·9359	·9512	·9666	·9818	·9970	1·0121	1·0271	1·0420	1·0569	1·0717	48
49	·9361	·9515	·9668	·9821	·9972	1·0123	1·0273	1·0423	1·0571	1·0719	49
50	·9364	·9518	·9671	·9823	·9975	1·0126	1·0276	1·0425	1·0574	1·0721	50
51	·9366	·9520	·9673	·9826	·9977	1·0128	1·0278	1·0428	1·0576	1·0724	51
52	·9369	·9523	·9676	·9828	·9980	1·0131	1·0281	1·0430	1·0579	1·0726	52
53	·9371	·9525	·9678	·9831	·9982	1·0133	1·0283	1·0433	1·0581	1·0729	53
54	·9374	·9528	·9681	·9833	·9985	1·0136	1·0286	1·0435	1·0584	1·0731	54
55	·9377	·9530	·9683	·9836	·9987	1·0138	1·0288	1·0438	1·0586	1·0734	55
56	·9379	·9533	·9686	·9838	·9990	1·0141	1·0291	1·0440	1·0589	1·0736	56
57	·9382	·9536	·9689	·9841	·9992	1·0143	1·0293	1·0443	1·0591	1·0739	57
58	·9384	·9538	·9691	·9843	·9995	1·0146	1·0296	1·0445	1·0593	1·0741	58
59	·9387	·9541	·9694	·9846	·9998	1·0148	1·0298	1·0447	1·0596	1·0744	59
60	·9389	·9543	·9696	·9848	10000	1·0151	1·0301	1·0450	1·0598	1·0746	60

TABLE OF CHORDS: [Radius = 1.0000].

M.	65°	66°	67°	68°	69°	70°	71°	72°	73°	M.
0′	1·0746	1·0893	1·1039	1·1184	1·1328	1·1472	1·1614	1·1756	1·1896	0′
1	1·0748	1·0895	1·1041	1·1186	1·1331	1·1474	1·1616	1·1758	1·1899	1
2	1·0751	1·0898	1·1044	1·1189	1·1333	1·1476	1·1619	1·1760	1·1901	2
3	1·0753	1·0900	1·1046	1·1191	1·1335	1·1479	1·1621	1·1763	1·1903	3
4	1·0756	1·0903	1·1048	1·1194	1·1338	1·1481	1·1624	1·1765	1·1906	4
5	1·0758	1·0905	1·1051	1·1196	1·1340	1·1483	1·1626	1·1767	1·1908	5
6	1·0761	1·0907	1·1053	1·1198	1·1342	1·1486	1·1628	1·1770	1·1910	6
7	1·0763	1·0910	1·1056	1·1201	1·1345	1·1488	1·1631	1·1772	1·1913	7
8	1·0766	1·0912	1·1058	1·1203	1·1347	1·1491	1·1633	1·1775	1·1915	8
9	1·0768	1·0915	1·1061	1·1206	1·1350	1·1493	1·1635	1·1777	1·1917	9
10	1·0771	1·0917	1·1063	1·1208	1·1352	1·1495	1·1638	1·1779	1·1920	10
11	1·0773	1·0920	1·1065	1·1210	1·1354	1·1498	1·1640	1·1782	1·1922	11
12	1·0775	1·0922	1·1068	1·1213	1·1357	1·1500	1·1642	1·1784	1·1924	12
13	1·0778	1·0924	1·1070	1·1215	1·1359	1·1502	1·1645	1·1786	1·1927	13
14	1·0780	1·0927	1·1073	1·1218	1·1362	1·1505	1·1647	1·1789	1·1929	14
15	1·0783	1·0929	1·1075	1·1220	1·1364	1·1507	1·1650	1·1791	1·1931	15
16	1·0785	1·0932	1·1078	1·1222	1·1366	1·1510	1·1652	1·1793	1·1934	16
17	1·0788	1·0934	1·1080	1·1225	1·1369	1·1512	1·1654	1·1796	1·1936	17
18	1·0790	1·0937	1·1082	1·1227	1·1371	1·1514	1·1657	1·1798	1·1938	18
19	1·0793	1·0939	1·1085	1·1230	1·1374	1·1517	1·1659	1·1800	1·1941	19
20	1·0795	1·0942	1·1087	1·1232	1·1376	1·1519	1·1661	1·1803	1·1943	20
21	1·0797	1·0944	1·1090	1·1234	1·1378	1·1522	1·1664	1·1805	1·1946	21
22	1·0800	1·0946	1·1092	1·1237	1·1381	1·1524	1·1666	1·1807	1·1948	22
23	1·0802	1·0949	1·1094	1·1239	1·1383	1·1526	1·1668	1·1810	1·1950	23
24	1·0805	1·0951	1·1097	1·1242	1·1386	1·1529	1·1671	1·1812	1·1952	24
25	1·0807	1·0954	1·1099	1·1244	1·1388	1·1531	1·1673	1·1814	1·1955	25
26	1·0810	1·0956	1·1102	1·1246	1·1390	1·1533	1·1676	1·1817	1·1957	26
27	1·0812	1·0959	1·1104	1·1249	1·1393	1·1536	1·1678	1·1819	1·1959	27
28	1·0815	1·0961	1·1107	1·1251	1·1395	1·1538	1·1680	1·1821	1·1962	28
29	1·0817	1·0963	1·1109	1·1254	1·1398	1·1541	1·1683	1·1824	1·1964	29
30	1·0820	1·0966	1·1111	1·1256	1·1400	1·1543	1·1685	1·1826	1·1966	30
31	1·0822	1·0968	1·1114	1·1258	1·1402	1·1545	1·1687	1·1829	1·1969	31
32	1·0824	1·0971	1·1116	1·1261	1·1405	1·1548	1·1690	1·1831	1·1971	32
33	1·0827	1·0973	1·1119	1·1263	1·1407	1·1550	1·1692	1·1833	1·1973	33
34	1·0829	1·0976	1·1121	1·1266	1·1409	1·1552	1·1694	1·1836	1·1976	34
35	1·0832	1·0978	1·1123	1·1268	1·1412	1·1555	1·1697	1·1838	1·1978	35
36	1·0834	1·0980	1·1126	1·1271	1·1414	1·1557	1·1699	1·1840	1·1980	36
37	1·0837	1·0983	1·1128	1·1273	1·1417	1·1560	1·1702	1·1843	1·1983	37
38	1·0839	1·0985	1·1131	1·1275	1·1419	1·1562	1·1704	1·1845	1·1985	38
39	1·0841	1·0988	1·1133	1·1278	1·1421	1·1564	1·1706	1·1847	1·1987	39
40	1·0844	1·0990	1·1136	1·1280	1·1424	1·1567	1·1709	1·1850	1·1990	40
41	1·0846	1·0993	1·1138	1·1283	1·1426	1·1569	1·1711	1·1852	1·1992	41
42	1·0849	1·0995	1·1140	1·1285	1·1429	1·1571	1·1713	1·1854	1·1994	42
43	1·0851	1·0997	1·1143	1·1287	1·1431	1·1574	1·1716	1·1857	1·1997	43
44	1·0854	1·1000	1·1145	1·1290	1·1433	1·1576	1·1718	1·1859	1·1999	44
45	1·0856	1·1002	1·1148	1·1292	1·1436	1·1579	1·1720	1·1861	1·2001	45
46	1·0859	1·1005	1·1150	1·1295	1·1438	1·1581	1·1723	1·1864	1·2004	46
47	1·0861	1·1007	1·1152	1·1297	1·1441	1·1583	1·1725	1·1866	1·2006	47
48	1·0863	1·1010	1·1155	1·1299	1·1443	1·1586	1·1727	1·1868	1·2008	48
49	1·0866	1·1012	1·1157	1·1302	1·1445	1·1588	1·1730	1·1871	1·2011	49
50	1·0868	1·1014	1·1160	1·1304	1·1448	1·1590	1·1732	1·1873	1·2013	50
51	1·0871	1·1017	1·1162	1·1307	1·1450	1·1593	1·1735	1·1875	1·2015	51
52	1·0873	1·1019	1·1165	1·1309	1·1452	1·1595	1·1737	1·1878	1·2018	52
53	1·0876	1·1022	1·1167	1·1311	1·1455	1·1598	1·1739	1·1880	1·2020	53
54	1·0878	1·1024	1·1169	1·1314	1·1457	1·1600	1·1742	1·1882	1·2022	54
55	1·0881	1·1027	1·1172	1·1316	1·1460	1·1602	1·1744	1·1885	1·2025	55
56	1·0883	1·1029	1·1174	1·1319	1·1462	1·1605	1·1746	1·1887	1·2027	56
57	1·0885	1·1031	1·1177	1·1321	1·1464	1·1607	1·1749	1·1889	1·2029	57
58	1·0888	1·1034	1·1179	1·1323	1·1467	1·1609	1·1751	1·1892	1·2032	58
59	1·0890	1·1036	1·1181	1·1326	1·1469	1·1612	1·1753	1·1894	1·2034	59
60	1·0893	1·1039	1·1184	1·1328	1·1472	1·1614	1·1756	1·1896	1·2036	60

TABLE OF CHORDS: [Radius = 1.0000].

M.	74°	75°	76°	77°	78°	79°	80°	81°	82°	M.
0′	1·2036	1·2175	1·2313	1·2450	1·2586	1·2722	1·2856	1·2989	1·3121	0′
1	1·2039	1·2178	1·2316	1·2453	1·2589	1·2724	1·2858	1·2991	1·3123	1
2	1·2041	1·2180	1·2318	1·2455	1·2591	1·2726	1·2860	1·2993	1·3126	2
3	1·2043	1·2182	1·2320	1·2457	1·2593	1·2728	1·2862	1·2996	1·3128	3
4	1·2046	1·2184	1·2322	1·2459	1·2595	1·2731	1·2865	1·2998	1·3130	4
5	1·2048	1·2187	1·2325	1·2462	1·2598	1·2733	1·2867	1·3000	1·3132	5
6	1·2050	1·2189	1·2327	1·2464	1·2600	1·2735	1·2869	1·3002	1·3134	6
7	1·2053	1·2191	1·2329	1·2466	1·2602	1·2737	1·2871	1·3004	1·3137	7
8	1·2055	1·2194	1·2332	1·2468	1·2604	1·2740	1·2874	1·3007	1·3139	8
9	1·2057	1·2196	1·2334	1·2471	1·2607	1·2742	1·2876	1·3009	1·3141	9
10	1·2060	1·2198	1·2336	1·2473	1·2609	1·2744	1·2878	1·3011	1·3143	10
11	1·2062	1·2201	1·2338	1·2475	1·2611	1·2746	1·2880	1·3013	1·3145	11
12	1·2064	1·2203	1·2341	1·2478	1·2614	1·2748	1·2882	1·3015	1·3147	12
13	1·2066	1·2205	1·2343	1·2480	1·2616	1·2751	1·2885	1·3018	1·3150	13
14	1·2069	1·2208	1·2345	1·2482	1·2618	1·2753	1·2887	1·3020	1·3152	14
15	1·2071	1·2210	1·2348	1·2484	1·2620	1·2755	1·2889	1·3022	1·3154	15
16	1·2073	1·2212	1·2350	1·2487	1·2623	1·2757	1·2891	1·3024	1·3156	16
17	1·2076	1·2214	1·2352	1·2489	1·2625	1·2760	1·2894	1·3027	1·3158	17
18	1·2078	1·2217	1·2354	1·2491	1·2627	1·2762	1·2896	1·3029	1·3161	18
19	1·2080	1·2219	1·2357	1·2493	1·2629	1·2764	1·2898	1·3031	1·3163	19
20	1·2083	1·2221	1·2359	1·2496	1·2632	1·2766	1·2900	1·3033	1·3165	20
21	1·2085	1·2224	1·2361	1·2498	1·2634	1·2769	1·2903	1·3035	1·3167	21
22	1·2087	1·2226	1·2364	1·2500	1·2636	1·2771	1·2905	1·3038	1·3169	22
23	1·2090	1·2228	1·2366	1·2503	1·2638	1·2773	1·2907	1·3040	1·3172	23
24	1·2092	1·2231	1·2368	1·2505	1·2641	1·2775	1·2909	1·3042	1·3174	24
25	1·2094	1·2233	1·2370	1·2507	1·2643	1·2778	1·2911	1·3044	1·3176	25
26	1·2097	1·2235	1·2373	1·2509	1·2645	1·2780	1·2914	1·3046	1·3178	26
27	1·2099	1·2237	1·2375	1·2512	1·2648	1·2782	1·2916	1·3049	1·3180	27
28	1·2101	1·2240	1·2377	1·2514	1·2650	1·2784	1·2918	1·3051	1·3183	28
29	1·2104	1·2242	1·2380	1·2516	1·2652	1·2787	1·2920	1·3053	1·3185	29
30	1·2106	1·2244	1·2382	1·2518	1·2654	1·2789	1·2922	1·3055	1·3187	30
31	1·2108	1·2247	1·2384	1·2521	1·2656	1·2791	1·2925	1·3057	1·3189	31
32	1·2111	1·2249	1·2386	1·2523	1·2659	1·2793	1·2927	1·3060	1·3191	32
33	1·2113	1·2251	1·2389	1·2525	1·2661	1·2795	1·2929	1·3062	1·3193	33
34	1·2115	1·2254	1·2391	1·2528	1·2663	1·2798	1·2931	1·3064	1·3196	34
35	1·2117	1·2256	1·2393	1·2530	1·2665	1·2800	1·2934	1·3066	1·3198	35
36	1·2120	1·2258	1·2396	1·2532	1·2668	1·2802	1·2936	1·3068	1·3200	36
37	1·2122	1·2260	1·2398	1·2534	1·2670	1·2804	1·2938	1·3071	1·3202	37
38	1·2124	1·2263	1·2400	1·2537	1·2672	1·2807	1·2940	1·3073	1·3204	38
39	1·2127	1·2265	1·2402	1·2539	1·2674	1·2809	1·2942	1·3075	1·3207	39
40	1·2129	1·2267	1·2405	1·2541	1·2677	1·2811	1·2945	1·3077	1·3209	40
41	1·2131	1·2270	1·2407	1·2543	1·2679	1·2813	1·2947	1·3079	1·3211	41
42	1·2134	1·2272	1·2409	1·2546	1·2681	1·2816	1·2949	1·3082	1·3213	42
43	1·2136	1·2274	1·2412	1·2548	1·2683	1·2818	1·2951	1·3084	1·3215	43
44	1·2138	1·2277	1·2414	1·2550	1·2686	1·2820	1·2954	1·3086	1·3218	44
45	1·2141	1·2279	1·2416	1·2552	1·2688	1·2822	1·2956	1·3088	1·3220	45
46	1·2143	1·2281	1·2418	1·2555	1·2690	1·2825	1·2958	1·3090	1·3222	46
47	1·2145	1·2283	1·2421	1·2557	1·2692	1·2827	1·2960	1·3093	1·3224	47
48	1·2148	1·2286	1·2423	1·2559	1·2695	1·2829	1·2962	1·3095	1·3226	48
49	1·2150	1·2288	1·2425	1·2562	1·2697	1·2831	1·2965	1·3097	1·3228	49
50	1·2152	1·2290	1·2428	1·2564	1·2699	1·2833	1·2967	1·3099	1·3231	50
51	1·2154	1·2293	1·2430	1·2566	1·2701	1·2836	1·2969	1·3101	1·3233	51
52	1·2157	1·2295	1·2432	1·2568	1·2704	1·2838	1·2971	1·3104	1·3235	52
53	1·2159	1·2297	1·2434	1·2571	1·2706	1·2840	1·2973	1·3106	1·3237	53
54	1·2161	1·2299	1·2437	1·2573	1·2708	1·2842	1·2976	1·3108	1·3239	54
55	1·2164	1·2302	1·2439	1·2575	1·2710	1·2845	1·2978	1·3110	1·3242	55
56	1·2166	1·2304	1·2441	1·2577	1·2713	1·2847	1·2980	1·3112	1·3244	56
57	1·2168	1·2306	1·2443	1·2580	1·2715	1·2849	1·2982	1·3115	1·3246	57
58	1·2171	1·2309	1·2446	1·2582	1·2717	1·2851	1·2985	1·3117	1·3248	58
59	1·2173	1·2311	1·2448	1·2584	1·2719	1·2854	1·2987	1·3119	1·3250	59
60	1·2175	1·2313	1·2450	1·2586	1·2722	1·2856	1·2989	1·3121	1·3252	60

TABLE OF CHORDS: [Radius = 1.0000].

M.	83°	84°	85°	86°	87°	88°	89°	M.
0'	1·3252	1·3383	1·3512	1·3640	1·3767	1·3893	1·4018	0'
1	1·3255	1·3385	1·3514	1·3642	1·3769	1·3895	1·4020	1
2	1·3257	1·3387	1·3516	1·3644	1·3771	1·3897	1·4022	2
3	1·3259	1·3389	1·3518	1·3646	1·3773	1·3899	1·4024	3
4	1·3261	1·3391	1·3520	1·3648	1·3776	1·3902	1·4026	4
5	1·3263	1·3393	1·3523	1·3651	1·3778	1·3904	1·4029	5
6	1·3265	1·3396	1·3525	1·3653	1·3780	1·3906	1·4031	6
7	1·3268	1·3398	1·3527	1·3655	1·3782	1·3908	1·4033	7
8	1·3270	1·3400	1·3529	1·3657	1·3784	1·3910	1·4035	8
9	1·3272	1·3402	1·3531	1·3659	1·3786	1·3912	1·4037	9
10	1·3274	1·3404	1·3533	1·3661	1·3788	1·3914	1·4039	10
11	1·3276	1·3406	1·3535	1·3663	1·3790	1·3916	1·4041	11
12	1·3279	1·3409	1·3538	1·3665	1·3792	1·3918	1·4043	12
13	1·3281	1·3411	1·3540	1·3668	1·3794	1·3920	1·4045	13
14	1·3283	1·3413	1·3542	1·3670	1·3797	1·3922	1·4047	14
15	1·3285	1·3415	1·3544	1·3672	1·3799	1·3925	1·4049	15
16	1·3287	1·3417	1·3546	1·3674	1·3801	1·3927	1·4051	16
17	1·3289	1·3419	1·3548	1·3676	1·3803	1·3929	1·4053	17
18	1·3292	1·3421	1·3550	1·3678	1·3805	1·3931	1·4055	18
19	1·3294	1·3424	1·3552	1·3680	1·3807	1·3933	1·4058	19
20	1·3296	1·3426	1·3555	1·3682	1·3809	1·3935	1·4060	20
21	1·3298	1·3428	1·3557	1·3685	1·3811	1·3937	1·4062	21
22	1·3300	1·3430	1·3559	1·3687	1·3813	1·3939	1·4064	22
23	1·3302	1·3432	1·3561	1·3689	1·3816	1·3941	1·4066	23
24	1·3305	1·3434	1·3563	1·3691	1·3818	1·3943	1·4068	24
25	1·3307	1·3437	1·3565	1·3693	1·3820	1·3945	1·4070	25
26	1·3309	1·3439	1·3567	1·3695	1·3822	1·3947	1·4072	26
27	1·3311	1·3441	1·3570	1·3697	1·3824	1·3950	1·4074	27
28	1·3313	1·3443	1·3572	1·3699	1·3826	1·3952	1·4076	28
29	1·3315	1·3445	1·3574	1·3702	1·3828	1·3954	1·4078	29
30	1·3318	1·3447	1·3576	1·3704	1·3830	1·3956	1·4080	30
31	1·3320	1·3449	1·3578	1·3706	1·3832	1·3958	1·4082	31
32	1·3322	1·3452	1·3580	1·3708	1·3834	1·3960	1·4084	32
33	1·3324	1·3454	1·3582	1·3710	1·3837	1·3962	1·4086	33
34	1·3326	1·3456	1·3585	1·3712	1·3839	1·3964	1·4089	34
35	1·3328	1·3458	1·3587	1·3714	1·3841	1·3966	1·4091	35
36	1·3331	1·3460	1·3589	1·3716	1·3843	1·3968	1·4093	36
37	1·3333	1·3462	1·3591	1·3718	1·3845	1·3970	1·4095	37
38	1·3335	1·3465	1·3593	1·3721	1·3847	1·3972	1·4097	38
39	1·3337	1·3467	1·3595	1·3723	1·3849	1·3975	1·4099	39
40	1·3339	1·3469	1·3597	1·3725	1·3851	1·3977	1·4101	40
41	1·3341	1·3471	1·3599	1·3727	1·3853	1·3979	1·4103	41
42	1·3344	1·3473	1·3602	1·3729	1·3855	1·3981	1·4105	42
43	1·3346	1·3475	1·3604	1·3731	1·3858	1·3983	1·4107	43
44	1·3348	1·3477	1·3606	1·3733	1·3860	1·3985	1·4109	44
45	1·3350	1·3480	1·3608	1·3735	1·3862	1·3987	1·4111	45
46	1·3352	1·3482	1·3610	1·3738	1·3864	1·3989	1·4113	46
47	1·3354	1·3484	1·3612	1·3740	1·3866	1·3991	1·4115	47
48	1·3357	1·3486	1·3614	1·3742	1·3868	1·3993	1·4117	48
49	1·3359	1·3488	1·3617	1·3744	1·3870	1·3995	1·4119	49
50	1·3361	1·3490	1·3619	1·3746	1·3872	1·3997	1·4122	50
51	1·3363	1·3492	1·3621	1·3748	1·3874	1·3999	1·4124	51
52	1·3365	1·3495	1·3623	1·3750	1·3876	1·4002	1·4126	52
53	1·3367	1·3497	1·3625	1·3752	1·3879	1·4004	1·4128	53
54	1·3370	1·3499	1·3627	1·3754	1·3881	1·4006	1·4130	54
55	1·3372	1·3501	1·3629	1·3757	1·3883	1·4008	1·4132	55
56	1·3374	1·3503	1·3631	1·3759	1·3885	1·4010	1·4134	56
57	1·3376	1·3505	1·3634	1·3761	1·3887	1·4012	1·4136	57
58	1·3378	1·3508	1·3636	1·3763	1·3889	1·4014	1·4138	58
59	1·3380	1·3510	1·3638	1·3765	1·3891	1·4016	1·4140	59
60	1·3383	1·3512	1·3640	1·3767	1·3893	1·4018	1·4142	60

TABLE I.,

OF

LOGARITHMS OF NUMBERS

FROM

1 TO 10000.

N.	Log.	N.	Log.	N.	Log.	N.	Log.
1	0·000000	26	1·414973	51	1·707570	76	1·880814
2	0·301030	27	1·431364	52	1·716003	77	1·886491
3	0·477121	28	1·447158	53	1·724276	78	1·892095
4	0·602060	29	1·462398	54	1·732394	79	1·897627
5	0·698970	30	1·477121	55	1·740363	80	1·903090
6	0·778151	31	1·491362	56	1·748188	81	1·908485
7	0·845098	32	1·505150	57	1·755875	82	1·913814
8	0·903090	33	1·518514	58	1·763428	83	1·919078
9	0·954243	34	1·531479	59	1·770852	84	1·924279
10	1·000000	35	1·544068	60	1·778151	85	1·929419
11	1·041393	36	1·556303	61	1·785330	86	1·934498
12	1·079181	37	1·568202	62	1·792392	87	1·939519
13	1·113943	38	1·579784	63	1·799341	88	1·944483
14	1·146128	39	1·591065	64	1·806180	89	1·949390
15	1·176091	40	1·602060	65	1·812913	90	1·954243
16	1·204120	41	1·612784	66	1·819544	91	1·959041
17	1·230449	42	1·623249	67	1·826075	92	1·963788
18	1·255273	43	1·633468	68	1·832509	93	1·968483
19	1·278754	44	1·643453	69	1·838849	94	1·973128
20	1·301030	45	1·653213	70	1·845098	95	1·977724
21	1·322219	46	1·662758	71	1·851258	96	1·982271
22	1·342423	47	1·672098	72	1·857333	97	1·986772
23	1·361728	48	1·681241	73	1·863323	98	1·991226
24	1·380211	49	1·690196	74	1·869232	99	1·995635
25	1·397940	50	1·698970	75	1·875061	100	2·000000

N. B. In the following table, in the last nine columns of each page, where the first or leading figures change from 9's to 0's, the character ⧫ is introduced instead of the 0's, to catch the eye, and to indicate that from thence the annexed first two figures of the Logarithm in the second column stand in the next lower line, directly under the *asterisk*.

N.	0	1	2	3	4	5	6	7	8	9	D.
100	00 0000	0434	0868	1301	1734	2166	2598	3029	3461	3891	432
101	4321	4751	5181	5609	6038	6466	6894	7321	7748	8174	428
102	*8600	9026	9451	9876	✦300	0724	1147	1570	1993	2415	424
103	01 2837	3259	3680	4100	4521	4940	5360	5779	6197	6616	419
104	*7033	7451	7868	8284	8700	9116	9532	9947	✦361	0775	416
105	02 1189	1603	2016	2428	2841	3252	3664	4075	4486	4896	412
106	5306	5715	6125	6533	6942	7350	7757	8164	8571	8978	408
107	*9384	9789	✦195	0600	1004	1408	1812	2216	2619	3021	404
108	03 3424	3826	4227	4628	5029	5430	5830	6230	6629	7028	400
109	*7426	7825	8223	8620	9017	9414	9811	✦207	0602	0998	396
110	04 1393	1787	2182	2576	2969	3362	3755	4148	4540	4932	393
111	5323	5714	6105	6495	6885	7275	7664	8053	8442	8830	389
112	*9218	9606	9993	✦380	0766	1153	1538	1924	2309	2694	386
113	05 3078	3463	3846	4230	4613	4996	5378	5760	6142	6524	382
114	*6905	7286	7666	8046	8426	8805	9185	9563	9942	✦320	379
115	06 0698	1075	1452	1829	2206	2582	2958	3333	3709	4083	376
116	4458	4832	5206	5580	5953	6326	6699	7071	7443	7815	372
117	*8186	8557	8928	9298	9668	✦038	0407	0776	1145	1514	369
118	07 1882	2250	2617	2985	3352	3718	4085	4451	4816	5182	366
119	5547	5912	6276	6640	7004	7368	7731	8094	8457	8819	363
120	*9181	9543	9904	✦266	0626	0987	1347	1707	2067	2426	360
121	08 2785	3144	3503	3861	4219	4576	4934	5291	5647	6004	357
122	6360	6716	7071	7426	7781	8136	8490	8845	9198	9552	355
123	*9905	✦258	0611	0963	1315	1667	2018	2370	2721	3071	351
124	09 3422	3772	4122	4471	4820	5169	5518	5866	6215	6562	349
125	*6910	7257	7604	7951	8298	8644	8990	9335	9681	✦026	346
126	10 0371	0715	1059	1403	1747	2091	2434	2777	3119	3462	343
127	3804	4146	4487	4828	5169	5510	5851	6191	6531	6871	340
128	*7210	7549	7888	8227	8565	8903	9241	9579	9916	✦253	338
129	11 0590	0926	1263	1599	1934	2270	2605	2940	3275	3609	335
130	3943	4277	4611	4944	5278	5611	5943	6276	6608	6940	333
131	*7271	7603	7934	8265	8595	8926	9256	9586	9915	✦245	330
132	12 0574	0903	1231	1560	1888	2216	2544	2871	3198	3525	328
133	3852	4178	4504	4830	5156	5481	5806	6131	6456	6781	325
134	*7105	7429	7753	8076	8399	8722	9045	9368	9690	✦012	323
135	13 0334	0655	0977	1298	1619	1939	2260	2580	2900	3219	321
136	3539	3858	4177	4496	4814	5133	5451	5769	6086	6403	318
137	6721	7037	7354	7671	7987	8303	8618	8934	9249	9564	315
138	*9879	✦194	0508	0822	1136	1450	1763	2076	2389	2702	314
139	14 3015	3327	3639	3951	4263	4574	4885	5196	5507	5818	311
140	6128	6438	6748	7058	7367	7676	7985	8294	8603	8911	309
141	*9219	9527	9835	✦142	0449	0756	1063	1370	1676	1982	307
142	15 2288	2594	2900	3205	3510	3815	4120	4424	4728	5032	305
143	5336	5640	5943	6246	6549	6852	7154	7457	7759	8061	303
144	*8362	8664	8965	9266	9567	9868	✦168	0469	0769	1068	301
145	16 1368	1667	1967	2266	2564	2863	3161	3460	3758	4055	299
146	4353	4650	4947	5244	5541	5838	6134	6430	6726	7022	297
147	7317	7613	7908	8203	8497	8792	9086	9380	9674	9968	295
148	17 0262	0555	0848	1141	1434	1726	2019	2311	2603	2895	293
149	3186	3478	3769	4060	4351	4641	4932	5222	5512	5802	291
150	6091	6381	6670	6959	7248	7536	7825	8113	8401	8689	289
151	*8977	9264	9552	9839	✦126	0413	0699	0985	1272	1558	287
152	18 1844	2129	2415	2700	2985	3270	3555	3839	4123	4407	285
153	4691	4975	5259	5542	5825	6108	6391	6674	6956	7239	283
154	*7521	7803	8084	8366	8647	8928	9209	9490	9771	✦051	281
155	19 0332	0612	0892	1171	1451	1730	2010	2289	2567	2846	279
156	3125	3403	3681	3959	4237	4514	4792	5069	5346	5623	278
157	5900	6176	6453	6729	7005	7281	7556	7832	8107	8382	276
158	*8657	8932	9206	9481	9755	✦029	0303	0577	0850	1124	274
159	20 1397	1670	1943	2216	2488	2761	3033	3305	3577	3848	272
N.	0	1	2	3	4	5	6	7	8	9	D.

N.	0	1	2	3	4	5	6	7	8	9	D.
160	20 4120	4391	4663	4934	5204	5475	5746	6016	6286	6556	271
161	6826	7096	7365	7634	7904	8173	8441	8710	8979	9247	269
162	*9515	9783	*051	0319	0586	0853	1121	1388	1654	1921	267
163	21 2188	2454	2720	2986	3252	3518	3783	4049	4314	4579	266
164	4844	5109	5373	5638	5902	6166	6430	6694	6957	7221	264
165	7484	7747	8010	8273	8536	8798	9060	9323	9585	9846	262
166	22 0108	0370	0631	0892	1153	1414	1675	1936	2196	2456	261
167	2716	2976	3236	3496	3755	4015	4274	4533	4792	5051	259
168	5309	5568	5826	6084	6342	6600	6858	7115	7372	7630	258
169	*7887	8144	8400	8657	8913	9170	9426	9682	9938	*193	256
170	23 0449	0704	0960	1215	1470	1724	1979	2234	2488	2742	254
171	2996	3250	3504	3757	4011	4264	4517	4770	5023	5276	253
172	5528	5781	6033	6285	6537	6789	7041	7292	7544	7795	252
173	*8046	8297	8548	8799	9049	9299	9550	9800	*050	0300	250
174	24 0549	0799	1048	1297	1546	1795	2044	2293	2541	2790	249
175	3038	3286	3534	3782	4030	4277	4525	4772	5019	5266	248
176	5513	5759	6006	6252	6499	6745	6991	7237	7482	7728	246
177	*7973	8219	8464	8709	8954	9198	9443	9687	9932	*176	245
178	25 0420	0664	0908	1151	1395	1638	1881	2125	2368	2610	243
179	2853	3096	3338	3580	3822	4064	4306	4548	4790	5031	242
180	5273	5514	5755	5996	6237	6477	6718	6958	7198	7439	241
181	7679	7918	8158	8398	8637	8877	9116	9355	9594	9833	239
182	26 0071	0310	0548	0787	1025	1263	1501	1739	1976	2214	238
183	2451	2688	2925	3162	3399	3636	3873	4109	4346	4582	237
184	4818	5054	5290	5525	5761	5996	6232	6467	6702	6937	235
185	7172	7406	7641	7875	8110	8344	8578	8812	9046	9279	234
186	*9513	9746	9980	*213	0446	0679	0912	1144	1377	1609	233
187	27 1842	2074	2306	2538	2770	3001	3233	3464	3696	3927	232
188	4158	4389	4620	4850	5081	5311	5542	5772	6002	6232	230
189	6462	6692	6921	7151	7380	7609	7838	8067	8296	8525	229
190	*8754	8982	9211	9439	9667	9895	*123	0351	0578	0806	228
191	28 1033	1261	1488	1715	1942	2169	2396	2622	2849	3075	227
192	3301	3527	3753	3979	4205	4431	4656	4882	5107	5332	226
193	5557	5782	6007	6232	6456	6681	6905	7130	7354	7578	225
194	7802	8026	8249	8473	8696	8920	9143	9366	9589	9812	223
195	29 0035	0257	0480	0702	0925	1147	1369	1591	1813	2034	222
196	2256	2478	2699	2920	3141	3363	3584	3804	4025	4246	221
197	4466	4687	4907	5127	5347	5567	5787	6007	6226	6446	220
198	6665	6884	7104	7323	7542	7761	7979	8198	8416	8635	219
199	*8853	9071	9289	9507	9725	9943	*161	0378	0595	0813	218
200	30 1030	1247	1464	1681	1898	2114	2331	2547	2764	2980	217
201	3196	3412	3628	3844	4059	4275	4491	4706	4921	5136	216
202	5351	5566	5781	5996	6211	6425	6639	6854	7068	7282	215
203	7496	7710	7924	8137	8351	8564	8778	8991	9204	9417	213
204	*9630	9843	*056	0268	0481	0693	0906	1118	1330	1542	212
205	31 1754	1966	2177	2389	2600	2812	3023	3234	3445	3656	211
206	3867	4078	4289	4499	4710	4920	5130	5340	5551	5760	210
207	5970	6180	6390	6599	6809	7018	7227	7436	7646	7854	209
208	8063	8272	8481	8689	8898	9106	9314	9522	9730	9938	208
209	32 0146	0354	0562	0769	0977	1184	1391	1598	1805	2012	207
210	2219	2426	2633	2839	3046	3252	3458	3665	3871	4077	206
211	4282	4488	4694	4899	5105	5310	5516	5721	5926	6131	205
212	6336	6541	6745	6950	7155	7359	7563	7767	7972	8176	204
213	*8380	8583	8787	8991	9194	9398	9601	9805	*008	0211	203
214	33 0414	0617	0819	1022	1225	1427	1630	1832	2034	2236	202
215	2438	2640	2842	3044	3246	3447	3649	3850	4051	4253	202
216	4454	4655	4856	5057	5257	5458	5658	5859	6059	6260	201
217	6460	6660	6860	7060	7260	7459	7659	7858	8058	8257	200
218	*8456	8656	8855	9054	9253	9451	9650	9849	*047	0246	199
219	34 0444	0642	0841	1039	1237	1435	1632	1830	2028	2225	198
N.	0	1	2	3	4	5	6	7	8	9	D.

N.	0	1	2	3	4	5	6	7	8	9	D.
220	34 2423	2620	2817	3014	3212	3409	3606	3802	3999	4196	197
221	4392	4589	4785	4981	5178	5374	5570	5766	5962	6157	196
222	6353	6549	6744	6939	7135	7330	7525	7720	7915	8110	195
223	*8305	8500	8694	8889	9083	9278	9472	9666	9860	+054	194
224	35 0248	0442	0636	0829	1023	1216	1410	1603	1796	1989	193
225	2183	2375	2568	2761	2954	3147	3339	3532	3724	3916	193
226	4108	4301	4493	4685	4876	5068	5260	5452	5643	5834	192
227	6026	6217	6408	6599	6790	6981	7172	7363	7554	7744	191
228	7935	8125	8316	8506	8696	8886	9076	9266	9456	9646	190
229	*9835	+025	0215	0404	0593	0783	0972	1161	1350	1539	189
230	36 1728	1917	2105	2294	2482	2671	2859	3048	3236	3424	188
231	3612	3800	3988	4176	4363	4551	4739	4926	5113	5301	188
232	5488	5675	5862	6049	6236	6423	6610	6796	6983	7169	187
233	7356	7542	7729	7915	8101	8287	8473	8659	8845	9030	186
234	*9216	9401	9587	9772	9958	+143	0328	0513	0698	0883	185
235	37 1068	1253	1437	1622	1806	1991	2175	2360	2544	2728	184
236	2912	3096	3280	3464	3647	3831	4015	4198	4382	4565	184
237	4748	4932	5115	5298	5481	5664	5846	6029	6212	6394	183
238	6577	6759	6942	7124	7306	7488	7670	7852	8034	8216	182
239	*8398	8580	8761	8943	9124	9306	9487	9668	9849	+030	181
240	38 0211	0392	0573	0754	0934	1115	1296	1476	1656	1837	181
241	2017	2197	2377	2557	2737	2917	3097	3277	3456	3636	180
242	3815	3995	4174	4353	4533	4712	4891	5070	5249	5428	179
243	5606	5785	5964	6142	6321	6499	6677	6856	7034	7212	178
244	7390	7568	7746	7923	8101	8279	8456	8634	8811	8989	178
245	*9166	9343	9520	9698	9875	+051	0228	0405	0582	0759	177
246	39 0935	1112	1288	1464	1641	1817	1993	2169	2345	2521	176
247	2697	2873	3048	3224	3400	3575	3751	3926	4101	4277	176
248	4452	4627	4802	4977	5152	5326	5501	5676	5850	6025	175
249	6199	6374	6548	6722	6896	7071	7245	7419	7592	7766	174
250	7940	8114	8287	8461	8634	8808	8981	9154	9328	9501	173
251	*9674	9847	+020	0192	0365	0538	0711	0883	1056	1228	173
252	40 1401	1573	1745	1917	2089	2261	2433	2605	2777	2949	172
253	3121	3292	3464	3635	3807	3978	4149	4320	4492	4663	171
254	4834	5005	5176	5346	5517	5688	5858	6029	6199	6370	171
255	6540	6710	6881	7051	7221	7391	7561	7731	7901	8070	170
256	8240	8410	8579	8749	8918	9087	9257	9426	9595	9764	169
257	*9933	+102	0271	0440	0609	0777	0946	1114	1283	1451	169
258	41 1620	1788	1956	2124	2293	2461	2629	2796	2964	3132	168
259	3300	3467	3635	3803	3970	4137	4305	4472	4639	4806	167
260	4973	5140	5307	5474	5641	5808	5974	6141	6308	6474	167
261	6641	6807	6973	7139	7306	7472	7638	7804	7970	8135	166
262	8301	8467	8633	8798	8964	9129	9295	9460	9625	9791	165
263	*9956	+121	0286	0451	0616	0781	0945	1110	1275	1439	165
264	42 1604	1768	1933	2097	2261	2426	2590	2754	2918	3082	164
265	3246	3410	3574	3737	3901	4065	4228	4392	4555	4718	164
266	4882	5045	5208	5371	5534	5697	5860	6023	6186	6349	163
267	6511	6674	6836	6999	7161	7324	7486	7648	7811	7973	162
268	8135	8297	8459	8621	8783	8944	9106	9268	9429	9591	162
269	*9752	9914	+075	0236	0398	0559	0720	0881	1042	1203	161
270	43 1364	1525	1685	1846	2007	2167	2328	2488	2649	2809	161
271	2969	3130	3290	3450	3610	3770	3930	4090	4249	4409	160
272	4569	4729	4888	5048	5207	5367	5526	5685	5844	6004	159
273	6163	6322	6481	6640	6799	6957	7116	7275	7433	7592	159
274	7751	7909	8067	8226	8384	8542	8701	8859	9017	9175	158
275	*9333	9491	9648	9806	9964	+122	0279	0437	0594	0752	158
276	44 0909	1066	1224	1381	1538	1695	1852	2009	2166	2323	157
277	2480	2637	2793	2950	3106	3263	3419	3576	3732	3889	157
278	4045	4201	4357	4513	4669	4825	4981	5137	5293	5449	156
279	5604	5760	5915	6071	6226	6382	6537	6692	6848	7003	155
N.	0	1	2	3	4	5	6	7	8	9	D.

N.	0	1	2	3	4	5	6	7	8	9	D.
280	44 7158	7313	7468	7623	7778	7933	8088	8242	8397	8552	155
281	*8706	8861	9015	9170	9324	9478	9633	9787	9941	*095	154
282	45 0249	0403	0557	0711	0865	1018	1172	1326	1479	1633	154
283	1786	1940	2093	2247	2400	2553	2706	2859	3012	3165	153
284	3318	3471	3624	3777	3930	4082	4235	4387	4540	4692	153
285	4845	4997	5150	5302	5454	5606	5758	5910	6062	6214	152
286	6366	6518	6670	6821	6973	7125	7276	7428	7579	7731	152
287	7882	8033	8184	8336	8487	8638	8789	8940	9091	9242	151
288	*9392	9543	9694	9845	9995	*146	0296	0447	0597	0748	151
289	46 0898	1048	1198	1348	1499	1649	1799	1948	2098	2248	150
290	2398	2548	2697	2847	2997	3146	3296	3445	3594	3744	150
291	3893	4042	4191	4340	4490	4639	4788	4936	5085	5234	149
292	5383	5532	5680	5829	5977	6126	6274	6423	6571	6719	149
293	6868	7016	7164	7312	7460	7608	7756	7904	8052	8200	148
294	8347	8495	8643	8790	8938	9085	9233	9380	9527	9675	148
295	*9822	9969	*116	0263	0410	0557	0704	0851	0998	1145	147
296	47 1292	1438	1585	1732	1878	2025	2171	2318	2464	2610	146
297	2756	2903	3049	3195	3341	3487	3633	3779	3925	4071	146
298	4216	4362	4508	4653	4799	4944	5090	5235	5381	5526	146
299	5671	5816	5962	6107	6252	6397	6542	6687	6832	6976	145
300	7121	7266	7411	7555	7700	7844	7989	8133	8278	8422	145
301	8566	8711	8855	8999	9143	9287	9431	9575	9719	9863	144
302	48 0007	0151	0294	0438	0582	0725	0869	1012	1156	1299	144
303	1443	1586	1729	1872	2016	2159	2302	2445	2588	2731	143
304	2874	3016	3159	3302	3445	3587	3730	3872	4015	4157	143
305	4300	4442	4585	4727	4869	5011	5153	5295	5437	5579	142
306	5721	5863	6005	6147	6289	6430	6572	6714	6855	6997	142
307	7138	7280	7421	7563	7704	7845	7986	8127	8269	8410	141
308	8551	8692	8833	8974	9114	9255	9396	9537	9677	9818	141
309	*9958	*099	0239	0380	0520	0661	0801	0941	1081	1222	140
310	49 1362	1502	1642	1782	1922	2062	2201	2341	2481	2621	140
311	2760	2900	3040	3179	3319	3458	3597	3737	3876	4015	139
312	4155	4294	4433	4572	4711	4850	4989	5128	5267	5406	139
313	5544	5683	5822	5960	6099	6238	6376	6515	6653	6791	139
314	6930	7068	7206	7344	7483	7621	7759	7897	8035	8173	138
315	8311	8448	8586	8724	8862	8999	9137	9275	9412	9550	138
316	*9687	9824	9962	*099	0236	0374	0511	0648	0785	0922	137
317	50 1059	1196	1333	1470	1607	1744	1880	2017	2154	2291	137
318	2427	2564	2700	2837	2973	3109	3246	3382	3518	3655	136
319	3791	3927	4063	4199	4335	4471	4607	4743	4878	5014	136
320	5150	5286	5421	5557	5693	5828	5964	6099	6234	6370	136
321	6505	6640	6776	6911	7046	7181	7316	7451	7586	7721	135
322	7856	7991	8126	8260	8395	8530	8664	8799	8934	9068	135
323	*9203	9337	9471	9606	9740	9874	*009	0143	0277	0411	134
324	51 0545	0679	0813	0947	1081	1215	1349	1482	1616	1750	134
325	1883	2017	2151	2284	2418	2551	2684	2818	2951	3084	133
326	3218	3351	3484	3617	3750	3883	4016	4149	4282	4414	133
327	4548	4681	4813	4946	5079	5211	5344	5476	5609	5741	133
328	5874	6006	6139	6271	6403	6535	6668	6800	6932	7064	132
329	7196	7328	7460	7592	7724	7855	7987	8119	8251	8382	132
330	8514	8646	8777	8909	9040	9171	9303	9434	9566	9697	131
331	*9828	9959	*090	0221	0353	0484	0615	0745	0876	1007	131
332	52 1138	1269	1400	1530	1661	1792	1922	2053	2183	2314	131
333	2444	2575	2705	2835	2966	3096	3226	3356	3486	3616	130
334	3746	3876	4006	4136	4266	4396	4526	4656	4785	4915	130
335	5045	5174	5304	5434	5563	5693	5822	5951	6081	6210	129
336	6339	6469	6598	6727	6856	6985	7114	7243	7372	7501	129
337	7630	7759	7888	8016	8145	8274	8402	8531	8660	8788	129
338	*8917	9045	9174	9302	9430	9559	9687	9815	9943	*072	128
339	53 0200	0328	0456	0584	0712	0840	0968	1096	1223	1351	128

N. | 0 | 1 | 2 | 3 | 4 | 5 | 6 | 7 | 8 | 9 | D.

N.	0	1	2	3	4	5	6	7	8	9	D.
340	53 1479	1607	1734	1862	1990	2117	2245	2372	2500	2627	128
341	2754	2882	3009	3136	3264	3391	3518	3645	3772	3899	127
342	4026	4153	4280	4407	4534	4661	4787	4914	5041	5167	127
343	5294	5421	5547	5674	5800	5927	6053	6180	6306	6432	126
344	6558	6685	6811	6937	7063	7189	7315	7441	7567	7693	126
345	7819	7945	8071	8197	8322	8448	8574	8699	8825	8951	126
346	*9076	9202	9327	9452	9578	9703	9829	9954	*079	0204	125
347	54 0329	0455	0580	0705	0830	0955	1080	1205	1330	1454	125
348	1579	1704	1829	1953	2078	2203	2327	2452	2576	2701	125
349	2825	2950	3074	3199	3323	3447	3571	3696	3820	3944	124
350	4068	4192	4316	4440	4564	4688	4812	4936	5060	5183	124
351	5307	5431	5555	5678	5802	5925	6049	6172	6296	6419	124
352	6543	6666	6789	6913	7036	7159	7282	7405	7529	7652	123
353	7775	7898	8021	8144	8267	8389	8512	8635	8758	8881	123
354	*9003	9126	9249	9371	9494	9616	9739	9861	9984	*106	123
355	55 0228	0351	0473	0595	0717	0840	0962	1084	1206	1328	122
356	1450	1572	1694	1816	1938	2060	2181	2303	2425	2547	122
357	2668	2790	2911	3033	3155	3276	3398	3519	3640	3762	121
358	3883	4004	4126	4247	4368	4489	4610	4731	4852	4973	121
359	5094	5215	5336	5457	5578	5699	5820	5940	6061	6182	121
360	6303	6423	6544	6664	6785	6905	7026	7146	7267	7387	120
361	7507	7627	7748	7868	7988	8108	8228	8349	8469	8589	120
362	8709	8829	8948	9068	9188	9308	9428	9548	9667	9787	120
363	*9907	*026	0146	0265	0385	0504	0624	0743	0863	0982	119
364	56 1101	1221	1340	1459	1578	1698	1817	1936	2055	2174	119
365	2293	2412	2531	2650	2769	2887	3006	3125	3244	3362	119
366	3481	3600	3718	3837	3955	4074	4192	4311	4429	4548	119
367	4666	4784	4903	5021	5139	5257	5376	5494	5612	5730	118
368	5848	5966	6084	6202	6320	6437	6555	6673	6791	6909	118
369	7026	7144	7262	7379	7497	7614	7732	7849	7967	8084	118
370	8202	8319	8436	8554	8671	8788	8905	9023	9140	9257	117
371	*9374	9491	9608	9725	9842	9959	*076	0193	0309	0426	117
372	57 0543	0660	0776	0893	1010	1126	1243	1359	1476	1592	117
373	1709	1825	1942	2058	2174	2291	2407	2523	2639	2755	116
374	2872	2988	3104	3220	3336	3452	3568	3684	3800	3915	116
375	4031	4147	4263	4379	4494	4610	4726	4841	4957	5072	116
376	5188	5303	5419	5534	5650	5765	5880	5996	6111	6226	115
377	6341	6457	6572	6687	6802	6917	7032	7147	7262	7377	115
378	7492	7607	7722	7836	7951	8066	8181	8295	8410	8525	115
379	8639	8754	8868	8983	9097	9212	9326	9441	9555	9669	114
380	*9784	9898	*012	0126	0241	0355	0469	0583	0697	0811	114
381	58 0925	1039	1153	1267	1381	1495	1608	1722	1836	1950	114
382	2063	2177	2291	2404	2518	2631	2745	2858	2972	3085	114
383	3199	3312	3426	3539	3652	3765	3879	3992	4105	4218	113
384	4331	4444	4557	4670	4783	4896	5009	5122	5235	5348	113
385	5461	5574	5686	5799	5912	6024	6137	6250	6362	6475	113
386	6587	6700	6812	6925	7037	7149	7262	7374	7486	7599	112
387	7711	7823	7935	8047	8160	8272	8384	8496	8608	8720	112
388	8832	8944	9056	9167	9279	9391	9503	9615	9726	9838	112
389	*9950	*061	0173	0284	0396	0507	0619	0730	0842	0953	112
390	59 1065	1176	1287	1399	1510	1621	1732	1843	1955	2066	111
391	2177	2288	2399	2510	2621	2732	2843	2954	3064	3175	111
392	3286	3397	3508	3618	3729	3840	3950	4061	4171	4282	111
393	4393	4503	4614	4724	4834	4945	5055	5165	5276	5386	110
394	5496	5606	5717	5827	5937	6047	6157	6267	6377	6487	110
395	6597	6707	6817	6927	7037	7146	7256	7366	7476	7586	110
396	7695	7805	7914	8024	8134	8243	8353	8462	8572	8681	110
397	8791	8900	9009	9119	9228	9337	9446	9556	9665	9774	109
398	*9883	9992	*101	0210	0319	0428	0537	0646	0755	0864	109
399	60 0973	1082	1191	1299	1408	1517	1625	1734	1843	1951	109
N.	0	1	2	3	4	5	6	7	8	9	D.

N.	0	1	2	3	4	5	6	7	8	9	D.
400	60 2060	2169	2277	2386	2494	2603	2711	2819	2928	3036	108
401	3144	3253	3361	3469	3577	3686	3794	3902	4010	4118	108
402	4226	4334	4442	4550	4658	4766	4874	4982	5089	5197	108
403	5305	5413	5521	5628	5736	5844	5951	6059	6166	6274	108
404	6381	6489	6596	6704	6811	6919	7026	7133	7241	7348	107
405	7455	7562	7669	7777	7884	7991	8098	8205	8312	8419	107
406	8526	8633	8740	8847	8954	9061	9167	9274	9381	9488	107
407	*9594	9701	9808	9914	•021	0128	0234	0341	0447	0554	107
408	61 0660	0767	0873	0979	1086	1192	1298	1405	1511	1617	106
409	1723	1829	1936	2042	2148	2254	2360	2466	2572	2678	106
410	2784	2890	2996	3102	3207	3313	3419	3525	3630	3736	106
411	3842	3947	4053	4159	4264	4370	4475	4581	4686	4792	106
412	4897	5003	5108	5213	5319	5424	5529	5634	5740	5845	105
413	5950	6055	6160	6265	6370	6476	6581	6686	6790	6895	105
414	7000	7105	7210	7315	7420	7525	7629	7734	7839	7943	105
415	8048	8153	8257	8362	8466	8571	8676	8780	8884	8989	105
416	*9093	9198	9302	9406	9511	9615	9719	9824	9928	•032	104
417	62 0136	0240	0344	0448	0552	0656	0760	0864	0968	1072	104
418	1176	1280	1384	1488	1592	1695	1799	1903	2007	2110	104
419	2214	2318	2421	2525	2628	2732	2835	2939	3042	3146	104
420	3249	3353	3456	3559	3663	3766	3869	3973	4076	4179	103
421	4282	4385	4488	4591	4695	4798	4901	5004	5107	5210	103
422	5312	5415	5518	5621	5724	5827	5929	6032	6135	6238	103
423	6340	6443	6546	6648	6751	6853	6956	7058	7161	7263	103
424	7366	7468	7571	7673	7775	7878	7980	8082	8185	8287	102
425	8389	8491	8593	8695	8797	8900	9002	9104	9206	9308	102
426	*9410	9512	9613	9715	9817	9919	•021	0123	0224	0326	102
427	63 0428	0530	0631	0733	0835	0936	1038	1139	1241	1342	102
428	1444	1545	1647	1748	1849	1951	2052	2153	2255	2356	101
429	2457	2559	2660	2761	2862	2963	3064	3165	3266	3367	101
430	3468	3569	3670	3771	3872	3973	4074	4175	4276	4376	100
431	4477	4578	4679	4779	4880	4981	5081	5182	5283	5383	100
432	5484	5584	5685	5785	5886	5986	6087	6187	6287	6388	100
433	6488	6588	6688	6789	6889	6989	7089	7189	7290	7390	100
434	7490	7590	7690	7790	7890	7990	8090	8190	8290	8389	99
435	8489	8589	8689	8789	8888	8988	9088	9188	9287	9387	99
436	*9486	9586	9686	9785	9885	9984	•084	0183	0283	0382	99
437	64 0481	0581	0680	0779	0879	0978	1077	1177	1276	1375	99
438	1474	1573	1672	1771	1871	1970	2069	2168	2267	2366	99
439	2465	2563	2662	2761	2860	2959	3058	3156	3255	3354	99
440	3453	3551	3650	3749	3847	3946	4044	4143	4242	4340	98
441	4439	4537	4636	4734	4832	4931	5029	5127	5226	5324	98
442	5422	5521	5619	5717	5815	5913	6011	6110	6208	6306	98
443	6404	6502	6600	6698	6796	6894	6992	7089	7187	7285	98
444	7383	7481	7579	7676	7774	7872	7969	8067	8165	8262	98
445	8360	8458	8555	8653	8750	8848	8945	9043	9140	9237	97
446	*9335	9432	9530	9627	9724	9821	9919	•016	0113	0210	97
447	65 0308	0405	0502	0599	0696	0793	0890	0987	1084	1181	97
448	1278	1375	1472	1569	1666	1762	1859	1956	2053	2150	97
449	2246	2343	2440	2536	2633	2730	2826	2923	3019	3116	97
450	3213	3309	3405	3502	3598	3695	3791	3888	3984	4080	96
451	4177	4273	4369	4465	4562	4658	4754	4850	4946	5042	96
452	5138	5235	5331	5427	5523	5619	5715	5810	5906	6002	96
453	6098	6194	6290	6386	6482	6577	6673	6769	6864	6960	96
454	7056	7152	7247	7343	7438	7534	7629	7725	7820	7916	96
455	8011	8107	8202	8298	8393	8488	8584	8679	8774	8870	95
456	8965	9060	9155	9250	9346	9441	9536	9631	9726	9821	95
457	*9916	•011	0106	0201	0296	0391	0486	0581	0676	0771	95
458	66 0865	0960	1055	1150	1245	1339	1434	1529	1623	1718	95
459	1813	1907	2002	2096	2191	2286	2380	2475	2569	2663	95
N.	0	1	2	3	4	5	6	7	8	9	D.

N.	0	1	2	3	4	5	6	7	8	9	D.
460	66 2758	2852	2947	3041	3135	3230	3324	3418	3512	3607	94
461	3701	3795	3889	3983	4078	4172	4266	4360	4454	4548	94
462	4642	4736	4830	4924	5018	5112	5206	5299	5393	5487	94
463	5581	5675	5769	5862	5956	6050	6143	6237	6331	6424	94
464	6518	6612	6705	6799	6892	6986	7079	7173	7266	7360	94
465	7453	7546	7640	7733	7826	7920	8013	8106	8199	8293	93
466	8386	8479	8572	8665	8759	8852	8945	9038	9131	9224	93
467	*9317	9410	9503	9596	9689	9782	9875	9967	*060	0153	93
468	67 0246	0339	0431	0524	0617	0710	0802	0895	0988	1080	93
469	1173	1265	1358	1451	1543	1636	1728	1821	1913	2005	93
470	2098	2190	2283	2375	2467	2560	2652	2744	2836	2929	92
471	3021	3113	3205	3297	3390	3482	3574	3666	3758	3850	92
472	3942	4034	4126	4218	4310	4402	4494	4586	4677	4769	92
473	4861	4953	5045	5137	5228	5320	5412	5503	5595	5687	92
474	5778	5870	5962	6053	6145	6236	6328	6419	6511	6602	92
475	6694	6785	6876	6968	7059	7151	7242	7333	7424	7516	91
476	7607	7698	7789	7881	7972	8063	8154	8245	8336	8427	91
477	8518	8609	8700	8791	8882	8973	9064	9155	9246	9337	91
478	*9428	9519	9610	9700	9791	9882	9973	*063	0154	0245	91
479	68 0336	0426	0517	0607	0698	0789	0879	0970	1060	1151	91
480	1241	1332	1422	1513	1603	1693	1784	1874	1964	2055	90
481	2145	2235	2326	2416	2506	2596	2686	2777	2867	2957	90
482	3047	3137	3227	3317	3407	3497	3587	3677	3767	3857	90
483	3947	4037	4127	4217	4307	4396	4486	4576	4666	4756	90
484	4845	4935	5025	5114	5204	5294	5383	5473	5563	5652	90
485	5742	5831	5921	6010	6100	6189	6279	6368	6458	6547	89
486	6636	6726	6815	6904	6994	7083	7172	7261	7351	7440	89
487	7529	7618	7707	7796	7886	7975	8064	8153	8242	8331	89
488	8420	8509	8598	8687	8776	8865	8953	9042	9131	9220	89
489	*9309	9398	9486	9575	9664	9753	9841	9930	*019	0107	89
490	69 0196	0285	0373	0462	0550	0639	0728	0816	0905	0993	89
491	1081	1170	1258	1347	1435	1524	1612	1700	1789	1877	88
492	1965	2053	2142	2230	2318	2406	2494	2583	2671	2759	88
493	2847	2935	3023	3111	3199	3287	3375	3463	3551	3639	88
494	3727	3815	3903	3991	4078	4166	4254	4342	4430	4517	88
495	4605	4693	4781	4868	4956	5044	5131	5219	5307	5394	88
496	5482	5569	5657	5744	5832	5919	6007	6094	6182	6269	87
497	6356	6444	6531	6618	6706	6793	6880	6968	7055	7142	87
498	7229	7317	7404	7491	7578	7665	7752	7839	7926	8014	87
499	8101	8188	8275	8362	8449	8535	8622	8709	8796	8883	87
500	8970	9057	9144	9231	9317	9404	9491	9578	9664	9751	87
501	*9838	9924	*011	0098	0184	0271	0358	0444	0531	0617	87
502	70 0704	0790	0877	0963	1050	1136	1222	1309	1395	1482	86
503	1568	1654	1741	1827	1913	1999	2086	2172	2258	2344	86
504	2431	2517	2603	2689	2775	2861	2947	3033	3119	3205	86
505	3291	3377	3463	3549	3635	3721	3807	3895	3979	4065	86
506	4151	4236	4322	4408	4494	4579	4665	4751	4837	4922	86
507	5008	5094	5179	5265	5350	5436	5522	5607	5693	5778	86
508	5864	5949	6035	6120	6206	6291	6376	6462	6547	6632	85
509	6718	6803	6888	6974	7059	7144	7229	7315	7400	7485	85
510	7570	7655	7740	7826	7911	7996	8081	8166	8251	8336	85
511	8421	8506	8591	8676	8761	8846	8931	9015	9100	9185	85
512	*9270	9355	9440	9524	9609	9694	9779	9863	9948	*033	85
513	71 0117	0202	0287	0371	0456	0540	0625	0710	0794	0879	85
514	0963	1048	1132	1217	1301	1385	1470	1554	1639	1723	84
515	1807	1892	1976	2060	2144	2229	2313	2397	2481	2566	84
516	2650	2734	2818	2902	2986	3070	3154	3238	3323	3407	84
517	3491	3575	3650	3742	3826	3910	3994	4078	4162	4246	84
518	4330	4414	4497	4581	4665	4749	4833	4916	5000	5084	84
519	5167	5251	5335	5418	5502	5586	5669	5753	5836	5920	84
N.	0	1	2	3	4	5	6	7	8	9	D.

N.	0	1	2	3	4	5	6	7	8	9	D.
520	71 6003	6087	6170	6254	6337	6421	6504	6588	6671	6754	83
521	6838	6921	7004	7088	7171	7254	7338	7421	7504	7587	83
522	7671	7754	7837	7920	8003	8086	8169	8253	8336	8419	83
523	8502	8585	8668	8751	8834	8917	9000	9083	9165	9248	83
524	*9331	9414	9497	9580	9663	9745	9828	9911	9994	*077	83
525	72 0159	0242	0325	0407	0490	0573	0655	0738	0821	0903	83
526	0986	1068	1151	1233	1316	1398	1481	1563	1646	1728	82
527	1811	1893	1975	2058	2140	2222	2305	2387	2469	2552	82
528	2634	2716	2798	2881	2963	3045	3127	3209	3291	3374	82
529	3456	3538	3620	3702	3784	3866	3948	4030	4112	4194	82
530	4276	4358	4440	4522	4604	4685	4767	4849	4931	5013	82
531	5095	5176	5258	5340	5422	5503	5585	5667	5748	5830	82
532	5912	5993	6075	6156	6238	6320	6401	6483	6564	6646	82
533	6727	6809	6890	6972	7053	7134	7216	7297	7379	7460	81
534	7541	7623	7704	7785	7866	7948	8029	8110	8191	8273	81
535	8354	8435	8516	8597	8678	8759	8841	8922	9003	9084	81
536	9165	9246	9327	9408	9489	9570	9651	9732	9813	9893	81
537	*9974	*055	0136	0217	0298	0378	0459	0540	0621	0702	81
538	73 0782	0863	0944	1024	1105	1186	1266	1347	1428	1508	81
539	1589	1669	1750	1830	1911	1991	2072	2152	2233	2313	81
540	2394	2474	2555	2635	2715	2796	2876	2956	3037	3117	80
541	3197	3278	3358	3438	3518	3598	3679	3759	3839	3919	80
542	3999	4079	4160	4240	4320	4400	4480	4560	4640	4720	80
543	4800	4880	4960	5040	5120	5200	5279	5359	5439	5519	80
544	5599	5679	5759	5838	5918	5998	6078	6157	6237	6317	80
545	6397	6476	6556	6635	6715	6795	6874	6954	7034	7113	80
546	7193	7272	7352	7431	7511	7590	7670	7749	7829	7908	79
547	7987	8067	8146	8225	8305	8384	8463	8543	8622	8701	79
548	8781	8860	8939	9018	9097	9177	9256	9335	9414	9493	79
549	*9572	9651	9731	9810	9889	9968	*047	0126	0205	0284	79
550	74 0363	0442	0521	0600	0678	0757	0836	0915	0994	1073	79
551	1152	1230	1309	1388	1467	1546	1624	1703	1782	1860	79
552	1939	2018	2096	2175	2254	2332	2411	2489	2568	2646	79
553	2725	2804	2882	2961	3039	3118	3196	3275	3353	3431	78
554	3510	3588	3667	3745	3823	3902	3980	4058	4136	4215	78
555	4293	4371	4449	4528	4606	4684	4762	4840	4919	4997	78
556	5075	5153	5231	5309	5387	5465	5543	5621	5699	5777	78
557	5855	5933	6011	6089	6167	6245	6323	6401	6479	6556	78
558	6634	6712	6790	6868	6945	7023	7101	7179	7256	7334	78
559	7412	7489	7567	7645	7722	7800	7878	7955	8033	8110	78
560	8188	8266	8343	8421	8498	8576	8653	8731	8808	8885	77
561	8963	9040	9118	9195	9272	9350	9427	9504	9582	9659	77
562	*9736	9814	9891	9968	*045	0123	0200	0277	0354	0431	77
563	75 0508	0586	0663	0740	0817	0894	0971	1048	1125	1202	77
564	1279	1356	1433	1510	1587	1664	1741	1818	1895	1972	77
565	2048	2125	2202	2279	2356	2433	2509	2586	2663	2740	77
566	2816	2893	2970	3047	3123	3200	3277	3353	3430	3506	77
567	3583	3660	3736	3813	3889	3966	4042	4119	4195	4272	77
568	4348	4425	4501	4578	4654	4730	4807	4883	4960	5036	76
569	5112	5189	5265	5341	5417	5494	5570	5646	5722	5799	76
570	5875	5951	6027	6103	6180	6256	6332	6408	6484	6560	76
571	6636	6712	6788	6864	6940	7016	7092	7168	7244	7320	76
572	7396	7472	7548	7624	7700	7775	7851	7927	8003	8079	76
573	8155	8230	8306	8382	8458	8533	8609	8685	8761	8836	76
574	8912	8988	9063	9139	9214	9290	9366	9441	9517	9592	76
575	*9668	9743	9819	9894	9970	*045	0121	0196	0272	0347	75
576	76 0422	0498	0573	0649	0724	0799	0875	0950	1025	1101	75
577	1176	1251	1326	1402	1477	1552	1627	1702	1778	1853	75
578	1928	2003	2078	2153	2228	2303	2378	2453	2529	2604	75
579	2679	2754	2829	2904	2978	3053	3128	3203	3278	3353	75
N.	0	1	2	3	4	5	6	7	8	9	D.

N.	0	1	2	3	4	5	6	7	8	9	D.
580	76 3428	3503	3578	3653	3727	3802	3877	3952	4027	4101	75
581	4176	4251	4326	4400	4475	4550	4624	4699	4774	4848	75
582	4923	4998	5072	5147	5221	5296	5370	5445	5520	5594	75
583	5669	5743	5818	5892	5966	6041	6115	6190	6264	6338	74
584	6413	6487	6562	6636	6710	6785	6859	6933	7007	7082	74
585	7156	7230	7304	7379	7453	7527	7601	7675	7749	7823	74
586	7898	7972	8046	8120	8194	8268	8342	8416	8490	8564	74
587	8638	8712	8786	8860	8934	9008	9082	9156	9230	9303	74
588	*9377	9451	9525	9599	9673	9746	9820	9894	9968	*042	74
589	77 0115	0189	0263	0336	0410	0484	0557	0631	0705	0778	74
590	0852	0926	0999	1073	1146	1220	1293	1367	1440	1514	74
591	1587	1661	1734	1808	1881	1955	2028	2102	2175	2248	73
592	2322	2395	2468	2542	2615	2688	2762	2835	2908	2981	73
593	3055	3128	3201	3274	3348	3421	3494	3567	3640	3713	73
594	3786	3860	3933	4006	4079	4152	4225	4298	4371	4444	73
595	4517	4590	4663	4736	4809	4882	4955	5028	5100	5173	73
596	5246	5319	5392	5465	5538	5610	5683	5756	5829	5902	73
597	5974	6047	6120	6193	6265	6338	6411	6483	6556	6629	73
598	6701	6774	6846	6919	6992	7064	7137	7209	7282	7354	73
599	7427	7499	7572	7644	7717	7789	7862	7934	8006	8079	72
600	8151	8224	8296	8368	8441	8513	8585	8658	8730	8802	72
601	8874	8947	9019	9091	9163	9236	9308	9380	9452	9524	72
602	*9596	9669	9741	9813	9885	9957	*029	0101	0173	0245	72
603	78 0317	0389	0461	0533	0605	0677	0749	0821	0893	0965	72
604	1037	1109	1181	1253	1324	1396	1468	1540	1612	1684	72
605	1755	1827	1899	1971	2042	2114	2186	2258	2329	2401	72
606	2473	2544	2616	2688	2759	2831	2902	2974	3046	3117	72
607	3189	3260	3332	3403	3475	3546	3618	3689	3761	3832	71
608	3904	3975	4046	4118	4189	4261	4332	4403	4475	4546	71
609	4617	4689	4760	4831	4902	4974	5045	5116	5187	5259	71
610	5330	5401	5472	5543	5615	5686	5757	5828	5899	5970	71
611	6041	6112	6183	6254	6325	6396	6467	6538	6609	6680	71
612	6751	6822	6893	6964	7035	7106	7177	7248	7319	7390	71
613	7460	7531	7602	7673	7744	7815	7885	7956	8027	8098	71
614	8168	8239	8310	8381	8451	8522	8593	8663	8734	8804	71
615	8875	8946	9016	9087	9157	9228	9299	9369	9440	9510	71
616	*9581	9651	9722	9792	9863	9933	*004	0074	0144	0215	70
617	79 0285	0356	0426	0496	0567	0637	0707	0778	0848	0918	70
618	0988	1059	1129	1199	1269	1340	1410	1480	1550	1620	70
619	1691	1761	1831	1901	1971	2041	2111	2181	2252	2322	70
620	2392	2462	2532	2602	2672	2742	2812	2882	2952	3022	70
621	3092	3162	3231	3301	3371	3441	3511	3581	3651	3721	70
622	3790	3860	3930	4000	4070	4139	4209	4279	4349	4418	70
623	4488	4558	4627	4697	4767	4836	4906	4976	5045	5115	70
624	5185	5254	5324	5393	5463	5532	5602	5672	5741	5811	70
625	5880	5949	6019	6088	6158	6227	6297	6366	6436	6505	69
626	6574	6644	6713	6782	6852	6921	6990	7060	7129	7198	69
627	7268	7337	7406	7475	7545	7614	7683	7752	7821	7890	69
628	7960	8029	8098	8167	8236	8305	8374	8443	8513	8582	69
629	8651	8720	8789	8858	8927	8996	9065	9134	9203	9272	69
630	9341	9409	9478	9547	9616	9685	9754	9823	9892	9961	69
631	80 0029	0098	0167	0236	0305	0373	0442	0511	0580	0648	69
632	0717	0786	0854	0923	0992	1061	1129	1198	1266	1335	69
633	1404	1472	1541	1609	1678	1747	1815	1884	1952	2021	69
634	2089	2158	2226	2295	2363	2432	2500	2568	2637	2705	69
635	2774	2842	2910	2979	3047	3116	3184	3252	3321	3389	68
636	3457	3525	3594	3662	3730	3798	3867	3935	4003	4071	68
637	4139	4208	4276	4344	4412	4480	4548	4616	4685	4753	68
638	4821	4889	4957	5025	5093	5161	5229	5297	5365	5433	68
639	5501	5569	5637	5705	5773	5841	5908	5976	6044	6112	68
N.	0	1	2	3	4	5	6	7	8	9	D.

N.	0	1	2	3	4	5	6	7	8	9	D.
640	80 6180	6248	6316	6384	6451	6519	6587	6655	6723	6790	68
641	6858	6926	6994	7061	7129	7197	7264	7332	7400	7467	68
642	7535	7603	7670	7738	7806	7873	7941	8008	8076	8143	68
643	8211	8279	8346	8414	8481	8549	8616	8684	8751	8818	67
644	8886	8953	9021	9088	9156	9223	9290	9358	9425	9492	67
645	*9560	9627	9694	9762	9829	9896	9964	*031	0098	0165	67
646	81 0233	0300	0367	0434	0501	0569	0636	0703	0770	0837	67
647	0904	0971	1039	1106	1173	1240	1307	1374	1441	1508	67
648	1575	1642	1709	1776	1843	1910	1977	2044	2111	2178	67
649	2245	2312	2379	2445	2512	2579	2646	2713	2780	2847	67
650	2913	2980	3047	3114	3181	3247	3314	3381	3448	3514	67
651	3581	3648	3714	3781	3848	3914	3981	4048	4114	4181	67
652	4248	4314	4381	4447	4514	4581	4647	4714	4780	4847	67
653	4913	4980	5046	5113	5179	5246	5312	5378	5445	5511	66
654	5578	5644	5711	5777	5843	5910	5976	6042	6109	6175	66
655	6241	6308	6374	6440	6506	6573	6639	6705	6771	6838	66
656	6904	6970	7036	7102	7169	7235	7301	7367	7433	7499	66
657	7565	7631	7698	7764	7830	7896	7962	8028	8094	8160	66
658	8226	8292	8358	8424	8490	8556	8622	8688	8754	8820	66
659	8885	8951	9017	9083	9149	9215	9281	9346	9412	9478	66
660	*9544	9610	9676	9741	9807	9873	9939	*004	0070	0136	66
661	82 0201	0267	0333	0399	0464	0530	0595	0661	0727	0792	66
662	0858	0924	0989	1055	1120	1186	1251	1317	1382	1448	66
663	1514	1579	1645	1710	1775	1841	1906	1972	2037	2103	65
664	2168	2233	2299	2364	2430	2495	2560	2626	2691	2756	65
665	2822	2887	2952	3018	3083	3148	3213	3279	3344	3409	65
666	3474	3539	3605	3670	3735	3800	3865	3930	3996	4061	65
667	4126	4191	4256	4321	4386	4451	4516	4581	4646	4711	65
668	4776	4841	4906	4971	5036	5101	5166	5231	5296	5361	65
669	5426	5491	5556	5621	5686	5751	5815	5880	5945	6010	65
670	6075	6140	6204	6269	6334	6399	6464	6528	6593	6658	65
671	6723	6787	6852	6917	6981	7046	7111	7175	7240	7305	65
672	7369	7434	7499	7563	7628	7692	7757	7821	7886	7951	65
673	8015	8080	8144	8209	8273	8338	8402	8467	8531	8595	64
674	8660	8724	8789	8853	8918	8982	9046	9111	9175	9239	64
675	9304	9368	9432	9497	9561	9625	9690	9754	9818	9882	64
676	*9947	*011	0075	0139	0204	0268	0332	0396	0460	0525	64
677	83 0589	0653	0717	0781	0845	0909	0973	1037	1102	1166	64
678	1230	1294	1358	1422	1486	1550	1614	1678	1742	1806	64
679	1870	1934	1998	2062	2126	2189	2253	2317	2381	2445	64
680	2509	2573	2637	2700	2764	2828	2892	2956	3020	3083	64
681	3147	3211	3275	3338	3402	3466	3530	3593	3657	3721	64
682	3784	3848	3912	3975	4039	4103	4166	4230	4294	4357	64
683	4421	4484	4548	4611	4675	4739	4802	4866	4929	4993	64
684	5056	5120	5183	5247	5310	5373	5437	5500	5564	5627	63
685	5691	5754	5817	5881	5944	6007	6071	6134	6197	6261	63
686	6324	6387	6451	6514	6577	6641	6704	6767	6830	6894	63
687	6957	7020	7083	7146	7210	7273	7336	7399	7462	7525	63
688	7588	7652	7715	7778	7841	7904	7967	8030	8093	8156	63
689	8219	8282	8345	8408	8471	8534	8597	8660	8723	8786	63
690	8849	8912	8975	9038	9101	9164	9227	9289	9352	9415	63
691	*9478	9541	9604	9667	9729	9792	9855	9918	9981	*043	63
692	84 0106	0169	0232	0294	0357	0420	0482	0545	0608	0671	63
693	0733	0796	0859	0921	0984	1046	1109	1172	1234	1297	63
694	1359	1422	1485	1547	1610	1672	1735	1797	1860	1922	63
695	1985	2047	2110	2172	2235	2297	2360	2422	2484	2547	62
696	2609	2672	2734	2796	2859	2921	2983	3046	3108	3170	62
697	3233	3295	3357	3420	3482	3544	3606	3669	3731	3793	62
698	3855	3918	3980	4042	4104	4166	4229	4291	4353	4415	62
699	4477	4539	4601	4664	4726	4788	4850	4912	4974	5036	62
N.	0	1	2	3	4	5	6	7	8	9	D.

N.	0	1	2	3	4	5	6	7	8	9	D.
700	84 5098	5160	5222	5284	5346	5408	5470	5532	5594	5656	62
701	5718	5780	5842	5904	5966	6028	6090	6151	6213	6275	62
702	6337	6399	6461	6523	6585	6646	6708	6770	6832	6894	62
703	6955	7017	7079	7141	7202	7264	7326	7388	7449	7511	62
704	7573	7634	7696	7758	7819	7881	7943	8004	8066	8128	62
705	8189	8251	8312	8374	8435	8497	8559	8620	8682	8743	62
706	8805	8866	8928	8989	9051	9112	9174	9235	9297	9358	61
707	9419	9481	9542	9604	9665	9726	9788	9849	9911	9972	61
708	85 0033	0095	0156	0217	0279	0340	0401	0462	0524	0585	61
709	0646	0707	0769	0830	0891	0952	1014	1075	1136	1197	61
710	1258	1320	1381	1442	1503	1564	1625	1686	1747	1809	61
711	1870	1931	1992	2053	2114	2175	2236	2297	2358	2419	61
712	2480	2541	2602	2663	2724	2785	2846	2907	2968	3029	61
713	3090	3150	3211	3272	3333	3394	3455	3516	3577	3637	61
714	3698	3759	3820	3881	3941	4002	4063	4124	4185	4245	61
715	4306	4367	4428	4488	4549	4610	4670	4731	4792	4852	61
716	4913	4974	5034	5095	5156	5216	5277	5337	5398	5459	61
717	5519	5580	5640	5701	5761	5822	5882	5943	6003	6064	61
718	6124	6185	6245	6306	6366	6427	6487	6548	6608	6668	60
719	6729	6789	6850	6910	6970	7031	7091	7152	7212	7272	60
720	7332	7393	7453	7513	7574	7634	7694	7755	7815	7875	60
721	7935	7995	8056	8116	8176	8236	8297	8357	8417	8477	60
722	8537	8597	8657	8718	8778	8838	8898	8958	9018	9078	60
723	9138	9198	9258	9318	9379	9439	9499	9559	9619	9679	60
724	*9739	9799	9859	9918	9978	*038	0098	0158	0218	0278	60
725	86 0338	0398	0458	0518	0578	0637	0697	0757	0817	0877	60
726	0937	0996	1056	1116	1176	1236	1295	1355	1415	1475	60
727	1534	1594	1654	1714	1773	1833	1893	1952	2012	2072	60
728	2131	2191	2251	2310	2370	2430	2489	2549	2608	2668	60
729	2728	2787	2847	2906	2966	3025	3085	3144	3204	3263	60
730	3323	3382	3442	3501	3561	3620	3680	3739	3799	3858	59
731	3917	3977	4036	4096	4155	4214	4274	4333	4392	4452	59
732	4511	4570	4630	4689	4748	4808	4867	4926	4985	5045	59
733	5104	5163	5222	5282	5341	5400	5459	5519	5578	5637	59
734	5696	5755	5814	5874	5933	5992	6051	6110	6169	6228	59
735	6287	6346	6405	6465	6524	6583	6642	6701	6760	6819	59
736	6878	6937	6996	7055	7114	7173	7232	7291	7350	7409	59
737	7467	7526	7585	7644	7703	7762	7821	7880	7939	7998	59
738	8056	8115	8174	8233	8292	8350	8409	8468	8527	8586	59
739	8644	8703	8762	8821	8879	8938	8997	9056	9114	9173	59
740	9232	9290	9349	9408	9466	9525	9584	9642	9701	9760	59
741	*9818	9877	9935	9994	*053	0111	0170	0228	0287	0345	59
742	87 0404	0462	0521	0579	0638	0696	0755	0813	0872	0930	58
743	0989	1047	1106	1164	1223	1281	1339	1398	1456	1515	58
744	1573	1631	1690	1748	1806	1865	1923	1981	2040	2098	58
745	2156	2215	2273	2331	2389	2448	2506	2564	2622	2681	58
746	2739	2797	2855	2913	2972	3030	3088	3146	3204	3262	58
747	3321	3379	3437	3495	3553	3611	3669	3727	3785	3844	58
748	3902	3960	4018	4076	4134	4192	4250	4308	4366	4424	58
749	4482	4540	4598	4656	4714	4772	4830	4888	4945	5003	58
750	5061	5119	5177	5235	5293	5351	5409	5466	5524	5582	58
751	5640	5698	5756	5813	5871	5929	5987	6045	6102	6160	58
752	6218	6276	6333	6391	6449	6507	6564	6622	6680	6737	58
753	6795	6853	6910	6968	7026	7083	7141	7199	7256	7314	58
754	7371	7429	7487	7544	7602	7659	7717	7774	7832	7889	58
755	7947	8004	8062	8119	8177	8234	8292	8349	8407	8464	57
756	8522	8579	8637	8694	8752	8809	8866	8924	8981	9039	57
757	9096	9153	9211	9268	9325	9383	9440	9497	9555	9612	57
758	*9669	9726	9784	9841	9898	9956	*013	0070	0127	0185	57
759	88 0242	0299	0356	0413	0471	0528	0585	0642	0699	0756	57
N.	0	1	2	3	4	5	6	7	8	9	D.

N.	0	1	2	3	4	5	6	7	8	9	D.
760	88 0814	0871	0928	0985	1042	1099	1156	1213	1271	1328	57
761	1385	1442	1499	1556	1613	1670	1727	1784	1841	1898	57
762	1955	2012	2069	2126	2183	2240	2297	2354	2411	2468	57
763	2525	2581	2638	2695	2752	2809	2866	2923	2980	3037	57
764	3093	3150	3207	3264	3321	3377	3434	3491	3548	3605	57
765	3661	3718	3775	3832	3888	3945	4002	4059	4115	4172	57
766	4229	4285	4342	4399	4455	4512	4569	4625	4682	4739	57
767	4795	4852	4909	4965	5022	5078	5135	5192	5248	5305	57
768	5361	5418	5474	5531	5587	5644	5700	5757	5813	5870	57
769	5926	5983	6039	6096	6152	6209	6265	6321	6378	6434	56
770	6491	6547	6604	6660	6716	6773	6829	6885	6942	6998	56
771	7054	7111	7167	7223	7280	7336	7392	7449	7505	7561	56
772	7617	7674	7730	7786	7842	7898	7955	8011	8067	8123	56
773	8179	8236	8292	8348	8404	8460	8516	8573	8629	8685	56
774	8741	8797	8853	8909	8965	9021	9077	9134	9190	9246	56
775	9302	9358	9414	9470	9526	9582	9638	9694	9750	9806	56
776	*9862	9918	9974	*030	0086	0141	0197	0253	0309	0365	56
777	89 0421	0477	0533	0589	0645	0700	0756	0812	0868	0924	56
778	0980	1035	1091	1147	1203	1259	1314	1370	1426	1482	56
779	1537	1593	1649	1705	1760	1816	1872	1928	1983	2039	56
780	2095	2150	2206	2262	2317	2373	2429	2484	2540	2595	56
781	2651	2707	2762	2818	2873	2929	2985	3040	3096	3151	56
782	3207	3262	3318	3373	3429	3484	3540	3595	3651	3706	56
783	3762	3817	3873	3928	3984	4039	4094	4150	4205	4261	55
784	4316	4371	4427	4482	4538	4593	4648	4704	4759	4814	55
785	4870	4925	4980	5036	5091	5146	5201	5257	5312	5367	55
786	5423	5478	5533	5588	5644	5699	5754	5809	5864	5920	55
787	5975	6030	6085	6140	6195	6251	6306	6361	6416	6471	55
788	6526	6581	6636	6692	6747	6802	6857	6912	6967	7022	55
789	7077	7132	7187	7242	7297	7352	7407	7462	7517	7572	55
790	7627	7682	7737	7792	7847	7902	7957	8012	8067	8122	55
791	8176	8231	8286	8341	8396	8451	8506	8561	8615	8670	55
792	8725	8780	8835	8890	8944	8999	9054	9109	9164	9218	55
793	9273	9328	9383	9437	9492	9547	9602	9656	9711	9766	55
794	*9821	9875	9930	9985	*039	0094	0149	0203	0258	0312	55
795	90 0367	0422	0476	0531	0586	0640	0695	0749	0804	0859	55
796	0913	0968	1022	1077	1131	1186	1240	1295	1349	1404	55
797	1458	1513	1567	1622	1676	1731	1785	1840	1894	1948	54
798	2003	2057	2112	2166	2221	2275	2329	2384	2438	2492	54
799	2547	2601	2655	2710	2764	2818	2873	2927	2981	3036	54
800	3090	3144	3199	3253	3307	3361	3416	3470	3524	3578	54
801	3633	3687	3741	3795	3849	3904	3958	4012	4066	4120	54
802	4174	4229	4283	4337	4391	4445	4499	4553	4607	4661	54
803	4716	4770	4824	4878	4932	4986	5040	5094	5148	5202	54
804	5256	5310	5364	5418	5472	5526	5580	5634	5688	5742	54
805	5796	5850	5904	5958	6012	6066	6119	6173	6227	6281	54
806	6335	6389	6443	6497	6551	6604	6658	6712	6766	6820	54
807	6874	6927	6981	7035	7089	7143	7196	7250	7304	7358	54
808	7411	7465	7519	7573	7626	7680	7734	7787	7841	7895	54
809	7949	8002	8056	8110	8163	8217	8270	8324	8378	8431	54
810	8485	8539	8592	8646	8699	8753	8807	8860	8914	8967	54
811	9021	9074	9128	9181	9235	9289	9342	9396	9449	9503	54
812	*9556	9610	9663	9716	9770	9823	9877	9930	9984	*037	53
813	91 0091	0144	0197	0251	0304	0358	0411	0464	0518	0571	53
814	0624	0678	0731	0784	0838	0891	0944	0998	1051	1104	53
815	1158	1211	1264	1317	1371	1424	1477	1530	1584	1637	53
816	1690	1743	1797	1850	1903	1956	2009	2063	2116	2169	53
817	2222	2275	2328	2381	2435	2488	2541	2594	2647	2700	53
818	2753	2806	2859	2913	2966	3019	3072	3125	3178	3231	53
819	3284	3337	3390	3443	3496	3549	3602	3655	3708	3761	53
N.	0	1	2	3	4	5	6	7	8	9	D.

N.	0	1	2	3	4	5	6	7	8	9	D.
820	91 3814	3867	3920	3973	4026	4079	4132	4184	4237	4290	53
821	4343	4396	4449	4502	4555	4608	4660	4713	4766	4819	53
822	4872	4925	4977	5030	5083	5136	5189	5241	5294	5347	53
823	5400	5453	5505	5558	5611	5664	5716	5769	5822	5875	53
824	5927	5980	6033	6085	6138	6191	6243	6296	6349	6401	53
825	6454	6507	6559	6612	6664	6717	6770	6822	6875	6927	53
826	6980	7033	7085	7138	7190	7243	7295	7348	7400	7453	53
827	7506	7558	7611	7663	7716	7768	7820	7873	7925	7978	52
828	8030	8083	8135	8188	8240	8293	8345	8397	8450	8502	52
829	8555	8607	8659	8712	8764	8816	8869	8921	8973	9026	52
830	9078	9130	9183	9235	9287	9340	9392	9444	9496	9549	52
831	*9601	9653	9706	9758	9810	9862	9914	9967	*019	0071	52
832	92 0123	0176	0228	0280	0332	0384	0436	0489	0541	0593	52
833	0645	0697	0749	0801	0853	0906	0958	1010	1062	1114	52
834	1166	1218	1270	1322	1374	1426	1478	1530	1582	1634	52
835	1686	1738	1790	1842	1894	1946	1998	2050	2102	2154	52
836	2206	2258	2310	2362	2414	2466	2518	2570	2622	2674	52
837	2725	2777	2829	2881	2933	2985	3037	3089	3140	3192	52
838	3244	3296	3348	3399	345[illegible]	3503	3555	3607	3658	3710	52
839	3762	3814	3865	3917	3969	4021	4072	4124	4176	4228	52
840	4279	4331	4383	4434	4486	4538	4589	4641	4693	4744	52
841	4796	4848	4899	4951	5003	5054	5106	5157	5209	5261	52
842	5312	5364	5415	5467	5518	5570	5621	5673	5725	5776	52
843	5828	5879	5931	5982	6034	6085	6137	6188	6240	6291	51
844	6342	6394	6445	6497	6548	6600	6651	6702	6754	6805	51
845	6857	6908	6959	7011	7062	7114	7165	7216	7268	7319	51
846	7370	7422	7473	7524	7576	7627	7678	7730	7781	7832	51
847	7883	7935	7986	8037	8088	8140	8191	8242	8293	8345	51
848	8396	8447	8498	8549	8601	8652	8703	8754	8805	8857	51
849	8908	8959	9010	9061	9112	9163	9215	9266	9317	9368	51
850	9419	9470	9521	9572	9623	9674	9725	9776	9827	9879	51
851	*9930	9981	*032	0083	0134	0185	0236	0287	0338	0389	51
852	93 0440	0491	0542	0592	0643	0694	0745	0796	0847	0898	51
853	0949	1000	1051	1102	1153	1204	1254	1305	1356	1407	51
854	1458	1509	1560	1610	1661	1712	1763	1814	1865	1915	51
855	1966	2017	2068	2118	2169	2220	2271	2322	2372	2423	51
856	2474	2524	2575	2626	2677	2727	2778	2829	2879	2930	51
857	2981	3031	3082	3133	3183	3234	3285	3335	3386	3437	51
858	3487	3538	3589	3639	3690	3740	3791	3841	3892	3943	51
859	3993	4044	4094	4145	4195	4246	4296	4347	4397	4448	51
860	4498	4549	4599	4650	4700	4751	4801	4852	4902	4953	50
861	5003	5054	5104	5154	5205	5255	5306	5356	5406	5457	50
862	5507	5558	5608	5658	5709	5759	5809	5860	5910	5960	50
863	6011	6061	6111	6162	6212	6262	6313	6363	6413	6463	50
864	6514	6564	6614	6665	6715	6765	6815	6865	6916	6966	50
865	7016	7066	7117	7167	7217	7267	7317	7367	7418	7468	50
866	7518	7568	7618	7668	7718	7769	7819	7869	7919	7969	50
867	8019	8069	8119	8169	8219	8269	8320	8370	8420	8470	50
868	8520	8570	8620	8670	8720	8770	8820	8870	8920	8970	50
869	9020	9070	9120	9170	9220	9270	9320	9369	9419	9469	50
870	9519	9569	9619	9669	9719	9769	9819	9869	9918	9968	50
871	94 0018	0068	0118	0168	0218	0267	0317	0367	0417	0467	50
872	0516	0566	0616	0666	0716	0765	0815	0865	0915	0964	50
873	1014	1064	1114	1163	1213	1263	1313	1362	1412	1462	50
874	1511	1561	1611	1660	1710	1760	1809	1859	1909	1958	50
875	2008	2058	2107	2157	2207	2256	2306	2355	2405	2455	50
876	2504	2554	2603	2653	2702	2752	2801	2851	2901	2950	50
877	3000	3049	3099	3148	3198	3247	3297	3346	3396	3445	49
878	3495	3544	3593	3643	3692	3742	3791	3841	3890	3939	49
879	3989	4038	4088	4137	4186	4236	4285	4335	4384	4433	49
N.	0	1	2	3	4	5	6	7	8	9	D.

N.	0	1	2	3	4	5	6	7	8	9	D.
880	94 4483	4532	4581	4631	4680	4729	4779	4828	4877	4927	49
881	4976	5025	5074	5124	5173	5222	5272	5321	5370	5419	49
882	5469	5518	5567	5616	5665	5715	5764	5813	5862	5912	49
883	5961	6010	6059	6108	6157	6207	6256	6305	6354	6403	49
884	6452	6501	6551	6600	6649	6698	6747	6796	6845	6894	49
885	6943	6992	7041	7090	7140	7189	7238	7287	7336	7385	49
886	7434	7483	7532	7581	7630	7679	7728	7777	7826	7875	49
887	7924	7973	8022	8070	8119	8168	8217	8266	8315	8364	49
888	8413	8462	8511	8560	8609	8657	8706	8755	8804	8853	49
889	8902	8951	8999	9048	9097	9146	9195	9244	9292	9341	49
890	9390	9439	9488	9536	9585	9634	9683	9731	9780	9829	49
891	*9878	9926	9975	•024	0073	0121	0170	0219	0267	0316	49
892	95 0365	0414	0462	0511	0560	0608	0657	0706	0754	0803	49
893	0851	0900	0949	0997	1046	1095	1143	1192	1240	1289	49
894	1338	1386	1435	1483	1532	1580	1629	1677	1726	1775	49
895	1823	1872	1920	1969	2017	2066	2114	2163	2211	2260	48
896	2308	2356	2405	2453	2502	2550	2599	2647	2696	2744	48
897	2792	2841	2889	2938	2986	3034	3083	3131	3180	3228	48
898	3276	3325	3373	3421	3470	3518	3566	3615	3663	3711	48
899	3760	3808	3856	3905	3953	4001	4049	4098	4146	4194	48
900	4243	4291	4339	4387	4435	4484	4532	4580	4628	4677	48
901	4725	4773	4821	4869	4918	4966	5014	5062	5110	5158	48
902	5207	5255	5303	5351	5399	5447	5495	5543	5592	5640	48
903	5688	5736	5784	5832	5880	5928	5976	6024	6072	6120	48
904	6168	6216	6265	6313	6361	6409	6457	6505	6553	6601	48
905	6649	6697	6745	6793	6840	6888	6936	6984	7032	7080	48
906	7128	7176	7224	7272	7320	7368	7416	7464	7512	7559	48
907	7607	7655	7703	7751	7799	7847	7894	7942	7990	8038	48
908	8086	8134	8181	8229	8277	8325	8373	8421	8468	8516	48
909	8564	8612	8659	8707	8755	8803	8850	8898	8946	8994	48
910	9041	9089	9137	9185	9232	9280	9328	9375	9423	9471	48
911	9518	9566	9614	9661	9709	9757	9804	9852	9900	9947	48
912	*9995	•042	0090	0138	0185	0233	0280	0328	0376	0423	48
913	96 0471	0518	0566	0613	0661	0709	0756	0804	0851	0899	48
914	0946	0994	1041	1089	1136	1184	1231	1279	1326	1374	47
915	1421	1469	1516	1563	1611	1658	1706	1753	1801	1848	47
916	1895	1943	1990	2038	2085	2132	2180	2227	2275	2322	47
917	2369	2417	2464	2511	2559	2606	2653	2701	2748	2795	47
918	2843	2890	2937	2985	3032	3079	3126	3174	3221	3268	47
919	3316	3363	3410	3457	3504	3552	3599	3646	3693	3741	47
920	3788	3835	3882	3929	3977	4024	4071	4118	4165	4212	47
921	4260	4307	4354	4401	4448	4495	4542	4590	4637	4684	47
922	4731	4778	4825	4872	4919	4966	5013	5061	5108	5155	47
923	5202	5249	5296	5343	5390	5437	5484	5531	5578	5625	47
924	5672	5719	5766	5813	5860	5907	5954	6001	6048	6095	47
925	6142	6189	6236	6283	6329	6376	6423	6470	6517	6564	47
926	6611	6658	6705	6752	6799	6845	6892	6939	6986	7033	47
927	7080	7127	7173	7220	7267	7314	7361	7408	7454	7501	47
928	7548	7595	7642	7688	7735	7782	7829	7875	7922	7969	47
929	8016	8062	8109	8156	8203	8249	8296	8343	8390	8436	47
930	8483	8530	8576	8623	8670	8716	8763	8810	8856	8903	47
931	8950	8996	9043	9090	9136	9183	9229	9276	9323	9369	47
932	9416	9463	9509	9556	9602	9649	9695	9742	9789	9835	47
933	*9882	9928	9975	•021	0068	0114	0161	0207	0254	0300	47
934	97 0347	0393	0440	0486	0533	0579	0626	0672	0719	0765	46
935	0812	0858	0904	0951	0997	1044	1090	1137	1183	1229	46
936	1276	1322	1369	1415	1461	1508	1554	1601	1647	1693	46
937	1740	1786	1832	1879	1925	1971	2018	2064	2110	2157	46
938	2203	2249	2295	2342	2388	2434	2481	2527	2573	2619	46
939	2666	2712	2758	2804	2851	2897	2943	2989	3035	3082	46
N.	0	1	2	3	4	5	6	7	8	9	D.

N.	0	1	2	3	4	5	6	7	8	9	D.
940	97 3128	3174	3220	3266	3313	3359	3405	3451	3497	3543	46
941	3590	3636	3682	3728	3774	3820	3866	3913	3959	4005	46
942	4051	4097	4143	4189	4235	4281	4327	4374	4420	4466	46
943	4512	4558	4604	4650	4696	4742	4788	4834	4880	4926	46
944	4972	5018	5064	5110	5156	5202	5248	5294	5340	5386	46
945	5432	5478	5524	5570	5616	5662	5707	5753	5799	5845	46
946	5891	5937	5983	6029	6075	6121	6167	6212	6258	6304	46
947	6350	6396	6442	6488	6533	6579	6625	6671	6717	6763	46
948	6808	6854	6900	6946	6992	7037	7083	7129	7175	7220	46
949	7266	7312	7358	7403	7449	7495	7541	7586	7632	7678	46
950	7724	7769	7815	7861	7906	7952	7998	8043	8089	8135	46
951	8181	8226	8272	8317	8363	8409	8454	8500	8546	8591	46
952	8637	8683	8728	8774	8819	8865	8911	8956	9002	9047	46
953	9093	9138	9184	9230	9275	9321	9366	9412	9457	9503	46
954	9548	9594	9639	9685	9730	9776	9821	9867	9912	9958	46
955	98 0003	0049	0094	0140	0185	0231	0276	0322	0367	0412	45
956	0458	0503	0549	0594	0640	0685	0730	0776	0821	0867	45
957	0912	0957	1003	1048	1093	1139	1184	1229	1275	1320	45
958	1366	1411	1456	1501	1547	1592	1637	1683	1728	1773	45
959	1819	1864	1909	1954	2000	2045	2090	2135	2181	2226	45
960	2271	2316	2362	2407	2452	2497	2543	2588	2633	2678	45
961	2723	2769	2814	2859	2904	2949	2994	3040	3085	3130	45
962	3175	3220	3265	3310	3356	3401	3446	3491	3536	3581	45
963	3626	3671	3716	3762	3807	3852	3897	3942	3987	4032	45
964	4077	4122	4167	4212	4257	4302	4347	4392	4437	4482	45
965	4527	4572	4617	4662	4707	4752	4797	4842	4887	4932	45
966	4977	5022	5067	5112	5157	5202	5247	5292	5337	5382	45
967	5426	5471	5516	5561	5606	5651	5696	5741	5786	5830	45
968	5875	5920	5965	6010	6055	6100	6144	6189	6234	6279	45
969	6324	6369	6413	6458	6503	6548	6593	6637	6682	6727	45
970	6772	6817	6861	6906	6951	6996	7040	7085	7130	7175	45
971	7219	7264	7309	7353	7398	7443	7488	7532	7577	7622	45
972	7666	7711	7756	7800	7845	7890	7934	7979	8024	8068	45
973	8113	8157	8202	8247	8291	8336	8381	8425	8470	8514	45
974	8559	8604	8648	8693	8737	8782	8826	8871	8916	8960	45
975	9005	9049	9094	9138	9183	9227	9272	9316	9361	9405	45
976	9450	9494	9539	9583	9628	9672	9717	9761	9806	9850	44
977	*9895	9939	9983	*028	0072	0117	0161	0206	0250	0294	44
978	99 0339	0383	0428	0472	0516	0561	0605	0650	0694	0738	44
979	0783	0827	0871	0916	0960	1004	1049	1093	1137	1182	44
980	1226	1270	1315	1359	1403	1448	1492	1536	1580	1625	44
981	1669	1713	1758	1802	1846	1890	1935	1979	2023	2067	44
982	2111	2156	2200	2244	2288	2333	2377	2421	2465	2509	44
983	2554	2598	2642	2686	2730	2774	2819	2863	2907	2951	44
984	2995	3039	3083	3127	3172	3216	3260	3304	3348	3392	44
985	3436	3480	3524	3568	3613	3657	3701	3745	3789	3833	44
986	3877	3921	3965	4009	4053	4097	4141	4185	4229	4273	44
987	4317	4361	4405	4449	4493	4537	4581	4625	4669	4713	44
988	4757	4801	4845	4889	4933	4977	5021	5065	5108	5152	44
989	5196	5240	5284	5328	5372	5416	5460	5504	5547	5591	44
990	5635	5679	5723	5767	5811	5854	5898	5942	5986	6030	44
991	6074	6117	6161	6205	6249	6293	6337	6380	6424	6468	44
992	6512	6555	6599	6643	6687	6731	6774	6818	6862	6906	44
993	6949	6993	7037	7080	7124	7168	7212	7255	7299	7343	44
994	7386	7430	7474	7517	7561	7605	7648	7692	7736	7779	44
995	7823	7867	7910	7954	7998	8041	8085	8129	8172	8216	44
996	8259	8303	8347	8390	8434	8477	8521	8564	8608	8652	44
997	8695	8739	8782	8826	8869	8913	8956	9000	9043	9087	44
998	9131	9174	9218	9261	9305	9348	9392	9435	9479	9522	44
999	9565	9609	9652	9696	9739	9783	9826	9870	9913	9957	43
N.	0	1	2	3	4	5	6	7	8	9	D.

TABLE II.

LOGARITHMIC SINES AND TANGENTS,

FOR

EVERY DEGREE AND MINUTE OF THE QUADRANT.

If the logarithms of the values in Table III. be each increased by 10, the results will be the values of this table.

The logarithmic Secants and Cosecants are not given. They may be readily obtained, as follows:—Subtract the logarithmic Cosine from 20, and the remainder will be the logarithmic Secant; subtract the logarithmic Sine from 20, and the remainder will be the logarithmic Cosecant.

0° 179°

′	Sine.	D.	Cosine.	D.	Tang.	D.	Cotang.	′
0	Inf. Neg.		10·000000		Inf. Neg.		Infinite.	60
1	6·463726	501717	000000	00	6·463726	501717	13·536274	59
2	764756	293485	000000	00	764756	293483	235244	58
3	940847	208231	000000	00	940847	208231	059153	57
4	7·065786	161517	000000	00	7·065786	161517	12·934214	56
5	162696	131968	000000	00	162696	131969	837304	55
6	241877	111575	9·999999	01	241878	111578	758122	54
7	308824	96653	999999	01	308825	96653	691175	53
8	366816	85254	999999	01	366817	85254	633183	52
9	417968	76263	999999	01	417970	76263	582030	51
10	463726	68988	999998	01	463727	68988	536273	50
11	7·505118	62981	9·999998	01	7·505120	62981	12·494880	49
12	542906	57936	999997	01	542909	57933	457091	48
13	577668	53641	999997	01	577672	53642	422328	47
14	609853	49938	999996	01	609857	49939	390143	46
15	639816	46714	999996	01	639820	46715	360180	45
16	667845	43881	999995	01	667849	43882	332151	44
17	694173	41372	999995	01	694179	41373	305821	43
18	718997	39135	999994	01	719003	39136	280997	42
19	742478	37127	999993	01	742484	37128	257516	41
20	764754	35315	999993	01	764761	35136	235239	40
21	7·785943	33672	9·999992	01	7·785951	33673	12·214049	39
22	806146	32175	999991	01	806155	32176	193845	38
23	825451	30805	999990	01	825460	30806	174540	37
24	843934	29547	999989	02	843944	29549	156056	36
25	861662	28388	999989	02	861674	28390	138326	35
26	878695	27317	999988	02	878708	27318	121292	34
27	895085	26323	999987	02	895099	26325	104901	33
28	910879	25399	999986	02	910894	25401	089106	32
29	926119	24538	999985	02	926134	24540	073866	31
30	940842	23733	999983	02	940858	23735	059142	30
31	7·955082	22980	9·999982	02	7·955100	22981	12·044900	29
32	968870	22273	999981	02	968889	22275	031111	28
33	982233	21608	999980	02	982253	21610	017747	27
34	995198	20981	999979	02	995219	20983	004781	26
35	8·007787	20390	999977	02	8·007809	20392	11·992191	25
36	020021	19831	999976	02	020044	19833	979956	24
37	031919	19302	999975	02	031945	19305	968055	23
38	043501	18801	999973	02	043527	18803	956473	22
39	054781	18325	999972	02	054809	18327	945191	21
40	065776	17872	999971	02	065806	17874	934194	20
41	8·076500	17441	9·999969	02	8·076531	17444	11·923469	19
42	086965	17031	999968	02	086997	17034	913003	18
43	097183	16639	999966	02	097217	16642	902783	17
44	107167	16265	999964	03	107203	16268	892797	16
45	116926	15908	999963	03	116963	15910	883037	15
46	126471	15566	999961	03	126510	15568	873490	14
47	135810	15238	999959	03	135851	15241	864149	13
48	144953	14924	999958	03	144996	14927	855004	12
49	153907	14622	999956	03	153952	14627	846048	11
50	162681	14333	999954	03	162727	14336	837273	10
51	8·171280	14054	9·999952	03	8·171328	14057	11·828672	9
52	179713	13786	999950	03	179763	13790	820237	8
53	187985	13529	999948	03	188036	13532	811964	7
54	196102	13280	999946	03	196156	13284	803844	6
55	204070	13041	999944	03	204126	13044	795874	5
56	211895	12810	999942	04	211953	12814	788047	4
57	219581	12587	999940	04	219641	12590	780359	3
58	227134	12372	999938	04	227195	12376	772805	2
59	234557	12164	999936	04	234621	12168	765379	1
60	241855	11963	999934	04	241921	11967	758079	0
′	Cosine.	D.	Sine.	D.	Cotang.	D.	Tang.	′

90° 89°

1° 178°

′	Sine.	D.	Cosine.	D.	Tang.	D.	Cotang.	′
0	8·241855	11963	9·999934	04	8·241921	11967	11·758079	60
1	249033	11768	999932	04	249102	11772	750898	59
2	256094	11580	999929	04	256165	11584	743835	58
3	263042	11398	999927	04	263115	11402	736885	57
4	269881	11221	999925	04	269956	11225	730044	56
5	276614	11050	999922	04	276691	11054	723309	55
6	283243	10883	999920	04	283323	10887	716677	54
7	289773	10721	999918	04	289856	10726	710144	53
8	296207	10565	999915	04	296292	10570	703708	52
9	302546	10413	999913	04	302634	10418	697366	51
10	308794	10266	999910	04	308884	10270	691116	50
11	8·314954	10122	9·999907	04	8·315046	10126	11·684954	49
12	321027	9982	999905	04	321122	9987	678878	48
13	327016	9847	999902	04	327114	9851	672886	47
14	332924	9714	999899	05	333025	9719	666975	46
15	338753	9586	999897	05	338856	9590	661144	45
16	344504	9460	999894	05	344610	9465	655390	44
17	350181	9338	999891	05	350289	9343	649711	43
18	355783	9219	999888	05	355895	9224	644105	42
19	361315	9103	999885	05	361430	9108	638570	41
20	366777	8990	999882	05	366895	8995	633105	40
21	8·372171	8880	9·999879	05	8·372292	8885	11·627708	39
22	377499	8772	999876	05	377622	8777	622378	38
23	382762	8667	999873	05	382889	8672	617111	37
24	387962	8564	999870	05	388092	8570	611908	36
25	393101	8464	999867	05	393234	8470	606766	35
26	398179	8366	999864	05	398315	8371	601685	34
27	403199	8271	999861	05	403338	8276	596662	33
28	408161	8177	999858	05	408304	8182	591696	32
29	413068	8086	999854	05	413213	8091	586787	31
30	417919	7996	999851	06	418068	8002	581932	30
31	8·422717	7909	9·999848	06	8·422869	7914	11·577131	29
32	427462	7823	999844	06	427618	7830	572382	28
33	432156	7740	999841	06	432315	7745	567685	27
34	436800	7657	999838	06	436962	7663	563038	26
35	441394	7577	999834	06	441560	7583	558440	25
36	445941	7499	999831	06	446110	7505	553890	24
37	450440	7422	999827	06	450613	7428	549387	23
38	454893	7346	999824	06	455070	7352	544930	22
39	459301	7273	999820	06	459481	7279	540519	21
40	463665	7200	999816	06	463849	7206	536151	20
41	8·467985	7129	9·999813	06	8·468172	7135	11·531828	19
42	472263	7060	999809	06	472454	7066	527546	18
43	476498	6991	999805	06	476693	6998	523307	17
44	480693	6924	999801	06	480892	6931	519108	16
45	484848	6859	999797	07	485050	6865	514950	15
46	488963	6794	999794	07	489170	6801	510830	14
47	493040	6731	999790	07	493250	6738	506750	13
48	497078	6669	999786	07	497293	6676	502707	12
49	501080	6608	999782	07	501298	6615	498702	11
50	505045	6548	999778	07	505267	6555	494733	10
51	8·508974	6489	9·999774	07	8·509200	6496	11·490800	9
52	512867	6431	999769	07	513098	6439	486902	8
53	516726	6375	999765	07	516961	6382	483039	7
54	520551	6319	999761	07	520790	6326	479210	6
55	524343	6264	999757	07	524586	6272	475414	5
56	528102	6211	999753	07	528349	6218	471651	4
57	531828	6158	999748	07	532080	6165	467920	3
58	535523	6106	999744	07	535779	6113	464221	2
59	539186	6055	999740	07	539447	6062	460553	1
60	542819	6004	999735	07	543084	6012	456916	0
′	Cosine.	D.	Sine.	D.	Cotang.	D.	Tang.	′

91° 88°

2° | 177°

′	Sine.	D.	Cosine.	D.	Tang.	D.	Cotang.	′
0	8·542819	6004	9·999735	07	8·543084	6012	11·456916	60
1	546422	5955	999731	07	546691	5962	453309	59
2	549995	5906	999726	07	550268	5914	449732	58
3	553539	5858	999722	08	553817	5866	446183	57
4	557054	5811	999717	08	557336	5819	442664	56
5	560540	5765	999713	08	560828	5773	439172	55
6	563999	5719	999708	08	564291	5727	435709	54
7	567431	5674	999704	08	567727	5682	432273	53
8	570836	5630	999699	08	571137	5638	428863	52
9	574214	5587	999694	08	574520	5595	425480	51
10	577566	5544	999689	08	577877	5552	422123	50
11	8·580892	5502	9·999685	08	8·581208	5510	11·418792	49
12	584193	5460	999680	08	584514	5468	415486	48
13	587469	5419	999675	08	587795	5427	412205	47
14	590721	5379	999670	08	591051	5387	408949	46
15	593948	5339	999665	08	594283	5347	405717	45
16	597152	5300	999660	08	597492	5308	402508	44
17	600332	5261	999655	08	600677	5270	399323	43
18	603489	5223	999650	08	603839	5232	396161	42
19	606623	5186	999645	09	606978	5194	393022	41
20	609734	5149	999640	09	610094	5158	389906	40
21	8·612823	5112	9·999635	09	8·613189	5121	11·386811	39
22	615891	5076	999629	09	616262	5085	383738	38
23	618937	5041	999624	09	619313	5050	380687	37
24	621962	5006	999619	09	622343	5015	377657	36
25	624965	4972	999614	09	625352	4981	374648	35
26	627948	4938	999608	09	628340	4947	371660	34
27	630911	4904	999603	09	631308	4913	368692	33
28	633854	4871	999597	09	634256	4880	365744	32
29	636776	4839	999592	09	637184	4848	362816	31
30	639680	4806	999586	09	640093	4816	359907	30
31	8·642563	4775	9·999581	09	8·642982	4784	11·357018	29
32	645428	4743	999575	09	645853	4753	354147	28
33	648274	4712	999570	09	648704	4722	351296	27
34	651102	4682	999564	09	651537	4691	348463	26
35	653911	4652	999558	10	654352	4661	345648	25
36	656702	4622	999553	10	657149	4631	342851	24
37	659475	4592	999547	10	659928	4602	340072	23
38	662230	4563	999541	10	662689	4573	337311	22
39	664968	4535	999535	10	665433	4544	334567	21
40	667689	4506	999529	10	668160	4526	331840	20
41	8·670393	4479	9·999524	10	8·670870	4488	11·329130	19
42	673080	4451	999518	10	673563	4461	326437	18
43	675751	4424	999512	10	676239	4434	323761	17
44	678405	4397	999506	10	678900	4417	321100	16
45	681043	4370	999500	10	681544	4380	318456	15
46	683665	4344	999493	10	684172	4354	315828	14
47	686272	4318	999487	10	686784	4328	313216	13
48	688863	4292	999481	10	689381	4303	310619	12
49	691438	4267	999475	10	691963	4277	308037	11
50	693998	4242	999469	10	694529	4252	305471	10
51	8·696543	4217	9·999463	11	8·697081	4228	11·302919	9
52	699073	4192	999456	11	699617	4203	300383	8
53	701589	4168	999450	11	702139	4179	297861	7
54	704090	4144	999443	11	704646	4155	295354	6
55	706577	4121	999437	11	707140	4132	292860	5
56	709049	4097	999431	11	709618	4108	290382	4
57	711507	4074	999424	11	712083	4085	287917	3
58	713952	4051	999418	11	714534	4062	285466	2
59	716383	4029	999411	11	716972	4040	283028	1
60	718800	4006	999404	11	719396	4017	280604	0
′	Cosine.	D.	Sine.	D.	Cotang.	D.	Tang.	′

92° | 87°

3°								176°
′	Sine.	D.	Cosine.	D.	Tang.	D.	Cotang.	′
0	8·718800	4006	9·999404	11	8·719396	4017	11·280604	60
1	721204	3984	999398	11	721806	3995	278194	59
2	723595	3962	999391	11	724204	3974	275796	58
3	725972	3941	999384	11	726588	3952	273412	57
4	728337	3919	999378	11	728959	3930	271041	56
5	730688	3898	999371	11	731317	3909	268683	55
6	733027	3877	999364	12	733663	3889	266337	54
7	735354	3857	999357	12	735996	3868	264004	53
8	737667	3836	999350	12	738317	3848	261683	52
9	739969	3816	999343	12	740626	3827	259374	51
10	742259	3796	999336	12	742922	3807	257078	50
11	8·744536	3776	9·999329	12	8·745207	3787	11·254793	49
12	746802	3756	999322	12	747479	3768	252521	48
13	749055	3737	999315	12	749740	3749	250260	47
14	751297	3717	999308	12	751989	3729	248011	46
15	753528	3698	999301	12	754227	3710	245773	45
16	755747	3679	999294	12	756453	3692	243547	44
17	757955	3661	999287	12	758668	3673	241332	43
18	760151	3642	999279	12	760872	3655	239128	42
19	762337	3624	999272	12	763065	3636	236935	41
20	764511	3606	999265	12	765246	3618	234754	40
21	8·766675	3588	9·999257	12	8·767417	3600	11·232583	39
22	768828	3570	999250	13	769578	3583	230422	38
23	770970	3553	999242	13	771727	3565	228273	37
24	773101	3535	999235	13	773866	3548	226134	36
25	775223	3518	999227	13	775995	3531	224005	35
26	777333	3501	999220	13	778114	3514	221886	34
27	779434	3484	999212	13	780222	3497	219778	33
28	781524	3467	999205	13	782320	3480	217680	32
29	783605	3451	999197	13	784408	3464	215592	31
30	785675	3431	999189	13	786486	3447	213514	30
31	8·787736	3418	9·999181	13	8·788554	3431	11·211446	29
32	789787	3402	999174	13	790613	3414	209387	28
33	791828	3386	999166	13	792662	3399	207338	27
34	793859	3370	999158	13	794701	3383	205299	26
35	795881	3354	999150	13	796731	3368	203269	25
36	797894	3339	999142	13	798752	3352	201248	24
37	799897	3323	999134	13	800763	3337	199237	23
38	801892	3308	999126	13	802765	3322	197235	22
39	803876	3293	999118	13	804758	3307	195242	21
40	805852	3278	999110	13	806742	3292	193258	20
41	8·807819	3263	9·999102	13	8·808717	3278	11·191283	19
42	809777	3249	999094	14	810683	3262	189317	18
43	811726	3234	999086	14	812641	3248	187359	17
44	813667	3219	999077	14	814589	3233	185411	16
45	815599	3205	999069	14	816529	3219	183471	15
46	817522	3191	999061	14	818461	3205	181539	14
47	819436	3177	999053	14	820384	3191	179616	13
48	821343	3163	999044	14	822298	3177	177702	12
49	823240	3149	999036	14	824205	3163	175795	11
50	825130	3135	999027	14	826103	3150	173897	10
51	8·827011	3122	9·999019	14	8·827992	3136	11·172008	9
52	828884	3108	999010	14	829874	3123	170126	8
53	830749	3095	999002	14	831748	3110	168252	7
54	832607	3082	998993	14	833613	3096	166387	6
55	834456	3069	998984	14	835471	3083	164529	5
56	836297	3056	998976	14	837321	3070	162679	4
57	838130	3043	998967	15	839163	3057	160837	3
58	839956	3030	998958	15	840998	3045	159002	2
59	841774	3017	998950	15	842825	3032	157175	1
60	843585	3000	998941	15	844644	3019	155356	0
′	Cosine.	D.	Sine.	D.	Cotang.	D.	Tang.	′
93°								86°

4° 175°

′	Sine.	D.	Cosine.	D.	Tang.	D.	Cotang.	′
0	8·843585	3005	9·998941	15	8·844644	3019	11·155356	60
1	845387	2992	998932	15	846455	3007	153545	59
2	847183	2980	998923	15	848260	2995	151740	58
3	848971	2967	998914	15	850057	2982	149943	57
4	850751	2955	998905	15	851846	2970	148154	56
5	852525	2943	998896	15	853628	2958	146372	55
6	854291	2931	998887	15	855403	2946	144597	54
7	856049	2919	998878	15	857171	2935	142829	53
8	857801	2907	998869	15	858932	2923	141068	52
9	859546	2896	998860	15	860686	2911	139314	51
10	861283	2884	998851	15	862433	2900	137567	50
11	8·863014	2873	9·998841	15	8·864173	2888	11·135827	49
12	864738	2861	998832	15	865906	2877	134094	48
13	866455	2850	998823	16	867632	2866	132368	47
14	868165	2839	998813	16	869351	2854	130649	46
15	869868	2828	998804	16	871064	2843	128936	45
16	871565	2817	998795	16	872770	2832	127230	44
17	873255	2806	998785	16	874469	2821	125531	43
18	874938	2795	998776	16	876162	2811	123838	42
19	876615	2786	998766	16	877849	2800	122151	41
20	878285	2773	998757	16	879529	2789	120471	40
21	8·879949	2763	9·998747	16	8·881202	2779	11·118798	39
22	881607	2752	998738	16	882869	2768	117131	38
23	883258	2742	998728	16	884530	2758	115470	37
24	884903	2731	998718	16	886185	2747	113815	36
25	886542	2721	998708	16	887833	2737	112167	35
26	888174	2711	998699	16	889476	2727	110524	34
27	889801	2700	998689	16	891112	2717	108888	33
28	891421	2690	998679	16	892742	2707	107258	32
29	893035	2680	998669	17	894366	2697	105634	31
30	894643	2670	998659	17	895984	2687	104016	30
31	8·896246	2660	9·998649	17	8·897596	2677	11·102404	29
32	897842	2651	998639	17	899203	2667	160797	28
33	899432	2641	998629	17	900803	2658	099197	27
34	901017	2631	998619	17	902398	2648	097602	26
35	902596	2622	998609	17	903987	2638	096013	25
36	904169	2612	998599	17	905570	2629	094430	24
37	905736	2603	998589	17	907147	2620	092853	23
38	907297	2593	998578	17	908719	2610	091281	22
39	908853	2584	998568	17	910285	2601	089715	21
40	910404	2575	998558	17	911846	2592	088154	20
41	8·911949	2566	9·998548	17	8·913401	2583	11·086599	19
42	913488	2556	998537	17	914951	2574	085049	18
43	915022	2547	998527	17	916495	2565	083505	17
44	916550	2538	998516	18	918034	2556	081966	16
45	918073	2529	998506	18	919568	2547	080432	15
46	919591	2520	998495	18	921096	2538	078904	14
47	921103	2512	998485	18	922619	2530	077381	13
48	922610	2503	998474	18	924136	2521	075864	12
49	924112	2494	998464	18	925649	2512	074351	11
50	925609	2486	998453	18	927156	2503	072844	10
51	8·927100	2477	9·998442	18	8·928658	2495	11·071342	9
52	928587	2469	998431	18	930155	2486	069845	8
53	930068	2460	998421	18	931647	2478	068353	7
54	931544	2452	998410	18	933134	2470	066866	6
55	933015	2443	998399	18	934616	2461	065384	5
56	934481	2435	998388	18	936093	2453	063907	4
57	935942	2427	998377	18	937565	2445	062435	3
58	937398	2419	998366	18	939032	2437	060968	2
59	938850	2411	998355	18	940494	2430	059506	1
60	940296	2403	998344	18	941952	2421	058048	0
′	Cosine.	D.	Sine.	D.	Cotang.	D.	Tang.	′

94° 85°

5°								174°
′	Sine.	D.	Cosine.	D.	Tang.	D.	Cotang.	′
0	8·940296	2403	9·998344	19	8·941952	2421	11·058048	60
1	941738	2394	998333	19	943404	2413	056596	59
2	943174	2387	998322	19	944852	2405	055148	58
3	944606	2379	998311	19	946295	2397	053705	57
4	946034	2371	998300	19	947734	2390	052266	56
5	947456	2363	998289	19	949168	2382	050832	55
6	948874	2355	998277	19	950597	2374	049403	54
7	950287	2348	998266	19	952021	2366	047979	53
8	951696	2340	998255	19	953441	2360	046559	52
9	953100	2332	998243	19	954856	2351	045144	51
10	954499	2325	998232	19	956267	2344	043733	50
11	8·955894	2317	9·998220	19	8·957674	2337	11·042326	49
12	957284	2310	998209	19	959075	2329	040925	48
13	958670	2302	998197	19	960473	2323	039527	47
14	960052	2295	998186	19	961866	2314	038134	46
15	961429	2288	998174	19	963255	2307	036745	45
16	962801	2280	998163	19	964639	2300	035361	44
17	964170	2273	998151	19	966019	2293	033981	43
18	965534	2266	998139	20	967394	2286	032606	42
19	966893	2259	998128	20	968766	2279	031234	41
20	968249	2252	998116	20	970133	2271	029867	40
21	8·969600	2244	9·998104	20	8·971496	2265	11·028504	39
22	970947	2238	998092	20	972855	2257	027145	38
23	972289	2231	998080	20	974209	2251	025791	37
24	973628	2224	998068	20	975560	2244	024440	36
25	974962	2217	998056	20	976906	2237	023094	35
26	976293	2210	998044	20	978248	2230	021752	34
27	977619	2203	998032	20	979586	2223	020414	33
28	978941	2197	998020	20	980921	2217	019079	32
29	980259	2190	998008	20	982251	2210	017749	31
30	981573	2183	997996	20	983577	2204	016423	30
31	8·982883	2177	9·997984	20	8·984899	2197	11·015101	29
32	984189	2170	997972	20	986217	2191	013783	28
33	985491	2163	997959	20	987532	2184	012468	27
34	986789	2157	997947	20	988842	2178	011158	26
35	988083	2150	997935	21	990149	2171	009851	25
36	989374	2144	997922	21	991451	2165	008549	24
37	990660	2138	997910	21	992750	2158	007250	23
38	991943	2131	997897	21	994045	2152	005955	22
39	993222	2125	997885	21	995337	2146	004663	21
40	994497	2119	997872	21	996624	2140	003376	20
41	8·995768	2112	9·997860	21	8·997908	2134	11·002092	19
42	997036	2106	997847	21	999188	2127	000812	18
43	998299	2100	997835	21	9·000465	2121	10·999535	17
44	999560	2094	997822	21	001738	2115	998262	16
45	9·000816	2087	997809	21	003007	2109	996993	15
46	002069	2082	997797	21	004272	2103	995728	14
47	003318	2076	997784	21	005534	2097	994466	13
48	004563	2070	997771	21	006792	2091	993208	12
49	005805	2064	997758	21	008047	2085	991953	11
50	007044	2058	997745	21	009298	2080	990702	10
51	9·008278	2052	9·997732	21	9·010546	2074	10·989454	9
52	009510	2046	997719	21	011790	2068	988210	8
53	010737	2040	997706	21	013031	2062	986969	7
54	011962	2034	997693	22	014268	2056	985732	6
55	013182	2029	997680	22	015502	2051	984498	5
56	014400	2023	997667	22	016732	2045	983268	4
57	015613	2017	997654	22	017959	2040	982041	3
58	016824	2012	997641	22	019183	2033	980817	2
59	018031	2006	997628	22	020403	2028	979597	1
60	019235	2000	997614	22	021620	2023	978380	0
′	Cosine.	D.	Sine.	D.	Cotang.	D.	Tang.	′
95°								84°

6° 173°

′	Sine.	D.	Cosine.	D.	Tang.	D.	Cotang.	′
0	9·019235	2000	9·997614	22	9·021620	2023	10·978380	60
1	020435	1995	997601	22	022834	2017	977166	59
2	021632	1989	997588	22	024044	2011	975956	58
3	022825	1984	997574	22	025251	2006	974749	57
4	024016	1978	997561	22	026455	2000	973545	56
5	025203	1973	997547	22	027655	1995	972345	55
6	026386	1967	997534	23	028852	1990	971148	54
7	027567	1962	997520	23	030046	1985	969954	53
8	028744	1957	997507	23	031237	1979	968763	52
9	029918	1951	997493	23	032425	1974	967575	51
10	031089	1947	997480	23	033609	1969	966391	50
11	9·032257	1941	9·997466	23	9·034791	1964	10·965209	49
12	033421	1936	997452	23	035969	1958	964031	48
13	034582	1930	997439	23	037144	1953	962856	47
14	035741	1925	997425	23	038316	1948	961684	46
15	036896	1920	997411	23	039485	1943	960515	45
16	038048	1915	997397	23	040651	1938	959349	44
17	039197	1910	997383	23	041813	1933	958187	43
18	040342	1905	997369	23	042973	1928	957027	42
19	041485	1899	997355	23	044130	1923	955870	41
20	042625	1894	997341	23	045284	1918	954716	40
21	9·043762	1889	9·997327	24	9·046434	1913	10·953566	39
22	044895	1884	997313	24	047582	1908	952418	38
23	046026	1879	997299	24	048727	1903	951273	37
24	047154	1875	997285	24	049869	1898	950131	36
25	048279	1870	997271	24	051008	1893	948992	35
26	049400	1865	997257	24	052144	1889	947856	34
27	050519	1860	997242	24	053277	1884	946723	33
28	051635	1855	997228	24	054407	1879	945593	32
29	952749	1850	997214	24	055535	1874	944465	31
30	053859	1845	997199	24	056659	1870	943341	30
31	9·054966	1841	9·997185	24	9·057781	1865	10·942219	29
32	056071	1836	997170	24	058900	1869	941100	28
33	057172	1831	997156	24	060016	1855	939984	27
34	058271	1827	997141	24	061130	1851	938870	26
35	059367	1822	997127	24	062240	1846	937760	25
36	060460	1817	997112	24	063348	1842	936652	24
37	061551	1813	997098	24	064453	1837	935547	23
38	062639	1808	997083	25	065556	1833	934444	22
39	063724	1804	997068	25	066655	1828	933345	21
40	064806	1799	997053	25	067752	1824	932248	20
41	9·065885	1794	9·997039	25	9·068846	1819	10·931154	19
42	066962	1790	997024	25	069938	1815	930062	18
43	068036	1786	997009	25	071027	1810	928973	17
44	069107	1781	996994	25	072113	1806	927887	16
45	070176	1777	996979	25	073197	1802	926803	15
46	071242	1772	996964	25	074278	1797	925722	14
47	072306	1768	996949	25	075356	1793	924644	13
48	073366	1763	996934	25	076432	1789	923568	12
49	074424	1759	996919	25	077505	1784	922495	11
50	075480	1755	996904	25	078576	1780	921424	10
51	9·076533	1750	9·996889	25	9·079644	1776	10·920356	9
52	077583	1746	996874	25	080710	1772	919290	8
53	078631	1742	996858	25	081773	1767	918227	7
54	079676	1738	996843	25	082833	1763	917167	6
55	080719	1733	996828	25	083891	1759	916109	5
56	081759	1729	996812	26	084947	1755	915053	4
57	082797	1725	996797	26	086000	1751	914000	3
58	083832	1721	996782	26	087050	1747	912950	2
59	084864	1717	996766	26	088098	1743	911902	1
60	085894	1713	996751	26	089144	1738	910856	0
′	Cosine.	D.	Sine.	D.	Cotang.	D.	Tang.	′

96° 83°

7°								172°
′	Sine.	D.	Cosine.	D.	Tang.	D.	Cotang.	′
0	9·085894	1713	9·996751	26	9·089144	1738	10·910856	60
1	086922	1709	996735	26	090187	1734	909813	59
2	087947	1704	996720	26	091228	1730	908772	58
3	088970	1700	996704	26	092266	1727	907734	57
4	089990	1696	996688	26	093302	1722	906698	56
5	091008	1692	996673	26	094336	1719	905664	55
6	092024	1688	996657	26	095367	1715	904633	54
7	093037	1684	996641	26	096395	1711	903605	53
8	094047	1680	996625	26	097422	1707	902578	52
9	095056	1676	996610	26	098446	1703	901554	51
10	096062	1673	996594	26	099468	1699	900532	50
11	9·097065	1668	9·996578	27	9·100487	1695	10·899513	49
12	098066	1665	996562	27	101504	1691	898496	48
13	099065	1661	996546	27	102519	1687	897481	47
14	100062	1657	996530	27	103532	1684	896468	46
15	101056	1653	996514	27	104542	1680	895458	45
16	102048	1649	996498	27	105550	1676	894450	44
17	103037	1645	996482	27	106556	1672	893444	43
18	104025	1641	996465	27	107559	1669	892441	42
19	105010	1638	996449	27	108560	1665	891440	41
20	105992	1634	996433	27	109559	1661	890441	40
21	9·106973	1630	9·996417	27	9·110556	1658	10·889444	39
22	107951	1627	996400	27	111551	1654	888449	38
23	108927	1623	996384	27	112543	1650	887457	37
24	109901	1619	996368	27	113533	1646	886467	36
25	110873	1616	996351	27	114521	1643	885479	35
26	111842	1612	996335	27	115507	1639	884493	34
27	112809	1608	996318	27	116491	1636	883509	33
28	113774	1605	996302	28	117472	1632	882528	32
29	114737	1601	996285	28	118452	1629	881548	31
30	115698	1597	996269	28	119429	1625	880571	30
31	9·116656	1594	9·996252	28	9·120404	1622	10·879596	29
32	117613	1590	996235	28	121377	1618	878623	28
33	118567	1587	996219	28	122348	1615	877652	27
34	119519	1583	996202	28	123317	1611	876683	26
35	120469	1580	996185	28	124284	1607	875716	25
36	121417	1576	996168	28	125249	1604	874751	24
37	122362	1573	996151	28	126211	1601	873789	23
38	123306	1569	996134	28	127172	1597	872828	22
39	124248	1566	996117	28	128130	1594	871870	21
40	125187	1562	996100	28	129087	1591	870913	20
41	9·126125	1559	9·996083	29	9·130041	1587	10·869959	19
42	127060	1556	996066	29	130994	1584	869006	18
43	127993	1552	996049	29	131944	1581	868056	17
44	128925	1549	996032	29	132893	1577	867107	16
45	129854	1545	996015	29	133839	1574	866161	15
46	130781	1542	995998	29	134784	1571	865216	14
47	131706	1539	995980	29	135726	1567	864274	13
48	132630	1535	995963	29	136667	1564	863333	12
49	133551	1532	995946	29	137605	1561	862395	11
50	134470	1529	995928	29	138542	1558	861458	10
51	9·135387	1525	9·995911	29	9·139476	1555	10·860524	9
52	136303	1522	995894	29	140409	1551	859591	8
53	137216	1519	995876	29	141340	1548	858660	7
54	138128	1516	995859	29	142269	1545	857731	6
55	139037	1512	995841	29	143196	1542	856804	5
56	139944	1509	995823	29	144121	1539	855879	4
57	140850	1506	995806	29	145044	1535	854956	3
58	141754	1503	995788	29	145966	1532	854034	2
59	142655	1500	995771	29	146885	1529	853115	1
60	143555	1496	995753	29	147803	1526	852197	0
′	Cosine.	D.	Sine.	D.	Cotang.	D.	Tang.	′
97°								82°

8° 171°

′	Sine.	D.	Cosine.	D.	Tang.	D.	Cotang.	′
0	9·143555	1496	9·995753	30	9·147803	1526	10·852197	60
1	144453	1493	995735	30	148718	1523	851282	59
2	145349	1490	995717	30	149632	1520	850368	58
3	146243	1487	995699	30	150544	1517	849456	57
4	147136	1484	995681	30	151454	1514	848546	56
5	148026	1481	995664	30	152363	1511	847637	55
6	148915	1478	995646	30	153269	1508	846731	54
7	149802	1475	995628	30	154174	1505	845826	53
8	150686	1472	995610	30	155077	1502	844923	52
9	151569	1469	995591	30	155978	1499	844022	51
10	152451	1466	995573	30	156877	1496	843123	50
11	9·153330	1463	9·995555	30	9·157775	1493	10·842225	49
12	154208	1460	995537	30	158671	1490	841329	48
13	155083	1457	995519	30	159565	1487	840435	47
14	155957	1454	995501	31	160457	1484	839543	46
15	156830	1451	995482	31	161347	1481	838653	45
16	157700	1448	995464	31	162236	1479	837764	44
17	158569	1445	995446	31	163123	1476	836877	43
18	159435	1442	995427	31	164008	1473	835992	42
19	160301	1439	995409	31	164892	1470	835108	41
20	161164	1436	995390	31	165774	1467	834226	40
21	9·162025	1433	9·995372	31	9·166654	1464	10·833346	39
22	162885	1430	995353	31	167532	1461	832468	38
23	163743	1427	995334	31	168409	1458	831591	37
24	164600	1424	995316	31	169284	1455	830716	36
25	165454	1422	995297	31	170157	1453	829843	35
26	166307	1419	995278	31	171029	1450	828971	34
27	167159	1416	995260	31	171899	1447	828101	33
28	168008	1413	995241	32	172767	1444	827233	32
29	168856	1410	995222	32	173634	1442	826366	31
30	169702	1407	995203	32	174499	1439	825501	30
31	9·170547	1405	9·995184	32	9·175362	1436	10·824638	29
32	171389	1402	995165	32	176224	1433	823776	28
33	172230	1399	995146	32	177084	1431	822916	27
34	173070	1396	995127	32	177942	1428	822058	26
35	173908	1394	995108	32	178799	1425	821201	25
36	174744	1391	995089	32	179655	1423	820345	24
37	175578	1388	995070	32	180508	1420	819492	23
38	176411	1386	995051	32	181360	1417	818640	22
39	177242	1383	995032	32	182211	1415	817789	21
40	178072	1380	995013	32	183059	1412	816941	20
41	9·178900	1377	9·994993	32	9·183907	1409	10·816093	19
42	179726	1374	994974	32	184752	1407	815248	18
43	180551	1372	994955	32	185597	1404	814403	17
44	181374	1369	994935	32	186439	1402	813561	16
45	182196	1366	994916	33	187280	1399	812720	15
46	183016	1364	994896	33	188120	1396	811880	14
47	183834	1361	994877	33	188958	1393	811042	13
48	184651	1359	994857	33	189794	1391	810206	12
49	185466	1356	994838	33	190629	1389	809371	11
50	186280	1353	994818	33	191462	1386	808538	10
51	9·187092	1351	9·994798	33	9·192294	1384	10·807706	9
52	187903	1348	994779	33	193124	1381	806876	8
53	188712	1346	994759	33	193953	1379	806047	7
54	189519	1343	994739	33	194780	1376	805220	6
55	190325	1341	994720	33	195606	1374	804394	5
56	191130	1338	994700	33	196430	1371	803570	4
57	191933	1336	994680	33	197253	1369	802747	3
58	192734	1333	994660	33	198074	1366	801926	2
59	193534	1330	994640	33	198894	1364	801106	1
60	194332	1328	994620	33	199713	1361	800287	0
′	Cosine.	D.	Sine.	D.	Cotang.	D.	Tang.	′

98° 81°

9°								170°
′	Sine.	D.	Cosine.	D.	Tang.	D.	Cotang.	′
0	9·194332	1328	9·994620	33	9·199713	1361	10·800287	60
1	195129	1326	994600	33	200529	1359	799471	59
2	195925	1323	994580	33	201345	1356	798655	58
3	196719	1321	994560	34	202159	1354	797841	57
4	197511	1318	994540	34	202971	1352	797029	56
5	198302	1316	994519	34	203782	1349	796218	55
6	199091	1313	994499	34	204592	1347	795408	54
7	199879	1311	994479	34	205400	1345	794600	53
8	200666	1308	994459	34	206207	1342	793793	52
9	201451	1306	994438	34	207013	1340	792987	51
10	202234	1304	994418	34	207817	1338	792183	50
11	9·203017	1301	9·994398	34	9·208619	1335	10·791381	49
12	203797	1299	994377	34	209420	1333	790580	48
13	204577	1296	994357	34	210220	1331	789780	47
14	205354	1294	994336	34	211018	1328	788982	46
15	206131	1292	994316	34	211815	1326	788185	45
16	206906	1289	994295	34	212611	1324	787389	44
17	207679	1287	994274	35	213405	1321	786595	43
18	208452	1285	994254	35	214198	1319	785802	42
19	209222	1282	994233	35	214989	1317	785011	41
20	209992	1280	994212	35	215780	1315	784220	40
21	9·210760	1278	9·994191	35	9·216568	1312	10·783432	39
22	211526	1275	994171	35	217356	1310	782644	38
23	212291	1273	994150	35	218142	1308	781858	37
24	213055	1271	994129	35	218926	1305	781074	36
25	213818	1268	994108	35	219710	1303	780290	35
26	214579	1266	994087	35	220492	1301	779508	34
27	215338	1264	994066	35	221272	1299	778728	33
28	216097	1261	994045	35	222052	1297	777948	32
29	216854	1259	994024	35	222830	1294	777170	31
30	217609	1257	994003	35	223607	1292	776393	30
31	9·218363	1255	9·993982	35	9·224382	1290	10·775618	29
32	219116	1253	993960	35	225156	1288	774844	28
33	219868	1250	993939	35	225929	1286	774071	27
34	220618	1248	993918	35	226700	1284	773300	26
35	221367	1246	993897	36	227471	1281	772529	25
36	222115	1244	993875	36	228239	1279	771761	24
37	222861	1242	993854	36	229007	1277	770993	23
38	223606	1239	993832	36	229773	1275	770227	22
39	224349	1237	993811	36	230539	1273	769461	21
40	225092	1235	993789	36	231302	1271	768698	20
41	9·225833	1233	9·993768	36	9·232065	1269	10·767935	19
42	226573	1231	993746	36	232826	1267	767174	18
43	227311	1228	993725	36	233586	1265	766414	17
44	228048	1226	993703	36	234345	1262	765655	16
45	228784	1224	993681	36	235103	1260	764897	15
46	229518	1222	993660	36	235859	1258	764141	14
47	230252	1220	993638	36	236614	1256	763386	13
48	230984	1218	993616	36	237368	1254	762632	12
49	231715	1216	993594	37	238120	1252	761880	11
50	232444	1214	993572	37	238872	1250	761128	10
51	9·233172	1212	9·993550	37	9·239622	1248	10·760378	9
52	233899	1209	993528	37	240371	1246	759629	8
53	234625	1207	993506	37	241118	1244	758882	7
54	235349	1205	993484	37	241865	1242	758135	6
55	236073	1203	993462	37	242610	1240	757390	5
56	236795	1201	993440	37	243354	1238	756646	4
57	237515	1199	993418	37	244097	1236	755903	3
58	238235	1197	993396	37	244839	1234	755161	2
59	238953	1195	993374	37	245579	1232	754421	1
60	239670	1193	993351	37	246319	1230	753681	0
′	Cosine.	D.	Sine.	D.	Cotang.	D.	Tang.	′
99°								80°

10° 169°

′	Sine.	D.	Cosine.	D.	Tang.	D.	Cotang.	′
0	9·239670	1193	9·993351	37	9·246319	1230	10·753681	60
1	240386	1191	993329	37	247057	1228	752943	59
2	241101	1189	993307	37	247794	1226	752206	58
3	241814	1187	993284	37	248530	1224	751470	57
4	242526	1185	993262	37	249264	1222	750736	56
5	243237	1183	993240	37	249998	1220	750002	55
6	243947	1181	993217	38	250730	1218	749270	54
7	244656	1179	993195	38	251461	1217	748539	53
8	245363	1177	993172	38	252191	1215	747809	52
9	246069	1175	993149	38	252920	1213	747080	51
10	246775	1173	993127	38	253648	1211	746352	50
11	9·247478	1171	9·993104	38	9·254374	1209	10·745626	49
12	248181	1169	993081	38	255100	1207	744900	48
13	248883	1167	993059	38	255824	1205	744176	47
14	249583	1165	993036	38	256547	1203	743453	46
15	250282	1163	993013	38	257269	1201	742731	45
16	250980	1161	992990	38	257990	1200	742010	44
17	251677	1159	992967	38	258710	1198	741290	43
18	252373	1158	992944	38	259429	1196	740571	42
19	253067	1156	992921	38	260146	1194	739854	41
20	253761	1154	992898	38	260863	1192	739137	40
21	9·254453	1152	9·992875	38	9·261578	1190	10·738422	39
22	255144	1150	992852	38	262292	1189	737708	38
23	255834	1148	992829	39	263005	1187	736995	37
24	256523	1146	992806	39	263717	1185	736283	36
25	257211	1144	992783	39	264428	1183	735572	35
26	257898	1142	992759	39	265138	1181	734862	34
27	258583	1141	992736	39	265847	1179	734153	33
28	259268	1139	992713	39	266555	1178	733445	32
29	259951	1137	992690	39	267261	1176	732739	31
30	260633	1135	992666	39	267967	1174	732033	30
31	9·261314	1133	9·992643	39	9·268671	1172	10·731329	29
32	261994	1131	992619	39	269375	1170	730625	28
33	262673	1130	992596	39	270077	1169	729923	27
34	263351	1128	992572	39	270779	1167	729221	26
35	264027	1126	992549	39	271479	1165	728521	25
36	264703	1124	992525	39	272178	1164	727822	24
37	265377	1122	992501	39	272876	1162	727124	23
38	266051	1120	992478	40	273573	1160	726427	22
39	266723	1119	992454	40	274269	1158	725731	21
40	267395	1117	992430	40	274964	1157	725036	20
41	9·268065	1115	9·992406	40	9·275658	1155	10·724342	19
42	268734	1113	992382	40	276351	1153	723649	18
43	269402	1111	992359	40	277043	1151	722957	17
44	270069	1110	992335	40	277734	1150	722266	16
45	270735	1108	992311	40	278424	1148	721576	15
46	271400	1106	992287	40	279113	1147	720887	14
47	272064	1105	992263	40	279801	1145	720199	13
48	272726	1103	992239	40	280488	1143	719512	12
49	273388	1101	992214	40	281174	1141	718826	11
50	274049	1099	992190	40	281858	1140	718142	10
51	9·274708	1098	9·992166	40	9·282542	1138	10·717458	9
52	275367	1096	992142	40	283225	1136	716775	8
53	276025	1094	992118	41	283907	1135	716093	7
54	276681	1092	992093	41	284588	1133	715412	6
55	277337	1091	992069	41	285268	1131	714732	5
56	277991	1089	992044	41	285947	1130	714053	4
57	278645	1087	992020	41	286624	1128	713376	3
58	279297	1086	991996	41	287301	1126	712699	2
59	279948	1084	991971	41	287977	1125	712023	1
60	280599	1082	991947	41	288652	1123	711348	0
′	Cosine.	D.	Sine.	D.	Cotang.	D.	Tang.	′

100° 79°

11° 168°

′	Sine.	D.	Cosine.	D.	Tang.	D.	Cotang.	′
0	9·280599	1082	9·991947	41	9·288652	1123	10·711348	60
1	281248	1081	991922	41	289326	1122	710674	59
2	281897	1079	991897	41	289999	1120	710001	58
3	282544	1077	991873	41	290671	1118	709329	57
4	283190	1076	991848	41	291342	1117	708658	56
5	283836	1074	991823	41	292013	1115	707987	55
6	284480	1072	991799	41	292682	1114	707318	54
7	285124	1071	991774	42	293350	1112	706650	53
8	285766	1069	991749	42	294017	1111	705983	52
9	286408	1067	991724	42	294684	1109	705316	51
10	287048	1066	991699	42	295349	1107	704651	50
11	9·287688	1064	9·991674	42	9·296013	1106	10·703987	49
12	288326	1063	991649	42	296677	1104	703323	48
13	288964	1061	991624	42	297339	1103	702661	47
14	289600	1059	991599	42	298001	1101	701999	46
15	290236	1058	991574	42	298662	1100	701338	45
16	290870	1056	991549	42	299322	1098	700678	44
17	291504	1054	991524	42	299980	1096	700020	43
18	292137	1053	991498	42	300638	1095	699362	42
19	292768	1051	991473	42	301295	1093	698705	41
20	293399	1050	991448	42	301951	1092	698049	40
21	9·294029	1048	9·991422	42	9·302607	1090	10·697393	39
22	294658	1046	991397	42	303261	1089	696739	38
23	295286	1045	991372	43	303914	1087	696086	37
24	295913	1043	991346	43	304567	1086	695433	36
25	296539	1042	991321	43	305218	1084	694782	35
26	297164	1040	991295	43	305869	1083	694131	34
27	297788	1039	991270	43	306519	1081	693481	33
28	298412	1037	991244	43	307168	1080	692832	32
29	299034	1036	991218	43	307816	1078	692184	31
30	299655	1034	991193	43	308463	1077	691537	30
31	9·300276	1032	9·991167	43	9·309109	1075	10·690891	29
32	300895	1031	991141	43	309754	1074	690246	28
33	301514	1029	991115	43	310399	1073	689601	27
34	302132	1028	991090	43	311042	1071	688958	26
35	302748	1026	991064	43	311685	1070	688315	25
36	303364	1025	991038	43	312327	1068	687673	24
37	303979	1023	991012	43	312968	1067	687032	23
38	304593	1022	990986	43	313608	1065	686392	22
39	305207	1020	990960	43	314247	1064	685753	21
40	305819	1019	990934	44	314885	1062	685115	20
41	9·306430	1017	9·990908	44	9·315523	1061	10·684477	19
42	307041	1016	990882	44	316159	1060	683841	18
43	307650	1014	990855	44	316795	1058	683205	17
44	308259	1013	990829	44	317430	1057	682570	16
45	308867	1011	990803	44	318064	1055	681936	15
46	309474	1010	990777	44	318697	1054	681303	14
47	310080	1008	990750	44	319330	1053	680670	13
48	310685	1007	990724	44	319961	1051	680039	12
49	311289	1005	990697	44	320592	1050	679408	11
50	311893	1004	990671	44	321222	1048	678778	10
51	9·312495	1003	9·990645	44	9·321851	1047	10·678149	9
52	313097	1001	990618	44	322479	1045	677521	8
53	313698	1000	990591	44	323106	1044	676894	7
54	314297	998	990565	44	323733	1043	676267	6
55	314897	997	990538	44	324358	1041	675642	5
56	315495	996	990511	45	324983	1040	675017	4
57	316092	994	990485	45	325607	1039	674393	3
58	316689	993	990458	45	326231	1037	673769	2
59	317284	991	990431	45	326853	1036	673147	1
60	317879	990	990404	45	327475	1035	672525	0
′	Cosine.	D.	Sine.	D.	Cotang.	D.	Tang.	′

101° 78°

12°								167°
′	Sine.	D.	Cosine.	D.	Tang.	D.	Cotang.	′
0	9·317879	990	9·990404	45	9·327475	1035	10·672525	60
1	318473	988	990378	45	328095	1033	671905	59
2	319066	987	990351	45	328715	1032	671285	58
3	319658	986	990324	45	329334	1030	670666	57
4	320249	984	990297	45	329953	1029	670047	56
5	320840	983	990270	45	330570	1028	669430	55
6	321430	982	990243	45	331187	1026	668813	54
7	322019	980	990215	45	331803	1025	668197	53
8	322607	979	990188	45	332418	1024	667582	52
9	323194	977	990161	45	333033	1023	666967	51
10	323780	976	990134	45	333646	1021	666354	50
11	9·324366	975	9·990107	46	9·334259	1020	10·665741	49
12	324950	973	990079	46	334871	1019	665129	48
13	325534	972	990052	46	335482	1017	664518	47
14	326117	970	990025	46	336093	1016	663907	46
15	326700	969	989997	46	336702	1015	663298	45
16	327281	968	989970	46	337311	1013	662689	44
17	327862	966	989942	46	337919	1012	662081	43
18	328442	965	989915	46	338527	1011	661473	42
19	329021	964	989887	46	339133	1010	660867	41
20	329599	962	989860	46	339739	1008	660261	40
21	9·330176	961	9·989832	46	9·340344	1007	10·659656	39
22	330753	960	989804	46	340948	1006	659052	38
23	331329	958	989777	46	341552	1004	658448	37
24	331903	957	989749	47	342155	1003	657845	36
25	332478	956	989721	47	342757	1002	657243	35
26	333051	954	989693	47	343358	1000	656642	34
27	333624	953	989665	47	343958	999	656042	33
28	334195	952	989637	47	344558	998	655442	32
29	334767	950	989610	47	345157	997	654843	31
30	335337	949	989582	47	345755	996	654245	30
31	9·335906	948	9·989553	47	9·346353	994	10·653647	29
32	336475	946	989525	47	346949	993	653051	28
33	337043	945	989497	47	347545	992	652455	27
34	337610	944	989469	47	348141	991	651859	26
35	338176	943	989441	47	348735	990	651265	25
36	338742	941	989413	47	349329	988	650671	24
37	339307	940	989385	47	349922	987	650078	23
38	339871	939	989356	47	350514	986	649486	22
39	340434	937	989328	47	351106	985	648894	21
40	340996	936	989300	47	351697	983	648303	20
41	9·341558	935	9·989271	47	9·352287	982	10·647713	19
42	342119	934	989243	47	352876	981	647124	18
43	342679	932	989214	47	353465	980	646535	17
44	343239	931	989186	47	354053	979	645947	16
45	343797	930	989157	47	354640	977	645360	15
46	344355	929	989128	48	355227	976	644773	14
47	344912	927	989100	48	355813	975	644187	13
48	345469	926	989071	48	356398	974	643602	12
49	346024	925	989042	48	356982	973	643018	11
50	346579	924	989014	48	357566	971	642434	10
51	9·347134	922	9·988985	48	9·358149	970	10·641851	9
52	347687	921	988956	48	358731	969	641269	8
53	348240	920	988927	48	359313	968	640687	7
54	348792	919	988898	48	359893	967	640107	6
55	349343	917	988869	48	360474	966	639526	5
56	349893	916	988840	48	361053	965	638947	4
57	350443	915	988811	49	361632	963	638368	3
58	350992	914	988782	49	362210	962	637790	2
59	351540	913	988753	49	362787	961	637213	1
60	352088	911	988724	49	363364	960	636636	0
′	Cosine.	D.	Sine.	D.	Cotang.	D.	Tang.	′
102°								77°

13°								166°
′	Sine.	D.	Cosine.	D.	Tang.	D.	Cotang.	′
0	9·352088	911	9·988724	49	9·363364	960	10·636636	60
1	352635	910	988695	49	363940	959	636060	59
2	353181	909	988666	49	364515	958	635485	58
3	353726	908	988636	49	365090	957	634910	57
4	354271	907	988607	49	365664	955	634336	56
5	354815	905	988578	49	366237	954	633763	55
6	355358	904	988548	49	366810	953	633190	54
7	355901	903	988519	49	367382	952	632618	53
8	356443	902	988489	49	367953	951	632047	52
9	356984	901	988460	49	368524	950	631476	51
10	357524	899	988430	49	369094	949	630906	50
11	9·358064	898	9·988401	49	9·369663	948	10·630337	49
12	358603	897	988371	49	370232	946	629768	48
13	359141	896	988342	49	370799	945	629201	47
14	359678	895	988312	50	371367	944	628633	46
15	360215	893	988282	50	371933	943	628067	45
16	360752	892	988252	50	372499	942	627501	44
17	361287	891	988223	50	373064	941	626936	43
18	361822	890	988193	50	373629	940	626371	42
19	362356	889	988163	50	374193	939	625807	41
20	362889	888	988133	50	374756	938	625244	40
21	9·363422	887	9·988103	50	9·375319	937	10·624681	39
22	363954	885	988073	50	375881	935	624119	38
23	364485	884	988043	50	376442	934	623558	37
24	365016	883	988013	50	377003	933	622997	36
25	365546	882	987983	50	377563	932	622437	35
26	366075	881	987953	50	378122	931	621878	34
27	366604	880	987922	50	378681	930	621319	33
28	367131	879	987892	50	379239	929	620761	32
29	367659	877	987862	50	379797	928	620203	31
30	368185	876	987832	51	380354	927	619646	30
31	9·368711	875	9·987801	51	9·380910	926	10·619090	29
32	369236	874	987771	51	381466	925	618534	28
33	369761	873	987740	51	382020	924	617980	27
34	370285	872	987710	51	382575	923	617425	26
35	370808	871	987679	51	383129	922	616871	25
36	371330	870	987649	51	383682	921	616318	24
37	371852	869	987618	51	384234	920	615766	23
38	372373	867	987588	51	384786	919	615214	22
39	372894	866	987557	51	385337	918	614663	21
40	373414	865	987526	51	385888	917	614112	20
41	9·373933	864	9·987496	51	9·386438	915	10·613562	19
42	374452	863	987465	51	386987	914	613013	18
43	374970	862	987434	51	387536	913	612464	17
44	375487	861	987403	52	388084	912	611916	16
45	376003	860	987372	52	388631	911	611369	15
46	376519	859	987341	52	389178	910	610822	14
47	377035	858	987310	52	389724	909	610276	13
48	377549	857	987279	52	390270	908	609730	12
49	378063	856	987248	52	390815	907	609185	11
50	378577	854	987217	52	391360	906	608640	10
51	9·379089	853	9·987186	52	9·391903	905	10·608097	9
52	379601	852	987155	52	392447	904	607553	8
53	380113	851	987124	52	392989	903	607011	7
54	380624	850	987092	52	393531	902	606469	6
55	381134	849	987061	52	394073	901	605927	5
56	381643	848	987030	52	394614	900	605386	4
57	382152	847	986998	52	395154	899	604846	3
58	382661	846	986967	52	395694	898	604306	2
59	383168	845	986936	52	396233	897	603767	1
60	383675	844	986904	52	396771	896	603229	0
′	Cosine.	D.	Sine.	D.	Cotang.	D.	Tang.	′
103°								76°

14°								165°
′	Sine.	D.	Cosine.	D.	Tang.	D.	Cotang.	′
0	9·383675	844	9·986904	52	9·396771	896	10·603229	60
1	384182	843	986873	53	397309	896	602691	59
2	384687	842	986841	53	397846	895	602154	58
3	385192	841	986809	53	398383	894	601617	57
4	385697	840	986778	53	398919	893	601081	56
5	386201	839	986746	53	399455	892	600545	55
6	386704	838	986714	53	399990	891	600010	54
7	387207	837	986683	53	400524	890	599476	53
8	387709	836	986651	53	401058	889	598942	52
9	388210	835	986619	53	401591	888	598409	51
10	388711	834	986587	53	402124	887	597876	50
11	9·389211	833	9·986555	53	9·402656	886	10·597344	49
12	389711	832	986523	53	403187	885	596813	48
13	390210	831	986491	53	403718	884	596282	47
14	390708	830	986459	53	404249	883	595751	46
15	391206	828	986427	53	404778	882	595222	45
16	391703	827	986395	53	405308	881	594692	44
17	392199	826	986363	54	405836	880	594164	43
18	392695	825	986331	54	406364	879	593636	42
19	393191	824	986299	54	406892	878	593108	41
20	393685	823	986266	54	407419	877	592581	40
21	9·394179	822	9·986234	54	9·407945	876	10·592055	39
22	394673	821	986202	54	408471	875	591529	38
23	395166	820	986169	54	408996	874	591004	37
24	395658	819	986137	54	409521	874	590479	36
25	396150	818	986104	54	410045	873	589955	35
26	396641	817	986072	54	410569	872	589431	34
27	397132	817	986039	54	411092	871	588908	33
28	397621	816	986007	54	411615	870	588385	32
29	398111	815	985974	54	412137	869	587863	31
30	398600	814	985942	54	412658	868	587342	30
31	9·399088	813	9·985909	55	9·413179	867	10·586821	29
32	399575	812	985876	55	413699	866	586301	28
33	400062	811	985843	55	414219	865	585781	27
34	400549	810	985811	55	414738	864	585262	26
35	401035	809	985778	55	415257	864	584743	25
36	401520	808	985745	55	415775	863	584225	24
37	402005	807	985712	55	416293	862	583707	23
38	402489	806	985679	55	416810	861	583190	22
39	402972	805	985646	55	417326	860	582674	21
40	403455	804	985613	55	417842	859	582158	20
41	9·403938	803	9·985580	55	9·418358	858	10·581642	19
42	404420	802	985547	55	418873	857	581127	18
43	404901	801	985514	55	419387	856	580613	17
44	405382	800	985480	55	419901	855	580099	16
45	405862	799	985447	55	420415	855	579585	15
46	406341	798	985414	56	420927	854	579073	14
47	406820	797	985381	56	421440	853	578560	13
48	407299	796	985347	56	421952	852	578048	12
49	407777	795	985314	56	422463	851	577537	11
50	408254	794	985280	56	422974	850	577026	10
51	9·408731	794	9·985247	56	9·423484	849	10·576516	9
52	409207	793	985213	56	423993	848	576007	8
53	409682	792	985180	56	424503	848	575497	7
54	410157	791	985146	56	425011	847	574989	6
55	410632	790	985113	56	425519	846	574481	5
56	411106	789	985079	56	426027	845	573973	4
57	411579	788	985045	56	426534	844	573466	3
58	412052	787	985011	56	427041	843	572959	2
59	412524	786	984978	56	427547	843	572453	1
60	412996	785	984944	56	428052	842	571948	0
′	Cosine.	D.	Sine.	D.	Cotang.	D.	Tang.	′
104°								75°

15° 164°

′	Sine.	D.	Cosine.	D.	Tang.	D.	Cotang.	′
0	9·412996	785	9·984944	57	9·428052	842	10·571948	60
1	413467	784	984910	57	428558	841	571442	59
2	413938	783	984876	57	429062	840	570938	58
3	414408	783	984842	57	429566	839	570434	57
4	414878	782	984808	57	430070	838	569930	56
5	415347	781	984774	57	430573	838	569427	55
6	415815	780	984740	57	431075	837	568925	54
7	416283	779	984706	57	431577	836	568423	53
8	416751	778	984672	57	432079	835	567921	52
9	417217	777	984638	57	432580	834	567420	51
10	417684	776	984603	57	433080	833	566920	50
11	9·418150	775	9·984569	57	9·433580	832	10·566420	49
12	418615	774	984535	57	434080	832	565920	48
13	419079	773	984500	57	434579	831	565421	47
14	419544	773	984466	57	435078	830	564922	46
15	420007	772	984432	58	435576	829	564424	45
16	420470	771	984397	58	436073	828	563927	44
17	420933	770	984363	58	436570	828	563430	43
18	421395	769	984328	58	437067	827	562933	42
19	421857	768	984294	58	437563	826	562437	41
20	422318	767	984259	58	438059	825	561941	40
21	9·422778	767	9·984224	58	9·438554	824	10·561446	39
22	423238	766	984190	58	439048	823	560952	38
23	423697	765	984155	58	439543	823	560457	37
24	424156	764	984120	58	440036	822	559964	36
25	424615	763	984085	58	440529	821	559471	35
26	425073	762	984050	58	441022	820	558978	34
27	425530	761	984015	58	441514	819	558486	33
28	425987	760	983981	58	442006	819	557994	32
29	426443	760	983946	58	442497	818	557503	31
30	426899	759	983911	58	442988	817	557012	30
31	9·427354	758	9·983875	58	9·443479	816	10·556521	29
32	427809	757	983840	59	443968	816	556032	28
33	428263	756	983805	59	444458	815	555542	27
34	428717	755	983770	59	444947	814	555053	26
35	429170	754	983735	59	445435	813	554565	25
36	429623	753	983700	59	445923	812	554077	24
37	430075	752	983664	59	446411	812	553589	23
38	430527	752	983629	59	446898	811	553102	22
39	430978	751	983594	59	447384	810	552616	21
40	431429	750	983558	59	447870	809	552130	20
41	9·431879	749	9·983523	59	9·448356	809	10·551644	19
42	432329	749	983487	59	448841	808	551159	18
43	432778	748	983452	59	449326	807	550674	17
44	433226	747	983416	59	449810	806	550190	16
45	433675	746	983381	59	450294	806	549706	15
46	434122	745	983345	59	450777	805	549223	14
47	434569	744	983309	59	451260	804	548740	13
48	435016	744	983273	60	451743	803	548257	12
49	435462	743	983238	60	452225	802	547775	11
50	435908	742	983202	60	452706	802	547294	10
51	9·436353	741	9·983166	60	9·453187	801	10·546813	9
52	436798	740	983130	60	453668	800	546332	8
53	437242	740	983094	60	454148	799	545852	7
54	437686	739	983058	60	454628	799	545372	6
55	438129	738	983022	60	455107	798	544893	5
56	438572	737	982986	60	455586	797	544414	4
57	439014	736	982950	60	456064	796	543936	3
58	439456	736	982914	60	456542	796	543458	2
59	439897	735	982878	60	457019	795	542981	1
60	440338	734	982842	60	457496	794	542504	0
′	Cosine.	D.	Sine.	D.	Cotang.	D.	Tang.	′

105° 74°

16° 163°

′	Sine.	D.	Cosine.	D.	Tang.	D.	Cotang.	′
0	9·440338	734	9·982842	60	9·457496	794	10·542504	60
1	440778	733	982805	60	457973	793	542027	59
2	441218	732	982769	61	458449	793	541551	58
3	441658	731	982733	61	458925	792	541075	57
4	442096	731	982696	61	459400	791	540600	56
5	442535	730	982660	61	459875	790	540125	55
6	442973	729	982624	61	460349	790	539651	54
7	443410	728	982587	61	460823	789	539177	53
8	443847	727	982551	61	461297	788	538703	52
9	444284	727	982514	61	461770	788	538230	51
10	444720	726	982477	61	462242	787	537758	50
11	9·445155	725	9·982441	61	9·462715	786	10·537285	49
12	445590	724	982404	61	463186	785	536814	48
13	446025	723	982367	61	463658	785	536342	47
14	446459	723	982331	61	464128	784	535872	46
15	446893	722	982294	61	464599	783	535401	45
16	447326	721	982257	61	465069	783	534931	44
17	447759	720	982220	62	465539	782	534461	43
18	448191	720	982183	62	466008	781	533992	42
19	448623	719	982146	62	466477	780	533523	41
20	449054	718	982109	62	466945	780	533055	40
21	9·449485	717	9·982072	62	9·467413	779	10·532587	39
22	449915	716	982035	62	467880	778	532120	38
23	450345	716	981998	62	468347	778	531653	37
24	450775	715	981961	62	468814	777	531186	36
25	451204	714	981924	62	469280	776	530720	35
26	451632	713	981886	62	469746	775	530254	34
27	452060	713	981849	62	470211	775	529789	33
28	452488	712	981812	62	470676	774	529324	32
29	452915	711	981774	62	471141	773	528859	31
30	453342	710	981737	62	471605	773	528395	30
31	9·453768	710	9·981700	63	9·472069	772	10·527931	29
32	454194	709	981662	63	472532	771	527468	28
33	454619	708	981625	63	472995	771	527005	27
34	455044	707	981587	63	473457	770	526543	26
35	455469	707	981549	63	473919	769	526081	25
36	455893	706	981512	63	474381	769	525619	24
37	456316	705	981474	63	474842	768	525158	23
38	456739	704	981436	63	475303	767	524697	22
39	457162	704	981399	63	475763	767	524237	21
40	457584	703	981361	63	476223	766	523777	20
41	9·458006	702	9·981323	63	9·476683	765	10·523317	19
42	458427	701	981285	63	477142	765	522858	18
43	458848	701	981247	63	477601	764	522399	17
44	459268	700	981209	63	478059	763	521941	16
45	459688	699	981171	63	478517	763	521483	15
46	460108	698	981133	64	478975	762	521025	14
47	460527	698	981095	64	479432	761	520568	13
48	460946	697	981057	64	479889	761	520111	12
49	461364	696	981019	64	480345	760	519655	11
50	461782	695	980981	64	480801	759	519199	10
51	9·462199	695	9·980942	64	9·481257	759	10·518743	9
52	462616	694	980904	64	481712	758	518288	8
53	463032	693	980866	64	482167	757	517833	7
54	463448	693	980827	64	482621	757	517379	6
55	463864	692	980789	64	483075	756	516925	5
56	464279	691	980750	64	483529	755	516471	4
57	464694	690	980712	64	483982	755	516018	3
58	465108	690	980673	64	484435	754	515565	2
59	465522	689	980635	64	484887	753	515113	1
60	465935	688	980596	64	485339	753	514661	0
′	Cosine.	D.	Sine.	D.	Cotang.	D.	Tang.	′

106° 73°

17°								162°
′	Sine.	D.	Cosine.	D.	Tang.	D.	Cotang.	′
0	9·465935	688	9·980596	64	9·485339	755	10·514661	60
1	466348	688	980558	64	485791	752	514209	59
2	466761	687	980519	65	486242	751	513758	58
3	467173	686	980480	65	486693	751	513307	57
4	467585	685	980442	65	487143	750	512857	56
5	467996	685	980403	65	487593	749	512407	55
6	468407	684	980364	65	488043	749	511957	54
7	468817	683	980325	65	488492	748	511508	53
8	469227	683	980286	65	488941	747	511059	52
9	469637	682	980247	65	489390	747	510610	51
10	470046	681	980208	65	489838	746	510162	50
11	9·470455	680	9·980169	65	9·490286	746	10·509714	49
12	470863	680	980130	65	490733	745	509267	48
13	471271	679	980091	65	491180	744	508820	47
14	471679	678	980052	65	491627	744	508373	46
15	472086	678	980012	65	492073	743	507927	45
16	472492	677	979973	65	492519	743	507481	44
17	472898	676	979934	66	492965	742	507035	43
18	473304	676	979895	66	493410	741	506590	42
19	473710	675	979855	66	493854	740	506146	41
20	474115	674	979816	66	494299	740	505701	40
21	9·474519	674	9·979776	66	9·494743	740	10·505257	39
22	474923	673	979737	66	495186	739	504814	38
23	475327	672	979697	66	495630	738	504370	37
24	475730	672	979658	66	496073	737	503927	36
25	476133	671	979618	66	496515	737	503485	35
26	476536	670	979579	66	496957	736	503043	34
27	476938	669	979539	66	497399	736	502601	33
28	477340	669	979499	66	497841	735	502159	32
29	477741	668	979459	66	498282	734	501718	31
30	478142	667	979420	66	498722	734	501278	30
31	9·478542	667	9·979380	66	9·499163	733	10·500837	29
32	478942	666	979340	66	499603	733	500397	28
33	479342	665	979300	67	500042	732	499958	27
34	479741	665	979260	67	500481	731	499519	26
35	480140	664	979220	67	500920	731	499080	25
36	480539	663	979180	67	501359	730	498641	24
37	480937	663	979140	67	501797	730	498203	23
38	481334	662	979100	67	502235	729	497765	22
39	481731	661	979059	67	502672	728	497328	21
40	482128	661	979019	67	503109	728	496891	20
41	9·482525	660	9·978979	67	9·503546	727	10·496454	19
42	482921	659	978939	67	503982	727	496018	18
43	483316	659	978898	67	504418	726	495582	17
44	483712	658	978858	67	504854	725	495146	16
45	484107	657	978817	67	505289	725	494711	15
46	484501	657	978777	67	505724	724	494276	14
47	484895	656	978737	67	506159	724	493841	13
48	485289	655	978696	68	506593	723	493407	12
49	485682	655	978655	68	507027	722	492973	11
50	486075	654	978615	68	507460	722	492540	10
51	9·486467	653	9·978574	68	9·507893	721	10·492107	9
52	486860	653	978533	68	508326	721	491674	8
53	487251	652	978493	68	508759	720	491241	7
54	487643	651	978452	68	509191	719	490809	6
55	488034	651	978411	68	509622	719	490378	5
56	488424	650	978370	68	510054	718	489946	4
57	488814	650	978329	68	510485	718	489515	3
58	489204	649	978288	68	510916	717	489084	2
59	489593	648	978247	68	511346	716	488654	1
60	489982	648	978206	68	511776	716	488224	0
′	Cosine.	D.	Sine.	D.	Cotang.	D.	Tang.	′
107°								72°

18° | 161°

′	Sine.	D.	Cosine.	D.	Tang.	D.	Cotang.	′
0	9·489982	648	9·978206	68	9·511776	716	10·488224	60
1	490371	648	978165	68	512206	716	487794	59
2	490759	647	978124	68	512635	715	487365	58
3	491147	646	978083	69	513064	714	486936	57
4	491535	646	978042	69	513493	714	486507	56
5	491922	645	978001	69	513921	713	486079	55
6	492308	644	977959	69	514349	713	485651	54
7	492695	644	977918	69	514777	712	485223	53
8	493081	643	977877	69	515204	712	484796	52
9	493466	642	977835	69	515631	711	484369	51
10	493851	642	977794	69	516057	710	483943	50
11	9·494236	641	9·977752	69	9·516484	710	10·483516	49
12	494621	641	977711	69	516910	709	483090	48
13	495005	640	977669	69	517335	709	482665	47
14	495388	639	977628	69	517761	708	482239	46
15	495772	639	977586	69	518186	708	481814	45
16	496154	638	977544	70	518610	707	481390	44
17	496537	637	977503	70	519034	706	480966	43
18	496919	637	977461	70	519458	706	480542	42
19	497301	636	977419	70	519882	705	480118	41
20	497682	636	977377	70	520305	705	479695	40
21	9·498064	635	9·977335	70	9·520728	704	10·479272	39
22	498444	634	977293	70	521151	703	478849	38
23	498825	634	977251	70	521573	703	478427	37
24	499204	633	977209	70	521995	703	478005	36
25	499584	632	977167	70	522417	702	477583	35
26	499963	632	977125	70	522838	702	477162	34
27	500342	631	977083	70	523259	701	476741	33
28	500721	631	977041	70	523680	701	476320	32
29	501099	630	976999	70	524100	700	475900	31
30	501476	629	976957	70	524520	699	475480	30
31	9·501854	629	9·976914	70	9·524940	699	10·475060	29
32	502231	628	976872	71	525359	698	474641	28
33	502607	628	976830	71	525778	698	474222	27
34	502984	627	976787	71	526197	697	473803	26
35	503360	626	976745	71	526615	697	473385	25
36	503735	626	976702	71	527033	696	472967	24
37	504110	625	976660	71	527451	696	472549	23
38	504485	625	976617	71	527868	695	472132	22
39	504860	624	976574	71	528285	695	471715	21
40	505234	623	976532	71	528702	694	471298	20
41	9·505608	623	9·976489	71	9·529119	693	10·470881	19
42	505981	622	976446	71	529535	693	470465	18
43	506354	622	976404	71	529951	693	470049	17
44	506727	621	976361	71	530366	692	469634	16
45	507099	620	976318	71	530781	691	469219	15
46	507471	620	976275	71	531196	691	468804	14
47	507843	619	976232	72	531611	690	468389	13
48	508214	619	976189	72	532025	690	467975	12
49	508585	618	976146	72	532439	689	467561	11
50	508956	618	976103	72	532853	689	467147	10
51	9·509326	617	9·976060	72	9·533266	688	10·466734	9
52	509696	616	976017	72	533679	688	466321	8
53	510065	616	975974	72	534092	687	465908	7
54	510434	615	975930	72	534504	687	465496	6
55	510803	615	975887	72	534916	686	465084	5
56	511172	614	975844	72	535328	686	464672	4
57	511540	613	975800	72	535739	685	464261	3
58	511907	613	975757	72	536150	685	463850	2
59	512275	612	975714	72	536561	684	463439	1
60	512642	612	975670	72	536972	684	463028	0
′	Cosine.	D.	Sine.	D.	Cotang.	D.	Tang.	′

108° | 71°

19°								160°
′	Sine.	D.	Cosine.	D.	Tang.	D.	Cotang.	′
0	9·512642	612	9·975670	73	9·536972	684	10·463028	60
1	513009	·611	975627	73	537382	683	462618	59
2	513375	611	975583	73	537792	683	462208	58
3	513741	610	975539	73	538202	682	461798	57
4	514107	609	975496	73	538611	682	461389	56
5	514472	609	975452	73	539020	681	460980	55
6	514837	608	975408	73	539429	681	460571	54
7	515202	608	975365	73	539837	680	460163	53
8	515566	607	975321	73	540245	680	459755	52
9	515930	607	975277	73	540653	679	459347	51
10	516294	606	975233	73	541061	679	458939	50
11	9·516657	605	9·975189	73	9·541468	678	10·458532	49
12	517020	605	975145	73	541875	678	458125	48
13	517382	604	975101	73	542281	677	457719	47
14	517745	604	975057	73	542688	677	457312	46
15	518107	603	975013	73	543094	676	456906	45
16	518468	603	974969	74	543499	676	456501	44
17	518829	602	974925	74	543905	675	456095	43
18	519190	601	974880	74	544310	675	455690	42
19	519551	601	974836	74	544715	674	455285	41
20	519911	600	974792	74	545119	674	454881	40
21	9·520271	600	9·974748	74	9·545524	673	10·454476	39
22	520631	599	974703	74	545928	673	454072	38
23	520990	599	974659	74	546331	672	453669	37
24	521349	598	974614	74	546735	672	453265	36
25	521707	598	974570	74	547138	671	452862	35
26	522066	597	974525	74	547540	671	452460	34
27	522424	596	974481	74	547943	670	452057	33
28	522781	596	974436	74	548345	670	451655	32
29	523138	595	974391	74	548747	669	451253	31
30	523495	595	974347	75	549149	669	450851	30
31	9·523852	594	9·974302	75	9·549550	668	10·450450	29
32	524208	594	974257	75	549951	668	450049	28
33	524564	593	974212	75	550352	667	449648	27
34	524920	593	974167	75	550752	667	449248	26
35	525275	592	974122	75	551153	666	448847	25
36	525630	591	974077	75	551552	666	448448	24
37	525984	591	974032	75	551952	665	448048	23
38	526339	590	973987	75	552351	665	447649	22
39	526693	590	973942	75	552750	665	447250	21
40	527046	589	973897	75	553149	664	446851	20
41	9·527400	589	9·973852	75	9·553548	664	10·446452	19
42	527753	588	973807	75	553946	663	446054	18
43	528105	588	973761	75	554344	663	445656	17
44	528458	587	973716	76	554741	662	445259	16
45	528810	587	973671	76	555139	662	444861	15
46	529161	586	973625	76	555536	661	444464	14
47	529513	586	973580	76	555933	661	444067	13
48	529864	585	973535	76	556329	660	443671	12
49	530215	585	973489	76	556725	660	443275	11
50	530565	584	973444	76	557121	659	442879	10
51	9·530915	584	9·973398	76	9·557517	659	10·442483	9
52	531265	583	973352	76	557913	659	442087	8
53	531614	582	973307	76	558308	658	441692	7
54	531963	582	973261	76	558703	658	441297	6
55	532312	581	973215	76	559097	657	440903	5
56	532661	581	973169	76	559491	657	440509	4
57	533009	580	973124	76	559885	656	440115	3
58	533357	580	973078	76	560279	656	439721	2
59	533704	579	973032	77	560673	655	439327	1
60	534052	578	972986	77	561066	655	438934	0
′	Cosine.	D.	Sine.	D.	Cotang.	D.	Tang.	′
109°								70°

20°								159°
′	Sine.	D.	Cosine.	D.	Tang.	D.	Cotang.	′
0	9·534052	578	9·972986	77	9·561066	655	10·438934	60
1	534399	577	972940	77	561459	654	438541	59
2	534745	577	972894	77	561851	654	438149	58
3	535092	577	972848	77	562244	653	437756	57
4	535438	576	972802	77	562636	653	437364	56
5	535783	576	972755	77	563028	653	436972	55
6	536129	575	972709	77	563419	652	436581	54
7	536474	574	972663	77	563811	652	436189	53
8	536818	574	972617	77	564202	651	435798	52
9	537163	573	972570	77	564593	651	435407	51
10	537507	573	972524	77	564983	650	435017	50
11	9·537851	572	9·972478	77	9·565373	650	10·434627	49
12	538194	572	972431	78	565763	649	434237	48
13	538538	571	972385	78	566153	649	433847	47
14	538880	571	972338	78	566542	649	433458	46
15	539223	570	972291	78	566932	648	433068	45
16	539565	570	972245	78	567320	648	432680	44
17	539907	569	972198	78	567709	647	432291	43
18	540249	569	972151	78	568098	647	431902	42
19	540590	568	972105	78	568486	646	431514	41
20	540931	568	972058	78	568873	646	431127	40
21	9·541272	567	9·972011	78	9·569261	645	10·430739	39
22	541613	567	971964	78	569648	645	430352	38
23	541953	566	971917	78	570035	645	429965	37
24	542293	566	971870	78	570422	644	429578	36
25	542632	565	971823	78	570809	644	429191	35
26	542971	565	971776	78	571195	643	428805	34
27	543310	564	971729	79	571581	643	428419	33
28	543649	564	971682	79	571967	642	428033	32
29	543987	563	971635	79	572352	642	427648	31
30	544325	563	971588	79	572738	642	427262	30
31	9·544663	562	9·971540	79	9·573123	641	10·426877	29
32	545000	562	971493	79	573507	641	426493	28
33	545338	561	971446	79	573892	640	426108	27
34	545674	561	971398	79	574276	640	425724	26
35	546011	560	971351	79	574660	639	425340	25
36	546347	560	971303	79	575044	639	424956	24
37	546683	559	971256	79	575427	639	424573	23
38	547019	559	971208	79	575810	638	424190	22
39	547354	558	971161	79	576193	638	423807	21
40	547689	558	971113	79	576576	637	423424	20
41	9·548024	557	9·971066	80	9·576959	637	10·423041	19
42	548359	557	971018	80	577341	636	422659	18
43	548693	556	970970	80	577723	636	422277	17
44	549027	556	970922	80	578104	636	421896	16
45	549360	555	970874	80	578486	635	421514	15
46	549693	555	970827	80	578867	635	421133	14
47	550026	554	970779	80	579248	634	420752	13
48	550359	554	970731	80	579629	634	420371	12
49	550692	553	970683	80	580009	634	419991	11
50	551024	553	970635	80	580389	633	419611	10
51	9·551356	552	9·970586	80	9·580769	633	10·419231	9
52	551687	552	970538	80	581149	632	418851	8
53	552018	552	970490	80	581528	632	418472	7
54	552349	551	970442	80	581907	632	418093	6
55	552680	551	970394	80	582286	631	417714	5
56	553010	550	970345	81	582665	631	417335	4
57	553341	550	970297	81	583044	630	416956	3
58	553670	549	970249	81	583422	630	416578	2
59	554000	549	970200	81	583800	629	416200	1
60	554329	548	970152	81	584177	629	415823	0
′	Cosine.	D.	Sine.	D.	Cotang.	D.	Tang.	′
110°								69°

21° 158°

′	Sine.	D.	Cosine.	D.	Tang.	D.	Cotang.	′
0	9·554329	548	9·970152	81	9·584177	629	10·415823	60
1	554658	548	970103	81	584555	629	415445	59
2	554987	547	970055	81	584932	628	415068	58
3	555315	547	970006	81	585309	628	414691	57
4	555643	546	969957	81	585686	627	414314	56
5	555971	546	969909	81	586062	627	413938	55
6	556299	545	969860	81	586439	627	413561	54
7	556626	545	969811	81	586815	626	413185	53
8	556953	544	969762	81	587190	626	412810	52
9	557280	544	969714	81	587566	625	412434	51
10	557606	543	969665	81	587941	625	412059	50
11	9·557932	543	9·969616	82	9·588316	625	10·411684	49
12	558258	543	969567	82	588691	624	411309	48
13	558583	542	969518	82	589066	624	410934	47
14	558909	542	969469	82	589440	623	410560	46
15	559234	541	969420	82	589814	623	410186	45
16	559558	541	969370	82	590188	623	409812	44
17	559883	540	969321	82	590562	622	409438	43
18	560207	540	969272	82	590935	622	409065	42
19	560531	539	969223	82	591308	622	408692	41
20	560855	539	969173	82	591681	621	408319	40
21	9·561178	538	9·969124	82	9·592054	621	10·407946	39
22	561501	538	969075	82	592426	620	407574	38
23	561824	537	969025	82	592799	620	407201	37
24	562146	537	968976	82	593171	619	406829	36
25	562468	536	968926	83	593542	619	406458	35
26	562790	536	968877	83	593914	618	406086	34
27	563112	536	968827	83	594285	618	405715	33
28	563433	535	968777	83	594656	618	405344	32
29	563755	535	968728	83	595027	617	404973	31
30	564075	534	968678	83	595398	617	404602	30
31	9·564396	534	9·968628	83	9·595768	617	10·404232	29
32	564716	533	968578	83	596138	616	403862	28
33	565036	533	968528	83	596508	616	403492	27
34	565356	532	968479	83	596878	616	403122	26
35	565676	532	968429	83	597247	615	402753	25
36	565995	531	968379	83	597616	615	402384	24
37	566314	531	968329	83	597985	615	402015	23
38	566632	531	968278	83	598354	614	401646	22
39	566951	530	968228	84	598722	614	401278	21
40	567269	530	968178	84	599091	613	400909	20
41	9·567587	529	9·968128	84	9·599459	613	10·400541	19
42	567904	529	968078	84	599827	613	400173	18
43	568222	528	968027	84	600194	612	399806	17
44	568539	528	967977	84	600562	612	399438	16
45	568856	528	967927	84	600929	611	399071	15
46	569172	527	967876	84	601296	611	398704	14
47	569488	527	967826	84	601663	611	398337	13
48	569804	526	967775	84	602029	610	397971	12
49	570120	526	967725	84	602395	610	397605	11
50	570435	525	967674	84	602761	610	397239	10
51	9·570751	525	9·967624	84	9·603127	609	10·396873	9
52	571066	524	967573	84	603493	609	396507	8
53	571380	524	967522	85	603858	609	396142	7
54	571695	523	967471	85	604223	608	395777	6
55	572009	523	967421	85	604588	608	395412	5
56	572323	523	967370	85	604953	607	395047	4
57	572636	522	967319	85	605317	607	394683	3
58	572950	522	967268	85	605682	607	394318	2
59	573263	521	967217	85	606046	606	393954	1
60	573575	521	967166	85	606410	606	393590	0
′	Cosine.	D.	Sine.	D.	Cotang.	D.	Tang.	′

111° 68°

22° 157°

′	Sine.	D.	Cosine.	D.	Tang.	D.	Cotang.	′
0	9·573575	521	9·967166	85	9·606410	606	10·393590	60
1	573888	520	967115	85	606773	606	393227	59
2	574200	520	967064	85	607137	605	392863	58
3	574512	519	967013	85	607500	605	392500	57
4	574824	519	966961	85	607863	604	392137	56
5	575136	519	966910	85	608225	604	391775	55
6	575447	518	966859	85	608588	604	391412	54
7	575758	518	966808	85	608950	603	391050	53
8	576069	517	966756	86	609312	603	390688	52
9	576379	517	966705	86	609674	603	390326	51
10	576689	516	966653	86	610036	602	389964	50
11	9·576999	516	9·966602	86	9·610397	602	10·389603	49
12	577309	516	966550	86	610759	602	389241	48
13	577618	515	966499	86	611120	601	388880	47
14	577927	515	966447	86	611480	601	388520	46
15	578236	514	966395	86	611841	601	388159	45
16	578545	514	966344	86	612201	600	387799	44
17	578853	513	966292	86	612561	600	387439	43
18	579162	513	966240	86	612921	600	387079	42
19	579470	513	966188	86	613281	599	386719	41
20	579777	512	966136	86	613641	599	386359	40
21	9·580085	512	9·966085	87	9·614000	598	10·386000	39
22	580392	511	966033	87	614359	598	385641	38
23	580699	511	965981	87	614718	598	385282	37
24	581005	511	965928	87	615077	597	384923	36
25	581312	510	965876	87	615435	597	384565	35
26	581618	510	965824	87	615793	597	384207	34
27	581924	509	965772	87	616151	596	383849	33
28	582229	509	965720	87	616509	596	383491	32
29	582535	509	965668	87	616867	596	383133	31
30	582840	508	965615	87	617224	595	382776	30
31	9·583145	508	9·965563	87	9·617582	595	10·382418	29
32	583449	507	965511	87	617939	595	382061	28
33	583754	507	965458	87	618295	594	381705	27
34	584058	506	965406	87	618652	594	381348	26
35	584361	506	965353	88	619008	594	380992	25
36	584665	506	965301	88	619364	593	380636	24
37	584968	505	965248	88	619720	593	380280	23
38	585272	505	965195	88	620076	593	379924	22
39	585574	504	965143	88	620432	592	379568	21
40	585877	504	965090	88	620787	592	379213	20
41	9·586179	503	9·965037	88	9·621142	592	10·378858	19
42	586482	503	964984	88	621497	591	378503	18
43	586783	503	964931	88	621852	591	378148	17
44	587085	502	964879	88	622207	590	377793	16
45	587386	502	964826	88	622561	590	377439	15
46	587688	501	964773	88	622915	590	377085	14
47	587989	501	964720	88	623269	589	376731	13
48	588289	501	964666	89	623623	589	376377	12
49	588590	500	964613	89	623976	589	376024	11
50	588890	500	964560	89	624330	588	375670	10
51	9·589190	499	9·964507	89	9·624683	588	10·375317	9
52	589489	499	964454	89	625036	588	374964	8
53	589789	499	964400	89	625388	587	374612	7
54	590088	498	964347	89	625741	587	374259	6
55	590387	498	964294	89	626093	587	373907	5
56	590686	497	964240	89	626445	586	373555	4
57	590984	497	964187	89	626797	586	373203	3
58	591282	497	964133	89	627149	586	372851	2
59	591580	496	964080	89	627501	585	372499	1
60	591878	496	964026	89	627852	585	372148	0
′	Cosine.	D.	Sine.	D.	Cotang.	D.	Tang.	′

112° 67°

23°								156°
′	Sine.	D.	Cosine.	D.	Tang.	D.	Cotang.	′
0	9·591878	496	9·964026	89	9·627852	585	10·372148	60
1	592176	495	963972	89	628203	585	371797	59
2	592473	495	963919	89	628554	585	371446	58
3	592770	495	963865	90	628905	584	371095	57
4	593067	494	963811	90	629255	584	370745	56
5	593363	494	963757	90	629606	583	370394	55
6	593659	493	963704	90	629956	583	370044	54
7	593955	493	963650	90	630306	583	369694	53
8	594251	493	963596	90	630656	583	369344	52
9	594547	492	963542	90	631005	582	368995	51
10	594842	492	963488	90	631355	582	368645	50
11	9·595137	491	9·963434	90	9·631704	582	10·368296	49
12	595432	491	963379	90	632053	581	367947	48
13	595727	491	963325	90	632402	581	367598	47
14	596021	490	963271	90	632750	581	367250	46
15	596315	490	963217	90	633099	580	366901	45
16	596609	489	963163	90	633447	580	366553	44
17	596903	489	963108	91	633795	580	366205	43
18	597196	489	963054	91	634143	579	365857	42
19	597490	488	962999	91	634490	579	365510	41
20	597783	488	962945	91	634838	579	365162	40
21	9·598075	487	9·962890	91	9·635185	578	10·364815	39
22	598368	487	962836	91	635532	578	364468	38
23	598660	487	962781	91	635879	578	364121	37
24	598952	486	962727	91	636226	577	363774	36
25	599244	486	962672	91	636572	577	363428	35
26	599536	485	962617	91	636919	577	363081	34
27	599827	485	962562	91	637265	577	362735	33
28	600118	485	962508	91	637611	576	362389	32
29	600409	484	962453	91	637956	576	362044	31
30	600700	484	962398	92	638302	576	361698	30
31	9·600990	484	9·962343	92	9·638647	575	10·361353	29
32	601280	483	962288	92	638992	575	361008	28
33	601570	483	962233	92	639337	575	360663	27
34	601860	482	962178	92	639682	574	360318	26
35	602150	482	962123	92	640027	574	359973	25
36	602439	482	962067	92	640371	574	359629	24
37	602728	481	962012	92	640716	573	359284	23
38	603017	481	961957	92	641060	573	358940	22
39	603305	481	961902	92	641404	573	358596	21
40	603594	480	961846	92	641747	572	358253	20
41	9·603882	480	9·961791	92	9·642091	572	10·357909	19
42	604170	479	961735	92	642434	572	357566	18
43	604457	479	961680	92	642777	572	357223	17
44	604745	479	961624	93	643120	571	356880	16
45	605032	478	961569	93	643463	571	356537	15
46	605319	478	961513	93	643806	571	356194	14
47	605606	478	961458	93	644148	570	355852	13
48	605892	477	961402	93	644490	570	355510	12
49	606179	477	961346	93	644832	570	355168	11
50	606465	476	961290	93	645174	569	354826	10
51	9·606751	476	9·961235	93	9·645516	569	10·354484	9
52	607036	476	961179	93	645857	569	354143	8
53	607322	475	961123	93	646199	569	353801	7
54	607607	475	961067	93	646540	568	353460	6
55	607892	474	961011	93	646881	568	353119	5
56	608177	474	960955	93	647222	568	352778	4
57	608461	474	960899	93	647562	567	352438	3
58	608745	473	960843	94	647903	567	352097	2
59	609029	473	960786	94	648243	567	351757	1
60	609313	473	960730	94	648583	566	351417	0
′	Cosine.	D.	Sine.	D.	Cotang.	D.	Tang.	′
113°								66°

24°								155°
′	Sine.	D.	Cosine.	D.	Tang.	D.	Cotang.	′
0	9·609313	473	9·960730	94	9·648583	566	10·351417	60
1	609597	472	960674	94	648923	566	351077	59
2	609880	472	960618	94	649263	566	350737	58
3	610164	472	960561	94	649602	566	350398	57
4	610447	471	960505	94	649942	565	350058	56
5	610729	471	960448	94	650281	565	349719	55
6	611012	470	960392	94	650620	565	349380	54
7	611294	470	960335	94	650959	564	349041	53
8	611576	470	960279	94	651297	564	348703	52
9	611858	469	960222	94	651636	564	348364	51
10	612140	469	960165	94	651974	563	348026	50
11	9·612421	469	9·960109	95	9·652312	563	10·347688	49
12	612702	468	960052	95	652650	563	347350	48
13	612983	468	959995	95	652988	563	347012	47
14	613264	467	959938	95	653326	562	346674	46
15	613545	467	959882	95	653663	562	346337	45
16	613825	467	959825	95	654000	562	346000	44
17	614105	466	959768	95	654337	561	345663	43
18	614385	466	959711	95	654674	561	345326	42
19	614665	466	959654	95	655011	561	344989	41
20	614944	465	959596	95	655348	561	344652	40
21	9·615223	465	9·959539	95	9·655684	560	10·344316	39
22	615502	465	959482	95	656020	560	343980	38
23	615781	464	959425	95	656356	560	343644	37
24	616060	464	959368	95	656692	559	343308	36
25	616338	464	959310	96	657028	559	342972	35
26	616616	463	959253	96	657364	559	342636	34
27	616894	463	959195	96	657699	559	342301	33
28	617172	462	959138	96	658034	558	341966	32
29	617450	462	959080	96	658369	558	341631	31
30	617727	462	959023	96	658704	558	341296	30
31	9·618004	461	9·958965	96	9·659039	558	10·340961	29
32	618281	461	958908	96	659373	557	340627	28
33	618558	461	958850	96	659708	557	340292	27
34	618834	460	958792	96	660042	557	339958	26
35	619110	460	958734	66	660376	557	339624	25
36	619386	460	958677	96	660710	556	339290	24
37	619662	459	958619	96	661043	556	338957	23
38	619938	459	958561	96	661377	556	338623	22
39	620213	459	958503	97	661710	555	338290	21
40	620488	458	958445	97	662043	555	337957	20
41	9·620763	458	9·958387	97	9·662376	555	10·337624	19
42	621038	457	958329	97	662709	554	337291	18
43	621313	457	958271	97	663042	554	336958	17
44	621587	457	958213	97	663375	554	336625	16
45	621861	456	958154	97	663707	554	336293	15
46	622135	456	958096	97	664039	553	335961	14
47	622409	456	958038	97	664371	553	335629	13
48	622682	455	957979	97	664703	553	335297	12
49	622956	455	957921	97	665035	553	334965	11
50	623229	455	957863	97	665366	552	334634	10
51	9·623502	454	9·957804	97	9·665698	552	10·334302	9
52	623774	454	957746	98	666029	552	333971	8
53	624047	454	957687	98	666360	551	333640	7
54	624319	453	957628	98	666691	551	333309	6
55	624591	453	957570	98	667021	551	332979	5
56	624863	453	957511	98	667352	551	332648	4
57	625135	452	957452	98	667682	550	332318	3
58	625406	452	957393	98	668013	550	331987	2
59	625677	452	957335	98	668343	550	331657	1
60	625948	451	957276	98	668673	550	331327	0
′	Cosine.	D.	Sine.	D.	Cotang.	D.	Tang.	′
114°								65°

25°								154°
′	Sine.	D.	Cosine.	D.	Tang.	D.	Cotang.	′
0	9·625948	451	9·957276	98	9·668673	550	10·331327	60
1	626219	451	957217	98	669002	549	330998	59
2	626490	451	957158	98	669332	549	330668	58
3	626760	450	957099	98	669661	549	330339	57
4	627030	450	957040	98	669991	548	330009	56
5	627300	450	956981	98	670320	548	329680	55
6	627570	449	956921	99	670649	548	329351	54
7	627840	449	956862	99	670977	548	329023	53
8	628109	449	956803	99	671306	547	328694	52
9	628378	448	956744	99	671635	547	328365	51
10	628647	448	956684	99	671963	547	328037	50
11	9·628916	457	9·956625	99	9·672291	547	10·327709	49
12	629185	447	956566	99	672619	546	327381	48
13	629453	447	956506	99	672947	546	327053	47
14	629721	446	956447	99	673274	546	326726	46
15	629989	446	956387	99	673602	546	326398	45
16	630257	446	956327	99	673929	545	326071	44
17	630524	446	956268	99	674257	545	325743	43
18	630792	445	956208	100	674584	545	325416	42
19	631059	445	956148	100	674911	544	325089	41
20	631326	445	956089	100	675237	544	324763	40
21	9·631593	444	9·956029	100	9·675564	544	10·324436	39
22	631859	444	955969	100	675890	544	324110	38
23	632125	444	955909	100	676217	543	323783	37
24	632392	443	955849	100	676543	543	323457	36
25	632658	443	955789	100	676869	543	323131	35
26	632923	443	955729	100	677194	543	322806	34
27	633189	442	955669	100	677520	542	322480	33
28	633454	442	955609	100	677846	542	322154	32
29	633719	442	955548	100	678171	542	321829	31
30	633984	441	955488	100	678496	542	321504	30
31	9·634249	441	9·955428	101	9·678821	541	10·321179	29
32	634514	440	955368	101	679146	541	320854	28
33	634778	440	955307	101	679471	541	320529	27
34	635042	440	955247	101	679795	541	320205	26
35	635306	439	955186	101	680120	540	319880	25
36	635570	439	955126	101	680444	540	319556	24
37	635834	439	955065	101	680768	540	319232	23
38	636097	438	955005	101	681092	540	318908	22
39	636360	438	954944	101	681416	539	318584	21
40	636623	438	954883	101	681740	539	318260	20
41	9·636886	437	9·954823	101	9·682063	539	10·317937	19
42	637148	437	954762	101	682387	539	317613	18
43	637411	437	954701	101	682710	538	317290	17
44	637673	437	954640	101	683033	538	316967	16
45	637935	436	954579	101	683356	538	316644	15
46	638197	436	954518	102	683679	538	316321	14
47	638458	436	954457	102	684001	537	315999	13
48	638720	435	954396	102	684324	537	315676	12
49	638981	435	954335	102	684646	537	315354	11
50	639242	435	954274	102	684968	537	315032	10
51	9·639503	434	9·954213	102	9·685290	536	10·314710	9
52	639764	434	954152	102	685612	536	314388	8
53	640024	434	954090	102	685934	536	314066	7
54	640284	433	954029	102	686255	536	313745	6
55	640544	433	953968	102	686577	535	313423	5
56	640804	433	953906	102	686898	535	313102	4
57	641064	432	953845	102	687219	535	312781	3
58	641324	432	953783	102	687540	535	312460	2
59	641583	432	953722	103	687861	534	312139	1
60	641842	431	953660	103	688182	534	311818	0
′	Cosine.	D.	Sine.	D.	Cotang.	D.	Tang.	′
115°								64°

26° 153°

′	Sine.	D.	Cosine.	D.	Tang.	D.	Cotang.	′
0	9·641842	431	9·953660	103	9·688182	534	10·311818	60
1	642101	431	953599	103	688502	534	311498	59
2	642360	431	953537	103	688823	534	311177	58
3	642618	430	953475	103	689143	533	310857	57
4	642877	430	953413	103	689463	533	310537	56
5	643135	430	953352	103	689783	533	310217	55
6	643393	430	953290	103	690103	533	309897	54
7	643650	429	953228	103	690423	533	309577	53
8	643908	429	953166	103	690742	532	309258	52
9	644165	429	953104	103	691062	532	308938	51
10	644423	428	953042	103	691381	532	308619	50
11	9·644680	428	9·952980	104	9·691700	531	10·308300	49
12	644936	428	952918	104	692019	531	307981	48
13	645193	427	952855	104	692338	531	307662	47
14	645450	427	952793	104	692656	531	307344	46
15	645706	427	952731	104	692975	531	307025	45
16	645962	426	952669	104	693293	530	306707	44
17	646218	426	952606	104	693612	530	306388	43
18	646474	426	952544	104	693930	530	306070	42
19	646729	425	952481	104	694248	530	305752	41
20	646984	425	952419	104	694566	529	305434	40
21	9·647240	425	9·952356	104	9·694883	529	10·305117	39
22	647494	424	952294	104	695201	529	304799	38
23	647749	424	952231	104	695518	529	304482	37
24	648004	424	952168	105	695836	529	304164	36
25	648258	424	952106	105	696153	528	303847	35
26	648512	423	952043	105	696470	528	303530	34
27	648766	423	951980	105	696787	528	303213	33
28	649020	423	951917	105	697103	528	302897	32
29	649274	422	951854	105	697420	527	302580	31
30	649527	422	951791	105	697736	527	302264	30
31	9·649781	422	9·951728	105	9·698053	527	10·301947	29
32	650034	422	951665	105	698369	527	301631	28
33	650287	421	951602	105	698685	526	301315	27
34	650539	421	951539	105	699001	526	300999	26
35	650792	421	951476	105	699316	526	300684	25
36	651044	420	951412	105	699632	526	300368	24
37	651297	420	951349	106	699947	526	300053	23
38	651549	420	951286	106	700263	525	299737	22
39	651800	419	951222	106	700578	525	299422	21
40	652052	419	951159	106	700893	525	299107	20
41	9·652304	419	9·951096	106	9·701208	524	10·298792	19
42	652555	418	951032	106	701523	524	298477	18
43	652806	418	950968	106	701837	524	298163	17
44	653057	418	950905	106	702152	524	297848	16
45	653308	418	950841	106	702466	524	297534	15
46	653558	417	950778	106	702781	523	297219	14
47	653808	417	950714	106	703095	523	296905	13
48	654059	417	950650	106	703409	523	296591	12
49	654309	416	950586	106	703722	523	296278	11
50	654558	416	950522	107	704036	522	295964	10
51	9·654808	416	9·950458	107	9·704350	522	10·295650	9
52	655058	416	950394	107	704663	522	295337	8
53	655307	415	950330	107	704976	522	295024	7
54	655556	415	950266	107	705290	522	294710	6
55	655805	415	950202	107	705603	521	294397	5
56	656054	414	950138	107	705916	521	294084	4
57	656302	414	950074	107	706228	521	293772	3
58	656551	414	950010	107	706541	521	293459	2
59	656799	413	949945	107	706854	521	293146	1
60	657047	413	949881	107	707166	520	292834	0
′	Cosine.	D.	Sine.	D.	Cotang.	D.	Tang.	′

116° 63°

27° 152°

′	Sine.	D.	Cosine.	D.	Tang.	D.	Cotang.	′
0	9·657047	413	9·949881	107	9·707166	520	10·292834	60
1	657295	413	949816	107	707478	520	292522	59
2	657542	412	949752	107	707790	520	292210	58
3	657790	412	949688	108	708102	520	291898	57
4	658037	412	949623	108	708414	519	291586	56
5	658284	412	949558	108	708726	519	291274	55
6	658531	411	949494	108	709037	519	290963	54
7	658778	411	949429	108	709349	519	290651	53
8	659025	411	949364	108	709660	519	290340	52
9	659271	410	949300	108	709971	518	290029	51
10	659517	410	949235	108	710282	518	289718	50
11	9·659763	410	9·949170	108	9·710593	518	10·289407	49
12	660009	409	949105	108	710904	518	289096	48
13	660255	409	949040	108	711215	518	288785	47
14	660501	409	948975	108	711525	517	288475	46
15	660746	409	948910	108	711836	517	288164	45
16	660991	408	948845	108	712146	517	287854	44
17	661236	408	948780	109	712456	517	287544	43
18	661481	408	948715	109	712766	516	287234	42
19	661726	407	948650	109	713076	516	286924	41
20	661970	407	948584	109	713386	516	286614	40
21	9·662214	407	9·948519	109	9·713696	516	10·286304	39
22	662459	407	948454	109	714005	516	285995	38
23	662703	406	948388	109	714314	515	285686	37
24	662946	406	948323	109	714624	515	285376	36
25	663190	406	948257	109	714933	515	285067	35
26	663433	405	948192	109	715242	515	284758	34
27	663677	405	948126	109	715551	514	284449	33
28	663920	405	948060	109	715860	514	284140	32
29	664163	405	947995	110	716168	514	283832	31
30	664406	404	947929	110	716477	514	283523	30
31	9·664648	404	9·947863	110	9·716785	514	10·283215	29
32	664891	404	947797	110	717093	513	282907	28
33	665133	403	947731	110	717401	513	282599	27
34	665375	403	947665	110	717709	513	282291	26
35	665617	403	947600	110	718017	513	281983	25
36	665859	402	947533	110	718325	513	281675	24
37	666100	402	947467	110	718633	512	281367	23
38	666342	402	947401	110	718940	512	281060	22
39	666583	402	947335	110	719248	512	280752	21
40	666824	401	947269	110	719555	512	280445	20
41	9·667065	401	9·947203	110	9·719862	512	10·280138	19
42	667305	401	947136	111	720169	511	279831	18
43	667546	401	947070	111	720476	511	279524	17
44	667786	400	947004	111	720783	511	279217	16
45	668027	400	946937	111	721089	511	278911	15
46	668267	400	946871	111	721396	511	278604	14
47	668506	399	946804	111	721702	510	278298	13
48	668746	399	946738	111	722009	510	277991	12
49	668986	399	946671	111	722315	510	277685	11
50	669225	399	946604	111	722621	510	277379	10
51	9·669464	398	9·946538	111	9·722927	510	10·277073	9
52	669703	398	946471	111	723232	509	276768	8
53	669942	398	946404	111	723538	509	276462	7
54	670181	397	946337	111	723844	509	276156	6
55	670419	397	946270	112	724149	509	275851	5
56	670658	397	946203	112	724454	509	275546	4
57	670896	397	946136	112	724760	508	275240	3
58	671134	396	946069	112	725065	508	274935	2
59	671372	396	946002	112	725370	508	274630	1
60	671609	396	945935	112	725674	508	274326	0
′	Cosine.	D.	Sine.	D.	Cotang.	D.	Tang.	′

117° 62°

28°								151°
′	Sine.	D.	Cosine.	D.	Tang.	D.	Cotang.	′
0	9·671609	396	9·945935	112	9·725674	508	10·274326	60
1	671847	395	945868	112	725979	508	274021	59
2	672084	395	945800	112	726284	507	273716	58
3	672321	395	945733	112	726588	507	273412	57
4	672558	395	945666	112	726892	507	273108	56
5	672795	394	945598	112	727197	507	272803	55
6	673032	394	945531	112	727501	507	272499	54
7	673268	394	945464	113	727805	506	272195	53
8	673505	394	945396	113	728109	506	271891	52
9	673741	393	945328	113	728412	506	271588	51
10	673977	393	945261	113	728716	506	271284	50
11	9·674213	393	9·945193	113	9·729020	506	10·270980	49
12	674448	392	945125	113	729323	505	270677	48
13	674684	392	945058	113	729626	505	270374	47
14	674919	392	944990	113	729929	505	270071	46
15	675155	392	944922	113	730233	505	269767	45
16	675390	391	944854	113	730535	505	269465	44
17	675624	391	944786	113	730838	504	269162	43
18	675859	391	944718	113	731141	504	268859	42
19	676094	391	944650	113	731444	504	268556	41
20	676328	390	944582	114	731746	504	268254	40
21	9·676562	390	9·944514	114	9·732048	504	10·267952	39
22	676796	390	944446	114	732351	503	267649	38
23	677030	390	944377	114	732653	503	267347	37
24	677264	389	944309	114	732955	503	267045	36
25	677498	389	944241	114	733257	503	266743	35
26	677731	389	944172	114	733558	503	266442	34
27	677964	388	944104	114	733860	502	266140	33
28	678197	388	944036	114	734162	502	265838	32
29	678430	388	943967	114	734463	502	265537	31
30	678663	388	943899	114	734764	502	265236	30
31	9·678895	387	9·943830	114	9·735066	502	10·264934	29
32	679128	387	943761	114	735367	502	264633	28
33	679360	387	943693	115	735668	501	264332	27
34	679592	387	943624	115	735969	501	264031	26
35	679824	386	943555	115	736269	501	263731	25
36	680056	386	943486	115	736570	501	263430	24
37	680288	386	943417	115	736870	501	263130	23
38	680519	385	943348	115	737171	500	262829	22
39	680750	385	943279	115	737471	500	262529	21
40	680982	385	943210	115	737771	500	262229	20
41	9·681213	385	9·943141	115	9·738071	500	10·261929	19
42	681443	384	943072	115	738371	500	261629	18
43	681674	384	943003	115	738671	499	261329	17
44	681905	384	942934	115	738971	499	261029	16
45	682135	384	942864	115	739271	499	260729	15
46	682365	383	942795	116	739570	499	260430	14
47	682595	383	942726	116	739870	499	260130	13
48	682825	383	942656	116	740169	499	259831	12
49	683055	383	942587	116	740468	498	259532	11
50	683284	382	942517	116	740767	498	259233	10
51	9·683514	382	9·942448	116	9·741066	498	10·258934	9
52	683743	382	942378	116	741365	498	258635	8
53	683972	382	942308	116	741664	498	258336	7
54	684201	381	942239	116	741962	497	258038	6
55	684430	381	942169	116	742261	497	257739	5
56	684658	381	942099	116	742559	497	257441	4
57	684887	380	942029	116	742858	497	257142	3
58	685115	380	941959	116	743156	497	256844	2
59	685343	380	941889	117	743454	497	256546	1
60	685571	380	941819	117	743752	496	256248	0
′	Cosine.	D.	Sine.	D.	Cotang.	D.	Tang.	′
118°								61°

29°								150°
′	Sine.	D.	Cosine.	D.	Tang.	D.	Cotang.	′
0	9·685571	380	9·941819	117	9·743752	496	10·256248	60
1	685799	379	941749	117	744050	496	255950	59
2	686027	379	941679	117	744348	496	255652	58
3	686254	379	941609	117	744645	496	255355	57
4	686482	379	941539	117	744943	496	255057	56
5	686709	378	941469	117	745240	496	254760	55
6	686936	378	941398	117	745538	495	254462	54
7	687163	378	941328	117	745835	495	254165	53
8	687389	378	941258	117	746132	495	253868	52
9	687616	377	941187	117	746429	495	253571	51
10	687843	377	941117	117	746726	495	253274	50
11	9·688069	377	9·941046	118	9·747023	494	10·252977	49
12	688295	377	940975	118	747319	494	252681	48
13	688521	376	940905	118	747616	494	252384	47
14	688747	376	940834	118	747913	494	252087	46
15	688972	376	940763	118	748209	494	251791	45
16	689198	376	940693	118	748505	493	251495	44
17	689423	375	940622	118	748801	493	251199	43
18	689648	375	940551	118	749097	493	250903	42
19	689873	375	940480	118	749393	493	250607	41
20	690098	375	940409	118	749689	493	250311	40
21	9·690323	374	9·940338	118	9·749985	493	10·250015	39
22	690548	374	940267	118	750281	492	249719	38
23	690772	374	940196	118	750576	492	249424	37
24	690996	374	940125	119	750872	492	249128	36
25	691220	373	940054	119	751167	492	248833	35
26	691444	373	939982	119	751462	492	248538	34
27	691668	373	939911	119	751757	492	248243	33
28	691892	373	939840	119	752052	491	247948	32
29	692115	372	939768	119	752347	491	247653	31
30	692339	372	939697	119	752642	491	247358	30
31	9·692562	372	9·939625	119	9·752937	491	10·247063	29
32	692785	371	939554	119	753231	491	246769	28
33	693008	371	939482	119	753526	491	246474	27
34	693231	371	939410	119	753820	490	246180	26
35	693453	371	939339	119	754115	490	245885	25
36	693676	370	939267	120	754409	490	245591	24
37	693898	370	939195	120	754703	490	245297	23
38	694120	370	939123	120	754997	490	245003	22
39	694342	370	939052	120	755291	490	244709	21
40	694564	369	938980	120	755585	489	244415	20
41	9·694786	369	9·938908	120	9·755878	489	10·244122	19
42	695007	369	938836	120	756172	489	243828	18
43	695229	369	938763	120	756465	489	243535	17
44	695450	368	938691	120	756759	489	243241	16
45	695671	368	938619	120	757052	489	242948	15
46	695892	368	938547	120	757345	488	242655	14
47	696113	368	938475	120	757638	488	242362	13
48	696334	367	938402	121	757931	488	242069	12
49	696554	367	938330	121	758224	488	241776	11
50	696775	367	938258	121	758517	488	241483	10
51	9·696995	367	9·938185	121	9·758810	488	10·241190	9
52	697215	366	938113	121	759102	487	240898	8
53	697435	366	938040	121	759395	487	240605	7
54	697654	366	937967	121	759687	487	240313	6
55	697874	366	937895	121	759979	487	240021	5
56	698094	365	937822	121	760272	487	239728	4
57	698313	365	937749	121	760564	487	239436	3
58	698532	365	937676	121	760856	486	239144	2
59	698751	365	937604	121	761148	486	238852	1
60	698970	364	937531	121	761439	486	238561	0
′	Cosine.	D.	Sine.	D.	Cotang.	D.	Tang.	′
119°								60°

30° | 149°

′	Sine.	D.	Cosine.	D.	Tang.	D.	Cotang.	′
0	9·698970	364	9·937531	121	9·761439	486	10·238561	60
1	699189	364	937458	122	761731	486	238269	59
2	699407	364	937385	122	762023	486	237977	58
3	699626	364	937312	122	762314	486	237686	57
4	699844	363	937238	122	762606	485	237394	56
5	700062	363	937165	122	762897	485	237103	55
6	700280	363	937092	122	763188	485	236812	54
7	700498	363	937019	122	763479	485	236521	53
8	700716	363	936946	122	763770	485	236230	52
9	700933	362	936872	122	764061	485	235939	51
10	701151	362	936799	122	764352	484	235648	50
11	9·701368	362	9·936725	122	9·764643	484	10·235357	49
12	701585	362	936652	123	764933	484	235067	48
13	701802	361	936578	123	765224	484	234776	47
14	702019	361	936505	123	765514	484	234486	46
15	702236	361	936431	123	765805	484	234195	45
16	702452	361	936357	123	766095	484	233905	44
17	702669	360	936284	123	766385	483	233615	43
18	702885	360	936210	123	766675	483	233325	42
19	703101	360	936136	123	766965	483	233035	41
20	703317	360	936062	123	767255	483	232745	40
21	9·703533	359	9·935988	123	9·767545	483	10·232455	39
22	703749	359	935914	123	767834	483	232166	38
23	703964	359	935840	123	768124	482	231876	37
24	704179	359	935766	124	768414	482	231586	36
25	704395	359	935692	124	768703	482	231297	35
26	704610	358	935618	124	768992	482	231008	34
27	704825	358	935543	124	769281	482	230719	33
28	705040	358	935469	124	769571	482	230429	32
29	705254	358	935395	124	769860	481	230140	31
30	705469	357	935320	124	770148	481	229852	30
31	9·705683	357	9·935246	124	9·770437	481	10·229563	29
32	705898	357	935171	124	770726	481	229274	28
33	706112	357	935097	124	771015	481	228985	27
34	706326	356	935022	124	771303	481	228697	26
35	706539	356	934948	124	771592	481	228408	25
36	706753	356	934873	124	771880	480	228120	24
37	706967	356	934798	125	772168	480	227832	23
38	707180	355	934723	125	772457	480	227543	22
39	707393	355	934649	125	772745	480	227255	21
40	707606	355	934574	125	773033	480	226967	20
41	9·707819	355	9·934499	125	9·773321	480	10·226679	19
42	708032	354	934424	125	773608	479	226392	18
43	708245	354	934349	125	773896	479	226104	17
44	708458	354	934274	125	774184	479	225816	16
45	708670	354	934199	125	774471	479	225529	15
46	708882	353	934123	125	774759	479	225241	14
47	709094	353	934048	125	775046	479	224954	13
48	709306	353	933973	125	775333	479	224667	12
49	709518	353	933898	126	775621	478	224379	11
50	709730	353	933822	126	775908	478	224092	10
51	9·709941	352	9·933747	126	9·776195	478	10·223805	9
52	710153	352	933671	126	776482	478	223518	8
53	710364	352	933596	126	776768	478	223232	7
54	710575	352	933520	126	777055	478	222945	6
55	710786	351	933445	126	777342	478	222658	5
56	710997	351	933369	126	777628	477	222372	4
57	711208	351	933293	126	777915	477	222085	3
58	711419	351	933217	126	778201	477	221799	2
59	711629	350	933141	126	778488	477	221512	1
60	711839	350	933066	126	778774	477	221226	0
′	Cosine.	D.	Sine.	D.	Cotang.	D.	Tang.	′

120° | 59°

31°								148°
′	Sine.	D.	Cosine.	D.	Tang.	D.	Cotang.	′
0	9·711839	350	9·933066	126	9·778774	477	10·221226	60
1	712050	350	932990	127	779060	477	220940	59
2	712260	350	932914	127	779346	476	220654	58
3	712469	349	932838	127	779632	476	220368	57
4	712679	349	932762	127	779918	476	220082	56
5	712889	349	932685	127	780203	476	219797	55
6	713098	349	932609	127	780489	476	219511	54
7	713308	349	932533	127	780775	476	219225	53
8	713517	348	932457	127	781060	476	218940	52
9	713726	348	932380	127	781346	475	218654	51
10	713935	348	932304	127	781631	475	218369	50
11	9·714144	348	9·932228	127	9·781916	475	10·218084	49
12	714352	347	932151	127	782201	475	217799	48
13	714561	347	932075	128	782486	475	217514	47
14	714769	347	931998	128	782771	475	217229	46
15	714978	347	931921	128	783056	475	216944	45
16	715186	347	931845	128	783341	475	216659	44
17	715394	346	931768	128	783626	474	216374	43
18	715602	346	931691	128	783910	474	216090	42
19	715809	346	931614	128	784195	474	215805	41
20	716017	346	931537	128	784479	474	215521	40
21	9·716224	345	9·931460	128	9·784764	474	10·215236	39
22	716432	345	931383	128	785048	474	214952	38
23	716639	345	931306	128	785332	473	214668	37
24	716846	345	931229	129	785616	473	214384	36
25	717053	345	931152	129	785900	473	214100	35
26	717259	344	931075	129	786184	473	213816	34
27	717466	344	930998	129	786468	473	213532	33
28	717673	344	930921	129	786752	473	213248	32
29	717879	344	930843	129	787036	473	212964	31
30	718085	343	930766	129	787319	472	212681	30
31	9·718291	343	9·930688	129	9·787603	472	10·212397	29
32	718497	343	930611	129	787886	472	212114	28
33	718703	343	930533	129	788170	472	211830	27
34	718909	343	930456	129	788453	472	211547	26
35	719114	342	930378	129	788736	472	211264	25
36	719320	342	930300	130	789019	472	210981	24
37	719525	342	930223	130	789302	471	210698	23
38	719730	342	930145	130	789585	471	210415	22
39	719935	341	930067	130	789868	471	210132	21
40	720140	341	929989	130	790151	471	209849	20
41	9·720345	341	9·929911	130	9·790434	471	10·209566	19
42	720549	341	929833	130	790716	471	209284	18
43	720754	340	929755	130	790999	471	209001	17
44	720958	340	929677	130	791281	471	208719	16
45	721162	340	929599	130	791563	470	208437	15
46	721366	340	929521	130	791846	470	208154	14
47	721570	340	929442	130	792128	470	207872	13
48	721774	339	929364	131	792410	470	207590	12
49	721978	339	929286	131	792692	470	207308	11
50	722181	339	929207	131	792974	470	207026	10
51	9·722385	339	9·929129	131	9·793256	470	10·206744	9
52	722588	339	929050	131	793538	469	206462	8
53	722791	338	928972	131	793819	469	206181	7
54	722994	338	928893	131	794101	469	205899	6
55	723197	338	928815	131	794383	469	205617	5
56	723400	338	928736	131	794664	469	205336	4
57	723603	337	928657	131	794946	469	205054	3
58	723805	337	928578	131	795227	469	204773	2
59	724007	337	928499	131	795508	468	204492	1
60	724210	337	928420	131	795789	468	204211	0
′	Cosine.	D.	Sine.	D.	Cotang.	D.	Tang.	′
121°								58°

32° 147°

′	Sine.	D.	Cosine.	D.	Tang.	D.	Cotang.	′
0	9·724210	337	9·928420	132	9·795789	468	10·204211	60
1	724412	337	928342	132	796070	468	203930	59
2	724614	336	928263	132	796351	468	203649	58
3	724816	336	928183	132	796632	468	203368	57
4	725017	336	928104	132	796913	468	203087	56
5	725219	336	928025	132	797194	468	202806	55
6	725420	335	927946	132	797474	468	202526	54
7	725622	335	927867	132	797755	468	202245	53
8	725823	335	927787	132	798036	467	201964	52
9	726024	335	927708	132	798316	467	201684	51
10	726225	335	927629	132	798596	467	201404	50
11	9·726426	334	9·927549	132	9·798877	467	10·201123	49
12	726626	334	927470	133	799157	467	200843	48
13	726827	334	927390	133	799437	467	200563	47
14	727027	334	927310	133	799717	467	200283	46
15	727228	334	927231	133	799997	466	200003	45
16	727428	333	927151	133	800277	466	199723	44
17	727628	333	927071	133	800557	466	199443	43
18	727828	333	926991	133	800836	466	199164	42
19	728027	333	926911	133	801116	466	198884	41
20	728227	333	926831	133	801396	466	198604	40
21	9·728427	332	9·926751	133	9·801675	466	10·198325	39
22	728626	332	926671	133	801955	466	198045	38
23	728825	332	926591	133	802234	465	197766	37
24	729024	332	926511	134	802513	465	197487	36
25	729223	331	926431	134	802792	465	197208	35
26	729422	331	926351	134	803072	465	196928	34
27	729621	331	926270	134	803351	465	196649	33
28	729820	331	926190	134	803630	465	196370	32
29	730018	330	926110	134	803909	465	196091	31
30	730217	330	926029	134	804187	465	195813	30
31	9·730415	330	9·925949	134	9·804466	464	10·195534	29
32	730613	330	925868	134	804745	464	195255	28
33	730811	330	925788	134	805023	464	194977	27
34	731009	329	925707	134	805302	464	194698	26
35	731206	329	925626	134	805580	464	194420	25
36	731404	329	925545	135	805859	464	194141	24
37	731602	329	925465	135	806137	464	193863	23
38	731799	329	925384	135	806415	463	193585	22
39	731996	328	925303	135	806693	463	193307	21
40	732193	328	925222	135	806971	463	193029	20
41	9·732390	328	9·925141	135	9·807249	463	10·192751	19
42	732587	328	925060	135	807527	463	192473	18
43	732784	328	924979	135	807805	463	192195	17
44	732980	327	924897	135	808083	463	191917	16
45	733177	327	924816	135	808361	463	191639	15
46	733373	327	924735	136	808638	462	191362	14
47	733569	327	924654	136	808916	462	191084	13
48	733765	327	924572	136	809193	462	190807	12
49	733961	326	924491	136	809471	462	190529	11
50	734157	326	924409	136	809748	462	190252	10
51	9·734353	326	9·924328	136	9·810025	462	10·189975	9
52	734549	326	924246	136	810302	462	189698	8
53	734744	325	924164	136	810580	462	189420	7
54	734939	325	924083	136	810857	462	189143	6
55	735135	325	924001	136	811134	461	188866	5
56	735330	325	923919	136	811410	461	188590	4
57	735525	325	923837	136	811687	461	188313	3
58	735719	324	923755	137	811964	461	188036	2
59	735914	324	923673	137	812241	461	187759	1
60	736109	324	923591	137	812517	461	187483	0
′	Cosine.	D.	Sine.	D.	Cotang.	D.	Tang.	′

122° 57°

33°								146°
′	Sine.	D.	Cosine.	D.	Tang.	D.	Cotang.	′
0	9·736109	324	9·923591	137	9·812517	461	10·187483	60
1	736303	324	923509	137	812794	461	187206	59
2	736498	324	923427	137	813070	461	186930	58
3	736692	323	923345	137	813347	460	186653	57
4	736886	323	923263	137	813623	460	186377	56
5	737080	323	923181	137	813899	460	186101	55
6	737274	323	923098	137	814176	460	185824	54
7	737467	323	923016	137	814452	460	185548	53
8	737661	322	922933	137	814728	460	185272	52
9	737855	322	922851	137	815004	460	184996	51
10	738048	322	922768	138	815280	460	184720	50
11	9·738241	322	9·922686	138	9·815555	459	10·184445	49
12	738434	322	922603	138	815831	459	184169	48
13	738627	321	922520	138	816107	459	183893	47
14	738820	321	922438	138	816382	459	183618	46
15	739013	321	922355	138	816658	459	183342	45
16	739206	321	922272	138	816933	459	183067	44
17	739398	321	922189	138	817209	459	182791	43
18	739590	320	922106	138	817484	459	182516	42
19	739783	320	922023	138	817759	459	182241	41
20	739975	320	921940	138	818035	458	181965	40
21	9·740167	320	9·921857	139	9·818310	458	10·181690	39
22	740359	320	921774	139	818585	458	181415	38
23	740550	319	921691	139	818860	458	181140	37
24	740742	319	921607	139	819135	458	180865	36
25	740934	319	921524	139	819410	458	180590	35
26	741125	319	921441	139	819684	458	180316	34
27	741316	319	921357	139	819959	458	180041	33
28	741508	318	921274	139	820234	458	179766	32
29	741699	318	921190	139	820508	457	179492	31
30	741889	318	921107	139	820783	457	179217	30
31	9·742080	318	9·921023	139	9·821057	457	10·178943	29
32	742271	318	920939	140	821332	457	178668	28
33	742462	317	920856	140	821606	457	178394	27
34	742652	317	920772	140	821880	457	178120	26
35	742842	317	920688	140	822154	457	177846	25
36	743033	317	920604	140	822429	457	177571	24
37	743223	317	920520	140	822703	457	177297	23
38	743413	316	920436	140	822977	456	177023	22
39	743602	316	920352	140	823251	456	176749	21
40	743792	316	920268	140	823524	456	176476	20
41	9·743982	316	9·920184	140	9·823798	456	10·176202	19
42	744171	316	920099	140	824072	456	175928	18
43	744361	315	920015	140	824345	456	175655	17
44	744550	315	919931	141	824619	456	175381	16
45	744739	315	919846	141	824893	456	175107	15
46	744928	315	919762	141	825166	456	174834	14
47	745117	315	919677	141	825439	455	174561	13
48	745306	314	919593	141	825713	455	174287	12
49	745494	314	919508	141	825986	455	174014	11
50	745683	314	919424	141	826259	455	173741	10
51	9·745871	314	9·919339	141	9·826532	455	10·173468	9
52	746060	314	919254	141	826805	455	173195	8
53	746248	313	919169	141	827078	455	172922	7
54	746436	313	919085	141	827351	455	172649	6
55	746624	313	919000	141	827624	455	172376	5
56	746812	313	918915	142	827897	454	172103	4
57	746999	313	918830	142	828170	454	171830	3
58	747187	312	918745	142	828442	454	171558	2
59	747374	312	918659	142	828715	454	171285	1
60	747562	312	918574	142	828987	454	171013	0
′	Cosine.	D.	Sine.	D.	Cotang.	D.	Tang.	′
123°								56°

34° 145°

′	Sine.	D.	Cosine.	D.	Tang.	D.	Cotang.	′
0	9·747562	312	9·918574	142	9·828987	454	10·171013	60
1	747749	312	918489	142	829260	454	170740	59
2	747936	312	918404	142	829532	454	170468	58
3	748123	311	918318	142	829805	454	170195	57
4	748310	311	918233	142	830077	454	169923	56
5	748497	311	918147	142	830349	453	169651	55
6	748683	311	918062	142	830621	453	169379	54
7	748870	311	917976	143	830893	453	169107	53
8	749056	310	917891	143	831165	453	168835	52
9	749243	310	917805	143	831437	453	168563	51
10	749429	310	917719	143	831709	453	168291	50
11	9·749615	310	9·917634	143	9·831981	453	10·168019	49
12	749801	310	917548	143	832253	453	167747	48
13	749987	309	917462	143	832525	453	167475	47
14	750172	309	917376	143	832796	453	167204	46
15	750358	309	917290	143	833068	452	166932	45
16	750543	309	917204	143	833339	452	166661	44
17	750729	309	917118	144	833611	452	166389	43
18	750914	308	917032	144	833882	452	166118	42
19	751099	308	916946	144	834154	452	165846	41
20	751284	308	916859	144	834425	452	165575	40
21	9·751469	308	9·916773	144	9·834696	452	10·165304	39
22	751654	308	916687	144	834967	452	165033	38
23	751839	308	916600	144	835238	452	164762	37
24	752023	307	916514	144	835509	452	164491	36
25	752208	307	916427	144	835780	451	164220	35
26	752392	307	916341	144	836051	451	163949	34
27	752576	307	916254	144	836322	451	163678	33
28	752760	307	916167	145	836593	451	163407	32
29	752944	306	916081	145	836864	451	163136	31
30	753128	306	915994	145	837134	451	162866	30
31	9·753312	306	9·915907	145	9·837405	451	10·162595	29
32	753495	306	915820	145	837675	451	162325	28
33	753679	306	915733	145	837946	451	162054	27
34	753862	305	915646	145	838216	451	161784	26
35	754046	305	915559	145	838487	450	161513	25
36	754229	305	915472	145	838757	450	161243	24
37	754412	305	915385	145	839027	450	160973	23
38	754595	305	915297	145	839297	450	160703	22
39	754778	304	915210	145	839568	450	160432	21
40	754960	304	915123	146	839838	450	160162	20
41	9·755143	304	9·915035	146	9·840108	450	10·159892	19
42	755326	304	914948	146	840378	450	159622	18
43	755508	304	914860	146	840648	450	159352	17
44	755690	304	914773	146	840917	449	159083	16
45	755872	303	914685	146	841187	449	158813	15
46	756054	303	914598	146	841457	449	158543	14
47	756236	303	914510	146	841727	449	158273	13
48	756418	303	914422	146	841996	449	158004	12
49	756600	303	914334	146	842266	449	157734	11
50	756782	302	914246	147	842535	449	157465	10
51	9·756963	302	9·914158	147	9·842805	449	10·157195	9
52	757144	302	914070	147	843074	449	156926	8
53	757326	302	913982	147	843343	449	156657	7
54	757507	302	913894	147	843612	449	156388	6
55	757688	301	913806	147	843882	448	156118	5
56	757869	301	913718	147	844151	448	155849	4
57	758050	301	913630	147	844420	448	155580	3
58	758230	301	913541	147	844689	448	155311	2
59	758411	301	913453	147	844958	448	155042	1
60	758591	301	913365	147	845227	448	154773	0
′	Cosine.	D.	Sine.	D.	Cotang.	D.	Tang.	′

124° 55°

35° 144°

′	Sine.	D.	Cosine.	D.	Tang.	D.	Cotang.	′
0	9·758591	301	9·913365	147	9·845227	448	10·154773	60
1	758772	300	913276	147	845496	448	154504	59
2	758952	300	913187	148	845764	448	154236	58
3	759132	300	913099	148	846033	448	153967	57
4	759312	300	913010	148	846302	448	153698	56
5	759492	300	912922	148	846570	447	153430	55
6	759672	299	912833	148	846839	447	153161	54
7	759852	299	912744	148	847108	447	152892	53
8	760031	299	912655	148	847376	447	152624	52
9	760211	299	912566	148	847644	447	152356	51
10	760390	299	912477	148	847913	447	152087	50
11	9·760569	298	9·912388	148	9·848181	447	10·151819	49
12	760748	298	912299	149	848449	447	151551	48
13	760927	298	912210	149	848717	447	151283	47
14	761106	298	912121	149	848986	447	151014	46
15	761285	298	912031	149	849254	447	150746	45
16	761464	298	911942	149	849522	447	150478	44
17	761642	297	911853	149	849790	446	150210	43
18	761821	297	911763	149	850057	446	149943	42
19	761999	297	911674	149	850325	446	149675	41
20	762177	297	911584	149	850593	446	149407	40
21	9·762356	297	9·911495	149	9·850861	446	10·149139	39
22	762534	296	911405	149	851129	446	148871	38
23	762712	296	911315	150	851396	446	148604	37
24	762889	296	911226	150	851664	446	148336	36
25	763067	296	911136	150	851931	446	148069	35
26	763245	296	911046	150	852199	446	147801	34
27	763422	296	910956	150	852466	446	147534	33
28	763600	295	910866	150	852733	445	147267	32
29	763777	295	910776	150	853001	445	146999	31
30	763954	295	910686	150	853268	445	146732	30
31	9·764131	295	9·910596	150	9·853535	445	10·146465	29
32	764308	295	910506	150	853802	445	146198	28
33	764485	294	910415	150	854069	445	145931	27
34	764662	294	910325	151	854336	445	145664	26
35	764838	294	910235	151	854603	445	145397	25
36	765015	294	910144	151	854870	445	145130	24
37	765191	294	910054	151	855137	445	144863	23
38	765367	294	909963	151	855404	445	144596	22
39	765544	293	909873	151	855671	444	144329	21
40	765720	293	909782	151	855938	444	144062	20
41	9·765896	293	9·909691	151	9·856204	444	10·143796	19
42	766072	293	909601	151	856471	444	143529	18
43	766247	293	909510	151	856737	444	143263	17
44	766423	293	909419	151	857004	444	142996	16
45	766598	292	909328	152	857270	444	142730	15
46	766774	292	909237	152	857537	444	142463	14
47	766949	292	909146	152	857803	444	142197	13
48	767124	292	909055	152	858069	444	141931	12
49	767300	292	908964	152	858336	444	141664	11
50	767475	291	908873	152	858602	443	141398	10
51	9·767649	291	9·908781	152	9·858868	443	10·141132	9
52	767824	291	908690	152	859134	443	140866	8
53	767999	291	908599	152	859400	443	140600	7
54	768173	291	908507	152	859666	443	140334	6
55	768348	290	908416	153	859932	443	140068	5
56	768522	290	908324	153	860198	443	139802	4
57	768697	290	908233	153	860464	443	139536	3
58	768871	290	908141	153	860730	443	139270	2
59	769045	290	908049	153	860995	443	139005	1
60	769219	290	907958	153	861261	443	138739	0
′	Cosine.	D.	Sine.	D.	Cotang.	D.	Tang.	′

125° 54°

36°								143°
′	Sine.	D.	Cosine.	D.	Tang.	D.	Cotang.	′
0	9·769219	290	9·907958	153	9·861261	443	10·138739	60
1	769393	289	907866	153	861527	443	138473	59
2	769566	289	907774	153	861792	442	138208	58
3	769740	289	907682	153	862058	442	137942	57
4	769913	289	907590	153	862323	442	137677	56
5	770087	289	907498	153	862589	442	137411	55
6	770260	288	907406	153	862854	442	137146	54
7	770433	288	907314	154	863119	442	136881	53
8	770606	288	907222	154	863385	442	136615	52
9	770779	288	907129	154	863650	442	136350	51
10	770952	288	907037	144	863915	442	136085	50
11	9·771125	288	9·906945	154	9·864180	442	10·135820	49
12	771298	287	906852	154	864445	442	135555	48
13	771470	287	906760	154	864710	442	135290	47
14	771643	287	906667	154	864975	441	135025	46
15	771815	287	906575	154	865240	441	134760	45
16	771987	287	906482	154	865505	441	134495	44
17	772159	287	906389	155	865770	441	134230	43
18	772331	286	906296	155	866035	441	133965	42
19	772503	286	906204	155	866300	441	133700	41
20	772675	286	906111	155	866564	441	133436	40
21	9·772847	286	9·906018	155	9·866829	441	10·133171	39
22	773018	286	905925	155	867094	441	132906	38
23	773190	286	905832	155	867358	441	132642	37
24	773361	285	905739	155	867623	441	132377	36
25	773533	285	905645	155	867887	441	132113	35
26	773704	285	905552	155	868152	440	131848	34
27	773875	285	905459	155	868416	440	131584	33
28	774046	285	905366	156	868680	440	131320	32
29	774217	285	905272	156	868945	440	131055	31
30	774388	284	905179	156	869209	440	130791	30
31	9·774558	284	9·905085	156	9·869473	440	10·130527	29
32	774729	284	904992	156	869737	440	130263	28
33	774899	284	904898	156	870001	440	129999	27
34	775070	284	904804	156	870265	440	129735	26
35	775240	284	904711	156	870529	440	129471	25
36	775410	283	904617	156	870793	440	129207	24
37	775580	283	904523	156	871057	440	128943	23
38	775750	283	904429	157	871321	440	128679	22
39	775920	283	904335	157	871585	440	128415	21
40	776090	283	904241	157	871849	439	128151	20
41	9·776259	283	9·904147	157	9·872112	439	10·127888	19
42	776429	282	904053	157	872376	439	127624	18
43	776598	282	903959	157	872640	439	127360	17
44	776768	282	903864	157	872903	439	127097	16
45	776937	282	903770	157	873167	439	126833	15
46	777106	282	903676	157	873430	439	126570	14
47	777275	281	903581	167	873694	439	126306	13
48	777444	281	903487	157	873957	439	126043	12
49	777613	281	903392	158	874220	439	125780	11
50	777781	281	903298	158	874484	439	125516	10
51	9·777950	281	9·903203	158	9·874747	439	10·125253	9
52	778119	281	903108	158	875010	439	124990	8
53	778287	280	903014	158	875273	438	124727	7
54	778455	280	902919	158	875537	438	124463	6
55	778624	280	902824	158	875800	438	124200	5
56	778792	280	902729	158	876063	438	123937	4
57	778960	280	902634	158	876326	438	123674	3
58	779128	280	902539	159	876589	438	123411	2
59	779295	279	902444	159	876852	438	123148	1
60	779463	279	902349	159	877114	438	122886	0
′	Cosine.	D.	Sine.	D.	Cotang.	D.	Tang.	′
126°								53°

37° | 142°

′	Sine.	D.	Cosine.	D.	Tang.	D.	Cotang.	′
0	9·779463	279	9·902349	159	9·877114	438	10·122886	60
1	779631	279	902253	159	877377	438	122623	59
2	779798	279	902158	159	877640	438	122360	58
3	779966	279	902063	159	877903	438	122097	57
4	780133	279	901967	159	878165	438	121835	56
5	780300	278	901872	159	878428	438	121572	55
6	780467	278	901776	159	878691	438	121309	54
7	780634	278	901681	159	878953	437	121047	53
8	780801	278	901585	159	879216	437	120784	52
9	780968	278	901490	159	879478	437	120522	51
10	781134	278	901394	160	879741	437	120259	50
11	9·781301	277	9·901298	160	9·880003	437	10·119997	49
12	781468	277	901202	160	880265	437	119735	48
13	781634	277	901106	160	880528	437	119472	47
14	781800	277	901010	160	880790	437	119210	46
15	781966	277	900914	160	881052	437	118948	45
16	782132	277	900818	160	881314	437	118686	44
17	782298	276	900722	160	881577	437	118423	43
18	782464	276	900626	160	881839	437	118161	42
19	782630	276	900529	160	882101	437	117899	41
20	782796	276	900433	161	882363	436	117637	40
21	9·782961	276	9·900337	161	9·882625	436	10·117375	39
22	783127	276	900240	161	882887	436	117113	38
23	783292	275	900144	161	883148	436	116852	37
24	783458	275	900047	161	883410	436	116590	36
25	783623	275	899951	161	883672	436	116328	35
26	783788	275	899854	161	883934	436	116066	34
27	783953	275	899757	161	884196	436	115804	33
28	784118	275	899660	161	884457	436	115543	32
29	784282	274	899564	161	884719	436	115281	31
30	784447	274	899467	162	884980	436	115020	30
31	9·784612	274	9·899370	162	9·885242	436	10·114758	29
32	784776	274	899273	162	885504	436	114496	28
33	784941	274	899176	162	885765	436	114235	27
34	785105	274	899078	162	886026	436	113974	26
35	785269	273	898981	162	886288	436	113712	25
36	785433	273	898884	162	886549	435	113451	24
37	785597	273	898787	162	886811	435	113189	23
38	785761	273	898689	162	887072	435	112928	22
39	785925	273	898592	162	887333	435	112667	21
40	786089	273	898494	163	887594	435	112406	20
41	9·786252	272	9·898397	163	9·887855	435	10·112145	19
42	786416	272	898299	163	888116	435	111884	18
43	786579	272	898202	163	888378	435	111622	17
44	786742	272	898104	163	888639	435	111361	16
45	786906	272	898006	163	888900	435	111100	15
46	787069	272	897908	163	889161	435	110839	14
47	787232	271	897810	163	889421	435	110579	13
48	787395	271	897712	163	889682	435	110318	12
49	787557	271	897614	163	889943	435	110057	11
50	787720	271	897516	163	890204	434	109796	10
51	9·787883	271	9·897418	164	9·890465	434	10·109535	9
52	788045	271	897320	164	890725	434	109275	8
53	788208	271	897222	164	890986	434	109014	7
54	788370	270	897123	164	891247	434	108753	6
55	788532	270	897025	164	891507	434	108493	5
56	788694	270	896926	164	891768	434	108232	4
57	788856	270	896828	164	892028	434	107972	3
58	789018	270	896729	164	892289	434	107711	2
59	789180	270	896631	164	892549	434	107451	1
60	789342	269	896532	164	892810	434	107190	0
′	Cosine.	D.	Sine.	D.	Cotang.	D.	Tang.	′

127° | 52°

38° | 141°

′	Sine.	D.	Cosine.	D.	Tang.	D.	Cotang.	′
0	9·789342	269	9·896532	164	9·892810	434	10·107190	60
1	789504	269	896433	165	893070	434	106930	59
2	789665	269	896335	165	893331	434	106669	58
3	789827	269	896236	165	893591	434	106409	57
4	789988	269	896137	165	893851	434	106149	56
5	790149	269	896038	165	894111	434	105889	55
6	790310	268	895939	165	894372	434	105628	54
7	790471	268	895840	165	894632	433	105368	53
8	790632	268	895741	165	894892	433	105108	52
9	790793	268	895641	165	895152	433	104848	51
10	790954	268	895542	165	895412	433	104588	50
11	9·791115	268	9·895443	166	9·895672	433	10·104328	49
12	791275	267	895343	166	895932	433	104068	48
13	791436	267	895244	166	896192	433	103808	47
14	791596	267	895145	166	896452	433	103548	46
15	791757	267	895045	166	896712	433	103288	45
16	791917	267	894945	166	896971	433	103029	44
17	792077	267	894846	166	897231	433	102769	43
18	792237	266	894746	166	897491	433	102509	42
19	792397	266	894646	166	897751	433	102249	41
20	792557	266	894546	166	898010	433	101990	40
21	9·792716	266	9·894446	167	9·898270	433	10·101730	39
22	792876	266	894346	167	898530	433	101470	38
23	793035	266	894246	167	898789	433	101211	37
24	793195	265	894146	167	899049	432	100951	36
25	793354	265	894046	167	899308	432	100692	35
26	793514	265	893946	167	899568	432	100432	34
27	793673	265	893846	167	899827	432	100173	33
28	793832	265	893745	167	900087	432	099913	32
29	793991	265	893645	167	900346	432	099654	31
30	794150	264	893544	167	900605	432	099395	30
31	9·794308	264	9·893444	168	9·900864	432	10·099136	29
32	794467	264	893343	168	901124	432	098876	28
33	794626	264	893243	168	901383	432	098617	27
34	794784	264	893142	168	901642	432	098358	26
35	794942	264	893041	168	901901	432	098099	25
36	795101	264	892940	168	902160	432	097840	24
37	795259	263	892839	168	902420	432	097580	23
38	795417	263	892739	168	902679	432	097321	22
39	795575	263	892638	168	902938	432	097062	21
40	795733	263	892536	168	903197	431	096803	20
41	9·795891	263	9·892435	169	9·903456	431	10·096544	19
42	796049	263	892334	169	903714	431	096286	18
43	796206	263	892233	169	903973	431	096027	17
44	796364	262	892132	169	904232	431	095768	16
45	796521	262	892030	169	904491	431	095509	15
46	796679	262	891929	169	904750	431	095250	14
47	796836	262	891827	169	905008	431	094992	13
48	796993	262	891726	169	905267	431	094733	12
49	797150	261	891624	169	905526	431	094474	11
50	797307	261	891523	170	905785	431	094215	10
51	9·797464	261	9·891421	170	9·906043	431	10·093957	9
52	797621	261	891319	170	906302	431	093698	8
53	797777	261	891217	170	906560	431	093440	7
54	797934	261	891115	170	906819	431	093181	6
55	798091	261	891013	170	907077	431	092923	5
56	798247	261	890911	170	907336	431	092664	4
57	798403	260	890809	170	907594	431	092406	3
58	798560	260	890707	170	907853	431	092147	2
59	798716	260	890605	170	908111	430	091889	1
60	798872	260	890503	170	908369	430	091631	0
′	Cosine.	D.	Sine.	D.	Cotang.	D.	Tang.	′

128° | 51°

39° 140°

′	Sine.	D.	Cosine.	D.	Tang.	D.	Cotang.	′
0	9·798872	260	9·890503	170	9·908369	430	10·091631	60
1	799028	260	890400	171	908628	430	091372	59
2	799184	260	890298	171	908886	430	091114	58
3	799339	259	890195	171	909144	430	090856	57
4	799495	259	890093	171	909402	430	090598	56
5	799651	259	889990	171	909660	430	090340	55
6	799806	259	889888	171	909918	430	090082	54
7	799962	259	889785	171	910177	430	089823	53
8	800117	259	889682	171	910435	430	089565	52
9	800272	258	889579	171	910693	430	089307	51
10	800427	258	889477	171	910951	430	089049	50
11	9·800582	258	9·889374	172	9·911209	430	10·088791	49
12	800737	258	889271	172	911467	430	088533	48
13	800892	258	889168	172	911725	430	088275	47
14	801047	258	889064	172	911982	430	088018	46
15	801201	258	888961	172	912240	430	087760	45
16	801356	257	888858	172	912498	430	087502	44
17	801511	257	888755	172	912756	430	087244	43
18	801665	257	888651	172	913014	429	086986	42
19	801819	257	888548	172	913271	429	086729	41
20	801973	257	888444	173	913529	429	086471	40
21	9·802128	257	9·888341	173	9·913787	429	10·086213	39
22	802282	256	888237	173	914044	429	085956	38
23	802436	256	888134	173	914302	429	085698	37
24	802589	256	888030	173	914560	429	085440	36
25	802743	256	887926	173	914817	429	085183	35
26	802897	256	887822	173	915075	429	084925	34
27	803050	256	887718	173	915332	429	084668	33
28	803204	256	887614	173	915590	429	084410	32
29	803357	255	887510	173	915847	429	084153	31
30	803511	255	887406	174	916104	429	083896	30
31	9·803664	255	9·887302	174	9·916362	429	10·083638	29
32	803817	255	887198	174	916619	429	083381	28
33	803970	255	887093	174	916877	429	083123	27
34	804123	255	886989	174	917134	429	082866	26
35	804276	254	886885	174	917391	429	082609	25
36	804428	254	886780	174	917648	429	082352	24
37	804581	254	886676	174	917906	429	082094	23
38	804734	254	886571	174	918163	428	081837	22
39	804886	254	886466	174	918420	428	081580	21
40	805039	254	886362	175	918677	428	081323	20
41	9·805191	254	9·886257	175	9·918934	428	10·081066	19
42	805343	253	886152	175	919191	428	080809	18
43	805495	253	886047	175	919448	428	080552	17
44	805647	253	885942	175	919705	428	080295	16
45	805799	253	885837	175	919962	428	080038	15
46	805951	253	885732	175	920219	428	079781	14
47	806103	253	885627	175	920476	428	079524	13
48	806254	253	885522	175	920733	428	079267	12
49	806406	252	885416	175	920990	428	079010	11
50	806557	252	885311	176	921247	428	078753	10
51	9·806709	252	9·885205	176	9·921503	428	10·078497	9
52	806860	252	885100	176	921760	428	078240	8
53	807011	252	884994	176	922017	428	077983	7
54	807163	252	884889	176	922274	428	077726	6
55	807314	252	884783	176	922530	428	077470	5
56	807465	251	884677	176	922787	428	077213	4
57	807615	251	884572	176	923044	428	076956	3
58	807766	251	884466	176	923300	428	076700	2
59	807917	251	884360	176	923557	427	076443	1
60	808067	251	884254	177	923814	427	076186	0
′	Cosine.	D.	Sine.	D.	Cotang.	D.	Tang.	′

129° 50°

40° 139°

′	Sine.	D.	Cosine.	D.	Tang.	D.	Cotang.	′
0	9·808067	251	9·884254	177	9·923814	427	10·076186	60
1	808218	251	884148	177	924070	427	075930	59
2	808368	251	884042	177	924327	427	075673	58
3	808519	250	883936	177	924583	427	075417	57
4	808669	250	883829	177	924840	427	075160	56
5	808819	250	883723	177	925096	427	074904	55
6	808969	250	883617	177	925352	427	074648	54
7	809119	250	883510	177	925609	427	074391	53
8	809269	250	883404	177	925865	427	074135	52
9	809419	249	883297	178	926122	427	073878	51
10	809569	249	883191	178	926378	427	073622	50
11	9·809718	249	9·883084	178	9·926634	427	10·073366	49
12	809868	249	882977	178	926890	427	073110	48
13	810017	249	882871	178	927147	427	072853	47
14	810167	249	882764	178	927403	427	072597	46
15	810316	248	882657	178	927659	427	072341	45
16	810465	248	882550	178	927915	427	072085	44
17	810614	248	882443	178	928171	427	071829	43
18	810763	248	882336	179	928427	427	071573	42
19	810912	248	882229	179	928684	427	071316	41
20	811061	248	882121	179	928940	427	071060	40
21	9·811210	248	9·882014	179	9·929196	427	10·070804	39
22	811358	247	881907	179	929452	427	070548	38
23	811507	247	881799	179	929708	427	070292	37
24	811655	247	881692	179	029964	426	070036	36
25	811804	247	881584	179	930220	426	069780	35
26	811952	247	881477	179	930475	426	069525	34
27	812100	247	881369	179	930731	426	069269	33
28	812248	247	881261	180	930987	426	069013	32
29	812396	246	881153	180	931243	426	068757	31
30	812544	246	881046	180	931499	426	068501	30
31	9·812692	246	9·880938	180	9·931755	426	10·068245	29
32	812840	246	880830	180	932010	426	067990	28
33	812988	246	880722	180	932266	426	067734	27
34	813135	246	880613	180	932522	426	067478	26
35	813283	246	880505	180	932778	426	067222	25
36	813430	245	880397	180	933033	426	066967	24
37	813578	245	880289	r81	933289	426	066711	23
38	813725	245	880180	181	933545	426	066455	22
39	813872	245	880072	181	933800	426	066200	21
40	814019	245	879963	181	934056	426	065944	20
41	9·814166	245	9·879855	181	9·934311	426	10·065689	19
42	814313	245	879746	181	934567	426	065433	18
43	814460	244	879637	181	934822	426	065178	17
44	814607	244	879529	181	935078	426	064922	16
45	814753	244	879420	181	935333	426	064667	15
46	814900	244	879311	181	935589	426	064411	14
47	815046	244	879202	182	935844	426	064156	13
48	815193	244	879093	182	936100	426	063900	12
49	815339	244	878984	182	936355	426	063645	11
50	815485	243	878875	182	936611	426	063389	10
51	9·815631	243	9·878766	182	9·936866	425	10·063134	9
52	815778	243	878656	182	937121	425	062879	8
53	815924	243	878547	182	937377	425	062623	7
54	816069	243	878438	182	937632	425	062368	6
55	816215	243	878328	182	937887	425	062113	5
56	816361	243	878219	183	938142	425	061858	4
57	816507	242	878109	183	938398	425	061602	3
58	816652	242	877999	183	938653	425	061347	2
59	816798	242	877890	183	938908	425	061092	1
60	816943	242	877780	183	939163	425	060837	0
′	Cosine.	D.	Sine.	D.	Cotang.	D.	Tang.	′

130° 49°

41° | 138°

′	Sine.	D.	Cosine.	D.	Tang.	D.	Cotang.	′
0	9·816943	242	9·877780	183	9·939163	425	10·060837	60
1	817088	242	877670	183	939418	425	060582	59
2	817233	242	877560	183	939673	425	060327	58
3	817379	242	877450	183	939928	425	060072	57
4	817524	241	877340	183	940183	425	059817	56
5	817668	241	877230	184	940439	425	059561	55
6	817813	241	877120	184	940694	425	059306	54
7	817958	241	877010	184	940949	425	059051	53
8	818103	241	876899	184	941204	425	058796	52
9	818247	241	876789	184	941459	425	058541	51
10	818392	241	876678	184	941713	425	058287	50
11	9·818536	240	9·876568	184	9·941968	425	10·058032	49
12	818681	240	876457	184	942223	425	057777	48
13	818825	240	876347	184	942478	425	057522	47
14	818969	240	876236	185	942733	425	057267	46
15	819113	240	876125	185	942988	425	057012	45
16	819257	240	876014	185	943243	425	056757	44
17	819401	240	875904	185	943498	425	056502	43
18	819545	239	875793	185	943752	425	056248	42
19	819689	239	875682	185	944007	425	055993	41
20	819832	239	875571	185	944262	425	055738	40
21	9·819976	239	9·875459	185	9·944517	425	10·055483	39
22	820120	239	875348	185	944771	424	055229	38
23	820263	239	875237	185	945026	424	054974	37
24	820406	239	875126	186	945281	424	054719	36
25	820550	238	875014	186	945535	424	054465	35
26	820693	238	874903	186	945790	424	054210	34
27	820836	238	874791	186	946045	424	053955	33
28	820979	238	874680	186	946299	424	053701	32
29	821122	238	874568	186	946554	424	053446	31
30	821265	238	874456	186	946808	424	053192	30
31	9·821407	238	9·874344	186	9·947063	424	10·052937	29
32	821550	238	874232	187	947318	424	052682	28
33	821693	237	874121	187	947572	424	052428	27
34	821835	237	874009	187	947827	424	052173	26
35	821977	237	873896	187	948081	424	051919	25
36	822120	237	873784	187	948335	424	051665	24
37	822262	237	873672	187	948590	424	051410	23
38	822404	237	873560	187	948844	424	051156	22
39	822546	237	873448	187	949099	424	050901	21
40	822688	236	873335	187	949353	424	050647	20
41	9·822830	236	9·873223	187	9·949608	424	10·050392	19
42	822972	236	873110	188	949862	424	050138	18
43	823114	236	872998	188	950116	424	049884	17
44	823255	236	872885	188	950371	424	049629	16
45	823397	236	872772	188	950625	424	049375	15
46	823539	236	872659	188	950879	424	049121	14
47	823680	235	872547	188	951133	424	048867	13
48	823821	235	872434	188	951388	424	048612	12
49	823963	235	872321	188	951642	424	048358	11
50	824104	235	872208	188	951896	424	048104	10
51	9·824245	235	9·872095	189	9·952150	424	10·047850	9
52	824386	235	871981	189	952405	424	047595	8
53	824527	235	871868	189	952659	424	047341	7
54	824668	234	871755	189	952913	424	047087	6
55	824808	234	871641	189	953167	423	046833	5
56	824949	234	871528	189	953421	423	046579	4
57	825090	234	871414	189	953675	423	046325	3
58	825230	234	871301	189	953929	423	046071	2
59	825371	234	871187	189	954183	423	045817	1
60	825511	234	871073	190	954437	423	045563	0
′	Cosine.	D.	Sine.	D.	Cotang.	D.	Tang.	′

131° | 48°

42° 137°

′	Sine.	D.	Cosine.	D.	Tang.	D.	Cotang.	′
0	9·825511	234	9·871073	190	9·954437	423	10·045563	60
1	825651	233	870960	190	954691	423	045309	59
2	825791	233	870846	190	954946	423	045054	58
3	825931	233	870732	190	955200	423	044800	57
4	826071	233	870618	190	955454	423	044546	56
5	826211	233	870504	190	955708	423	044292	55
6	826351	233	870390	190	955961	423	044039	54
7	826491	233	870276	190	956215	423	043785	53
8	826631	233	870161	190	956469	423	043531	52
9	826770	232	870047	191	956723	423	043277	51
10	826910	232	869933	191	956977	423	043023	50
11	9·827049	232	9·869818	191	9·957231	423	10·042769	49
12	827189	232	869704	191	957485	423	042515	48
13	827328	232	869589	191	957739	423	042261	47
14	827467	232	869474	191	957993	423	042007	46
15	827606	232	869360	191	958247	423	041753	45
16	827745	232	869245	191	958500	423	041500	44
17	827884	231	869130	191	958754	423	041246	43
18	828023	231	869015	192	959008	423	040992	42
19	828162	231	868900	192	959262	423	040738	41
20	828301	231	868785	192	959516	423	040484	40
21	9·828439	231	9·868670	192	9·959769	423	10·040231	39
22	828578	231	868555	192	960023	423	039977	38
23	828716	231	868440	192	960277	423	039723	37
24	828855	230	868324	192	960530	423	039470	36
25	828993	230	868209	192	960784	423	039216	35
26	829131	230	868093	192	961038	423	038962	34
27	829269	230	867978	193	961292	423	038708	33
28	829407	230	867862	193	961545	423	038455	32
29	829545	230	867747	193	961799	423	038201	31
30	829683	230	867631	193	962052	423	037948	30
31	9·829821	229	9·867515	193	9·962306	423	10·037694	29
32	829959	229	867399	193	962560	423	037440	28
33	830097	229	867283	193	962813	423	037187	27
34	830234	229	867167	193	963067	423	036933	26
35	830372	229	867051	193	963320	423	036680	25
36	830509	229	866935	194	963574	423	036426	24
37	830646	229	866819	194	963828	423	036172	23
38	830784	229	866703	194	964081	423	035919	22
39	830921	228	866586	194	964335	423	035665	21
40	831058	228	866470	194	964588	422	035412	20
41	9·831195	228	9·866353	194	9·964842	422	10·035158	19
42	831332	228	866237	194	965095	422	034905	18
43	831469	228	866120	194	965349	422	034651	17
44	831606	228	866004	195	965602	422	034398	16
45	831742	228	865887	195	965855	422	034145	15
46	831879	228	865770	195	966109	422	033891	14
47	832015	227	865653	195	966362	422	033638	13
48	832152	227	865536	195	966616	422	033384	12
49	832288	227	865419	195	966869	422	033131	11
50	832425	227	865302	195	967123	422	032877	10
51	9·832561	227	9·865185	195	9·967376	422	10·032624	9
52	832697	227	865068	195	967629	422	032371	8
53	832833	227	864950	195	967883	422	032117	7
54	832969	226	864833	196	968136	422	031864	6
55	833105	226	864716	196	968389	422	031611	5
56	833241	226	864598	196	968643	422	031357	4
57	833377	226	864481	196	968896	422	031104	3
58	833512	226	864363	196	969149	422	030851	2
59	833648	226	864245	196	969403	422	030597	1
60	833783	226	864127	196	969656	422	030344	0
′	Cosine.	D.	Sine.	D.	Cotang.	D.	Tang.	′

132° 47°

43° | 136°

′	Sine.	D.	Cosine.	D.	Tang.	D.	Cotang.	′
0	9·833783	226	9·864127	196	9·969656	422	10·030344	60
1	833919	225	864010	196	969909	422	030091	59
2	834054	225	863892	197	970162	422	029838	58
3	834189	225	863774	197	970416	422	029584	57
4	834325	225	863656	197	970669	422	029331	56
5	834460	225	863538	197	970922	422	029078	55
6	834595	225	863419	197	971175	422	028825	54
7	834730	225	863301	197	971429	422	028571	53
8	834865	225	863183	197	971682	422	028318	52
9	834999	224	863064	197	971935	422	028065	51
10	835134	224	862946	198	972188	422	027812	50
11	9·835269	224	9·862827	198	9·972441	422	10·027559	49
12	835403	224	862709	198	972695	422	027305	48
13	835538	224	862590	198	972948	422	027052	47
14	835672	224	862471	198	973201	422	026799	46
15	835807	224	862353	198	973454	422	026546	45
16	835941	224	862234	198	973707	422	026293	44
17	836075	223	862115	198	973960	422	026040	43
18	836209	223	861996	198	974213	422	025787	42
19	836343	223	861877	198	974466	422	025534	41
20	836477	223	861758	199	974720	422	025280	40
21	9·836611	223	9·861638	199	9·974973	422	10·025027	39
22	836745	223	861519	199	975226	422	024774	38
23	836878	223	861400	199	975479	422	024521	37
24	837012	222	861280	199	975732	422	024268	36
25	837146	222	861161	199	975985	422	024015	35
26	837279	222	861041	199	976238	422	023762	34
27	837412	222	860922	199	976491	422	023509	33
28	837546	222	860802	199	976744	422	023256	32
29	837679	222	860682	200	976997	422	023003	31
30	837812	222	860562	200	977250	422	022750	30
31	9·837945	222	9·860442	200	9·977503	422	10·022497	29
32	838078	221	860322	200	977756	422	022244	28
33	838211	221	860202	200	978009	422	021991	27
34	838344	221	860082	200	978262	422	021738	26
35	838477	221	859962	200	978515	422	021485	25
36	838610	221	859842	200	978768	422	021232	24
37	838742	221	859721	201	979021	422	020979	23
38	838875	221	859601	201	979274	422	020726	22
39	839007	221	859480	201	979527	422	020473	21
40	839140	220	859360	201	979780	422	020220	20
41	9·839272	220	9·859239	201	9·980033	422	10·019967	19
42	839404	220	859119	201	980286	422	019714	18
43	839536	220	858998	201	980538	422	019462	17
44	839668	220	858877	201	980791	421	019209	16
45	839800	220	858756	202	981044	421	018956	15
46	839932	220	858635	202	981297	421	018703	14
47	840064	219	858514	202	981550	421	018450	13
48	840196	219	858393	202	981803	421	018197	12
49	840328	219	858272	202	982056	421	017944	11
50	840459	219	858151	202	982309	421	017691	10
51	9·840591	219	9·858029	202	9·982562	421	10·017438	9
52	840722	219	857908	202	982814	421	017186	8
53	840854	219	857786	202	983067	421	016933	7
54	840985	219	857665	203	983320	421	016680	6
55	841116	218	857543	203	983573	421	016427	5
56	841247	218	857422	203	983826	421	016174	4
57	841378	218	857300	203	984079	421	015921	3
58	841509	218	857178	203	984332	421	015668	2
59	841640	218	857056	203	984584	421	015416	1
60	841771	218	856934	203	984837	421	015163	0
′	Cosine.	D.	Sine.	D.	Cotang.	D.	Tang.	′

133° | 46°

44° 135°

′	Sine.	D.	Cosine.	D.	Tang.	D.	Cotang.	′
0	9·841771	218	9·856934	203	9·984837	421	10·015163	60
1	841902	218	856812	203	985090	421	014910	59
2	842033	218	856690	204	985343	421	014657	58
3	842163	217	856568	204	985596	421	014404	57
4	842294	217	856446	204	985848	421	014152	56
5	842424	217	856323	204	986101	421	013899	55
6	842555	217	856201	204	986354	421	013646	54
7	842685	217	856078	204	986607	421	013393	53
8	842815	217	855956	204	986860	421	013140	52
9	842946	217	855833	204	987112	421	012888	51
10	843076	217	855711	205	987365	421	012635	50
11	9·843206	216	9·855588	205	9·987618	421	10·012382	49
12	843336	216	855465	205	987871	421	012129	48
13	843466	216	855342	205	988123	421	011877	47
14	843595	216	855219	205	988376	421	011624	46
15	843725	216	855096	205	988629	421	011371	45
16	843855	216	854973	205	988882	421	011118	44
17	843984	216	854850	205	989134	421	010866	43
18	844114	215	854727	206	989387	421	010613	42
19	844243	215	854603	206	989640	421	010360	41
20	844372	215	854480	206	989893	421	010107	40
21	9·844502	215	9·854356	206	9·990145	421	10·009855	39
22	844631	215	854233	206	990398	421	009602	38
23	844760	215	854109	206	990651	421	009349	37
24	844889	215	853986	206	990903	421	009097	36
25	845018	215	853862	206	991156	421	008844	35
26	845147	215	853738	206	991409	421	008591	34
27	845276	214	853614	207	991662	421	008338	33
28	845405	214	853490	207	991914	421	008086	32
29	845533	214	853366	207	992167	421	007833	31
30	845662	214	853242	207	992420	421	007580	30
31	9·845790	214	9·853118	207	9·992672	421	10·007328	29
32	845919	214	852994	207	992925	421	007075	28
33	846047	214	852869	207	993178	421	006822	27
34	846175	214	852745	207	993431	421	006569	26
35	846304	214	852620	207	993683	421	006317	25
36	846432	213	852496	208	993936	421	006064	24
37	846560	213	852371	208	994189	421	005811	23
38	846688	213	852247	208	994441	421	005559	22
39	846816	213	852122	208	994694	421	005306	21
40	846944	213	851997	208	994947	421	005053	20
41	9·847071	213	9·851872	208	9·995199	421	10·004801	19
42	847199	213	851747	208	995452	421	004548	18
43	847327	213	851622	208	995705	421	004295	17
44	847454	212	851497	209	995957	421	004043	16
45	847582	212	851372	209	996210	421	003790	15
46	847709	212	851246	209	996463	421	003537	14
47	847836	212	851121	209	996715	421	003285	13
48	847964	212	850996	209	996968	421	003032	12
49	848091	212	850870	209	997221	421	002779	11
50	848218	212	850745	209	997473	421	002527	10
51	9·848345	212	9·850619	209	9·997726	421	10·002274	9
52	848472	211	850493	210	997979	421	002021	8
53	848599	211	850368	210	998231	421	001769	7
54	848726	211	850242	210	998484	421	001516	6
55	848852	211	850116	210	998737	421	001263	5
56	848979	211	849990	210	998989	421	001011	4
57	849106	211	849864	210	999242	421	000758	3
58	849232	211	849738	210	999495	421	000505	2
59	849359	211	849611	210	999747	421	000253	1
60	849485	211	849485	210	10·000000	421	10·000000	0
′	Cosine.	D.	Sine.	D.	Cotang.	D.	Tang.	′

134° 45°

TABLE III.,

OF

NATURAL SINES AND TANGENTS;

TO

EVERY DEGREE AND MINUTE OF THE QUADRANT.

If the given angle is less than 45°, look for the degrees and the title of the column, at the *top* of the page; and for the minutes on the *left*. But if the angle is between 45° and 90°, look for the degrees and the title of the column, at the *bottom*; and for the minutes on the *right*.

The *Secants and Cosecants*, which are not inserted in this table, may be easily supplied. If 1 be divided by the cosine of an arc, the quotient will be the secant of that arc. And if 1 be divided by the sine, the quotient will be the cosecant.

The values of the Sines and Cosines are less than a unit, and are given in decimals, although the decimal point is not printed. So also, the tangents of arcs less than 45°, and cotangents of arcs greater than 45°, are less than a unit and are expressed in decimals with the decimal point omitted.

′	0°		1°		2°		3°		4°		′
	Sine.	Cosine.	Sine.	Cosine.	Sine.	Cosine.	Sine.	Cosine.	Sine.	Cosine.	
0	00000	Unit.	01745	99985	03490	99939	05234	99863	06976	99756	60
1	00029	Unit.	01774	99984	03519	99938	05263	99861	07005	99754	59
2	00058	Unit.	01803	99984	03548	99937	05292	99860	07034	99752	58
3	00087	Unit.	01832	99983	03577	99936	05321	99858	07063	99750	57
4	00116	Unit.	01862	99983	03606	99935	05350	99857	07092	99748	56
5	00145	Unit.	01891	99982	03635	99934	05379	99855	07121	99746	55
6	00175	Unit.	01920	99982	03664	99933	05408	99854	07150	99744	54
7	00204	Unit.	01949	99981	03693	99932	05437	99852	07179	99742	53
8	00233	Unit.	01978	99980	03723	99931	05466	99851	07208	99740	52
9	00262	Unit.	02007	99980	03752	99930	05495	99849	07237	99738	51
10	00291	Unit.	02036	99979	03781	99929	05524	99847	07266	99736	50
11	00320	99999	02065	99979	03810	99927	05553	99846	07295	99734	49
12	00349	99999	02094	99978	03839	99926	05582	99844	07324	99731	48
13	00378	99999	02123	99977	03868	99925	05611	99842	07353	99729	47
14	00407	99999	02152	99977	03897	99924	05640	99841	07382	99727	46
15	00436	99999	02181	99976	03926	99923	05669	99839	07411	99725	45
16	00465	99999	02211	99976	03955	99922	05698	99838	07440	99723	44
17	00495	99999	02240	99975	03984	99921	05727	99836	07469	99721	43
18	00524	99999	02269	99974	04013	99919	05756	99834	07498	99719	42
19	00553	99998	02298	99974	04042	99918	05785	99833	07527	99716	41
20	00582	99998	02327	99973	04071	99917	05814	99831	07556	99714	40
21	00611	99998	02356	99972	04100	99916	05844	99829	07585	99712	39
22	00640	99998	02385	99972	04129	99915	05873	99827	07614	99710	38
23	00669	99998	02414	99971	04159	99913	05902	99826	07643	99708	37
24	00698	99998	02443	99970	04188	99912	05931	99824	07672	99705	36
25	00727	99997	02472	99969	04217	99911	05960	99822	07701	99703	35
26	00756	99997	02501	99969	04246	99910	05989	99821	07730	99701	34
27	00785	99997	02530	99968	04275	99909	06018	99819	07759	99699	33
28	00814	99997	02560	99967	04304	99907	06047	99817	07788	99696	32
29	00844	99996	02589	99966	04333	99906	06076	99815	07817	99694	31
30	00873	99996	02618	99966	04362	99905	06105	99813	07846	99692	30
31	00902	99996	02647	99965	04391	99904	06134	99812	07875	99689	29
32	00931	99996	02676	99964	04420	99902	06163	99810	07904	99687	28
33	00960	99995	02705	99963	04449	99901	06192	99808	07933	99685	27
34	00989	99995	02734	99963	04478	99900	06221	99806	07962	99683	26
35	01018	99995	02763	99962	04507	99898	06250	99804	07991	99680	25
36	01047	99995	02792	99961	04536	99897	06279	99803	08020	99678	24
37	01076	99994	02821	99960	04565	99896	06308	99801	08049	99676	23
38	01105	99994	02850	99959	04594	99894	06337	99799	08078	99673	22
39	01134	99994	02879	99959	04623	99893	06366	99797	08107	99671	21
40	01164	99993	02908	99958	04653	99892	06395	99795	08136	99668	20
41	01193	99993	02938	99957	04682	99890	06424	99793	08165	99666	19
42	01222	99993	02967	99956	04711	99889	06453	99792	08194	99664	18
43	01251	99992	02996	99955	04740	99888	06482	99790	08223	99661	17
44	01280	99992	03025	99954	04769	99886	06511	99788	08252	99659	16
45	01309	99991	03054	99953	04798	99885	06540	99786	08281	99657	15
46	01338	99991	03083	99952	04827	99883	06569	99784	08310	99654	14
47	01367	99991	03112	99952	04856	99882	06598	99782	08339	99652	13
48	01396	99990	03141	99951	04885	99881	06627	99780	08368	99649	12
49	01425	99990	03170	99950	04914	99879	06656	99778	08397	99647	11
50	01454	99989	03199	99949	04943	99878	06685	99776	08426	99644	10
51	01483	99989	03228	99948	04972	99876	06714	99774	08455	99642	9
52	01513	99989	03257	99947	05001	99875	06743	99772	08484	99639	8
53	01542	99988	03286	99946	05030	99873	06773	99770	08513	99637	7
54	01571	99988	03316	99945	05059	99872	06802	99768	08542	99635	6
55	01600	99987	03345	99944	05088	99870	06831	99766	08571	99632	5
56	01629	99987	03374	99943	05117	99869	06860	99764	08600	99630	4
57	01658	99986	03403	99942	05146	99867	06889	99762	08629	99627	3
58	01687	99986	03432	99941	05175	99866	06918	99760	08658	99625	2
59	01716	99985	03461	99940	05205	99864	06947	99758	08687	99622	1
60	01745	99985	03490	99939	05234	99863	06976	99756	08716	99619	0
	Cosine.	Sine.	Cosine.	Sine.	Cosine.	Sine.	Cosine.	Sine.	Cosine.	Sine.	
′	89°		88°		87°		86°		85°		′

′	5° Sine	5° Cosine.	6° Sine.	6° Cosine.	7° Sine.	7° Cosine.	8° Sine.	8° Cosine.	9° Sine.	9° Cosine.	′
0	08716	99619	10453	99452	12187	99255	13917	99027	15643	98769	60
1	08745	99617	10482	99449	12216	99251	13946	99023	15672	98764	59
2	08774	99614	10511	99446	12245	99248	13975	99019	15701	98760	58
3	08803	99612	10540	99443	12274	99244	14004	99015	15730	98755	57
4	08831	99609	10569	99440	12302	99240	14033	99011	15758	98751	56
5	08860	99607	10597	99437	12331	99237	14061	99006	15787	98746	55
6	08889	99604	10626	99434	12360	99233	14090	99002	15816	98741	54
7	08918	99602	10655	99431	12389	99230	14119	98998	15845	98737	53
8	08947	99599	10684	99428	12418	99226	14148	98994	15873	98732	52
9	08976	99596	10713	99424	12447	99222	14177	98990	15902	98728	51
10	09005	99594	10742	99421	12476	99219	14205	98986	15931	98723	50
11	09034	99591	10771	99418	12504	99215	14234	98982	15959	98718	49
12	09063	99588	10800	99415	12533	99211	14263	98978	15988	98714	48
13	09092	99586	10829	99412	12562	99208	14292	98973	16017	98709	47
14	09121	99583	10858	99409	12591	99204	14320	98969	16046	98704	46
15	09150	99580	10887	99406	12620	99200	14349	98965	16074	98700	45
16	09179	99578	10916	99402	12649	99197	14378	98961	16103	98695	44
17	09208	99575	10945	99399	12678	99193	14407	98957	16132	98690	43
18	09237	99572	10973	99396	12706	99189	14436	98953	16160	98686	42
19	09266	99570	11002	99393	12735	99186	14464	98948	16189	98681	41
20	09295	99567	11031	99390	12764	99182	14493	98944	16218	98676	40
21	09324	99564	11060	99386	12793	99178	14522	98940	16246	98671	39
22	09353	99562	11089	99383	12822	99175	14551	98936	16275	98667	38
23	09382	99559	11118	99380	12851	99171	14580	98931	16304	98662	37
24	09411	99556	11147	99377	12880	99167	14608	98927	16333	98657	36
25	09440	99553	11176	99374	12908	99163	14637	98923	16361	98652	35
26	09469	99551	11205	99370	12937	99160	14666	98919	16390	98648	34
27	09498	99548	11234	99367	12966	99156	14695	98914	16419	98643	33
28	09527	99545	11263	99364	12995	99152	14723	98910	16447	98638	32
29	09556	99542	11291	99360	13024	99148	14752	98906	16476	98633	31
30	09585	99540	11320	99357	13053	99144	14781	98902	16505	98629	30
31	09614	99537	11349	99354	13081	99141	14810	98897	16533	98624	29
32	09642	99534	11378	99351	13110	99137	14838	98893	16562	98619	28
33	09671	99531	11407	99347	13139	99133	14867	98889	16591	98614	27
34	09700	99528	11436	99344	13168	99129	14896	98884	16620	98609	26
35	09729	99526	11465	99341	13197	99125	14925	98880	16648	98604	25
36	09758	99523	11494	99337	13226	99122	14954	98876	16677	98600	24
37	09787	99520	11523	99334	13254	99118	14982	98871	16706	98595	23
38	09816	99517	11552	99331	13283	99114	15011	98867	16734	98590	22
39	09845	99514	11580	99327	13312	99110	15040	98863	16763	98585	21
40	09874	99511	11609	69324	13341	99106	15069	98858	16792	98580	20
41	09903	99508	11638	99320	13370	99102	15097	98854	16820	98575	19
42	09932	99506	11667	99317	13399	99098	15126	98849	16849	98570	18
43	09961	99503	11696	99314	13427	99094	15155	98845	16878	98565	17
44	09990	99500	11725	99310	13456	99091	15184	98841	16906	98561	16
45	10019	99497	11754	99307	13485	99087	15212	98836	16935	98556	15
46	10048	99494	11783	99303	13514	99083	15241	98832	16964	98551	14
47	10077	99491	11812	99300	13543	99079	15270	98827	16992	98546	13
48	10106	99488	11840	99297	13572	99075	15299	98823	17021	98541	12
49	10135	99485	11869	99293	13600	99071	15327	98818	17050	98536	11
50	10164	99482	11898	99290	13629	99067	15356	98814	17078	98531	10
51	10192	99479	11927	99286	13658	99063	15385	98809	17107	98526	9
52	10221	99476	11956	99283	13687	99059	15414	98805	17136	98521	8
53	10250	99473	11985	99279	13716	99055	15442	98800	17164	98516	7
54	10279	99470	12014	99276	13744	99051	15471	98796	17193	98511	6
55	10308	99467	12043	99272	13773	99047	15500	98791	17222	98506	5
56	10337	99464	12071	99269	13802	99043	15529	98787	17250	98501	4
57	10366	99461	12100	99265	13831	99039	15557	98782	17279	98496	3
58	10395	99458	12129	99262	13860	99035	15586	98778	17308	98491	2
59	10424	99455	12158	99258	13889	99031	15615	98773	17336	98486	1
60	10453	99452	12187	99255	13917	99027	15643	98769	17365	98481	0
′	Cosine.	Sine.	Cosine.	Sine.	Cosine.	Sine.	Cosine.	Sine.	Cosine.	Sine.	′
	84°		83°		82°		81°		80°		

′	10°		11°		12°		13°		14°		′
	Sine.	Cosine.	Sine.	Cosine.	Sine.	Cosine.	Sine.	Cosine.	Sine.	Cosine.	
0	17365	98481	19081	98163	20791	97815	22495	97437	24192	97030	60
1	17393	98476	19109	98157	20820	97809	22523	97430	24220	97023	59
2	17422	98471	19138	98152	20848	97803	22552	97424	24249	97015	58
3	17451	98466	19167	98146	20877	97797	22580	97417	24277	97008	57
4	17479	98461	19195	98140	20905	97791	22608	97411	24305	97001	56
5	17508	98455	19224	98135	20933	97784	22637	97404	24333	96994	55
6	17537	98450	19252	98129	20962	97778	22665	97398	24362	96987	54
7	17565	98445	19281	98124	20990	97772	22693	97391	24390	96980	53
8	17594	98440	19309	98118	21019	97766	22722	97384	24418	96973	52
9	17623	98435	19338	98112	21047	97760	22750	97378	24446	96966	51
10	17651	98430	19366	98107	21076	97754	22778	97371	24474	96959	50
11	17680	98425	19395	98101	21104	97748	22807	97365	24503	96952	49
12	17708	98420	19423	98096	21132	97742	22835	97358	24531	96945	48
13	17737	98414	19452	98090	21161	97735	22863	97351	24559	96937	47
14	17766	98409	19481	98084	21189	97729	22892	97345	24587	96930	46
15	17794	98404	19509	98079	21218	97723	22920	97338	24615	96923	45
16	17823	98399	19538	98073	21246	97717	22948	97331	24644	96916	44
17	17852	98394	19566	98067	21275	97711	22977	97325	24672	96909	43
18	17880	98389	19595	98061	21303	97705	23005	97318	24700	96902	42
19	17909	98383	19623	98056	21331	97698	23033	97311	24728	96894	41
20	17937	98378	19652	98050	21360	97692	23062	97304	24756	96887	40
21	17966	98373	19680	98044	21388	97686	23090	97298	24784	96880	39
22	17995	98368	19709	98039	21417	97680	23118	97291	24813	96873	38
23	18023	98362	19737	98033	21445	97673	23146	97284	24841	96866	37
24	18052	98357	19766	98027	21474	97667	23175	97278	24869	96858	36
25	18081	98352	19794	98021	21502	97661	23203	97271	24897	96851	35
26	18109	98347	19823	98016	21530	97655	23231	97264	24925	96844	34
27	18138	98341	19851	98010	21559	97648	23260	97257	24954	96837	33
28	18166	98336	19880	98004	21587	97642	23288	97251	24982	96829	32
29	18195	98331	19908	97998	21616	97636	23316	97244	25010	96822	31
30	18224	98325	19937	97992	21644	97630	23345	97237	25038	96815	30
31	18252	98320	19965	97987	21672	97623	23373	97230	25066	96807	29
32	18281	98315	19994	97981	21701	97617	23401	97223	25094	96800	28
33	18309	98310	20022	97975	21729	97611	23429	97217	25122	96793	27
34	18338	98304	20051	97969	21758	97604	23458	97210	25151	96786	26
35	18367	98299	20079	97963	21786	97598	23486	97203	25179	96778	25
36	18395	98294	20108	97958	21814	97592	23514	97196	25207	96771	24
37	18424	98288	20136	97952	21843	97585	23542	97189	25235	96764	23
38	18452	98283	20165	97946	21871	97579	23571	97182	25263	96756	22
39	18481	98277	20193	97940	21899	97573	23599	97176	25291	96749	21
40	18509	98272	20222	97934	21928	97566	23627	97169	25320	96742	20
41	18538	98267	20250	97928	21956	97560	23656	97162	25348	96734	19
42	18567	98261	20279	97922	21985	97553	23684	97155	25376	96727	18
43	18595	98256	20307	97916	22013	97547	23712	97148	25404	96719	17
44	18624	98250	20336	97910	22041	97541	23740	97141	25432	96712	16
45	18652	98245	20364	97905	22070	97534	23769	97134	25460	96705	15
46	18681	98240	20393	97899	22098	97528	23797	97127	25488	96697	14
47	18710	98234	20421	97893	22126	97521	23825	97120	25516	96690	13
48	18738	98229	20450	97887	22155	97515	23853	97113	25545	96682	12
49	18767	98223	20478	97881	22183	97508	23882	97106	25573	96675	11
50	18795	98218	20507	97875	22212	97502	23910	97100	25601	96667	10
51	18824	98212	20535	97869	22240	97496	23938	97093	25629	96660	9
52	18852	98207	20563	97863	22268	97489	23966	97086	25657	96653	8
53	18881	98201	20592	97857	22297	97483	23995	97079	25685	96645	7
54	18910	98196	20620	97851	22325	97476	24023	97072	25713	96638	6
55	18938	98190	20649	97845	22353	97470	24051	97065	25741	96630	5
56	18967	98185	20677	97839	22382	97463	24079	97058	25769	96623	4
57	18995	98179	20706	97833	22410	97457	24108	97051	25798	96615	3
58	19024	98174	20734	97827	22438	97450	24136	97044	25826	96608	2
59	19052	98168	20763	97821	22467	97444	24164	97037	25854	96600	1
60	19081	98163	20791	97815	22495	97437	24192	97030	25882	96593	0
	Cosine.	Sine.	Cosine.	Sine.	Cosine.	Sine.	Cosine.	Sine.	Cosine.	Sine.	
′	79°		78°		77°		76°		75°		′

′	15°		16°		17°		18°		19°		′
	Sine.	Cosine.	Sine.	Cosine.	Sine.	Cosine.	Sine.	Cosine.	Sine.	Cosine.	
0	25882	96593	27564	96126	29237	95630	30902	95106	32557	94552	60
1	25910	96585	27592	96118	29265	95622	30929	95097	32584	94542	59
2	25938	96578	27620	96110	29293	95613	30957	95088	32612	94533	58
3	25966	96570	27648	96102	29321	95605	30985	95079	32639	94523	57
4	25994	96562	27676	96094	29348	95596	31012	95070	32667	94514	56
5	26022	96555	27704	96086	29376	95588	31040	95061	32694	94504	55
6	26050	96547	27731	96078	29404	95579	31068	95052	32722	94495	54
7	26079	96540	27759	96070	29432	95571	31095	95043	32749	94485	53
8	26107	96532	27787	96062	29460	95562	31123	95033	32777	94476	52
9	26135	96524	27815	96054	29487	95554	31151	95024	32804	94466	51
10	26163	96517	27843	96046	29515	95545	31178	95015	32832	94457	50
11	26191	96509	27871	96037	29543	95536	31206	95006	32859	94447	49
12	26219	96502	27899	96029	29571	95528	31233	94997	32887	94438	48
13	26247	96494	27927	96021	29599	95519	31261	94988	32914	94428	47
14	26275	96486	27955	96013	29626	95511	31289	94979	32942	94418	46
15	26303	96479	27983	96005	29654	95502	31316	94970	32969	94409	45
16	26331	96471	28011	95997	29682	95493	31344	94961	32997	94399	44
17	26359	96463	28039	95989	29710	95485	31372	94952	33024	94390	43
18	26387	96456	28067	95981	29737	95476	31399	94943	33051	94380	42
19	26415	96448	28095	95972	29765	95467	31427	94933	33079	94370	41
20	26443	96440	28123	95964	29793	95459	31454	94924	33106	94361	40
21	26471	96433	28150	95956	29821	95450	31482	94915	33134	94351	39
22	26500	96425	28178	95948	29849	95441	31510	94906	33161	94342	38
23	26528	96417	28206	95940	29876	95433	31537	94897	33189	94332	37
24	26556	96410	28234	95931	29904	95424	31565	94888	33216	94322	36
25	26584	96402	28262	95923	29932	95415	31593	94878	33244	94313	35
26	26612	96394	28290	95915	29960	95407	31620	94869	33271	94303	34
27	26640	96386	28318	95907	29987	95398	31648	94860	33298	94293	33
28	26668	96379	28346	95898	30015	95389	31675	94851	33326	94284	32
29	26696	96371	28374	95890	30043	95380	31703	94842	33353	94274	31
30	26724	96363	28402	95882	30071	95372	31730	94832	33381	94264	30
31	26752	96355	28429	95874	30098	95363	31758	94823	33408	94254	29
32	26780	96347	28457	95865	30126	95354	31786	94814	33436	94245	28
33	26808	96340	28485	95857	30154	95345	31813	94805	33463	94235	27
34	26836	96332	28513	95849	30182	95337	31841	94795	33490	94225	26
35	26864	96324	28541	95841	30209	95328	31868	94786	33518	94215	25
36	26892	96316	28569	95832	30237	95319	31896	94777	33545	94206	24
37	26920	96308	28597	95824	30265	95310	31923	94768	33573	94196	23
38	26948	96301	28625	95816	30292	95301	31951	94758	33600	94186	22
39	26976	96293	28652	95807	30320	95293	31979	94749	33627	94176	21
40	27004	96285	28680	95799	30348	95284	32006	94740	33655	94167	20
41	27032	96277	28708	95791	30376	95275	32034	94730	33682	94157	19
42	27060	96269	28736	95782	30403	95266	32061	94721	33710	94147	18
43	27088	96261	28764	95774	30431	95257	32089	94712	33737	94137	17
44	27116	96253	28792	95766	30459	95248	32116	94702	33764	94127	16
45	27144	96246	28820	95757	30486	95240	32144	94693	33792	94118	15
46	27172	96238	28847	95749	30514	95231	32171	94684	33819	94108	14
47	27200	96230	28875	95740	30542	95222	32199	94674	33846	94098	13
48	27228	96222	28903	95732	30570	95213	32227	94665	33874	94088	12
49	27256	96214	28931	95724	30597	95204	32254	94656	33901	94078	11
50	27284	96206	28959	95715	30625	95195	32282	94646	33929	94068	10
51	27312	96198	28987	95707	30653	95186	32309	94637	33956	94058	9
52	27340	96190	29015	95698	30680	95177	32337	94627	33983	94049	8
53	27368	96182	29042	95690	30708	95168	32364	94618	34011	94039	7
54	27396	96174	29070	95681	30736	95159	32392	94609	34038	94029	6
55	27424	96166	29098	95673	30763	95150	32419	94599	34065	94019	5
56	27452	96158	29126	95664	30791	95142	32447	94590	34093	94009	4
57	27480	96150	29154	95656	30819	95133	32474	94580	34120	93999	3
58	27508	96142	29182	95647	30846	95124	32502	94571	34147	93989	2
59	27536	96134	29209	95639	30874	95115	32529	94561	34175	93979	1
60	27564	96126	29237	95630	30902	95106	32557	94552	34202	93969	0
	Cosine.	Sine.	Cosine.	Sine.	Cosine.	Sine.	Cosine.	Sine.	Cosine.	Sine.	
′	74°		73°		72°		71°		70°		′

′	20°		21°		22°		23°		24°		′
	Sine.	Cosine.	Sine.	Cosine.	Sine.	Cosine.	Sine.	Cosine.	Sine.	Cosine.	
0	34202	93969	35837	93358	37461	92718	39073	92050	40674	91355	60
1	34229	93959	35864	93348	37488	92707	39100	92039	40700	91343	59
2	34257	93949	35891	93337	37515	92697	39127	92028	40727	91331	58
3	34284	93939	35918	93327	37542	92686	39153	92016	40753	91319	57
4	34311	93929	35945	93316	37569	92675	39180	92005	40780	91307	56
5	34339	93919	35973	93306	37595	92664	39207	91994	40806	91295	55
6	34366	93909	36000	93295	37622	92653	39234	91982	40833	91283	54
7	34393	93899	36027	93285	37649	92642	39260	91971	40860	91272	53
8	34421	93889	36054	93274	37676	92631	39287	91959	40886	91260	52
9	34448	93879	36081	93264	37703	92620	39314	91948	40913	91248	51
10	34475	93869	36108	93253	37730	92609	39341	91936	40939	91236	50
11	34503	93859	36135	93243	37757	92598	39367	91925	40966	91224	49
12	34530	93849	36162	93232	37784	92587	39394	91914	40992	91212	48
13	34557	93839	36190	93222	37811	92576	39421	91902	41019	91200	47
14	34584	93829	36217	93211	37838	92565	39448	91891	41045	91188	46
15	34612	93819	36244	93201	37865	92554	39474	91879	41072	91176	45
16	34639	93809	36271	93190	37892	92543	39501	91868	41098	91164	44
17	34666	93799	36298	93180	37919	92532	39528	91856	41125	91152	43
18	34694	93789	36325	93169	37946	92521	39555	91845	41151	91140	42
19	34721	93779	36352	93159	37973	92510	39581	91833	41178	91128	41
20	34748	93769	36379	93148	37999	92499	39608	91822	41204	91116	40
21	34775	93759	36406	93137	38026	92488	39635	91810	41231	91104	39
22	34803	93748	36434	93127	38053	92477	39661	91799	41257	91092	38
23	34830	93738	36461	93116	38080	92466	39688	91787	41284	91080	37
24	34857	93728	36488	93106	38107	92455	39715	91775	41310	91068	36
25	34884	93718	36515	93095	38134	92444	39741	91764	41337	91056	35
26	34912	93708	36542	93084	38161	92432	39768	91752	41363	91044	34
27	34939	93698	36569	93074	38188	92421	39795	91741	41390	91032	33
28	34966	93688	36596	93063	38215	92410	39822	91729	41416	91020	32
29	34993	93677	36623	93052	38241	92399	39848	91718	41443	91008	31
30	35021	93667	36650	93042	38268	92388	39875	91706	41469	90996	30
31	35048	93657	36677	93031	38295	92377	39902	91694	41496	90984	29
32	35075	93647	36704	93020	38322	92366	39928	91683	41522	90972	28
33	35102	93637	36731	93010	38349	92355	39955	91671	41549	90960	27
34	35130	93626	36758	92999	38376	92343	39982	91660	41575	90948	26
35	35157	93616	36785	92988	38403	92332	40008	91648	41602	90936	25
36	35184	93606	36812	92978	38430	92321	40035	91636	41628	90924	24
37	35211	93596	36839	92967	38456	92310	40062	91625	41655	90911	23
38	35239	93585	36867	92956	38483	92299	40088	91613	41681	90899	22
39	35266	93575	36894	92945	38510	92287	40115	91601	41707	90887	21
40	35293	93565	36921	92935	38537	92276	40141	91590	41734	90875	20
41	35320	93555	36948	92924	38564	92265	40168	91578	41760	90863	19
42	35347	93544	36975	92913	38591	92254	40195	91566	41787	90851	18
43	35375	93534	37002	92902	38617	92243	40221	91555	41813	90839	17
44	35402	93524	37029	92892	38644	92231	40248	91543	41840	90826	16
45	35429	93514	37056	92881	38671	92220	40275	91531	41866	90814	15
46	35456	93503	37083	92870	38698	92209	40301	91519	41892	90802	14
47	35484	93493	37110	92859	38725	92198	40328	91508	41919	90790	13
48	35511	93483	37137	92849	38752	92186	40355	91496	41945	90778	12
49	35538	93472	37164	92838	38778	92175	40381	91484	41972	90766	11
50	35565	93462	37191	92827	38805	92164	40408	91472	41998	90753	10
51	35592	93452	37218	92816	38832	92152	40434	91461	42024	90741	9
52	35619	93441	37245	92805	38859	92141	40461	91449	42051	90729	8
53	35647	93431	37272	92794	38886	92130	40488	91437	42077	90717	7
54	35674	93420	37299	92784	38912	92119	40514	91425	42104	90704	6
55	35701	93410	37326	92773	38939	92107	40541	91414	42130	90692	5
56	35728	93400	37353	92762	38966	92096	40567	91402	42156	90680	4
57	35755	93389	37380	92751	38993	92085	40594	91390	42183	90668	3
58	35782	93379	37407	92740	39020	92073	40621	91378	42209	90655	2
59	35810	93368	37434	92729	39046	92062	40647	91366	42235	90643	1
60	35837	93358	37461	92718	39073	92050	40674	91355	42262	90631	0
	Cosine.	Sine.	Cosine.	Sine.	Cosine.	Sine.	Cosine.	Sine.	Cosine.	Sine.	
′	69°		68°		67°		66°		65°		′

′	25° Sine.	25° Cosine.	26° Sine.	26° Cosine.	27° Sine.	27° Cosine.	28° Sine.	28° Cosine.	29° Sine.	29° Cosine.	′
0	42262	90631	43837	89879	45399	89101	46947	88295	48481	87462	60
1	42288	90618	43863	89867	45425	89087	46973	88281	48506	87448	59
2	42315	90606	43889	89854	45451	89074	46999	88267	48532	87434	58
3	42341	90594	43916	89841	45477	89061	47024	88254	48557	87420	57
4	42367	90582	43942	89828	45503	89048	47050	88240	48583	87406	56
5	42394	90569	43968	89816	45529	89035	47076	88226	48608	87391	55
6	42420	90557	43994	89803	45554	89021	47101	88213	48634	87377	54
7	42446	90545	44020	89790	45580	89008	47127	88199	48659	87363	53
8	42473	90532	44046	89777	45606	88995	47153	88185	48684	87349	52
9	42499	90520	44072	89764	45632	88981	47178	88172	48710	87335	51
10	42525	90507	44098	89752	45658	88968	47204	88158	48735	87321	50
11	42552	90495	44124	89739	45684	88955	47229	88144	48761	87306	49
12	42578	90483	44151	89726	45710	88942	47255	88130	48786	87292	48
13	42604	90470	44177	89713	45736	88928	47281	88117	48811	87278	47
14	42631	90458	44203	89700	45762	88915	47306	88103	48837	87264	46
15	42657	90446	44229	89687	45787	88902	47332	88089	48862	87250	45
16	42683	90433	44255	89674	45813	88888	47358	88075	48888	87235	44
17	42709	90421	44281	89662	45839	88875	47383	88062	48913	87221	43
18	42736	90408	44307	89649	45865	88862	47409	88048	48938	87207	42
19	42762	90396	44333	89636	45891	88848	47434	88034	48964	87193	41
20	42788	90383	44359	89623	45917	88835	47460	88020	48989	87178	40
21	42815	90371	44385	89610	45942	88822	47486	88006	49014	87164	39
22	42841	90358	44411	89597	45968	88808	47511	87993	49040	87150	38
23	42867	90346	44437	89584	45994	88795	47537	87979	49065	87136	37
24	42894	90334	44464	89571	46020	88782	47562	87965	49090	87121	36
25	42920	90321	44490	89558	46046	88768	47588	87951	49116	87107	35
26	42946	90309	44516	89545	46072	88755	47614	87937	49141	87093	34
27	42972	90296	44542	89532	46097	88741	47639	87923	49166	87079	33
28	42999	90284	44568	89519	46123	88728	47665	87909	49192	87064	32
29	43025	90271	44594	89506	46149	88715	47690	87896	49217	87050	31
30	43051	90259	44620	89493	46175	88701	47716	87882	49242	87036	30
31	43077	90246	44646	89480	46201	88688	47741	87868	49268	87021	29
32	43104	90233	44672	89467	46226	88674	47767	87854	49293	87007	28
33	43130	90221	44698	89454	46252	88661	47793	87840	49318	86993	27
34	43156	90208	44724	89441	46278	88647	47818	87826	49344	86978	26
35	43182	90196	44750	89428	46304	88634	47844	87812	49369	86964	25
36	43209	90183	44776	89415	46330	88620	47869	87798	49394	86949	24
37	43235	90171	44802	89402	46355	88607	47895	87784	49419	86935	23
38	43261	90158	44828	89389	46381	88593	47920	87770	49445	86921	22
39	43287	90146	44854	89376	46407	88580	47946	87756	49470	86906	21
40	43313	90133	44880	89363	46433	88566	47971	87743	49495	86892	20
41	43340	90120	44906	89350	46458	88553	47997	87729	49521	86878	19
42	43366	90108	44932	89337	46484	88539	48022	87715	49546	86863	18
43	43392	90095	44958	89324	46510	88526	48048	87701	49571	86849	17
44	43418	90082	44984	89311	46536	88512	48073	87687	49596	86834	16
45	43445	90070	45010	89298	46561	88499	48099	87673	49622	86820	15
46	43471	90057	45036	89285	46587	88485	48124	87659	49647	86805	14
47	43497	90045	45062	89272	46613	88472	48150	87645	49672	86791	13
48	43523	90032	45088	89259	46639	88458	48175	87631	49697	86777	12
49	43549	90019	45114	89245	46664	88445	48201	87617	49723	86762	11
50	43575	90007	45140	89232	46690	88431	48226	87603	49748	86748	10
51	43602	89994	45166	89219	46716	88417	48252	87589	49773	86733	9
52	43628	89981	45192	89206	46742	88404	48277	87575	49798	86719	8
53	43654	89968	45218	89193	46767	88390	48303	87561	49824	86704	7
54	43680	89956	45243	89180	46793	88377	48328	87546	49849	86690	6
55	43706	89943	45269	89167	46819	88363	48354	87532	49874	86675	5
56	43733	89930	45295	89153	46844	88349	48379	87518	49899	86661	4
57	43759	89918	45321	89140	46870	88336	48405	87504	49924	86646	3
58	43785	89905	45347	89127	46896	88322	48430	87490	49950	86632	2
59	43811	89892	45373	89114	46921	88308	48456	87476	49975	86617	1
60	43837	89879	45399	89101	46947	88295	48481	87462	50000	86603	0
′	64° Cosine.	64° Sine.	63° Cosine.	63° Sine.	62° Cosine.	62° Sine.	61° Cosine.	61° Sine.	60° Cosine.	60° Sine.	′

′	30° Sine.	30° Cosine.	31° Sine.	31° Cosine.	32° Sine.	32° Cosine.	33° Sine.	33° Cosine.	34° Sine.	34° Cosine.	′
0	50000	86603	51504	85717	52992	84805	54464	83867	55919	82904	60
1	50025	86588	51529	85702	53017	84789	54488	83851	55943	82887	59
2	50050	86573	51554	85687	53041	84774	54513	83835	55968	82871	58
3	50076	86559	51579	85672	53066	84759	54537	83819	55992	82855	57
4	50101	86544	51604	85657	53091	84743	54561	83804	56016	82839	56
5	50126	86530	51628	85642	53115	84728	54586	83788	56040	82822	55
6	50151	86515	51653	85627	53140	84712	54610	83772	56064	82806	54
7	50176	86501	51678	85612	53164	84697	54635	83756	56088	82790	53
8	50201	86486	51703	85597	53189	84681	54659	83740	56112	82773	52
9	50227	86471	51728	85582	53214	84666	54683	83724	56136	82757	51
10	50252	86457	51753	85567	53238	84650	54708	83708	56160	82741	50
11	50277	86442	51778	85551	53263	84635	54732	83692	56184	82724	49
12	50302	86427	51803	85536	53288	84619	54756	83676	56208	82708	48
13	50327	86413	51828	85521	53312	84604	54781	83660	56232	82692	47
14	50352	86398	51852	85506	53337	84588	54805	83645	56256	82675	46
15	50377	86384	51877	85491	53361	84573	54829	83629	56280	82659	45
16	50403	86369	51902	85476	53386	84557	54854	83613	56305	82643	44
17	50428	86354	51927	85461	53411	84542	54878	83597	56329	82626	43
18	50453	86340	51952	85446	53435	84526	54902	83581	56353	82610	42
19	50478	86325	51977	85431	53460	84511	54927	83565	56377	82593	41
20	50503	86310	52002	85416	53484	84495	54951	83549	56401	82577	40
21	50528	86295	52026	85401	53509	84480	54975	83533	56425	82561	39
22	50553	86281	52051	85385	53534	84464	54999	83517	56449	82544	38
23	50578	86266	52076	85370	53558	84448	55024	83501	56473	82528	37
24	50603	86251	52101	85355	53583	84433	55048	83485	56497	82511	36
25	50628	86237	52126	85340	53607	84417	55072	83469	56521	82495	35
26	50654	86222	52151	85325	53632	84402	55097	83453	56545	82478	34
27	50679	86207	52175	85310	53656	84386	55121	83437	56569	82462	33
28	50704	86192	52200	85294	53681	84370	55145	83421	56593	82446	32
29	50729	86178	52225	85279	53705	84355	55169	83405	56617	82429	31
30	50754	86163	52250	85264	53730	84339	55194	83389	56641	82413	30
31	50779	86148	52275	85249	53754	84324	55218	83373	56665	82396	29
32	50804	86133	52299	85234	53779	84308	55242	83356	56689	82380	28
33	50829	86119	52324	85218	53804	84292	55266	83340	56713	82363	27
34	50854	86104	52349	85203	53828	84277	55291	83324	56736	82347	26
35	50879	86089	52374	85188	53853	84261	55315	83308	56760	82330	25
36	50904	86074	52399	85173	53877	84245	55339	83292	56784	82314	24
37	50929	86059	52423	85157	53902	84230	55363	83276	56808	82297	23
38	50954	86045	52448	85142	53926	84214	55388	83260	56832	82281	22
39	50979	86030	52473	85127	53951	84198	55412	83244	56856	82264	21
40	51004	86015	52498	85112	53975	84182	55436	83228	56880	82248	20
41	51029	86000	52522	85096	54000	84167	55460	83212	56904	82231	19
42	51054	85985	52547	85081	54024	84151	55484	83195	56928	82214	18
43	51079	85970	52572	85066	54049	84135	55509	83179	56952	82198	17
44	51104	85956	52597	85051	54073	84120	55533	83163	56976	82181	16
45	51129	85941	52621	85035	54097	84104	55557	83147	57000	82165	15
46	51154	85926	52646	85020	54122	84088	55581	83131	57024	82148	14
47	51179	85911	52671	85005	54146	84072	55605	83115	57047	82132	13
48	51204	85896	52696	84989	54171	84057	55630	83098	57071	82115	12
49	51229	85881	52720	84974	54195	84041	55654	83082	57095	82098	11
50	51254	85866	52745	84959	54220	84025	55678	83066	57119	82082	10
51	51279	85851	52770	84943	54244	84009	55702	83050	57143	82065	9
52	51304	85836	52794	84928	54269	83994	55726	83034	57167	82048	8
53	51329	85821	52819	84913	54293	83978	55750	83017	57191	82032	7
54	51354	85806	52844	84897	54317	83962	55775	83001	57215	82015	6
55	51379	85792	52869	84882	54342	83946	55799	82985	57238	81999	5
56	51404	85777	52893	84866	54366	83930	55823	82969	57262	81982	4
57	51429	85762	52918	84851	54391	83915	55847	82953	57286	81965	3
58	51454	85747	52943	84836	54415	83899	55871	82936	57310	81949	2
59	51479	85732	52967	84820	54440	83883	55895	82920	57334	81932	1
60	51504	85717	52992	84805	54464	83867	55919	82904	57358	81915	0
′	Cosine.	Sine.	Cosine.	Sine.	Cosine.	Sine.	Cosine.	Sine.	Cosine.	Sine.	′
	59°		58°		57°		56°		55°		

′	35° Sine.	35° Cosine.	36° Sine.	36° Cosine.	37° Sine.	37° Cosine.	38° Sine.	38° Cosine.	39° Sine.	39° Cosine.	′
0	57358	81915	58779	80902	60182	79864	61566	78801	62932	77715	60
1	57381	81899	58802	80885	60205	79846	61589	78783	62955	77696	59
2	57405	81882	58826	80867	60228	79829	61612	78765	62977	77678	58
3	57429	81865	58849	80850	60251	79811	61635	78747	63000	77660	57
4	57453	81848	58873	80833	60274	79793	61658	78729	63022	77641	56
5	57477	81832	58896	80816	60298	79776	61681	78711	63045	77623	55
6	57501	81815	58920	80799	60321	79758	61704	78694	63068	77605	54
7	57524	81798	58943	80782	60344	79741	61726	78676	63090	77586	53
8	57548	81782	58967	80765	60367	79723	61749	78658	63113	77568	52
9	57572	81765	58990	80748	60390	79706	61772	78640	63135	77550	51
10	57596	81748	59014	80730	60414	79688	61795	78622	63158	77531	50
11	57619	81731	59037	80713	60437	79671	61818	78604	63180	77513	49
12	57643	81714	59061	80696	60460	79653	61841	78586	63203	77494	48
13	57667	81698	59084	80679	60483	79635	61864	78568	63225	77476	47
14	57691	81681	59108	80662	60506	79618	61887	78550	63248	77458	46
15	57715	81664	59131	80644	60529	79600	61909	78532	63271	77439	45
16	57738	81647	59154	80627	60553	79583	61932	78514	63293	77421	44
17	57762	81631	59178	80610	60576	79565	61955	78496	63316	77402	43
18	57786	81614	59201	80593	60599	79547	61978	78478	63338	77384	42
19	57810	81597	59225	80576	60622	79530	62001	78460	63361	77366	41
20	57833	81580	59248	80558	60645	79512	62024	78442	63383	77347	40
21	57857	81563	59272	80541	60668	79494	62046	78424	63406	77329	39
22	57881	81546	59295	80524	60691	79477	62069	78405	63428	77310	38
23	57904	81530	59318	80507	60714	79459	62092	78387	63451	77292	37
24	57928	81513	59342	80489	60738	79441	62115	78369	63473	77273	36
25	57952	81496	59365	80472	60761	79424	62138	78351	63496	77255	35
26	57976	81479	59389	80455	60784	79406	62160	78333	63518	77236	34
27	57999	81462	59412	80438	60807	79388	62183	78315	63540	77218	33
28	58023	81445	59436	80420	60830	79371	62206	78297	63563	77199	32
29	58047	81428	59459	80403	60853	79353	62229	78279	63585	77181	31
30	58070	81412	59482	80386	60876	79335	62251	78261	63608	77162	30
31	58094	81395	59506	80368	60899	79318	62274	78243	63630	77144	29
32	58118	81378	59529	80351	60922	79300	62297	78225	63653	77125	28
33	58141	81361	59552	80334	60945	79282	62320	78206	63675	77107	27
34	58165	81344	59576	80316	60968	79264	62342	78188	63698	77088	26
35	58189	81327	59599	80299	60991	79247	62365	78170	63720	77070	25
36	58212	81310	59622	80282	61015	79229	62388	78152	63742	77051	24
37	58236	81293	59646	80264	61038	79211	62411	78134	63765	77033	23
38	58260	81276	59669	80247	61061	79193	62433	78116	63787	77014	22
39	58283	81259	59693	80230	61084	79176	62456	78098	63810	76996	21
40	58307	81242	59716	80212	61107	79158	62479	78079	63832	76977	20
41	58330	81225	59739	80195	61130	79140	62502	78061	63854	76959	19
42	58354	81208	59763	80178	61153	79122	62524	78043	63877	76940	18
43	58378	81191	59786	80160	61176	79105	62547	78025	63899	76921	17
44	58401	81174	59809	80143	61199	79087	62570	78007	63922	76903	16
45	58425	81157	59832	80125	61222	79069	62592	77988	63944	76884	15
46	58449	81140	59856	80108	61245	79051	62615	77970	63966	76866	14
47	58472	81123	59879	80091	61268	79033	62638	77952	63989	76847	13
48	58496	81106	59902	80073	61291	79016	62660	77934	64011	76828	12
49	58519	81089	59926	80056	61314	78998	62683	77916	64033	76810	11
50	58543	81072	59949	80038	61337	78980	62706	77897	64056	76791	10
51	58567	81055	59972	80021	61360	78962	62728	77879	64078	76772	9
52	58590	81038	59995	80003	61383	78944	62751	77861	64100	76754	8
53	58614	81021	60019	79986	61406	78926	62774	77843	64123	76735	7
54	58637	81004	60042	79968	61429	78908	62796	77824	64145	76717	6
55	58661	80987	60065	79951	61451	78891	62819	77806	64167	76698	5
56	58684	80970	60089	79934	61474	78873	62842	77788	64190	76679	4
57	58708	80953	60112	79916	61497	78855	62864	77769	64212	76661	3
58	58731	80936	60135	79899	61520	78837	62887	77751	64234	76642	2
59	58755	80919	60158	79881	61543	78819	62909	77733	64256	76623	1
60	58779	80902	60182	79864	61566	78801	62932	77715	64279	76604	0
′	Cosine	Sine.	Cosine.	Sine.	Cosine.	Sine.	Cosine.	Sine.	Cosine.	Sine.	′
	54°		53°		52°		51°		50°		

′	40°		41°		42°		43°		44°		′
	Sine.	Cosine.	Sine.	Cosine.	Sine.	Cosine.	Sine.	Cosine.	Sine.	Cosine.	
0	64279	76604	65606	75471	66913	74314	68200	73135	69466	71934	60
1	64301	76586	65628	75452	66935	74295	68221	73116	69487	71914	59
2	64323	76567	65650	75433	66956	74276	68242	73096	69508	71894	58
3	64346	76548	65672	75414	66978	74256	68264	73076	69529	71873	57
4	64368	76530	65694	75395	66999	74237	68285	73056	69549	71853	56
5	64390	76511	65716	75375	67021	74217	68306	73036	69570	71833	55
6	64412	76492	65738	75356	67043	74198	68327	73016	69591	71813	54
7	64435	76473	65759	75337	67064	74178	68349	72996	69612	71792	53
8	64457	76455	65781	75318	67086	74159	68370	72976	69633	71772	52
9	64479	76436	65803	75299	67107	74139	68391	72957	69654	71752	51
10	64501	76417	65825	75280	67129	74120	68412	72937	69675	71732	50
11	64524	76398	65847	75261	67151	74100	68434	72917	69696	71711	49
12	64546	76380	65869	75241	67172	74080	68455	72897	69717	71691	48
13	64568	76361	65891	75222	67194	74061	68476	72877	69737	71671	47
14	64590	76342	65913	75203	67215	74041	68497	72857	69758	71650	46
15	64612	76323	65935	75184	67237	74022	68518	72837	69779	71630	45
16	64635	76304	65956	75165	67258	74002	68539	72817	69800	71610	44
17	64657	76286	65978	75146	67280	73983	68561	72797	69821	71590	43
18	64679	76267	66000	75126	67301	73963	68582	72777	69842	71569	42
19	64701	76248	66022	75107	67323	73944	68603	72757	69862	71549	41
20	64723	76229	66044	75088	67344	73924	68624	72737	69883	71529	40
21	64746	76210	66066	75069	67366	73904	68645	72717	69904	71508	39
22	64768	76192	66088	75050	67387	73885	68666	72697	69925	71488	38
23	64790	76173	66109	75030	67409	73865	68688	72677	69946	71468	37
24	64812	76154	66131	75011	67430	73846	68709	72657	69966	71447	36
25	64834	76135	66153	74992	67452	73826	68730	72637	69987	71427	35
26	64856	76116	66175	74973	67473	73806	68751	72617	70008	71407	34
27	64878	76097	66197	74953	67495	73787	68772	72597	70029	71386	33
28	64901	76078	66218	74934	67516	73767	68793	72577	70049	71366	32
29	64923	76059	66240	74915	67538	73747	68814	72557	70070	71345	31
30	64945	76041	66262	74896	67559	73728	68835	72537	70091	71325	30
31	64967	76022	66284	74876	67580	73708	68857	72517	70112	71305	29
32	64989	76003	66306	74857	67602	73688	68878	72497	70132	71284	28
33	65011	75984	66327	74838	67623	73669	68899	72477	70153	71264	27
34	65033	75965	66349	74818	67645	73649	68920	72457	70174	71243	26
35	65055	75946	66371	74799	67666	73629	68941	72437	70195	71223	25
36	65077	75927	66393	74780	67688	73610	68962	72417	70215	71203	24
37	65100	75908	66414	74760	67709	73590	68983	72397	70236	71182	23
38	65122	75889	66436	74741	67730	73570	69004	72377	70257	71162	22
39	65144	75870	66458	74722	67752	73551	69025	72357	70277	71141	21
40	65166	75851	66480	74703	67773	73531	69046	72337	70298	71121	20
41	65188	75832	66501	74683	67795	73511	69067	72317	70319	71100	19
42	65210	75813	66523	74664	67816	73491	69088	72297	70339	71080	18
43	65232	75794	66545	74644	67837	73472	69109	72277	70360	71059	17
44	65254	75775	66566	74625	67859	73452	69130	72257	70381	71039	16
45	65276	75756	66588	74606	67880	73432	69151	72236	70401	71019	15
46	65298	75738	66610	74586	67901	73413	69172	72216	70422	70998	14
47	65320	75719	66632	74567	67923	73393	69193	72196	70443	70978	13
48	65342	75700	66653	74548	67944	73373	69214	72176	70463	70957	12
49	65364	75680	66675	74528	67965	73353	69235	72156	70484	70937	11
50	65386	75661	66697	74509	67987	73333	69256	72136	70505	70916	10
51	65408	75642	66718	74489	68008	73314	69277	72116	70525	70896	9
52	65430	75623	66740	74470	68029	73294	69298	72095	70546	70875	8
53	65452	75604	66762	74451	68051	73274	69319	72075	70567	70855	7
54	65474	75585	66783	74431	68072	73254	69340	72055	70587	70834	6
55	65496	75566	66805	74412	68093	73234	69361	72035	70608	70813	5
56	65518	75547	66827	74392	68115	73215	69382	72015	70628	70793	4
57	65540	75528	66848	74373	68136	73195	69403	71995	70649	70772	3
58	65562	75509	66870	74353	68157	73175	69424	71974	70670	70752	2
59	65584	75490	66891	74334	68179	73155	69445	71954	70690	70731	1
60	65606	75471	66913	74314	68200	73135	69466	71934	70711	70711	0
	Cosine.	Sine.	Cosine.	Sine.	Cosine.	Sine.	Cosine.	Sine.	Cosine.	Sine.	
′	49°		48°		47°		46°		45°		′

′	0°		1°		2°		3°		′
	Tangent.	Cotang.	Tangent.	Cotang.	Tangent.	Cotang.	Tangent.	Cotang.	
0	00000	Infinite.	01746	57·2900	03492	28·6363	05241	19·0811	60
1	00029	3437·75	01775	56·3506	03521	28·3994	05270	18·9755	59
2	00058	1718·87	01804	55·4415	03550	28·1664	05299	18·8711	58
3	00087	1145·92	01833	54·5613	03579	27·9372	05328	18·7678	57
4	00116	859·436	01862	53·7086	03609	27·7117	05357	18·6656	56
5	00145	687·549	01891	52·8821	03638	27·4899	05387	18·5645	55
6	00175	572·957	01920	52·0807	03667	27·2715	05416	18·4645	54
7	00204	491·106	01949	51·3032	03696	27·0566	05445	18·3655	53
8	00233	429·718	01978	50·5485	03725	26·8450	05474	18·2677	52
9	00262	381·971	02007	49·8157	03754	26·6367	05503	18·1708	51
10	00291	343·774	02036	49·1039	03783	26·4316	05533	18·0750	50
11	00320	312·521	02066	48·4121	03812	26·2296	05562	17·9802	49
12	00349	286·478	02095	47·7395	03842	26·0307	05591	17·8863	48
13	00378	264·441	02124	47·0853	03871	25·8348	05620	17·7934	47
14	00407	245·552	02153	46·4489	03900	25·6418	05649	17·7015	46
15	00436	229·182	02182	45·8294	03929	25·4517	05678	17·6106	45
16	00465	214·858	02211	45·2261	03958	25·2644	05708	17·5205	44
17	00495	202·219	02240	44·6386	03987	25·0798	05737	17·4314	43
18	00524	190·984	02269	44·0661	04016	24·8978	05766	17·3432	42
19	00553	180·932	02298	43·5081	04046	24·7185	05795	17·2558	41
20	00582	171·885	02328	42·9641	04075	24·5418	05824	17·1693	40
21	00611	163·700	02357	42·4335	04104	24·3675	05854	17·0837	39
22	00640	156·259	02386	41·9158	04133	24·1957	05883	16·9990	38
23	00669	149·465	02415	41·4106	04162	24·0263	05912	16·9150	37
24	00698	143·237	02444	40·9174	04191	23·8593	05941	16·8319	36
25	00727	137·507	02473	40·4358	04220	23·6945	05970	16·7496	35
26	00756	132·219	02502	39·9655	04250	23·5321	05999	16·6681	34
27	00785	127·321	02531	39·5059	04279	23·3718	06029	16·5874	33
28	00814	122·774	02560	39·0568	04308	23·2137	06058	16·5075	32
29	00844	118·540	02589	38·6177	04337	23·0577	06087	16·4283	31
30	00873	114·589	02619	38·1885	04366	22·9038	06116	16·3499	30
31	00902	110·892	02648	37·7686	04395	22·7519	06145	16·2722	29
32	00931	107·426	02677	37·3579	04424	22·6020	06175	16·1952	28
33	00960	104·171	02706	36·9560	04454	22·4541	06204	16·1190	27
34	00989	101·107	02735	36·5627	04483	22·3081	06233	16·0435	26
35	01018	98·2179	02764	36·1776	04512	22·1640	06262	15·9687	25
36	01047	95·4895	02793	35·8006	04541	22·0217	06291	15·8945	24
37	01076	92·9085	02822	35·4313	04570	21·8813	06321	15·8211	23
38	01105	90·4633	02851	35·0695	04599	21·7426	06350	15·7483	22
39	01135	88·1436	02881	34·7151	04628	21·6056	06379	15·6762	21
40	01164	85·9398	02910	34·3678	04658	21·4704	06408	15·6048	20
41	01193	83·8435	02939	34·0273	04687	21·3369	06437	15·5340	19
42	01222	81·8470	02968	33·6935	04716	21·2049	06467	15·4638	18
43	01251	79·9434	02997	33·3662	04745	21·0747	06496	15·3943	17
44	01280	78·1263	03026	33·0452	04774	20·9460	06525	15·3254	16
45	01309	76·3900	03055	32·7303	04803	20·8188	06554	15·2571	15
46	01338	74·7292	03084	32·4213	04832	20·6932	06584	15·1893	14
47	01367	73·1390	03114	32·1181	04862	20·5691	06613	15·1222	13
48	01396	71·6151	03143	31·8205	04891	20·4465	06642	15·0557	12
49	01425	70·1533	03172	31·5284	04920	20·3253	06671	14·9898	11
50	01455	68·7501	03201	31·2416	04949	20·2056	06700	14·9244	10
51	01484	67·4019	03230	30·9599	04978	20·0872	06730	14·8596	9
52	01513	66·1055	03259	30·6833	05007	19·9702	06759	14·7954	8
53	01542	64·8580	03288	30·4116	05037	19·8546	06788	14·7317	7
54	01571	63·6567	03317	30·1446	05066	19·7403	06817	14·6685	6
55	01600	62·4992	03346	29·8823	05095	19·6273	06847	14·6059	5
56	01629	61·3829	03376	29·6245	05124	19·5156	06876	14·5438	4
57	01658	60·3058	03405	29·3711	05153	19·4051	06905	14·4823	3
58	01687	59·2659	03434	29·1220	05182	19·2959	06934	14·4212	2
59	01716	58·2612	03463	28·8771	05212	19·1879	06963	14·3607	1
60	01746	57·2900	03492	28·6363	05241	19·0811	06993	14·3007	0
′	Cotang.	Tangent.	Cotang.	Tangent.	Cotang.	Tangent.	Cotang.	Tangent.	′
	89°		88°		87°		86°		

′	4°		5°		6°		7°		′
	Tangent.	Cotang.	Tangent.	Cotang.	Tangent.	Cotang.	Tangent.	Cotang.	
0	06993	14·3007	08749	11·4301	10510	9·51436	12278	8·14435	60
1	07022	14·2411	08778	11·3919	10540	9·48781	12308	8·12481	59
2	07051	14·1821	08807	11·3540	10569	9·46141	12338	8·10536	58
3	07080	14·1235	08837	11·3163	10599	9·43515	12367	8·08600	57
4	07110	14·0655	08866	11·2789	10628	9·40904	12397	8·06674	56
5	07139	14·0079	08895	11·2417	10657	9·38307	12426	8·04756	55
6	07168	13·9507	08925	11·2048	10687	9·35724	12456	8·02848	54
7	07197	13·8940	08954	11·1681	10716	9·33154	12485	8·00948	53
8	07227	13·8378	08983	11·1316	10746	9·30599	12515	7·99058	52
9	07256	13·7821	09013	11·0954	10775	9·28058	12544	7·97176	51
10	07285	13·7267	09042	11·0594	10805	9·25530	12574	7·95302	50
11	07314	13·6719	09071	11·0237	10834	9·23016	12603	7·93438	49
12	07344	13·6174	09101	10·9882	10863	9·20516	12633	7·91582	48
13	07373	13·5634	09130	10·9529	10893	9·18028	12662	7·89734	47
14	07402	13·5098	09159	10·9178	10922	9·15554	12692	7·87895	46
15	07431	13·4566	09189	10·8829	10952	9·13093	12722	7·86064	45
16	07461	13·4039	09218	10·8483	10981	9·10646	12751	7·84242	44
17	07490	13·3515	09247	10·8139	11011	9·08211	12781	7·82428	43
18	07519	13·2996	09277	10·7797	11040	9·05789	12810	7·80622	42
19	07548	13·2480	09306	10·7457	11070	9·03379	12840	7·78825	41
20	07578	13·1969	09335	10·7119	11099	9·00983	12869	7·77035	40
21	07607	13·1461	09365	10·6783	11128	8·98598	12899	7·75254	39
22	07636	13·0958	09394	10·6450	11158	8·96227	12929	7·73480	38
23	07665	13·0458	09423	10·6118	11187	8·93867	12958	7·71715	37
24	07695	12·9962	09453	10·5789	11217	8·91520	12988	7·69957	36
25	07724	12·9469	09482	10·5462	11246	8·89185	13017	7·68208	35
26	07753	12·8981	09511	10·5136	11276	8·86862	13047	7·66466	34
27	07782	12·8496	09541	10·4813	11305	8·84551	13076	7·64732	33
28	07812	12·8014	09570	10·4491	11335	8·82252	13106	7·63005	32
29	07841	12·7536	09600	10·4172	11364	8·79964	13136	7·61287	31
30	07870	12·7062	09629	10·3854	11394	8·77689	13165	7·59575	30
31	07899	12·6591	09658	10·3538	11423	8·75425	13195	7·57872	29
32	07929	12·6124	09688	10·3224	11452	8·73172	13224	7·56176	28
33	07958	12·5660	09717	10·2913	11482	8·70931	13254	7·54487	27
34	07987	12·5199	09746	10·2602	11511	8·68701	13284	7·52806	26
35	08017	12·4742	09776	10·2294	11541	8·66482	13313	7·51132	25
36	08046	12·4288	09805	10·1988	11570	8·64275	13343	7·49465	24
37	08075	12·3838	09834	10·1683	11600	8·62078	13372	7·47806	23
38	08104	12·3390	09864	10·1381	11629	8·59893	13402	7·46154	22
39	08134	12·2946	09893	10·1080	11659	8·57718	13432	7·44509	21
40	08163	12·2505	09923	10·0780	11688	8·55555	13461	7·42871	20
41	08192	12·2067	09952	10·0483	11718	8·53402	13491	7·41240	19
42	08221	12·1632	09981	10·0187	11747	8·51259	13521	7·39616	18
43	08251	12·1201	10011	9·98930	11777	8·49128	13550	7·37999	17
44	08280	12·0772	10040	9·96007	11806	8·47007	13580	7·36389	16
45	08309	12·0346	10069	9·93101	11836	8·44896	13609	7·34786	15
46	08339	11·9923	10099	9·90211	11865	8·42795	13639	7·33190	14
47	08368	11·9504	10128	9·87338	11895	8·40705	13669	7·31600	13
48	08397	11·9087	10158	9·84482	11924	8·38625	13698	7·30018	12
49	08427	11·8673	10187	9·81641	11954	8·36555	13728	7·28442	11
50	08456	11·8262	10216	9·78817	11983	8·34496	13758	7·26873	10
51	08485	11·7853	10246	9·76009	12013	8·32446	13787	7·25310	9
52	08514	11·7448	10275	9·73217	12042	8·30406	13817	7·23754	8
53	08544	11·7045	10305	9·70441	12072	8·28376	13846	7·22204	7
54	08573	11·6645	10334	9·67680	12101	8·26355	13876	7·20661	6
55	08602	11·6248	10363	9·64935	12131	8·24345	13906	7·19125	5
56	08632	11·5853	10393	9·62205	12160	8·22344	13935	7·17594	4
57	08661	11·5461	10422	9·59490	12190	8·20352	13965	7·16071	3
58	08690	11·5072	10452	9·56791	12219	8·18370	13995	7·14553	2
59	08720	11·4685	10481	9·54106	12249	8·16398	14024	7·13042	1
60	08749	11·4301	10510	9·51436	12278	8·14435	14054	7·11537	0
	Cotang.	Tangent.	Cotang.	Tangent.	Cotang.	Tangent.	Cotang.	Tangent.	
′	85°		84°		83°		82°		′

′	8°		9°		10°		11°		′
	Tangent.	Cotang.	Tangent.	Cotang.	Tangent.	Cotang.	Tangent.	Cotang.	
0	14054	7·11537	15838	6·31375	17633	5·67128	19438	5·14455	60
1	14084	7·10038	15868	6·30189	17663	5·66165	19468	5·13658	59
2	14113	7·08546	15898	6·29007	17693	5·65205	19498	5·12862	58
3	14143	7·07059	15928	6·27829	17723	5·64248	19529	5·12069	57
4	14173	7·05579	15958	6·26655	17753	5·63295	19559	5·11279	56
5	14202	7·04105	15988	6·25486	17783	5·62344	19589	5·10490	55
6	14232	7·02637	16017	6·24321	17813	5·61397	19619	5·09704	54
7	14262	7·01174	16047	6·23160	17843	5·60452	19649	5·08921	53
8	14291	6·99718	16077	6·22003	17873	5·59511	19680	5·08139	52
9	14321	6·98268	16107	6·20851	17903	5·58573	19710	5·07360	51
10	14351	6·96823	16137	6·19703	17933	5·57638	19740	5·06584	50
11	14381	6·95385	16167	6·18559	17963	5·56706	19770	5·05809	49
12	14410	6·93952	16196	6·17419	17993	5·55777	19801	5·05037	48
13	14440	6·92525	16226	6·16283	18023	5·54851	19831	5·04267	47
14	14470	6·91104	16256	6·15151	18053	5·53927	19861	5·03499	46
15	14499	6·89688	16286	6·14023	18083	5·53007	19891	5·02734	45
16	14529	6·88278	16316	6·12899	18113	5·52090	19921	5·01971	44
17	14559	6·86874	16346	6·11779	18143	5·51176	19952	5·01210	43
18	14588	6·85475	16376	6·10664	18173	5·50264	19982	5·00451	42
19	14618	6·84082	16405	6·09552	18203	5·49356	20012	4·99695	41
20	14648	6·82694	16435	6·08444	18233	5·48451	20042	4·98940	40
21	14678	6·81312	16465	6·07340	18263	5·47548	20073	4·98188	39
22	14707	6·79936	16495	6·06240	18293	5·46648	20103	4·97438	38
23	14737	6·78564	16525	6·05143	18323	5·45751	20133	4·96690	37
24	14767	6·77199	16555	6·04051	18353	5·44857	20164	4·95945	36
25	14796	6·75838	16585	6·02962	18383	5·43966	20194	4·95201	35
26	14826	6·74483	16615	6·01878	18414	5·43077	20224	4·94460	34
27	14856	6·73133	16645	6·00797	18444	5·42192	20254	4·93721	33
28	14886	6·71789	16674	5·99720	18474	5·41309	20285	4·92984	32
29	14915	6·70450	16704	5·98646	18504	5·40429	20315	4·92249	31
30	14945	6·69116	16734	5·97576	18534	5·39552	20345	4·91516	30
31	14975	6·67787	16764	5·96510	18564	5·38677	20376	4·90785	29
32	15005	6·66463	16794	5·95448	18594	5·37805	20406	4·90056	28
33	15034	6·65144	16824	5·94390	18624	5·36936	20436	4·89330	27
34	15064	6·63831	16854	5·93335	18654	5·36070	20466	4·88605	26
35	15094	6·62523	16884	5·92283	18684	5·35206	20497	4·87882	25
36	15124	6·61219	16914	5·91235	18714	5·34345	20527	4·87162	24
37	15153	6·59921	16944	5·90191	18745	5·33487	20557	4·86444	23
38	15183	6·58627	16974	5·89151	18775	5·32631	20588	4·85727	22
39	15213	6·57339	17004	5·88114	18805	5·31778	20618	4·85013	21
40	15243	6·56055	17033	5·87080	18835	5·30928	20648	4·84300	20
41	15272	6·54777	17063	5·86051	18865	5·30080	20679	4·83590	19
42	15302	6·53503	17093	5·85024	18895	5·29235	20709	4·82882	18
43	15332	6·52234	17123	5·84001	18925	5·28393	20739	4·82175	17
44	15362	6·50970	17153	5·82982	18955	5·27553	20770	4·81471	16
45	15391	6·49710	17183	5·81966	18986	5·26715	20800	4·80769	15
46	15421	6·48456	17213	5·80953	19016	5·25880	20830	4·80068	14
47	15451	6·47206	17243	5·79944	19046	5·25048	20861	4·79370	13
48	15481	6·45961	17273	5·78938	19076	5·24218	20891	4·78673	12
49	15511	6·44720	17303	5·77936	19106	5·23391	20921	4·77978	11
50	15540	6·43484	17333	5·76937	19136	5·22566	20952	4·77286	10
51	15570	6·42253	17363	5·75941	19166	5·21744	20982	4·76595	9
52	15600	6·41026	17393	5·74949	19197	5·20925	21013	4·75906	8
53	15630	6·39804	17423	5·73960	19227	5·20107	21043	4·75219	7
54	15660	6·38587	17453	5·72974	19257	5·19293	21073	4·74534	6
55	15689	6·37374	17483	5·71992	19287	5·18480	21104	4·73851	5
56	15719	6·36165	17513	5·71013	19317	5·17671	21134	4·73170	4
57	15749	6·34961	17543	5·70037	19347	5·16863	21164	4·72490	3
58	15779	6·33761	17573	5·69064	19378	5·16058	21195	4·71813	2
59	15809	6·32566	17603	5·68094	19408	5·15256	21225	4·71137	1
60	15838	6·31375	17633	5·67128	19438	5·14455	21256	4·70463	0
′	Cotang.	Tangent.	Cotang.	Tangent.	Cotang.	Tangent.	Cotang.	Tangent.	′
	81°		80°		79°		78°		

′	12°		13°		14°		15°		′
	Tangent.	Cotang.	Tangent.	Cotang.	Tangent.	Cotang.	Tangent.	Cotang.	
0	21256	4·70463	23087	4·33148	24933	4·01078	26795	3·73205	60
1	21286	4·69791	23117	4·32573	24964	4·00582	26826	3·72771	59
2	21316	4·69121	23148	4·32001	24995	4·00086	26857	3·72338	58
3	21347	4·68452	23179	4·31430	25026	3·99592	26888	3·71907	57
4	21377	4·67786	23209	4·30860	25056	3·99099	26920	3·71476	56
5	21408	4·67121	23240	4·30291	25087	3·98607	26951	3·71046	55
6	21438	4·66458	23271	4·29724	25118	3·98117	26982	3·70616	54
7	21469	4·65797	23301	4·29159	25149	3·97627	27013	3·70188	53
8	21499	4·65138	23332	4·28595	25180	3·97139	27044	3·69761	52
9	21529	4·64480	23363	4·28032	25211	3·96651	27076	3·69335	51
10	21560	4·63825	23393	4·27471	25242	3·96165	27107	3·68909	50
11	21590	4·63171	23424	4·26911	25273	3·95680	27138	3·68485	49
12	21621	4·62518	23455	4·26352	25304	3·95196	27169	3·68061	48
13	21651	4·61868	23485	4·25795	25335	3·94713	27201	3·67638	47
14	21682	4·61219	23516	4·25239	25366	3·94232	27232	3·67217	46
15	21712	4·60572	23547	4·24685	25397	3·93751	27263	3·66796	45
16	21743	4·59927	23578	4·24132	25428	3·93271	27294	3·66376	44
17	21773	4·59283	23608	4·23580	25459	3·92793	27326	3·65957	43
18	21804	4·58641	23639	4·23030	25490	3·92316	27357	3·65538	42
19	21834	4·58001	23670	4·22481	25521	3·91839	27388	3·65121	41
20	21864	4·57363	23700	4·21933	25552	3·91364	27419	3·64705	40
21	21895	4·56726	23731	4·21387	25583	3·90890	27451	3·64289	39
22	21925	4·56091	23762	4·20842	25614	3·90417	27482	3·63874	38
23	21956	4·55458	23793	4·20298	25645	3·89945	27513	3·63461	37
24	21986	4·54826	23823	4·19756	25676	3·89474	27545	3·63048	36
25	22017	4·54196	23854	4·19215	25707	3·89004	27576	3·62636	35
26	22047	4·53568	23885	4·18675	25738	3·88536	27607	3·62224	34
27	22078	4·52941	23916	4·18137	25769	3·88068	27638	3·61814	33
28	22108	4·52316	23946	4·17600	25800	3·87601	27670	3·61405	32
29	22139	4·51693	23977	4·17064	25831	3·87136	27701	3·60996	31
30	22169	4·51071	24008	4·16530	25862	3·86671	27732	3·60588	30
31	22200	4·50451	24039	4·15997	25893	3·86208	27764	3·60181	29
32	22231	4·49832	24069	4·15465	25924	3·85745	27795	3·59775	28
33	22261	4·49215	24100	4·14934	25955	3·85284	27826	3·59370	27
34	22292	4·48600	24131	4·14405	25986	3·84824	27858	3·58966	26
35	22322	4·47986	24162	4·13877	26017	3·84364	27889	3·58562	25
36	22353	4·47374	24193	4·13350	26048	3·83906	27920	3·58160	24
37	22383	4·46764	24223	4·12825	26079	3·83449	27952	3·57758	23
38	22414	4·46155	24254	4·12301	26110	3·82992	27983	3·57357	22
39	22444	4·45548	24285	4·11778	26141	3·82537	28015	3·56957	21
40	22475	4·44942	24316	4·11256	26172	3·82083	28046	3·56557	20
41	22505	4·44338	24347	4·10736	26203	3·81630	28077	3·56159	19
42	22536	4·43735	24377	4·10216	26235	3·81177	28109	3·55761	18
43	22567	4·43134	24408	4·09699	26266	3·80726	28140	3·55364	17
44	22597	4·42534	24439	4·09182	26297	3·80276	28172	3·54968	16
45	22628	4·41936	24470	4·08666	26328	3·79827	28203	3·54573	15
46	22658	4·41340	24501	4·08152	26359	3·79378	28234	3·54179	14
47	22689	4·40745	24532	4·07639	26390	3·78931	28266	3·53785	13
48	22719	4·40152	24562	4·07127	26421	3·78485	28297	3·53393	12
49	22750	4·39560	24593	4·06616	26452	3·78040	28329	3·53001	11
50	22781	4·38969	24624	4·06107	26483	3·77595	28360	3·52609	10
51	22811	4·38381	24655	4·05599	26515	3·77152	28391	3·52219	9
52	22842	4·37793	24686	4·05092	26546	3·76709	28423	3·51829	8
53	22872	4·37207	24717	4·04586	26577	3·76268	28454	3·51441	7
54	22903	4·36623	24747	4·04081	26608	3·75828	28486	3·51053	6
55	22934	4·36040	24778	4·03578	26639	3·75388	28517	3·50666	5
56	22964	4·35459	24809	4·03075	26670	3·74950	28549	3·50279	4
57	22995	4·34879	24840	4·02574	26701	3·74512	28580	3·49894	3
58	23026	4·34300	24871	4·02074	26733	3·74075	28612	3·49509	2
59	23056	4·33723	24902	4·01576	26764	3·73640	28643	3·49125	1
60	23087	4·33148	24933	4·01078	26795	3·73205	28675	3·48741	0
′	Cotang.	Tangent.	Cotang.	Tangent.	Cotang.	Tangent.	Cotang.	Tangent.	′
	77°		76°		75°		74°		

′	16°		17°		18°		19°		′
	Tangent.	Cotang.	Tangent.	Cotang.	Tangent.	Cotang.	Tangent.	Cotang.	
0	28675	3·48741	30573	3·27085	32492	3·07768	34433	2·90421	60
1	28706	3·48359	30605	3·26745	32524	3·07464	34465	2·90147	59
2	28738	3·47977	30637	3·26406	32556	3·07160	34498	2·89873	58
3	28769	3·47596	30669	3·26067	32588	3·06857	34530	2·89600	57
4	28800	3·47216	30700	3·25729	32621	3·06554	34563	2·89327	56
5	28832	3·46837	30732	3·25392	32653	3·06252	34596	2·89055	55
6	28864	3·46458	30764	3·25055	32685	3·05950	34628	2·88783	54
7	28895	3·46080	30796	3·24719	32717	3·05649	34661	2·88511	53
8	28927	3·45703	30828	3·24383	32749	3·05349	34693	2·88240	52
9	28958	3·45327	30860	3·24049	32782	3·05049	34726	2·87970	51
10	28990	3·44951	30891	3·23714	32814	3·04749	34758	2·87700	50
11	29021	3·44576	30923	3·23381	32846	3·04450	34791	2·87430	49
12	29053	3·44202	30955	3·23048	32878	3·04152	34824	2·87161	48
13	29084	3·43829	30987	3·22715	32911	3·03854	34856	2·86892	47
14	29116	3·43456	31019	3·22384	32943	3·03556	34889	2·86624	46
15	29147	3·43084	31051	3·22053	32975	3·03260	34922	2·86356	45
16	29179	3·42713	31083	3·21722	33007	3·02963	34954	2·86089	44
17	29210	3·42343	31115	3·21392	33040	3·02667	34987	2·85822	43
18	29242	3·41973	31147	3·21063	33072	3·02372	35019	2·85555	42
19	29274	3·41604	31178	3·20734	33104	3·02077	35052	2·85289	41
20	29305	3·41236	31210	3·20406	33136	3·01783	35085	2·85023	40
21	29337	3·40869	31242	3·20079	33169	3·01489	35117	2·84758	39
22	29368	3·40502	31274	3·19752	33201	3·01196	35150	2·84494	38
23	29400	3·40136	31306	3·19426	33233	3·00903	35183	2·84229	37
24	29432	3·39771	31338	3·19100	33266	3·00611	35216	2·83965	36
25	29463	3·39406	31370	3·18775	33298	3·00319	35248	2·83702	35
26	29495	3·39042	31402	3·18451	33330	3·00028	35281	2·83439	34
27	29526	3·38679	31434	3·18127	33363	2·99738	35314	2·83176	33
28	29558	3·38317	31466	3·17804	33395	2·99447	35346	2·82914	32
29	29590	3·37955	31498	3·17481	33427	2·99158	35379	2·82653	31
30	29621	3·37594	31530	3·17159	33460	2·98868	35412	2·82391	30
31	29653	3·37234	31562	3·16838	33492	2·98580	35445	2·82130	29
32	29685	3·36875	31594	3·16517	33524	2·98292	35477	2·81870	28
33	29716	3·36516	31626	3·16197	33557	2·98004	35510	2·81610	27
34	29748	3·36158	31658	3·15877	33589	2·97717	35543	2·81350	26
35	29780	3·35800	31690	3·15558	33621	2·97430	35576	2·81091	25
36	29811	3·35443	31722	3·15240	33654	2·97144	35608	2·80833	24
37	29843	3·35087	31754	3·14922	33686	2·96858	35641	2·80574	23
38	29875	3·34732	31786	3·14605	33718	2·96573	35674	2·80316	22
39	29906	3·34377	31818	3·14288	33751	2·96288	35707	2·80059	21
40	29938	3·34023	31850	3·13972	33783	2·96004	35740	2·79802	20
41	29970	3·33670	31882	3·13656	33816	2·95721	35772	2·79545	19
42	30001	3·33317	31914	3·13341	33848	2·95437	35805	2·79289	18
43	30033	3·32965	31946	3·13027	33881	2·95155	35838	2·79033	17
44	30065	3·32614	31978	3·12713	33913	2·94872	35871	2·78778	16
45	30097	3·32264	32010	3·12400	33945	2·94590	35904	2·78523	15
46	30128	3·31914	32042	3·12087	33978	2·94309	35937	2·78269	14
47	30160	3·31565	32074	3·11775	34010	2·94028	35969	2·78014	13
48	30192	3·31216	32106	3·11464	34043	2·93748	36002	2·77761	12
49	30224	3·30868	32139	3·11153	34075	2·93468	36035	2·77507	11
50	30255	3·30521	32171	3·10842	34108	2·93189	36068	2·77254	10
51	30287	3·30174	32203	3·10532	34140	2·92910	36101	2·77002	9
52	30319	3·29829	32235	3·10223	34173	2·92632	36134	2·76750	8
53	30351	3·29483	32267	3·09914	34205	2·92354	36167	2·76498	7
54	30382	3·29139	32299	3·09606	34238	2·92076	36199	2·76247	6
55	30414	3·28795	32331	3·09298	34270	2·91799	36232	2·75996	5
56	30446	3·28452	32363	3·08991	34303	2·91523	36265	2·75746	4
57	30478	3·28109	32396	3·08685	34335	2·91246	36298	2·75496	3
58	30509	3·27767	32428	3·08379	34368	2·90971	36331	2·75246	2
59	30541	3·27426	32460	3·08073	34400	2·90696	36364	2·74997	1
60	30573	3·27085	32492	3·07768	34433	2·90421	36397	2·74748	0
	Cotang.	Tangent.	Cotang.	Tangent.	Cotang.	Tangent.	Cotang.	Tangent.	
′	73°		72°		71°		70°		′

′	20°		21°		22°		23°		′
	Tangent.	Cotang.	Tangent.	Cotang.	Tangent.	Cotang.	Tangent.	Cotang.	
0	36397	2·74748	38386	2·60509	40403	2·47509	42447	2·35585	60
1	36430	2·74499	38420	2·60283	40436	2·47302	42482	2·35395	59
2	36463	2·74251	38453	2·60057	40470	2·47095	42516	2·35205	58
3	36496	2·74004	38487	2·59831	40504	2·46888	42551	2·35015	57
4	36529	2·73756	38520	2·59606	40538	2·46682	42585	2·34825	56
5	36562	2·73509	38553	2·59381	40572	2·46476	42619	2·34636	55
6	36595	2·73263	38587	2·59156	40606	2·46270	42654	2·34447	54
7	36628	2·73017	38620	2·58932	40640	2·46065	42688	2·34258	53
8	36661	2·72771	38654	2·58708	40674	2·45860	42722	2·34069	52
9	36694	2·72526	38687	2·58484	40707	2·45655	42757	2·33881	51
10	36727	2·72281	38721	2·58261	40741	2·45451	42791	2·33693	50
11	36760	2·72036	38754	2·58038	40775	2·45246	42826	2·33505	49
12	36793	2·71792	38787	2·57815	40809	2·45043	42860	2·33317	48
13	36826	2·71548	38821	2·57593	40843	2·44839	42894	2·33130	47
14	36859	2·71305	38854	2·57371	40877	2·44636	42929	2·32943	46
15	36892	2·71062	38888	2·57150	40911	2·44433	42963	2·32756	45
16	36925	2·70819	38921	2·56928	40945	2·44230	42998	2·32570	44
17	36958	2·70577	38955	2·56707	40979	2·44027	43032	2·32383	43
18	36991	2·70335	38988	2·56487	41013	2·43825	43067	2·32197	42
19	37024	2·70094	39022	2·56266	41047	2·43623	43101	2·32012	41
20	37057	2·69853	39055	2·56046	41081	2·43422	43136	2·31826	40
21	37090	2·69612	39089	2·55827	41115	2·43220	43170	2·31641	39
22	37124	2·69371	39122	2·55608	41149	2·43019	43205	2·31456	38
23	37157	2·69131	39156	2·55389	41183	2·42819	43239	2·31271	37
24	37190	2·68892	39190	2·55170	41217	2·42618	43274	2·31086	36
25	37223	2·68653	39223	2·54952	41251	2·42418	43308	2·30902	35
26	37256	2·68414	39257	2·54734	41285	2·42218	43343	2·30718	34
27	37289	2·68175	39290	2·54516	41319	2·42019	43378	2·30534	33
28	37322	2·67937	39324	2·54299	41353	2·41819	43412	2·30351	32
29	37355	2·67700	39357	2·54082	41387	2·41620	43447	2·30167	31
30	37388	2·67462	39391	2·53865	41421	2·41421	43481	2·29984	30
31	37422	2·67225	39425	2·53648	41455	2·41223	43516	2·29801	29
32	37455	2·66989	39458	2·53432	41490	2·41025	43550	2·29619	28
33	37488	2·66752	39492	2·53217	41524	2·40827	43585	2·29437	27
34	37521	2·66516	39526	2·53001	41558	2·40629	43620	2·29254	26
35	37554	2·66281	39559	2·52786	41592	2·40432	43654	2·29073	25
36	37588	2·66046	39593	2·52571	41626	2·40235	43689	2·28891	24
37	37621	2·65811	39626	2·52357	41660	2·40038	43724	2·28710	23
38	37654	2·65576	39660	2·52142	41694	2·39841	43758	2·28528	22
39	37687	2·65342	39694	2·51929	41728	2·39645	43793	2·28348	21
40	37720	2·65109	39727	2·51715	41763	2·39449	43828	2·28167	20
41	37754	2·64875	39761	2·51502	41797	2·39253	43862	2·27987	19
42	37787	2·64642	39795	2·51289	41831	2·39058	43897	2·27806	18
43	37820	2·64410	39829	2·51076	41865	2·38862	43932	2·27626	17
44	37853	2·64177	39862	2·50864	41899	2·38668	43966	2·27447	16
45	37887	2·63945	39896	2·50652	41933	2·38473	44001	2·27267	15
46	37920	2·63714	39930	2·50440	41968	2·38279	44036	2·27088	14
47	37953	2·63483	39963	2·50229	42002	2·38084	44071	2·26909	13
48	37986	2·63252	39997	2·50018	42036	2·37891	44105	2·26730	12
49	38020	2·63021	40031	2·49807	42070	2·37697	44140	2·26552	11
50	38053	2·62791	40065	2·49597	42105	2·37504	44175	2·26374	10
51	38086	2·62561	40098	2·49386	42139	2·37311	44210	2·26196	9
52	38120	2·62332	40132	2·49177	42173	2·37118	44244	2·26018	8
53	38153	2·62103	40166	2·48967	42207	2·36925	44279	2·25840	7
54	38186	2·61874	40200	2·48758	42242	2·36733	44314	2·25663	6
55	38220	2·61646	40234	2·48549	42276	2·36541	44349	2·25486	5
56	38253	2·61418	40267	2·48340	42310	2·36349	44384	2·25309	4
57	38286	2·61190	40301	2·48132	42345	2·36158	44418	2·25132	3
58	38320	2·60963	40335	2·47924	42379	2·35967	44453	2·24956	2
59	38353	2·60736	40369	2·47716	42413	2·35776	44488	2·24780	1
60	38386	2·60509	40403	2·47509	42447	2·35585	44523	2·24604	0
′	Cotang.	Tangent.	Cotang.	Tangent.	Cotang.	Tangent.	Cotang.	Tangent.	′
	69°		68°		67°		66°		

′	24°		25°		26°		27°		′
	Tangent.	Cotang.	Tangent.	Cotang.	Tangent.	Cotang.	Tangent.	Cotang.	
0	44523	2·24604	46631	2·14451	48773	2·05030	50953	1·96261	60
1	44558	2·24428	46666	2·14288	48809	2·04879	50989	1·96120	59
2	44593	2·24252	46702	2·14125	48845	2·04728	51026	1·95979	58
3	44627	2·24077	46737	2·13963	48881	2·04577	51063	1·95838	57
4	44662	2·23902	46772	2·13801	48917	2·04426	51099	1·95698	56
5	44697	2·23727	46808	2·13639	48953	2·04276	51136	1·95557	55
6	44732	2·23553	46843	2·13477	48989	2·04125	51173	1·95417	54
7	44767	2·23378	46879	2·13316	49026	2·03975	51209	1·95277	53
8	44802	2·23204	46914	2·13154	49062	2·03825	51246	1·95137	52
9	44837	2·23030	46950	2·12993	49098	2·03675	51283	1·94997	51
10	44872	2·22857	46985	2·12832	49134	2·03526	51319	1·94858	50
11	44907	2·22683	47021	2·12671	49170	2·03376	51356	1·94718	49
12	44942	2·22510	47056	2·12511	49206	2·03227	51393	1·94579	48
13	44977	2·22337	47092	2·12350	49242	2·03078	51430	1·94440	47
14	45012	2·22164	47128	2·12190	49278	2·02929	51467	1·94301	46
15	45047	2·21992	47163	2·12030	49315	2·02780	51503	1·94162	45
16	45082	2·21819	47199	2·11871	49351	2·02631	51540	1·94023	44
17	45117	2·21647	47234	2·11711	49387	2·02483	51577	1·93885	43
18	45152	2·21475	47270	2·11552	49423	2·02335	51614	1·93746	42
19	45187	2·21304	47305	2·11392	49459	2·02187	51651	1·93608	41
20	45222	2·21132	47341	2·11233	49495	2·02039	51688	1·93470	40
21	45257	2·20961	47377	2·11075	49532	2·01891	51724	1·93332	39
22	45292	2·20790	47412	2·10916	49568	2·01743	51761	1·93195	38
23	45327	2·20619	47448	2·10758	49604	2·01596	51798	1·93057	37
24	45362	2·20449	47483	2·10600	49640	2·01449	51835	1·92920	36
25	45397	2·20278	47519	2·10442	49677	2·01302	51872	1·92782	35
26	45432	2·20108	47555	2·10284	49713	2·01155	51909	1·92645	34
27	45467	2·19938	47590	2·10126	49749	2·01008	51946	1·92508	33
28	45502	2·19769	47626	2·09969	49786	2·00862	51983	1·92371	32
29	45537	2·19599	47662	2·09811	49822	2·00715	52020	1·92235	31
30	45573	2·19430	47698	2·09654	49858	2·00569	52057	1·92098	30
31	45608	2·19261	47733	2·09498	49894	2·00423	52094	1·91962	29
32	45643	2·19092	47769	2·09341	49931	2·00277	52131	1·91826	28
33	45678	2·18923	47805	2·09184	49967	2·00131	52168	1·91690	27
34	45713	2·18755	47840	2·09028	50004	1·99986	52205	1·91554	26
35	45748	2·18587	47876	2·08872	50040	1·99841	52242	1·91418	25
36	45784	2·18419	47912	2·08716	50076	1·99695	52279	1·91282	24
37	45819	2·18251	47948	2·08560	50113	1·99550	52316	1·91147	23
38	45854	2·18084	47984	2·08405	50149	1·99406	52353	1·91012	22
39	45889	2·17916	48019	2·08250	50185	1·99261	52390	1·90876	21
40	45924	2·17749	48055	2·08094	50222	1·99116	52427	1·90741	20
41	45960	2·17582	48091	2·07939	50258	1·98972	52464	1·90607	19
42	45995	2·17416	48127	2·07785	50295	1·98828	52501	1·90472	18
43	46030	2·17249	48163	2·07630	50331	1·98684	52538	1·90337	17
44	46065	2·17083	48198	2·07476	50368	1·98540	52575	1·90203	16
45	46101	2·16917	48234	2·07321	50404	1·98396	52613	1·90069	15
46	46136	2·16751	48270	2·07167	50441	1·98253	52650	1·89935	14
47	46171	2·16585	48306	2·07014	50477	1·98110	52687	1·89801	13
48	46206	2·16420	48342	2·06860	50514	1·97966	52724	1·89667	12
49	46242	2·16255	48378	2·06706	50550	1·97823	52761	1·89533	11
50	46277	2·16090	48414	2·06553	50587	1·97680	52798	1·89400	10
51	46312	2·15925	48450	2·06400	50623	1·97538	52836	1·89266	9
52	46348	2·15760	48486	2·06247	50660	1·97395	52873	1·89133	8
53	46383	2·15596	48521	2·06094	50696	1·97253	52910	1·89000	7
54	46418	2·15432	48557	2·05942	50733	1·97111	52947	1·88867	6
55	46454	2·15268	48593	2·05790	50769	1·96969	52984	1·88734	5
56	46489	2·15104	48629	2·05637	50806	1·96827	53022	1·88602	4
57	46525	2·14940	48665	2·05485	50843	1·96685	53059	1·88469	3
58	46560	2·14777	48701	2·05333	50879	1·96544	53096	1·88337	2
59	46595	2·14614	48737	2·05182	50916	1·96402	53134	1·88205	1
60	46631	2·14451	48773	2·05030	50953	1·96261	53171	1·88073	0
′	Cotang.	Tangent.	Cotang.	Tangent.	Cotang.	Tangent.	Cotang.	Tangent.	′
	65°		64°		63°		62°		

′	28°		29°		30°		31°		′
	Tangent.	Cotang.	Tangent.	Cotang.	Tangent.	Cotang.	Tangent.	Cotang.	
0	53171	1·88073	55431	1·80405	57735	1·73205	60086	1·66428	60
1	53208	1·87941	55469	1·80281	57774	1·73089	60126	1·66318	59
2	53246	1·87809	55507	1·80158	57813	1·72973	60165	1·66209	58
3	53283	1·87677	55545	1·80034	57851	1·72857	60205	1·66099	57
4	53320	1·87546	55583	1·79911	57890	1·72741	60245	1·65990	56
5	53358	1·87415	55621	1·79788	57929	1·72625	60284	1·65881	55
6	53395	1·87283	55659	1·79665	57968	1·72509	60324	1·65772	54
7	53432	1·87152	55697	1·79542	58007	1·72393	60364	1·65663	53
8	53470	1·87021	55736	1·79419	58046	1·72278	60403	1·65554	52
9	53507	1·86891	55774	1·79296	58085	1·72163	60443	1·65445	51
10	53545	1·86760	55812	1·79174	58124	1·72047	60483	1·65337	50
11	53582	1·86630	55850	1·79051	58162	1·71932	60522	1·65228	49
12	53620	1·86499	55888	1·78929	58201	1·71817	60562	1·65120	48
13	53657	1·86369	55926	1·78807	58240	1·71702	60602	1·65011	47
14	53694	1·86239	55964	1·78685	58279	1·71588	60642	1·64903	46
15	53732	1·86109	56003	1·78563	58318	1·71473	60681	1·64795	45
16	53769	1·85979	56041	1·78441	58357	1·71358	60721	1·64687	44
17	53807	1·85850	56079	1·78319	58396	1·71244	60761	1·64579	43
18	53844	1·85720	56117	1·78198	58435	1·71129	60801	1·64471	42
19	53882	1·85591	56156	1·78077	58474	1·71015	60841	1·64363	41
20	53920	1·85462	56194	1·77955	58513	1·70901	60881	1·64256	40
21	53957	1·85333	56232	1·77834	58552	1·70787	60921	1·64148	39
22	53995	1·85204	56270	1·77713	58591	1·70673	60960	1·64041	38
23	54032	1·85075	56309	1·77592	58631	1·70560	61000	1·63934	37
24	54070	1·84946	56347	1·77471	58670	1·70446	61040	1·63826	36
25	54107	1·84818	56385	1·77351	58709	1·70332	61080	1·63719	35
26	54145	1·84689	56424	1·77230	58748	1·70219	61120	1·63612	34
27	54183	1·84561	56462	1·77110	58787	1·70106	61160	1·63505	33
28	54220	1·84433	56500	1·76990	58826	1·69992	61200	1·63398	32
29	54258	1·84305	56539	1·76869	58865	1·69879	61240	1·63292	31
30	54296	1·84177	56577	1·76749	58904	1·69766	61280	1·63185	30
31	54333	1·84049	56616	1·76630	58944	1·69653	61320	1·63079	29
32	54371	1·83922	56654	1·76510	58983	1·69541	61360	1·62972	28
33	54409	1·83794	56693	1·76390	59022	1·69428	61400	1·62866	27
34	54446	1·83667	56731	1·76271	59061	1·69316	61440	1·62760	26
35	54484	1·83540	56769	1·76151	59101	1·69203	61480	1·62654	25
36	54522	1·83413	56808	1·76032	59140	1·69091	61520	1·62548	24
37	54560	1·83286	56846	1·75913	59179	1·68979	61561	1·62442	23
38	54597	1·83159	56885	1·75794	59218	1·68866	61601	1·62336	22
39	54635	1·83033	56923	1·75675	59258	1·68754	61641	1·62230	21
40	54673	1·82906	56962	1·75556	59297	1·68643	61681	1·62125	20
41	54711	1·82780	57000	1·75437	59336	1·68531	61721	1·62019	19
42	54748	1·82654	57039	1·75319	59376	1·68419	61761	1·61914	18
43	54786	1·82528	57078	1·75200	59415	1·68308	61801	1·61808	17
44	54824	1·82402	57116	1·75082	59454	1·68196	61842	1·61703	16
45	54862	1·82276	57155	1·74964	59494	1·68085	61882	1·61598	15
46	54900	1·82150	57193	1·74846	59533	1·67974	61922	1·61493	14
47	54938	1·82025	57232	1·74728	59573	1·67863	61962	1·61388	13
48	54975	1·81899	57271	1·74610	59612	1·67752	62003	1·61283	12
49	55013	1·81774	57309	1·74492	59651	1·67641	62043	1·61179	11
50	55051	1·81649	57348	1·74375	59691	1·67530	62083	1·61074	10
51	55089	1·81524	57386	1·74257	59730	1·67419	62124	1·60970	9
52	55127	1·81399	57425	1·74140	59770	1·67309	62164	1·60865	8
53	55165	1·81274	57464	1·74022	59809	1·67198	62204	1·60761	7
54	55203	1·81150	57503	1·73905	59849	1·67088	62245	1·60657	6
55	55241	1·81025	57541	1·73788	59888	1·66978	62285	1·60553	5
56	55279	1·80901	57580	1·73671	59928	1·66867	62325	1·60449	4
57	55317	1·80777	57619	1·73555	59967	1·66757	62366	1·60345	3
58	55355	1·80653	57657	1·73438	60007	1·66647	62406	1·60241	2
59	55393	1·80529	57696	1·73321	60046	1·66538	62446	1·60137	1
60	55431	1·80405	57735	1·73205	60086	1·66428	62487	1·60033	0
′	Cotang.	Tangent.	Cotang.	Tangent.	Cotang.	Tangent.	Cotang.	Tangent.	′
	61°		60°		59°		58°		

′	32°		33°		34°		35°		′
	Tangent.	Cotang.	Tangent.	Cotang.	Tangent.	Cotang.	Tangent.	Cotang.	
0	62487	1·60033	64941	1·53986	67451	1·48256	70021	1·42815	60
1	62527	1·59930	64982	1·53888	67493	1·48163	70064	1·42726	59
2	62568	1·59826	65023	1·53791	67536	1·48070	70107	1·42638	58
3	62608	1·59723	65065	1·53693	67578	1·47977	70151	1·42550	57
4	62649	1·59620	65106	1·53595	67620	1·47885	70194	1·42462	56
5	62689	1·59517	65148	1·53497	67663	1·47792	70238	1·42374	55
6	62730	1·59414	65189	1·53400	67705	1·47699	70281	1·42286	54
7	62770	1·59311	65231	1·53302	67748	1·47607	70325	1·42198	53
8	62811	1·59208	65272	1·53205	67790	1·47514	70368	1·42110	52
9	62852	1·59105	65314	1·53107	67832	1·47422	70412	1·42022	51
10	62892	1·59002	65355	1·53010	67875	1·47330	70455	1·41934	50
11	62933	1·58900	65397	1·52913	67917	1·47238	70499	1·41847	49
12	62973	1·58797	65438	1·52816	67960	1·47146	70542	1·41759	48
13	63014	1·58695	65480	1·52719	68002	1·47053	70586	1·41672	47
14	63055	1·58593	65521	1·52622	68045	1·46962	70629	1·41584	46
15	63095	1·58490	65563	1·52525	68088	1·46870	70673	1·41497	45
16	63136	1·58388	65604	1·52429	68130	1·46778	70717	1·41409	44
17	63177	1·58286	65646	1·52332	68173	1·46686	70760	1·41322	43
18	63217	1·58184	65688	1·52235	68215	1·46595	70804	1·41235	42
19	63258	1·58083	65729	1·52139	68258	1·46503	70848	1·41148	41
20	63299	1·57981	65771	1·52043	68301	1·46411	70891	1·41061	40
21	63340	1·57879	65813	1·51946	68343	1·46320	70935	1·40974	39
22	63380	1·57778	65854	1·51850	68386	1·46229	70979	1·40887	38
23	63421	1·57676	65896	1·51754	68429	1·46137	71023	1·40800	37
24	63462	1·57575	65938	1·51658	68471	1·46046	71066	1·40714	36
25	63503	1·57474	65980	1·51562	68514	1·45955	71110	1·40627	35
26	63544	1·57372	66021	1·51466	98557	1·45864	71154	1·40540	34
27	63584	1·57271	66063	1·51370	68600	1·45773	71198	1·40454	33
28	63625	1·57170	66105	1·51275	68642	1·45682	71242	1·40367	32
29	63666	1·57069	66147	1·51179	68685	1·45592	71285	1·40281	31
30	63707	1·56969	66189	1·51084	68728	1·45501	71329	1·40195	30
31	63748	1·56868	66230	1·50988	68771	1·45410	71373	1·40109	29
32	63789	1·56767	66272	1·50893	68814	1·45320	71417	1·40022	28
33	63830	1·56667	66314	1·50797	68857	1·45229	71461	1·39936	27
34	63871	1·56566	66356	1·50702	68900	1·45139	71505	1·39850	26
35	63912	1·56466	66398	1·50607	68942	1·45049	71549	1·39764	25
36	63953	1·56366	66440	1·50512	68985	1·44958	71593	1·39679	24
37	63994	1·56265	66482	1·50417	69028	1·44868	71637	1·39593	23
38	64035	1·56165	66524	1·50322	69071	1·44778	71681	1·39507	22
39	64076	1·56065	66566	1·50228	69114	1·44688	71725	1·39421	21
40	64117	1·55966	66608	1·50133	69157	1·44598	71769	1·39336	20
41	64158	1·55866	66650	1·50038	69200	1·44508	71813	1·39250	19
42	64199	1·55766	66692	1·49944	69243	1·44418	71857	1·39165	18
43	64240	1·55666	66734	1·49849	69286	1·44329	71901	1·39079	17
44	64281	1·55567	66776	1·49755	69329	1·44239	71946	1·38994	16
45	64322	1·55467	66818	1·49661	69372	1·44149	71990	1·38909	15
46	64363	1·55368	66860	1·49566	69416	1·44060	72034	1·38824	14
47	64404	1·55269	66902	1·49472	69459	1·43970	72078	1·38738	13
48	64446	1·55170	66944	1·49378	69502	1·43881	72122	1·38653	12
49	64487	1·55071	66986	1·49284	69545	1·43792	72166	1·38568	11
50	64528	1·54972	67028	1·49190	69588	1·43703	72211	1·38484	10
51	64569	1·54873	67071	1·49097	69631	1·43614	72255	1·38399	9
52	64610	1·54774	67113	1·49003	69675	1·43525	72299	1·38314	8
53	64652	1·54675	67155	1·48909	69718	1·43436	72344	1·38229	7
54	64693	1·54576	67197	1·48816	69761	1·43347	72388	1·38145	6
55	64734	1·54478	67239	1·48722	69804	1·43258	72432	1·38060	5
56	64775	1·54379	67282	1·48629	69847	1·43169	72477	1·37976	4
57	64817	1·54281	67324	1·48536	69891	1·43080	72521	1·37891	3
58	64858	1·54183	67366	1·48442	69934	1·42992	72565	1·37807	2
59	64899	1·54085	67409	1·48349	69977	1·42903	72610	1·37722	1
60	64941	1·53986	67451	1·48256	70021	1·42815	72654	1·37638	0
′	Cotang.	Tangent.	Cotang.	Tangent.	Cotang.	Tangent.	Cotang.	Tangent.	′
	57°		56°		55°		54°		

′	36°		37°		38°		39°		′
	Tangent.	Cotang.	Tangent.	Cotang.	Tangent.	Cotang.	Tangent.	Cotang.	
0	72654	1·37638	75355	1·32704	78129	1·27994	80978	1·23490	60
1	72699	1·37554	75401	1·32624	78175	1·27917	81027	1·23416	59
2	72743	1·37470	75447	1·32544	78222	1·27841	81075	1·23343	58
3	72788	1·37386	75492	1·32464	78269	1·27764	81123	1·23270	57
4	72832	1·37302	75538	1·32384	78316	1·27688	81171	1·23196	56
5	72877	1·37218	75584	1·32304	78363	1·27611	81220	1·23123	55
6	72921	1·37134	75629	1·32224	78410	1·27535	81268	1·23050	54
7	72966	1·37050	75675	1·32144	78457	1·27458	81316	1·22977	53
8	73010	1·36967	75721	1·32064	78504	1·27382	81364	1·22904	52
9	73055	1·36883	75767	1·31984	78551	1·27306	81413	1·22831	51
10	73100	1·36800	75812	1·31904	78598	1·27230	81461	1·22758	50
11	73144	1·36716	75858	1·31825	78645	1·27153	81510	1·22685	49
12	73189	1·36633	75904	1·31745	78692	1·27077	81558	1·22612	48
13	73234	1·36549	75950	1·31666	78739	1·27001	81606	1·22539	47
14	73278	1·36466	75996	1·31586	78786	1·26925	81655	1·22467	46
15	73323	1·36383	76042	1·31507	78834	1·26849	81703	1·22394	45
16	73368	1·36300	76088	1·31427	78881	1·26774	81752	1·22321	44
17	73413	1·36217	76134	1·31348	78928	1·26698	81800	1·22249	43
18	73457	1·36133	76180	1·31269	78975	1·26622	81849	1·22176	42
19	73502	1·36051	76226	1·31190	79022	1·26546	81898	1·22104	41
20	73547	1·35968	76272	1·31110	79070	1·26471	81946	1·22031	40
21	73592	1·35885	76318	1·31031	79117	1·26395	81995	1·21959	39
22	73637	1·35802	76364	1·30952	79164	1·26319	82044	1·21886	38
23	73681	1·35719	76410	1·30873	79212	1·26244	82092	1·21814	37
24	73726	1·35637	76456	1·30795	79259	1·26169	82141	1·21742	36
25	73771	1·35554	76502	1·30716	79306	1·26093	82190	1·21670	35
26	73816	1·35472	76548	1·30637	79354	1·26018	82238	1·21598	34
27	73861	1·35389	76594	1·30558	79401	1·25943	82287	1·21526	33
28	73906	1·35307	76640	1·30480	79449	1·25867	82336	1·21454	32
29	73951	1·35224	76686	1·30401	79496	1·25792	82385	1·21382	31
30	73996	1·35142	76733	1·30323	79544	1·25717	82434	1·21310	30
31	74041	1·35060	76779	1·30244	79591	1·25642	82483	1·21238	29
32	74086	1·34978	76825	1·30166	79639	1·25567	82531	1·21166	28
33	74131	1·34896	76871	1·30087	79686	1·25492	82580	1·21094	27
34	74176	1·34814	76918	1·30009	79734	1·25417	82629	1·21023	26
35	74221	1·34732	76964	1·29931	79781	1·25343	82678	1·20951	25
36	74267	1·34650	77010	1·29853	79829	1·25268	82727	1·20879	24
37	74312	1·34568	77057	1·29775	79877	1·25193	82776	1·20808	23
38	74357	1·34487	77103	1·29696	79924	1·25118	82825	1·20736	22
39	74402	1·34405	77149	1·29618	79972	1·25044	82874	1·20665	21
40	74447	1·34323	77196	1·29541	80020	1·24969	82923	1·20593	20
41	74492	1·34242	77242	1·29463	80067	1·24895	82972	1·20522	19
42	74538	1·34160	77289	1·29385	80115	1·24820	83022	1·20451	18
43	74583	1·34079	77335	1·29307	80163	1·24746	83071	1·20379	17
44	74628	1·33998	77382	1·29229	80211	1·24672	83120	1·20308	16
45	74674	1·33916	77428	1·29152	80258	1·24597	83169	1·20237	15
46	74719	1·33835	77475	1·29074	80306	1·24523	83218	1·20166	14
47	74764	1·33754	77521	1·28997	80354	1·24449	83268	1·20095	13
48	74810	1·33673	77568	1·28919	80402	1·24375	83317	1·20024	12
49	74855	1·33592	77615	1·28842	80450	1·24301	83366	1·19953	11
50	74900	1·33511	77661	1·28764	80498	1·24227	83415	1·19882	10
51	74946	1·33430	77708	1·28687	80546	1·24153	83465	1·19811	9
52	74991	1·33349	77754	1·28610	80594	1·24079	83514	1·19740	8
53	75037	1·33268	77801	1·28533	80642	1·24005	83564	1·19669	7
54	75082	1·33187	77848	1·28456	80690	1·23931	83613	1·19599	6
55	75128	1·33107	77895	1·28379	80738	1·23858	83662	1·19528	5
56	75173	1·33026	77941	1·28302	80786	1·23784	83712	1·19457	4
57	75219	1·32946	77988	1·28225	80834	1·23710	83761	1·19387	3
58	75264	1·32865	78035	1·28148	80882	1·23637	83811	1·19316	2
59	75310	1·32785	78082	1·28071	80930	1·23563	83860	1·19246	1
60	75355	1·32704	78129	1·27994	80978	1·23490	83910	1·19175	0
′	Cotang.	Tangent.	Cotang.	Tangent.	Cotang.	Tangent.	Cotang.	Tangent.	′
	53°		52°		51°		50°		

′	40°		41°		42°		43°		′
	Tangent.	Cotang.	Tangent.	Cotang.	Tangent.	Cotang.	Tangent.	Cotang.	
0	83910	1·19175	86929	1·15037	90040	1·11061	93252	1·07237	60
1	83960	1·19105	86980	1·14969	90093	1·10996	93306	1·07174	59
2	84009	1·19035	87031	1·14902	90146	1·10931	93360	1·07112	58
3	84059	1·18964	87082	1·14834	90199	1·10867	93415	1·07049	57
4	84108	1·18894	87133	1·14767	90251	1·10802	93469	1·06987	56
5	84158	1·18824	87184	1·14699	90304	1·10737	93524	1·06925	55
6	84208	1·18754	87236	1·14632	90357	1·10672	93578	1·06862	54
7	84258	1·18684	87287	1·14565	90410	1·10607	93633	1·06800	53
8	84307	1·18614	87338	1·14498	90463	1·10543	93688	1·06738	52
9	84357	1·18544	87389	1·14430	90516	1·10478	93742	1·06676	51
10	84407	1·18474	87441	1·14363	90569	1·10414	93797	1·06613	50
11	84457	1·18404	87492	1·14296	90621	1·10349	93852	1·06551	49
12	84507	1·18334	87543	1·14229	90674	1·10285	93906	1·06489	48
13	84556	1·18264	87595	1·14162	90727	1·10220	93961	1·06427	47
14	84606	1·18194	87646	1·14095	90781	1·10156	94016	1·06365	46
15	84656	1·18125	87698	1·14028	90834	1·10091	94071	1·06303	45
16	84706	1·18055	87749	1·13961	90887	1·10027	94125	1·06241	44
17	84756	1·17986	87801	1·13894	90940	1·09963	94180	1·06179	43
18	84806	1·17916	87852	1·13828	90993	1·09899	94235	1·06117	42
19	84856	1·17846	87904	1·13761	91046	1·09834	94290	1·06056	41
20	84906	1·17777	87955	1·13694	91099	1·09770	94345	1·05994	40
21	84956	1·17708	88007	1·13627	91153	1·09706	94400	1·05932	39
22	85006	1·17638	88059	1·13561	91206	1·09642	94455	1·05870	38
23	85057	1·17569	88110	1·13494	91259	1·09578	94510	1·05809	37
24	85107	1·17500	88162	1·13428	91313	1·09514	94565	1·05747	36
25	85157	1·17430	88214	1·13361	91366	1·09450	94620	1·05685	35
26	85207	1·17361	88265	1·13295	91419	1·09386	94676	1·05624	34
27	85257	1·17292	88317	1·13228	91473	1·09322	94731	1·05562	33
28	85307	1·17223	88369	1·13162	91526	1·09258	94786	1·05501	32
29	85358	1·17154	88421	1·13096	91580	1·09195	94841	1·05439	31
30	85408	1·17085	88473	1·13029	91633	1·09131	94896	1·05378	30
31	85458	1·17016	88524	1·12963	91687	1·09067	94952	1·05317	29
32	85509	1·16947	88576	1·12897	91740	1·09003	95007	1·05255	28
33	85559	1·16878	88628	1·12831	91794	1·08940	95062	1·05194	27
34	85609	1·16809	88680	1·12765	91847	1·08876	95118	1·05133	26
35	85660	1·16741	88732	1·12699	91901	1·08813	95173	1·05072	25
36	85710	1·16672	88784	1·12633	91955	1·08749	95229	1·05010	24
37	85761	1·16603	88836	1·12567	92008	1·08686	95284	1·04949	23
38	85811	1·16535	88888	1·12501	92062	1·08622	95340	1·04888	22
39	85862	1·16466	88940	1·12435	92116	1·08559	95395	1·04827	21
40	85912	1·16398	88992	1·12369	92170	1·08496	95451	1·04766	20
41	85963	1·16329	89045	1·12303	92223	1·08432	95506	1·04705	19
42	86014	1·16261	89097	1·12238	92277	1·08369	95562	1·04644	18
43	86064	1·16192	89149	1·12172	92331	1·08306	95618	1·04583	17
44	86115	1·16124	89201	1·12106	92385	1·08243	95673	1·04522	16
45	86166	1·16056	89253	1·12041	92439	1·08179	95729	1·04461	15
46	86216	1·15987	89306	1·11975	92493	1·08116	95785	1·04401	14
47	86267	1·15919	89358	1·11909	92547	1·08053	95841	1·04340	13
48	86318	1·15851	89410	1·11844	92601	1·07990	95897	1·04279	12
49	86368	1·15783	89463	1·11778	92655	1·07927	95952	1·04218	11
50	86419	1·15715	89515	1·11713	92709	1·07864	96008	1·04158	10
51	86470	1·15647	89567	1·11648	92763	1·07801	96064	1·04097	9
52	86521	1·15579	89620	1·11582	92817	1·07738	96120	1·04036	8
53	86572	1·15511	89672	1·11517	92872	1·07676	96176	1·03976	7
54	86623	1·15443	89725	1·11452	92926	1·07613	96232	1·03915	6
55	86674	1·15375	89777	1·11387	92980	1·07550	96288	1·03855	5
56	86725	1·15308	89830	1·11321	93034	1·07487	96344	1·03794	4
57	86776	1·15240	89883	1·11256	93088	1·07425	96400	1·03734	3
58	86827	1·15172	89935	1·11191	93143	1·07362	96457	1·03674	2
59	86878	1·15104	89988	1·11126	93197	1·07299	96513	1·03613	1
60	86929	1·15037	90040	1·11061	93252	1·07237	96569	1·03553	0
′	Cotang.	Tangent.	Cotang.	Tangent.	Cotang.	Tangent.	Cotang.	Tangent.	′
	49°		48°		47°		46°		

′	44° Tangent.	44° Cotang.	′	′	44° Tangent.	44° Cotang.	′
0	96569	1·03553	60	31	98327	1·01702	29
1	96625	1·03493	59	32	98384	1·01642	28
2	96681	1·03433	58	33	98441	1·01583	27
3	96738	1·03372	57	34	98499	1·01524	26
4	96794	1·03312	56	35	98556	1·01465	25
5	96850	1·03252	55	36	98613	1·01406	24
6	96907	1·03192	54	37	98671	1·01347	23
7	96963	1·03132	53	38	98728	1·01288	22
8	97020	1·03072	52	39	98786	1·01229	21
9	97076	1·03012	51	40	98843	1·01170	20
10	97133	1·02952	50	41	98901	1·01112	19
11	97189	1·02892	49	42	98958	1·01053	18
12	97246	1·02832	48	43	99016	1·00994	17
13	97302	1·02772	47	44	99073	1·00935	16
14	97359	1·02713	46	45	99131	1·00876	15
15	97416	1·02653	45	46	99189	1·00818	14
16	97472	1·02593	44	47	99247	1·00759	13
17	97529	1·02533	43	48	99304	1·00701	12
18	97586	1·02474	42	49	99362	1·00642	11
19	97643	1·02414	41	50	99420	1·00583	10
20	97700	1·02355	40	51	99478	1·00525	9
21	97756	1·02295	39	52	99536	1·00467	8
22	97813	1·02236	38	53	99594	1·00408	7
23	97870	1·02176	37	54	99652	1·00350	6
24	97927	1·02117	36	55	99710	1·00291	5
25	97984	1·02057	35	56	99768	1·00233	4
26	98041	1·01998	34	57	99826	1·00175	3
27	98098	1·01939	33	58	99884	1·00116	2
28	98155	1·01879	32	59	99942	1·00058	1
29	98213	1·01820	31	60	Unit.	Unit.	0
30	98270	1·01761	30				
′	45° Cotang.	45° Tangent.	′	′	45° Cotang.	45° Tangent.	′

TABLE OF CONSTANTS.

Base of Napier's system of logarithms = ...ε = 2·718281828459

Mod. of common syst. of logarithms = ... com. log. ε = M = 0·434294481903

Ratio of circumference to diameter of a circle = ...π = 3·141592653590

log. π = 0·497149872694

π² = 9·869604401089 .... √π = 1·772453850906

Arc of same length as radius = ...180° ÷ π = 10800′ ÷ π = 648000″ ÷ π

180° ÷ π = 57°·2957795130, ...log. = 1·758122632409

10800′ ÷ π = 3437′·7467707849, ...log. = 3·536273882793

648000″ ÷ π = 206264″·8062470964, ...log. = 5·314425133176

Tropical year = 365d. 5h. 48m. 47s. ·588 = 365d. ·242217456, log. = 2·5625810

Sidereal year = 365d. 6h. 9m. 10s. ·742 = 365d. ·256374332, log. = 2·5625978

24h. sol. t.=24h. 3m. 56s. ·555335 sid. t.=24h.×1·00273791, log. 1·002=0·0011874

24h. sid. t.=24h. −(3m.55s.·90944) sol. t.=24h.×0·9972696, log. 0·997=9·9988126

British imperial gallon = 277·274 cubic inches, ...log. = 2·4429091

Length of sec. pend., in inches, at London, 39·13929; Paris, 39·1285; New York, 39·1285.

French *metre* = 3·2808992 English *feet* = 39·3707904 *inches.*

1 cubic inch of water (bar. 30 inches, Fahr. therm. 62°) = 252·458 Troy grains.

www.ingramcontent.com/pod-product-compliance
Lightning Source LLC
LaVergne TN
LVHW021306110826
845150LV00003B/500

* 9 7 8 1 4 2 5 5 5 8 9 5 6 *